Hoover Institution Publications

CONSTITUTIONS
OF THE
COMMUNIST PARTY-STATES

Constitutions
of the
Communist Party-States

Edited by JAN F. TRISKA

The Hoover Institution
on War, Revolution and Peace
Stanford University

Hoover Institution Publications [70]

PREFACE

THIS volume is a collection of the texts, past and present, of the constitutions (fundamental laws) of the Communist party-states,* as well as of constitutional amendments and/or amended constitutional texts. In one case—that of the USSR, for which a new constitution has been embarrassingly overdue—a set of proposals prepared by P. S. Romashkin, a Soviet legal theoretician and Corresponding Member of the Academy of Sciences of the USSR, has been added.

Not included here are constitutions of these states *before* they had become Communist party-states, even if such traditional constitutions, adapted to changed political conditions, were used initially by the new Communist-ruled governments.

Although it is now almost ten years since the Communist seizure of power in Cuba, that nation still has not adopted a new constitution, and hence is the only party-state for which a constitutional text does not appear in this volume. Instead, a brief statement prepared by my distinguished colleague and friend, Theodore Draper, introduces three items which are intended to help to explain the peculiar Cuban case: (1) 'The Constitutional Legislation of Cuba' is an authoritative analysis of the Cuban constitutional situation excerpted from *Cuba and the Rule of Law*, which was published by the International Commission of Jurists in Geneva, in 1962; and (2) 'Questions and Answers Concerning Constitutional Principles Applied' and (3) 'The Development of the Socialist Countries.' The last two items first appeared in *Hoy*, the Cuban daily, and deal respectively with the questions, 'What is the Cuban constitution?' and 'Is Cuba a socialist state?'

The materials for the present volume, prepared for publication by the Hoover Institution, were compiled under the auspices of the Stanford University *Studies of the Communist System* project, a systematic study of the Communist world as a system—a delineated and interacting universe whose characteristics and behavior affect, and in turn are affected by, its several parts. We view the Communist system as a large transformation process in which demands and supports are processed and outputs produced in ways that are typical to the system.

We attempted to secure official English translations of all documents included in this volume. When official translations were not available, we searched for and used the most authoritative translations. Where no English translations were available at all, as in the cases of the 1924 Mongolian constitution and the 1952 Rumanian constitution, the documents were translated especially for this work.

---

* By 'Communist party-states' are meant the fourteen states ruled by their respective Communist party elites, or according to *Pravda* (February 10, 1963, page 2), where the Communist parties are 'at the helm'—namely, the USSR, People's Republic of China, People's Republic of Albania, People's Republic of Bulgaria, Hungarian People's Republic, Democratic Republic of Vietnam, German Democratic Republic, People's Republic of Korea, 'Heroic People of Cuba,' Mongolian People's Republic, Polish People's Republic, Socialist Republic of Rumania, Czechoslovak Socialist Republic, and Socialist Federal Republic of Yugoslavia. Both the CPSU and the Chinese Communist Party recognize Cuba as one of the Communist party-states; China excludes Yugoslavia.

Inasmuch as the documents cited here have not previously been readily available in English or in one up-to-date source, we hope this collection will fill a need and be of service to the scholarly community.

JAN F. TRISKA

Stanford University
Institute of Political Studies
January 1966

ACKNOWLEDGMENTS

THE Bulgarian, Czechoslovak, Polish, Rumanian, Soviet and Yugoslav embassies, and the Hungarian Legation, all in Washington, D.C., and the Albanian and Mongolian permanent missions to the United Nations in New York kindly supplied the most recent versions of their respective constitutions. In addition, Mr. Michael C. Proshev of the Cyril and Methodius National Library in Sofia found and promptly made available an original official copy of the 1947 Bulgarian constitution.

The Hoover Institution staff, and in particular Messrs. Karol Maichel and Witold Sworakowski, contributed generous advice and assistance; Mrs. Eva Nyqvist kindly translated the 1924 Mongolian constitution and Mr. Ladis Kristof the 1952 Rumanian constitution; but this volume would not have reached the printer as early as it has, and in the present form, without the sustained, imaginative and painstaking work of Mrs. Carole Norton, editor for the Institution's Publications Department.

Drs. Dennis Doolin, David Finley, and John Rue, and Mr. Wallace Berry, all of the *Studies of the Communist System*, offered suggestions and rendered valuable help in preparation of this volume. I am grateful to them all.

TABLE OF CONTENTS

INTRODUCTION

As in Western political systems, a constitution (or fundamental law, as it is often called) in the Communist setting is the formal basis of and for all law, enacted and adopted with special formalities, changed only according to special processes. As in the West, Communist party-state constitutions provide for (1) a definition of the basic philosophy and/or fundamental social and political principles of the political system; (2) a legislature, its composition and powers; (3) an executive and the exercise of executive powers; (4) local government and organs; (5) courts and the judicial functions; (6) the rights of the individual citizens; and (7) a method of constitutional amendment. In the federal Communist party-states, (8) the federal organs and the definition and division of authority between the federation and its members is also provided for, as is (9) the instrumentality of conflict-solving between them.

As in the West, Communist party-state constitutions establish fundamental *principles* for all law, thereby unifying the legal system of the state. But unlike the Western concept, these fundamental principles, embodied in the constitution 'and other major *instruments* of the state,' are the result of 'scientific generalization of state development.'

In the tradition of Western civilization, constitutionalism is a venerated concept: it defines a political scheme in which *law, rather than men, is supreme.* Political authority is exercised according to law, which is to be obeyed by all, *including the governors*, who cannot depart from it at whim. By definition, then, a constitutional government is *limited* government, deliberately adopted by the people governed by it. A cherished symbol of *freedom*, constitutionalism is held in esteem because it ensures the *equality* of all citizens before law. The constitution limits the powers of the constituent organs; its authority and sanction is highest in the political system. The constitution thus is endowed with a superior *moral* binding force. And as the will of the people ('a constitution is not the act of a government but of a people constituting a government,' wrote Thomas Paine), the constitution receives broad societal support.

Communist party-state constitutions do not limit the respective governments; instead, they are themselves limited by the ruling party's principal decision-makers, whether in the government or not. Men are supreme, not law; hence the Communist party-state constitutions are not the symbols of freedom they are in Western democracies. They have no great moral force nor are they broadly supported. As major instrumentalities of the rulers they are obeyed, but they are not cherished. And because they serve the rulers, rather than limiting them, the norms which they contain are interpreted from the sole point of view of *the interest of the state* as determined by the rulers.

Constitutions function both to legitimize the rule within the state and to socialize the citizens into their political and social roles. In the Communist party-states, the constitutions formulate the theory of state and law current at the time of enactment among the leadership, and periodic changes in official theory demand repeated, periodic changes in constitutions. As the bases of both legitimation and socialization functions change, constitutional amendments become insufficient for the purpose. The need for complete rewriting of the constitutional document becomes imperative. Hence the sustained need for constant rewriting of Communist party-state constitutions that will conform to new demands.

The distinction between people's democracy, socialist republic, and 'heroic people' forms of government rests on the stage of development the decision-makers of a given Communist party-state assume that state has achieved. This assumption in turn depends upon the assessment concerning 'the correlation of forces' in the state—i.e., the class structure of society and 'the degree of forms of democracy' in various spheres of activity. The Communist party-state constitutions, which record the state development, thus must reflect this assessment. And because the social reality within which the correlation of forces changes is alleged to be the only blueprint for constitutions (which record 'what has already been achieved'), the sustained need for up-to-date constitutions in all the Communist party-states becomes obvious. Amendments can keep the constitutions in accord with the assessed changing social structure only so far; for major societal changes, nothing but new constitutions can answer the need for the basic legal mirror-image of the social reality which a true constitution is said to represent.

For this reason, in the last eight years five new Communist party-state constitutions—Vietnamese, Mongolian, Czechoslovak, Yugoslav, and Rumanian—have been adopted; Soviet leaders and constitutional lawyers have been increasingly vocal in emphasizing the great urgency of replacing the much-amended, obsolete Soviet (Stalin) 1936 constitution by a new one; and in Bulgaria, Hungary and East Germany (and Cuba), official discussions have been held on the same subject. The sustained demand for constitutions to conform to the changing rationale of societal development as assessed by the various Communist parties' élites—and the changing 'degree and forms of democracy'—has been the fundamental cause of this development.

The social order of the Communist party-states then, may be described broadly as a dichotomous system. Two structures, both fundamental and prescriptive, exist. On the one hand, there is the formal and exalted *constitutional* superstructure with all the attractive, convenient and necessary paraphernalia which in their sum stand for the government of the people: universal, equal and direct vote by secret ballot; broad civil and human rights of citizens, constitutionally guaranteed, and including much-emulated economic rights (right to work, to rest and leisure, to old age maintenance, to education, etc.);* a complete and exemplary judicial system; central (regional) and local law-giving bodies, elected by and responsible to the people (bodies which in turn elect executive organs whom they supervise

---

* As 'welfare of the individual depends on the welfare of the people,' citizens' rights in the respective party-state constitutions are matched by their duties to the state. Like the rights, the duties extend 'equally' to all citizens. In addition to such usual civic duties as the observance of the constitution and the laws, service in the armed forces, and defense of the country, they include duty to work, to maintain labor discipline, to safeguard socialist property, and to respect the rules of socialist intercourse.

and control on the people's behalf); and plenty of local autonomy, with vertical autonomy in the more structurally complex party-states, guaranteed by the constitution. The supreme law-articulating function of the constitution is thus very elaborate, entirely democratic, and quite complete.

On the other hand, there is the effective and existential *political* infra-structure which institutionally—though not decisionally—often coincides with the formal legal order. The only locus of important decision-making and policy-articulation, rule-implementation and conflict-containment in the Communist party-states, this other realm of the system possesses all the perquisites of effective rule: the decision-makers and the policy-articulators in the party élite; the rest of the party which, with other specialized large coercive agencies, enforce the rulers' decisions; and the all-pervasive and sustained control mechanisms and check systems. In this scheme, the constitution, one of the lesser tools of the rulers, serves as a rule-implementing mechanism.

Lately, however, the formal, formerly neglected constitutional order has been somewhat gaining in ascendancy in the process of practical politics in several of the Communist party-states. Not only has the 'domino theory' worked, on the whole, from the case of Yugoslavia to what is presently referred to as 'polycentrism' in the world Communist system. But the repudiation of Stalin's practices by Khrushchev in 1956 and by many of the Communist party-state leaders in their countries; the repudiation of Khrushchev by Brezhnev and Kosygin; and the increasing attention to issues of (socialist) legality in the several party-states (more often than not motivated by the search for future legal security of present lawful endeavor, greater social stability and less arbitrariness and extra-legal Communist intervention) all suggest that with the growing aspirations of party-states as national entities, matched by the changing role of the ruling Communist parties at home as well as in the world Communist system, the formal order may show a propensity to impress itself more and more (largely because it is simply there) on the political decision-making process.

The party-state constitutions, patterned on and emulating Western constitutions, were adopted, following the model of the 1936 Stalin constitution, partly for display purposes, to show how truly democratic these states were. However, the spirit of constitutionalism which they contained was bound, it seems, to produce a degree of schizophrenia which has proved increasingly difficult to sustain and which the above-mentioned tendency now seems to relieve. The kind of probing for new boundaries by the young and the articulate, encouraged by default through the ruling parties' difficulties of coping with new, unexpected conditions and situations, has been going on now for years. Should past justifications for the monopoly of the rule by the party élites continue to evaporate—as this writer thinks they will—the several constitutions may indeed become the *ultima ratio* of the Communist party-states in their difficult search for self-maintenance under adverse conditions.

SECTION I

USSR

CONSTITUTION
(FUNDAMENTAL LAW)
OF THE RUSSIAN SOCIALIST
FEDERATED SOVIET REPUBLIC (RSFSR)[1]

Adopted by the Fifth All-Russian Congress of Soviets
July 10, 1918

THE declaration of rights of the laboring and exploited people (approved by the Third All-Russian Congress of Soviets in January 1918), together with the Constitution of the Soviet Republic, approved by the fifth congress, constitutes a single fundamental law of the Russian Socialist Federated Soviet Republic.

This fundamental law becomes effective upon the publication of the same in its entirety in the 'Izvestia of the All-Russian General Executive Committee.' It must be published by all organs of the Soviet Government and must be posted in a prominent place in every soviet institution.

The fifth congress instructs the People's Commissariat of Education to introduce in all schools and educational institutions of the Russian Republic the study and explanation of the basic principles of this Constitution.

ARTICLE ONE

DECLARATION OF RIGHTS OF THE
LABORING AND EXPLOITED PEOPLE

CHAPTER ONE

1. Russia is declared to be a republic of the Soviets of Workers', Soldiers', and Peasants' Deputies. All the central and local power belongs to these soviets.

2. The Russian Soviet Republic is organized on the basis of a free union of free nations, as a federation of soviet national republics.

CHAPTER TWO

3. Bearing in mind as its fundamental problem the abolition of the exploitation of men by men, the entire abolition of the division of the people into classes, the suppression of exploiters, the establishment of a socialist society, and the victory of socialism in all lands, the Third All-Russian Congress of Soviets of Workers', Soldiers', and Peasants' Deputies further resolves:

---

[1] Revised reprint from *The Nation*, CVIII (January 4, 1919), pp. 8–12.

(*a*) For the purpose of attaining the socialization of land, all private property in land is abolished, and the entire land is declared to be national property and is to be apportioned among agriculturists without compensation to the former owners, in the measure of each one's ability to till it.

(*b*) All forests, treasures of the earth, and waters of general public utility, all equipment whether animate or inanimate, model farms and agricultural enterprises, are declared to be national property.

(*c*) As a first step toward complete transfer of ownership to the Soviet Republic of all factories, mills, mines, railways, and other means of production and transportation, the soviet law for the control of workmen and the establishment of a Supreme Soviet of National Economy is hereby confirmed so as to insure the power of the workers over the exploiters.

(*d*) With reference to international banking and finance, the Third Congress of Soviets is discussing the soviet decree regarding the annulment of loans made by the Government of the Czar, by landowners and the bourgeoisie, and it trusts that the Soviet Government will firmly follow this course until the final victory of the international workers' revolt against the oppression of capital.

(*e*) The transfer of all banks to the ownership of the Workers' and Peasants' Government, as one of the conditions of the liberation of the toiling masses from the yoke of capital, is confirmed.

(*f*) Universal obligation to work is introduced for the purpose of eliminating the parasitic strata of society and organizing the economic life of the country.

(*g*) For the purpose of securing the working class in the possession of complete power, and in order to eliminate all possibility of restoring the power of the exploiters, it is decreed that all workers be armed, and that a Socialist Red Army be organized and the propertied class disarmed.

CHAPTER THREE

4. Expressing its fixed resolve to liberate mankind from the grip of capital and imperialism, which flooded the earth with blood in its present most criminal of all wars, the Third Congress of Soviets fully agrees with the Soviet Government in its policy of abrogating secret treaties, of organizing on a wide scale the fraternization of the workers and peasants of the belligerent armies, and of making all efforts to conclude a general democratic peace without annexations or indemnities, upon the basis of the free determination of peoples.

5. It is also to this end that the Third Congress of Soviets insists upon putting an end to the barbarous policy of the bourgeois civilization which enables the exploiters of a few chosen nations to enslave hundreds of millions of the working population of Asia, of the colonies, and of small countries generally.

6.   The Third Congress of Soviets hails the policy of the Council of People's Commissars in proclaiming the full independence of Finland, in withdrawing troops from Persia, and in proclaiming the right of Armenia to self-determination.

CHAPTER FOUR

7.   The Third All-Russian Congress of Soviets of Workers', Soldiers', and Peasants' Deputies believes that now, during the progress of the decisive battle between the proletariat and its exploiters, the exploiters should not hold a position in any branch of the Soviet Government. The power must belong entirely to the toiling masses and to their plenipotentiary representatives—the Soviets of Workers', Soldiers', and Peasants' Deputies.

8.   In its effort to create a league—free and voluntary, and for that reason all the more complete and secure—of the working classes of all the peoples of Russia, the Third Congress of Soviets merely establishes the fundamental principles of the Federation of Russian Soviet Republics, leaving to the workers and peasants of every people to decide the following question at their plenary sessions of their soviets, namely, whether or not they desire to participate, and on what basis, in the Federal government and other Federal soviet institutions.

ARTICLE TWO

GENERAL PROVISIONS OF THE CONSTITUTION OF THE RUSSIAN SOCIALIST FEDERATED SOVIET REPUBLIC

CHAPTER FIVE

9.   The fundamental problem of the constitution of the Russian Socialist Federated Soviet Republic involves, in view of the present transition period, the establishment of a dictatorship of the urban and rural proletariat and the poorest peasantry in the form of a powerful All-Russian soviet authority, for the purpose of abolishing the exploitation of men by men and of introducing socialism, in which there will be neither a division into classes nor a state of autocracy.

10.   The Russian Republic is a free socialist society of all the working people of Russia. The entire power, within the boundaries of the Russian Socialist Federated Soviet Republic, belongs to all the working people of Russia, united in urban and rural soviets.

11.   The soviets of those regions which differentiate themselves by a special form of existence and national character may unite in autonomous regional unions, ruled by the local congress of the soviets and their executive organs.

These autonomous regional unions participate in the Russian Socialist Federated Soviet Republic upon a Federal basis.

12.   The supreme power of the Russian Socialist Federated Soviet Republic belongs to the All-Russian Congress of Soviets, and, in periods between the convocation of the congress, to the All-Russian Central Executive Committee.

13. For the purpose of securing to the workers real freedom of conscience, the church is to be separated from the state and the school from the church, and the right of religious and antireligious propaganda is accorded to every citizen.

14. For the purpose of securing freedom of expression to the toiling masses, the Russian Socialist Federated Soviet Republic abolishes all dependence of the Press upon capital, and turns over to the working people and the poorest peasantry all technical and material means for the publication of newspapers, pamphlets, books, etc., and guarantees their free circulation throughout the country.

15. For the purpose of enabling the workers to hold free meetings, the Russian Socialist Federated Soviet Republic offers to the working class and to the poorest peasantry furnished halls, and takes care of their heating and lighting appliances.

16. The Russian Socialist Federated Soviet Republic, having crushed the economic and political power of the propertied classes, and having thus abolished all obstacles which interfered with the freedom of organization and action of the workers and peasants, offers assistance, material and other, to the workers and the poorest peasantry in their effort to unite and organize.

17. For the purpose of guaranteeing to the workers real access to knowledge, the Russian Socialist Federated Soviet Republic sets itself the task of furnishing full and general free education to the workers and the poorest peasantry.

18. The Russian Socialist Federated Soviet Republic considers work the duty of every citizen of the Republic, and proclaims as its motto: 'He shall not eat who does not work.'

19. For the purpose of defending the victory of the great peasants' and workers' revolution, the Russian Socialist Federated Soviet Republic recognizes the duty of all citizens of the Republic to come to the defense of their socialist fatherland, and it therefore introduces universal military training. The honor of defending the revolution with arms is accorded only to the workers, and the non-working elements are charged with the performance of other military duties.

20. In consequence of the solidarity of the workers of all nations, the Russian Socialist Federated Soviet Republic grants all political rights of Russian citizens to foreigners who live in the territory of the Russian Republic and are engaged in work and who belong to the working class. The Russian Socialist Federated Soviet Republic also recognizes the right of local soviets to grant citizenship to such foreigners without complicated formality.

21. The Russian Socialist Federated Soviet Republic offers shelter to all foreigners who seek refuge from political or religious persecution.

22. The Russian Socialist Federated Soviet Republic, recognizing the equal rights of all citizens, irrespective of their racial or national connections, proclaims all privileges on this ground, as well as oppression of national minorities, to be contrary to the fundamental laws of the Republic.

23. Being guided by the interests of the working class as a whole, the Russian Socialist Federated Soviet Republic deprives all individuals and groups of rights which could be utilized by them to the detriment of the socialist revolution.

ARTICLE THREE

ORGANIZATION OF THE SOVIET POWER

A. *Organization of the Central Power*

CHAPTER SIX

THE ALL-RUSSIAN CONGRESS OF SOVIETS OF WORKERS', PEASANTS', COSSACKS', AND RED ARMY DEPUTIES

24. The All-Russian Congress of Soviets is the supreme power of the Russian Socialist Federated Soviet Republic.

25. The All-Russian Congress of Soviets is composed of representatives of urban soviets (one delegate for 25,000 voters), and of representatives of the provincial (gubernia) congresses of soviets (one delegate for 125,000 inhabitants).

NOTE 1: In case the provincial congress is not called before the All-Russian Congress is convoked, delegates for the latter are sent directly from the county (uyezd) congress.

NOTE 2: In case the regional (oblast) congress is convoked indirectly, previous to the convocation of the All-Russian Congress, delegates for the latter may be sent by the regional congress.

26. The All-Russian Congress is convoked by the All-Russian Central Executive Committee at least twice a year.

27. A special All-Russian Congress is convoked by the All-Russian Central Executive Committee upon its own initiative, or upon the request of local soviets having not less than one-third of the entire population of the Republic.

28. The All-Russian Congress elects an All-Russian Central Executive Committee of not more than 200 members.

29. The All-Russian Central Executive Committee is entirely responsible to the All-Russian Congress of Soviets.

30. In the periods between the convocation of the congresses, the All-Russian Central Executive Committee is the supreme power of the Republic.

CHAPTER SEVEN

THE ALL-RUSSIAN CENTRAL EXECUTIVE COMMITTEE

31. The All-Russian Central Executive Committee is the supreme legislative, executive and controlling organ of the Russian Socialist Federated Soviet Republic.

32. The All-Russian Central Executive Committee directs in a general way the activity of the Workers' and Peasants' Government and of all organs of the soviet authority in the country, and it coordinates and regulates the operation of the Soviet Constitution and of the resolutions of the all-Russian congresses and of the central organs of the soviet power.

33. The All-Russian Central Executive Committee considers and enacts all measures and proposals introduced by the Soviet of People's Commissars or by the various departments, and it also issues its own decrees and regulations.

34. The All-Russian Central Executive Committee convokes the All-Russian Congress of Soviets, at which time the Executive Committee reports on its activity and on general questions.

35. The All-Russian Central Executive Committee forms a Council of People's Commissars for the purpose of general management of the affairs of the Russian Socialist Federated Soviet Republic, and it also forms departments (People's Commissariats) for the purpose of conducting various branches.

36. The members of the All-Russian Central Executive Committee work in the various departments (People's Commissariats) or execute special orders of the All-Russian Central Executive Committee.

CHAPTER EIGHT

THE COUNCIL OF PEOPLE'S COMMISSARS

37. The Council of People's Commissars is entrusted with the general management of the affairs of the Russian Socialist Federated Soviet Republic.

38. For the accomplishment of this task the Council of People's Commissars issues decrees, resolutions, orders, and, in general, takes all steps necessary for the proper and rapid conduct of governmental affairs.

39. The Council of People's Commissars notifies immediately the All-Russian Central Executive Committee of all its orders and resolutions.

40. The All-Russian Central Executive Committee has the right to revoke or suspend all orders and resolutions of the Council of People's Commissars.

41. All orders and resolutions of the Council of People's Commissars of great political significance are referred for consideration and final approval to the All-Russian Central Executive Committee.

NOTE: Measures requiring immediate execution may be enacted directly by the Council of People's Commissars.

42. The members of the Council of People's Commissars stand at the head of the various People's Commissariats.

43. There are seventeen [sic] People's Commissars: (a) Foreign Affairs; (b) Army; (c) Navy; (d) Interior; (e) Justice; (f) Labor; (g) Social Welfare; (h) Education; (i) Post and Telegraph; (j) National Affairs; (k) Finances; (l) Ways of Communication; (m) Agriculture; (n) Commerce and Industry; (o) National Supplies; (p) State Control; (q) Supreme Soviet of National Economy; (r) Public Health.

44. Every commissar has a collegium (committee) of which he is the president, and the members of which are appointed by the Council of People's Commissars.

45. A People's Commissar has the individual right to decide on all questions under the jurisdiction of his commissariat, and he is to report on his decision to the collegium. If the collegium does not agree with the commissar on some decisions, the former may, without stopping the execution of the decision, complain of it to the executive members of the Council of People's Commissars or to the All-Russian Central Executive Committee.

Individual members of the collegium have this right also.

46. The Council of People's Commissars is entirely responsible to the All-Russian Congress of Soviets and the All-Russian Central Executive Committee.

47. The People's Commissars and the collegia of the People's Commissariats are entirely responsible to the Council of People's Commissars and the All-Russian Central Executive Committee.

48. The title of People's Commissar belongs only to the members of the Council of People's Commissars, which is in charge of general affairs of the Russian Socialist Federated Soviet Republic, and it cannot be used by any other representative of the Soviet power, either central or local.

CHAPTER NINE

AFFAIRS IN THE JURISDICTION OF THE ALL-RUSSIAN CONGRESS AND THE ALL-RUSSIAN CENTRAL EXECUTIVE COMMITTEE

49. The All-Russian Congress and the All-Russian Central Executive Committee deal with questions of state, such as:

(a) Ratification and amendment of the Constitution of the Russian Socialist Federated Soviet Republic;

(b) General direction of the entire interior and foreign policy of the Russian Socialist Federated Soviet Republic;

(c) Establishing and changing boundaries, also ceding territory belonging to the Russian Socialist Federated Soviet Republics;

(d) Establishing boundaries for regional soviet unions belonging to the Russian Socialist Federated Soviet Republic, also settling disputes among them;

(e) Admission of new members to the Russian Socialist Federated Soviet Republic, and recognition of the secession of any parts of it;

(f) The general administrative division of the territory of the Russian Socialist Federated Soviet Republic and the approval of regional unions;

(g) Establishing and changing weights, measures, and money denominations in the Russian Socialist Federated Soviet Republic;

(h) Foreign relations, declaration of war, and ratification of peace treaties;

(i) Making loans, signing commercial treaties and financial agreements;

(j) Working out a basis and a general plan for the national economy and for its various branches in the Russian Socialist Federated Soviet Republic;

(k) Approval of the budget of the Russian Socialist Federated Soviet Republic;

(l) Levying taxes and establishing the duties of citizens to the state;

(m) Establishing the bases for the organization of armed forces;

(n) State legislation, judicial organization and procedure, civil and criminal legislation, etc.;

(o) Appointment and dismissal of the individual People's Commissars or the entire council, also approval of the president of the Council of People's Commissars;

(p) Granting and cancelling Russian citizenship and fixing rights of foreigners;

(q) The right to declare individual and general amnesty.

50. Besides the above-mentioned questions, the All-Russian Congress and the All-Russian Central Executive Committee have charge of all other affairs which, according to their decision, require their attention.

51. The following questions are solely under the jurisdiction of the All-Russian Congress:

(a) Ratification and amendment of the fundamental principles of the Soviet Constitution;

(b) Ratification of peace treaties.

52. The decision of questions indicated in paragraphs *(c)* and *(h)* of Section 49 may be made by the All-Russian Central Executive Committee only in case it is impossible to convoke the Congress.

B. *Organization of Local Soviets*

CHAPTER TEN
THE CONGRESSES OF THE SOVIETS

53. Congresses of Soviets are composed as follows:

(a) *Regional:* of representatives of the urban and county soviets, one representative for 25,000 inhabitants of the county, and one representative for 5,000 voters of the cities—but not more than 500 representatives for the entire region—or of representatives of the provincial congresses, chosen on the same basis, if such a congress meets before the regional congress.

(b) *Provincial* (gubernia): of representatives of urban and rural (volost) soviets, one representative for 10,000 inhabitants from the rural districts, and one representative for 2,000 voters in the city; altogether not more than 300 representatives for the entire province. In case the county congress meets before the provincial, election takes place on the same basis, but by the county congress instead of the rural.

(c) *County:* of representatives of rural soviets, one delegate for each 1,000 inhabitants, but not more than 300 delegates for the entire county.

(d) Rural (volost): of representatives of all village soviets in the volost, one delegate for ten members of the soviet.

NOTE 1:   Representatives of urban soviets which have a population of not more than 10,000 persons participate in the county congress; village soviets of districts of less than 10,000 inhabitants unite for the purpose of electing delegates to the county congress.

NOTE 2:   Rural soviets of less than ten members send one delegate to the rural (volost) congress.

54.   Congresses of the soviets are convoked by the respective executive committees upon their own initiative, or upon request of local soviets comprising not less than one-third of the entire population of the given district. In any case they are convoked at least twice a year for regions, every three months for provinces and counties, and once a month for rural districts.

55.   Every congress of soviets (regional, provincial, county, or rural) elects its executive organ—an executive committee the membership of which shall not exceed *(a)* for regions and provinces, twenty-five; *(b)* for a county, twenty; *(c)* for a rural district, ten. The executive committee is responsible to the congress which elected it.

56.   In the boundaries of the respective territories the congress is the supreme power; during intervals between the convocations of the congress, the executive committee is the supreme power.

CHAPTER ELEVEN

THE SOVIET OF DEPUTIES

57.   Soviets of Deputies are formed

(a) In cities, one deputy for each 1,000 inhabitants; the total to be not less than fifty and not more than 1,000 members.

(b) All other settlements (towns, villages, hamlets, etc.) of less than 10,000 inhabitants, one deputy for each 100 inhabitants; the total to be not less than three and not more than fifty deputies for each settlement.

Term of the deputy, three months.

NOTE: In small rural sections, whenever possible, all questions shall be decided at general meetings of voters.

58.   The Soviet of Deputies elects an executive committee to deal with current affairs; not more than five members for rural districts, one for every fifty members of the soviets of cities, but not more than fifteen and not less than three in the aggregate (Petrograd and Moscow not more than forty). The executive committee is entirely responsible to the soviet which elected it.

59.   The Soviet of Deputies is convoked by the executive committee upon its own initiative, or upon the request of not less than one-half of the membership of the soviet; in any case at least once a week in cities, and twice a week in rural sections.

60. Within its jurisdiction the soviet, and in cases mentioned in Section 57, NOTE, the meeting of the voters is the supreme power in the given district.

CHAPTER TWELVE
JURISDICTION OF THE LOCAL ORGANS OF THE SOVIETS

61. Regional, provincial, county, and rural organs of the soviet power and also the Soviets of Deputies have to perform the following duties:

(a) Carry out all orders of the respective higher organs of the soviet power;

(b) Take all steps for raising the cultural and economic standard of the given territory;

(c) Decide all questions of local importance within their respective territories;

(d) Coordinate all soviet activity in their respective territories.

62. The congresses of soviets and their executive committees have the right to control the activity of the local soviets (i.e., the regional congress controls all soviets of the respective region; the provincial, of the respective province, with the exception of the urban soviets, etc.); and the regional and provincial congresses and their executive committees have in addition the right to overrule the decisions of the soviets of their districts, giving notice in important cases to the central soviet authority.

63. For the purpose of performing their duties, the local soviets, rural and urban, and the executive committees form sections respectively.

ARTICLE FOUR
THE RIGHT TO VOTE

CHAPTER THIRTEEN

64. The right to vote and to be elected to the soviets is enjoyed by the following citizens of both sexes, irrespective of religion, nationality, domicile, etc., of the Russian Socialist Federated Soviet Republic, who shall have completed their eighteenth year by the day of election:

(a) All who have acquired the means of livelihood through labor that is productive and useful to society, and also persons engaged in housekeeping which enables the former to do productive work, i.e., laborers and employees of all classes who are employed in industry, trade, agriculture, etc., and peasants and Cossack agricultural laborers who employ no help for the purpose of making profits.

(b) Soldiers of the army and navy of the soviets.

(c) Citizens of the two preceding categories who have in any degree lost their capacity to work.

NOTE 1: Local soviets may, upon approval of the central power, lower the age standard mentioned herein.

NOTE 2: Non-citizens mentioned in Section 20 (Article Two, Chapter 5) have the right to vote.

65.   The following persons enjoy neither the right to vote nor the right to be voted for, even though they belong to one of the categories enumerated above, namely:

(a) Persons who employ hired labor in order to obtain from it an increase in profits;

(b) Persons who have an income without doing any work, such as interest from capital, receipts from property, etc.;

(c) Private merchants, trade and commercial brokers;

(d) Monks and clergy of all denominations;

(e) Employees and agents of the former police, the gendarme corps, and the Okhrana (Czar's secret service), also members of the former reigning dynasty;

(f) Persons who have in legal form been declared demented or mentally deficient, and also persons under guardianship;

(g) Persons who have been deprived by a soviet of their rights of citizenship because of selfish or dishonorable offenses, for the period fixed by the sentence.

CHAPTER FOURTEEN

ELECTIONS

66.   Elections are conducted according to custom on days fixed by the local soviets.

67.   Election takes place in the presence of an election committee and the representation of the local soviet.

68.   In case the representative of the soviet cannot for valid causes be present, the chairman of the election committee takes his place, and in case the latter is absent, the chairman of the election meeting replaces him.

69.   Minutes of the proceedings and results of elections are to be compiled and signed by the members of the election committee and the representative of the soviet.

70.   Detailed instructions regarding the election proceedings and the participation in them of professional and other workers' organizations are to be issued by the local soviets, according to the instructions of the All-Russian Central Executive Committee.

CHAPTER FIFTEEN

THE CHECKING AND CANCELLATION OF ELECTIONS
AND RECALL OF THE DEPUTIES

71.   The respective soviets receive all the records of the proceedings of the election.

72.   The soviet appoints a commission to verify the election.

73.   This commission reports the results to the soviet.

74.   The soviet decides the question when there is doubt as to which candidate is elected.

75.   The soviet announces a new election if the election of one candidate or another cannot be determined.

76.   If an election was irregularly carried on in its entirety, it may be declared void by a higher soviet authority.

77.   The highest authority in relation to questions of elections is the All-Russian Central Executive Committee.

78.   Voters who have sent a deputy to the soviet have the right to recall him, and to have a new election, according to general provisions.

ARTICLE FIVE

THE BUDGET

CHAPTER SIXTEEN

79.   The financial policy of the Russian Socialist Federated Soviet Republic in the present transition period of dictatorship of the proletariat facilitates the fundamental purpose of expropriation of the bourgeoisie and the preparation of conditions necessary for the equality of all citizens of Russia in the production and distribution of wealth. To this end it sets forth as its task the supplying of the organs of the soviet power with all necessary funds for local and state needs of the Soviet Republic, without regard to private property rights.

80.   The state expenditure and income of the Russian Socialist Federated Soviet Republic are combined in the state budget.

81.   The All-Russian Congress of Soviets or the All-Russian Central Executive Committee determine what matters of income and taxation shall go to the state budget and what shall go to the local soviets; they also set the limits of taxes.

82.   The soviets levy taxes only for the local needs. The state needs are covered by the funds of the state treasury.

83.   No expenditures out of the state treasury not set forth in the budget of income and expense shall be made without a special order of the central power.

84. The local soviets shall receive credits from the proper People's Commissars out of the state treasury, for the purpose of making expenditures for general state needs.

85. All credits allotted to the soviets from the state treasury, and also credits approved for local needs, must be expended according to the estimates, and cannot be used for any other purposes without a special order of the All-Russian Central Executive Committee and the Soviet of People's Commissars.

86. Local soviets draw up semi-annual and annual estimates of income and expenditure for local needs. The estimates of urban and rural soviets participating in county congresses, and also the estimates of the county organs of the soviet power, are to be approved by provincial and regional congresses or by their executive committees; the estimates of the urban, provincial, and regional organs of the soviets are to be approved by the All-Russian Central Executive Committee and the Council of People's Commissars.

87. The soviets may ask for additional credits from the respective People's Commissariats for expenditures not set forth in the estimate, or where the allotted sum is insufficient.

88. In case of an insufficiency of local funds for local needs, the necessary subsidy may be obtained from the state treasury by applying to the All-Russian Central Executive Committee or the Council of People's Commissars.

ARTICLE SIX

THE COAT OF ARMS AND FLAG OF THE RUSSIAN SOCIALIST FEDERATED SOVIET REPUBLIC

CHAPTER SEVENTEEN

89. The coat of arms of the Russian Socialist Federated Soviet Republic consists of a red background on which a golden scythe and a hammer are placed (crosswise, handles downward) in sun-rays and surrounded by a wreath, inscribed:

Russian Socialist Federated Soviet Republic

Workers of the World, Unite!

90. The commercial, naval, and army flag of the Russian Socialist Federated Soviet Republic consists of a red cloth, in the left corner of which (on top, near the pole) are in golden characters the letters R.S.F.S.R., or the inscription: Russian Socialist Federated Soviet Republic.

Chairman of the fifth All-Russian Congress of Soviets and of the All-Russian Central Executive Committee—J. Sverdlov.

Executive Officers, All-Russian Central Executive Committee—T. I. Teodorovitch, F. A. Rosin, A. P. Rosenholz, A. C. Mitrofanov, K. G. Maximov.

Secretary of the All-Russian Central Executive Committee—V. A. Avamessov.

1.1.1   AMENDMENTS TO THE RSFSR CONSTITUTION OF 1918[1]

In the period of the Civil War and military intervention of the imperialist states some amendments and addenda to the Constitution of the R.S.F.S.R. were adopted. For instance, the seventh All-Russian Congress of Soviets, held in December 1919, legislatively sanctioned the formation of the Presidium of the All-Russian Central Executive Committee, defined its powers and established that the sessions of the All-Russian Central Executive Committee were to be convened every two months.

The Presidium of the All-Russian Central Executive Committee directed the sittings of the All-Russian Central Executive Committee, supervised the execution of decisions adopted by the latter, guided the activity both of the central and local state organs, exercised the right of pardon, and decided a number of other administrative questions. In the intervals between the sessions of the All-Russian Central Executive Committee the Presidium had the right to approve or annul decisions of the Council of People's Commissars, to appoint People's Commissars on the recommendation of the Council of People's Commissars, to decide questions relating to administrative-territorial division and to make preparations for the convocation of all-Russian congresses of Soviets and sessions of the All-Russian Central Executive Committee.

According to the decision of the seventh All-Russian Congress of Soviets, the Executive Committees were elected by the gubernia, uyezd and volost congresses of Soviets and were considered the highest organs of Soviet state power within the territories of the gubernias, uyezds and volosts in the intervals between the sessions of the corresponding congresses of Soviets. The gubernia Executive Committees were empowered to supervise and inspect the activity of all governmental institutions on the territories under their jurisdiction (except institutions belonging to the Army in the Field), and were obliged to report back immediately to the respective central organs on the results of such supervision and inspection.

The decision of the eighth All-Russian Congress of Soviets 'Concerning Further Development of the Soviets,' adopted on December 29, 1920, extended the powers of the Presidium of the All-Russian Central Executive Committee. The latter was vested with the authority to annul decisions of the Council of People's Commissars, and to adopt necessary administrative decisions on behalf of the All-Russian Central Executive Committee; at the same time it was obliged to submit reports on its activity to the regular sessions of the All-Russian Central Executive Committee.

The eighth All-Russian Congress of Soviets also extended the powers of the Council of People's Commissars. The decision of the congress stated that all urgent decrees and measures of nationwide importance, including legislative acts relating to military affairs, as well as measures in the sphere of foreign relations which might impose certain commitments upon the Russian Socialist Federated Soviet Republic, were to be considered and approved by the Council of People's Commissars. The latter had the right to adopt legislative acts of nationwide importance, along with the All-Russian Congress of Soviets, All-Russian Central Executive Committee

---

[1] Excerpted from A. Denisov and M. Kirichenko, *Soviet State Law* (Moscow: Foreign Languages Publishing House, 1960), pp. 50–52.

and Presidium of the All-Russian Central Executive Committee. The People's Commissariats had the rights to issue decisions and orders only within the limits of their jurisdiction strictly defined in corresponding decrees of the All-Russian Central Executive Committee, its Presidium and the Council of People's Commissars.

By a decision of the eighth All-Russian Congress of Soviets, the gubernia executive committees had the right only in extraordinary cases to suspend the execution of certain orders issued by individual People's Commissars.[2]

All the aforementioned amendments in no way affected the fundamental principles of the Constitution of the R.S.F.S.R. as a whole.

---

[2] Similar rights were granted to the uyezd executive committees with regard to the instructions of the gubernia executive committees [authors' note].

1. 2

CONSTITUTION
(FUNDAMENTAL LAW)
OF THE UNION OF THE SOVIET
SOCIALIST REPUBLICS[1]

Adopted by the Central Executive Committee of the USSR
at its Second Session

July 6, 1923

SECTION ONE

DECLARATION OF UNION

SINCE the formation of the Soviet Republics, the world has become divided into two camps—that of capitalism and that of socialism.

Within the capitalist camp, national hatred and inequality, colonial bondage and chauvinism, national oppression and massacres, imperialist brutalities and wars prevail, while here, within the camp of socialism, mutual trust and peace, national freedom and equality, peaceful coexistence and fraternal collaboration of peoples is to be found.

The efforts of the capitalist regime, in the course of the decades, to solve the question of nationalities by the joint methods of the free development of peoples and the exploitation of man by man have proven vain. On the contrary, the web of national antagonism is becoming even more entangled until it threatens the very existence of capitalism itself. The bourgeoisie has proven impotent of bringing about cooperation among peoples.

Only within the camps of the soviets, only under the prevalence of the proletarian dictatorship around which the majority of the population has rallied, has it become possible to destroy national oppression root and branch, to create an atmosphere of mutual trust and to lay the foundations for the brotherly cooperation of peoples.

Owing to that—and to that only—it [has been] possible for the Soviet Republics to repel the external as well as the internal attacks of world imperialism. Solely because of these conditions were they able successfully to end the civil war, [to] become secure in their existence and to pass to the tasks of peaceful economic reconstruction.

But the years of war have left their scars. The devastated fields and idle factories, the breakdown of productive forces and the depletion of economic resources—this

---

[1] Reprinted from *The Constitution (Fundamental Law) of the Union of Socialist Soviet Republics (USSR)*, (Washington, D.C.: Russian Information Bureau, 1924).

legacy of the war makes the isolated efforts of individual republics toward economic reconstruction inadequate. The rebirth of economic welfare was found impossible as long as the separate republics maintained a divided existence. At the same time the unsettled state of international affairs and the danger of new attacks point to the necessity of creating a common front of the Soviet Republics against the surrounding capitalist world.

Finally, the very structure of the soviet power, which is international in its class character, calls the toiling masses of the Soviet Republics toward a unity of one socialist family.

All these circumstances imperatively demand the unification of the Soviet Republics into one federal state, powerful enough of warding off foreign attacks and of [securing] internal economic welfare, as well as the unhampered existence of the various nations [sic].

The will of the peoples of the Soviet Republics, unanimously proclaimed at their recent Soviet Congresses in their decision for the formation of the 'Union of the Soviet Socialist Republics,' stands as the unimpeachable guarantee that this Union shall be the voluntary association of these sovereign nations on a basis of equality, each republic reserving to itself the right of free withdrawal from the Union, that admission to this Union shall be open to all Soviet Socialist Republics such as are now existing and such as shall arise in the future, that the new united state is a fitting consummation of the beginnings which had their inception in November 1917, toward the tranquil and cooperative existence and mutual bond of the peoples, that it shall stand as the firm bulwark against world capitalism and form a decisive step toward the union of the toilers of all countries into one World Soviet Socialist Republic.

SECTION TWO

COVENANT

The Russian Socialist Federated Soviet Republic (R.S.F.S.R.), the Ukrainian Socialist Soviet Republic (U.S.S.R.), the White Russian Socialist Soviet Republic (W.S.S.R.), and the Transcaucasian Socialist Federated Soviet Republic (T.C.S. F.S.R.), consisting of the Socialist Soviet Republic of Azerbaijan, the Soviet Socialist Republic of Georgia, and the Soviet Socialist Republic of Armenia, by this covenant enter into a single federal state to be known as UNION OF SOVIET SOCIALIST REPUBLICS.

ARTICLE ONE

SCOPE OF AUTHORITY OF THE UNION

1. The sovereignty of the Union of Soviet Socialist Republics, as exercised through the supreme governing departments, shall include:

> (a) The representation of the Union in international affairs, the conduct of all diplomatic intercourse and the conclusion of political and other treaties with foreign states;

(b) The modification of the frontiers of the Union and the regulation of questions dealing with the alteration of boundaries between the constituent Republics;

(c) The conclusion of treaties for the admission of new Republics into the Union;

(d) The declaration of war and conclusion of peace;

(e) The contracting of foreign and domestic loans by the Union of Soviet Socialist Republics and the sanctioning of foreign and domestic loans by the several constituent Republics;

(f) The ratification of international treaties;

(g) Control of foreign trade, and establishment of a system of internal trade;

(h) Establishment of the basic principles and of a general plan for the whole economic system of the Union; determination of the branches of industry and of separate industrial undertakings which are of importance to the whole Union; and the conclusion of concession agreements, both those relating to the Union as a whole [and] those relating only to the constituent Republics;

(i) The regulation and control of transport, posts and telegraphs;

(j) The organization and control of the armed forces of the Union;

(k) Adoption of a single State budget for the Union, comprising the budgets of the constituent Republics; determination of the general Union taxes and revenues, as [well as] deductions therefrom and additions thereto for the budgets of the constituent Republics; authorization of additional taxes and dues for the budgets of the constituent Republics;

(l) Establishment of a single currency and credit system;

(m) Establishment of general principles governing the distribution and use of land, and the exploitation of mineral wealth, forests and waterways throughout the whole territory of the Union;

(n) General Union legislation on migration from one Republic to another, and establishment of a colonization fund;

(o) Establishment of basic principles for the composition and procedure of the courts and the civil and criminal legislation of the Union;

(p) The enactment of fundamental laws dealing with the rights of labor;

(q) Establishment of the general principles of national education;

(r) Adoption of measures for the protection of public health;

(s) Establishment of a common system of weights and measures;

(t) The organization of census for the entire Union;

(u) Fundamental legislation as to the rights of foreigners to citizenship of the Union;

(v) The right of general amnesty within the territory of the entire Union;

(w) The right to vote all decrees made by the different soviet congresses and by central executive committees of the several constituent republics which shall be in violation of the within Constitution;

(x) Settlement of controversies arising between the several constituent Republics.

2. The ratification and amendment of the Constitution shall be exclusively delegated to the Soviet Congress of the Union of S.S.R.

ARTICLE TWO

THE SOVEREIGNTY OF THE SEVERAL CONSTITUENT REPUBLICS AND FEDERAL CITIZENSHIP

3. The Union of the Soviet Socialist Republics shall guarantee the sovereignty of each and every constituent Republic of the Union. Except as delegated in the herein Constitution, the sovereign rights of the several Republics constituting this Union shall not be restricted or impaired.

4. Each of the constituent Republics shall have the right to withdraw freely from the Federal Union.

5. Each of the several constituent Republics shall pass such amendments to its respective constitutions as will bring it in conformity with the Federal Constitution.

6. The territory of each of the constituent Republics shall not be altered without its consent and no amendment, modification, limitation or repeal of [paragraph 4] of the Federal Constitution shall be made without the consent of all the constituent Republics of the Union.

7. Federal citizenship of the Union shall replace the citizenships of the several constituent Republics.

ARTICLE THREE

SOVIET CONGRESS OF THE UNION OF THE SOVIET SOCIALIST REPUBLICS

8. The supreme authority of the Union of the Soviet Socialist Republics shall be vested in the Soviet Congress and, during the intervals of sessions of the said Congress, in the Central Executive Committee of the Union of Soviet Socialist Republics, which shall consist of the Council of the Union and the Council of Nationalities.

9. The Soviet Congress of the Union of the Soviet Socialist Republics shall be composed of the representatives of city and township soviets on the basis of one deputy for each 25,000 electors, and of representatives of provincial soviet congresses on the basis of one deputy for each 125,000 inhabitants.

10. The representatives to the Soviet Congress of the Union of the Soviet Socialist Republics shall be elected at the provincial soviet congresses. In those

Republics which have no provincial units, the delegates shall be elected directly at the Soviet Congresses of the respective republics.

11. The regular session of the Soviet Congresses of the Union of the Soviet Socialist Republics shall be convened by the Central Executive Committee of the Union of the Soviet Socialist Republics once a year; extraordinary sessions shall be convened by the Central Executive Committee of the Union of the Soviet Socialist Republics either on its own initiative or on the demand of the Council of the Union or Council of Nationalities or of any two of the constituent Republics.

12. Under extraordinary circumstances preventing the convening of the Soviet Congress at the appointed time, the Central Executive Committee of the Union of Soviet Socialist Republics shall have the right to postpone the convening of the Soviet Congress.

ARTICLE FOUR
THE CENTRAL EXECUTIVE COMMITTEE OF THE UNION OF SOVIET SOCIALIST REPUBLICS

13. The Central Executive Committee of the Union shall consist of the Council of the Union and the Council of Nationalities.

14. The Soviet Congress of the Union shall elect the Council of the Union, which shall consist of 371 members from among the representatives of the several constituent Republics counted in proportion to the population of each republic.

15. The Council of Nationalities shall be formed of the representatives of the constituent and autonomous Soviet Socialist Republics on the basis of five representatives from each; and of representatives of the autonomous territories of the Russian Socialist Federated Soviet Republic on the basis of one representative thereof. The composition of the Council of Nationalities as a whole shall be subject to confirmation by the Soviet Congress of the Union of Soviet Socialist Republics.

> NOTE: The autonomous Republics of Adjaria and Abkhazia and the autonomous Territory of Southern Ossetia shall send one representative each to the Council of Nationalities.

16. The Union Council and Council of Nationalities shall examine all decrees, codes and regulations submitted to them by the Presidium of the Central Executive Committee and the Council of People's Commissars of the Union, by separate People's Commissars of the Union, or by the central executive committees of the constituent republics, also when the question of such decrees, codes and regulations is raised on the initiative of the Union Council or the Council of Nationalities.

17. The Union Central Executive Committee issues codes, decrees, regulations and orders, and forms a single legislative and executive body for the Union; it further defines the work of the Presidium of the Central Executive Committee and the Council of People's Commissars of the Union.

18. All decrees and ordinances concerning political and economic life of the Union of Soviet Socialist Republics and also those which introduce fundamental

changes in the existing practice of the state departments of the Union, must be submitted for the examination and ratification of the Central Executive Committee of the Union of Soviet Socialist Republics.

19. All decrees, regulations and orders issued by the Central Executive Committee shall be compulsory throughout the territory of the Union.

20. The Central Executive Committee of the Union of Soviet Socialist Republics shall have the right to veto or suspend all decrees, regulations and ordinances of the Presidium of the Central Executive Committee of the Union of Soviet Socialist Republics, of the soviet congresses and of the central executive committees of all the constituent republics, and of all other governmental organs within the territory of the Union.

21. The regular sessions of the Central Executive Committee of the Union of Soviet Socialist Republics shall be convened by the Presidium of the Central Executive Committee three times a year. The extraordinary sessions shall be convened upon the demand of the Presidium of the Council of the Union, or the Presidium of the Council of Nationalities, and also upon the demand of the central executive committee of any one of the constituent Republics.

22. Legislative bills submitted for consideration by the Central Executive Committee of the Union of Soviet Socialist Republics shall become laws only after having been passed by both the Council of the Union and the Council of Nationalities; they are published in the name of the Central Executive Committee of the Union of Soviet Socialist Republics.

23. In case of disagreement between the Council of the Union and the Council of Nationalities, the question at issue shall be referred to a Conciliation Commission appointed by these two organs.

24. If no agreement be reached in the Conciliation Commission, the question shall be referred to a joint session of the Council of the Union and of the Council of Nationalities, wherein, in the event that no majority vote of the Union Council or of the Council of Nationalities can be obtained the question may be referred, on the demand of either of these bodies, for decision to either the regular or extraordinary Congress of the Union of Soviet Socialist Republics.

25. The Union Council and [the] Council of Nationalities each elect a presidium of seven . . . members to arrange . . . sessions and conduct the work. . . .

26. In the intervals between sessions of the Union Central Executive Committee, supreme authority is vested in its Presidium, formed by the Union Central Executive Committee of twenty-one members, among whom are included the whole of the Union Council Presidium and the Presidium of the Council of Nationalities.

27. The Central Executive Committee elects, in accordance with the number of contracting Republics, four chairmen of the Union Central Executive Committee from members of its presidium.

28.   The Central Executive Committee of the Union shall be responsible to the Congress of Soviets of the Union of the Soviet Socialist Republics.

THE PRESIDIUM OF THE
UNION CENTRAL EXECUTIVE COMMITTEE

29.   The Presidium of the Central Executive Committee of the Union of Soviet Socialist Republics shall during the intervals between the sessions of the Central Executive Committee of the Union of Soviet Socialist Republics be the highest legislative, executive and administrative organ in the Union of Soviet Socialist Republics.

30.   The Presidium of the Union Central Executive Committee shall have the power to enforce the application of the Union constitution and the carrying out by all departmental authorities of all decisions of the Union Congress of Soviets and of the Union Central Executive Committee.

31.   The Presidium of the Central Executive Committee of the Union of Soviet Socialist Republics shall have the power to suspend or to veto the decisions of the Council of the People's Commissars and of the individual People's Commissariats of the Union; and of the central executive committees and the Councils of People's Commissars of the constituent Republics.

32.   The Presidium of the Central Executive Committee of the Union shall have the power to suspend the decisions of the soviet congresses of the constituent Republics, but it shall subsequently thereto submit such decision for examination and ratification to the Central Executive Committee of the Union of the Soviet Socialist Republics.

33.   The Presidium of the Central Executive Committee of the Union shall pass decrees, regulations and ordinances [and] shall examine and ratify draft decrees and resolutions submitted to it by the Council of the People's Commissars, by the separate departments of the Union of S.S.R., or by the central executive committees of the constituent Republics, their presidia and by other governmental departments.

34.   The decrees and decisions of the Central Executive Committee of the Union, of its Presidium, and of the Council of People's Commissars of the Union shall be printed in all languages in popular use within the constituent Republics (Russian, Ukrainian, White Russian, Georgian, Armenian, Turko-Tartar).

35.   The Presidium of the Central Executive Committee of the Union shall have the power to decide all questions pertaining to the interrelations between the Council of the People's Commissars of the Union and the People's Commissariats of the Union on the one hand, and the central executive committees of the constituent Republics and their presidia, on the other hand.

36.   The Presidium of the Central Executive Committee of the Union shall be responsible to the Central Executive Committee of the Union.

THE COUNCIL OF THE PEOPLE'S COMMISSARS OF THE
UNION OF THE SOVIET SOCIALIST REPUBLICS

37. The Council of the People's Commissars of the Union shall be the executive and administrative organ of the Central Executive Committee of the Union and it shall be constituted by it in the following order:

Chairman of the Council of the People's Commissars of the Union of the Soviet Socialist Republics; Vice-Chairman of the Council of People's Commissars of the Soviet Socialist Republics; People's Commissar for Foreign Affairs; People's Commissar for Army and Navy; People's Commissar for Foreign Trade; People's Commissar for Transport; People's Commissar for Posts and Telegraphs; People's Commissar for Workers' and Peasants' Inspection; People's Commissar for Labor; People's Commissar for Food; People's Commissar for Finance; and the Chairman of the Supreme Council of National Economy.

38. The Council of People's Commissars of the Union shall issue decrees and regulations, which, within the limits of the powers conferred upon it by the Central Executive Committee of the Union, and by virtue of the statute establishing it, shall be compulsory throughout the territory of the Union.

39. The Council of the People's Commissars of the Union shall examine decrees and regulations submitted to it by the individual People's Commissariats of the Union or by the central executive committees of the constituent Republics and by their presidia.

40. The Council of the People's Commissariats of the Union shall be, in all of its work, responsible to the Central Executive Committee of the Union and to its Presidium.

41. All decrees and orders made by the Council of the People's Commissars of the Union may be suspended or vetoed only by the Central Executive Committee of the Union or its Presidium.

42. The Central Executive Committees of the constituent Republics and their presidia may appeal against the decrees and decisions of the Council of the People's Commissars of the Union to the Presidium of the Central Executive Committee of the Union, but in the meantime such decrees and decisions shall not be suspended.

THE SUPREME COURT OF THE UNION

43. In order to firmly maintain revolutionary law throughout the territory of the Union, there shall be created a Supreme Court of the Union which shall be attached to the Union Central Executive Committee. The said court shall have the power and jurisdiction:

(a) To promulgate authoritative opinions on questions concerning general Federal legislation to the constituent Republics.

(b) On the motion of the Attorney General of the Union, the Supreme Court shall review the regulations, decisions and sentences of the supreme courts of the constituent Republics and appeal against them to the Central Executive Committee of the Union whenever such decisions violate the general legislation of the Union or whenever they are prejudicial to the interests of other Republics of the Union.

(c) To render decisions at the request of the Central Executive Committee of the Union on the constitutionality of any regulations made by the constituent Republics.

(d) To adjudicate all judiciable controversies between the constituent Republics.

(e) To try the charges against high officials of the Union for offenses committed in the discharge of their duties.

44.   The Supreme Court of the Union shall function through:

(a) Plenary sessions;

(b) Civil and Criminal Departments;

(c) Military and Military Transport Divisions.

45.   In its plenary sessions the Supreme Court shall consist of eleven members, including one chairman, one vice-chairman, the four chairmen of the plenary sessions of the supreme courts of the constituent Republics, and a representative of the political department of the Union (see Section [paragraph] 61). The chairman, vice-chairman, [and] the other five members shall be appointed by the Presidium of the Central Executive Committee of the Union.

46.   The Attorney General of the Union and his deputy shall be appointed by the Presidium of the Central Executive Committee of the Union. The duties of the Attorney General of the Supreme Court of the Union shall include the rendering of opinions on all questions submitted to the Supreme Court of the Union and the arguing for the validity of such opinion rendered at the session of the Court. Whenever the Supreme Court of the Union at its plenary sessions shall render a decision in disagreement with his opinion, the Attorney General shall have the right of appealing from such decision of the court to the Presidium of the Central Executive Committee of the Union.

47.   The right to submit questions specified in Section [paragraph] 43 to the plenary sessions of the Supreme Court of the Union may be exercised only by the Central Executive Committee of the Union, its Presidium, the Attorney General of the Union Supreme Court, the attorneys general of the constituent Republics and the Political Department of the Union.

48.   The Supreme Court of the Union, at the plenary session thereof, shall have jurisdiction, sitting as a trial Court, in

(a) Criminal and civil cases of exceptional importance affecting the safety of two or more of the constituent Republics.

(b) Cases of impeachment and liability of the members of the Central Executive Committee of the Union and the Council of the People's Commissars of the Union.

No such cases, however, shall be tried by the Supreme Court of the Union, except upon a motion in each case made by the Central Executive Committee of the Union or the Presidium thereof.

ARTICLE EIGHT

THE PEOPLE'S COMMISSARIATS OF THE UNION OF SOVIET SOCIALIST REPUBLICS

49. There shall be formed in accordance with Section [paragraph] 37 of the within Constitution, ten People's Commissariats which shall conduct the branches of the state administration reserved to them herein. The regulations regarding the functions of the said People's Commissariats shall be made by the Central Executive Committee of the Union of Soviet Socialist Republics.

50. The People's Commissariats of the Union shall be divided into:

(a) People's Commissariats (Federal) for the entire Union of Soviet Socialist Republics, and

(b) Joint (Mixed) People's Commissariats of the Union of Soviet Socialist Republics.

51. The People's Commissariats (Federal) for the Union of Soviet Socialist Republics shall be the following: Foreign Affairs; Army and Navy; Foreign Trade; Transport; Posts and Telegraphs.

52. The Joint (Mixed) People's Commissariats of the Union of Soviet Socialist Republics shall be the following: Supreme Council of National Economy; Food; Labor; Finances; Workers' and Peasants' Inspection.

53. The People's Commissariats of the Union of Soviet Socialist Republics (Federal), shall have their representatives in the constituent Republics, who shall be directly subordinated to them.

54. The Joint (Mixed) People's Commissariats of the Union of Soviet Socialist Republics shall exercise their functions through the department of the corresponding commissariats of the several constituent Republics on the territory of the aforesaid Republics.

55. Each member of the Council of People's Commissars shall constitute the head of his respective department within the Commissariats of the Union of Soviet Socialist Republics.

56. Within each People's Commissariat, a board (collegium) shall be created which shall be presided over by the People's Commissar. The said board shall be appointed by the Council of People's Commissars of the Union.

57. The People's Commissar shall have the right independently to decide all questions within the scope of his authority, provided, however, that he informs the board (collegium) of his decision.

In the event that the board, or any member thereof, disagrees with the decision of the People's Commissar, a protest may be filed by him or them with the Council of People's Commissars. Such protest, however, shall in no way affect or suspend the execution of the decision in dispute.

58. Any decree issued by an individual commissariat of the Union of Soviet Socialist Republics may be annulled by the Central Executive Committee of the Union or by the Council of People's Commissars of the Union of Soviet Socialist Republics.

59. The decisions of the People's Commissariats of the Union of Soviet Socialist Republics may be suspended by the central executive committees or the presidia of the central executive committees of the different Republics, whenever such decisions are in manifest conflict with the Constitution of the Union, with Federal legislation or with the legislation of the respective Republics. Upon such suspension a notification thereof shall immediately be made by the Central Executive Committee to the Council of People's Commissars of the Union of Soviet Socialist Republics and to the Union Commissariat concerned.

60. The People's Commissars of the Union of Soviet Socialist Republics shall be responsible to the Council of People's Commissars, to the Central Executive Committee of the Union of Soviet Socialist Republics and the Presidium thereof.

ARTICLE NINE
THE STATE POLITICAL DEPARTMENT OF THE UNION

61. In order to unite the efforts of the constituent Republics in their struggle against the political and economic counter-revolution and against espionage and brigandage, there shall be created a joint State Political Department attached to the Council of People's Commissars of the Union, the chairman of this department entering the Council of People's Commissars of the Union with the right of advisory vote.

62. The State Political Department of the Union shall direct the activities of the local branches of the State Political Department through its representatives in the Councils of the People's Commissariats of the constituent Republics, acting in accordance with special rules and regulations duly ratified.

63. The control of the legality of the acts of the State Political Department of the Union shall be exercised by the Attorney General of the Union in accordance with a special decree made by the Central Executive Committee of the Union of Soviet Socialist Republics.

ARTICLE TEN
THE CONSTITUENT REPUBLICS

64. Within the territory of each constituent Republic the supreme organ of governmental authority shall be the soviet congress of the Republic, and during the intervals between congresses, its central executive committee.

65.   The interrelations between the supreme organs of governmental authority of the several constituent Republics and the supreme organs of the Federal Government are defined in the within Constitution.

66.   The central executive committees of the several constituent Republics shall elect from among their number their presidia, which during the intervals between the central executive committee sessions shall constitute the supreme organs of governmental authority.

67.   The central executive committees of the constituent Republics shall establish their own respective executive organs which shall be the Councils of People's Commissars, consisting of the following: Chairman of the Council of People's Commissars, Vice-Chairman, Chairman of the Supreme Council of National Economy, People's Commissar for Agriculture, People's Commissar for Finance, People's Commissar for Food, People's Commissar for Labor, People's Commissar for Internal Affairs, People's Commissar for Justice; People's Commissar for Workers' and Peasants' Inspection, People's Commissar for Education, People's Commissar for Health, People's Commissar for Social Welfare; and also, with an advisory or deciding vote, according to the decisions of the respective central executive committees of the several Republics, the representatives of the People's Commissariats of Foreign Affairs, Army and Navy, Foreign Trade, Transport, and of Posts and Telegraphs.

68.   The Supreme Council of National Economy and the People's Commissariat for Food, Finance, Labor, [or] Workers' and Peasants' Inspection of each constituent Republic, while subordinate to its respective central executive committee and Council of People's Commissariats of [its] constituent Republic, shall at the same time carry out decrees of the corresponding People's Commissariat (Federal).

69.   The right of amnesty, as well as the right of pardon and restoration of citizenship of citizens condemned by the judicial or administrative organs of the constituent Republics, shall be the prerogative of the central executive committees of these Republics.

ARTICLE ELEVEN

THE ARMS, THE FLAG AND THE CAPITAL OF THE UNION OF SOVIET SOCIALIST REPUBLICS

70.   The insignia of the Union of the Soviet Socialist Republics shall consist of a sickle and hammer mounted upon a terrestrial globe surrounded by sheaves of grain, bearing the inscription, in the six languages mentioned in Section [paragraph] 34, 'Proletarians of all countries, unite!' The upper portion of the insignia shall be surmounted by a five-pointed star.

71.   The flag of state of the Union of Soviet Socialist Republics shall be made of red or scarlet cloth and shall bear the insignia of the Union thereon.

72.   The capital city of the Union of Soviet Socialist Republics shall be the city of Moscow.

1.2.1 AMENDMENTS TO THE USSR CONSTITUTION OF 1924[1]

3.   The sovereignty of the Union Republics shall be restricted only to the extent set forth in the present Constitution, which restrictions shall be confined to the subject matters delegated to the jurisdiction of the Union. Except as so restricted, every Union Republic shall enjoy the rights of an independent state. The Union of the Soviet Socialist Republics shall protect the sovereign rights of the Union Republics.

10.   The delegates to the Congress of Soviets of the Union of Soviet Socialist Republics shall be elected as follows:

(a) Directly at the congresses of soviets of the Union Republics, which are not divided into krais or oblasts;

(b) At the krai or oblast congresses of soviets in those Union Republics which are divided into krais or oblasts;

(c) At the congresses of soviets of the Soviet Socialist Republics of Azerbaijan, Georgia, and Armenia and at the congresses of soviets of the Autonomous Republics and oblasts, both those which form and those which do not form part of the krai or oblast federations.

11.   The regular congresses of the soviets of the Union of Soviet Socialist Republics shall be convened by the Central Executive Committee of the Union of Soviet Socialist Republics once every two years; special congresses shall be convened by the Central Executive Committee of the Union of Soviet Socialist Republics on its own resolution to do so or at the demand of the Union Council, of the Council of Nationalities or of the Union Republics.

14.   The Congress of Soviets of the Union of Soviet Socialist Republics shall elect a Union Council to consist of representatives of the Union Republics in proportion to the population of each of them and in such number as shall be determined by the Congress of Soviets of the Union of Soviet Socialist Republics.

15.   No NOTE.

21.   The regular sessions of the Central Executive Committee of the Union of the Soviet Socialist Republics shall be called by the Presidium of the Central Executive Committee at least three times during the interval between two regular Congresses of Soviets of the Union of Soviet Socialist Republics.

Special sessions shall be called by decision of the presidium of the Central Executive Committee of the Union of Soviet Socialist Republics, at the demand of the Presidium of the Union Council or of the Presidium of the Council of Nationalities, or at the demand of the central executive committee of one of the Union Republics.

23.   If the Union Council of Nationalities shall fail to agree on any question, the question shall be referred to a conciliation committee to be appointed by them.

---

[1] Excerpted from *The Fundamental Law (Constitution) of the USSR* (Moscow: Co-Operative Publishing Society of Foreign Workers in the USSR, 1932).

26.   During the intervals between the sessions of the Central Executive Committee of the Union of Soviet Socialist Republics [supreme authority is vested in its Presidium], which shall be formed by the Central Executive Committee and shall consist of twenty-seven members, which number shall include all the members of the Presidiums of both the Union Council and the Council of Nationalities.

A joint meeting of the Union Council and of the Council of Nationalities shall be held for the purpose of forming the Presidium of the Central Executive Committee and of the Council of People's Commissars by Articles [paragraphs] 26 and 37 of the present Constitution. The Union Council and the Council of Nationalities shall vote separately at the joint meeting of the Union Council and of the Council of Nationalities.

27.   The Central Executive Committee shall elect as many chairmen of the Central Executive Committee of the Union of Soviet Socialist Republics as there are Union Republics from among the members of the Presidium of the Central Executive Committee of the Union of Soviet Socialist Republics.

37.   The executive and administrative organs of the Central Executive Committee of the Union of Soviet Socialist Republics shall be the Council of People's Commissars of the Union of Soviet Socialist Republics, which shall be formed by the Central Executive Committee of the Union of Soviet Socialist Republics and shall consist of the following members:

The President of the Council of People's Commissars of the Union of Soviet Socialist Republics and of the Council of Labor and Defense; the vice-presidents; the President of the State Planning Commission; the People's Commissar of Foreign Affairs; the People's Commissar of the Army and Navy; the People's Commissar of Foreign Trade; the People's Commissar of Ways and Communication; the People's Commissar of Water Transport; the People's Commissar of Posts and Telegraphs; the People's Commissar of the Workers' and Peasants' Inspection; the President of the Supreme Council of National Economy; the People's Commissar of Agriculture; the People's Commissar of Labor; the People's Commissar of Supplies; the People's Commissar of Finance.

49.   The twelve People's Commissariats indicated in Article [paragraph] 37 of the present Constitution shall be established for the purpose of giving direct guidance to the separate branches of the State administration which are under the jurisdiction of the Council of People's Commissars of the Union of Soviet Socialist Republics. These People's Commissariats shall function in accordance with the provisions of the statute concerning the People's Commissariats, approved by the Central Executive Committee of the Union of the Soviet Socialist Republics.

51.   The following shall be the All-Union People's Commissariats of the Union of the Soviet Socialist Republics:

The Commissariats of Foreign Affairs, of the Army and Navy, of Foreign Trade, of Ways and Communications, of Water Transport, and of Posts and Telegraphs.

52.   The following shall be the Federated People's Commissariats of the Union of the Soviet Socialist Republics:

The Supreme Council of National Economy; the People's Commissariats of Agriculture, of Labor, of Supplies, of Finance, and of the Workers' and Peasants' Inspection.

58. Any order of the respective People's Commissariats of the Union of Soviet Socialist Republics may be annulled by the Presidium of the Central Executive Committee or by the Council of People's Commissars of the Union of Soviet Socialist Republics.

59. Any order of the respective People's Commissariats of the Union of Soviet Socialist Republics may be suspended by the respective central executive committee or the respective presidium of such central executive committee of the Union Republics if such order is palpably in violation of the Union Constitution or of the laws of the Union or of the laws of the Union Republics. The central executive committees, or the presidiums of the central executive committees of the Union Republics, as the case may be, shall immediately inform the Council of People's Commissars of the Union of Soviet Socialist Republics and the corresponding People's Commissar of the Union of Soviet Socialist Republics of the suspension of such order.

62. The United State Political Department of the Union of the Soviet Socialist Republics shall direct the work of the local authorities of the State Political Department (S.P.U.) through its plenipotentiary representative attached to the Councils of the People's Commissars of the Union Republics, which shall function in accordance with the provisions of a special statute duly enacted and approved.

65. The mutual relations between the supreme authorities of the Union Republics and the supreme authorities of the Union of Soviet Socialist Republics shall be defined in the present Constitution.

67. The central executive committees of the Union Republics shall form Councils of People's Commissars which shall be their executive organs and shall each consist of the following members:

The President of the Council of People's Commissars, the Vice-President, the President of the State Planning Commission, the President of the Supreme Council of National Economy, the People's Commissar of Agriculture, the People's Commissar of Finance, the People's Commissar of Supplies, the People's Commissar of Labor, the People's Commissar of Justice, the People's Commissar of Education, the People's Commissar of Public Health, the People's Commissar of Social Maintenance; and also the following members who shall have a consultative or a full vote, as the central executive committees of the Union Republics may decide:

The plenipotentiary representatives of the People's Commissariats of the Union of Soviet Socialist Republics of Foreign Affairs, of the Army and Navy, of Foreign Trade, of Ways and Communications, [of] Water Transport, of Posts and Telegraphs.

68. The supreme councils of National Economy, the People's Commissariats of Agriculture, of Supplies, of Finance, of Labor and of the Workers' and Peasants' Inspection of the Union Republics shall be subordinate to the central executive committees and the Councils of People's Commissars of the Union Republics in every respect and shall carry out the directives of the respective People's Commissariats of the Union of Soviet Socialist Republics in their activities.

71.   The state flag of the Union of Soviet Socialist Republics shall consist of a field of red or crimson with the image of a golden sickle and hammer in the upper corner near the staff and above them the image of a red five-pointed star bordered with gold edging; the proportion of the length to the width shall be two to one.

1.2.2   AMENDMENTS AND ADDENDA TO THE USSR CONSTITUTION OF 1924[1]

By 1924 the territory of Soviet Central Asia included the Turkestan Autonomous S.S.R. (which entered the R.S.F.S.R.) and the independent Soviet people's republics of Bukhara and Khorezm (the latter were turned into socialist republics). The boundaries of these republics did not correspond to the boundaries of the territories inhabited by Kazakhs, Tajiks, Turkmens, Uzbeks, Kara-Kalpaks and Kirghiz. It was necessary to put an end to this incongruity through the national and state delimitation of Central Asia. This was done in 1924 and 1925 on the basis of the decision of the Central Committee of the Russian Communist Party (Bolsheviks) 'Concerning National and State Delimitation' adopted in June 1924, and in accordance with the expressed will of the peoples of Central Asia.

In September 1924 the highest organs of state power of the Turkestan Autonomous S.S.R. and the Republics of Bukhara and Khorezm passed a decision concerning the delimitation of these republics on the national principle.

On December 5, 1924,[2] the Revolutionary Committee of Uzbekistan issued an appeal to the Uzbek people. In February 1925 the First All-Bukhara Congress of Soviets of Workers', Dehkans' (Peasants') and Red Army men's deputies adopted a declaration on the formation of the Uzbek S.S.R. and on its voluntary entry into the U.S.S.R. as an equal Union Republic.

In October 1924, the Turkmen S.S.R. was formed; it included the former Turkestan Autonomous S.S.R. and parts of the Bukhara and Khorezm republics. In 1925 the Uzbek and Turkmen republics were admitted to the U.S.S.R. as equal Union Republics. Later, in 1929, the Tajik S.S.R. entered the Soviet Union.[3] Thus, as a result of the national delimitation of Central Asia, the number of Union Republics increased from four to seven. This found reflection in the Constitution of the U.S.S.R.

A number of autonomous republics and autonomous regions (the Adygei, Jewish, Oirot and others) were formed within the R.S.F.S.R. after 1920. Also a new form of state organization of small nationalities was created, namely, National Areas, whose number reached ten by the end of 1936. Autonomous republics were also formed in Transcaucasia (the Abkhazian, Ajarian and Nakhichevan republics)

---

[1] Excerpted from A. Denisov and M. Kirichenko, *Soviet State Law* (Moscow: Foreign Languages Publishing House, 1960), pp. 83–91.

[2] This date is considered [to be] the date of the formation of the Uzbek Soviet Socialist Republic, which included the Tashkent, Samarkand, Ferghana, Kashka-Darya, Zeravshan, Surkhan-Darya and Khorezm regions, as well as the Tajik Autonomous S.S.R. (the latter was formed on October 27, 1924). The aforementioned regions and the Tajik A.S.S.R. included territories which formerly belonged to the Turkestan, Bukhara and Khorezm republics.

[3] On December 5, 1929, the Tajik Republic was turned from an autonomous into a sovereign republic. The Central Executive Committee of the Uzbek S.S.R. sanctioned the secession of Tajikistan from the Uzbek S.S.R.

and in the Ukrainian S.S.R. (the Moldavian Republic). The total number of autonomous republics within the U.S.S.R. reached 22 by the end of 1936. This necessitated corresponding amendments in the Constitution of the U.S.S.R. and in the constitutions of the Union Republics.

Amendments were also introduced into the aforementioned constitutions with a view to specifying the jurisdiction of the U.S.S.R. and of the Union Republics. For example, according to Article 1 of the Constitution of the U.S.S.R., the jurisdiction of the Soviet Union in the field of criminal legislation was originally confined to the basic principles of such legislation. Practice, however, showed that it was expedient to extend the powers of the U.S.S.R. in the sphere of combating criminal offenses. Accordingly, on October 29, 1924, the Presidium of the Central Executive Committee of the U.S.S.R. was empowered—in conformity with the Basic Principles of Criminal Legislation—to specify those types and categories of offenses which required a common punitive policy on the part of all the Union Republics. In this connection special all-Union legislative acts, such as 'Ordinance on State Offenses' and 'Ordinance on Military Offenses' were issued in 1927.

In civil legislation, too, it was found expedient to extend the powers of the U.S.S.R. until then confined to the determination of the basic principles of civil legislation. A number of all-Union legislative acts concerning copyright, housing relationships, insurance, negotiable instrument law, etc., were therefore passed at different periods.

The jurisdiction of the U.S.S.R. in the field of labor legislation was also extended (along with general legislative acts relating to labor, a number of other special all-Union laws were issued—for example, 'Temporary Rules for the Use of Auxiliary Hired Labor in Farm Households').

According to the Constitution, the jurisdiction of the U.S.S.R. embraced approval of the state budget of the U.S.S.R. (which covered the budgets of the Union Republics); determination of all-Union taxes and revenues, as well as various deductions from them and additions to them which went to make up the budgets of the Union Republics, authorization of additional taxes and dues which were likewise designed for the republican budgets. The general principles of the Constitution of the U.S.S.R. relating to this branch of state administration were further developed in the 'Ordinance on the Budgetary Rights of the U.S.S.R. and of the Union Republics,' which was adopted on October 29, 1924. In particular, a single budgetary system was established (under this system the revenues and expenditures of the U.S.S.R. and of all the Union and Autonomous Republics were united within a single budget). According to the 'Ordinance on Local Budgets' approved in April 1926, the local finances were also included into the single financial system of the U.S.S.R. Since then the budget of the U.S.S.R., which includes the republican and local budgets, has been approved by the highest organ of state power of the Soviet Union.

The task of building socialism, and particularly of industrializing the country and collectivizing agriculture, necessitated a partial reorganization of the system of state administration (extension and greater specialization in the management of industry, agriculture, trade, municipal economy, etc.). It also necessitated a new administrative-territorial division of the country.

With every passing year the old People's Commissariats were being divided up and new ones were being created. In May 1924, the People's Commissariat of Food Supply, which had played a signal part in the implementation of the Soviet Government's food policy, was abolished. At the same time the Commission for Internal Trade set up in July 1923 under the Council of Labor and Defense, was reorganized into the People's Commissariat of Internal Trade.

In November 1925, the People's Commissariat of Foreign Trade of the U.S.S.R. and the People's Commissariat of Internal Trade of the U.S.S.R. merged into a single People's Commissariat of Foreign and Internal Trade of the U.S.S.R. In November 1930, this Commissariat was again divided into two independent Commissariats—of Supply and of Foreign Trade; this was due to the considerably increased volume of the country's foreign trade and the steady extension of planned supply.

The republican People's Commissariats of Agriculture were reorganized into Union-republican Commissariats; the following factors conditioned this reorganization: steady growth of collective and state farms, a higher level of organization of agricultural production, ever-increasing requirements of Soviet industry in raw materials and food supplies as a result of the rapid rate of industrialization, the growing role of industry in the reorganization of agriculture, etc.

The municipal economy acquired particular importance in the socialist reconstruction of the entire national economy; it called for planned guidance and strict coordination both with the development of the local economy, and with the rate of industrialization of the country as a whole. The People's Commissariats of Internal Affairs of the Union and Autonomous Republics, which were responsible for the municipal economy of the republics, the militia, criminal investigation departments, prisons, etc., could no longer cope with their tasks and were therefore abolished in December 1930. Their functions passed to a number of other departments.[4]

At the end of January 1931, the People's Commissariat of Inland Water Transport of the U.S.S.R. was set up.

In August 1931, the Chief Departments of Municipal Economy of the Union Republics were replaced by Commissariats of Municipal Economy; the latter were also set up in the Autonomous Republics. An All-Union Council of Municipal Economy was formed under the Central Executive Committee of the U.S.S.R.; it was empowered to direct and supervise the municipal economy of the U.S.S.R. as a whole.[5]

In January 1932, the All-Union Council of National Economy (in charge of both all-Union and local industry) was reorganized. Two new all-Union commissariats were formed—the Commissariat of the Forestry and Timber Industry and

---

[4] The management of the municipal economy passed to special Departments of Municipal Economy set up under the Councils of People's Commissariats of the Union Republics; the management of the militia and of the organs of criminal investigation was accordingly entrusted to the Chief Departments of the Militia and Criminal Investigation under the Councils of People's Commissariats of the Union Republics; the general guidance of the correctional labor policy, implementation of correctional labor legislation, organization and management of prisons, etc., passed to the People's Commissariats of Justice.

[5] This Council existed up to August 10, 1937.

the Commissariat of Light Industry.[6] The Council of National Economy itself was reorganized into the All-Union People's Commissariat of Heavy Industry.[7] At the same time the People's Commissariat of Posts and Telegraphs was renamed the People's Commissariat of Communications.

In October 1932, the All-Union People's Commissariat of Grain-Growing and Cattle-Breeding State Farms was formed.

In response to numerous proposals made by trade-union organizations and for the purpose of ensuring the more efficient fulfillment of the duties vested in the People's Commissariat of Labor, the Central Executive Committee and the Council of People's Commissars of the U.S.S.R. passed a decision on June 23, 1933, to amalgamate this commissariat with the apparatus of the All-Union Central Council of Trade Unions and to charge the latter with the duties previously performed by the Commissariat of Labor and by its organs.

In June 1934, the People's Commissariat of the Army and Navy was renamed the People's Commissariat of Defense.

In July of the same year, the People's Commissariat of Supply was divided into two Commissariats—of the Food Industry and Internal Trade.

In August 1934, the republican People's Commissariat of Local Industry was set up. The purpose of the Commissariat was to develop local industry and its production of articles of mass consumption, and to ensure that it was supplied with the necessary raw materials and funds.

The apparatus of Workers' and Peasants' Inspection was reorganized, the Soviet Government passing from the method of inspection to the method of verifying fulfillment of decisions passed by the central state bodies. This measure was necessitated by the fact that economic activity in the country was steadily growing and becoming more and more manifold. Inspection from a single center, i.e., from the People's Commissariat of Workers' and Peasants' Inspection, was no longer adequate. In accordance with this, the seventeenth congress of the Party adopted a decision on the expediency of abolishing the aforementioned commissariat. On the basis of this decision the Central Executive Committee and the Council of People's Commissars of the U.S.S.R. on February 11, 1934, issued a decree which liquidated the system of workers' and peasants' inspection and reorganized the Commission of Fulfillment[8] into the Commission of Soviet Control under the Council of People's Commissars of the U.S.S.R.; the whole apparatus of the former People's Commissariat of Workers' and Peasants' Inspection was transferred to this commission.

On July 10, 1934, the People's Commissariat of Internal Affairs was created. It was entrusted with the duties of safeguarding revolutionary order and state security, protecting the state frontiers, and managing the civil registrar's office.

The local apparatus directing the various branches of state administration also underwent corresponding changes; the reasons, in the main, were the same [as those]

---

[6] Later the Commissariat of Light Industry was divided into the Commissariats of Food Industry, Fish Industry, Textile Industry, and others.

[7] Later it was divided into a number of Commissariats: of the Defense Industry, Iron and Steel Industry, Non-Ferrous Industry, Chemical Industry, Aircraft Industry and others.

[8] This commission was set up by the Central Executive Committee and the Council of People's Commissars of the U.S.S.R. on December 24, 1930.

which necessitated the reorganization of the central state administrative organs; another reason was the new administrative-territorial division of the country.

Of great importance was the extension of the functions of the Supreme Court of the U.S.S.R. in the system of the Soviet state organs. The Supreme Court of the U.S.S.R. was empowered to supervise the constitutionality of all acts issued by the central institutions and People's Commissariats of the U.S.S.R. It was also authorized to submit (at the request of the Central Executive Committee of the U.S.S.R.) its conclusions concerning the validity of decisions passed by the organs of state power and state administration of the Union Republics.

The period of the operation of the first Constitution of the U.S.S.R. saw the complete reorganization of the administrative-territorial division of the country. Actually this was a new administrative-territorial division based on socialist principles (with due regard for the economic potentialities and requirements of different parts of the country, as well as the national composition and mode of life of the population). As a result of the economic division and national delimitation of the country, the old volosts, uyezds and gubernias were abolished, and districts, areas[9] and regions (or territories) were set up in their place. The material basis of the new administrative-territorial formations was appreciably extended.

Thus, in the period from 1924 to 1936 a number of amendments and addenda were introduced into the Constitution of the U.S.S.R. and the constitutions of the Union Republics. They reflected, firstly, the development of the national and state organization of the U.S.S.R. (admission of new republics into the U.S.S.R., delimitation between the jurisdiction of the U.S.S.R. and that of the Union Republics, formation of Autonomous Republics, Regions and National Areas); secondly, the radical changes carried out in the administrative-territorial division of the republics; thirdly, the reorganization of the organs of state administration (structural and functional changes). All these amendments and addenda, however, did not affect the fundamental principles of the Soviet Constitution.

---

[9] Later, the administrative areas were abolished and the districts were considerably enlarged. This contributed to closer contacts between the Soviet state apparatus and the countryside, the collective and state farms, the broad masses of the people.

1. 3

CONSTITUTION (FUNDAMENTAL LAW) OF THE UNION OF SOVIET SOCIALIST REPUBLICS[1]

Adopted at the Extraordinary Eighth Congress of the
Soviets of the USSR

December 5, 1936

CHAPTER I

THE ORGANIZATION OF SOCIETY

ARTICLE 1. The Union of Soviet Socialist Republics is a socialist state of workers and peasants.

ARTICLE 2. The political foundation of the U.S.S.R. is the Soviets of Toilers' Deputies, which developed and grew strong as a result of the overthrow of the power of the landlords and capitalists and the winning of the dictatorship of the proletariat.

ARTICLE 3. All power in the U.S.S.R. belongs to the toilers of town and country as represented by the Soviets of Toilers' Deputies.

ARTICLE 4. The economic foundation of the U.S.S.R. is the socialist system of economy and the socialist ownership of the implements and means of production firmly established as a result of the liquidation of the capitalist system of economy, the abolition of private property in the implements and means of production, and the abolition of exploitation of man by man.

ARTICLE 5. Socialist property in the U.S.S.R. bears either the form of state property (property of the whole people) or the form of cooperative and collective farm (kolkhoz) property (property of individual collective farms and property of cooperative associations).

ARTICLE 6. The land, mineral deposits, waters, forests, mills, factories, mines, railways, water and air transport, banks, means of communication, large state-organized agricultural enterprises such as state farms (sovkhoz), machine and tractor stations and the like, as well as municipal enterprises and the principal

---

[1] Reprinted from *Constitution (Fundamental Law) of the Union of Soviet Socialist Republics* (New York: International Publishers, 1936).

dwelling house properties in the cities and industrial localities, are state property, that is, the property of the whole people.

ARTICLE 7. Public enterprises in collective farms and cooperative organizations, with their livestock and implements, products raised or manufactured by the collective farms and cooperative organizations, as well as their public structures, constitute the public, socialist property of the collective farms and cooperative organizations.

Every collective farm household, in addition to its basic income from the public collective farm enterprise, has for its own use a plot of land attached to the house and, as personal property, an auxiliary establishment on the plot, a house, produce animals and poultry, and minor agricultural implements—in accordance with the statutes of the agricultural artel.

ARTICLE 8. The land occupied by collective farms is secured to them for their free use for an unlimited time, that is, forever.

ARTICLE 9. Alongside the socialist system of economy, which is the predominant form of economy in the U.S.S.R., the law permits small private economy of individual peasants and handicraftsmen based on their personal labor and precluding the exploitation of the labor of others.

ARTICLE 10. The right of personal property of citizens in their income from work and in their savings, in their dwelling houses and auxiliary household economy, their domestic furniture and utensils and objects of personal use and comfort, as well as the right of inheritance of personal property of citizens, are protected by law.

ARTICLE 11. The economic life of the U.S.S.R. is determined and directed by the state plan of national economy for the purpose of increasing the public wealth, of steadily raising the material and cultural level of the toilers, and of strengthening the independence of the U.S.S.R. and its power of defense.

ARTICLE 12. In the U.S.S.R. work is the obligation and honorable duty of every able-bodied citizen, in accordance with the principle: 'He who does not work, neither shall he eat.'

In the U.S.S.R. the principle of socialism is realized: 'From each according to his ability, to each according to the work performed.'

CHAPTER II

THE ORGANIZATION OF THE STATE

ARTICLE 13. The Union of Soviet Socialist Republics is a federated state, formed on the basis of the voluntary association of the followng Soviet Socialist Republics possessing equal rights:

The Russian Soviet Federative Socialist Republic

The Ukrainian Soviet Socialist Republic

The Byelorussian Soviet Socialist Republic

The Azerbaijan Soviet Socialist Republic

The Georgian Soviet Socialist Republic

The Armenian Soviet Socialist Republic

The Turkmen Soviet Socialist Republic

The Uzbek Soviet Socialist Republic

The Tadjik Soviet Socialist Republic

The Kazakh Soviet Socialist Republic

The Kirghiz Soviet Socialist Republic.

ARTICLE 14. The jurisdiction of the Union of Soviet Socialist Republics, as represented by its highest organs of power and organs of state administration, covers:

(a) Representation of the Union in international relations, conclusion and ratification of treaties with other states;

(b) Question of war and peace;

(c) Admission of new republics into the U.S.S.R.;

(d) Supervision over the observance of the Constitution of the U.S.S.R. and ensuring that the Constitutions of the Union Republics conform with the Constitution of the U.S.S.R.;

(e) Ratification of alterations of boundaries between Union Republics;

(f) Ratification of the formation of new Territories and Regions and also of new Autonomous Republics within the Union Republics;

(g) Organization of the defense of the U.S.S.R. and the direction of all the armed forces of the U.S.S.R.;

(h) Foreign trade on the basis of state monopoly;

(i) Safeguarding the security of the state;

(j) Determining the plans of national economy of the U.S.S.R.;

(k) Approbation of the unified state budget of the U.S.S.R. as well as of the taxes and revenues which go to form the Union, Republican and local budgets;

(l) Administration of the banks, industrial and agricultural establishments and enterprises and trading enterprises of all-Union importance;

(m) Administration of transport and communications;

(n) Direction of the monetary and credit system;

(o) Organization of state insurance;

(p) Contracting and granting loans;

(q) Determining the basic principles of land tenure and tenure of mineral deposits, forests and waters;

(r) Determining the basic principles in the spheres of education and public health;

(s) Organization of a uniform system of national economic accounting;

(t) Determining the principles of labor legislation;

(u) Legislation governing the judicial system and judicial procedure, [and] criminal and civil codes;

(v) Laws governing citizenship of the Union; laws governing the rights of foreigners;

(w) Passing of amnesty acts for the entire Union.

ARTICLE 15. The sovereignty of the Union Republics is restricted only within the limits set forth in Article 14 of the Constitution of the U.S.S.R. Outside of these limits, each Union Republic exercises state power independently. The U.S.S.R. protects the sovereign rights of the Union Republics.

ARTICLE 16. Each Union Republic has its own Constitution which takes into account the specific features of the Republic and is drawn up in full conformity with the Constitution of the U.S.S.R.

ARTICLE 17. To every Union Republic is reserved the right freely to secede from the U.S.S.R.

ARTICLE 18. The territory of the Union Republics may not be altered without their consent.

ARTICLE 19. The laws of the U.S.S.R. have equal force in the territory of all Union Republics.

ARTICLE 20. In the event of a discrepancy between a law of a Union Republic and the law of the Union, the all-Union law prevails.

ARTICLE 21. Single Union citizenship is established for all citizens of the U.S.S.R. Every citizen of a Union Republic is a citizen of the U.S.S.R.

ARTICLE 22. The Russian Soviet Federative Socialist Republic consists of the Azov-Black Sea, Far Eastern, West Siberian, Krassnoyarsk and North Caucasian Territories; the Voronezh, East Siberian, Gorky, Western, Ivanevo, Kalinin, Kirov, Kuibyshev, Kursk, Leningrad, Moscow, Omsk, Orenburg, Saratov, Sverdlovsk, Northern, Stalingrad, Chelyabinsk and Yaroslav Regions; the Tatar, Bashkir, Daghestan, Buryat-Mongolian, Kabardino-Balkarian, Kalmyk, Karelian, Komi, Crimean, Mari, Mordovian, Volga German, North Ossetian, Udmurt, Chechen-Ingush, Chuvash and Yakut Autonomous Soviet Socialist Republics; the Adygei, Jewish, Karachai, Oirot, Khahass and Cherkess Autonomous Regions.

ARTICLE 23. The Ukrainian Soviet Socialist Republic consists of the Vinnitsa, Dniepropetrovsk, Donetz, Kiev, Odessa, Kharkov and Chernigov Regions and the Moldavian Autonomous Soviet Socialist Republic.

ARTICLE 24. The Azerbaidjan Soviet Socialist Republic includes the Nakhichevan Autonomous Soviet Socialist Republic and the Nagorno-Karabakh Autonomous Region.

ARTICLE 25. The Georgian Soviet Socialist Republic includes the Abkhazian Autonomous Soviet Socialist Republic, the Adjar Autonomous Soviet Socialist Republic and the South Ossetian Autonomous Region.

ARTICLE 26. The Uzbek Soviet Socialist Republic includes the Kara-Kalpak Autonomous Soviet Socialist Republic.

ARTICLE 27. The Tadjik Soviet Socialist Republic includes the Gorno-Badakhshan Autonomous Region.

ARTICLE 28. The Kazakh Soviet Socialist Republic consists of the Aktyubinsk, Alma-Ata, East Kazakhstan, West Kazakhstan, Karaganda, Kustanai, North Kazakhstan and South Kazakhstan Regions.

ARTICLE 29. The Armenian Soviet Socialist Republic, the Byelorussian Soviet Socialist Republic, the Turkmen Soviet Socialist Republic and the Kirghiz Soviet Socialist Republic contain no Autonomous Republics or Territories and Regions.

CHAPTER III

THE HIGHEST ORGANS OF STATE POWER OF THE UNION OF SOVIET SOCIALIST REPUBLICS

ARTICLE 30. The highest organ of state power of the U.S.S.R. is the Supreme Soviet of the U.S.S.R.

ARTICLE 31. The Supreme Soviet of the U.S.S.R. exercises all rights vested in the Union of Soviet Socialist Republics in accordance with Article 14 of the Constitution, insofar as, by virtue of the Constitution, they do not come within the jurisdiction of organs of the U.S.S.R. which are accountable to the Supreme Soviet of the U.S.S.R., i.e., the Presidium of the Supreme Soviet of the U.S.S.R., the Council of People's Commissars of the U.S.S.R. and the People's Commissariats of the U.S.S.R.

ARTICLE 32. The legislative power of the U.S.S.R. is exercised exclusively by the Supreme Soviet of the U.S.S.R.

ARTICLE 33. The Supreme Soviet of the U.S.S.R. consists of two Chambers: the Soviet of the Union and the Soviet of Nationalities.

ARTICLE 34. The Soviet of the Union is elected by the citizens of the U.S.S.R. according to electoral areas on the basis of one deputy for every 300,000 of the population.

ARTICLE 35. The Soviet of Nationalities is elected by the citizens of the U.S.S.R. according to Union and Autonomous Republics, Autonomous Regions and national areas on the basis of twenty-five deputies from each Union Republic, eleven deputies from each Autonomous Republic, five deputies from each Autonomous Region and one deputy from each national area.

ARTICLE 36. The Supreme Soviet of the U.S.S.R. is elected for a term of four years.

ARTICLE 37. The two Chambers of the Supreme Soviet of the U.S.S.R., the Soviet of the Union and the Soviet of Nationalities, have equal rights.

Article 38. The Soviet of the Union and the Soviet of Nationalities enjoy equal right to initiate legislation.

Article 39. A law is considered adopted if passed by both Chambers of the Supreme Soviet of the U.S.S.R., by a simple majority in each.

Article 40. Laws adopted by the Supreme Soviet of the U.S.S.R. are published in the languages of the Union Republics over the signatures of the Chairman and Secretary of the Presidium of the Supreme Soviet of the U.S.S.R.

Article 41. Sessions of the Soviet of the Union and the Soviet of Nationalities begin and terminate simultaneously.

Article 42. The Soviet of the Union elects a Chairman of the Soviet of the Union and two Vice-Chairmen.

Article 43. The Soviet of Nationalities elects a Chairman of the Soviet of Nationalities and two Vice-Chairmen.

Article 44. The Chairmen of the Soviet of the Union and of the Soviet of Nationalities preside over the meetings of the respective Chambers and are in charge of the procedure of these bodies.

Article 45. Joint sessions of both Chambers of the Supreme Soviet of the U.S.S.R. are presided over alternately by the Chairman of the Soviet of the Union and the Chairman of the Soviet of Nationalities.

Article 46. Sessions of the Supreme Soviet of the U.S.S.R. are convened by the Presidium of the Supreme Soviet of the U.S.S.R. twice a year.

Extraordinary sessions are convened by the Presidium of the Supreme Soviet of the U.S.S.R. at its discretion or on the demand of one of the Union Republics.

Article 47. In the event of disagreement between the Soviet of the Union and the Soviet of Nationalities the question is referred for settlement to a conciliation commission established on a parity basis. If the conciliation commission fails to arrive at an agreed decision, or if its decision fails to satisfy one of the Chambers, the question is considered for a second time by the Chambers. Failing an agreed decision of the two Chambers, the Presidium of the Supreme Soviet of the U.S.S.R. dissolves the Supreme Soviet of the U.S.S.R. and appoints new elections.

Article 48. The Supreme Soviet of the U.S.S.R. at a joint sitting of both Chambers elects the Presidium of the Supreme Soviet of the U.S.S.R., consisting of the Chairman of the Presidium of the Supreme Soviet of the U.S.S.R., eleven Vice-Chairmen, the Secretary of the Presidium and twenty-four members of the Presidium.

The Presidium of the Supreme Soviet of the U.S.S.R. is accountable to the Supreme Soviet of the U.S.S.R. for all its activities.

Article 49. The Presidium of the Supreme Soviet of the U.S.S.R.

(a) Convenes the sessions of the Supreme Soviet of the U.S.S.R.;

(b) Interprets existing laws of the U.S.S.R., promulgates orders;

(c) Dissolves the Supreme Soviet of the U.S.S.R. in conformity with Article 47 of the Constitution of the U.S.S.R. and appoints new elections;

(d) Conducts a popular canvass (referendum) on its own initiative or on the demand of one of the Union Republics;

(e) Annuls such decisions and orders of the Council of People's Commissars of the U.S.S.R. and the Councils of People's Commissars of the Union Republics as do not conform to law;

(f) In the intervals between sessions of the Supreme Soviet of the U.S.S.R., dismisses and appoints People's Commissars of the U.S.S.R. on the recommendation of the Chairman of the Council of People's Commissars of the U.S.S.R., subject to subsequent confirmation by the Supreme Soviet of the U.S.S.R.;

(g) Awards decorations and titles of honor of the U.S.S.R.;

(h) Exercises the right of pardon;

(i) Appoints and dismisses the High Command of the armed forces of the U.S.S.R.;

(j) In the intervals between sessions of the Supreme Soviet of the U.S.S.R., proclaims a state of war in the event of armed attack on the U.S.S.R., or whenever required to fulfill international treaty obligations concerning mutual defense against aggression;

(k) Proclaims general or partial mobilization;

(l) Ratifies international treaties;

(m) Appoints and recalls plenipotentiary representatives of the U.S.S.R. to foreign states;

(n) Accepts the credentials and letters of recall of diplomatic representatives of foreign states accredited to it.

ARTICLE 50. The Soviet of the Union and the Soviet of Nationalities elect Credentials Commissions which examine the credentials of the members of the respective Chambers.

On the recommendations of the Credentials Commissions the Chambers decide either to endorse the credentials or to annul the election of the deputies concerned.

ARTICLE 51. The Supreme Soviet of the U.S.S.R., when it deems necessary, appoints commissions of enquiry and investigation on any matter.

It is the duty of all institutions and officials to comply with the demands of these commissions and to submit to them the necessary materials and documents.

ARTICLE 52. A member of the Supreme Soviet of the U.S.S.R. may not be prosecuted or arrested without the consent of the Supreme Soviet of the U.S.S.R., and in the period when the Supreme Soviet of the U.S.S.R. is not in session, without the consent of the Presidium of the Supreme Soviet of the U.S.S.R.

ARTICLE 53. On the expiration of the term of office of the Supreme Soviet of the U.S.S.R., or after the Supreme Soviet has been dissolved prior to the expiration of its term of office, the Presidium of the Supreme Soviet of the U.S.S.R. retains its powers until the formation of a new Presidium of the Supreme Soviet of the U.S.S.R. by the newly elected Supreme Soviet of the U.S.S.R.

ARTICLE 54. On the expiration of the term of office of the Supreme Soviet of the U.S.S.R., or in the event of its dissolution prior to the expiration of its term of office, the Presidium of the Supreme Soviet of the U.S.S.R. appoints new elections to be held within a period not exceeding two months from the date of expiration of the term of office or the dissolution of the Supreme Soviet of the U.S.S.R.

ARTICLE 55. The newly elected Supreme Soviet of the U.S.S.R. is convened by the outgoing Presidium of the Supreme Soviet of the U.S.S.R. not later than one month after the elections.

ARTICLE 56. The Supreme Soviet of the U.S.S.R., at a joint sitting of both Chambers, forms the Government of the U.S.S.R.—the Council of People's Commissars of the U.S.S.R.

CHAPTER IV

THE HIGHEST ORGANS OF STATE POWER
OF THE UNION REPUBLICS

ARTICLE 57. The highest organ of state power of a Union Republic is the Supreme Soviet of the Union Republic.

ARTICLE 58. The Supreme Soviet of a Union Republic is elected by the citizens of the Republic for a term of four years.

The rates of representation are determined by the Constitutions of the Union Republics.

ARTICLE 59. The Supreme Soviet of a Union Republic is the sole legislative organ of the Republic.

ARTICLE 60. The Supreme Soviet of a Union Republic

(a) Adopts the Constitution of the Republic and amends it in conformity with Article 16 of the Constitution of the U.S.S.R.;

(b) Ratifies the Constitutions of the Autonomous Republics belonging to it and defines the boundaries of their territories;

(c) Approves the plan of national economy and the budget of the Republic;

(d) Exercises the right to amnesty and [to] pardon citizens sentenced by the judicial organs of the Union Republic.

ARTICLE 61. The Supreme Soviet of a Union Republic elects a Presidium of the Supreme Soviet of the Union Republic consisting of the Chairman of the Presidium of the Supreme Soviet of the Union Republic, Vice-Chairman, the Secretary of the Presidium and members of the Presidium of the Supreme Soviet of the Union Republic.

The powers of the Presidium of the Supreme Soviet of a Union Republic are defined by the Constitution of the Union Republic.

ARTICLE 62. The Supreme Soviet of a Union Republic elects a Chairman and Vice-Chairman to conduct its meetings.

ARTICLE 63. The Supreme Soviet of a Union Republic forms the Government of a Union Republic—the Council of People's Commissars of the Union Republic.

CHAPTER V

THE ORGANS OF STATE ADMINISTRATION OF THE UNION OF SOVIET SOCIALIST REPUBLICS

ARTICLE 64. The highest executive and administrative organ of state power of the Union of Soviet Socialist Republics is the Council of People's Commissars of the U.S.S.R.

ARTICLE 65. The Council of People's Commissars of the U.S.S.R. is responsible to the Supreme Soviet of the U.S.S.R. and accountable to it; and in the intervals between sessions of the Supreme Soviet it is responsible and accountable to the Presidium of the Supreme Soviet of the U.S.S.R.

ARTICLE 66. The Council of People's Commissars of the U.S.S.R. issues decisions and orders on the basis and in pursuance of the laws in operation, and supervises their execution.

ARTICLE 67. Decisions and orders of the Council of People's Commissars of the U.S.S.R. are binding throughout the entire territory of the U.S.S.R.

ARTICLE 68. The Council of People's Commissars of the U.S.S.R.

(a) Coordinates and directs the work of the All-Union and Union-Republic People's Commissariats of the U.S.S.R. and of other economic and cultural institutions under its jurisdiction;

(b) Adopts measures to carry out the plan of national economy and the state budget and to strengthen the credit and monetary system;

(c) Adopts measures for the maintenance of public order, for the protection of the interests of the state, and for safeguarding the rights of citizens;

(d) Exercises general control in the sphere of relations with foreign states;

(e) Determines the annual contingent of citizens to be called up for military service and directs the general organization and development of the armed forces of the country;

(f) Forms, whenever necessary, special committees and central boards under the Council of People's Commissars of the U.S.S.R. for matters concerning the development of economy, culture and defense.

ARTICLE 69. The Council of People's Commissars of the U.S.S.R. has the right, in respect to those branches of administration and economy which come within the jurisdiction of the U.S.S.R., to suspend decisions and orders of the Councils of People's Commissars of the Union Republics and to annul orders and instructions of People's Commissars of the U.S.S.R.

ARTICLE 70. The Council of People's Commissars of the U.S.S.R. is formed by the Supreme Soviet of the U.S.S.R. and consists of the Chairman of the Council of People's Commissars of the U.S.S.R., the Vice-Chairman of the Council of People's Commissars of the U.S.S.R., the Chairman of the State Planning Commission of the U.S.S.R., the Chairman of the Commission of Soviet Control, the People's Commissars of the U.S.S.R., the Chairman of the Committee of Agricultural Stocks, the Chairman of the Committee of Higher Education, [and] the Chairman of the Committee of Arts.

ARTICLE 71. The Government of the U.S.S.R. or a People's Commissar of the U.S.S.R. to whom a question of a member of the Supreme Soviet of the U.S.S.R. is addressed must give a verbal or written reply in the respective Chamber within a period not exceeding three days.

ARTICLE 72. The People's Commissars of the U.S.S.R. direct the branches of state administration which come within the jurisdiction of the U.S.S.R.

ARTICLE 73. The People's Commissars of the U.S.S.R. issue, within the limits of the jurisdiction of the respective People's Commissariats, orders and instructions on the basis and in pursuance of the laws in operation and also of decisions and orders of the Council of People's Commissars of the U.S.S.R., and supervise their execution.

ARTICLE 74. The People's Commissariats of the U.S.S.R. are either All-Union or Union-Republic Commissariats.

ARTICLE 75. The All-Union People's Commissariats direct the branches of state administration entrusted to them throughout the territory of the U.S.S.R. either directly or through bodies appointed by them.

ARTICLE 76. The Union-Republic People's Commissariats direct the branches of state administration entrusted to them as a rule through the medium of identically named People's Commissariats of the Union Republics; under their immediate direction they have only a definite and limited number of enterprises according to a list confirmed by the Presidium of the Supreme Soviet of the U.S.S.R.

ARTICLE 77. The following People's Commissariats are All-Union People's Commissariats: Defense, Foreign Affairs, Foreign Trade, Railways, Postal and Electrical Communications, Water Transport, Heavy Industry, Defense Industry.

ARTICLE 78. The following People's Commissariats are Union-Republic People's Commissariats: Food Industry, Light Industry, Timber Industry, Agriculture, State Grain and Livestock Farms, Finance, Internal Trade, Internal Affairs, Justice, Public Health.

CHAPTER VI

THE ORGANS OF STATE ADMINISTRATION
OF THE UNION REPUBLICS

ARTICLE 79. The highest executive and administrative organ of state power of a Union Republic is the Council of People's Commissars of the Union Republic.

ARTICLE 80. The Council of People's Commissars of a Union Republic is responsible to the Supreme Soviet of the Union Republic and accountable to it; and in the intervals between sessions of the Supreme Soviet of the Union Republics it is responsible and accountable to the Presidium of the Supreme Soviet of the respective Union Republic.

ARTICLE 81. The Council of People's Commissars of a Union Republic issues decisions and orders on the basis and in pursuance of the laws in operation in the U.S.S.R. and the Union Republic, and of decisions and orders of the Council of People's Commissars of the U.S.S.R., and supervises their execution.

ARTICLE 82. The Council of People's Commissars of a Union Republic has the right to suspend decisions and orders of Councils of People's Commissars of Autonomous Republics and to annul decisions and orders of Executive Committees of Soviets of Toilers' Deputies of Territories, Regions and Autonomous Regions.

ARTICLE 83. The Council of People's Commissars of a Union Republic is formed by the Supreme Soviet of the Union Republic and consists of

The Chairman of the Council of People's Commissars of the Union Republic;

The Vice-Chairmen;

The Chairman of the State Planning Commission;

The People's Commissars of Food Industry, Light Industry, Timber Industry, Agriculture, State Grain and Livestock Farms, Finance, Internal Trade, Internal Affairs, Justice, Public Health, Education, Local Industry, Municipal Economy, and Social Maintenance;

The Representative of the Committee of Agricultural Stocks;

Chief of the Board of Arts;

The Representative of the All-Union People's Commissariats.

ARTICLE 84. The People's Commissars of a Union Republic direct the branches of the state administration which come within the jurisdiction of the Union Republic.

ARTICLE 85. The People's Commissars of a Union Republic issue, within the limits of the jurisdiction of the respective People's Commissariats, orders and instructions on the basis and in pursuance of the laws of the U.S.S.R. and the Union Republic, of decisions and orders of the Council of People's Commissars of the U.S.S.R. and that of the Union Republic, and of orders and instructions of the Union-Republic People's Commissariats of the U.S.S.R.

ARTICLE 86. The People's Commissariats of a Union Republic are either Union Republic or Republic Commissariats.

ARTICLE 87. The Union Republic People's Commissariats direct the branches of state administration entrusted to them, and are subordinate both to the Council of People's Commissars of the Union Republic and to the corresponding Union Republic People's Commissariats of the U.S.S.R.

ARTICLE 88.   The Republic People's Commissariats direct the branches of state administration entrusted to them, and are directly subordinate to the Council of People's Commissars of the Union Republic.

CHAPTER VII

THE HIGHEST ORGANS OF STATE POWER OF THE AUTONOMOUS SOVIET SOCIALIST REPUBLICS

ARTICLE 89.   The highest organ of state power of an Autonomous Republic is the Supreme Soviet of the Autonomous Soviet Socialist Republic.

ARTICLE 90.   The Supreme Soviet of an Autonomous Republic is elected by the citizens of the Republic for a term of four years at the rate of representation determined by the Constitution of the Autonomous Republic.

ARTICLE 91.   The Supreme Soviet of an Autonomous Republic is the sole legislative organ of the Autonomous Soviet Socialist Republic.

ARTICLE 92.   Each Autonomous Republic has its own Constitution, which takes into account the specific features of the Autonomous Republic and is drawn up in full conformity with the Constitution of the Union Republic.

ARTICLE 93.   The Supreme Soviet of an Autonomous Republic elects a Presidium of the Supreme Soviet of the Autonomous Republic and forms a Council of People's Commissars of the Autonomous Republic, in accordance with its Constitution.

CHAPTER VIII

THE LOCAL ORGANS OF STATE POWER

ARTICLE 94.   The organs of state power in territories, regions, autonomous regions, areas, districts, cities and rural localities (stanitsa, village, hamlet, kishlak, aul) are the Soviets of Toilers' Deputies.

ARTICLE 95.   The Soviets of Toilers' Deputies of territories, regions, autonomous regions, areas, districts, cities or rural localities (stanitsa, village, hamlet, kishlak, aul) are elected by the toilers in the respective territories, regions, autonomous regions, areas, districts, cities or rural localities for a term of two years.

ARTICLE 96.   The rates of representation for Soviets of Toilers' Deputies are determined by the Constitutions of the Union Republics.

ARTICLE 97.   The Soviets of Toilers' Deputies direct the activities of the organs of administration subordinate to them; ensure the maintenance of public order, the observance of the laws and the protection of the rights of citizens; direct local economic and cultural development; and determine the local budgets.

ARTICLE 98.   The Soviets of Toilers' Deputies adopt decisions and issue orders within the limits of the powers vested in them by the laws of the U.S.S.R. and the Union Republic.

ARTICLE 99. The executive and administrative organs of the Soviets of Toilers' Deputies of the territories, regions, autonomous regions, areas, districts, cities and rural localities are the Executive Committees elected by them, consisting of a Chairman, Vice-Chairmen, Secretary and members.

ARTICLE 100. The executive and administrative organ of rural Soviets of Toiler's Deputies in small localities, in accordance with the Constitutions of the Union Republics, is the Chairman, the Vice-Chairman and Secretary elected by them.

ARTICLE 101. The executive organs of the Soviets of Toilers' Deputies are directly accountable both to the Soviets of Toilers' Deputies which elected them and to the executive organ of the superior Soviet of Toilers' Deputies.

CHAPTER IX
THE COURTS AND THE STATE ATTORNEY'S OFFICE

ARTICLE 102. Justice in the U.S.S.R. is administered by the Supreme Court of the U.S.S.R., the Supreme Courts of the Union Republics, the Territorial and Regional courts, the courts of the Autonomous Republics and Autonomous Regions, Area courts, special courts of the U.S.S.R. established by decision of the Supreme Soviet of the U.S.S.R., and the People's Courts.

ARTICLE 103. In all courts cases are tried with the assistance of the people's assessors, except in cases specially provided for by law.

ARTICLE 104. The Supreme Court of the U.S.S.R. is the highest judicial organ. The Supreme Court of the U.S.S.R. is charged with the function of supervising the judicial activities of all the judicial organs of the U.S.S.R. and of the Union Republics.

ARTICLE 105. The Supreme Court of the U.S.S.R. and the special courts of the U.S.S.R. are elected by the Supreme Soviet of the U.S.S.R. for a term of five years.

ARTICLE 106. The Supreme Courts of the Union Republics are elected by the Supreme Soviets of the Union Republics for a term [of] five years.

ARTICLE 107. The Supreme Courts of the Autonomous Republics are elected by the Supreme Soviets of the Autonomous Republics for a term of five years.

ARTICLE 108. Territorial and Regional courts, the courts of Autonomous Regions and Area courts are elected by the Territorial, Regional or Area Soviets of Toilers' Deputies or by the Soviets of Toilers' Deputies of the Autonomous Regions for a term of five years.

ARTICLE 109. People's Courts are elected by the citizens of the district on the basis of universal, direct and equal suffrage and secret ballot, for a term of three years.

ARTICLE 110. Court proceedings are conducted in the language of the Union Republic, Autonomous Republic or Autonomous Region, persons not knowing this language being ensured every opportunity of fully acquainting themselves with the material pertaining to the case through an interpreter and the right to speak in court in their own language.

ARTICLE 111. In all courts of the U.S.S.R. cases are heard in public, unless otherwise provided for by law, and the accused is guaranteed the right of defense.

ARTICLE 112. Judges are independent and subject only to the law.

ARTICLE 113. Highest supervision over the strict execution of the laws by all People's Commissariats and institutions subordinated to them, as well as by official persons and by citizens of the U.S.S.R., is vested in the State Attorney of the U.S.S.R.

ARTICLE 114. The State Attorney of the U.S.S.R. is appointed by the Supreme Soviet of the U.S.S.R. for a term of seven years.

ARTICLE 115. State Attorneys of Republics, Territories and Regions, as well as State Attorneys of Autonomous Republics and Autonomous Regions, are appointed by the State Attorney of the U.S.S.R. for a term of five years.

ARTICLE 116. Area, district and city state attorneys are appointed for a term of five years by the State Attorney of the Union Republics and confirmed by the State Attorney of the U.S.S.R.

ARTICLE 117. The State Attorney's offices perform their functions independently of any local organs whatsoever and are subordinate solely to the State Attorney of the U.S.S.R.

CHAPTER X

THE FUNDAMENTAL RIGHTS AND DUTIES OF CITIZENS

ARTICLE 118. Citizens of the U.S.S.R. have the right to work, i.e., the right to guaranteed employment and payment for their work in accordance with its quantity and quality.

The right to work is ensured by the socialist organization of national economy, the steady growth of the productive forces of Soviet society, the preclusion of the possibility of economic crises, and the abolition of unemployment.

ARTICLE 119. Citizens of the U.S.S.R. have the right to rest and leisure.

The right to rest and leisure is ensured by the reduction of the working day to seven hours for the overwhelming majority of the workers, the institution of annual vacations with pay for workers and other employees and the provision of a wide network of sanatoria, rest homes and clubs for the accommodation of the toilers.

ARTICLE 120. Citizens of the U.S.S.R. have the right to maintenance in old age and also in case of sickness or loss of capacity to work.

This right is ensured by the wide development of social insurance of workers and other employees at state expense, free medical service, and the provision of a wide network of health resorts for the accommodation of the toilers.

ARTICLE 121. Citizens of the U.S.S.R. have the right to education.

This right is ensured by universal, compulsory elementary education; by the fact that education, including higher (university) education is free of charge: by the system of state scholarships for the overwhelming majority of students in the higher schools; by instruction in schools being conducted in the native language, and by the organization of free vocational, technical and agronomic training for the toilers in the factories, state farms, machine and tractor stations and collective farms.

ARTICLE 122. Women in the U.S.S.R. are accorded equal rights with men in all spheres of economic, state, cultural, social and political life.

The possibility of exercising these rights of women is ensured by affording women equally with men the right to work, payment for work, rest and leisure; social insurance and education, and by state protection of the interests of mother and child, maternity leave with pay, and the provision of a wide network of maternity homes, nurseries and kindergartens.

ARTICLE 123. The equality of the rights of citizens of the U.S.S.R., irrespective of their nationality or race, in all spheres of economic, state, cultural, social and political life, is an indefensible law.

Any direct or indirect restriction of the rights of, or, conversely, the establishment of direct or indirect privileges for citizens on account of their race or nationality, as well as the advocacy of racial or national exclusiveness or hatred and contempt, is punishable by law.

ARTICLE 124. In order to ensure to citizens freedom of conscience, the church in the U.S.S.R. is separated from the state, and the school from the church. Freedom of religious worship and freedom of anti-religious propaganda are recognized for all citizens.

ARTICLE 125. In conformity with the interests of the toilers, and in order to strengthen the socialist system, the citizens of the U.S.S.R. are guaranteed by law: (a) freedom of speech; (b) freedom of the press; (c) freedom of assembly and of holding mass meetings; (d) freedom of street processions and demonstrations.

These rights of the citizens are ensured by placing at the disposal of the toilers and their organizations printing presses, stocks of paper, public buildings, the streets, means of communication and other material requisites for the exercise of these rights.

ARTICLE 126. In conformity with the interests of the toilers, and in order to develop the organizational initiative and political activity of the masses of the people, citizens of the U.S.S.R. are ensured the right to unite in public organizations—trade unions, cooperative associations, youth organizations, sport and defense organizations, cultural, technical and scientific societies; and the most active and politically conscious citizens in the ranks of working class and other strata of the toilers unite in the Communist Party of the U.S.S.R., which is the vanguard of the toilers in their struggle to strengthen and develop the socialist system and which represents the leading core of all organizations of the toilers, both public and state.

ARTICLE 127. The citizens of the U.S.S.R. are guaranteed inviolability of person. No person may be placed under arrest except by decision of court or with the sanction of a state attorney.

Article 128. The inviolability of the homes of citizens and secrecy of correspondence are protected by law.

Article 129. The U.S.S.R. grants the right of asylum to foreign citizens persecuted for defending the interests of the toilers or for their scientific activities or for their struggle for national liberation.

Article 130. It is the duty of every citizen of the U.S.S.R. to abide by the Constitution of the Union of Soviet Socialist Republics, to observe the laws, to maintain labor discipline, honestly to perform public duties, and to respect the rules of socialist human intercourse.

Article 131. It is the duty of every citizen of the U.S.S.R. to safeguard and fortify public, socialist property as the sacred and inviolable foundation of the Soviet system, as the source of the wealth and might of the country, as the source of the prosperous and cultural life of all the toilers.

Persons encroaching upon public, socialist property are enemies of the people.

Article 132. Universal military service is a law. Military service in the workers' and peasants' Red Army is an honorable duty of the citizens of the U.S.S.R.

Article 133. To defend the fatherland is the sacred duty of every citizen of the U.S.S.R. Treason to the country—violation of the oath, desertion to the enemy, impairing the military power of the state, or espionage—is punishable with all the severity of the law as the worst of crimes.

CHAPTER XI

THE ELECTORAL SYSTEM

Article 134. Members of all Soviets of Toilers' Deputies—of the Supreme Soviet of the U.S.S.R., the Supreme Soviets of the Union Republics, the Soviets of Toilers' Deputies of the Territories and Regions, the Supreme Soviets of the Autonomous Republics, the Soviets of Toilers' Deputies of Autonomous Regions, area, district, city and rural (stanitsa, village, hamlet, kishlak, aul) Soviets of Toilers' Deputies— are elected by the electors on the basis of universal, equal and direct suffrage by secret ballot.

Article 135. Elections of deputies are universal; All citizens of the U.S.S.R. who have reached the age of eighteen, irrespective of race or nationality, religion, standard of education, domicile, social origin, property status or past activities, have the right to vote in the election of deputies and to be elected, with the exception of the insane and persons convicted by court of law to sentences including deprivation of rights.

Article 136. Elections of deputies are equal: Every citizen is entitled to one vote; all citizens participate in elections on an equality footing.

Article 137. Women have the right to elect and be elected on equal terms with men.

Article 138. Citizens serving in the Red Army have the right to elect and be elected on equal terms with all other citizens.

ARTICLE 139. Elections of deputies are direct: All Soviets of Toilers' Deputies, from rural and city Soviets of Toilers' Deputies up to and including the Supreme Soviet of the U.S.S.R., are elected by the citizens by direct vote.

ARTICLE 140. Voting at elections of deputies is secret.

ARTICLE 141. Candidates are nominated for election according to electoral areas.

The right to nominate candidates is ensured to public organizations and societies of toilers: Communist Party organizations, trade unions, cooperatives, youth organizations and cultural societies.

ARTICLE 142. It is the duty of every deputy to report to the electors on his work and on the work of the Soviet of Toilers' Deputies, and he is liable to be recalled at any time in the manner established by law upon decision of a majority of the electors.

CHAPTER XII

EMBLEM, FLAG, CAPITAL

ARTICLE 143. The state emblem of the Union of Soviet Socialist Republics consists of a sickle and hammer against a glove depicted in the rays of the sun and surrounded by ears of wheat with the inscription in the languages of the Union Republics: 'Workers of the World, Unite!' Above the emblem is a five-pointed star.

ARTICLE 144. The state flag of the Union of Soviet Socialist Republics is of red cloth with the sickle and hammer depicted in gold in the upper corner near the staff and above them a five-pointed red star bordered in gold. The relation of the width to the length is 1 : 2.

ARTICLE 145. The capital of the Union of Soviet Socialist Republics is the City of Moscow.

CHAPTER XIII

THE PROCEDURE FOR AMENDING THE CONSTITUTION

ARTICLE 146. The Constitution of the U.S.S.R. may be amended only by decision of the Supreme Soviet of the U.S.S.R. adopted by a majority of not less than two-thirds of the votes cast in each of its Chambers.

1.3.1 AMENDMENTS TO THE USSR CONSTITUTION OF 1936[1]

ARTICLE 13. [In addition to the Republics listed are the following:]

The Lithuanian Soviet Socialist Republic

The Latvian Soviet Socialist Republic

The Moldavian Soviet Socialist Republic

The Estonian Soviet Socialist Republic

ARTICLE 14.

(a) Representation of the U.S.S.R. in international relations, conclusions, ratification and denunciation of treaties of the U.S.S.R. with other states, establishment of general procedure governing the relations of Union Republics with foreign states;

(f) Confirmation of the formation of new Autonomous Republics and Autonomous Regions within Union Republics;

(g) Organization of the defense of the U.S.S.R., direction of all the Armed Forces of the U.S.S.R., determination of directing principles governing the organization of the military formations of the Union Republics;

(k) Approval of the consolidated state budget of the U.S.S.R. and of the report on its fulfillment; determination of the taxes and revenues which go to the Union, the Republican and the local budgets;

(l) Administration of the banks, industrial and agricultural institutions and enterprises, and trading enterprises of all-Union jurisdiction; general guidance of industry and construction under Union Republican jurisdiction;

(m) Administration of transport and communications of all-Union importance;

(w) Determination of the principles of legislation concerning marriage and the family;

(x) Issuing of all-Union acts of amnesty.

ARTICLE 18a. Each Union Republic has the right to enter into direct relations with foreign states and to conclude agreements and exchange diplomatic and consular representatives with them.

ARTICLE 18b. Each Union Republic has its own Republican military formations.

ARTICLE 22. The Russian Soviet Federative Socialist Republic includes the Bashkirian, Buryst, Daghestan, Kabardinian-Balkar, Kalmyk, Karelian, Komi, Mari, Mordovian, North Ossetian, Tatar, Udmurt, Checheno-Ingush, Chuvash and Yakut Autonomous Soviet Socialist Republics; and the Adygei, Gorny Altai, Jewish, Karachai-Cherkess, Tuva and Khakass regions.

ARTICLE 23. [Repealed.]

---

[1] Excerpted from A. Denisov and M. Kirichenko, *Soviet State Law* (Moscow: Foreign Languages Publishing House, 1960), pp. 375–409.

ARTICLE 29. [Repealed.]

ARTICLE 31. [Council of Ministers instead of Council of People's Commissars in the last sentence—and throughout the Constitution.]

ARTICLE 42. The Soviet of the Union elects a Chairman of the Soviet of the Union and four vice-chairmen.

ARTICLE 43. The Soviet of Nationalities elects a Chairman of the Soviet of Nationalities and four vice-chairmen.

ARTICLE 47. In the event of disagreement between the Soviet of the Union and the Soviet of Nationalities, the question is referred for settlement to a conciliation commission formed by the Chambers on a parity basis. If the conciliation commission fails to arrive at an agreement or if its decision fails to satisfy one of the Chambers, the question is considered for a second time by the Chambers. Failing agreement between the two Chambers, the Presidium of the Supreme Soviet of the U.S.S.R. dissolves the Supreme Soviet of the U.S.S.R. and orders new elections.

ARTICLE 48. The Supreme Soviet of the U.S.S.R. at a joint sitting of the two Chambers elects the Presidium of the Supreme Soviet of the U.S.S.R., consisting of a President of the Presidium of the Supreme Soviet of the U.S.S.R., fifteen vice-presidents—one from each Union Republic—a Secretary of the Presidium, and sixteen members of the Presidium of the Supreme Soviet of the U.S.S.R.

The Presidium of the Supreme Soviet of the U.S.S.R. is accountable to the Supreme Soviet of the U.S.S.R. for all its activities.

ARTICLE 49.

(b) Issues decrees;

(c) Gives interpretations of the laws of the U.S.S.R. in operation;

(h) Institutes decorations (orders and medals) and titles of honor of the U.S.S.R.;

(k) Institutes military titles, diplomatic ranks and other special titles;

(r) Proclaims martial law in separate localities or throughout the U.S.S.R. in the interests of the defense of the U.S.S.R. or of the maintenance of public order and the security of the state.

ARTICLE 55. The newly elected Supreme Soviet of the U.S.S.R. is convened by the outgoing Presidium of the Supreme Soviet of the U.S.S.R. not later than three months after the elections.

ARTICLE 60. (c) Approves the national-economic plan and the budget of the Republic and forms economic administration areas;

ARTICLE 68. The Council of Ministers of the U.S.S.R.

(a) Coordinates and directs the work of the All-Union and Union-Republican Ministries of the U.S.S.R. and of other institutions under its jurisdiction, exercises guidance of the Economic Councils of the economic administration areas through the Councils of Ministers of the Union Republics.

ARTICLE 69.   The Council of Ministers of the U.S.S.R. has the right, in respect of those branches of administration and economy which come within the jurisdiction of the U.S.S.R., to suspend decisions and orders of the Councils of Ministers of the Union Republics and of the Economic Councils of the economic administration areas and to annul orders and instructions of Ministers of the U.S.S.R.

ARTICLE 70.   The Council of Ministers of the U.S.S.R. is appointed by the Supreme Soviet of the U.S.S.R. and consists of

The Chairman of the Council of Ministers of the U.S.S.R.;

The First Vice-Chairman of the Council of Ministers of the U.S.S.R.;

The vice-chairmen of the Council of Ministers of the U.S.S.R.;

The ministers of the U.S.S.R.;

The Chairman of the State Planning Committee of the Council of Ministers of the U.S.S.R.;

The Chairman of the Commission of Soviet Control of the Council of Ministers of the U.S.S.R.;

The Chairman of the State Labor and Wages Committee of the U.S.S.R. on Professional and Technical Training;

The Chairman of the State Committee of the Council of Ministers of the U.S.S.R. on Professional and Technical Training;

The Chairman of the State Scientific and Technical Committee of the Council of Ministers of the U.S.S.R.;

The Chairman of the State Committee of the Council of Ministers of the U.S.S.R. on Automation and Machine-Building;

The Chairman of the State Committee of the Council of Ministers of the U.S.S.R. on Aircraft Technique;

The Chairman of the State Committee of the Council of Ministers of the U.S.S.R. on Defense Technique;

The Chairman of the State Committee of the Council of Ministers of the U.S.S.R. on Radioelectronics;

The Chairman of the State Committee of the Council of Ministers of the U.S.S.R. on Shipbuilding;

The Chairman of the State Committee of the Council of Ministers of the U.S.S.R. on Chemistry;

The Chairman of the State Committee of the Council of Ministers of the U.S.S.R. on Construction;

The Chairman of the State Grain and Cereals Committee of the Council of Ministers of the U.S.S.R.;

The Chairman of the State Committee of the Council of Ministers of the U.S.S.R. on Foreign Economic Relations;

The Chairman of the State Security Committee under the Council of Ministers or the U.S.S.R;

The Chairman of the Administrative Board of the State Bank of the U.S.S.R.;

The chief of the Central Statistical Board under the Council of Ministers of the U.S.S.R.;

The Chairman of the State Council of Scientific and Economic Research of the Council of Ministers of the U.S.S.R.;

The Council of Ministers of the U.S.S.R. includes the Chairmen of the Councils of Ministers of the Union Republics by virtue of their office.

ARTICLE 77. The following ministries are all-Union ministries: the Ministry of Foreign Trade; The Ministry of Merchant Marine; the Ministry of Railways; the Ministry of Medium Machine-Building Industry; the Ministry for the Construction of Electric Power Stations; the Ministry of Transport Construction.

ARTICLE 78. The following ministries are Union-Republican ministries: the Ministry of Internal Affairs; the Ministry of Higher and Secondary Special Education; the Ministry of Geological Survey and Conservation of Mineral Resources; the Ministry of Public Health; the Ministry of Foreign Affairs; the Ministry of Culture; The Ministry of Defense; the Ministry of Communications; the Ministry of Agriculture; the Ministry of Finance.

ARTICLE 82. The council of ministers of a Union Republic has the right to suspend decisions and orders of the councils of ministers of its autonomous republics, and to annul decisions and orders of the executive committees of the soviets of working people's deputies of its territories, regions and autonomous regions, as well as decisions and orders of the economic councils of the economic administration areas.

ARTICLE 83. The council of ministers of a Union Republic is appointed by the supreme soviet of the Union Republic and consists of the chairman of the council of ministers of the Union Republic; the vice-chairmen of the council of ministers; the ministers; the chairmen of state committees, commissions, and the heads of other departments of the council of ministers set up by the supreme soviet of the Union Republic in conformity with the constitution of the Union Republic.

ARTICLE 88. The Economic Councils of the economic administration areas direct the branches of economic activity entrusted to them, and are directly subordinate to the Council of Ministers of the Union Republic.

The Economic Councils of the economic administration areas issue within their jurisdiction decisions and orders on the basis and in pursuance of the laws of the U.S.S.R. and the Union Republic and decisions and orders of the Council of Ministers of the U.S.S.R. and the Council of Ministers of the Union Republic.

ARTICLE 105. [This is added to the first sentence:]

The Supreme Court of the U.S.S.R. includes the chairmen of the Supreme Courts of the Union Republics by virtue of their office.

ARTICLE 109. People's judges of District (city) People's Courts are elected by the citizens of the districts (cities) on the basis of universal, direct and equal suffrage by secret ballot for a term of five years.

People's assessors of District (city) People's Courts are elected at general meetings of industrial, office and professional workers, and peasants in the place of their work or residence, and of servicemen in military units, for a term of two years.

ARTICLE 119. [This addition should be made:]

The right to rest and leisure is ensured by the establishment of an eight-hour day for industrial, office, and professional workers, the reduction of the working day to seven or six hours [for] arduous trades and to four hours in shops where conditions of work are particularly arduous; by the institution of annual vacations with full pay for industrial, office, and professional workers; and by the provision of a wide network of sanatoriums, holiday homes and clubs for the accommodation of the working people.

ARTICLE 121. Citizens of the U.S.S.R. have the right to education.

This right is ensured by universal compulsory eight-year education; by extensive development of secondary general polytechnical education, vocational-technical education, and secondary special and higher education on the basis of close links between school and life and production; by utmost development of evening and extramural education; by free education in all schools, by a system of state grants; by instruction in schools being conducted in the native language; and by the organization in the factories, state farms, and collective farms of free vocational, technical and agronomic training for the working people.

ARTICLE 135. Elections of deputies are universal: all citizens of the U.S.S.R. who have reached the age of eighteen, irrespective of race or nationality, sex, religion, education, domicile, social origin, property status or past activities, have the right to vote in the election of deputies, with the exception of persons who have been legally certified as insane.

Every citizen of the U.S.S.R. who has reached the age of twenty-three is eligible for election to the Supreme Soviet of the U.S.S.R., irrespective of race or nationality, sex, religion, education, domicile, social origin, property status or past activities.

1. 3. 2

CONSTITUTION
(FUNDAMENTAL LAW)
OF THE UNION
OF SOVIET SOCIALIST REPUBLICS[1]

As Amended by the Fifth Session of the Sixth Supreme Soviet
of the USSR

CHAPTER I

THE SOCIAL STRUCTURE

ARTICLE 1. The Union of Soviet Socialist Republics is a socialist state of workers and peasants.

ARTICLE 2. The political foundation of the U.S.S.R. is the Soviets of Working People's Deputies, which grew and became strong as a result of the overthrow of the power of the landlords and capitalists and the attainment of the dictatorship of the proletariat.

ARTICLE 3. All power in the U.S.S.R. is vested in the working people of town and country as represented by the Soviets of Working People's Deputies.

ARTICLE 4. The economic foundation of the U.S.S.R. is the socialist system of economy and the socialist ownership of the instruments and means of production, firmly established as a result of abolishing the capitalist system of economy, the private ownership of the instruments and means of production, and the exploitation of man by man.

ARTICLE 5. Socialist property in the U.S.S.R. exists either in the form of state property (belonging to the whole people) or in the form of cooperative and collective-farm property (the property of collective farms or cooperative societies).

ARTICLE 6. The land, its mineral wealth, waters, forests, the factories and mines, rail, water and air transport facilities, the banks, means of communication, large state-organized agricultural enterprises (state farms, machine and tractor stations, etc.), as well as municipal enterprises and the bulk of the dwelling-houses in the cities and industrial localities, are state property, that is, belong to the whole people.

---

[1] Reprinted from *Constitution (Fundamental Law) of the Union of Soviet Socialist Republics*, revised translation (Moscow: Progress Publishers, 1965).

ARTICLE 7. The enterprises of the collective farms and cooperative organizations, with their livestock, buildings, implements, and output are the common, socialist property of the collective farms and cooperative organizations.

Every collective-farm household, in addition to its basic income from the collective farm, has for its own use a small plot of land attached to the house and, as its own property, a dwelling-house, livestock, poultry, and minor agricultural implements—in conformity with the Rules of the Agricultural Artel.

ARTICLE 8. The land occupied by the collective farms is made over to them for their free use for an unlimited time, that is, in perpetuity.

ARTICLE 9. In addition to the socialist system of economy, which is the predominant form of economy in the U.S.S.R. the law permits the small private undertakings of individual peasants and handicraftsmen based on their own labor and precluding the exploitation of the labor of others.

ARTICLE 10. The right of citizens to own, as their personal property, income and savings derived from work, to own a dwellinghouse and a supplementary husbandry, articles of household and articles of personal use and convenience, is protected by law, as is also the right of citizens to inherit personal property.

ARTICLE 11. The economic life of the U.S.S.R. is determined and guided by the state economic plan for the purpose of increasing the wealth of society, steadily raising the material and cultural standards of the working people and strengthening the independence of the U.S.S.R. and its defense potential.

ARTICLE 12. Work in the U.S.S.R. is a duty and a matter of honor for every able-bodied citizen, in accordance with the principle: 'He who does not work, neither shall he eat.'

The principle applied in the U.S.S.R. is that of socialism: 'From each according to his ability, to each according to his work.'

CHAPTER II

THE STATE STRUCTURE

ARTICLE 13. The Union of Soviet Socialist Republics is a federal state, formed on the basis of a voluntary union of equal Soviet Socialist Republics, namely:

Russian Soviet Federative Socialist Republic, Ukrainian Soviet Socialist Republic, Byelorussian Soviet Socialist Republic, Uzbek Soviet Socialist Republic, Kazakh Soviet Socialist Republic, Georgian Soviet Socialist Republic, Azerbaijan Soviet Socialist Republic, Lithuanian Soviet Socialist Republic, Moldavian Soviet Socialist Republic, Latvian Soviet Socialist Republic, Kirghiz Soviet Socialist Republic, Tajik Soviet Socialist Republic, Armenian Soviet Socialist Republic, Turkmen Soviet Socialist Republic, Estonian Soviet Socialist Republic.

ARTICLE 14. The jurisdiction of the Union of Soviet Socialist Republics, as represented by its higher organs of state power and organs of state administration, covers:

(a) Representation of the U.S.S.R. in international relations; conclusion, ratification and denunciation of treaties of the U.S.S.R. with other states; establishment of general procedure governing the relations of the Union Republics with foreign states;

(b) Questions of war and peace;

(c) Admission of new republics into the U.S.S.R.;

(d) Control over the observance of the Constitution of the U.S.S.R., and ensuring conformity of the Constitutions of the Union Republics with the Constitution of the U.S.S.R.;

(e) Approval of changes to boundaries between Union Republics;

(f) Approval of the formation of new Autonomous Republics and Autonomous Regions within Union Republics;

(g) Organization of the defense of the U.S.S.R., direction of all the Armed Forces of the U.S.S.R., formulation of principles guiding the organization of the military formations of the Union Republics;

(h) Foreign trade on the basis of state monopoly;

(i) State security;

(j) Approval of the economic plans of the U.S.S.R.;

(k) Approval of the consolidated state budget of the U.S.S.R. and of the report on its implementation; fixing taxes and revenues that go to the Union, Republican and local budgets;

(l) Administration of banks and industrial, agricultural and trading enterprises and institutions under Union jurisdiction; general direction of industry and building under Union-Republican jurisdiction;

(m) Administration of transport and communications of all-Union importance;

(n) Direction of the monetary and credit system;

(o) Organization of state insurance;

(p) Contracting and granting of loans;

(q) Definition of the basic principles of land tenure and of the use of mineral wealth, forests and waters;

(r) Definition of the basic principles in the spheres of education and public health;

(s) Organization of a uniform system of economic statistics;

(t) Definition of the fundamentals of labor legislation;

(u) Definition of the fundamentals of legislation on the judicial system and judicial procedure and the fundamentals of civil and criminal legislation;

(v) Legislation on Union citizenship; legislation on rights of foreigners;

(w) Definition of the fundamentals of legislation on marriage and the family;

(x) Promulgation of all-Union acts of amnesty.

ARTICLE 15.   The sovereignty of the Union Republics is limited only in the spheres defined in Article 14 of the Constitution of the U.S.S.R. Outside of these spheres each Union Republic exercises state authority independently. The U.S.S.R. protects the sovereign rights of the Union Republics.

ARTICLE 16.   Each Union Republic has its own Constitution, which takes account of the specific features of the Republic and is drawn up in full conformity with the Constitution of the U.S.S.R.

ARTICLE 17.   The right freely to secede from the U.S.S.R. is reserved to every Union Republic.

ARTICLE 18.   The territory of a Union Republic may not be altered without its consent.

ARTICLE 18a.   Each Union Republic has the right to enter into direct relations with foreign states and to conclude agreements and exchange diplomatic and consular representatives with them.

ARTICLE 18b.   Each Union Republic has its own Republican military formations.

ARTICLE 19.   The laws of the U.S.S.R. have the same force within the territory of every Union Republic.

ARTICLE 20.   In the event of divergence between a law of a Union Republic and a law of the Union, the Union law shall prevail.

ARTICLE 21.   Uniform Union citizenship is established for citizens of the U.S.S.R. Every citizen of a Union Republic is a citizen of the U.S.S.R.

ARTICLE 22.   The Russian Soviet Federative Socialist Republic includes the Bashkirian, Buryat, Checheno-Ingush, Chuvash, Daghestan, Kabardinian-Balkar, Kalmyk, Karelian, Komi, Mari, Mordovian, North Ossetian, Tatar, Tuva, Udmurt and Yakut Autonomous Soviet Socialist Republics; and the Adygei, Gorny Altai, Jewish, Karachai-Cherkess and Khakass Autonomous Regions.

ARTICLE 23.   *Repealed.*

ARTICLE 24.   The Azerbaijan Soviet Socialist Republic includes the Nakhichevan Autonomous Soviet Socialist Republic and the Nagorny Karabakh Autonomous Region.

ARTICLE 25.   The Georgian Soviet Socialist Republic includes the Abkhazian and Ajarian Autonomous Soviet Socialist Republics and the South Ossetian Autonomous Region.

ARTICLE 26.   The Uzbek Soviet Socialist Republic includes the Kara-Kalpak Autonomous Soviet Socialist Republic.

ARTICLE 27.   The Tajik Soviet Socialist Republic includes the Gorny Badakhshan Autonomous Region.

ARTICLE 28.   The settlement of questions pertaining to the regional or territorial administrative division of the Union Republics comes within the jurisdiction of the Union Republics.

ARTICLE 29.   *Repealed.*

CHAPTER III

THE HIGHER ORGANS OF STATE POWER
IN THE UNION OF SOVIET SOCIALIST REPUBLICS

ARTICLE 30. The highest organ of state power in the U.S.S.R. is the Supreme Soviet of the U.S.S.R.

ARTICLE 31. The Supreme Soviet of the U.S.S.R. exercises all rights vested in the Union of Soviet Socialist Republics in accordance with Article 14 of the Constitution, insofar as they do not, by virtue of the Constitution, come within the jurisdiction of organs of the U.S.S.R. that are accountable to the Supreme Soviet of the U.S.S.R., that is, the Presidium of the Supreme Soviet of the U.S.S.R., the Council of Ministers of the U.S.S.R., and the Ministries of the U.S.S.R.

ARTICLE 32. The legislative power of the U.S.S.R. is exercised exclusively by the Supreme Soviet of the U.S.S.R.

ARTICLE 33. The Supreme Soviet of the U.S.S.R. consists of two Chambers: the Soviet of the Union and the Soviet of Nationalities.

ARTICLE 34. The Soviet of the Union is elected by the citizens of the U.S.S.R. voting by election districts on the basis of one deputy for every 300,000 of the population.

ARTICLE 35. The Soviet of Nationalities is elected by the citizens of the U.S.S.R. voting by Union Republics, Autonomous Republics, Autonomous Regions, and National Areas on the basis of twenty-five deputies from each Union Republic, eleven deputies from each Autonomous Republic, five deputies from each Autonomous Region, and one deputy from each National Area.

ARTICLE 36. The Supreme Soviet of the U.S.S.R. is elected for a term of four years.

ARTICLE 37. The two Chambers of the Supreme Soviet of the U.S.S.R., the Soviet of the Union and the Soviet of Nationalities, have equal rights.

ARTICLE 38. The Soviet of the Union and the Soviet of Nationalities have equal powers to initiate legislation.

ARTICLE 39. A law is considered adopted if passed by both Chambers of the Supreme Soviet of the U.S.S.R. by a simple majority vote in each.

ARTICLE 40. Laws passed by the Supreme Soviet of the U.S.S.R. are published in the languages of the Union Republics over the signatures of the President and Secretary of the Presidium of the Supreme Soviet of the U.S.S.R.

ARTICLE 41. Sessions of the Soviet of the Union and of the Soviet of Nationalities begin and terminate simultaneously.

ARTICLE 42. The Soviet of the Union elects a Chairman of the Soviet of the Union and four Vice-Chairman.

ARTICLE 43. The Soviet of Nationalities elects a Chairman of the Soviet of Nationalities and four Vice-Chairmen.

ARTICLE 44. The Chairmen of the Soviet of the Union and the Soviet of Nationalities preside at the sittings of the respective Chambers and have charge of the conduct of their business and proceedings.

ARTICLE 45. Joint sittings of the two Chambers of the Supreme Soviet of the U.S.S.R. are presided over alternately by the Chairman of the Soviet of the Union and the Chairman of the Soviet of Nationalities.

ARTICLE 46. Sessions of the Supreme Soviet of the U.S.S.R. are convened by the Presidium of the Supreme Soviet of the U.S.S.R. twice a year.

Extraordinary sessions are convened by the Presidium of the Supreme Soviet of the U.S.S.R. at its discretion or on the demand of one of the Union Republics.

ARTICLE 47. In the event of disagreement between the Soviet of the Union and the Soviet of Nationalities, the question is referred for settlement to a conciliation commission formed by the Chambers on a parity basis. If the conciliation commission fails to arrive at an agreement or if its decision fails to satisfy one of the Chambers, the question is considered for a second time by the Chambers. Failing agreement between the two Chambers, the Presidium of the Supreme Soviet of the U.S.S.R. dissolves the Supreme Soviet of the U.S.S.R. and orders new elections.

ARTICLE 48. The Supreme Soviet of the U.S.S.R. at a joint sitting of the two Chambers elects the Presidium of the Supreme Soviet of the U.S.S.R., consisting of a President of the Presidium of the Supreme Soviet of the U.S.S.R., fifteen vice-presidents—one from each Union Republic—a Secretary of the Presidium and sixteen members of the Presidium of the Supreme Soviet of the U.S.S.R.

The Presidium of the Supreme Soviet of the U.S.S.R. is accountable to the Supreme Soviet of the U.S.S.R. for all its activities.

ARTICLE 49. The Presidium of the Supreme Soviet of the U.S.S.R.

(a) Convenes the sessions of the Supreme Soviet of the U.S.S.R.;

(b) Issues ordinances;

(c) Interprets the laws of the U.S.S.R. in operation;

(d) Dissolves the Supreme Soviet of the U.S.S.R. in conformity with Article 47 of the Constitution of the U.S.S.R. and orders new elections;

(e) Conducts nationwide polls (referendums) on its own initiative or on the demand of one of the Union Republics;

(f) Annuls decisions and orders of the Council of Ministers of the U.S.S.R. and of the Councils of Ministers of the Union Republics if they do not conform to law;

(g) In the intervals between sessions of the Supreme Soviet of the U.S.S.R., appoints or removes Ministers of the U.S.S.R. on the recommendation of the Chairman of the Council of Ministers of the U.S.S.R., subject to subsequent confirmation by the Supreme Soviet of the U.S.S.R.;

(h) Institutes decorations (Orders and Medals) and titles of honor of the U.S.S.R.;

(i) Awards Orders and Medals and confers titles of honor of the U.S.S.R.;

(j) Exercises the right of pardon;

(k) Institutes military titles, diplomatic ranks and other special titles;

(l) Appoints and removes the high command of the Armed Forces of the U.S.S.R.;

(m) In the intervals between sessions of the Supreme Soviet of the U.S.S.R., proclaims a state of war in the event of an armed attack on the U.S.S.R., or when necessary to fulfill international treaty obligations providing for mutual defense against aggression;

(n) Orders general or partial mobilization;

(o) Ratifies and denounces international treaties of the U.S.S.R.;

(p) Appoints and recalls plenipotentiary representatives of the U.S.S.R. to foreign states;

(q) Receives the letters of credence and recall of diplomatic representatives accredited to it by foreign states;

(r) Proclaims martial law in separate localities or throughout the U.S.S.R. in the interests of the defense of the U.S.S.R. or of the maintenance of law and order and the security of the state.

ARTICLE 50.   The Soviet of the Union and the Soviet of Nationalities elect Credentials Committees to verify the credentials of the members of the respective Chambers.

On the report of the Credentials Committees, the Chambers decide whether to recognize the credentials of deputies or to annul their election.

ARTICLE 51.   The Supreme Soviet of the U.S.S.R., when it deems necessary, appoints commissions of inquiry and audit on any matter.

It is the duty of all institutions and officials to comply with the demands of such commissions and to submit to them all necessary materials and documents.

ARTICLE 52.   No member of the Supreme Soviet of the U.S.S.R. shall be prosecuted or arrested without the consent of the Supreme Soviet of the U.S.S.R., or, when the Supreme Soviet of the U.S.S.R. is not in session, without the consent of the Presidium of the Supreme Soviet of the U.S.S.R.

ARTICLE 53.   On the expiry of the term of office of the Supreme Soviet of the U.S.S.R., or on its dissolution prior to the expiry of its term of office, the Presidium of the Supreme Soviet of the U.S.S.R. retains its powers until the newly elected Supreme Soviet of the U.S.S.R. shall have formed a new Presidium of the Supreme Soviet of the U.S.S.R.

ARTICLE 54.   On the expiry of the term of office of the Supreme Soviet of the U.S.S.R., or in the event of its dissolution prior to the expiry of its term of office, the Presidium of the Supreme Soviet of the U.S.S.R. orders new elections to be held within a period not exceeding two months from the date of expiry of the term of office or dissolution of the Supreme Soviet of the U.S.S.R.

ARTICLE 55. The newly elected Supreme Soviet of the U.S.S.R. is convened by the outgoing Presidium of the Supreme Soviet of the U.S.S.R. not later than three months after the elections.

ARTICLE 56. The Supreme Soviet of the U.S.S.R., at a joint sitting of the two Chambers, appoints the Government of the U.S.S.R., namely, the Council of Ministers of the U.S.S.R.

CHAPTER IV

THE HIGHER ORGANS OF STATE POWER
IN THE UNION REPUBLICS

ARTICLE 57. The highest organ of state power in a Union Republic is the Supreme Soviet of the Union Republic.

ARTICLE 58. The Supreme Soviet of a Union Republic is elected by the citizens of the Republic for a term of four years.

The basis of representation is established by the Constitution of the Union Republic.

ARTICLE 59. The Supreme Soviet of a Union Republic is the sole legislative organ of the Republic.

ARTICLE 60. The Supreme Soviet of a Union Republic

(a) Adopts the Constitution of the Republic and amends it in conformity with Article 16 of the Constitution of the U.S.S.R.;

(b) Confirms the Constitutions of the Autonomous Republics forming part of it and defines the boundaries of their territory;

(c) Approves the economic plan and the budget of the Republic and forms economic administration areas;

(d) Exercises the right of amnesty and pardon of citizens sentenced by the judicial bodies of the Union Republic;

(e) Decides upon the representation of the Union Republic in its international relations;

(f) Determines the manner of organizing the Republic's military formations.

ARTICLE 61. The Supreme Soviet of a Union Republic elects the Presidium of the Supreme Soviet of the Union Republic, consisting of the President of the Presidium of the Supreme Soviet of the Union Republic, vice-presidents, a Secretary of the Presidium and members of the Presidium of the Supreme Soviet of the Union Republic.

The powers of the Presidium of the Supreme Soviet of a Union Republic are defined by the Constitution of the Union Republic.

ARTICLE 62. The Supreme Soviet of a Union Republic elects a Chairman and Vice-Chairmen to conduct its sittings.

ARTICLE 63. The Supreme Soviet of a Union Republic appoints the Government of the Union Republic, namely, the Council of Ministers of the Union Republic.

CHAPTER V

THE ORGANS OF STATE ADMINISTRATION
OF THE UNION OF SOVIET SOCIALIST REPUBLICS

ARTICLE 64. The highest executive and administrative organ of the state power of the Union of Soviet Socialist Republics is the Council of Ministers of the U.S.S.R.

ARTICLE 65. The Council of Ministers of the U.S.S.R. is responsible and accountable to the Supreme Soviet of the U.S.S.R., or, in the intervals between sessions of the Supreme Soviet, to the Presidium of the Supreme Soviet of the U.S.S.R.

ARTICLE 66. The Council of Ministers of the U.S.S.R. issues decisions and orders on the basis and in pursuance of the laws in operation, and verifies their execution.

ARTICLE 67. Decisions and orders of the Council of Ministers of the U.S.S.R. are binding throughout the territory of the U.S.S.R.

ARTICLE 68. The Council of Ministers of the U.S.S.R.

(a) Coordinates and directs the work of the Supreme Economic Council of the U.S.S.R. under the jurisdiction of the Council of Ministers of the U.S.S.R., the all-Union and Union-Republican Ministries of the U.S.S.R., the State Committees of the Council of Ministers of the U.S.S.R. and of other bodies under its jurisdiction;

(b) Adopts measures to carry out the economic plan and the state budget, and to strengthen the credit and monetary system;

(c) Adopts measures for the maintenance of law and order, for the protection of the interests of the state, and for the safeguarding of the rights of citizens;

(d) Exercises general guidance in the sphere of relations with foreign states;

(e) Fixes the annual contingent of citizens to be called up for military service and directs the general organization of the Armed Forces of the country;

(f) Sets up State Committees of the U.S.S.R., and, whenever necessary, special Committees and Central Boards under the Council of Ministers of the U.S.S.R. for economic and cultural affairs and defense.

ARTICLE 69. The Council of Ministers of the U.S.S.R. has the right, in respect of those branches of administration and economy which come within the jurisdiction of the U.S.S.R., to suspend decisions and orders of the Councils of Ministers of the Union Republics and to annul orders and instructions of Ministers of the U.S.S.R. and also statutory acts of other bodies under its jurisdiction.

ARTICLE 70. The Council of Ministers of the U.S.S.R. is appointed by the Supreme Soviet of the U.S.S.R. and consists of:

Chairman of the Council of Ministers of the U.S.S.R.;

First Vice-Chairmen of the Council of Ministers of the U.S.S.R.;

Vice-Chairmen of the Council of Ministers of the U.S.S.R.;

Chairman of the Supreme Economic Council of the Council of Ministers of the U.S.S.R.;

Ministers of the U.S.S.R.;

Chairman of the Economic Council of the U.S.S.R.;

Chairman of the State Building Committee of the U.S.S.R.;

Chairman of the State Planning Committee of the U.S.S.R.;

Chairman of the Party and State Control Committee of the Central Committee of the C.P.S.U. and the Council of Ministers of the U.S.S.R.;

Chairman of the State Labor and Wages Committee of the Council of Ministers of the U.S.S.R.;

Chairman of the State Committee of the U.S.S.R. for the Coordination of Research;

Chairman of the State Radio and Television Committee of the Council of Ministers of the U.S.S.R.;

Chairman of the State Cinematography Committee of the Council of Ministers of the U.S.S.R.;

Chairman of the State Press Committee of the Council of Ministers of the U.S.S.R.;

Chairman of the State Committee of the Council of Ministers of the U.S.S.R. on Trade;

Chairman of the State Committee of the Council of Ministers of the U.S.S.R. for Farm Produce Purchases;

Chairman of the State Foreign Economic Relations Committee of the Council of Ministers of the U.S.S.R.;

Chairman of the State Foreign Cultural Relations Committee of the Council of Ministers of the U.S.S.R.;

Chairman of the State Security Committee under the Council of Ministers of the U.S.S.R.;

Chairman of the Administrative Board of the State Bank of the U.S.S.R.;

Chief of the Central Statistical Board under the Council of Ministers of the U.S.S.R.;

The Council of Ministers of the U.S.S.R. includes the Chairmen of the Councils of Ministers of the Union Republics by virtue of their office.

ARTICLE 71. The Government of the U.S.S.R. or a Minister of the U.S.S.R. to whom a question of a member of the Supreme Soviet of the U.S.S.R. is addressed must give a verbal or written reply in the respective Chamber within a period not exceeding three days.

ARTICLE 72. The Ministers of the U.S.S.R. direct the branches of state administration which come within the jurisdiction of the U.S.S.R.

ARTICLE 73.   The Ministers of the U.S.S.R., within the limits of the jurisdiction of their respective Ministries, issue orders and instructions on the basis and in pursuance of the laws in operation, and also of decisions and orders of the Council of Ministers of the U.S.S.R., and verify their execution.

ARTICLE 74.   The Ministries of the U.S.S.R. are either all-Union or Union-Republican Ministries.

ARTICLE 75.   The all-Union Ministries direct the branch of state administration entrusted to them throughout the territory of the U.S.S.R. either directly or through bodies appointed by them.

ARTICLE 76.   The Union-Republican Ministries, as a rule, direct the branches of state administration entrusted to them through the relevant Ministries of the Union Republics; they administer directly only a certain limited number of enterprises according to a list approved by the Presidium of the Supreme Soviet of the U.S.S.R.

ARTICLE 77.   The following are all-Union Ministries: Ministry of Foreign Trade; Ministry of Civil Aviation; Ministry of the Merchant Marine; Ministry of Railways.

ARTICLE 78.   The following are Union-Republican Ministries: Ministry of Higher and Secondary Specialized Education; Ministry of Public Health; Ministry of Foreign Affairs; Ministry of Culture; Ministry of Defense; Ministry of Communications; Ministry of Agriculture; Ministry of Finance.

CHAPTER VI

THE ORGANS OF STATE ADMINISTRATION OF THE UNION REPUBLICS

ARTICLE 79.   The highest executive and administrative organ of the state power of a Union Republic is the Council of Ministers of the Union Republic.

ARTICLE 80.   The Council of Ministers of a Union Republic is responsible and accountable to the Supreme Soviet of the Union Republic, or, in the intervals between sessions of the Supreme Soviet of the Union Republic, to the Presidium of the Supreme Soviet of the Union Republic.

ARTICLE 81.   The Council of Ministers of a Union Republic issues decisions and orders on the basis and in pursuance of the laws in operation of the U.S.S.R. and of the Union Republic, and of the decisions and orders of the Council of Ministers of the U.S.S.R., and verifies their execution.

ARTICLE 82.   The Council of Ministers of a Union Republic has the right to suspend decisions and orders of the Councils of Ministers of its Autonomous Republics, and to annul decisions and orders of the Executive Committees of the Soviets of Working People's Deputies of its Territories, Regions and Autonomous Regions, as well as decisions and orders of the Economic Councils of the Union Republic and of the economic administration areas.

ARTICLE 83. The Council of Ministers of a Union Republic is appointed by the Supreme Soviet of the Union Republic and consists of:

The Chairman of the Council of Ministers of the Union Republic;

The Vice-Chairmen of the Council of Ministers;

The Ministers;

The Chairmen of State Committees, Commissions, and the heads of other departments of the Council of Ministers set up by the Supreme Soviet of the Union Republic in conformity with the Constitution of the Union Republic.

ARTICLE 84. The Ministers of a Union Republic direct the branches of state administration which come within the jurisdiction of the Union Republic.

ARTICLE 85. The Ministers of a Union Republic, within the limits of the jurisdiction of their respective Ministries, issue orders and instructions on the basis and in pursuance of the laws of the U.S.S.R. and of the Union Republic, of the decisions and orders of the Council of Ministers of the U.S.S.R. and the Council of Ministers of the Union Republic, and of the orders and instructions of the Union-Republican Ministries of the U.S.S.R.

ARTICLE 86. The Ministries of a Union Republic are either Union-Republican or Republican Ministries.

ARTICLE 87. Each Union-Republican Ministry directs the branch of state administration entrusted to it, and is subordinate both to the Council of Ministers of the Union Republic and to the corresponding Union-Republican Ministry of the U.S.S.R.

ARTICLE 88. Each Republican Ministry directs the branch of state administration entrusted to it, and is directly subordinate to the Council of Ministers of the Union Republic.

CHAPTER VII

THE HIGHER ORGANS OF STATE POWER
IN THE AUTONOMOUS SOVIET SOCIALIST REPUBLICS

ARTICLE 89. The highest organ of stage power in an Autonomous Republic is the Supreme Soviet of the Autonomous Republic.

ARTICLE 90. The Supreme Soviet of an Autonomous Republic is elected by the citizens of the Republic for a term of four years on a basis of representation established by the Constitution of the Autonomous Republic.

ARTICLE 91. The Supreme Soviet of an Autonomous Republic is the sole legislative organ of the Autonomous Republic.

ARTICLE 92. Each Autonomous Republic has its own Constitution, which takes account of the specific features of the Autonomous Republic and is drawn up in full conformity with the Constitution of the Union Republic.

ARTICLE 93. The Supreme Soviet of an Autonomous Republic elects the Presidium of the Supreme Soviet of the Autonomous Republic and appoints the Council of Ministers of the Autonomous Republic, in accordance with its Constitution.

CHAPTER VIII

THE LOCAL ORGANS OF STATE POWER

ARTICLE 94. The organs of state power in Territories, Regions, Autonomous Regions, Areas, Districts, cities and rural localities (stanitsas, villages, hamlets, kishlaks, auls) are the Soviets of Working People's Deputies.

ARTICLE 95. The Soviets of Working People's Deputies of Territories, Regions, Autonomous Regions, Areas, Districts, cities and rural localities (stanitsas, villages, hamlets, kishlaks, auls) are elected by the working people of the respective Territories, Regions, Autonomous Regions, Areas, Districts, cities and rural localities for a term of two years.

ARTICLE 96. The basis of representation for Soviets of Working People's Deputies is determined by the Constitutions of the Union Republics.

ARTICLE 97. The Soviets of Working People's Deputies direct the work of the organs of administration subordinate to them, ensure the maintenance of public order, the observance of the laws, protect the rights of citizens, direct local economic and cultural affairs and draw up and approve local budgets.

ARTICLE 98. The Soviets of Working People's Deputies adopt decisions and issue orders within the limits of the powers vested in them by the laws of the U.S.S.R. and of the Union Republic.

ARTICLE 99. The executive and administrative organ of the Soviet of Working People's Deputies of a Territory, Region, Autonomous Region, Area, District, city or rural locality is the Executive Committee elected by it, consisting of a Chairman, Vice-Chairmen, a Secretary and members.

ARTICLE 100. The executive and administrative organ of the Soviet of Working People's Deputies in a small locality, in accordance with the Constitution of the Union Republic, is the Chairman, the Vice-Chairman and the Secretary elected by the Soviet of Working People's Deputies.

ARTICLE 101. The executive organs of the Soviets of Working People's Deputies are directly accountable both to the Soviets of Working People's Deputies which elected them and to the executive organ of the superior Soviet of Working People's Deputies.

CHAPTER IX

THE COURTS AND THE PROCURATOR'S OFFICE

ARTICLE 102. In the U.S.S.R. justice is administered by the Supreme Court of the U.S.S.R., the Supreme Courts of the Union Republics, the Courts of the

Territories, Regions, Autonomous Republics, Autonomous Regions and Areas, the Special Courts of the U.S.S.R., established by decision of the Supreme Soviet of the U.S.S.R., and the People's Courts.

ARTICLE 103. In all Courts cases are tried with the participation of people's assessors, except in cases specially provided for by law.

ARTICLE 104. The Supreme Court of the U.S.S.R. is the highest judicial organ. The Supreme Court of the U.S.S.R. is charged with the supervision of the judicial activities of all the judicial bodies of the U.S.S.R. and of the Union Republics within the limits established by law.

ARTICLE 105. The Supreme Court of the U.S.S.R. is elected by the Supreme Soviet of the U.S.S.R. for a term of five years.

The Supreme Court of the U.S.S.R. includes the Chairmen of the Supreme Courts of the Union Republics by virtue of their office.

ARTICLE 106. The Supreme Courts of the Union Republics are elected by the Supreme Soviets of the Union Republics for a term of five years.

ARTICLE 107. The Supreme Courts of the Autonomous Republics are elected by the Supreme Soviets of the Autonomous Republics for a term of five years.

ARTICLE 108. The Courts of Territories, Regions, Autonomous Regions and Areas are elected by the Soviets of Working People's Deputies of the respective Territories, Regions, Autonomous Regions or Areas for a term of five years.

ARTICLE 109. People's judges of District (City) People's Courts are elected by the citizens of the districts (cities) on the basis of universal, equal, and direct suffrage by secret ballot for a term of five years.

People's Assessors of District (City) People's Courts are elected at general meetings of industrial, office and professional workers, and peasants in the place of their work or residence, and of servicemen in military units, for a term of two years.

ARTICLE 110. Judicial proceedings are conducted in the language of the Union Republic, Autonomous Republic or Autonomous Region, persons not knowing this language being guaranteed the opportunity of fully acquainting themselves with the material of the case through an interpreter and likewise the right to use their own language in court.

ARTICLE 111. In all Courts of the U.S.S.R. cases are heard in public, unless otherwise provided for by law, and the accused is guaranteed the right to defense.

ARTICLE 112. Judges are independent and subject only to the law.

ARTICLE 113. Supreme supervisory power to ensure the strict observance of the law by all Ministries and institutions subordinated to them, as well as by people in office and citizens of the U.S.S.R. generally, is vested in the Procurator-General of the U.S.S.R.

ARTICLE 114. The Procurator-General of the U.S.S.R. is appointed by the Supreme Soviet of the U.S.S.R. for a term of seven years.

ARTICLE 115. Procurators of Republics, Territories, Regions, Autonomous Republics and Autonomous Regions are appointed by the Procurator-General of the U.S.S.R. for a term of five years.

ARTICLE 116. Area, district and city procurators are appointed by the Procurators of the Union Republics, subject to the approval of the Procurator-General of the U.S.S.R., for a term of five years.

ARTICLE 117. The organs of the Procurator's Office perform their functions independently of all local bodies, being subordinate solely to the Procurator-General of the U.S.S.R.

CHAPTER X

FUNDAMENTAL RIGHTS AND DUTIES OF CITIZENS

ARTICLE 118. Citizens of the U.S.S.R. have the right to work, that is, the right to guaranteed employment and payment for their work in accordance with its quantity and quality.

The right to work is ensured by the socialist organization of the national economy, the steady growth of the productive forces of Soviet society, the elimination of the possibility of economic crises, and the abolition of unemployment.

ARTICLE 119. Citizens of the U.S.S.R. have the right to rest and leisure.

The right to rest and leisure is ensured by the establishment of a seven-hour day for industrial, office, and professional workers, the reduction of the working day to six hours for arduous trades and to four hours in shops where conditions of work are particularly arduous; by the institution of annual vacations with full pay for industrial, office, and professional workers, and by placing a wide network of sanatoriums, holiday homes and clubs at the disposal of the working people.

ARTICLE 120. Citizens of the U.S.S.R. have the right to maintenance in old age and also in case of sickness or disability.

This right is ensured by the extensive development of social insurance of industrial, office, and professional workers at state expense, free medical service for the working people, and the provision of a wide network of health resorts for the use of the working people.

ARTICLE 121. Citizens of the U.S.S.R. have the right to education.

This right is ensured by universal compulsory eight-year education; by extensive development of secondary polytechnical education, vocational-technical education, and secondary specialized and higher education based on close ties between the school, real life and production activities; by the utmost development of evening and extramural education; by free education in all schools; by a system of state scholarship grants; by instruction in schools in the native language, and by the organization of free vocational, technical and agronomic training for the working people in the factories, state farms, and collective farms.

ARTICLE 122. Women in the U.S.S.R. are accorded all rights on an equal footing with men in all spheres of economic, government, cultural, political, and other social activity.

The possibility of exercising these rights is ensured by women being accorded the same rights as men to work, payment for work, rest and leisure, social insurance and education, and also by state protection of the interests of mother and child, state aid to mothers of large families and to unmarried mothers, maternity leave with full pay, and the provision of a wide network of maternity homes, nurseries and kindergartens.

ARTICLE 123. Equality of rights of citizens of the U.S.S.R., irrespective of their nationality or race, in all spheres of economic, government, cultural, political and other social activity, is an indefeasible law.

Any direct or indirect restriction of the rights of, or, conversely, the establishment of any direct or indirect privileges for, citizens on account of their race or nationality, as well as any advocacy of racial or national exclusiveness or hatred and contempt, are punishable by law.

ARTICLE 124. In order to ensure to citizens freedom of conscience, the church in the U.S.S.R. is separated from the state, and the school from the church. Freedom of religious worship and freedom of anti-religious propaganda is recognized for all citizens.

ARTICLE 125. In conformity with the interests of the working people, and in order to strengthen the socialist system, the citizens of the U.S.S.R. are guaranteed by law:

(a) freedom of speech;

(b) freedom of the Press;

(c) freedom of assembly, including the holding of mass meetings;

(d) freedom of street processions and demonstrations.

These civil rights are ensured by placing at the disposal of the working people and their organizations printing presses, stocks of paper, public buildings, the streets, communications facilities and other material requisites for the exercise of these rights.

ARTICLE 126. In conformity with the interests of the working people, and in order to develop the initiative and political activity of the masses of the people, citizens of the U.S.S.R. are guaranteed the right to unite in mass organizations—trade unions, cooperative societies, youth organizations, sport and defense organizations, cultural, technical and scientific societies; and the most active and politically-conscious citizens in the ranks of the working class, working peasants and working intelligentsia voluntarily unite in the Communist Party of the Soviet Union, which is the vanguard of the working people in their struggle to build communist society and is the leading core of all organizations of the working people, both government and non-government.

ARTICLE 127. Citizens of the U.S.S.R. are guaranteed inviolability of the person. No person shall be placed under arrest except by decision of a court of law or with the sanction of a procurator.

ARTICLE 128. The inviolability of the homes of citizens and privacy of correspondence are protected by law.

ARTICLE 129. The U.S.S.R. affords the right of asylum to foreign citizens persecuted for defending the interests of the working people, or for scientific activities, or for struggling for national liberation.

ARTICLE 130.   It is the duty of every citizen of the U.S.S.R. to abide by the Constitution of the Union of Soviet Socialist Republics, to observe the laws, to maintain labor discipline, honestly to perform public duties, and to respect the rules of socialist society.

ARTICLE 131.   It is the duty of every citizen of the U.S.S.R. to safeguard and fortify public, socialist property as the sacred and inviolable foundation of the Soviet system, as the source of the wealth and might of the country, as the source of the prosperity and culture of all the working people.

Persons committing crimes in respect of public, socialist property are enemies of the people.

ARTICLE 132.   Universal military service is law.

Military service in the Armed Forces of the U.S.S.R. is the honorable duty of citizens of the U.S.S.R.

ARTICLE 133.   To defend the country is the sacred duty of every citizen of the U.S.S.R. Treason to the motherland—violation of the oath of allegiance, desertion to the enemy, impairing the military power of the state, espionage—is punishable with all the severity of the law as the most heinous of crimes.

CHAPTER XI

THE ELECTORAL SYSTEM

ARTICLE 134.   Members of all Soviets of Working People's Deputies—of the Supreme Soviet of the U.S.S.R., the Supreme Soviets of the Union Republics, the Soviets of Working People's Deputies of the Territories and Regions, the Supreme Soviets of the Autonomous Republics, the Soviets of Working People's Deputies of the Autonomous Regions, and the Area, District, city and rural localities (stanitsas, village, hamlet, kishlak, aul) Soviets of Working People's Deputies—are elected on the basis of universal, equal and direct suffrage by secret ballot.

ARTICLE 135.   Elections of deputies are universal: all citizens of the U.S.S.R. who have reached the age of eighteen, irrespective of race or nationality, sex, religion, education, domicile, social origin, property status or past activities, have the right to vote in the election of deputies, with the exception of persons who have been legally certified insane.

Every citizen of the U.S.S.R. who has reached the age of twenty-three is eligible for election to the Supreme Soviet of the U.S.S.R., irrespective of race or nationality, sex, religion, education, domicile, social origin, property status or past activities.

ARTICLE 136.   Elections of deputies are equal: each citizen has one vote; all citizens participate in elections on an equal footing.

ARTICLE 137.   Women have the right to elect and be elected on equal terms with men.

ARTICLE 138.   Citizens serving in the Armed Forces of the U.S.S.R. have the right to elect and be elected on equal terms with all other citizens.

ARTICLE 139. Elections of deputies are direct: all Soviets of Working People's Deputies, from rural and city Soviets of Working People's Deputies to the Supreme Soviet of the U.S.S.R., are elected by the citizens by direct vote.

ARTICLE 140. Voting at elections of deputies is secret.

ARTICLE 141. Candidates are nominated for each constituency.

The right to nominate candidates is secured to mass organizations and societies of the working people: Communist Party organizations, trade unions, cooperatives, youth organizations and cultural societies.

ARTICLE 142. It is the duty of every deputy to report to his electorate on his work and on the work of his Soviet of Working People's Deputies, and he may be recalled at any time upon decision of a majority of the electors in the manner established by law.

ARTICLE 143. The arms of the Union of Soviet Socialist Republics are a sickle and hammer against a globe depicted in the rays of the sun and surrounded by ears of grain, with the inscription 'Workers of All Countries, Unite!' in the languages of the Union Republics. At the top of the arms is a five-pointed star.

ARTICLE 144. The state flag of the Union of Soviet Socialist Republics is of red cloth with the sickle and hammer depicted in gold in the upper corner near the staff and above them a five-pointed red star bordered in gold. The ratio of width to length is 1:2.

ARTICLE 145. The capital of the Union of Soviet Socialist Republics is the City of Moscow.

CHAPTER XII

PROCEDURE FOR AMENDING THE CONSTITUTION

ARTICLE 146. Amendments to the Constitution of the U.S.S.R. shall be adopted by a majority of not less than two-thirds of the votes in each of the Chambers of the Supreme Soviet of the U.S.S.R.

1. 4

PROPOSALS FOR A NEW CONSTITUTION (FUNDAMENTAL LAW) OF THE UNION OF SOVIET SOCIALIST REPUBLICS (USSR)[1]

NEW STAGE IN THE DEVELOPMENT OF THE SOVIET STATE[2]

THE period of the transition from socialism to communism differs considerably in a number of essential features from the period of the transition from capitalism to socialism. In the latter case it was a question of a transition from one social-economic formation to another—and in connection with this of the crowding out and then the complete elimination of the capitalist structure and the bourgeois class—and of a fundamental alteration of the private-property peasant economy, its change over to the path of socialist production.

In the period of the transition from socialism to communism, however, it is a matter of the consistent development of two stages of one and the same social-economic formation, of the transformation of a society that already has its own economic basis in the form of an all-embracing socialist economy of undivided sway, with socialist ownership of the tools and means of production and a firm social base consisting of free toilers of town and countryside—workers, the collective farm peasantry and the intelligentsia. This signifies the final disappearance of antagonistic contradictions within Soviet society. Instead of the spasmodic development linked with a sharp class struggle, with the process of elimination of the economic basis of hostile classes and of the possibilities for exploitation and with a fundamental remaking of the nonproletarian masses of the working people who are allied with the working class, in this period the development of the state proceeds on a socialist economic foundation, without antagonistic classes.

Communist beginnings are created and ripen as the result of the internal laws of development of socialist society, and do not enter into irreconcilable struggle with it. The shoots of communism break through as the *outcome* of the socialist basis of society, as the appearance and further *development* of tendencies inherent in this society, as the necessary result of the disclosing of the laws characteristic of it.

---

[1] Translation from the *Current Digest of the Soviet Press*, published weekly at Columbia University by the Joint Committee on Slavic Studies, appointed by the American Council of Learned Societies and the Social Sciences Research Council. Copyright 1960. Vol. 12, No. 40, pp. 3–7. Reprinted by permission. Original source: P. S. Romashkin, *Sovetskoye gosudarstvo i pravo*, No. 10 (October 1960), 31–40.

[2] This article is based on the author's report at a scientific conference held by the Moscow City Party Committee and the U.S.S.R. Academy of Sciences' Institutes of Philosophy and of State and Law in July 1960.—TR.

These features of the building of communism were comprehensively disclosed and generalized by the Twenty-First Party Congress. In his report to the Congress, N. S. Khrushchev stressed that the transition from socialism to the highest stage—communism—is a law-governed and inevitable process and that communism is not separated by a kind of wall from socialism but develops from it and is its direct continuation. N. S. Khrushchev showed how the process of the evolution of socialism into communism would take place. The affirmation of socialist principles is accompanied by the development of communist beginnings. Thus the strengthening of collective farm property is accompanied by the process of its approximation to public property: this prepares the way for the future merging of the two into a single communist public property. The improvement of the socialist principle of distribution according to labor takes place parallel with an increase in the share of the social product distributed, regardless of the qualifications and result of the workers' labor, and the material stake in the results of labor is augmented by moral incentives to work, which are assuming increasing importance.

Does the law of the development of the political basis of society diverge from the general law of the development of socialism into communism? No, it does not. One must not think that the process of the withering away of the socialist state can begin only after the realization of total communism, and then only if the camp of imperialism has disappeared by that time. One must not counterpose the process of the uninterrupted strengthening of the socialist state to the process of its withering away. What does withering away of the state mean? As correctly noted in the textbook *Fundamentals of Marxism-Leninism*, withering away of the state means: 'In the first place, the gradual disappearance and dissolution in society of that *particular stratum of people* who are permanently engaged in state administration and who, strictly speaking, form the state. In other words, withering away of the state assumes a steady reduction and then complete elimination of the state apparatus and the transfer of its functions to society itself, i.e., to public organizations, to the entire population. Secondly, [it means] . . . the gradual disappearance of the need for coercion with respect to members of society.'[3]

Therefore, in his talk with Henry Shapiro, correspondent of the American news agency United Press, N. S. Khrushchev quite justifiably stated that the process of the withering away of the state in our country is, strictly speaking, already under way. In a talk with American labor union leaders on September 21, 1959, N. S. Khrushchev again stressed that as we move toward communism, measures leading to the withering away of the state are being carried out on an increasingly broader scale in our country: 'In our country—the Soviet Union—a number of far-reaching measures have already been carried out in this sphere: We are reducing the armed forces, we are reducing the militia and we are reducing the number of workers in state security agencies. More and more functions in the maintenance of public order and state administration are being transferred to public organizations.'[4]

---

[3] *Fundamentals of Marxism-Leninsim: A Textbook* (Moscow: State Political Literature Publishing House, 1959), pp. 720–21.

[4] *Pravda*, September 25, 1959.

Consequently, in order not to fall into error, it is necessary to proceed from the fact that the process of the withering away of the socialist state is already under way, that it began with the socialist transformation of society, [with] the liquidation of the exploiting classes, and [with] the disappearance from the work of the state of the dictatorship of the working class of such an essential feature as the function of suppressing the opposition of the exploiters. The disappearance of this function also testified to the unprecedented strengthening of the socialist state, which rid itself of irreconcilably hostile exploiting classes while the remaining friendly classes united even more on the basis of common interests in the struggle to build communism.

However, does this mean that in the future the withering away of the state will proceed only as a process of the disappearance of its remaining functions? In his report to the Twenty-First Party Congress, N. S. Khrushchev drew a conclusion of enormous theoretical and practical importance: 'If we approach it dialectically, the question of the withering away of the state is a question of the evolution of the socialist state system toward communist public self-government.' This profoundly dialectical formula, which embodies the true nature of the processes of the building of communist society that are now taking place, completely discards the dogmatic counterposing of the strengthening of the socialist state to its gradual withering away, i.e., as N. S. Khrushchev explained, to its development into communist public self-government.

The expansion of the political basis of society, the enlistment of broader and broader masses in government, the transfer of a number of functions of state agencies to public organizations, the participation of public organizations in carrying out other state functions, and the further development of socialist democracy mean the ever greater strengthening of the socialist state and at the same time its development into something that is no longer a state, i.e., into nationwide public self-government.

This course of development was foreseen even by the Eighth Party Congress: 'As the organization of the socialist economy proceeds, the Soviet class state will increasingly merge into the managerial apparatus of production and distribution and into cultural-administrative agencies. Freed of its class nature, the state will cease to be a state and will become an agency of economic and cultural self-government.'

It must be borne in mind that the term 'withering away' has a twofold meaning— withering away as a *gradual process* and withering away as the *final result* of this process. As a process, the withering away of the state begins with the socialist reorganization of society. As the final result, it can be achieved only under total communism, when there will not be an imperialist camp and the danger of aggression by the imperialist states will have disappeared. V. I. Lenin always made a clear distinction between the two meanings of this concept. He stated that the process of the withering away of the state stems inevitably from the very nature of the state of the dictatorship of the working class as a state carrying out the rule of the overwhelming majority of the working people over the numerically insignificant class of exploiters. However, as V. I. Lenin stressed, total communism is needed for the full withering away of the state.

The revisionists, wrenching out of context V. I. Lenin's words concerning the withering away process, interpret them to mean the necessity for the complete withering away of the state even in the period of transition from capitalism to socialism. They grossly distort the very essence of withering away: With them it is a matter not of the state's gradual loss of its class—i.e., political—character and its transformation into an organization of public self-government, but rather of the rejection of major, primarily economic functions and of the weakening of the socialist state. Yet in present-day conditions there can be no talk of the weakening of the state. Until a disarmament agreement is reached a strong army, a good intelligence service, etc., are needed.

Of course it would be incorrect to assert that the state of the dictatorship of the working class—at least up until the time of its complete transformation into public communist self-government—remains *immutable* and that a raising of the question of changes in its nature is out of order. The socialist state and communist public self-government are not one and the same thing. But just as the development of the first into the second takes place uninterruptedly, so is there a gradual *process of change in essential aspects* of the socialist state system.

It goes without saying that the nature of the socialist state system remains *stable* as long as state leadership of society by the working class is retained, as long as its highest principle—alliance with the peasantry—not only does not change but is further developed and as long as it has one and the same goal—the building of communist society.

But great achievements in the building of socialism in our country have brought about important changes in the development of the socialist state system. Whereas in the beginning a major task of the socialist state was that of suppressing the opposition of the exploiter classes, today the state has become in the full sense of the word a public organization, an organization of all society, and it functions as a great creative force, uniting and organizing the popular masses for accomplishment of the cherished goal—the building of communism. For the first time in the history of mankind, state authority, from the standpoint of its internal functions, has ceased to be a weapon of class suppression. It is clear that this change is very much one of *nature* and does not apply merely to the sphere of *phenomena*. This is an enormous step on the path of the transformation of the socialist state system into communist public self-government.

How will the change in the political *forms* of the socialist state take place in connection with the successes of communist construction and the process of its development into an organization of 'economic and cultural self-government'? In general terms, one might reply as follows: There will be a change in the content of the activities of existing organizations and their improvement and development, as well as the appearance of new forms.

Above all it is necessary to speak of a law of development of socialist society noted by N. S. Khrushchev—the growth of the role of the Communist Party, the vanguard of the entire Soviet people.

But what prospects face the Soviets? What will their fate be? In deciding this question it is necessary to bear in mind the feature stressed by N. S. Khrushchev in his speech at a meeting of voters of Kalinin Election District, Moscow, namely, that while the Soviets are elected agencies of state power, they are at the same time agencies of public self-government.[5] The Soviets are the broadest representative organizations of the working people, wholly carrying out their will. They are *state* organizations inasmuch as they exercise the people's authority, and they are also the broadest mass, all-encompassing *public* organizations. The elimination of the antagonism between society and the state characteristic of the exploiter system has found reflection in the Soviets. Therefore the transfer of a number of functions of the state apparatus to public organizations signifies also an enhancing of the role of the Soviets and the performance by Soviet Deputies of certain functions formerly carried out by employees of the state apparatus.

This means that the Soviets, together with Party, trade union and cooperative organizations, are fully capable of becoming a base on which organizations performing the functions of public self-government will arise and develop. This process will evidently be accompanied by a strengthening of the role of the Soviets themselves and a reduction of the role of their executive agencies, by an extension of the elective principle to all officials, by a reduction in the terms of office of elected officials and by the general participation of citizens in deciding and carrying out public matters.

The experience of communist construction and a clear understanding of the nature of the process of the development of socialist society into a communist one and the process of development and perspectives of the socialist state system make it possible to answer the question concerning what changes should be made in the U.S.S.R. Constitution (the need for which was noted by N. S. Khrushchev at the Twenty-First Party Congress)—what the Constitution of the Soviet state should be in the new historical period, the period of the comprehensive building of communism.

Let us set forth certain observations on this question that can be stated within the limits of this article.[6]

1.   Almost a quarter of a century has elapsed since the adoption and approval of the new U.S.S.R. Constitution by the Extraordinary Eighth All-Union Congress of Soviets in 1936. The Constitution incorporated the basic principles of the social and state structure of the U.S.S.R. in the initial stage of the period of the completion of socialist construction and the gradual transition to communism, and affirmed in legislative terms the basic foundations of socialism that had been firmly established in life.

Since that time events of world historic importance have taken place in the international and domestic position of the U.S.S.R. Socialism has broken out of the framework of a single country and become a powerful world system. Highly

----

[5] This fact is not considered by the authors of *Fundamentals of the Theory of State and Law* (see pp. 10 and 186), although on page 188 they cite the appropriate passage from N. S. Khrushchev's speech.—Tr.

[6] On this question see also articles in the press by V. F. Kotok and D. A. Gaidukov, staff members of the U.S.S.R. Academy of Sciences' Institute of State and Law, published in the magazine *Sovety deputatov trudyashchikhsya* (Soviet of Working People's Deputies), No. 9, 1959, pp. 111–116.—Tr.

important changes have taken place in the political and economic life of our state; these are linked with the entry of the U.S.S.R. into the period of the comprehensive building of communism, with the gigantic growth of the socialist economy and culture of the peoples of the Soviet Union, and with the beginning process of the fullest and most comprehensive development of socialist democracy along the path of the gradual transformation of the socialist state system into communist self-government.

All these enormously important qualitative changes in the international and domestic situation, which of course are not reflected in the present Constitution, dictate the necessity of introducing a number of changes in its text so as to bring it fully into line with the vital, urgent requirements and tasks of the period of the comprehensive building of communism.

First and foremost, it would be advisable to mention in the Constitution the greatest achievement of the working people—the full and final victory of socialism.

In drawing the major conclusion concerning the final victory of socialism in our country, N. S. Khrushchev has made an important contribution to the creative development of Marxism-Leninism. Formerly it was thought that the final victory of socialism required the complete elimination of external contradictions, i.e., the disappearance of the imperialist camp. Generalizing the experience and achievements of communist construction and realistically assessing the correlation of forces in the international arena, N. S. Khrushchev showed that the new social system in the camp of socialism, even though the external contradictions between it and the camp of imperialism remain, has stengthened to such an extent that there is no longer a force in the world capable of overturning it.

With the formation of a world system of socialism, the Soviet state acquired a new function—fraternal cooperation and mutual assistance among the socialist countries. Consequently, the U.S.S.R. Constitution should disclose and officially, on behalf of the Soviet people, proclaim the principle of close cooperation and fraternal mutual help among countries of the socialist camp in their struggle for the building of communism and for peace throughout the world. The Constitution should evidently elaborate and describe the basic principles of the unity and fraternal mutual help of the countries of socialism. It is also expedient to formulate in it the ideas of the defense and safeguarding of peace in the struggle against imperialist aggression and warmongers, in the spirit of the ideas expressed in the laws on the defense of peace adopted by the countries of the socialist camp, and also to set forth the principle of the peaceful coexistence of countries with different social systems, which underlies the foreign policy of the U.S.S.R.

2. In connection with the nature of the new Constitution, the question also arises as to whether the U.S.S.R. Constitution should be limited solely to a statement and juridical incorporation of gains already won or whether it should also include formulations of the direction and tasks of the development of the Soviet state along the path to communism. As is known, the present Constitution does not contain such indications and does not go beyond the framework of recording and incorporating in legislative terms what has already been achieved and won in actual fact. But the constitution of a society that has entered the period of the comprehensive

building of communism can in no way be confined, and should not be confined, simply to recording what has already been achieved.

Let us clarify this by examples.

The present Constitution speaks of the right of citizens to payment for their labor in accordance with its quantity and quality and also establishes certain forms of distribution of benefits regardless of the results of the work performed. As is known, the share and importance of this form of distribution are constantly growing and in the future will increase even more. Hence it is necessary to formulate a general principle concerning the means of development of distribution and to note new forms that have already been established and to state the prospects for their further development.

The present Constitution mentions two forms of socialist property: state (public) property and cooperative-collective farm property. However, even today there are mixed forms of property that signify the process of the approximation of these two forms of property on the basis of the gradual development of cooperative-collective farm property to the level of public property.

We think it is necessary not only to stipulate the new phenomena in the Constitution but also to offer a general formula that would show the direction of development and its prospects and would thereby begin to play an organizing and mobilizing role in the further comprehensive development of Soviet society.

Let us note that the first Constitutions of the Russian Republic and other republics, worked out under V. I. Lenin's leadership, in addition to stating achievements, also included programmatic points that contained formulations of the aims and paths of further development.

3. A number of changes and additions should be made in the articles of the Constitution defining the social structure of the U.S.S.R.

As is known, the U.S.S.R. Constitution states that the Soviets are the political basis of the U.S.S.R. Evidently it would be desirable to add to this proposition a formulation to the effect that, with time, the process of transfer of a number of functions of state agencies to public organizations will develop to an ever greater extent. At the same time, it is expedient to state that the Soviets are not only agencies of state authority but also the broadest organizations of public self-government of the working people in the spirit of V. I. Lenin's instructions and corresponding statements by N. S. Khrushchev at the meeting of voters of Kalinin District, Moscow.

There should run throughout the entire Constitution the idea, expressed by the Twenty-First Party Congress, of the constantly expanding and deepening participation of the people in the exercise of state authority, in the management of public affairs and the guidance of economic and cultural work.

Perhaps the Soviets of Working People's Deputies should be renamed Soviets of People's Deputies. This would underscore even more the historical fact that the Soviet people are linked by an indestructible moral and political unity and that they create their own representative agencies, which express the will of all the people. The new name would more precisely express the broad social base of the Soviets, which are elected not only by those who work in production and in institutions—

workers, collective farmers and the working intelligentsia—but also by those veterans of labor, the pensioners, by students in higher secondary educational institutions who have reached their majority, whose number runs into hundreds of thousands, and by servicemen. All the enumerated segments of Soviet society are taking an active part in the country's social-political life.

4. The existing Constitution touches upon the question of the Communist Party's directing role in Soviet society and the state only in the chapter on the basic rights and duties of citizens, where it speaks of the right of the working people to unite in public organizations. Yet the directing role of the Communist Party of the Soviet Union, the vanguard of the Soviet people and the guiding nucleus of all public and state organizations of the working people, is linked not only with the legal status of Soviet citizens but above all with the general characteristic of the socialist nature of the Soviet state.

With the transfer of a number of functions of state agencies to public organizations and enhancement of the importance of persuasion and the principles of communist morality in the activity of citizens, the growing role of the Communist Party in the life of the Soviet people and state is manifested even more vividly. This role of the Party and its growth in the future must be clearly and precisely stated perhaps in two or even three places in the Constitution—in the general, introductory part; in the chapter on the social structure of the U.S.S.R.; and in the chapter on the basic rights and duties of citizens.

5. The Constitution should include a new and more comprehensive formulation indicating the process of the gradual approximation of the present two forms of socialist property and the prospect of their subsequent merging into a single communist public property. The present Constitution defines cooperative-collective farm property as the property of individual collective farms and individual cooperative organizations. But now, in addition to the property of individual collective farms, there has also been extensive development of intercollective-farm property, which signifies a higher level of socialization of the collective farms' means and implements of production. There is no doubt that mixed and intercollective-farm forms of public property will continue to develop in the future.

6. As is known, the Twenty-First Party Congress outlined the prospect of the abolition of all taxes on the population. In his report to the fifth session of the Fifth U.S.S.R. Supreme Soviet in May 1960, N. S. Khrushchev noted that the Soviet state would completely abolish taxes by 1965 and that until that time the abolition of taxes would proceed in stages, gradually extending to more and more segments of the working people.

This measure of the Soviet state is directed at further raising the material living standard of the Soviet people; at the same time it expresses an essential feature of socialist society, which is that the income of the Soviet socialist state's budget derives not from funds received as a result of taxes on the population but in the main from resources coming into the state budget from the public economy. The time approaches when public tax receipts will entirely disappear from the income of the state budget. The soviet state will be the first state in the history of mankind to completely abandon the collection of taxes from the population.

In view of the above, it would be advisable to stipulate the abolition of public taxes in the text of the U.S.S.R. Constitution also. This would be not only of enormous political and practical importance but of the greatest theoretical importance as well, since the very fact of the abolition by the socialist state of public taxes would stress even more the fundamental contrast between the socialist state and all exploiter types of states, an inalienable hallmark of which is the levying of taxes on the population, the main burden of which falls on the working people.

As is known, Engels in his outstanding study, 'Origin of the Family, Private Property and the State,' pointed to two principal features distinguishing any state from the prestate tribal system: (1) the division of the population on the basis of the *territorial principle* instead of the principle of blood (tribal) ties; (2) the institution of public [publichnaya] authority, which is raised above society and for whose maintenance *taxes* on the population and loans are established.

It goes without saying that from the time of the victory of the Great October Socialist Revolution, the second feature of a state could no longer be extended to the state of a new and higher historical type that arose as a result of this revolution. The Soviet socialist state, in contrast to an exploiter state, was a political organization of the vast majority of society for rule over its insignificant minority—the overthrown exploiter classes. It is precisely in this sense that V. I. Lenin considered the Soviet socialist state a semistate, a 'transitional state,' 'not a state in the strict meaning of the word.' It is clear that this new state, in contrast to the old one, never was counterposed to society and was not raised above it but increasingly displayed the features of the *unity* of society and state. In the period of the comprehensive building of communism, when the socialist state system is gradually developing into communist public self-government, the unity of socialist society and the socialist state emerges in its obvious fullness. This is also underscored by the abolition of public taxes, since the apparatus of state authority and public self-government will be fully financed from income from the public economy alone. Public taxes will no longer be an indispensable feature of the socialist state.

7. The U.S.S.R. Constitution states that the economic life of the U.S.S.R. is determined by a state national economic plan. It would be advisable to add to this principle the formulation that at the present time the state planning of national economic development is not confined solely to the limits of the U.S.S.R., that it is carried out on the basis of the consideration, coordination and correlation of state planning in all the other countries of the world socialist system on the principles of comprehensive mutual help and the division of labor among them.

8. The present Constitution establishes that work in the U.S.S.R. is a duty and a matter of honor for every able-bodied citizen on the basis of the principle 'He who does not work, neither shall he eat.' The Constitution should evidently reflect the swift development of the mighty movement for communist labor, the movement of communist labor brigades and collectives, the new, higher forms of socialist competition. It is also necessary to point to the growing role of communist principles of distribution, to the ever increasing share of material and spiritual benefits distributed among the members of society free of charge, to the growing role of moral incentives to work, and to the prospect of transition from the socialist principle,

'From each according to his ability, to each according to his labor' to the communist principle: 'From each according to his abilities, to each according to his needs,' on the basis of the achievement of an abundance of material goods and the growth of the communist consciousness of the masses.

9. It seems to us that the chapter of the basic rights and duties of Soviet citizens should immediately follow the chapter on the social structure. This would emphasize in Constitutional terms the high position of the individual in the U.S.S.R. and would fully stem from the basic law of socialism. The working people, headed by the working class and led by the Communist Party, have created a socialist state for the purpose of eliminating the exploitation of man by man and building a classless society. Sovereignty in our country belongs fully and undividedly to the people. The people create their own agencies of authority, participate in their work, and control and check on them; they also have the decisive word in the discussion of the most important drafts of laws.

It would be desirable to have this chapter stipulate all the basic rights of citizens, including the right of personal property, the right to elect and be elected to agencies of state authority, and others. As is known, in the present Constitution these rights are dealt with not in the chapter on the basic rights and duties of citizens but in other chapters.

The chapter on the basic rights and duties of citizens requires serious elaboration taking into account the successes and achievements of recent years and especially such great prospects for the building of communism as ensuring the working people of the U.S.S.R. in the next few years the highest living standard in the world and creating the most favorable conditions for the creative development of each member of society. It should stress that the Soviet people, who have already won for themselves a seven- and six-hour working day, are moving toward the shortest working day in the world, and should stipulate the right of Soviet citizens to health protection and free medical care, the right to modern housing, the right to free maintenance of children in kindergartens and nurseries, general schools and boarding schools, etc.

Perhaps the Constitution should stipulate the right of citizens to submit to enterprises and other state agencies proposals, comments and complaints and charge these agencies with full responsibility for considering and satisfying them. It is also necessary to discuss the question of expanding the duties of citizens to include duties in the rearing of the growing generation in the spirit of communist morality and awareness of public duty, to show concern for the safeguarding of public order, etc.

10. In addition to a fuller and more comprehensive formulation of a number of new factors in the relations of the U.S.S.R. and the Union republics stemming from the implementation by the Communist Party and the Soviet state of the Leninist policy of all-round extension of the sovereign rights of the Union republics and the competence of their agencies, the Constitution should also note in particular that the united Soviet multinational state sets itself the aim of further developing friendship and mutual help among the Soviet nations in the name of the joint struggle for the full victory of communism, that its task is the systematic education

of the working people of all nations of the Soviet Union in the spirit of socialist internationalism and Soviet patriotism and the fostering of the process of the mutual enrichment and interrelation of the national cultures of the peoples of the U.S.S.R. and of the comprehensive drawing together of nations.

In addition, it would be desirable to make changes and additions in the Constitution the basic aim of which should be to stress even more the sovereignty of the Union republics and to eliminate from the existing Constitution elements of regulation with respect to the Union republics that are excessive and undesirable in present conditions. For example, the Union republics could be granted the right to determine themselves the range of powers of their Supreme Soviets, the composition of the Supreme Soviet Presidiums, the composition of the Union republic Councils of Ministers, etc.

It would be desirable if the chapter on the Soviet electoral system (which is now the next to last chapter) were to follow the chapter on the state structure of the U.S.S.R., so that it would precede the chapters on state agencies. This would be more correct, since it would emphasize that the source of the powers of all state agencies is the people who elect their own representative agencies under the control of and responsible to the people.

11.   Changes should be made in the Constitution stemming from the experience of the work of higher and local agencies of state authority and state administration, the courts and prosecutors' offices of the U.S.S.R. and Union and autonomus republics in recent years (activization of the work of local Soviets and expansion of their rights in the guidance of the economy and culture, the increased importance of sessions of Supreme Soviets and their Presidiums, the practice of the account of the U.S.S.R. government to the U.S.S.R. Supreme Soviet in the sphere of domestic and foreign policy, etc.). Particular mention should also be made of the democratic form of public discussion of the most important drafts of laws before they are submitted to the Supreme Soviet.

After the necessary additions and changes have been made in the U.S.S.R. Constitution, the Soviet people will receive a document of exceptional importance that will sum up the results of great victories, clearly state the prospects for development of the Soviet state and express the unswerving determination of the entire people to build the most just social system—communism.

CHINA*

---

* The Constitution of the Kiangsi Soviet Republic of November 1931 (Chinese Soviet Republic at Juichin, Kiangsi) was the first state constitution adopted in China for a Communist-led area. The complete text of that constitution is reprinted below for purposes of comparison with constitutions adopted after the Communist conquest of the Chinese mainland. (Reprinted by permission. Source of translation: Conrad Brandt, Benjamin Schwartz and John K. Fairbank, *A Documentary History of Chinese Communism* [Cambridge, Mass.: Harvard University Press, 1952; London: Allen & Unwin, Ltd., 1952], pp. 220–24.)

CONSTITUTION OF THE SOVIET REPUBLIC (November 7, 1931)

The First All-China Soviet Congress hereby proclaims before the toiling masses of China and of the whole world this Constitution of the Chinese Soviet Republic which recites the basic tasks to be accomplished throughout all China.

The accomplishment of these tasks has already begun in the existing Soviet districts. But the First All-China Soviet Congress holds that the complete realization of these tasks can come only after the overthrow of the rule of imperialism and the KMT [Kuomintang] and the establishment of the rule of the Soviet Republic throughout all China. Then alone will this outline Constitution of the Chinese Soviet Republic find more concrete application and become a more detailed constitution of the Chinese Soviet Republic.

2. 1

THE COMMON PROGRAM
OF THE CHINESE PEOPLE'S POLITICAL
CONSULTATIVE CONFERENCE[1]

Adopted by the First Plenary Session of the Chinese People's P.C.C.
September 29, 1949

PREAMBLE

THE great victories of the Chinese people's war of liberation and of the people's revolution have put an end to the era of the rule of imperialism, feudalism and bureaucratic capitalism in China. From the status of the oppressed, the Chinese people has attained that of the master in a new society and a new state, and has replaced the Kuomintang's reactionary rule of feudal, comprador, fascist dictatorship with the Republic of the People's Democratic Dictatorship.

The Chinese People's Democratic Dictatorship is the state power of the people's democratic united front composed of the Chinese working class, peasantry, petty bourgeoisie, national bourgeoisie and other patriotic democratic elements, based on the alliance of workers and peasants and led by the working class. The Chinese People's Political Consultative Conference, composed of the representatives of the Communist Party of China, of all democratic parties and groups and people's organizations, of all regions, of the People's Liberation Army, of all national minorities, overseas Chinese and other patriotic democratic elements, is the organizational form of the Chinese people's democratic united front.

---

[1] Translation from Otto B. Van der Sprenkel, Robert Guillain and Michael Lindsay, *New China: Three Views* (London: Turnstile Press, 1950), pp. 199–216. Reprinted by permission.

The First All-China Soviet Congress calls upon all Chinese workers, peasants, and toilers to proceed to struggle, under the guidance of the provisional government of the Soviet Republic, for the realization of these basic tasks:

1) It shall be the mission of the Constitution of the Chinese Soviet Republic to guarantee the democratic dictatorship of the proletariat and peasantry in the Soviet districts, and to secure the triumph of the dictatorship throughout the whole of China. It shall be the aim of this dictatorship to destroy all feudal remnants, eliminate the influence of the imperialist powers in China, to unite China, to limit systematically the development of capitalism, to carry out economic reconstruction of the state, to promote the class-consciousness and solidarity of the proletariat, and to rally to its banner the broad masses of poor peasants in order to effect the transition to the dictatorship of the proletariat.

2) The Chinese Soviet regime is setting up a state based on the democratic dictatorship of the workers and peasants. All power of the Soviet shall belong to the workers, peasants, and Red Army soldiers and the entire toiling population. Under the Soviet regime the workers, peasants, Red Army soldiers, and the entire toiling population shall have the right to elect their own deputies to give effect to their power. Only militarists, bureaucrats, landlords, the gentry, *t'u-hao* [village bosses], monks—all exploiting and counterrevolutionary elements—shall be deprived of the right to elect deputies to participate in the government and to enjoy political freedom.

The Chinese People's Political Consultative Conference, representing the will of the people of the whole country, proclaims the establishment of the People's Republic of China and is organizing the people's own central government. The Chinese People's Political Consultative Conference unanimously agrees that New Democracy, or People's Democracy, shall be the political foundation for the national construction of the People's Republic of China. It has also adopted the following Common Program which should be jointly observed by all units participating in the Conference, by the people's government of all levels, and by the people of the whole country.

CHAPTER I
GENERAL PRINCIPLES

ARTICLE 1. The People's Republic of China is a New Democratic or People's Democratic state. It carries out the people's democratic dictatorship led by the working class, based on the alliance of workers and peasants, and uniting all democratic classes and all nationalities in China. It opposes imperialism, feudalism and bureaucratic capitalism and strives for independence, democracy, peace, and the unity, prosperity and strength of China.

ARTICLE 2. The Central People's Government of the People's Republic of China must undertake to wage the people's war of liberation to the very end to liberate all the territory of China, and to achieve the unification of China.

ARTICLE 3. The People's Republic of China must abolish all the prerogatives of imperialist countries in China. It must confiscate bureaucratic capital and put it into the possession of the people's state. It must systematically transform the feudal and semifeudal land ownership system into a system of peasant land ownership; it must protect the public property of the state and of the cooperatives and must protect the economic interests and private property of workers, peasants, the petty bourgeoisie and the national bourgeoisie. It must develop the people's economy of New Democracy and steadily transform the country from an agricultural into an industrial one.

ARTICLE 4. The people of the People's Republic of China shall have the right to elect and to be elected according to law.

---

3) In the Chinese Soviet Republic supreme power shall be vested in the All-China Congress of Soviets of Workers', Peasants', and Soldiers' Deputies. In between Congresses, the supreme organ of power shall be the All-China C.E.C. [Central Executive Committee] of the Soviets; the C.E.C. shall appoint a Council of People's Commissars, which shall conduct all governmental affairs, and promulgate orders and resolutions.

4) All workers, peasants, Red Army soldiers, and all toilers and their families, without distinction of sex, religion, or nationality (Chinese, Manchurians, Mongolians, Moslems, Tibetans, Miao, Li as well as all Koreans, Formosans, Annamites, etc., living in China) shall be equal before the Soviet law, and shall be citizens of the Soviet Republic. In order that the workers, peasants, soldiers, and toiling masses may actually hold the reins of power, the following regulations concerning Soviet elections shall be established: All the above-mentioned Soviet citizens who shall have attained the age of sixteen shall be entitled to vote and to be voted for in the elections of the soviets. [They] shall elect deputies to all congresses of workers, peasants, and soldiers (soviets); they shall discuss and decide all national and local political questions. The method of electing deputies [is as follows]. The workers shall elect their deputies in the factories; the artisans, peasants, and urban poor shall elect deputies

ARTICLE 5. The people of the People's Republic of China shall have freedom of thought, speech, publication, assembly, association, correspondence, person, domicile, change of domicile, religious belief and the freedom of holding processions and demonstrations.

ARTICLE 6. The People's Republic of China shall abolish the feudal system which holds women in bondage. Women shall enjoy equal rights with men in political, economic, cultural, educational and social life. Freedom of marriage for men and women shall be put into effect.

ARTICLE 7. The People's Republic of China will suppress all counterrevolutionary activities, severely punish all Kuomintang counterrevolutionary war criminals and other leading incorrigible counterrevolutionary elements who collaborate with imperialism, commit treason against the fatherland and oppose the cause of people's democracy. Feudal landlords, bureaucratic capitalists and reactionary elements in general, after they have been disarmed and have had their special powers abolished, shall, in addition, be deprived of their political rights in accordance with law for a necessary period. But, at the same time, they shall be given some means of livelihood and shall be compelled to reform themselves through labor so as to become new men. If they continue their counterrevolutionary activities, they will be severely punished.

ARTICLE 8. It is the duty of every national of the People's Republic of China to defend the fatherland, to abide by the law, to observe labor discipline, to protect public property, to perform public and military service, and to pay taxes.

ARTICLE 9. All nationalities in the People's Republic of China shall have equal rights and duties.

ARTICLE 10. The armed forces of the People's Republic of China, namely, the People's Liberation Army, the people's public security forces and the people's police, belong to the people. It is the task of these armed forces to defend the independence, territorial integrity and sovereignty of China, and to defend the revolutionary gains and all legitimate rights and interests of the Chinese people. The Central People's Government of the People's Republic of China shall endeavor to consolidate and strengthen the people's armed forces, so as to enable them to accomplish their tasks effectively.

---

according to their place of residence. Deputies to the local soviets shall be elected by these basic units (i.e., factory districts) for a definite term; they shall participate in the work of one of the organizations or commissions attached to the town or village soviets and shall periodically submit reports to their electors concerning their activities. The electors shall have the right at all times to recall their deputies and demand new elections. Since only the proletariat can lead the broad masses to socialism, the Chinese Soviet regime grants special rights to the proletariat in the elections to the soviets by allowing it a greater number of deputies.

5) It shall be the purpose of the Soviet regime to improve thoroughly the living conditions of the working class, to pass labor legislation, to introduce the eight-hour working day, to fix a minimum wage, and to institute social insurance and state assistance to the unemployed as well as to grant the workers the right to supervise production.

6) In setting itself the task of abolishing feudalism and radically improving the living conditions of the peasants, the Soviet regime of China shall pass a land law, and shall order the confiscation of the land of all landlords and its distribution among the poor and middle peasants, with a view to the ultimate nationalization of the land.

ARTICLE 11. The People's Republic of China shall unite with all peace-loving and freedom-loving countries and peoples throughout the world first of all; with the U.S.S.R., all People's Democracies and all oppressed nations. It shall take its stand in the camp of international peace and democracy, to oppose imperialist aggression, to defend lasting world peace.

CHAPTER II
ORGANS OF STATE POWER

ARTICLE 12. The state power of the People's Republic of China belongs to the people. The people's congresses and the people's governments of all levels are the organs for the exercise of state power by the people. The people's congresses of all levels shall be popularly elected by universal franchise. The people's congresses of all levels shall elect the people's governments of their respective levels. The people's governments shall be the organs for exercising state power at their respective levels when the people's congresses of their respective levels are not in session.

The All-China People's Congress shall be the supreme organ of state power. The Central People's Government shall be the supreme organ for exercising state power when the All-China People's Congress is not in session.

ARTICLE 13. The Chinese People's Political Consultative Conference is the organizational form of the people's democratic united front. It shall be composed of the representatives of the working class, the peasantry, members of the revolutionary armed forces, intellectuals, the petty bourgeoisie, the national bourgeoisie, national minorities, the overseas Chinese and other patriotic democratic elements.

Pending the convocation of the All-China People's Congress elected by universal franchise, the plenary session of the Chinese People's Political Consultative Conference shall exercise the functions and powers of the All-China People's Congress, enact the Organic Law of the Central People's Government of the People's Republic of China, elect the Central People's Government Council of the People's Republic of China and vest it with the authority to exercise state power.

After the convocation of the All-China People's Congress, elected by universal franchise, the Chinese People's Political Consultative Conference may submit proposals on fundamental policies relating to national construction work and on other important measures to the All-China People's Congress or to the Central People's Government.

---

7) It shall be the purpose of the Soviet regime of China to defend the interests of the workers and peasants and restrict the development of capitalism, with a view to liberating the toiling masses from capitalist exploitation and leading them to the socialist order of society. [The Soviet government of China] shall announce the abolition of all burdensome taxation and miscellaneous levies introduced during the counterrevolutionary regime and shall put into effect a single progressive income tax. It shall harshly suppress all attempts at wrecking and sabotage on the part of either native or foreign capitalists; it shall pursue an economic policy which shall be beneficial to the workers and peasant masses, which shall be understood by these masses and which shall lead to socialism.

8) The Soviet regime of China shall set itself the goal of freeing China from the yoke of imperialism. It shall declare the complete sovereignty and independence of the Chinese people, shall refuse to recognize any political or economic privileges for the imperialists in China, and shall abolish all unequal treaties and foreign loans contracted by the counterrevolutionary governments. No foreign imperialist troops, whether land, sea, or air, shall be allowed to be stationed on any territory of the

ARTICLE 14. In all places newly liberated by the People's Liberation Army, military control shall be exercised and the Kuomintang reactionary organs of state power shall be abolished. The Central People's Government or military and political organs at the front shall appoint personnel to organize Military Control Committees and local People's Governments. These shall lead the people in establishing revolutionary order and suppressing counterrevolutionary activities and, when conditions permit, shall convene All-Circles Representative Conferences.

Pending the convocation of the local people's congresses elected by universal franchise, the local All-Circles Representative Conferences shall gradually assume the functions and powers of the local people's congresses.

The duration of military control shall be determined by the Central People's Government according to the military and political conditions prevailing in the different localities.

In all places where military operations have completely ended, agrarian reform has been thoroughly carried out, and people of all circles have been fully organized, elections based on universal franchise shall be held immediately for the purpose of convening local People's Congresses.

ARTICLE 15. The organs of state power at all levels shall practice democratic centralism. In doing this the main principles shall be: the People's Congresses shall be responsible and accountable to the people; the People's Government Councils shall be responsible and accountable to the People's Congresses. Within the People's Congresses and within the People's Government Councils, the minority shall abide by the decisions of the majority; the appointment of the People's Governments of each level shall be ratified by the People's Government of the higher level; the People's Governments of the lower levels shall obey the People's Governments of the higher levels and all local People's Governments throughout the country shall obey the Central People's Government.

ARTICLE 16. The jurisdiction of the Central People's Government and the local People's Governments shall be defined according to the nature of the various matters involved, and shall be prescribed by decrees of the Central People's Government Council so as to satisfy the requirements of both national unity and local expediency.

ARTICLE 17. All laws, decrees and judicial systems of the Kuomintang reactionary government, which oppresses the people, shall be abolished. Laws and decrees protecting the people shall be enacted and the people's judicial system shall be established.

Chinese Soviets. All concessions or territories leased by the imperialists in China shall be unconditionally returned to China. All custom houses, railways, steamship companies, mining enterprises, factories, etc., in the hands of the imperialists shall be confiscated and nationalized. It shall be permissible for foreign enterprises to renew their leases (for their various businesses) and to continue production, provided they shall fully comply with the laws of the Soviet government.

9) The Soviet government of China will do its utmost to bring about the culmination of the workers' and peasants' revolution in its final victory throughout the whole of China. It declares that it is incumbent upon the entire toiling masses to participate in the revolutionary class struggle. The gradual introduction of universal military service and the change from voluntary to compulsory military service shall be worked out especially. The right to bear arms in defense of the revolution shall be granted only to workers, peasants, and the toiling masses; all counterrevolutionary and exploiting elements must be completely disarmed.

ARTICLE 18. All state organs of the People's Republic of China must enforce a revolutionary style of working, embodying honesty, simplicity and service to the people: they must severely punish corruption, forbid extravagance and oppose the bureaucratic style of working which alienates the masses of the people.

ARTICLE 19. People's supervisory organs shall be set up in the People's Governments of county and municipal level and above, to supervise the performance of duties by the state organs of various levels and by public functionaries of all types, and to propose that disciplinary action be taken against state organs and public functionaries who violate the law or are negligent in the performance of their duties.

The people or people's organizations shall have the right to file charges with the people's supervisory organs or people's judicial organs against any state organs or any public functionaries that violate the law or are negligent in the performance of their duties.

CHAPTER III

MILITARY SYSTEM

ARTICLE 20. The People's Republic of China shall build up a unified army, the People's Liberation Army and people's public security forces, which shall be under the command of the People's Revolutionary Military Council of the Central People's Government; it shall institute unification of command, system, formation and discipline.

ARTICLE 21. The People's Liberation Army and the people's public security forces shall, in accordance with the principle of unity between the officers and the rank-and-file and between the army and the people, set up a system of political work and shall educate the commanders and rank-and-file of these forces in a revolutionary and patriotic spirit.

ARTICLE 22. The People's Republic of China shall strengthen its modernized army and shall establish an air force and a navy in order to consolidate national defense.

ARTICLE 23. The People's Republic of China shall put into effect the people's militia system to maintain local order and to lay the foundation for national mobilization. It shall make preparations to enforce a system of obligatory military service at the appropriate time.

---

10) The Soviet government of China guarantees to the workers, peasants, and toilers freedom of speech and the press as well as the right to assembly; it will be opposed to bourgeois and landlord democracy, but is in favor of the democracy of the workers and peasant masses. It breaks down the economic and political prerogatives of the bourgeoisie and the landlords, in order to remove all obstacles placed by the reactionaries on the workers' and peasants' road to freedom. The workers, peasants, and toiling masses shall enjoy the use of printing shops, meeting halls, and similar establishments by the power of a people's regime, as a material basis for the realization of these rights and liberties. Furthermore, under the Soviet regime, all propaganda and other similar activities by reactionaries shall be suppressed and all exploiters be deprived of all political liberties.

11) It is the purpose of the Soviet government of China to guarantee the thorough emancipation of women; it recognizes freedom of marriage and will put into operation various measures for the protection of women, to enable women gradually to attain to the material basis required for their emancipation from the bondage of domestic work, and to give them the possibility of participating in the social, economic, political, and cultural life of the entire society.

ARTICLE 24. The armed forces of the People's Republic of China shall, during peacetime, systematically take part in agricultural and industrial production in order to assist in national construction work, provided their military duties are not thereby hampered.

ARTICLE 25. Dependents of those who have given their lives for the revolution and of members of the revolutionary forces who are in need, shall receive preferential treatment from the state and from society. The People's Government shall make appropriate arrangements for disabled or retired servicemen who have participated in the revolutionary war, providing them with the means of livelihood or with occupations.

CHAPTER IV

ECONOMIC POLICY

ARTICLE 26. The basic principle for the economic construction of the People's Republic of China is to develop production and bring about a prosperous economy through the policies of taking into account both public and private interests, of benefiting both labor and capital, of mutual aid between the city and countryside, and circulation of goods between China and abroad. The state shall coordinate and regulate state-owned economy, cooperative economy, the individual economy of peasants and handicraftsmen, private capitalist economy and state capitalist economy, in their spheres of operations, supply of raw materials, marketing, labor conditions, technical equipment, policies of public and general finance, etc. In this way all components of the social economy can, under the leadership of the state-owned economy, carry out division and coordination of labor and play their respective parts in promoting the development of the social economy as a whole.

ARTICLE 27. Agrarian reform is the necessary condition for the development of the nation's productive power and for its industrialization. In all areas where agrarian reform has been carried out, the ownership of the land acquired by the peasants shall be protected. In areas where agrarian reform has not been carried out, the peasant masses must be set in motion to establish peasant organizations and to put into effect the policy of 'land to the tiller' through such measures as the elimination of local bandits and despots, the reduction of rent and interest and the distribution of land.

---

12) The Soviet government of China shall guarantee to all workers, peasants, and the toiling masses the right to education. The Soviet government will, as far as the conditions of internal revolutionary war allow, begin at once to introduce free universal education. Above all, the Soviet government shall defend the interests of laboring youth and give them every opportunity of participating in the political and cultural revolutionary life with a view to developing new social forces.

13) The Soviet government of China guarantees true religious freedom to the workers, peasants, and the toiling population. Adhering to the principle of the complete separation of church and state, the Soviet state neither favors nor grants any financial assistance to any religion whatsoever. All Soviet citizens shall enjoy the right to engage in antireligious propaganda. No religious institution of the imperialists shall be allowed to exist unless it shall comply with Soviet law.

14) The Soviet government of China recognizes the right of self-determination of the national minorities in China, their right to complete separation from China, and to the formation of an independent state for each national minority. All Mongolians, Tibetans, Miao, Yao, Koreans, and

ARTICLE 28. State-owned economy is of a socialist nature. All enterprises relating to the economic life of the country and exercising a dominant influence over the people's livelihood shall be under the unified operation of the state. All state-owned resources and enterprises are the public property of all the people and are the main material basis on which the People's Republic will develop production and bring about a prosperous economy. They are the leading force of the entire social economy.

ARTICLE 29. Cooperative economy is of a semi-socialist nature and is an important component of the people's economy as a whole. The People's Government shall foster its development and accord it preferential treatment.

ARTICLE 30. The People's Government shall encourage the active operation of all private economic enterprises beneficial to the national welfare and to the people's livelihood and shall assist in their development.

ARTICLE 31. The economy jointly operated by state and private capital is of a state-capitalist nature. Whenever necessary and possible, private capital shall be encouraged to develop in the direction of state-capitalism, in such ways as processing for state-owned enterprises and exploiting state-owned resources in the form of concessions.

ARTICLE 32. The system of workers' participation in the administration of production shall, for the present period, be established in state-owned enterprises. This means that factory administrative committees shall be set up under the leadership of the factory managers. In privately owned enterprises, in order to carry out the principle of benefiting both labor and capital, collective contracts shall be signed by the trade union, representing the workers and employees, and the employer. For the present period, an eight- to ten-hour day should in general be enforced in publicly- and privately-operated enterprises, but under special circumstances this matter may be dealt with at discretion. The People's Governments shall fix minimum wages according to the conditions prevailing in various localities and trades. Labor insurance shall be gradually established. The special interests of juvenile and women workers shall be safeguarded. Inspection of industries and mines shall be carried out in order to improve their safety devices and sanitary facilities.

ARTICLE 33. The Central People's Government shall strive to draw up, as soon as possible, a general plan for rehabilitating and developing the main departments

---

others living on the territory of China shall enjoy the full right to self-determination, i.e., they may either join the Union of Chinese Soviets or secede from it and form their own state as they may prefer. The Soviet regime of China will do its utmost to assist the national minorities in liberating themselves from the yoke of imperialists, the KMT militarists, *t'u-ssu* [tribal headmen], the princes, lamas, and others, and in achieving complete freedom and autonomy. The Soviet regime must encourage the development of the national cultures and of the respective national languages of these peoples.

15) The Chinese regime offers asylum to Chinese and foreign revolutionaries persecuted for their revolutionary activities; it will assist and lead them in recovering their strength so that they may fight with increased vigor for the victory of the revolution.

16) All foreign toilers living in districts under the jurisdiction of the Soviet regime shall enjoy equal rights as stipulated by Soviet law.

17) The Soviet regime of China declares its readiness to form a united revolutionary front with the world proletariat and all oppressed nations, and proclaims the Soviet Union, the land of proletarian dictatorship, to be its loyal ally.

of the public and private economy of the entire country. It shall also fix the scope of the division and coordination of labor between the central and local governments in economic construction, and shall undertake centralized regulation of the inter-relationship between the economic departments of the central and local governments. Under the unified leadership of the Central People's Government, the various economic departments of the central and local governments should give full play to their creativeness and initiative.

ARTICLE 34. Agriculture, forestry, fisheries and animal husbandry: In all areas where agrarian reform has been thoroughly carried out, the central task of the People's Government shall be the organization of the peasants and of all manpower available for allocation to the development of agricultural production and secondary occupations. The People's Government shall also guide the peasants, step by step, in the organization of various forms of mutual aid in labor and cooperation in production, according to the principle of willingness and mutual benefit. In newly liberated areas, every step in agrarian reform shall be linked up with reviving and developing agricultural production.

The People's Government shall, in accordance with the state plan and the requirements of the people's livelihood, strive to restore the output of grain, industrial raw materials and export goods to the prewar production level and to surpass it within the shortest possible time. Attention shall be paid to construction and repair of irrigation works, to prevention of floods and droughts, to restoration and development of animal husbandry, to increasing the supply of fertilizers, to improvement of farm implements and seeds, to prevention of pest damage and plant diseases, to relief work in the event of natural calamities, and to planned migration for land reclamation.

Forests shall be protected and forestation shall be developed according to plan.

Coastal fisheries shall be protected and the aquatic products industry shall be developed.

Livestock-raising shall be protected and developed, and preventive measures shall be taken against plague.

ARTICLE 35. Industry: In order to lay the foundation for the industrialization of the country, the central point of industrial work shall be the planned, systematic rehabilitation and development of heavy industry, such as mining, the iron and steel industry, power industry, machine-making industry, electrical industry and the main chemical industries, etc. At the same time, the production of the textile industry and other light industries beneficial to the national welfare and to the people's livelihood shall be restored and increased so as to meet the needs of the people's daily consumption.

ARTICLE 36. Communications: Railways and highways shall be swiftly restored and gradually extended. Rivers shall be dredged and water transportation expanded. Postal, telegraphic and telephone services shall be improved and developed. Various communications facilities shall be built up and civil aviation established step by step according to plan.

ARTICLE 37. Commerce: All legitimate public and private trade shall be protected. Control shall be exercised over foreign trade and the policy of protecting trade shall be adopted. Freedom of domestic trade shall be established under a unified economic state plan, but commercial speculation disturbing the market shall be strictly prohibited. State-owned trading organizations shall assume the responsibility of adjusting supply and demand, stabilizing commodity prices and assisting the people's cooperatives. The People's Government shall adopt the measures necessary to encourage the people in saving, to facilitate remittances from overseas Chinese, and to channel into industry and other productive enterprises all socially idle capital and commercial capital which is not beneficial to the national welfare and/or to the people's livelihood.

ARTICLE 38. Cooperatives: The broad masses of working people shall be encouraged and assisted to develop cooperatives according to the principle of willingness. Supply and marketing cooperatives, as well as consumers', credit, producers', and transport cooperatives shall be organized in towns and villages. Consumers' cooperatives shall first be organized in factories, institutions and schools.

ARTICLE 39. Currency and Banking: Financial enterprises shall be strictly controlled by the state. The right of issuing currency belongs to the state. The circulation of foreign currency within the country shall be prohibited. The buying and selling of foreign exchange, foreign currency, gold and silver, shall be handled by the state banks. Private financial enterprises operating in accordance with the law shall be subjected to supervision and direction by the state. All who engage in financial speculation and undermine the financial enterprises of the state shall be subjected to severe punishment.

ARTICLE 40. Public finance: A budget and financial statement system shall be instituted. The spheres of financial administration of central and local governments shall be defined. Economizing and frugality shall be enforced. The budget shall be steadily balanced and capital accumulated for the country's production.

The tax policy of the state shall be based on the principle of ensuring supplies for the revolutionary war and taking into account the rehabilitation and development of production and the requirements of national construction. The tax system shall be simplified and an equitable distribution of the tax burden effected.

CHAPTER V

CULTURAL AND EDUCATIONAL POLICY

ARTICLE 41. The culture and education of the People's Republic of China shall be New Democratic—national, scientific and popular. The main tasks of the People's Government in cultural and educational work shall be the raising of the cultural level of the people, the training of personnel for national construction work, the eradicating of feudal, comprador and fascist ideology and the developing of the ideology of service to the people.

ARTICLE 42. Love of the fatherland, love of the people, love of labor, love of science and care of public property shall be promoted as the public spirit of all nationals of the People's Republic of China.

ARTICLE 43. Efforts shall be made to develop the natural sciences in order to serve industrial, agricultural and national defence construction. Scientific discoveries and inventions shall be encouraged and rewarded and scientific knowledge shall be disseminated among the people.

ARTICLE 44. The application of a scientific-historical viewpoint to the study and interpretation of history, economics, politics, culture and international affairs shall be promoted. Outstanding works of social science shall be encouraged and rewarded.

ARTICLE 45. Literature and art shall be promoted to serve the people, to awaken their political consciousness, and to enhance their enthusiasm for labor. Outstanding works of literature and art shall be encouraged and rewarded. The people's drama and cinema shall be developed.

ARTICLE 46. The method of education of the People's Republic of China shall be the unification of theory and practice. The People's Government shall reform the old educational system, subject matter and teaching methods in a planned, systematic manner.

ARTICLE 47. In order to meet the extensive requirements of revolutionary and national construction work, universal education shall be carried out, secondary and higher education shall be strengthened, technical education shall be stressed, the education of workers during their spare time and that of cadres at their posts shall be strengthened, and revolutionary political education shall be accorded to both young- and old-type intellectuals. All this is to be done in a planned and systematic manner.

ARTICLE 48. National physical culture shall be promoted. Public health and medical work shall be expanded and attention shall be paid to the protection of the health of mothers, infants and children.

ARTICLE 49. Freedom of reporting truthful news shall be safeguarded. The utilization of the press for slander, for undermining the interests of the state and the people and for provoking world war shall be prohibited. The people's radio and publication work shall be developed. Attention shall be paid to publishing popular books and journals beneficial to the people.

CHAPTER VI

POLICY TOWARD NATIONALITIES

ARTICLE 50. All nationalities within the boundaries of the People's Republic of China are equal. They shall establish unity and mutual aid among themselves, and shall oppose imperialism and their own public enemies, so that the People's Republic of China will become a big fraternal and cooperative family composed of all its nationalities. Greater nationalism and chauvinism shall be opposed. Acts involving discrimination, oppression and splitting of the unity of the various nationalities shall be prohibited.

ARTICLE 51. Regional autonomy shall be exercised in areas where national minorities are concentrated and various kinds of autonomous organizations of the different nationalities shall be set up according to the size of the respective populations and regions. In places where different nationalities live together and in the autonomous areas of the national minorities, the different nationalities shall each have an appropriate number of representatives in the local organs of political power.

ARTICLE 52. All national minorities within the boundaries of the People's Republic of China shall have the right to join the People's Liberation Army and to organize local people's public security forces in accordance with the unified military system of the state.

ARTICLE 53. All national minorities shall have freedom to develop their dialects and languages, to preserve or reform their traditions, customs and religious beliefs. The People's Government shall assist the masses of the people of all national minorities to develop their political, economic, cultural and educational construction work.

CHAPTER VII

FOREIGN POLICY

ARTICLE 54. The principle of the foreign policy of the People's Republic of China is protection of the independence, freedom, integrity of territory and sovereignty of the country, upholding of lasting international peace and friendly cooperation between the peoples of all countries, and opposition to the imperialist policy of aggression and war.

ARTICLE 55. The Central People's Government of the People's Republic of China shall examine the treaties and agreements concluded between the Kuomintang and foreign governments, and shall recognize, abrogate, revise, or renegotiate them according to their respective contents.

ARTICLE 56. The Central People's Government of the People's Republic of China may, on the basis of equality, mutual benefit and mutual respect for territory and sovereignty, negotiate with foreign governments which have severed relations with the Kuomintang reactionary clique and which adopt a friendly attitude toward the People's Republic of China, and may establish diplomatic relations with them.

ARTICLE 57. The People's Republic of China may restore and develop commercial relations with foreign governments and peoples on a basis of equality and mutual benefit.

ARTICLE 58. The Central People's Government of the People's Republic of China shall do its utmost to protect the proper rights and interests of Chinese residing abroad.

ARTICLE 59. The People's Government of the People's Republic of China protects law-abiding foreign nationals in China.

ARTICLE 60. The People's Republic of China shall accord the right of asylum to foreign nationals who seek refuge in China because they have been oppressed by their own governments for supporting the people's interests and taking part in the struggle for peace and democracy.

2. 2

THE ORGANIC LAW OF THE CENTRAL PEOPLE'S GOVERNMENT OF THE PEOPLE'S REPUBLIC OF CHINA[1]

Adopted by the First Plenary Session of the Chinese People's P.C.C.
September 29, 1949

CHAPTER I
GENERAL PRINCIPLES

ARTICLE 1. The People's Republic of China is a state of the people's democratic dictatorship, led by the working class, based on the alliance of workers and peasants, and uniting all democratic classes and the various nationalities within the country.

ARTICLE 2. The Government of the People's Republic of China is a government of the people's congress system based on the principle of democratic centralism.

ARTICLE 3. Prior to the convocation of the All-China People's Congress by universal franchise, the Plenary Session of the Chinese People's Political Consultative Conference shall perform the functions and exercise the power of the All-China People's Congress, enact the Organic Law of the Central People's Government of the People's Republic of China, elect the Central People's Government Council of the People's Republic of China, and vest it with the authority to exercise state power.

ARTICLE 4. The Central People's Government Council represents the People's Republic of China in international relations and assumes the leadership of the state apparatus at home.

ARTICLE 5. The Central People's Government Council shall set up the Government Administration Council as the highest executive body for state administration; the People's Revolutionary Military Council as the supreme military command of the state; and the Supreme People's Court and the People's Procurator-General's Office as the highest judicial and supervisory bodies of the country.

CHAPTER II
THE CENTRAL PEOPLE'S GOVERNMENT COUNCIL

ARTICLE 6. The Central People's Government Council shall consist of the Chairman and six Vice-Chairmen of the Central People's Government and of fifty-six

---

[1] Translation from Otto B. Van der Sprenkel, Robert Guillain and Michael Lindsay, *New China: Three Views* (London: Turnstile Press, 1950), pp. 217–26.

Council Members elected by the Plenary Session of the Chinese People's Political Consultative Conference. It shall have a Secretary-General elected by and from the Central People's Government Council.

ARTICLE 7. The Central People's Government Council shall exercise the following authority, in accordance with the Common Program enacted by the Plenary Session of the Chinese People's Political Consultative Conference:

1. Enacting and interpreting the laws of the state, promulgating decrees and supervising their execution;

2. Determining the administrative policies of the state;

3. Annulling or revising any decisions and orders of the Government Administration Council, which do not conform to the laws and decrees of the state;

4. Ratifying, abrogating or revising treaties and agreements concluded by the People's Republic of China with foreign countries;

5. Dealing with questions of war and peace;

6. Approving or revising the state budget and financial statement;

7. Promulgating acts of general amnesty and pardon;

8. Instituting and awarding orders, medals, and titles of honor of the state;

9. Appointing or removing government personnel as follows:

(a) Appointment or removal of the Premier and Vice-Premiers and Members of the Government Administration Council; Secretary-General and Assistant Secretaries-General of the Government Administration Council; Chairmen, Vice-Chairmen and Members of the various Committees and Commissions; Ministers and Vice-Ministers of the various Ministries; President and Vice Presidents of the Academy of Sciences; Directors and Deputy Directors of the various Administrations; and Manager and Assistant Managers of the Bank;

(b) Appointment or removal or confirmation of the appointment or removal, on the recommendation of the Government Administration Council, of Chairmen, Vice-Chairmen and chief administrative personnel of People's Governments in various major administrative areas, provinces and municipalities;

(c) Appointment or removal of ambassadors, ministers and plenipotentiary representatives to foreign states;

(d) Appointment or removal of the Chairmen, Vice-Chairmen and Members of the People's Revolutionary Military Council; of the Commander-in-Chief, Deputy Commander-in-Chief, Chief of Staff, Deputy Chief of Staff, Director and Assistant Director of the General Political Department of the People's Liberation Army;

(e) Appointment or removal of the President and Vice Presidents and Committee Members of the Supreme People's Court, the Procurator-General, Deputy Procurators-General and Committee Members of the People's Procurator-General's Office;

10. Preparing for and convening the All-China People's Congress.

ARTICLE 8. The Chairman of the Central People's Government shall preside over the meetings of the Central People's Government Council and shall direct its work.

ARTICLE 9. The Vice-Chairmen and Secretary-General of the Central People's Government shall assist the Chairman in the discharge of his duties.

ARTICLE 10. Sessions of Central People's Government Council shall be convened by the Chairman once every two months. The Chairman may convene the session earlier or postpone it when conditions demand it or upon the request of more than one-third of the members of the Central People's Government Council or upon the request of the Government Administration Council. More than one-half of the Council Members constitute a quorum, and the adoption of any resolution demands the concurrence of over one-half of the Members present at the session.

ARTICLE 11. The Central People's Government Council shall have a Secretariat and may set up other subordinate working bodies when necessary.

ARTICLE 12. The Central People's Government Council shall enact its own organizational regulations.

CHAPTER III

THE GOVERNMENT ADMINISTRATION COUNCIL

ARTICLE 13. The Government Administration Council shall consist of a Premier, a number of Vice-Premiers, a Secretary-General and a number of Council Members appointed by the Central People's Government Council.

Members of the Government Administration Council may concurrently hold posts as Chairmen of the various Committees or Commissions or as Ministers of the various Ministries.

ARTICLE 14. The Government Administration Council shall be responsible and accountable to the Central People's Government Council. When the Central People's Government Council adjourns, the Government Administration Council shall be responsible and accountable to the Chairman of the Central People's Government.

ARTICLE 15. The Government Administration Council shall exercise the following authority on the basis and in application of the Common Program of the Chinese People's Political Consultative Conference, and of the laws and decrees of the state and of the administrative policies stipulated by the Central People's Government Council:

1. Issuing decisions and orders and verifying their execution;

2. Annulling or revising the decisions and orders of the Committees, Ministries, Commissions, Academy, Administrations, and Bank, and governments of all levels, which do not conform to the laws and decrees of the state and of the decisions and orders of the Government Administration Council;

3. Submitting bills to the Central People's Government Council;

4. Coordinating, unifying and directing the interrelations, the internal organization and the general work of the Committees, Ministries, Commissions, Academy, Administrations, and Bank, and other subordinate bodies;

5. Directing the work of local People's Governments throughout the country;

6. Appointing or removing, or confirming the appointment or removal of the chief administrative personnel at the county and municipal level and above, not included in Article 7, Section 9b.

ARTICLE 16. The Premier of the Government Administration Council shall direct the Council's affairs. The Vice-Premiers and the Secretary-General of the Government Administration Council shall assist the Premier in the discharge of his duties.

ARTICLE 17. Once a week the Government Administration Council shall hold meetings convened by the Premier. The Premier may convene the meeting earlier or postpone it when conditions demand it, or upon the request of over one-third of the Council Members. Over one-half of the Members of the Government Administration Council constitute a quorum, and the adoption of a resolution demands the concurrence of over one-half of the Members present at the meeting.

The decisions and orders of the Government Administration Council shall come into force when signed by the Premier or signed by the Premier and countersigned by the heads of the Committees, Ministries, Commissions, Academy, Administrations, or Bank concerned.

ARTICLE 18. The Government Administration Council shall set up Committees of Political and Legal Affairs, of Financial and Economic Affairs, of Cultural and Educational Affairs, of People's Control, and shall set up the following Ministries, Commissions, Academy, Administrations, and Bank, which shall direct their respective departments of state administration: Ministry of the Interior, Ministry of Foreign Affairs, Information Administration, Ministry of Public Security, Ministry of Finance, People's Bank, Ministry of Trade, Customs Administration, Ministry of Heavy Industry, Ministry of Fuel Industry, Ministry of Textile Industry, Ministry of Food Industry, Ministry of Light Industry (industries not included in the four mentioned above), Ministry of Railways, Ministry of Posts, Telegraph and Telephone, Ministry of Communications, Ministry of Agriculture, Ministry of Forestry and Land Reclamation, Ministry of Water Works, Ministry of Labor, Ministry of Cultural Affairs, Ministry of Education, Academy of Sciences, Press Administration, Publications Administration, Ministry of Public Health, Ministry of Justice, Commission of Legislative Affairs, Commission of Nationalities Affairs, Commission of Overseas Chinese Affairs.

The Committee of Political and Legal Affairs shall direct the work of the Ministry of the Interior, the Ministry of Public Security, the Ministry of Justice, the Commission of Legislative Affairs, and the Commission of the Nationalities Affairs.

The Committee of Financial and Economical Affairs shall direct the work of the Ministries of Finance, of Trade, of Heavy Industry, of Fuel Industry, of Textile Industry, of Food Industry, of Light Industry, of Railways, of Posts, Telegraphs and Telephones, of Communications, of Agriculture, of Forestry and Land Reclamation, of Water Works, of Labor, and of the People's Bank, and of the Customs Administration.

The Committee of Cultural and Educational Affairs shall direct the work of the Ministry of Cultural Affairs, the Ministry of Education, the Ministry of Public Health, the Academy of Sciences, the Press Administration, and the Publications Administration.

In order to carry out their work, the responsible Committees may issue decisions and orders to the Ministries, the Commissions, the Academy, the Administrations and the Bank under their direction and to other subordinate bodies and may verify their execution.

The Committee of People's Supervision shall be responsible for the supervision over the execution of duties by government institutions, and public functionaries.

ARTICLE 19. The Ministries, Commissions, Academy, Administrations and the Bank may announce decisions and issue orders within their jurisdiction and may verify their execution.

ARTICLE 20. The Government Administration Council shall have a Secretariat to deal with routine work and to take charge of the files, archives and seals of the Government Administration Council, etc.

ARTICLE 21. The organizational regulations of the Government Administration Council, the Committees, Ministries, Commissions, the Academy, the Administrations, the Bank and the Secretariat shall be enacted or ratified by the Central People's Government Council.

ARTICLE 22. The Central People's Government Council may, when necessary, decide on the increase or reduction of the number or on the merging of the Committees, Ministries, Commissions, the Academy, Administrations, the Bank and the Secretariat.

CHAPTER IV

THE PEOPLE'S REVOLUTIONARY MILITARY COUNCIL

ARTICLE 23. The People's Liberation Army and other people's armed forces throughout the country shall come under the unified control and command of the People's Revolutionary Military Council.

ARTICLE 24. The People's Revolutionary Military Council shall have a Chairman, a number of Vice-Chairmen, and a number of Council Members.

ARTICLE 25. The organization of the People's Revolutionary Military Council and the system of its administration and command shall be determined by the Central People's Government Council.

CHAPTER V

THE SUPREME PEOPLE'S COURT AND THE PEOPLE'S PROCURATOR-GENERAL'S OFFICE

ARTICLE 26. The Supreme People's Court is the highest judicial body of the country, and is charged with the direction and supervision of the judicial work of all levels of judicial bodies of the country.

ARTICLE 27. The Supreme People's Court shall have a President and a number of Vice Presidents and a number of Committee Members.

ARTICLE 28. The People's Procurator-General's Office shall have the supreme supervisory power to ensure the strict observance of the law by all government institutions and public functionaries as well as by nationals of the country.

ARTICLE 29. The People's Procurator-General's Office shall have a Procurator-General, a number of Deputy Procurators-General and a number of Committee Members.

ARTICLE 30. The organizational regulations of the Supreme People's Court and of the People's Procurator-General's Office shall be enacted by the Central People's Government Council.

CHAPTER VI

RIGHT OF AMENDMENT AND INTERPRETATION OF THIS ORGANIC LAW

ARTICLE 31. The right of amendment of the Organic Law of the Central People's Government belongs to the Plenary Session of the Chinese People's Political Consultative Conference; while the latter is not in session, it belongs to the Central People's Government Council. The right of interpretation of this Organic Law belongs to the Central People's Government Council.

2. 3

CONSTITUTION
OF THE PEOPLE'S REPUBLIC
OF CHINA[1]

Adopted by the First National People's Congress of the
People's Republic of China at its First Session
September 20, 1954

PREAMBLE

IN the year 1949, after more than a century of heroic struggle, the Chinese people, led by the Communist Party of China, finally won their great victory in the people's revolution against imperialism, feudalism and bureaucrat-capitalism, and thereby brought to an end the history of the oppression and enslavement they had undergone for so long and founded the People's Republic of China—a people's democratic dictatorship. The system of people's democracy—the system of new democracy—of the People's Republic of China guarantees that our country can in a peaceful way eliminate exploitation and poverty and build a prosperous and happy socialist society.

From the founding of the People's Republic of China to the attainment of a socialist society is a period of transition. The general tasks of the state during the transition period are, step by step, to bring about the socialist industrialization of the country and, step by step, to accomplish the socialist transformation of agriculture, handicrafts and capitalist industry and commerce. In the last few years our people have successfully carried out the reform of the agrarian system, resistance to United States aggression and aid to Korea, the suppression of counterrevolutionaries, the rehabilitation of the national economy, and other large-scale struggles, thereby preparing the necessary conditions for planned economic construction and the gradual transition to a socialist society.

The First National People's Congress of the People's Republic of China, at its First Session held in Peking, the capital, solemnly adopted the Constitution of the People's Republic of China on September 20, 1954. This Constitution is based on the Common Program of the Chinese People's Political Consultative Conference of 1949 and is a development of it. This Constitution consolidates the gains of the Chinese people's revolution and the new victories won in the political and economic fields since the founding of the People's Republic of China; and, moreover, it reflects the basic needs of the state in the period of transition, as well as the common desire of the broad masses of the people to build a socialist society.

In the course of the great struggle to establish the People's Republic of China, the people of our country forged a broad people's democratic united front led by

---

[1] *Constitution of the People's Republic of China* (Peking: Foreign Languages Press, 1961).

the Communist Party of China and composed of all democratic classes, democratic parties and groups, and people's organizations. This people's democratic united front will continue to play its part in mobilizing and rallying the whole people in the struggle to fulfill the general tasks of the state during the transition period and to oppose enemies within and without.

All the nationalities in our country have been united in one great family of free and equal nationalities. The unity of our country's nationalities will continue to gain in strength on the basis of the further development of the fraternal bonds and mutual aid among them, and on the basis of opposition to imperialism, opposition to public enemies within their own ranks, and opposition to both big-nation chauvinism and local nationalism. In the course of economic construction and cultural development, the state will concern itself with the needs of the different nationalities, and, in the matter of socialist transformation, pay full attention to the special characteristics in the development of each nationality.

Our country has already built an indestructible friendship with the great Union of Soviet Socialist Republics and the People's Democracies; and the friendship between our people and other peace-loving peoples all over the world is growing day by day. These friendships will continue to be developed and consolidated. Our country's policy of establishing and extending diplomatic relations with all countries on the principles of equality, mutual benefit and respect for each other's sovereignty and territorial integrity has already yielded success and will continue to be carried out. In international affairs the firm and consistent policy of our country is to strive for the noble aims of world peace and the progress of mankind.

CHAPTER ONE
GENERAL PRINCIPLES

ARTICLE 1.   The People's Republic of China is a people's democratic state led by the working class and based on the alliance of workers and peasants.

ARTICLE 2.   All power in the People's Republic of China belongs to the people. The organs through which the people exercise power are the National People's Congress and the local people's congresses at various levels.

The National People's Congress, the local people's congresses and other organs of state practice democratic centralism.

ARTICLE 3.   The People's Republic of China is a unitary multinational state.

All the nationalities are equal. Discrimination against or oppression of any nationality, and acts which undermine the unity of the nationalities, are prohibited.

All the nationalities have the freedom to use and develop their own spoken and written languages, and to preserve or reform their own customs and ways.

Regional autonomy applies in areas where a minority nationality live in a compact community. All the national autonomous areas are inseparable parts of the People's Republic of China.

ARTICLE 4.   The People's Republic of China, by relying on the organs of state and the social forces, and through socialist industrialization and socialist transformation, ensures the gradual abolition of systems of exploitation and the building of a socialist society.

ARTICLE 5.   At present, the main categories of ownership of means of production in the People's Republic of China are the following: state ownership, that is, ownership by the whole people; cooperative ownership, that is, collective ownership by the masses of working people; ownership by individual working people; and capitalist ownership.

ARTICLE 6.   The state sector of the economy is the socialist sector owned by the whole people. It is the leading force in the national economy and the material basis on which the state carries out socialist transformation. The state ensures priority for the development of the state sector of the economy.

All mineral resources and waters, as well as forests, undeveloped land and other resources which the state owns by law, are the property of the whole people.

ARTICLE 7.   The cooperative sector of the economy is either socialist, when collectively owned by the masses of working people, or semisocialist, when in part collectively owned by the masses of working people. Partial collective ownership by the masses of working people is a transitional form by means of which individual peasants, individual handicraftsmen and other individual working people organize themselves in their advance toward collective ownership by the masses of working people.

The state protects the property of the cooperatives, and encourages, guides and helps the development of the cooperative sector of the economy. It regards the development of cooperation in production as the chief means of the transformation of individual farming and individual handicrafts.

ARTICLE 8.   The state protects according to law the right of peasants to own land and other means of production.

The state guides and helps individual peasants to increase production and encourages them, on the voluntary principle, to organize cooperation in the fields of production, supply and marketing, and credit.

The policy of the state toward the rich-peasant economy is to restrict and gradually eliminate it.

ARTICLE 9.   The state protects according to law the right of handicraftsmen and other individual working people in nonagricultural pursuits to own means of production.

The state guides and helps individual handicraftsmen and other individual working people in nonagricultural pursuits to improve their operations, and encourages them, on the voluntary principle, to organize cooperation in production, and supply and marketing.

ARTICLE 10.   The state protects according to law the right of capitalists to own means of production and other capital.

The policy of the state toward capitalist industry and commerce is to use, restrict and transform them. Through control exercised by organs of state administration, leadership by the state sector of the economy, and supervision by the masses of the workers, the state makes use of the positive aspects of capitalist industry and commerce which are beneficial to national welfare and the people's livelihood, restricts their negative aspects which are detrimental to national welfare and the people's livelihood, and encourages and guides their transformation into various forms of state-capitalist economy, gradually replacing capitalist ownership with ownership by the whole people.

The state prohibits capitalists from engaging in any unlawful activities which injure the public interest, disturb the social-economic order, or undermine the economic plan of the state.

ARTICLE 11.   The state protects the right of citizens to own lawfully earned income, savings, houses and other means of subsistence.

ARTICLE 12.   The state protects according to law the right of citizens to inherit private property.

ARTICLE 13.   The state may, in the public interest, requisition by purchase, take over for use or nationalize both urban and rural land as well as other means of production on the conditions provided by law.

ARTICLE 14.   The state prohibits the use of private property by any person to the detriment of the public interest.

ARTICLE 15.   By economic planning, the state directs the growth and transformation of the national economy in order to bring about the constant increase of productive forces, thereby improving the material and cultural life of the people and consolidating the independence and security of the state.

ARTICLE 16.   Work is a matter of honor for every citizen of the People's Republic of China who is capable of working. The state encourages the working enthusiasm and creativeness of citizens.

ARTICLE 17.   All organs of state must rely on the masses of the people, constantly maintain close contact with them, heed their opinions and accept their supervision.

ARTICLE 18.   All personnel of organs of state must be loyal to the system of people's democracy, observe the Constitution and the law and strive to serve the people.

ARTICLE 19.   The People's Republic of China safeguards the system of people's democracy, suppresses all treasonable and counterrevolutionary activities and punishes all traitors and counterrevolutionaries.

The state deprives feudal landlords and bureaucrat-capitalists of political rights for a specific period of time according to law; at the same time it gives them a way to earn a living, in order to enable them to reform through labor and become citizens who earn their livelihood by their own labor.

ARTICLE 20.   The armed forces of the People's Republic of China belong to the people; their duty is to safeguard the gains of the people's revolution and the achievements of national construction, and to defend the sovereignty, territorial integrity and security of the state.

CHAPTER TWO

THE STATE STRUCTURE

SECTION I. THE NATIONAL PEOPLE'S CONGRESS

ARTICLE 21.   The National People's Congress of the People's Republic of China is the highest organ of state power.

ARTICLE 22. The National People's Congress is the sole organ exercising the legislative power of the state.

ARTICLE 23. The National People's Congress is composed of deputies elected by provinces, autonomous regions, cities directly under the central authority, the armed forces and Chinese who live abroad.

The number of deputies to the National People's Congress, including those representing minority nationalities, and the manner of their election, are prescribed by the electoral law.

ARTICLE 24. The National People's Congress is elected for a term of four years.

Two months before the term of office of the National People's Congress expires, its Standing Committee must complete the election of deputies to the succeeding National People's Congress. Should exceptional circumstances arise that prevent such an election, the term of office of the National People's Congress may be prolonged until the first session of the succeeding National People's Congress.

ARTICLE 25. The National People's Congress holds the session once a year, convened by its Standing Committee. It may also be convened whenever its Standing Committee deems this necessary or one-fifth of the deputies so propose.

ARTICLE 26. When the National People's Congress meets, it elects a presidium to conduct the session.

ARTICLE 27. The National People's Congress exercises the following functions and powers:

1) To amend the Constitution;

2) To make laws;

3) To supervise the enforcement of the Constitution;

4) To elect the Chairman and the Vice-Chairman of the People's Republic of China;

5) To decide on the choice of the Premier of the State Council upon recommendation by the Chairman of the People's Republic of China, and of the component members of the State Council upon recommendation by the Premier;

6) To decide on the choice of the Vice-Chairmen and members of the Council of National Defense upon recommendation by the Chairman of the People's Republic of China;

7) To elect the President of the Supreme People's Court;

8) To elect the Chief Procurator of the Supreme People's Procuratorate;

9) To decide on the national economic plan;

10) To examine and approve the state budget and the final state accounts;

11) To ratify the following administrative divisions: provinces, autonomous regions, and cities directly under the central authority;

12) To decide on amnesties;

13) To decide on questions of war and peace;

14) To exercise such other functions and powers as the National People's Congress considers it should exercise.

ARTICLE 28.   The National People's Congress has the power to remove from office

1) The Chairman and the Vice-Chairman of the People's Republic of China;

2) The Premier and Vice-Premiers, Ministers, Chairmen of Commissions and the Secretary-General of the State Council;

3) The Vice-Chairmen and members of the Council of National Defense;

4) The President of the Supreme People's Court;

5) The Chief Procurator of the Supreme People's Procuratorate.

ARTICLE 29.   Amendments to the Constitution require a two-thirds majority vote of all the deputies to the National People's Congress.

Decisions on laws and other proposals require a simple majority vote of all the deputies to the National People's Congress.

ARTICLE 30.   The Standing Committee of the National People's Congress is the permanent working organ of the National People's Congress.

The Standing Committee of the National People's Congress is composed of the following persons, elected by the National People's Congress: the Chairman; the Vice-Chairmen; the Secretary-General; the members.

ARTICLE 31.   The Standing Committee of the National People's Congress exercises the following functions and powers:

1) To conduct the election of deputies to the National People's Congress;

2) To convene the sessions of the National People's Congress;

3) To interpret laws;

4) To make decrees;

5) To supervise the work of the State Council, the Supreme People's Court and the Supreme People's Procuratorate;

6) To annul decisions and orders of the State Council which contravene the Constitution, laws or decrees;

7) To alter or annul inappropriate decisions of the organs of state power of provinces, autonomous regions, and cities directly under the central authority;

8) To decide on the individual appointment and removal of Vice-Premiers, Ministers, Chairmen of Commissions or the Secretary-General of the State Council when the National People's Congress is not in session;

9) To appoint and remove Vice Presidents and judges of the Supreme People's Court, and members of its Judicial Committee;

10) To appoint and remove Deputy Chief Procurators and procurators of the Supreme People's Procuratorate, and members of its Procuratorial Committee;

11) To decide on the appointment and removal of plenipotentiary representatives abroad;

12) To decide on the ratification and denunciation of treaties concluded with foreign states;

13) To institute military, diplomatic and other special titles and ranks;

14) To institute state orders and titles of honor and decide on their conferment;

15) To decide on the granting of pardons;

16) To decide, when the National People's Congress is not in session, on the proclamation of a state of war in the event of armed attack on the country or in case of necessity to execute an international treaty for joint defense against aggression;

17) To decide on general or partial mobilization;

18) To decide on the enforcement of martial law throughout the country or in certain areas;

19) To exercise such other functions and powers as are vested in it by the National People's Congress.

ARTICLE 32. The Standing Committee of the National People's Congress exercises its functions and powers until a new Standing Committee is elected by the succeeding National People's Congress.

ARTICLE 33. The Standing Committee of the National People's Congress is responsible and accountable to the National People's Congress.

The National People's Congress has the power to recall component members of its Standing Committee.

ARTICLE 34. The National People's Congress establishes a Nationalities Committee, a Bills Committee, a Budget Committee, a Credentials Committee and such other committees as may be necessary.

The Nationalities Committee and the Bills Committee are under the direction of the Standing Committee of the National People's Congress when the National People's Congress is not in session.

ARTICLE 35. The National People's Congress, or its Standing Committee when the National People's Congress is not in session, may, if it deems necessary, appoint commissions of investigation on specific questions.

All organs of state, people's organizations and citizens concerned are obliged to supply the necessary material to these commissions when they conduct investigations.

ARTICLE 36. Deputies to the National People's Congress have the right to address questions to the State Council, or to the Ministries and Commissions of the State Council, which are under obligation to answer.

ARTICLE 37. No deputy to the National People's Congress may be arrested or placed on trial without the consent of the National People's Congress or, when the National People's Congress is not in session, of its Standing Committee.

ARTICLE 38. Deputies to the National People's Congress are subject to the supervision of the units which elect them. These electoral units have the power to replace the deputies they elect at any time according to the procedure prescribed by law.

SECTION II. THE CHAIRMAN OF THE PEOPLE'S
REPUBLIC OF CHINA

ARTICLE 39. The Chairman of the People's Republic of China is elected by the National People's Congress. Any citizen of the People's Republic of China who has the right to vote and stand for election and has reached the age of thirty-five is eligible for election as Chairman of the People's Republic of China.

The term of office of the Chairman of the People's Republic of China is four years.

ARTICLE 40. The Chairman of the People's Republic of China, in pursuance of decisions of the National People's Congress or its Standing Committee, promulgates laws and decrees; appoints and removes the Premier, Vice-Premiers, Ministers, Chairmen of Commissions or the Secretary-General of the State Council; appoints and removes the Vice-Chairmen and members of the Council of National Defense; confers state orders and titles of honor; proclaims amnesties and grants pardons; proclaims martial law; proclaims a state of war; and orders mobilization.

ARTICLE 41. The Chairman of the People's Republic of China represents the People's Republic of China in its foreign relations, receives foreign diplomatic representatives and, in pursuance of decisions of the Standing Committee of the National People's Congress, dispatches and recalls plenipotentiary representatives abroad and ratifies treaties concluded with foreign states.

ARTICLE 42. The Chairman of the People's Republic of China commands the armed forces of the state, and is Chairman of the Council of National Defense.

ARTICLE 43. The Chairman of the People's Republic of China, whenever necessary, convenes a Supreme State Conference and acts as its chairman.

The Vice-Chairman of the People's Republic of China, the Chairman of the Standing Committee of the National People's Congress, the Premier of the State Council and other persons concerned take part in the Supreme State Conference.

The Chairman of the People's Republic of China submits the views of the Supreme State Conference on important affairs of state to the National People's Congress, its Standing Committee, the State Council, or other bodies concerned for their consideration and decision.

ARTICLE 44. The Vice-Chairman of the People's Republic of China assists the Chairman in his work. The Vice-Chairman may exercise such part of the functions and powers of the Chairman as the Chairman may entrust to him.

The provisions of Article 39 of the Constitution governing the election and term of office of the Chairman of the People's Republic of China apply also to the election and term of office of the Vice-Chairman of the People's Republic of China.

ARTICLE 45. The Chairman and the Vice-Chairman of the People's Republic of China exercise their functions and powers until the new Chairman and Vice-Chairman elected by the succeeding National People's Congress take office.

ARTICLE 46. Should the Chairman of the People's Republic of China be incapacitated for a prolonged period by reason of health, the functions and powers of Chairman shall be exercised by the Vice-Chairman.

Should the office of Chairman of the People's Republic of China fall vacant, the Vice-Chairman succeeds to the office of Chairman.

SECTION III. THE STATE COUNCIL

ARTICLE 47. The State Council of the People's Republic of China, that is, the Central People's Government, is the executive organ of the highest organ of state power; it is the highest organ of state administration.

ARTICLE 48. The State Council is composed of the following persons: the Premier; the Vice-Premiers; the Ministers; the Chairmen of Commissions; the Secretary-General.

The organization of the State Council is determined by law.

ARTICLE 49. The State Council exercises the following functions and powers:

1) To formulate administrative measures, issue decisions and orders and verify their execution in accordance with the Constitution, laws and decrees;

2) To submit proposals on laws and other matters to the National People's Congress or its Standing Committee;

3) To coordinate and lead the work of Ministries and Commissions;

4) To coordinate and lead the work of local organs of state administration at various levels throughout the country;

5) To alter or annul inappropriate orders and directives issued by Ministers or by Chairmen of Commissions;

6) To alter or annul inappropriate decisions and orders issued by local organs of state administration at various levels;

7) To put into effect the national economic plan and the state budget;

8) To administer foreign and domestic trade;

9) To administer cultural, educational and public health work;

10) To administer affairs concerning the nationalities;

11) To administer affairs concerning Chinese who live abroad;

12) To protect the interests of the state, to maintain public order and to safeguard the rights of citizens;

13) To administer the conduct of external affairs;

14) To direct the building up of the armed forces;

15) To ratify the following administrative divisions: autonomous *chou*, counties, autonomous counties, and cities;

16) To appoint and remove administrative personnel according to provisions of law;

17) To exercise such other functions and powers as are vested in it by the National People's Congress or its Standing Committee.

ARTICLE 50. The Premier directs the work of the State Council and presides over its meetings.

The Vice-Premiers assist the Premier in his work.

ARTICLE 51. The Ministers and Chairmen of Commissions direct the work of their respective departments. They may issue orders and directives within the jurisdiction of their respective departments and in accordance with laws and decrees and with the decisions and orders of the State Council.

ARTICLE 52. The State Council is responsible and accountable to the National People's Congress or, when the National People's Congress is not in session, to its Standing Committee.

SECTION IV. THE LOCAL PEOPLE'S CONGRESSES AND THE LOCAL PEOPLE'S COUNCILS

ARTICLE 53. The administrative division of the People's Republic of China is as follows:

1) The country is divided into provinces, autonomous regions, and cities directly under the central authority;

2) Provinces and autonomous regions are divided into autonomous *chou*, counties, autonomous counties, and cities;

3) Counties and autonomous counties are divided into *hsiang*, nationality *hsiang*, and towns.

Cities directly under the central authority and other large cities are divided into districts. Autonomous *chou* are divided into counties, autonomous counties, and cities.

Autonomous regions, autonomous *chou* and autonomous counties are all national autonomous areas.

ARTICLE 54. People's congresses and people's councils are established in provinces, cities directly under the central authority, counties, cities, city districts, *hsiang*, nationality *hsiang*, and towns.

Organs of self-government are established in autonomous regions, autonomous *chou* and autonomous counties. The organization and work of organs of self-government are specified in Chapter Two, Section V of the Constitution.

ARTICLE 55. Local people's congresses at various levels are local organs of state power.

ARTICLE 56. Deputies to the people's congresses of provinces, cities directly under the central authority, counties, and cities divided into districts are elected by people's congresses at the next lower level; deputies to the people's congresses of cities not divided into districts, and of city districts, *hsiang*, nationality *hsiang*, and towns are directly elected by the voters.

The number of deputies to local people's congresses at various levels and the manner of their election are prescribed by the electoral law.

ARTICLE 57. The term of office of the provincial people's congresses is four years. The term of office of the people's congresses of cities directly under the central authority, counties, cities, city districts, *hsiang*, nationality *hsiang*, and towns is two years.

ARTICLE 58. Local people's congresses in their respective administrative areas ensure the observance and execution of laws and decrees; make plans for local economic construction and cultural development and for public utilities; examine and approve local budgets and final accounts; protect public property; maintain public order; and safeguard the rights of citizens and the equal rights of minority nationalities.

ARTICLE 59. Local people's congresses elect, and have the power to remove, component members of people's councils at the corresponding levels.

People's congresses at county level and above elect, and have the power to remove, the presidents of people's courts at the corresponding levels.

ARTICLE 60. Local people's congresses adopt and issue decisions within the limits of their authority as prescribed by law.

The people's congresses of nationality *hsiang* may, within the limits of their authority as prescribed by law, take specific measures suited to the characteristics of the nationalities concerned.

Local people's congresses have the power to alter or annul inappropriate decisions and orders of people's councils at the corresponding levels.

People's congresses at county level and above have the power to alter or annul inappropriate decisions of people's congresses at the next lower level as well as inappropriate decisions and orders of people's councils at the next lower level.

ARTICLE 61. Deputies to the people's congresses of provinces, cities directly under the central authority, counties, and cities divided into districts are subject to supervision by the units which elect them; deputies to the people's congresses of cities not divided into districts, and of city districts, *hsiang*, nationality *hsiang*, and towns are subject to supervision by their electors. The electoral units and electorates which elect the deputies to the local people's congresses have the power to replace their deputies at any time according to the procedure prescribed by law.

ARTICLE 62. Local people's councils, that is, local people's governments, are the executive organs of local people's congresses at the corresponding levels, and are local organs of state administration.

ARTICLE 63. A local people's council is composed, according to its level, of the provincial governor and deputy provincial governors, or the mayor and deputy mayors of cities, or the county head and deputy county heads, or the district head and deputy district heads, or the *hsiang* head and deputy *hsiang* heads, or the mayor or deputy mayors of towns, as the case may be; together with council members.

The term of office of a local people's council is the same as that of the people's congress at the corresponding level.

The organization of local people's councils is determined by law.

ARTICLE 64. Local people's councils direct the administrative work of their respective areas within the limits of their authority as prescribed by law.

Local people's councils carry out decisions of people's congresses at the corresponding levels as well as decisions and orders of organs of state administration at the higher levels.

Local people's councils issue decisions and orders within the limits of their authority as prescribed by law.

ARTICLE 65. People's councils at county level and above direct the work of all their subordinate departments and of people's councils at the lower levels, as well as appoint and remove the personnel of organs of state according to provisions of law.

People's councils at county level and above have the power to suspend the carrying out of inappropriate decisions of people's congresses at the next lower level; and to alter or annul inappropriate orders and directives of their subordinate departments as well as inappropriate decisions and orders of people's councils at the lower levels.

ARTICLE 66. Local people's councils are responsible and accountable to people's congresses at the corresponding levels and to organs of state administration at the next higher level.

Local people's councils throughout the country are local organs of state administration under the coordinating leadership of the State Council and are subordinate to it.

SECTION V. THE ORGANS OF SELF-GOVERNMENT OF NATIONAL AUTONOMOUS AREAS

ARTICLE 67. The organization of the organs of self-government of autonomous regions, autonomous *chou* and autonomous counties should conform to the basic principles governing the organization of local organs of state as specified in Chapter Two, Section IV of the Constitution. The form of each organ of self-government may be determined in accordance with the wishes of the majority of the people of the nationality or nationalities enjoying regional autonomy in a given area.

ARTICLE 68. In autonomous regions, autonomous *chou* and autonomous counties where a number of nationalities live together, each nationality is entitled to appropriate representation in the organs of self-government.

ARTICLE 69. The organs of self-government of autonomous regions, autonomous *chou* and autonomous counties exercise the functions and powers of local organs of state as specified in Chapter Two, Section IV of the Constitution.

ARTICLE 70. The organs of self-government of autonomous regions, autonomous *chou* and autonomous counties exercise autonomy within the limits of their authority as prescribed by the Constitution and by law.

The organs of self-government of autonomous regions, autonomous *chou* and autonomous counties administer the finances of their areas within the limits of their authority as prescribed by law.

The organs of self-government of autonomous regions, autonomous *chou* and autonomous counties organize the public security forces of their areas in accordance with the military system of the state.

The organs of self-government of autonomous regions, autonomous *chou* and autonomous counties may, in the light of the political, economic and cultural characteristics of the nationality or nationalities in a given area, make regulations on the exercise of autonomy as well as specific regulations and submit them to the Standing Committee of the National People's Congress for approval.

ARTICLE 71. In performing their functions, organs of self-government of autonomous regions, autonomous *chou* and autonomous counties employ the spoken and written language or languages commonly used by the nationality or nationalities in the locality.

ARTICLE 72. The higher organs of state should fully safeguard the exercise of autonomy by organs of self-government of autonomous regions, autonomous *chou* and autonomous counties, and should assist all the minority nationalities in their political, economic and cultural development.

SECTION VI. THE PEOPLE'S COURTS AND THE PEOPLE'S PROCURATORATES

ARTICLE 73. The Supreme People's Court of the People's Republic of China, local people's courts at various levels and special people's courts exercise judicial authority.

ARTICLE 74. The term of office of the President of the Supreme People's Court and presidents of local people's courts is four years.

The organization of people's courts is determined by law.

ARTICLE 75. The people's courts, in administering justice, apply the system of people's assessors in accordance with law.

ARTICLE 76. All cases in the people's courts are heard in public except those involving special circumstances as prescribed by law. The accused has the right to defense.

ARTICLE 77. Citizens of all nationalities have the right to use their own spoken and written languages in judicial proceedings. The people's courts are required to provide interpretation for any party unacquainted with the spoken or written language commonly used in the locality.

In an area where people of a minority nationality live in a compact community or where a number of nationalities live together, hearings in people's courts should be conducted in the language commonly used in the locality, and judgments, notices and other documents of people's courts should be made public in that language.

ARTICLE 78. The people's courts administer justice independently and are subject only to the law.

ARTICLE 79. The Supreme People's Court is the highest judicial organ.

The Supreme People's Court supervises the administration of justice by local people's courts at various levels and special people's courts; people's courts at the higher levels supervise the administration of justice by people's courts at the lower levels.

ARTICLE 80. The Supreme People's Court is responsible and accountable to the National People's Congress or, when the National People's Congress is not in session, to its Standing Committee. Local people's courts are responsible and accountable to local people's congresses at the corresponding levels.

ARTICLE 81. The Supreme People's Procuratorate of the People's Republic of China exercises procuratorial authority to ensure observance of the law by all the departments under the State Council, local organs of state at various levels, persons working in organs of state and citizens. Local people's procuratorates and special people's procuratorates exercise procuratorial authority within the limits prescribed by law.

Local people's procuratorates and special people's procuratorates work under the leadership of people's procuratorates at the higher levels, and all of them work under the coordinating leadership of the Supreme People's Procuratorate.

ARTICLE 82. The term of office of the Chief Procurator of the Supreme People's Procuratorate is four years.

The organization of people's procuratorates is determined by law.

ARTICLE 83. Local people's procuratorates at various levels exercise their functions and powers independently and are not subject to interference by local organs of state.

ARTICLE 84. The Supreme People's Procuratorate is responsible and accountable to the National People's Congress or, when the National People's Congress is not in session, to its Standing Committee.

CHAPTER THREE
FUNDAMENTAL RIGHTS AND DUTIES OF CITIZENS

ARTICLE 85. All citizens of the People's Republic of China are equal before the law.

ARTICLE 86. All citizens of the People's Republic of China who have reached the age of eighteen have the right to vote and stand for election, irrespective of their nationality, race, sex, occupation, social origin, religious belief, education, property status, or length of residence, except insane persons and persons deprived by law of the right to vote and stand for election.

Women have equal rights with men to vote and stand for election.

ARTICLE 87. Citizens of the People's Republic of China enjoy freedom of speech, freedom of the press, freedom of assembly, freedom of association, freedom of procession and freedom of demonstration. To ensure that citizens can enjoy these freedoms, the state provides the necessary material facilities.

ARTICLE 88. Citizens of the People's Republic of China enjoy freedom of religious belief.

ARTICLE 89. The freedom of person of citizens of the People's Republic of China is inviolable. No citizen may be arrested except by decision of a people's court or with the sanction of a people's procuratorate.

ARTICLE 90. The homes of citizens of the People's Republic of China are inviolable, and privacy of correspondence is protected by law.

Citizens of the People's Republic of China enjoy freedom of residence and freedom to change their residence.

ARTICLE 91. Citizens of the People's Republic of China have the right to work. To ensure that citizens can enjoy this right, the state, by planned development of the national economy, gradually provides more employment, improves working conditions and increases wages, amenities and benefits.

ARTICLE 92. Working people in the People's Republic of China have the right to rest and leisure. To ensure that working people can enjoy this right, the state prescribes working hours and systems of vacations for workers and office personnel, and gradually expands material facilities for the working people to rest and build up their health.

ARTICLE 93. Working people in the People's Republic of China have the right to material assistance in old age, and in case of illness or disability. To ensure that working people can enjoy this right, the state provides social insurance, social assistance and public health services and gradually expands these facilities.

ARTICLE 94. Citizens of the People's Republic of China have the right to education. To ensure that citizens can enjoy this right, the state establishes and gradually expands schools of various types and other cultural and educational institutions.

The state pays special attention to the physical and mental development of young people.

ARTICLE 95. The People's Republic of China safeguards the freedom of citizens to engage in scientific research, literary and artistic creation and other cultural activities. The state encourages and assists the creative endeavors of citizens in science, education, literature, art and other cultural pursuits.

ARTICLE 96. Women in the People's Republic of China enjoy equal rights with men in all spheres of political, economic, cultural, social and family life.

The state protects marriage, the family, and the mother and child.

ARTICLE 97. Citizens of the People's Republic of China have the right to make written or oral complaints to organs of state at any level against any person working in an organ of state for transgression of law or neglect of duty. People suffering loss by reason of infringement of their rights as citizens by persons working in organs of state have the right to compensation.

ARTICLE 98. The People's Republic of China protects the just rights and interests of Chinese who live abroad.

ARTICLE 99. The People's Republic of China grants asylum to any foreign national persecuted for supporting a just cause, for taking part in the peace movement or for scientific activities.

ARTICLE 100. Citizens of the People's Republic of China must abide by the Constitution and the law, observe labor discipline, observe public order and respect public morality.

ARTICLE 101. The public property of the People's Republic of China is sacred and inviolable. It is the duty of every citizen to take care of and protect public property.

ARTICLE 102. Citizens of the People's Republic of China have the duty to pay taxes according to law.

ARTICLE 103. It is the sacred responsibility of every citizen of the People's Republic of China to defend the motherland.

It is the honorable duty of citizens of the People's Republic of China to perform military service according to law.

ARTICLE 104. The national flag of the People's Republic of China is a red flag with five stars.

ARTICLE 105. The national emblem of the People's Republic of China is: in the center, Tien An Men under the light of five stars, and encircled by ears of grain and a cogwheel.

ARTICLE 106. The capital of the People's Republic of China is Peking.

3. 1

CONSTITUTION OF THE PEOPLE'S REPUBLIC OF ALBANIA[1]

Adopted by the Presidium of the Constituent Assembly
March 15, 1946

PART ONE
FUNDAMENTAL LAWS

TITLE I

THE PEOPLE'S REPUBLIC OF ALBANIA

ARTICLE 1. Albania is a people's republic in which all powers are derived from and belong to the people.

ARTICLE 2. In the People's Republic of Albania the people rule by means of various representative organs of state, namely, the people's councils which came into existence during the struggle for national liberation against fascism and reaction and which represent the greatest victory of the large masses of the Albanian people.

These organs are freely elected by the people from the local councils to the People's Convention.

ARTICLE 3. All the representative organs of the state are elected by the citizens by free elections, and by universal, equal, direct, and secret ballot.

In all organs of the state the representatives of the people are responsible to their constituents.

The constituents have the right to recall their representatives at any time. The exercise of this right is to be regulated by a special law.

ARTICLE 4. All the organs of the state exercise their functions according to this constitution, and according to laws and regulations passed by the high organs of state.

All activities of the administrative organs of the state and courts must be based on law.

TITLE II

SOCIAL AND ECONOMIC MEASURES

ARTICLE 5. In the People's Republic of Albania the means of production comprises all the wealth of the people owned by the state, the cooperative organizations of the people, and private individuals whether real or legal entities.

---

[1] *Constitution of the People's Republic of Albania* (Boston: Committee for the Defense of Albania, n.d.). Reprinted by permission.

The wealth of the people includes mines and all other subsurface resources, as well as waterways, natural wealth, forests, pasture land, airways, postal service, telegraph, telephone, radio stations, and banks.

Foreign trade is under the control of the state.

ARTICLE 6.   In order to protect the vital interests of the people and to improve the standard of living, and in order to exploit all the economical forces, the state undertakes to direct the economic life and development by an overall planned economy. The state, by controlling its economy and the cooperatives, exercises a general control over private economy as well.

The state, in order to carry out the general economic plan, relies on the trade unions of the working men and civil servants, the cooperatives of the peasants, and other organizations of the laboring masses.

ARTICLE 7.   The state regulates and directs by law the use of the collective wealth of the people. The collective wealth of the people is especially favored by the state.

ARTICLE 8.   The state is especially interested in the cooperative movement of the people, which it favors and assists.

ARTICLE 9.   Private property and private initiative are guaranteed by the state. Private inheritance is guaranteed. Nobody may use private property to the detriment of the public.

Private property may be limited, and when the general welfare of the community calls for it, it may be expropriated by a law, which shall provide in each case what the amount of compensation shall be to the owner.

Likewise other branches of economy or enterprises may also be nationalized whenever the interest of the people demands or requires it.

Monopolies, trusts, cartels, etc., created for the purpose of imposing prices and monopolizing markets to the detriment of national economy, are prohibited.

ARTICLE 10.   The land belongs to those who till it. The conditions under which an institution or a person can own land which they do not cultivate shall be established by law.

Large estates may under no circumstances be owned by private individuals.

The maximum amount of land that may be owned individually is determined by law.

The state especially favors and protects the small and middle peasants by its economic policy, by means of credit, and by its taxation system.

ARTICLE 11.   The state, by means of economic and other measures, encourages the working classes to unite and organize themselves against economic exploitation.

The state protects the workers by guaranteeing them the right to organize, by limiting their hours of work, and by establishing minimum wages. The state supports the workers by means of social security laws and vacations with pay at the expense of the employers.

The state especially protects minors by regulating their employment.

RIGHTS AND DUTIES OF CITIZENS

ARTICLE 12. All citizens are equal before the law. They must obey the Constitution and all laws of the land.

No privilege because of family, position in life, wealth, or cultural level is recognized.

ARTICLE 13. All citizens are equal regardless of nationality, race or religion. Any act which grants privileges or takes away rights from any citizen because of nationality, race or religion is unconstitutional and carries with it punishments as provided by law. It is unconstitutional and punishable by law to stir up hatred and dissension among nationalities, races or religions.

ARTICLE 14. All citizens who have reached the age of eighteen are eligible to elect and be elected in all organs of state, regardless of sex, nationality, race, creed, cultural level or residence.

Members of the armed forces also have these rights.

The right to vote is universal, equal, direct and secret.

The right to vote is forfeited by those who have been disqualified by law.

ARTICLE 15. Women are equal to men in all walks of life, private, political or social.

Women shall receive the same pay as men for the same work. And women have similar rights with regard to social security.

The government especially protects the interests of mothers and young children, by assuring vacations with pay before and after childbirth and also by building maternity hospitals and nurseries.

ARTICLE 16. Freedom of conscience and religion is guaranteed to all citizens.

The church is separated from the state.

Religious communities are free to exercise and practise their creeds.

It is forbidden to use the church and religion for political purposes.

Likewise, political organizations based on religion are also forbidden.

The state may assist religious communities materially.

ARTICLE 17. Marriage and family are protected by the state. The legal conditions of marriage and family are fixed by law.

Legal marriages can be performed only by competent representatives of the government. After celebrating a civil marriage a citizen may celebrate a religious marriage according to the rules of his creed.

The courts of the state only are competent to determine all questions concerning marriage.

Parents have the same obligations toward their illegitimate children as to those born in wedlock. Illegitimate children have the same rights as those born in wedlock.

ARTICLE 18. Freedom of speech, freedom of press, freedom of organization, freedom of assembly and of public demonstration are guaranteed to all citizens.

ARTICLE 19. Personal inviolability is guaranteed to all citizens. Nobody can be arrested for more than three days without a court warrant or without the approval of the district attorney.

No person shall be punished for a crime without the decision of a competent judge in conformity with the law which defines the crime and the competence of the court.

No punishment shall be determined and inflicted except as prescribed by law.

No person shall be punished without a hearing or without being summoned to defend himself according to law, except in a case where his absence is legally established.

The administrative organs of the state may give jail sentences for common law misdemeanors as prescribed by law.

No citizen may be exiled or interned within the state except as prescribed by law.

The People's Republic of Albania protects the rights of its citizens in foreign lands.

ARTICLE 20. A home cannot be violated.

No person can enter a house and search it against the wishes of the owner, except when he holds a court order in his hands.

No search can be made except in the presence of two witnesses. The owner of the house also has a right to be present.

ARTICLE 21. The secrecy of mail and other correspondence cannot be violated except in cases of criminal investigations, military mobilization, or state of war.

ARTICLE 22. In the People's Republic of Albania work is a privilege and a duty.

Every citizen has a right to be paid according to his work and to receive from society as much as he gives to it.

ARTICLE 23. All citizens have a right to be employed in government work according to specific regulations laid down by law.

Citizens appointed or elected to public office are bound to perform their duties conscientiously.

ARTICLE 24. It is the duty of the state to adequately support disabled soldiers at public expense and to enable them to resume their work. The state shall support the families of those who died in battle and of all war victims.

ARTICLE 25. The state takes care of the health of the people by organizing and controlling health service, hospitals and sanatoriums.

ARTICLE 26. The state takes care of the physical education of the people, especially that of the youth, with a view to improving health and increasing the capacity of the people for work and the defense of the state.

ARTICLE 27. Freedom of scientific and artistic work is guaranteed. The state promotes science and the arts in such a way as to further the culture and welfare of the public.

The rights of authors are protected by law.

ARTICLE 28. In order to raise the cultural level, the state gives to all classes of people every chance to attend schools and other cultural institutions.

The state is particularly interested in the education of youth.

Minors are protected by law.

The schools belong to the state. Private schools can be opened only by special permission. All their activities are supervised by the state. Elementary education is free and obligatory.

Schools are separated from the church.

ARTICLE 29.   Citizens have the right to petition state organs for redress of wrongs.

Citizens have the right to complain against any illegal or irregular decision of an administrative organ of the state.

ARTICLE 30.   Every citizen can complain in competent courts against officials who have acted unjustly in the discharge of their duty.

ARTICLE 31.   Citizens are entitled to seek from the state or from an official compensation for damages incurred as a result of illegal or irregular punishment.

ARTICLE 32.   Defense of the country is the highest duty and greatest privilege of any citizen.

Treachery against the people is the greatest crime.

Military service is obligatory for all citizens.

ARTICLE 33.   Every citizen must pay taxes according to his income.

The state fixes taxes, and exemption from the same is determined by law.

ARTICLE 34.   Citizens cannot use the rights given them by this Constitution in order to change the constitutional regime of the People's Republic of Albania in an undemocratic manner. Any act of this kind is illegal and carries with it punishment as prescribed by law.

ARTICLE 35.   In the People's Republic of Albania national minorities enjoy all the rights enjoyed by other citizens as well as freedom to use their own language and develop their own culture.

ARTICLE 36.   The People's Republic of Albania gives the right of refuge to citizens of other countries who are persecuted for their activities in behalf of democracy, national liberation, rights of the workers, or scientific and cultural freedom.

PART TWO

STATE ORGANIZATIONS

TITLE I

HIGHEST ORGANS OF THE STATE

(a)   People's Convention

ARTICLE 37.   The People's Convention (Parliament) is the highest organ of the state of the People's Republic of Albania.

ARTICLE 38.   The People's Convention maintains the sovereignty of the nation and state, and exercises all the sovereign rights under the Constitution with the exception of those rights which the Constitution itself has assigned to the Presidium of the People's Convention or to the government.

ARTICLE 39. Legislative powers are exercised only by the People's Convention.

ARTICLE 40. The People's Convention is elected by all the citizens, with one representative for every 20,000 people.

ARTICLE 41. The People's Convention is elected for four years.

ARTICLE 42. At the beginning of each session the People's Convention elects a president, vice president and secretary. The president presides over the meetings according to the rules of procedure.

ARTICLE 43. The People's Convention is called by a decree of the Presidium in ordinary and extraordinary sessions.

Ordinary sessions meet twice annually, March 15 and October 15. If the People's Convention is not called on these two dates, it will meet on its own initiative and without a decree of the Presidium.

Extraordinary sessions of the People's Convention are called when the Presidium deems it necessary or when one-third of the members request its convocation.

ARTICLE 44. The People's Convention makes its own rules of procedure.

ARTICLE 45. No bill can become a law until it is passed by the relative majority in a session (at which) the majority of its members take part.

ARTICLE 46. Laws become effective fifteen days after they are promulgated in the official journal, except when it is designated otherwise in the law itself.

ARTICLE 47. The People's Convention appoints various committees for specific purposes.

The People's Convention appoints a committee to examine the credentials of the people's representatives in its first session.

Upon recommendation of this committee, the People's Convention approves or rejects the credentials of the people's representatives.

ARTICLE 48. The People's Convention may investigate matters of general interest through special committees.

All organs of the state must give facts and information when these committees demand it.

ARTICLE 49. All members of the People's Convention enjoy parliamentary immunity.

Members of the People's Convention and of the Presidium cannot be arrested or prosecuted without the approval of the People's Convention, except in case of *flagrante delicto.*

ARTICLE 50. In case of war or similar emergency the People's Convention may convene longer than its normal term so long as the emergency exists.

The People's Convention may also shorten its term.

ARTICLE 51. The date for new parliamentary election must be fixed before the convention dissolves.

The interval between the day of dissolution of the People's Convention and the day of the new elections must not exceed three months nor be less than two months.

ARTICLE 52. The Constitution can be changed or amended only by the People's Convention.

Bills for changes or amendments in the Constitution may be proposed by the Presidium, the Government, or by two-fifths of the members of the People's Convention.

Changes or amendments to the Constitution must be passed by an absolute majority of the members of the Convention.

(b) The Presidium of the People's Convention

ARTICLE 53. The People's Convention elects its own Presidium which shall consist of a president, two vice presidents, a secretary, and seven members.

ARTICLE 54. The Presidium of the People's Convention has the following duties:

1) It calls the People's Convention.

2) It designates the elections for the People's Convention.

3) It makes authentic interpretations as to the constitutionality of the laws. These interpretations are then submitted to the People's Convention for approval.

4) It makes authentic interpretations of the laws and issues decrees.

5) It promulgates the laws passed by the Convention.

6) It exercises the right of pardon in accordance with the prescriptions of the law.

7) It awards decorations and honorary titles upon recommendation of the Prime Minister.

8) It ratifies international treaties, except when it considers it necessary for ratification to be made by the People's Convention.

9) It appoints and recalls envoys extraordinary and ministers plenipotentiary to foreign countries upon recommendation of the government.

10) It accepts credentials and letters of recall from foreign diplomats.

11) It proclaims general mobilization and declares war in case of armed aggression against the People's Republic of Albania between the two sessions of the People's Convention; in case of urgent necessity it fulfills international obligations of the Republic to the international peace organizations or allied nations.

12) It appoints and dismisses ministers between the two sessions of the People's Convention upon recommendation of the Prime Minister.

13) It appoints assistant ministers upon recommendation of the Prime Minister.

14) It creates commissions within the government and designates their chairmen upon recommendation of the Prime Minister.

15) It assigns duties to a ministry or to a government commission.

16) On the basis of decisions made by the People's Convention or upon recommendation of the government, it submits various questions to a popular referendum.

The decrees of the Presidium of the People's Convention are signed by the president and by the secretary.

ARTICLE 55. The Presidium of the People's Convention is responsible for its activities to the People's Convention. The Convention may revoke its Presidium and replace it by another; it may dismiss some members and replace them by others before their term expires.

ARTICLE 56. When the People's Convention is dissolved, the Presidium continues in power until another People's Convention elects a new Presidium.

The Presidium convokes the People's Convention within one month after its election.

TITLE II

ADMINISTRATIVE ORGANS OF THE STATE

ARTICLE 57. The government is the highest executive and administrative organ of the People's Republic of Albania.

The government is appointed and dismissed by the People's Convention.

The government is responsible to the People's Convention and must account to it for its activities. Between the two sessions of the People's Convention the government is responsible to the Presidium of the Convention, before which it must render full account of its activities.

ARTICLE 58. The government performs its duties according to the Constitution and the laws. The government issues the decrees necessary for carrying out laws on the basis of a special authorization; it gives binding instructions for the execution of laws.

Orders, decrees, instructions and decisions of the government must be signed by the Prime Minister and the minister in charge of the department concerned.

ARTICLE 59. The government directs and coordinates the functioning of the ministries, committees, and all other institutions which come under its jurisdiction.

The government outlines the economic plan of the state, submits the annual budget to the People's Convention for its approval, and supervises its execution; directs the credit and monetary systems; takes all necessary measures to uphold the constitution and the rights of all citizens; directs all military forces; keeps in touch with foreign governments; carries out treaties with foreign countries and other international obligations; submits bills prepared by the government and by various ministries to the People's Convention; decides on how ministries and other government institutions shall be organized; and creates committees to execute economic, cultural and defensive measures on a national scale.

ARTICLE 60. The government is composed of the Prime Minister, the deputy prime minister, the ministers, the chairman of the Committee for Economic Planning, and the chairman of the Committee of Control.

The members of the government take the oath of office before the Presidium of the People's Convention.

ARTICLE 61. The Prime Minister represents the government, presides over all meetings, and directs all the activities of the government.

ARTICLE 62.   The members of the government head the various administrative departments of the state.

The cabinet may also have ministers without portfolio.

ARTICLE 63.   Members of the government are held criminally responsible for the violation of the Constitution or any other law in the performance of their duties.

They are also responsible for any damage they may cause the state for acting contrary to law.

The exact responsibilities of members of the government will be stated in a special law.

ARTICLE 64.   Ministers and government committees are authorized to issue orders, regulations, and instructions relating to laws and decrees of the government.

Each minister supervises the execution of the governmental laws, decrees, and instructions in his own department and is held responsible for their execution in his particular administrative branch.

ARTICLE 65.   The various ministries of the government are

1)   Ministry of Foreign Affairs,
2)   Ministry of the Interior,
3)   Ministry of National Defense,
4)   Ministry of Justice,
5)   Ministry of Finance,
6)   Ministry of Education,
7)   Ministry of Economy,
8)   Ministry of Agriculture and Forestry,
9)   Ministry of Public Works,
10)   Ministry of Health.

ARTICLE 66.   The government may appoint a special council of ministers to deal with questions of national economy and defense.

The decree by which this council is appointed shall determine its organization and scope.

TITLE III

ORGANS OF THE LOCAL GOVERNMENTAL UNITS

ARTICLE 67.   The people's councils are the governmental units in rural districts, communes, subprefectures and prefectures.

The people's councils are elected directly by the people; those of the rural districts for two years and those of the communes, subprefectures and prefectures, for three years.

The people's councils of the communes, subprefectures and prefectures hold regular meetings according to special regulations.

ARTICLE 68.   The people's councils direct their own administrative affairs, are responsible for economic and cultural matters within their jurisdiction, maintain order, see that the laws are carried out, uphold the rights of citizens, and pass local budgets.

The people's councils make decisions within their own jurisdiction in conformity with the Constitution and the laws, decrees and ordinances of high departments of government.

ARTICLE 69.   In the exercise of their local functions, the people's councils must cooperate with the people as well as the workers' organizations, and they should be inspired by their initiative.

ARTICLE 70.   With the exception of the rural districts, the executive committees elected by the people's councils are the executive and administrative organs of these councils.

The executive committee is composed of a chairman, a secretary, and members.

ARTICLE 71.   In the rural districts, the executive body of the people's council is composed of one chairman and one secretary.

ARTICLE 72.   The people's council of the rural district calls a convention to which it gives an account of its activities.

The rights and duties of the local convention are defined by law.

ARTICLE 73.   The executive organs of the people's council depend on the people's council and also on the executive and administrative organs of the state.

ARTICLE 74.   The people's councils may create special offices and sections to direct various administrative affairs.

The activities of these offices or subdivisions are directed by the executive committee and are under the jurisdiction of the people's council as well as the respective higher councils and ministries concerned.

TITLE IV

COURTS AND DEPARTMENT OF THE ATTORNEY-GENERAL

(a) Courts

ARTICLE 75.   The judicial organs of the People's Republic of Albania are the Supreme Court, the people's courts of the prefectures and subprefectures, and the military courts.

Special courts may be created by law for specific questions.

ARTICLE 76.   The courts give their decisions in the name of the people.

The courts are independent in the exercise of their own functions. They are separated from all the administrative branches of government. Their decisions cannot be altered except by higher courts.

The higher courts are empowered within the law to control lower courts.

The Ministry of Justice directs and controls all matters of judicial administration and organization.

ARTICLE 77.   The courts try cases according to law.

ARTICLE 78.   In principle, court sessions are open to the public.

ARTICLE 79.   In principle, the decisions of the courts are given for the entire bench. The judicial personnel of the subprefectures and prefectures sitting as a court of original jurisdiction is composed of permanent judges and juries, both of whom have equal rights.

Penal verdicts of more than ten years cannot be given by a court of original jurisdiction but only by a court of the prefecture or by a higher court.

ARTICLE 80. The official language in all courts is Albanian.

Any citizen who does not know Albanian may use his own language through an interpreter.

ARTICLE 81. The Supreme Court is elected for four years by the People's Convention of the republic and by secret ballot.

The courts of the prefectures are elected for three years by the people's council of the prefecture and by secret ballot.

The judges of the subprefectures are also elected for three years by the people's councils of the subprefectures and by secret ballot.

A person may be elected judge many times.

The manner of election to all courts will be defined by law.

ARTICLE 82. The Supreme Court is the highest judicial body of the People's Republic of Albania.

The Supreme Court can arbitrate any conflict of jurisdiction between the civil and military courts as well as between courts and any other bodies.

Cases in which the Supreme Court acts as a court of original or secondary jurisdiction will be defined by law.

ARTICLE 83. The Supreme Court passes on the legality of all court decisions of the republic.

Only the District Attorney may exercise an appeal against a summary decision of the courts. The decision given on such an appeal has no effect on the cause tried except when the law provides otherwise.

(b) Department of the Attorney-General

ARTICLE 84. The Department of the Attorney-General is the organ of the People's Convention which supervises the execution of the law by the ministries and other administrative bodies as well as by all public officials and citizens.

ARTICLE 85. The Attorney-General of the People's Republic of Albania and his assistants are appointed by the People's Convention.

District attorneys of the prefectures and subprefectures are appointed by the Attorney-General.

ARTICLE 86. All district attorneys are independent of the local governmental units and are responsible only to the Attorney-General, from whom they receive orders and instructions.

ARTICLE 87. District attorneys are authorized to initiate penal actions and also to exercise the right of appeal as well as the right to intervene during a judicial or administrative trial. District attorneys can exercise the right of appeal against summary decisions of the courts and other administrative organs when such decisions are illegal.

ARTICLE 88. The district attorney of the military courts of the national army of the People's Republic of Albania and other military attorneys are appointed by the commander-in-chief of the armed forces of the Republic.

TITLE V

RELATION BETWEEN THE EXECUTIVE AND ADMINISTRATIVE DEPARTMENTS

ARTICLE 89. The Presidium of the People's Convention may annul or suspend decrees, instructions, and decisions of the government when they are unconstitutional and illegal.

The government may annul or suspend decrees, ordinances, instructions and decisions of ministers when they are contrary to the laws, decrees, instructions and decisions of the government.

ARTICLE 90. The Presidium of the People's Convention and the higher people's councils may suspend any illegal or irregular act of the lower people's councils.

The government or the ministers may annul or suspend any illegal or irregular act of the executive committees. The higher executive committees have the same right over the lower executive committees.

The people's councils may annul or suspend any illegal or irregular act of their own executive committees.

The government and the executive committees of the higher people's councils may suspend the execution of every illegal or irregular act of the lower people's councils or may propose the annulment of such acts.

ARTICLE 91. The Presidium of the People's Convention and the higher people's councils may dissolve the lower people's councils and authorize new elections. Likewise they may suspend executive committees of the lower people's councils and order elections of new executive committees.

TITLE VI

THE NATIONAL ARMY

ARTICLE 92. The National Army is the armed force of the People's Republic of Albania. Its duty is to defend the independence of the state and the freedom of the people.

The army defends the frontiers of the state and guarantees internal peace and security.

ARTICLE 93. The Supreme Commander of the armed forces of the People's Republic of Albania is appointed by the People's Convention.

The Supreme Commander directs all the armed forces of the People's Republic of Albania.

PART THREE
THE SEAL, FLAG, AND CAPITAL CITY

ARTICLE 94.   The seal of the People's Republic of Albania depicts a field enclosed by two sheaves of wheat. The sheaves are tied at the bottom with a ribbon on which is written the date May 24, 1944.

Between the tips of the ears of wheat there is a red [five-pointed] star. In the center of the field is a black double-headed eagle.

ARTICLE 95.   The official flag of the People's Republic of Albania has a red field, in the center of which is a black double-headed eagle. Over the eagle is a [five-pointed] star, embroidered in gold. The length and breadth of the flag is one by one-and-forty.

ARTICLE 96.   The capital city of the People's Republic of Albania is Tirana.

Tirana, March 14, 1946

The Secretary
(signed) Sali Mborja

The President of the Constituent Assembly
(signed) Tuk Jakova

PRESIDIUM OF THE CONSTITUENT ASSEMBLY
Decree No. 24
Tirana, March 15, 1946
Promulgation of the Constitution of The People's Republic of Albania

According to Law No. 195 of January 12, 1946, the Presidium of the Constituent Assembly decrees the promulgation of the Constitution of the People's Republic of Albania, as approved by the Constituent Assembly of March 14, 1946.

Dr. Omer Nishani
General Lt. Kochi Xoxe
General Major Myslim Peza
Nako Spiru
Sami Baholli

General Col. Enver Hoxha
Dr. Medar Shtylla
Prof. S. Maleshova
Col. Ramadan Chitaku
Dr. Manol Konomi
Hasan Pulo
Qiriako Harito
Pandi Kristo

3.1. 1   CONSTITUTION OF THE PEOPLE'S REPUBLIC OF ALBANIA
AS AMENDED[1]

FIRST PART

BASIC PRINCIPLES

CHAPTER I

THE PEOPLE'S REPUBLIC OF ALBANIA

ARTICLE 1.   Albania is a people's republic.

ARTICLE 2.   The People's Republic of Albania is a state of workers and laboring peasants.

ARTICLE 3.   The political bases of the People's Republic of Albania are the people's councils which sprang up during the war of national liberation against fascism and reaction and were consolidated after the historic victory of this war and during the construction of the bases of socialism.

ARTICLE 4.   All power in the People's Republic of Albania belongs to the working people of town and countryside represented by the people's councils.

ARTICLE 5.   All the representative organs of state power are elected by the citizens in free elections and by general, equal, direct and secret ballots.

The representatives of the people in all the organs of state power are responsible to their electors.

The electors have a right to revoke their representatives at any time. The norms to exercise this power will be set by special law.

ARTICLE 6.   All the organs of state power exercise their functions on the basis of the Constitution, of the laws and general provisions issued by the high organs of state power.

CHAPTER II

THE SOCIAL AND ECONOMIC ORDER

ARTICLE 7.   The means of production in the People's Republic of Albania is made up of the common property of the people in the hands of the State, of the property of the people's cooperative organizations and of the property of the private persons, natural or legal.

All mines and other resources of the subsoil, waters, natural springs, forests and pasture grounds, the means of air, rail and maritime communication, posts, telegraph, telephone, broadcasting stations and banks make up the joint property of the people.

---

[1] *Constitution of the People's Republic of Albania* (Tirana: Albanian Committee for Cultural Relations and Friendship with Foreign Countries, 1964).

Foreign trade is under. . . . State control. The State also governs and controls the entire interior trade of the country.

ARTICLE 8. In order to safeguard the vital interests of the people and to raise the level of their well-being as well as to make full use of all the economic possibilities and powers, the State directs the economic life and development on the basis of a general economic plan. Relying on the state economic and cooperative sectors, it exercises a general control on the private sector of economy.

In fulfilling the general economic plan, the State lays its trust on the trade unions of the workers and employees, on the cooperatives of the peasants as well as on the other organizations of the laboring masses.

ARTICLE 9. The management of state property is governed by law.

State property enjoys special support by the State.

ARTICLE 10. The State shows special concern about the cooperative movement, sponsors and favors it.

ARTICLE 11. Private property and private enterprise in economy are guaranteed. The right of succession to private property is guaranteed. No one can use the right of private property to the prejudice of the community.

Private property may be limited and expropriated by law when the common good demands it.

In what cases and how much the proprietor will be remunerated will be specified by law.

Certain branches of economy or enterprises may be nationalized by the State under the same conditions if public interests demand it.

Monopolies, trusts, combines and so forth set up for the purpose of dictating prices and of monopolizing markets to the prejudice of national economy are prohibited.

ARTICLE 12. The land belongs to those who till it. When an institution or person who does not till the land may remain in possession of this land or of part of it, [the same] is specified by law.

Large estates can by no means be in the hands of private owners.

The maximum area of land that can be under private ownership is determined by law.

The State sponsors the socialist development of agriculture by setting up state agricultural enterprises, machine and tractor stations and by aiding agricultural cooperatives and other forms of union of laboring peasants created on the basis of free choice.

The State gives special protection and aid to the poor and medium peasants by its economic policy, its credits and its system of taxation.

ARTICLE 13. Work is the basis of the social order of the People's Republic of Albania.

Work is both a duty and an honor for all able-bodied citizens according to the principle of 'who works not, eats not.'

The socialist principle of 'from each according to his capacity and to each according to his work' is carried out in the People's Republic of Albania.

CHAPTER III

THE RIGHTS AND DUTIES OF CITIZENS

ARTICLE 14. All citizens are equal before the law. It is their duty to comply with the Constitution and the laws.

No privileges are recognized for reasons of origin, position, wealth or cultural standard.

ARTICLE 15. All citizens are equal with no differences of nationality, race or religion. Any act which brings about privileges in favor of citizens or limits their rights on account of differences of nationality, race or religion is contrary to the Constitution and incurs punishment foreseen by law. Any attempt to sow hatred and cause dissension among nationalities, races and religions is contrary to the Constitution and liable to punishment according to law.

ARTICLE 16. All citizens, without distinction of sex, nationality, belief, cultural standard or residence, and who have reached the age of 18 years, have the right to vote and stand for election to all the organs of state power.

These rights are enjoyed also by citizens serving in the army.

The right of the ballot is universal, equal, direct and secret.

The right of the ballot is refused to persons who are excluded by law.

ARTICLE 17. Women enjoy equal rights with men in all spheres of private, political and social life.

Women enjoy the rights of equal pay with men for the same work. They enjoy the same right in social insurances.

The State gives special protection to the interests of mother and child by securing the right for a paid leave before and after childbirth and by setting up homes for expectant mothers and homes for bringing up and sheltering children.

ARTICLE 18. All the citizens are guaranteed the freedom of conscience and of faith.

The church is separated from the State.

The religious communities are free in matters of their belief as well as in their outer exercise and practice.

It is prohibited to use the church and religion for political purposes.

Political organizations on a religious basis are likewise prohibited.

The State may give material aid to religious communities.

ARTICLE 19. Marriage and the family are under the protection of the State. The State determines by law the legal conditions of marriage and the family.

Lawful marriage can be contracted only before the competent organs of the State. After the celebration of lawful marriage the citizens may also celebrate religious marriage according to the rules of their religion.

Only the state courts have jurisdiction on all the matters connected with marriage.

Parents have the same obligations and duties toward the children born outside their marriage as they have toward children born within their marriage. Children born outside marriage enjoy the same rights as children born within marriage.

ARTICLE 20. All the citizens are guaranteed the freedom of speech, of the press, of organization, of meetings, of assembly and of public manifestations.

ARTICLE 21.   In order to develop the initiative of the working masses in the field of organization and their political activity, the State guarantees to the citizens the right to join in social organizations: the Democratic Front, the Trade Unions, the cooperatives, the organizations of Youth and of Women, the organizations of Sport and of Defense, cultural, scientific and technical societies; the more active and conscientious citizens of the working class and of the other working masses join the ranks of the Albanian Party of Labor, the vanguard organization of the working class and of all the working masses in their endeavors to build the bases of socialism and the leading nucleus of all the organizations of the working masses, . . . social as well as of the State.

ARTICLE 22.   All the citizens are guaranteed the inviolability of the person. No one can be detained under arrest more than three days without a decision of the court or without the approval of the public attorney.

Nobody can be condemned for a crime without a sentence of the court having jurisdiction according to the law which fixes the jurisdiction and specifies the crime.

No sentences can be passed except on the basis of law.

Nobody can be convicted without being heard and without being called to defend himself according to the provisions of law, except when his absence is legally verified.

The organs of the state administration may, within bounds specified by law, pass sentences to imprisonment for slight violations of common law.

No citizen can be banished abroad or within the State except in cases considered by law.

The People's Republic of Albania protects the Albanian citizens residing abroad.

ARTICLE 23.   Dwelling houses cannot be violated.

Nobody can enter one's domicile and make searchings without the consent of the owner of the house, except when he is in possession of a search warrant.

Searches cannot be made except in the presence of two witnesses. The owner of the house also has the right to be present.

ARTICLE 24.   The secrecy of correspondence and other means of communication cannot be violated, except in cases of inquiries on crimes, of mobilization and of a state of war.

ARTICLE 25.   The State guarantees to the citizens the right of work for a remuneration according to the amount and quality of the work they yield.

The State guarantees to the citizens the right to rest through a shortening of the hours of work, through granting an annual paid vacation, and through setting up sanatoria, rest homes, clubs, etc.

Through social insurance, the State [likewise] guarantees to the citizens . . . the material means of subsistence in old age and in case of illness and disability.

ARTICLE 26.   Under conditions specified by law, all the citizens have equal rights to be admitted to state posts.

The citizens charged with public functions or appointed to public service are bound to carry out their missions conscientiously.

ARTICLE 27.   The State is duty-bound to provide better living conditions to the invalids of the war and make them capable of work at its own expense. The State shows special concern for the children of the fighters fallen in the battlefield and of the other victims of the war.

ARTICLE 28. The State takes care of the health of the people by setting up and supervising health service, hospitals and sanatoria.

ARTICLE 29. The State takes care of the physical culture of the people, particularly of the youth, so that the health and the vigor of the people for work and the defense of the State may be improved.

ARTICLE 30. The freedom of scientific and art work is guaranteed. The State supports science and arts so that the culture and welfare of the people may develop.

Copyright is protected by law.

ARTICLE 31. In order to raise the general cultural standard of the people, the State provides opportunities to attend schools and other cultural institutions for all ranks of the people.

The State shows special concern for the education of youth.

Children of tender age are under the protection of the law.

The schools are under the dependence of the State. No private schools can be opened except by law. Their activity is under the supervision of the State.

Primary education is compulsory and is given free of charge.

The school is separated from the church.

ARTICLE 32. Citizens have a right to lodge petitions and complaints to the state organs.

Citizens have a right to complain against all decisions contrary to law or irregular, taken by the organs of state administration as well as when functionaries act unlawfully.

ARTICLE 33. Every citizen has the right to claim for damages before the competent courts against the state employees for unlawful deeds they incur in the exercise of their functions.

ARTICLE 34. Under conditions specified by law, citizens are entitled to indemnities from the State or its employees for damages incurred due to carrying out of services contrary to law or in an irregular way.

ARTICLE 35. Every citizen is duty-bound to safeguard and consolidate social property (state and cooperative property), the sacred and inviolable basis of the people's democracy, the source of power of the fatherland, of the welfare and culture of all the working people.

Those who lay hands on social property are enemies of the people.

ARTICLE 36. Protection of the fatherland is the supreme duty and the highest honor of every citizen.

Betrayal to the people is the greatest felony.

Military service is compulsory for all citizens.

ARTICLE 37. All citizens are obliged to pay taxes in proportion to their economic possibilities.

State taxes and exemptions from payment of taxes are stated by law.

ARTICLE 38. Citizens are not entitled to use the rights granted to them by this Constitution in order to change the constitutional order of the People's Republic of Albania for anti-democratic purposes.

Every act in this direction is considered contrary to law and incurs punishments foreseen by law.

ARTICLE 39. National minorities in the People's Republic of Albania enjoy all the rights [of citizenship], the protection of their cultural development and the free use of their language.

ARTICLE 40. The People's Republic of Albania grants the right to asylum in its territory to foreign citizens persecuted on account of their activity in favor of democracy, of the struggle for national liberation, of the rights of working people or in favor of . . . freedom in scientific and cultural work.

SECOND PART

ORGANIZATION OF THE STATE

CHAPTER I

THE HIGH ORGANS OF STATE POWER

(a)   The People's Assembly

ARTICLE 41. The People's Assembly is the highest organ of state power in the People's Republic of Albania.

ARTICLE 42. The sovereignty of the nation and of the State is invested in the People's Assembly, which exercises its sovereign rights on the basis of the Constitution, with the exception of those rights which the Constitution itself has left to the competence of the Presidium of the People's Assembly or of the Government.

ARTICLE 43. Legislative power is exercised only by the People's Assembly.

The Presidium of the People's Assembly, the Government and the representatives have the exclusive right of proposal of new laws.

ARTICLE 44. The People's Assembly is elected by universal suffrage in electoral districts in the ratio of one representative for every 8,000 inhabitants.

ARTICLE 45. The People's Assembly is elected for a term of four years.

ARTICLE 46. The People's Assembly elects one chairman, two vice-chairmen and a secretary. The chairman presides at the meetings in conformity with the rules.

ARTICLE 47. The People's Assembly is convened by decree of its Presidium into two regular sessions a year.

It may be convened into extraordinary sessions by decision of the Presidium of the People's Assembly or at the request of one-third of the representatives.

ARTICLE 48. The People's Assembly draw up their own rules and regulations.

ARTICLE 49. No draft law can have legal power if it is not voted upon by the relative majority of the representatives at a meeting of the People's Assembly attended by the majority of its members.

ARTICLE 50. Laws become effective fifteen days after they have been published in the Official Gazette, except when the law provides otherwise.

ARTICLE 51. The People's Assembly appoints special committees for specific missions.

At its first meeting, the People's Assembly appoints a committee to verify the mandates of the representatives.

On the proposal of this Committee, the People's Assembly confirms or annuls the mandates of the representatives.

ARTICLE 52. The People's Assembly may hold inquests on matters of general importance through a committee of investigation.

All organs of the State are obliged to respond to the queries of the Committee with regard to establishing facts and gathering evidences.

ARTICLE 53. The representatives to the People's Assembly enjoy parliamentary immunity.

They cannot be arrested or prosecuted without the approval of the People's Assembly or its Presidium, except when caught in the act.

ARTICLE 54. In case of war or in similar cases of emergency the People's Assembly may prolong their legislature beyond the normal term as long as the state of emergency lasts.

The People's Assembly may take a decision to dissolve itself before the end of the term for which it is elected.

ARTICLE 55. Elections for a new People's Assembly must be held not later than three months after the day of the dissolution of the People's Assembly.

ARTICLE 56. Amendments or additions to the Constitution can be made only by decision of the People's Assembly.

Bills on amendments or additions to the Constitution may be submitted by the Presidium of the People's Assembly, by the Government or by two-thirds of the number of representatives.

Bills on amendments or additions to the Constitution are adopted by a two-third majority of all the representatives of the People's Assembly.

(b) The Presidium of the People's Assembly

ARTICLE 57. The People's Assembly elects its Presidium which is made up of a President, two Vice Presidents, a secretary and ten members.

ARTICLE 58. The Presidium of the People's Assembly exercises the following functions:

1) Convenes the sessions of the People's Assembly;

2) Decrees the elections to the People's Assembly;

3) Decides on the conformity of laws to the Constitution provided that this decision is later approved by the People's Assembly;

4) Interprets laws;

5) Promulgates laws that have been enacted;

6) Issues decrees (when decrees contain juridical rules they must be submitted for approval to the People's Assembly at its next session);

7) Exercises the right of pardon in conformity with the provisions of the law;

8) Grants decorations and titles of honor;

9) Ratifies and denounces international treaties except in cases [wherein] it deems it advisable to have these ratifications or denunciations passed on by the People's Assembly;

10) Appoints or recalls envoys extraordinary and ministers plenipotentiary on the proposal of the Government;

11) Receives credential letters and letters of recall of the diplomatic representatives of foreign states;

12) Appoints and discharges the Supreme Command of the Armed Forces of the People's Republic of Albania;

13) During the interval between two sessions of the People's Republic of Albania, decrees general mobilization and a state of war in case of an armed aggression against the People's Republic of Albania or, when this is necessary, to fulfill the obligations that arise from international treaties of mutual defense against an aggression;

14) Appoints and discharges ministers between two sessions of the People's Assembly on the proposal of the Head of the Government;

15) On the proposal of the Head of the Government, it sets up committees within the Government and appoints their chairmen;

16) On the proposal of the Government, it designates which enterprises of general importance to the State should come under the direct supervision of a ministry or of a government committee;

17) Decrees people's referendums on various questions on the basis of the decision of the People's Assembly or on the proposal of the Government.

The decrees of the Presidium of the People's Assembly are signed by the President and the Secretary.

ARTICLE 59. The Presidium of the People's Assembly is responsible to the People's Assembly for its doings. The latter may revoke its Presidium and elect another, may revoke its members and may substitute them also before the end of the term for which they are elected.

ARTICLE 60. In case of the dissolution of the People's Assembly the Presidium remains in power until the new Presidium of the People's Assembly is elected.

The Presidium convenes the newly elected People's Assembly not later than three months after its election.

CHAPTER II

ORGANS OF THE STATE ADMINISTRATION

ARTICLE 61. The Government is the highest executive organ and authority of the People's Republic of Albania.

The Government is appointed and discharged by the People's Assembly.

The Government is responsible to the People's Assembly and should render account to it for its activity. During the interval between two sessions of the People's Assembly, it is responsible to the Presidium of the Assembly to which it should render account for its activity.

ARTICLE 62. The Government acts on the basis of the Constitution and in conformity with the laws.

The Government issues decisions and orders on the basis of and for the implementation of the laws in force and checks on their implementation.

The decisions and orders of the Government are signed by the Head of the Government and are published in the Official Gazette.

ARTICLE 63. The Government directs and coordinates the work of the Ministries, of the committees and of the services of other institutions which are under its direct supervision.

The Government draws up the general economic plan of the State and the general budget of the State, which it submits to the People's Assembly for approval, and supervises their implementation; directs the system of credits and the monetary system; takes all the necessary measures to assure and protect the constitutional order and the rights of citizens; directs the general organization of the army; maintains relations with foreign states; sees to it that international treaties and obligations are carried out; submits to the People's Assembly the drafts of laws drawn up by it or by the different ministers; determines the internal organization of the ministries and of the institutions dependent on it; sets up committees and institutions to carry out economic, cultural and national defense measures.

ARTICLE 64. The Government is made up of the chairman, the deputy chairmen, the ministers, the Chairman of the State Committee of Control and the Chairman of the Planning Committee.

The members of the Government take oath before the People's Assembly.

ARTICLE 65. The Head of the Government represents the Government, presides at its meetings and directs the affairs of the Government.

ARTICLE 66. The members of the Government head the various departments of the state administration.

The Government may also have ministers without portfolio.

ARTICLE 67. The members of the Government are penally responsible for the violation of the Constitution and the laws in force in connection with the exercise of their functions.

They are responsible also for damages they may cause to the State through their activities contrary to the law.

The norms on the responsibility of the members of the Government will be specified in detail by a special law.

ARTICLE 68. Within the bounds of the competence of their departments, the ministers issue orders and directions based on the laws and [aimed] at carrying out the laws in force, [and] the decisions and orders of the Government, and supervise their execution.

The orders and instructions of the ministers are published in the Official Gazette.

ARTICLE 69. The Ministries of the People's Republic of Albania are (1) The Ministry of Foreign Affairs; (2) The Ministry of Internal Affairs; (3) The Ministry of People's Defense; (4) The Ministry of Justice; (5) The Ministry of Finances; (6) The Ministry of Education and Culture; (7) The Ministry of Industry; (8) The Ministry of Commerce; (9) Ministry of Agriculture; (10) The Ministry of Health and Sanitation; (11) The Ministry of Construction; (12) The Ministry of Communications; (13) The Ministry of Mines and Geology.

The Committee of State Control and the State Planning Committee are of ministerial rank.

Other ministries may be set up, [but] those already in existence may be suppressed only by law.

ARTICLE 70. The Government may decide to charge a more restricted ministerial council to take up certain matters concerning economy and national defense.

The decision to set up a restricted ministerial council will determine its makeup and its competence.

CHAPTER III

ORGANS OF STATE POWER OF THE LOCAL ADMINISTRATIVE UNITS

ARTICLE 71. The people's councils are the organs of state power in villages, counties, cities, townships and districts.

The people's councils of villages, counties, cities, townships and districts are elected by the citizens for a term of three years.

The above administrative units may be suppressed or new administrative units may be set up . . . by law.

ARTICLE 72. The people's councils direct the affairs of the administrative organs dependent on them, . . . are charged with economic and cultural matters within the bounds of their competence, keep public order, supervise the implementation of laws, protect the rights of citizens, and draw up the local budgets.

ARTICLE 73. Within the bounds of their competence, the people's councils issue decrees and orders in conformity with the Constitution, [and with] the laws and general provisions of the higher organs of state power.

ARTICLE 74. In the exercise of their general and local functions, the people's councils must collaborate with the people and the organizations of the laboring masses and be inspired by their initiatives.

ARTICLE 75. The executive committees of the people's councils are the executive organs of authority of the people's councils.

The makeup and functions of the executive committees of the people's councils are specified by law.

The executive organs of authority in minor administrative units may be made up of the chairman and the secretary of the people's councils.

ARTICLE 76. The local people's councils call meetings of their electorate at the times set by law (and at such meetings) render account of their activity.

ARTICLE 77. The executive committees of the people's councils are dependent on both the people's councils which have elected them [and] the executive organs of authority of the higher organs of state power.

ARTICLE 78. In order to direct the various departments of administration, the people's councils may set up offices or sections. The activities of these offices or sections are directed by the executive committees and supervised by the people's councils and at the same time by the corresponding offices and sections of the higher people's councils and the competent ministry.

CHAPTER IV

COURTS OF JUSTICE AND PUBLIC ATTORNEYS

(a) Courts of Justice

ARTICLE 79. Justice in the People's Republic of Albania is administered by the High Court of the People's Republic of Albania, by district courts, by people's courts and by courts martial.

Special courts may also be set up by law for a given category of questions.

ARTICLE 80. Courts of justice are independent in the exercise of their functions. Courts of justice in all degrees are separated from the Administration. Their judgments and sentences cannot be changed except by the higher courts having jurisdiction.

Within the bounds of law, the higher courts of justice have the right to control the lower courts.

The Minister of Justice directs and supervises the activity of the judiciary administration and sees to it that the courts of justice are organized and function as they should.

ARTICLE 81. The courts of justice try cases on the basis of the law and pass sentences and judgments in the name of the people.

ARTICLE 82. The courts as a rule try their cases in public sittings.

The accused is assured the right of defense.

ARTICLE 83. The courts of justice try cases with the participation of the jury (assistant judges), except cases specifically envisaged by law.

ARTICLE 84. The Albanian language is used in all courts of justice. The citizens [who] do not speak Albanian may use their own language and make use of an interpreter.

ARTICLE 85. The High Court is elected by the People's Assembly for a four-year term.

Courts martial are elected by the People's Assembly and, between its two sessions, by the Presidium of the People's Assembly, for a three-year term.

District courts are elected by the people's councils of the district for a three-year term.

The people's courts are elected by citizens by universal, equal, direct and secret ballot for a three-year term.

ARTICLE 86. The High Court of Justice is the highest organ of justice in the People's Republic of Albania.

It is determined by law when the High Court of Justice will hold trials of the first or of the second grade.

ARTICLE 87. The High Court of Justice will decide whether the final judgments of all the courts of the Republic are lawful or not.

(b) Public Attorneys

ARTICLE 88. Public attorneys are organs of the People's Assembly, whose mission it is to check on the exact implementation of the law by the ministers and other administrative organs as well as by the public [servants] and by all the citizens.

ARTICLE 89. The Attorney-General of the People's Republic of Albania and his assistants are appointed by the People's Assembly.

Public attorneys are appointed by the Attorney-General.

ARTICLE 90. All public attorneys are independent toward all local organs and are dependent on the Attorney-General, from whom they receive orders and instructions.

CHAPTER V

RELATIONS BETWEEN THE ORGANS OF STATE POWER AND STATE ADMINISTRATION

ARTICLE 91. The Presidium of the People's Assembly may declare the decisions and the ordinances of the Government null and void when they are contrary to the Constitution and to the laws.

The Government may annul the orders and instructions of the Ministers when they are contrary to the Constitution and to the laws as well as to the decisions and orders of the Government.

ARTICLE 92. The Presidium of the People's Assembly and the higher people's councils may annul every unlawful or irregular act of the lower people's councils. The Government may annul all unlawful and irregular acts of the executive committees of the people's councils. The executive committees of the higher people's councils have the same right toward the lower executive committees.

The people's councils may quash every unlawful or irregular act of their executive committees.

The Government and the executive committees of the higher people's councils may suspend the execution of all unlawful and irregular acts of the lower people's councils and propose to their people's councils or to the Presidium of the People's Assembly to declare these acts null and void.

ARTICLE 93. The Presidium of the People's Assembly and the higher people's councils may dissolve the lower people's councils and order the election of new people's councils. They may likewise dismiss the executive committees of the lower people's councils and order the election of new executive committees.

CHAPTER VI

THE PEOPLE'S ARMY

ARTICLE 94.   The People's Army is the armed force of the People's Republic of Albania. Its function is to secure and protect the independence of the State and the freedom of the people.

It stands guard over the state boundaries so that they should not be violated and serves the cause of peace and security.

THIRD PART

NATIONAL EMBLEM, NATIONAL FLAG, CAPITAL

ARTICLE 95.   The national emblem of the People's Republic of Albania represents a field wrapped by two sheaves of ears of wheat. The sheaf of wheat is bound at the lower end with a ribbon which bears the inscription of the date May 24, 1944. A five-pointed red star stands among the tops of the tufts of the ears of wheat. A black double-headed eagle stands in the center of the field.

ARTICLE 96.   The national flag of the People's Republic of Albania represents a red field with a double-headed eagle in the center. Above the eagle there is a five-pointed red star, gold-embroidered all around. The ratio between the width and the length of the flag is one to one and forty-hundredths.

ARTICLE 97.   The Capital of the People's Republic of Albania is Tirana.

SECTION 4

BULGARIA

4. 1

CONSTITUTION OF THE PEOPLE'S REPUBLIC OF BULGARIA[1]

Approved by the Grand National Assembly
December 4, 1947

THE PEOPLE'S REPUBLIC OF BULGARIA

ARTICLE 1. Bulgaria is a People's Republic with a representative Government established and consolidated as a result of the heroic struggle of the Bulgarian people against the monarcho-fascist dictatorship, and of the victorious national uprising of September 9, 1944.

ARTICLE 2. In the People's Republic of Bulgaria all power emanates from the people and belongs to the people.

This power is exercised through freely elected representative organs and through referenda.

All representative organs of the state power are elected by the citizens, by a general, direct, and secret ballot.

ARTICLE 3. All citizens of the People's Republic who are above eighteen years of age, irrespective of sex, national origin, race, religion, education, profession, social status or material situation, with the exception of those under judicial disability or deprived of their civil and political rights, are eligible to vote and to be elected.

All persons serving in the ranks of the Bulgarian people's army can vote and can be elected on the same basis as all other Bulgarian citizens.

ARTICLE 4. The people's representatives in all representative organs are responsible to their electors. They may be recalled before the expiry of the term for which they have been elected.

The manner in which elections are held and the rules for recalling people's representatives are determined by law.

ARTICLE 5. The People's Republic of Bulgaria is governed in exact accordance with the Constitution and the laws of the country.

CHAPTER TWO
PUBLIC ECONOMIC ORGANIZATION

ARTICLE 6. The means of production of the People's Republic of Bulgaria belong to the state (national property), to cooperatives, or to private individuals or juridical persons.

---

[1] *Constitution of the People's Republic of Bulgaria* (Sofia, 1947). Translation supplied by the Methodius National Library, Sofia.

ARTICLE 7. All mineral and other underground natural resources, forests, waters, including mineral and curative springs, sources of natural power, railway and air communications, posts, telegraphs, telephones, and radio broadcasting are state, i.e. national, property. A special law shall regulate the utilization of forests by the population.

ARTICLE 8. National economy is the basis of the country's economic development and enjoys special protection.

The state can itself manage or give under concession its own means of production.

ARTICLE 9. The state aids and fosters cooperative enterprise.

ARTICLE 10. Private property and its inheritance, together with private enterprise in economy, are recognized and protected by law.

Private property acquired by labor and thrift and the right to inherit it enjoy special protection.

No one can exercise his right of ownership to the detriment of public interest.

Private monopolistic agreements and associations such as cartels, trusts, etc. are prohibited.

Private property may be subject to compulsory restrictions or expropriation only for state or public use and against fair indemnity.

The state can nationalize fully or in part industrial trade, transport or credit enterprises or branches thereof. The indemnity is determined by the Law for Nationalization.

ARTICLE 11. The land belongs to those who cultivate it.

The law determines how much land private persons may own and the cases in which nonagriculturists may own cultivable land. Private ownership of large landed estates is not permitted.

Cooperative-labor farms are fostered and aided by the state and enjoy its special protection.

The state may organize state farms.

ARTICLE 12. All state, cooperative, and private economic activity is directed by the state by means of a general economic plan with a view to the most rational development of the country's national economy and the promotion of the public welfare.

In preparing and implementing the national economic plan, the state avails itself of the active collaboration of professional, economic and public organizations and institutes.

ARTICLE 13. Foreign and domestic trade are directed and controlled by the state.

The state may reserve to itself the exclusive right to produce or trade in any goods which are of essential importance to the national economy and the needs of the people.

ARTICLE 14. Labor is recognized as a basic public and economic factor and is the object of the state's care in every aspect.

The state directly aids those who work—workers, peasants, craftsmen and intellectuals—by means of its general economic and social policy, tax system, cheap credits and cooperative organization.

With a view to improving the standard of living of the working classes, the state encourages their constructive initiative and enterprise.

CHAPTER THREE
SUPREME ORGANS OF THE STATE POWER

ARTICLE 15. The National Assembly is the supreme organ of the state power.

Within the framework of the Constitution it is repository of all state power insofar as certain particular functions do not fall within the competence of other and subordinate organs of the state power and of the state administration by virtue of the Constitution.

ARTICLE 16. The National Assembly is the only legislative organ of the People's Republic of Bulgaria.

ARTICLE 17. The National Assembly

1) Elects the Presidium of the National Assembly;

2) Appoints the Government of the People's Republic;

3) Amends the Constitution;

4) Decides on the establishment of new ministries and the abolition, fusion or renaming of existing ministries.

5) Decides questions of the cession, exchange or increase of the territory of the People's Republic;

6) Approves the state economic plan;

7) Approves the state budget and the laws for the application of the budget, and determines taxes and the method of their collection;

8) Decides on the nationalization of economic enterprises and the introduction of state monopolies;

9) Decides questions of war and peace;

10) Decides on the holding of referenda;

11) Grants amnesties.

ARTICLE 18. The National Assembly is elected for a term of four years.

It consists of deputies elected by the people, one for every 30,000 inhabitants.

ARTICLE 19. The National Assembly is summoned for ordinary sessions by an order of the National Assembly twice a year—on November 1 and on February 1. If the Presidium fails to summon the Assembly on these dates the latter can meet on its own.

The National Assembly may be summoned for an extraordinary session by a decision of the Presidium of the National Assembly or on the demand of at least one-third of the deputies.

ARTICLE 20. At its opening sitting, under the chairmanship of the oldest deputy, the National Assembly elects from its number a Bureau consisting of a president and three vice-presidents.

The president (or in his absence [one of] the vice presidents) conducts the proceedings in the National Assembly in accordance with the Rules of Procedure adopted by the National Assembly.

The National Assembly also elects the necessary number of secretaries and disciplinary officers in accordance with the Rules of Procedure.

ARTICLE 21. The deputies take the following oath:

'I swear in the name of the people and of the People's Republic that I will serve them devotedly and selflessly, that I will observe and hold sacred and inviolable the Constitution, that in my activity as a representative of the people I will keep in view only the interests of the nation and the state and will spare no effort in defense of the freedom and independence of my country. I have sworn.'

ARTICLE 22. Immediately after it has been constituted the National Assembly elects a commission for verifying the elections and within a period of not more than three months submits a report confirming or annulling the election of each deputy individually.

ARTICLE 23. Legislative initiative belongs to the Government and to the deputies.

Deputies can introduce bills if they are signed by at least one-fifth of the total number of deputies.

ARTICLE 24. After being passed by the National Assembly, each law is signed by the president and secretary of the Presidium of the National Assembly and is published in the State Gazette.

The law comes into effect three days after its publication unless a different term is set by the law itself.

ARTICLE 25. The National Assembly has the sole right to decide whether all the requirements of the Constitution have been observed for making a law and whether it is contradictory to the provisions of the Constitution.

ARTICLE 26. The National Assembly can hold a sitting if more than half of the total number of deputies are present. Decisions are then taken by a simple majority except in cases for which the Constitution has made special provision.

ARTICLE 27. The National Assembly's sittings are public, unless it decides that important state interests demand that they be held in camera.

ARTICLE 28. The National Assembly can make investigations and inquiries into any question through special commissions.

All organs of the state and private persons are obliged to supply the information and documents required by these commissions.

ARTICLE 29. Deputies cannot be detained or prosecuted except for grave offenses and with the consent of the National Assembly or, if it is not in session, with the consent of its Presidium. Such permission is not necessary if a deputy has been apprehended in the commission of a grave criminal offense, in which case it is sufficient to notify the Presidium of the National Assembly forthwith.

Deputies are immune from penal proceedings for their opinions expressed in the Assembly or for their votes.

ARTICLE 30. The National Assembly is dissolved on the expiry of its mandate, or earlier if it so decides.

In the event of war or other exceptional circumstances the National Assembly can prolong its mandate for their duration.

The dissolved National Assembly can be recalled by its Presidium and its mandate prolonged in the event of war or other exceptional circumstances.

ARTICLE 31. A new National Assembly is elected, at the latest, three months after the dissolution of the previous Assembly.

ARTICLE 32. Deputies receive remuneration determined by the National Assembly.

ARTICLE 33. The National Assembly by a majority of more than half of the total number of deputies elects the Presidium of the National Assembly consisting of a president, two vice presidents, a secretary and fifteen members.

ARTICLE 34. The Presidium of the National Assembly is responsible to the Assembly for all its activity.

The National Assembly may at any time change the Presidium or its individual members.

ARTICLE 35. The Presidium of the National Assembly has the following functions:

1) Summons the National Assembly;

2) Fixes the date of elections for the National Assembly;

3) Publishes the laws passed by the National Assembly;

4) Interprets the laws in a way binding on all;

5) Issues edicts;

6) Exercises the right of pardon and amnesty;

7) Institutes Orders and decorations and awards them;

8) Represents the People's Republic in its international relations, appoints and recalls diplomatic and consular representatives of the country abroad on the recommendation of the Government and receives foreign representatives accredited to it;

9) Ratifies and denounces international treaties concluded by the Government;

10) When the National Assembly is not in session, the Presidium can, on the recommendation of the Government, declare a state of war in the event of an armed aggression against the People's Republic, or in the event of an urgent necessity of fulfilling international obligations relating to common defense against aggression; in such a case the Presidium immediately summons the National Assembly to pronounce on the measure taken;

11) Proclaims, on the recommendation of the Government, a general or partial mobilization and a state of siege;

12) When the National Assembly is not in session, the Presidium may, on the recommendation of the Prime Minister, relieve of duty and appoint individual members of the Government; [however,] the Presidium is obliged to submit this to the ratification of the National Assembly at its earliest session;

13) Repeals the decisions and directives of the Government which do not conform to the Constitution or the laws of the country;

14) Fixes the date of a referendum on the decision of the National Assembly;

15) Appoints or discharges the staff of the high command of the armed forces of the People's Republic on the recommendation of the Government;

16) Appoints and discharges the commander-in-chief of the armed forces on the recommendation of the Government;

17) Remits uncollectable debts;

18) Decides questions with which the National Assembly has entrusted it;

19) Discharges all functions which have been assigned to it by law.

ARTICLE 36. Decrees issued by the Presidium of the National Assembly are signed by the President and the Secretary.

ARTICLE 37. After the expiry of the mandate of the National Assembly, or if it is dissolved before the expiry of its term, the Presidium which the Assembly has elected continues to exercise its functions until the newly elected National Assembly elects a new Presidium.

CHAPTER FOUR
ORGANS OF THE STATE EXECUTIVE

ARTICLE 38. The Government (Council of Ministers) is the supreme executive and administrative organ of the State in the People's Republic of Bulgaria.

ARTICLE 39. The Government consists of [the] president of the Council of Ministers, [the] vice-presidents of the Council of Ministers, [the] president of the State Planning Commission, [the] president of the Commission for State Control, [the] ministers, and [the] president of the Committee for Science, Arts and Culture.

The president and vice presidents of the Council of Ministers can hold the office of a ministry, of the State Planning Commission, the Commission for State Control or the Committee for Science, Arts and Culture, or they can be ministers without portfolio.

The ministries are

1) Ministry of Foreign Affairs,

2) Ministry of the Interior,

3) Ministry of National Education,

4) Ministry of Finance,

5) Ministry of Justice,

6) Ministry of National Defense,

7) Ministry of Trade and Supply,

8) Ministry of Agriculture and Forests,

9) Ministry of Construction and Roads,

10) Ministry of Communal Economy and Works,

11) Ministry of Railway, Road and Water Communications,

12) Ministry of Posts, Telegraphs and Telephones,

13) Ministry of Industry and Handicrafts,

14) Ministry of Electrification and Bonification,

15) Ministry of Mines and Mineral Wealth,

16) Ministry of Public Health,

17) Ministry of Labor and Social Security.

The National Assembly may by a vote of more than half of the total number of deputies establish new ministries, or abolish, fuse or rename the existing ministries.

The Presidium of the National Assembly can, on the recommendation of the Government, appoint assistant ministers to the various ministries.

ARTICLE 40. The National Assembly elects and relieves of their functions the Government or individual members of the Government.

The Government is responsible to the National Assembly and gives account of its activity to it.

When the National Assembly is not in session, the Government is responsible and gives account to the Presidium of the National Assembly.

ARTICLE 41. The members of the Government take the following oath before the National Assembly:

'I swear in the name of the people and of the People's Republic of Bulgaria that I will serve them devotedly and selflessly, that in my activity as a member of the Government I will keep in view only the interests of the nation and the state, that I will strictly observe the Constitution and the laws of the People's Republic and will spare no effort in defense of the freedom and independence of the People's Republic of Bulgaria. I have sworn.'

ARTICLE 42. Members of the Government may also be persons who are not deputies.

ARTICLE 43. The Government directs the state administration by unifying and coordinating the work of the various Ministries, the State Planning Commission, the Commission for State Control, and the Committee for Science, Arts and Culture; takes measures for the implementation of the state economic plan and of the state budget; it takes steps to ensure public order, to defend the interests of the state and the rights of the citizens; it directs the general line of the foreign policy of the People's Republic of Bulgaria and of national defense, and also supervises the observance of the laws and of governmental measures.

The various members of the Government direct their respective ministries within the framework and on the basis of the general policy and directives of the Council of Ministers.

The Council of Ministers can take under its direct control certain branches of the administration by forming for the purpose commissions, committees, councils, general directorates, directorates, or services directly subordinate to it.

ARTICLE 44. Each deputy has the right to question and interpellate the Government or its members.

The latter are obliged to answer questions within the period laid down by the Rules of Procedure, and [to reply to] interpellations—when put on the agenda.

ARTICLE 45. The members of the Government are penally responsible for any violation of the Constitution and the laws and for any criminal offense committed in the discharge of their functions.

They bear civil responsibility for damage caused by them to the state or to private citizens by their unlawful acts.

The responsibilities of the members of the Government and the procedure for their prosecution are regulated in detail by a special law.

ARTICLE 46. Officials must take an oath of loyalty to the People's Republic.

They bear disciplinary, penal and civil responsibility for offenses committed in the discharge of their duties.

CHAPTER FIVE

LOCAL ORGANS OF THE STATE POWER

ARTICLE 47. The territory of the People's Republic is divided into municipalities and counties.

Larger administrative units may be created by special laws.

ARTICLE 48. Organs of the state in the municipalities and counties are the municipal and county people's councils, which are elected by the local population for a term of three years.

ARTICLE 49. The municipal and county people's councils direct the implementation of all economic, social, and cultural undertakings of local significance in conformity with the laws of the country. They prepare the economic plan and budget of the municipality and the county within the frame of the state economic plan and the state budget and direct their implementation; they supervise the correct administration of state property and the economic enterprises in their area; they supervise the preservation of public order, the observance of the laws and the defense of the rights of the citizens; they direct the activity of their subordinate executive and administrative organs.

ARTICLE 50. Within the limits of their competence local people's councils take decisions and issue orders in compliance with the laws and general directives of the superior organs of the state power.

ARTICLE 51. Executive and administrative organs of the Municipal and County People's Council are the Municipal and County Executives consisting of a President, Vice Presidents, Secretary and members.

Municipal Executives in smaller inhabited localities may consist only of a President and Secretary.

ARTICLE 52. In the execution of their tasks municipal and county people's councils rely on the initiative and mass participation of the people and of their political, professional and other organizations.

At least once a year, in the manner regulated by law, municipal and county people's councils give an account of their past activity to the electors.

ARTICLE 53. The sessions of the municipal and county people's councils are regular or extraordinary. Municipal people's councils meet for a regular session every month and county people's councils every other month.

The municipal and county executives may summon the councils to an extraordinary session on their own initiative, on the demand of one-third of the [councilmen] or on the order of the corresponding superior state organ.

ARTICLE 54. Municipal and county executives are subordinate both to the people's councils which have elected them and to the superior organs of the state administration.

ARTICLE 55. Departments for the various branches of administration may be formed at the municipal and county people's councils; they are to be directed by the executives of the councils. In their work these departments are subordinate both to the executive of the people's council to which they are attached and to the corresponding department at the superior people's council and to the corresponding ministry or Government service of the People's Republic.

CHAPTER SIX

COURTS AND PROSECUTION

ARTICLE 56. The courts apply the law strictly and equally to all citizens.

Judges are independent; in giving their decisions they act only according to the dictates of the law. They pronounce their decisions and sentences in the name of the people.

ARTICLE 57. Assessors also take part in the administration of justice.

The occasions and procedure for their participation are determined by law.

ARTICLE 58. Judges, of all ranks, and assessors are elected, except in the cases explicitly laid down by law.

The law determines which judges and assessors are elected by the citizens in accordance with the rules and regulations of the general, equal, direct and secret ballot, and which by the local People's Councils or by the National Assembly, and the term for which they shall be elected.

ARTICLE 59. Special courts for specific lawsuits and crimes may only be created by a special law.

ARTICLE 60. The constitution of courts, their procedure, the conditions of eligibility of court officials, and the procedure for electing and recalling judges and assessors, as well as the grading of courts, are determined by law.

ARTICLE 61. Supreme judicial control over every kind and grade of court is exercised by the Supreme Court of the People's Republic, the members of which are elected by the National Assembly for a term of five years.

ARTICLE 62. Supreme control over the correct observance of the law by different Government organs and officials and by the citizens is exercised by the Attorney-General of the People's Republic.

It is the particular duty of the Attorney-General of the Republic to attend to the prosecution and punishment of crimes which affect the state, national and economic interests of the People's Republic, and crimes and actions detrimental to the independence and state sovereignty of the country.

ARTICLE 63. The Attorney-General of the People's Republic is elected by the National Assembly for a term of five years and is subordinate to it alone.

ARTICLE 64. All other prosecutors at courts of every grade are appointed and discharged by the Attorney-General of the People's Republic, and in the exercise of their duty are subordinate only to prosecutors directly over them, while all prosecutors are subordinate to the Attorney-General.

CHAPTER SEVEN

RELATIONS BETWEEN THE ORGANS OF THE STATE POWER AND THE ORGANS OF THE STATE ADMINISTRATION

ARTICLE 65. The Presidium of the National Assembly has the right to repeal all decisions and directives of the Council of Ministers which do not conform with the Constitution and the laws of the country.

The Council of Ministers has the right to repeal all decisions and orders of any of its members which do not conform with the Constitution, the laws, or the decisions and directives of the Government.

ARTICLE 66. The Presidium of the National Assembly and the superior local people's councils have the right to repeal unlawful or irregular acts of the inferior people's councils.

ARTICLE 67. The Government and each of its individual members have the right, within the limits of their competence, to repeal the unlawful or irregular acts of municipal and county executives.

The executives of superior people's councils have the same right with regard to the executives of inferior councils.

ARTICLE 68. Each municipal or county people's council can repeal unlawful and irregular acts of its executive.

ARTICLE 69. The Government or its individual members, within the limits of their competence, and similarly the executive of a superior local people's council, may suspend the execution of the unlawful and irregular acts of an inferior local people's council and refer the question of repeal to the Presidium of the National Assembly, or to the people's council of the same rank.

ARTICLE 70. A superior people's council as well as the Presidium of the National Assembly may dissolve an inferior people's council in its area and hold elections for a new people's council.

Superior people's councils as well as the Presidium of the National Assembly may discharge the executive of an inferior people's council in its area and hold elections for a new executive.

CHAPTER EIGHT

BASIC RIGHTS AND OBLIGATIONS OF CITIZENS

ARTICLE 71. All citizens of the People's Republic of Bulgaria are equal before the law.

No privileges based on nationality, origin, religion and material situation are recognized.

Every preaching of racial, national or religious hatred is punishable by law.

ARTICLE 72. Women have equal rights with men in all spheres of the state, private, economic, public, cultural and political life.

This equality is realized by guaranteeing to women on an equality with men the right to labor, equal pay for equal work, the right to rest, to social insurance, to pension and education.

Mothers enjoy special protection in respect to work. The state takes special care of mothers and their children by establishing maternity homes, creches, kindergartens and dispensaries, guarantees paid leave to mothers before and after childbirth, and free midwifery and medical aid.

ARTICLE 73. Citizens have a right to work.

The state guarantees this right to all citizens by planned economy, by systematically and continually developing the productive forces of the country and creating public works.

Labor is paid according to the amount and quality of the work done.

Labor is a duty and a point of honor for every able-bodied citizen. It is the duty of every citizen to engage in socially useful labor and to work according to his powers and ability.

Citizens' Labor Service obligations are determined by a special law.

ARTICLE 74. Citizens have a right to rest.

This right is guaranteed by limited working hours, by holiday with pay once a year, and by the establishment of a large system of rest homes, clubs, etc.

ARTICLE 75. Citizens have a right to pension, aid and compensation in the case of disease, accident, disablement, unemployment and old age.

This right is put into practical effect through social insurance and accessible medical aid guaranteed by the state.

ARTICLE 76. Marriage and the family are under state protection.

Only civil marriage performed by the competent organs is legally valid.

Children born out of wedlock have equal rights with the issue of lawful marriage.

ARTICLE 77. The state takes special care of the social, cultural, labor, physical and health education of the youth.

ARTICLE 78. Citizens are guaranteed freedom of conscience and religion, and of performing religious rites.

The church is separate from the state.

A special law regulates the legal status, the questions of material support, and the right to self-government and organization of the various religious communities.

It is prohibited to misuse the church and religion for political ends or to form political organizations with a religious basis.

ARTICLE 79. Citizens have a right to education. Education is secular, with a democratic and progressive spirit. National minorities have a right to be educated in their vernacular, and to develop their national culture, while the study of Bulgarian is obligatory.

Elementary education is compulsory and free of charge.

Schools are run by the state. The establishment of private schools may be allowed only by a special law, in which case the school in question is under state supervision.

The right to education is guaranteed by schools, educational institutes, [and] universities, as well as by scholarships, student hostels, material and other aid, and special encouragement for gifted students.

ARTICLE 80. The state cares for the development of science and art by establishing research institutions, publishing houses, libraries, theatres, museums, public reading clubs, art galleries, film studios, cinemas, etc., and by aiding persons who have shown ability in a given sphere.

ARTICLE 81. The state takes care of national health by organizing and directing health services and institutes, propagates health education among the people, and pays special attention to the physical culture of the people.

ARTICLE 82. The freedom and inviolability of the individual are guaranteed.

No one may be detained for more than forty-eight hours without a decision of the judicial authorities or the Prosecutor.

Punishment can be inflicted only on the basis of the existing laws.

Punishment is personal and corresponds to the crime committed.

Punishment for crimes can be inflicted only by the established courts.

The accused has a right to defense.

ARTICLE 83. All Bulgarian citizens abroad enjoy the protection of the People's Republic of Bulgaria.

ARTICLE 84. In the People's Republic of Bulgaria foreigners enjoy the right of sanctuary when they are prosecuted for defending democratic principles, for struggling for their national liberation, for the rights of the workers, or for the freedom of scientific and cultural activity.

ARTICLE 85. Homes are inviolable. Without the consent of the householder no one may enter his home or premises and conduct a search there unless conditions required by law are observed.

ARTICLE 86. The secrecy of correspondence is inviolable except in the event of mobilization, state of siege, or when special permission is given by the judicial authorities or the Prosecutor.

ARTICLE 87. Bulgarian citizens have the right to form societies, associations and organizations provided they are not contrary to the state and public order established by the present Constitution.

The law forbids and punishes the formation of and participation in organizations the aim of which is to deprive the Bulgarian people of the rights and liberties gained with the national uprising of September 9, 1944, and guaranteed by the present Constitution, or to encroach on these rights and liberties, or to imperil the national independence and state sovereignty of the country; or organizations which openly or secretly propagate fascist and antidemocratic ideology or facilitate imperialist aggression.

ARTICLE 88. The citizens of the People's Republic are guaranteed freedom of the press, of speech, of assembly, of meetings and demonstrations.

ARTICLE 89. Citizens have the right to make requests, complaints and petitions.

Every citizen has the right to demand court proceedings against officials for offenses committed in the discharge of their duties.

Citizens have a right to compensation from officials for damage caused them by the latter owing to unlawful or irregular execution of their duties.

ARTICLE 90. The defense of the country is a supreme duty and a point of honor for every citizen.

Treason to the motherland is the gravest crime against the people and is punished with the full severity of the law.

ARTICLE 91. Military service is obligatory for all citizens in accordance with the special laws.

ARTICLE 92. Citizens are bound to observe the Constitution and the laws of the country strictly and conscientiously.

ARTICLE 93. Citizens are bound to preserve national property and by all their actions to further the economic, cultural and defensive power of the country and the welfare of the people.

ARTICLE 94. The citizens' burden of taxation is distributed in accordance with their paying ability. These obligations and exemption from them are established only by law.

CHAPTER NINE

COAT OF ARMS, STATE SEAL, FLAG, CAPITAL

ARTICLE 95. The coat of arms of the People's Republic of Bulgaria is round, with a lion rampant in the center, ears of corn on either side of it, a five-pointed red star over its head and '9.IX.1944' in gold below.

ARTICLE 96. The state seal bears the state coat of arms.

ARTICLE 97. The flag of the People's Republic of Bulgaria is tricolored—white, red and green, placed horizontally. The upper left-hand corner of the white stripe bears the coat of arms of the People's Republic.

ARTICLE 98. The capital of the People's Republic of Bulgaria is Sofia.

CHAPTER TEN

AMENDMENT OF THE CONSTITUTION

ARTICLE 99. The Constitution may be amended on the proposal of the Government or of at least one-quarter of the deputies.

The Constitution Amendment Bill is put on the Agenda of the National Assembly within a week from its introduction in the Assembly.

It may be passed by a majority of two-thirds of the total number of deputies. The Law for the Amendment of the Constitution comes into effect on the day of its publication in the State Gazette.

CHAPTER ELEVEN

TEMPORARY PROVISIONS

ARTICLE 100. After the present Constitution comes into effect, the Grand National Assembly, elected on October 27, 1946, elects a Presidium of the Grand National Assembly in accordance with Article 33; the Presidium immediately assumes the functions provided for by the Constitution. This terminates the functions of the Presidium of the Grand National Assembly, elected in accordance with Article 2 of the Rules of Procedure of the Grand National Assembly. The deputies elect in accordance with Article 20 of the present Constitution a president and vice-president for conducting the proceedings in the Grand National Assembly.

ARTICLE 101. The Presidium of the Grand National Assembly appoints provisional municipal and county executives with the prerogatives of people's councils until municipal and county people's councils, provided for by the Constitution, are elected.

4. I. I CONSTITUTION OF THE PEOPLE'S REPUBLIC OF BULGARIA
AS AMENDED[1]

(Published in the *State Gazette* No. 284/1948, amended—*Izvestiia* No. 89/1961)

CHAPTER I
THE PEOPLE'S REPUBLIC OF BULGARIA

ARTICLE 1. Bulgaria is a People's Republic with a representative government, firmly established as a result of the heroic struggles of the Bulgarian peoples against the monarcho-fascist dictatorship and of the victorious people's uprising of September 9, 1944.

ARTICLE 2. All power in the People's Republic of Bulgaria derives from the people and belongs to the people.

This power is exercised through freely elected representative organs and through referenda.

All representative organs of the state authority are elected by the citizens on the basis of universal, equal and direct suffrage by secret ballot.

ARTICLE 3. All citizens of the People's Republic who have completed their eighteenth year of age, irrespective of sex, nationality, race, creed, education, occupation, social or property status have the right to vote and to be elected, with the exception of those placed under tutelage or deprived of civil and political rights.

ARTICLE 4. The representatives of the people in all representative bodies are responsible to the electors. They may be recalled before the end of the term for which they are elected.

The manner of holding elections as well as the order of recalling the people's elected candidates are established by law.

ARTICLE 5. The People's Republic of Bulgaria is governed in exact accordance with the Constitution and the laws of the country.

CHAPTER II
SOCIAL AND ECONOMIC STRUCTURE

ARTICLE 6. The means of production in the People's Republic of Bulgaria belong to the state (national property), to the cooperatives, or to private individuals or juridical persons.

ARTICLE 7. All mineral and other underground natural resources, forests, waters, including mineral and curative springs, sources of natural power, railways and communications, posts, telegraphs, telephones and radio broadcasting are state-owned, i.e., national property.

A special law shall regulate the exploitation of forests by the population.

---

[1] *Constitution of the People's Republic of Bulgaria* (Sofia: Foreign Languages Press, 1964).

ARTICLE 8. National property is the mainstay of the country's economic development and enjoys special protection.

The state can itself manage or concede to another the management of the means of production at its disposal.

ARTICLE 9. The state aids and fosters cooperative associations.

ARTICLE 10. Private property and its inheritance, as well as private initiative in economy, are recognized and protected by law.

Private property acquired by labor and thrift and the right to inherit it enjoy special protection.

No one can exercise his right of ownership to the detriment of the public interest.

Private monopoly agreements and associations, such as cartels, trusts and concerns, are prohibited. Private property may be subject to compulsory restrictions or expropriations solely for the state and public use and against fair indemnity.

The state can nationalize, fully or in part, certain branches or individual enterprises of industry, trade, transport and credit. The indemnity is determined by the Law on Nationalization.

ARTICLE 11. The land belongs to those who till it. The law determines how much land private persons may own, as well as the cases in which nonfarmers may own arable land. Private ownership of large landed estates is not permitted. Cooperative farms are fostered and aided by the state and enjoy special protection.

The state may organize state farms.

ARTICLE 12. All state, cooperative and private economic activity is directed by the state by means of a state economic plan, with a view to the most expedient development of the nation's economy and the promotion of the public welfare. In drawing up and implementing the state economic plan, the state avails itself of the active collaboration of professional, economic and social organizations and institutions.

ARTICLE 13. Foreign and domestic trade are directed and controlled by the state.

The state may reserve to itself the exclusive right to produce or trade in any goods which are of prime importance to the national economy and the needs of the people.

ARTICLE 14. Labor is recognized as a basic social and economic factor and is the object of the state's care in every respect.

The state directly aids the working people—workers, farmers, craftsmen and intellectuals—by means of its general economic and social policy, cheap credit, tax system and cooperative association.

For the all-round improvement of the life of the working people, the state encourages their associations, creative self-initiative and amateur art activities.

CHAPTER III
SUPREME ORGANS OF GOVERNMENT

ARTICLE 15. The National Assembly is the supreme organ of government.

Within the framework of the Constitution, it is the repository of government in its entirety, insofar as certain particular functions do not fall within the competence of other and subordinate organs of the government and of the state administration by virtue of the Constitution.

ARTICLE 16. The National Assembly is the sole legislative body of the People's Republic of Bulgaria.

ARTICLE 17. The National Assembly

1) Elects the Presidium of the National Assembly;

2) Appoints the Government of the People's Republic;

3) Amends the Constitution;

4) Resolves the establishment of new ministries and the abolition, fusion or renaming of existing ministries;

5) Resolves the question of the cession, exchange or increase of the territory of the People's Republic;

6) Votes the State Economic Plan;

7) Votes the state budget and the laws for the application of the budget program, determines taxes and tax collection procedure;

8) Resolves the nationalization of economic enterprises and the introduction of state monopolies;

9) Resolves questions of war and peace;

10) Resolves the holding of referenda;

11) Grants amnesties.

ARTICLE 18. The National Assembly is elected for a four-year term.

(New paragraph 2—*Izvestiia*, No. 89/1961).[2] It consists of national representatives elected by the people, one for every 25,000 inhabitants.

ARTICLE 19. (New article—*Izvestiia*, No. 89/1961).[3] The National Assembly is summoned for sessions by the Presidium of the National Assembly at least twice a year.

It may also be summoned on the demand of at least one-fifth of the national representatives.

The newly elected National Assembly is summoned for session two months at the latest after the date of the elections.

ARTICLE 20. Immediately after its opening, the National Assembly, under the chairmanship of the oldest national representative, elects from its number a bureau consisting of a president and three vice presidents.

The president, or in his absence the vice presidents, conducts the proceedings in the National Assembly in accordance with the Rules of Procedure worked out by the National Assembly.

---

[2] Old paragraph 2 of Article 18. It consists of national representatives, elected one for every 30,000 inhabitants.

[3] Old Article 19. The National Assembly is summoned for ordinary sessions by decree of the Presidium of the National Assembly twice a year, on November 1 and February 1. If the Presidium of the National Assembly fails to summon the National Assembly on these dates, it can assemble on its own.

The National Assembly may be summoned for an extraordinary session by decision of the Presidium of the National Assembly on the demand of at least one-third of the national representatives.

The National Assembly also elects the necessary number of secretaries and tellers in accordance with the Rules of Procedure.

ARTICLE 21. The National representatives take the following oath:

'I swear in the name of the people and of the People's Republic of Bulgaria that I will serve them devotedly and selflessly, that I will observe and hold sacred and inviolable the Constitution, that in my activity as national representative I will keep in view only the national and state interests and will spare no effort in defense of the freedom and independence of my country. I have sworn.'

ARTICLE 22. Immediately after it has been constituted, the National Assembly elects an auditing committee which, within a three-month period, reports the confirmation or annulment of the election of each national representative individually.

ARTICLE 23. Legislative initiative is vested in the Government and in the national representatives. National representatives can introduce bills if they bear the signature of at least one-fifth of their total number.

ARTICLE 24. Laws passed by the National Assembly are signed by the president and secretary of the Presidium of the National Assembly and published in the State Gazette.

A law enters into force three days after its publication unless a different term is set by the law itself.

ARTICLE 25. The National Assembly has the sole right to decide whether all the requirements of the Constitution have been observed for the issuance of a law and whether it is constitutional or not.

ARTICLE 26. The National Assembly can hold a session if more than half of the total number of representatives are present. Decisions are then taken by a simple majority of the national representatives except in cases for which the Constitution has made special provision.

ARTICLE 27. The sessions of the National Assembly are public unless it decides that important state interests call for the sitting to be secret.

ARTICLE 28. The National Assembly can make investigations and inquiries into any question through special committees.

All state organs and private persons are obliged to give the information and submit the documents requested by the inquiry committees.

ARTICLE 29. National representatives cannot be detained or prosecuted except for grave offenses and then with the consent of the National Assembly or, if it is not in session, with the consent of the Presidium. Such permission is not necessary if a deputy has been apprehended in the commission of a grave criminal offense, in which case it suffices to notify the Presidium of the National Assembly forthwith.

National representatives are immune from penal proceedings for their opinions expressed in the National Assembly or for their vote.

ARTICLE 30. The National Assembly is dissolved on the expiry of its mandate, or earlier if it so decides.

In case of war or other exceptional circumstances, the National Assembly can prolong its mandate for their duration.

The dissolved National Assembly can be recalled by its Presidium and its mandate prolonged in case of war or other exceptional circumstances.

ARTICLE 31. A new National Assembly is elected within three months after the dissolution of the previous Assembly.

ARTICLE 32. National representatives receive remuneration as determined by the National Assembly.

ARTICLE 33. The National Assembly, by a majority of more than half of the total number of national representatives, elects the Presidium of the National Assembly consisting of a president, two vice-presidents, a secretary and fifteen members.

ARTICLE 34. The Presidium of the National Assembly is responsible to the National Assembly for its entire activity.

The National Assembly may at any time change the Presidium or its individual members.

ARTICLE 35. The Presidium of the National Assembly has the following functions:

1) Summons the National Assembly;

2) Fixes the date of elections for the National Assembly;

3) Publishes the laws passed by the National Assembly;

4) Interprets the laws in a way binding to all;

5) Issues decrees;

6) Exercises the right of pardon;

7) Institutes medals and decorations and awards them;

8) Represents the People's Republic in its international relations, appoints and recalls diplomatic and consular representatives abroad on the recommendation of the Government and receives foreign representatives accredited to it;

9) Ratifies and denounces international treaties concluded by the Government;

10) When the National Assembly is not in session, the Presidium can, on the proposal of the Government, declare a state of war in the event of an armed aggression against the People's Republic, or in the event of an urgent necessity of fulfilling international obligations relating to common defense against aggression; in such a case the Presidium immediately summons the National Assembly to pronounce on the measure taken;

11) Proclaims, on the proposal of the Government, general or partial mobilization and martial law;

12) When the National Assembly is not in session, the Presidium may, on the proposal of the Prime Minister, relieve of duty and appoint individual members of the Government; the Presidium is obliged to submit this measure to the National Assembly for ratification at its nearest session;

13) Repeals the decisions and directives of the Government which do not conform to the Constitution or the laws;

14) Fixes the date of a referendum on the decision of the National Assembly;

15) Appoints and discharges, on the proposal of the Government, the staff of the high command of the armed forces of the People's Republic;

16) Appoints and discharges, on the proposal of the Government, the commander-in-chief of the armed forces;

17) Remits uncollectable debts;

18) Decides upon matters which the National Assembly has entrusted to it;

19) Discharges all functions which have been assigned to it by law.

ARTICLE 36. Edicts issued by the Presidium of the National Assembly are signed by its president and secretary.

ARTICLE 37. After the expiry of the mandate of the National Assembly, or if it is dissolved before the expiry of its term, the Presidium which it has elected continues to exercise its functions until the newly elected National Assembly elects a new Presidium.

CHAPTER IV

ORGANS OF THE STATE EXECUTIVE

ARTICLE 38. The Government (Council of Ministers) is the supreme executive and administrative organ of the state in the People's Republic of Bulgaria.

ARTICLE 39. The Government consists of [the] president of the Council of Ministers; vice presidents of the Council of Ministers; president of the State Planning Commission; president of the Commission for State Control; ministers; and president of the Committee for Science, Art and Culture.

The president and vice presidents of the Council of Ministers can head a ministry, as well as the State Planning Commission, the Commission for State Control, or the Committee for Science, Arts and Culture, or they can be ministers without portfolio.

The Ministries are

1) Ministry of Foreign Affairs
2) Ministry of the Interior
3) Ministry of Education
4) Ministry of Finance
5) Ministry of Justice
6) Ministry of National Defense
7) Ministry of Commerce and Supplies
8) Ministry of Agriculture and Forests
9) Ministry of Construction and Roads
10) Ministry of Communal Economy and Public Works
11) Ministry of Railway, Road and Water Communications
12) Ministry of Posts, Telegraphs and Telephones
13) Ministry of Industry and Handicrafts
14) Ministry of Electrification and Land Reclamation

15) Ministry of Mines and Mineral Wealth

16) Ministry of Public Health

17) Ministry of Labor and Social Welfare.

The National Assembly may, by a vote of more than half of the total number of national representatives, set up new ministries, or abolish, fuse or rename the existing ministries.

The Presidium of the National Assembly can, on the recommendation of the Government, appoint assistant ministers to the various ministries.

ARTICLE 40. The National Assembly elects and relieves of their functions the Government or individual members of the Government.

The Government is responsible to the National Assembly and gives account of its activity to it. When the National Assembly is not in session, the Government is responsible and gives account to the Presidium of the National Assembly.

ARTICLE 41. The members of the Government take the following oath before the National Assembly:

'I swear in the name of the people and the People's Republic of Bulgaria that I will serve them devotedly and selflessly, that in my activity as a member of the Government I will keep in view only the interests of the nation and the state, that I will strictly observe the Constitution and the laws of the People's Republic and will spare no effort in defense of the freedom and independence of the People's Republic of Bulgaria. I have sworn.'

ARTICLE 42. Members of the Government may also be persons who are not national representatives.

ARTICLE 43. The Government directs the state administration by unifying and coordinating the work of the various ministries, of the State Planning Commission, the Commission for State Control and the Committee for Science, Arts and Culture; takes measures for the implementation of the State Economic Plan and of the state budget, as well as for maintaining public order, defending the state interests and protecting the rights of the citizens; it exercises general guidance of the foreign policy of the People's Republic of Bulgaria and of national defense, and also supervises the execution of the laws and of various acts of the government.

The various members of the Government direct their respective Ministries within the framework and on the basis of the general policy and directives of the Council of Ministers.

The Council of Ministers may take under its direct control certain branches of the administration by setting up for the purpose commissions, committees, councils, head departments, departments, administrations and services directly subordinate to it.

ARTICLE 44. Every national representative has the right to question and interpellate the Government or its members.

The latter are obliged to answer the questions within the period set down by the rules of procedure, and interpellations—when put on the agenda.

ARTICLE 45. The members of the Government are penally responsible for any violation of the Constitution and the laws, and for any criminal offense committed in the discharge of their functions.

They bear civil responsibility for damage caused by them to the state or to private citizens by their unlawful acts.

The responsibilities of the members of the Government and the procedure for their prosecution are regulated in greater detail by a special law.

ARTICLE 46. Officials take an oath of loyalty to the People's Republic.

They bear disciplinary penal and civil responsibility for offenses committed in the discharge of their functions.

CHAPTER V
LOCAL ORGANS OF GOVERNMENT

ARTICLE 47. (New article—*Izvestiia*, No 89/1961).[4] The territory of the People's Republic of Bulgaria is divided into municipalities and districts.

Other administrative units may be established by law.

ARTICLE 48. Organs of Government in the municipalities are the municipal and district councils, which are elected by the local population for a three-year term.

ARTICLE 49. The municipal and district councils direct the implementation of all economic, social and cultural undertakings of local significance in accordance with the laws of the country. They draft the economic plan and budget of the municipality and the district within the frame of the State Economic Plan and the State budget and direct their implementation. They supervise the proper administration of state property and the economic enterprises in their area; they supervise the maintenance of public order for the observance of the laws and the defense of the citizens' rights; they direct the activity of the subordinate executive and administrative organs.

ARTICLE 50. Within the limits of their competence, the local people's councils take decisions and issue orders in conformity with the laws and general directives of the superior organs of government.

ARTICLE 51. Executive and administrative organs of the municipal and district councils are the municipal and district executives consisting of a president, vice presidents, a secretary and members.

ARTICLE 52. In the execution of their functions, the municipal and district councils rely on the initiative and broad participation of the people and their political, professional and other mass organizations.

At least once a year, in the manner and order regulated by law, municipal and district councils give an account of their past activity to the electors.

ARTICLE 53. The sessions of the municipal and district councils are regular or extraordinary. Municipal councils meet for a regular session every month, and

---

[4] Old Article 47. The territory of the People's Republic is divided into municipalities and districts. Larger administrative units may be established by special laws.

district councils every two months. The municipal and district executives may summon the councils to extraordinary session on their own initiative, on the demand of one-third of the councilors or on order of the respective superior state organ.

ARTICLE 54. Municipal and district executives are subordinate both to the people's councils which have elected them and to the superior state organs.

ARTICLE 55. Departments for the various administrative branches may be established at the municipal and district councils; they are then directed by the executives of the council. In their work these departments are subordinate both to the executive of the people's council to which they are attached and to the corresponding department at the superior people's councils and the corresponding Ministry or Government service of the People's Republic.

CHAPTER VI
PEOPLE'S COURTS AND PROSECUTION

ARTICLE 56. The courts apply the laws exactly and equally to all citizens.

Judges are independent: in issuing their warrants, they act only according to the dictates of the law. They pronounce their decisions and sentences in the name of the people.

ARTICLE 57. Assessors also take part in the dispensation of justice. The cases and procedure for their participation are determined by law.

ARTICLE 58. Judges of all ranks and assessors are elected except in the cases explicitly laid down by law.

The law determines which judges and assessors are directly elected by the citizens in accordance with the rules and regulations on the general, equal, direct and secret ballot, and which by the local people's councils, or by the National Assembly, as well as the term for which they shall be elected.

ARTICLE 59. Special courts for the judgment of specific lawsuits and crimes may be established only by law.

ARTICLE 60. The constitution of courts, legal proceedings, the conditions of eligibility of court officials and the procedure for electing and recalling judges and assessors, as well as the grading of courts, are determined by law.

ARTICLE 61. Supreme judicial control over every kind and grade of courts is exercised by the Supreme Court of the People's Republic, the members of which are elected by the National Assembly for a five-year term.

ARTICLE 62. Supreme supervision of the strict application of the laws by different government organs and officials and by the citizens is exercised by the Chief Prosecutor of the People's Republic.

The Chief Prosecutor of the People's Republic has the particular duty to attend to the prosecution and punishment of crimes against the state, national and economic interests of the People's Republic, as well as the crimes and acts detrimental to the independence and sovereignty of the nation.

ARTICLE 63. The Chief Prosecutor of the People's Republic is elected by the National Assembly for a five-year term and is subordinate to it alone.

ARTICLE 64. All other prosecutors at courts of every grade are appointed and discharged by the Chief Prosecutor of the People's Republic, and in the exercise of their duty are subordinate only to prosecutors who are their immediate superiors, while all prosecutors are subordinate to the Chief Prosecutor.

CHAPTER VII
RELATIONS BETWEEN GOVERNMENTAL AND ADMINISTRATIVE ORGANS

ARTICLE 65. The Presidium of the National Assembly may repeal all decisions and orders of the Council of Ministers which do not conform to the Constitution and the laws of the country. The Council of Ministers may repeal all decisions and orders of any one of its members which do not conform to the Constitution, the laws, or the decisions and orders of the Government.

ARTICLE 66. The Presidium of the National Assembly and the superior people's councils have the right to repeal unlawful and irregular acts of the inferior people's councils.

ARTICLE 67. The Government or its individual members may, within the limits of their competence, repeal the unlawful and irregular acts of the municipal and district executives.

The executives of superior people's councils have the same right with regard to the executives at the inferior councils.

ARTICLE 68. Each municipal and district council may repeal the unlawful and irregular acts of its own executive.

ARTICLE 69. The Government or its individual members, within the limits of their competence, as well as the executive of a superior people's council, may suspend the execution of the unlawful and irregular acts of an inferior local people's council and refer the question of repeal to the Presidium of the National Assembly, or to the people's council of the same rank.

ARTICLE 70. A superior local people's council, as well as the Presidium of the National Assembly, may dissolve an inferior people's council in its area and hold elections for a new people's council.

Superior people's councils as well as the Presidium of the National Assembly may discharge the executive of an inferior people's council in its area and hold elections for a new executive.

CHAPTER VIII
FUNDAMENTAL RIGHTS AND DUTIES OF CITIZENS

ARTICLE 71. All citizens of the People's Republic of Bulgaria are equal before the law.

No privileges based on nationality, origin, faith or property status shall be recognized.

Propagation of racial, national or religious hatred is punishable by law.

ARTICLE 72. Women enjoy equal rights with men in all spheres of state, private, economic, public, cultural and political life.

This equality is realized by guaranteeing to women, on an equality with men, the right to labor, equal pay for equal work, the right to rest, to social insurance, a pension and education.

Mothers enjoy special protection in respect to work. The state takes special care of mothers and their children by establishing maternity homes, nurseries, kindergartens, and outpatient clinics, guarantees paid leave to mothers before and after childbirth and free obstetrical and medical aid.

ARTICLE 73. Citizens have the right to work.

The state guarantees this right to all citizens by planning the national economy, by systematically and continually developing the forces of production and by creating public works.

Labor is paid according to the quantity and quality of the work done.

Work is a duty and a matter of honor for every ablebodied citizen. It is the duty of every citizen to engage in socially useful labor and work according to his powers and ability.

Citizens' labor service obligations are determined by a special law.

ARTICLE 74. Citizens have the right to rest.

This right is guaranteed by the limitation of the working day, by paid annual leave, and by the establishment of a wide network of rest homes, clubs, etc.

ARTICLE 75. Citizens have the right to pensions, aid and indemnities in case of illness, accident, disablement, unemployment and old age.

The state puts this right into practical effect through social insurance and medical aid.

ARTICLE 76. Marriage and the family are under state protection.

Only civil marriage performed by the competent organs is legally valid.

Children born out of wedlock enjoy equal rights with the issue of lawful marriage.

ARTICLE 77. The state takes special care of the social, cultural, labor, physical and health education of the youth.

ARTICLE 78. Citizens are guaranteed freedom of conscience and religion, and of performing religious rites.

The church is separated from the state.

A special law regulates the legal status, the questions of material support and the right of self-government of the various religious communities. Misusing the church and religion for political purposes, or forming political organizations on a religious basis is prohibited.

ARTICLE 79. Citizens have the right to education. Education is secular, democratic and progressive in spirit. National minorities have the right to be educated in their mother tongue and to develop their national culture, while the study of Bulgarian is compulsory.

Elementary education is compulsory and free.

The schools are state-owned. The establishment of private schools may be permitted only by law in which case they are under state supervision. The right to education is guaranteed by schools, educational institutions, universities, as well as by scholarships, student hostels, material aid and special encouragement for gifted students.

ARTICLE 80. The state promotes the development of science and arts by establishing research institutes, publishing houses, libraries, theatres, museums, reading clubs, art galleries, film studios, cinemas, etc. and by aiding persons who have shown ability in this field.

ARTICLE 81. The state promotes public health by organizing and directing health services and institutions, propagating health education among the people and paying special attention to the physical education of the people.

ARTICLE 82. The freedom and inviolability of the individual are guaranteed.

No one may be detained for more than forty-eight hours without a warrant of the judicial authorities or the prosecutor.

Punishment may be inflicted only in virtue of the existing laws.

Punishment is personal and corresponds to the crime committed.

Punishment for crimes may only be inflicted by the established courts.

The defendant has the right to defense.

ARTICLE 83. All Bulgarian citizens abroad enjoy the protection of the People's Republic of Bulgaria.

ARTICLE 84. Foreigners residing in the People's Republic of Bulgaria enjoy the right of sanctuary when they are persecuted for upholding democratic principles, for struggling for their national liberation, for the people's rights or for scientific and cultural freedom.

ARTICLE 85. Homes are inviolable. Without the consent of the householder no one may enter his home or premises and conduct a search there, unless all conditions required by law are observed.

ARTICLE 86. The secrecy of correspondence is inviolable, except in the event of mobilization, martial law, or special permission given by the judicial authorities or the prosecutor.

ARTICLE 87. Bulgarian citizens have the right to form societies, associations and organizations, provided they are not contrary to the state and public order established by the present Constitution.

The law forbids and punishes the formation of and participation in organizations aiming at depriving the Bulgarian people of their rights and liberties gained by the people's uprising of September 9, 1944, and guaranteed by the present Constitution or to encroach on these rights and liberties, or to imperil the nation's independence or sovereignty, or of organizations which openly or secretly propagate a fascist and antidemocratic ideology or facilitate imperialist aggression.

ARTICLE 88.   The citizens of the People's Republic are guaranteed freedom of the press, of speech and of assembly, including meetings and demonstrations.

ARTICLE 89.   Citizens have the right to make requests, complaints and petitions.

Every citizen has the right to demand court proceedings against officials for offenses committed in the discharge of their duties.

Citizens have a right to indemnity from officials for injury caused them by the latter, owing to unlawful or irregular execution of their duties.

ARTICLE 90.   The defense of the country is a supreme duty and a matter of honor for every citizen.

Treason to the country is the gravest crime against the people and is punished with the full severity of the law.

ARTICLE 91.   Military service is compulsory for all citizens in accordance with the special laws.

ARTICLE 92.   Citizens are bound to observe the Constitution and the laws of the country strictly and conscientiously.

ARTICLE 93.   Citizens are bound to protect national property and by all their actions to help promote the nation's economic, cultural and defensive power and the welfare of the people.

ARTICLE 94.   The citizens' tax obligations are repartitioned in accordance with their paying ability. These obligations and exemptions from them are established only by law.

CHAPTER IX

COAT OF ARMS, SEAL, FLAG, CAPITAL

ARTICLE 95.   The coat of arms of the People's Republic of Bulgaria is round; in the center, a lion rampant beset on both sides by ears of corn, above the lion a five-pointed red star, and below, in gold figures, 9.IX.1944.

ARTICLE 96.   The state seal bears the state coat of arms.

ARTICLE 97.   The flag of the People's Republic of Bulgaria is tricoloured—white, green and red, placed horizontally. The upper lefthand corner of the white strip bears the coat of arms of the People's Republic.

ARTICLE 98.   The capital of the People's Republic of Bulgaria is the city of Sofia.

CHAPTER X

AMENDMENT TO THE CONSTITUTION

ARTICLE 99.   The Constitution may be amended on the proposal of the Government or of at least one-quarter of the national representatives.

The Constitutional amendment bill is put on the agenda one week after its introduction in the Assembly at the earliest.

It may be passed by a majority of two-thirds of the total number of national representatives.

The Constitutional amendment law enters into force on the day of its publication in the State Gazette.

CHAPTER XI
TEMPORARY PROVISIONS

ARTICLE 100. After the present Constitution enters into force, the Grand National Assembly elected on October 27, 1946, elects a Presidium of the Grand National Assembly in accordance with Article 33; the Presidium immediately assumes the functions provided for by the Constitution. This terminates the functions of the presidency of the Grand National Assemby elected in accordance with Article 2 of the rules of procedure of the Grand National Assembly. The Grand National Assembly elects, in accordance with Article 20 of the present Constitution, a president and vice presidents for conducting the proceedings.

ARTICLE 101. The Presidium of the Grand National Assembly appoints temporary municipal and district administrations with the prerogatives of people's councils, until the municipal and district councils provided by the present Constitution are elected.

CONSTITUTION OF THE HUNGARIAN PEOPLE'S REPUBLIC AS AMENDED[1]

Promulgated on August 20, 1949

THE armed forces of the great Soviet Union liberated our country from the yoke of the German fascists, crushed the power of the great landowners and capitalists who were ever hostile to the people, and opened the road of democratic progress to our working people. Having acceded to power in hard struggles fought against the masters and defenders of the old order, the Hungarian working class, in alliance with the working peasantry and with the generous assistance of the Soviet Union, rebuilt our war-ravaged country. Led by our working class hardened in the struggles of several decades, enriched by the experiences of the socialist revolution of 1919 and supported by the Soviet Union, our people began to lay down the foundations of socialism, and now our country is advancing toward socialism along the road of people's democracy. The already realized achievements of this struggle and this constructive work, the fundamental changes effected in the economic and social structure of our country, are embodied in the Constitution of the Hungarian People's Republic, which also indicates the direction of our further advance.

SECTION ONE

THE HUNGARIAN PEOPLE'S REPUBLIC

ARTICLE 1. Hungary is a People's Republic.

ARTICLE 2. (1) The Hungarian People's Republic is a state of workers and working peasants.

(2) In the Hungarian People's Republic all power belongs to the working people. The workers of town and country exercise their power through their elected representatives, who are responsible and accountable to the people.

ARTICLE 3. The Hungarian People's Republic defends the power and liberty of the Hungarian working people and the independence of the country; it opposes every form of the exploitation of man by man and organizes the forces of society for socialist construction. In the Hungarian People's Republic the close alliance of the workers and working peasantry is made a reality under the leadership of the working class.

---

[1] *Constitution of the Hungarian People's Republic* (Budapest: University Press, 1959).

SECTION TWO
THE SOCIAL STRUCTURE

ARTICLE 4. (1) In the Hungarian People's Republic the bulk of the means of production is owned, as public property, by the state, by public bodies or by cooperative organizations. Means of production may also be privately owned.

(2) In the Hungarian People's Republic the force directing the national economy is the state power of the people. The working people gradually dislodge the capitalist elements and consistently build up a socialist system of economy.

ARTICLE 5. The economic life of the Hungarian People's Republic is determined by a state national-economic plan. Basing itself on the publicly owned enterprises, the state banking system and the agricultural machine stations, the state directs and controls the national economy with the object of expanding the forces of production, increasing the national wealth, raising to an ever higher level the material and cultural standards of the working people and strengthening the defenses of the country.

ARTICLE 6. The mineral resources; the forests; the waters; the natural sources of power; the mines; the large industrial enterprises; the means of communication, such as railways, road, water and air transports; the banks; the postal, telegraph and telephone services; the wireless; the state-sponsored agricultural enterprises, such as state farms, machine stations, irrigation works and the like, are the property of the state and of public bodies as trustees for the whole people. All foreign and all wholesale trade is carried on by state enterprises, all other trade is under state supervision.

ARTICLE 7. (1) The Hungarian People's Republic recognizes and guarantees the right of the working peasants to the land and regards it as its duty to assist the socialist development of agriculture by establishing state farms and machine stations and giving every support to productive cooperative societies based on voluntary association and joint work.

(2) The state recognizes and supports every genuine cooperative movement of the workers that is directed against exploitation.

ARTICLE 8. (1) The Constitution recognizes and protects all property acquired by labor.

(2) Private property and private enterprise must not be such as will run counter to the public interest.

(3) The Constitution guarantees the right of inheritance.

ARTICLE 9. (1) In the Hungarian People's Republic labor is the base of the social order.

(2) Every able-bodied citizen has the right and the duty to work to the best of his ability and is bound in honor to do so.

(3) By their labor, by participation in work competitions, by tightening labor discipline and improving working methods, the workers serve the cause of socialist construction.

(4) The Hungarian People's Republic strives to apply in practice the socialist principle: 'From each according to his ability, to each according to his work.'

SECTION THREE
THE HIGHEST ORGANS OF STATE AUTHORITY

ARTICLE 10. (1) The highest organ of state authority in the Hungarian People's Republic is Parliament.

(2) Parliament exercises all the rights deriving from the sovereignty of the people and determines the organization, direction and conditions of government.

(3) In accordance with this its competence, Parliament

(a) Enacts laws,

(b) Determines the state budget,

(c) Decides the national economic plan,

(d) Elects the Presidential Council of the People's Republic,

(e) Elects the Council of Ministers,

(f) Sets up and abolishes ministries and defines and changes the sphere of activity of the several ministries,

(g) Decides upon declaring war and concluding peace,

(h) Exercises the prerogative of amnesty.

ARTICLE 11. (1) Parliament is elected for a term of four years.

(2) Members of Parliament may not be arrested or prosecuted without the consent of Parliament, except when taken in the act.

(3) All political, economic or other activity or conduct detrimental to the interests of the workers is incompatible with the quality of a Member of Parliament.

ARTICLE 12. (1) Parliament meets in regular session not less than twice a year.

(2) Parliament must be convened at the written demand of one-third of its members or if the Presidential Council of the People's Republic so decides.

(3) Parliament elects a speaker, two deputy speakers and six recorders from among its own members.

(4) The sessions of Parliament are convened by the Presidential Council of the People's Republic.

(5) Parliament lays down its own rules of procedure and agenda.

ARTICLE 13. As a general rule, the sessions of Parliament are held in public. In exceptional cases Parliament may decide to hold a secret session.

ARTICLE 14. (1) The right of legislation is vested in Parliament.

(2) Legislation can be initiated by the Presidential Council of the People's Republic, by the Council of Ministers and by any member of Parliament.

ARTICLE 15. (1) Parliament can take valid decisions only if at least one-half of its members are present.

(2) Parliament decides issues by a simple majority.

(3) Changes in the Constitution require the votes of two-thirds of the members of Parliament.

ARTICLE 16. Acts passed by Parliament are signed by the president and secretary of the Presidential Council of the People's Republic. New acts are promulgated by the president of the Presidential Council. Promulgation is effected by publication in the official gazette.

ARTICLE 17. (1) Parliament may at need appoint, out of its own members, a committee to investigate any matter.

(2) It is the duty of all public authorities, offices and institutions as well as of all citizens to put at the disposal of such parliamentary committees all the data required by the committee and also to give evidence before the committee if required to do so.

ARTICLE 18. (1) Parliament may pronounce its dissolution before the expiration of its term.

(2) In the event of war or other emergency, Parliament can prolong its mandate for a stated length of time.

(3) In the event of war or other emergency, the Presidential Council of the People's Republic can reconvene a Parliament that has already been dissolved. A Parliament thus convened can itself decide the duration of its mandate.

(4) In the event of dissolution, a new Parliament must be elected within not more than three months from the day of dissolution.

(5) The newly elected Parliament must be convened by the Presidential Council of the People's Republic within one month of polling day.

ARTICLE 19. (1) At its first sitting, Parliament elects from among its own members the Presidential Council of the People's Republic, consisting of a president, two vice presidents, a secretary and seventeen members.

(2) The chairman of the Council of Ministers, its deputy chairmen and its members are ineligible for election to the Presidential Council of the People's Republic.

ARTICLE 20. (1) The competence of the Presidential Council of the People's Republic extends to

(a) Issuing the writ for a general election;

(b) Convening Parliament;

(c) Initiating legislation;

(d) Holding a plebiscite on matters of national importance;

(e) Directing on the highest level the work of the local organs of state power;

(f) Concluding international treaties on behalf of the Hungarian People's Republic;

(g) Appointing diplomatic representatives and receiving the letters of credence of foreign diplomatic representatives;

(h) Ratifying international treaties;

(i) Appointing the higher civil servants and the higher officers of the armed forces, in accordance with the provisions of the law;

(j) Awarding the orders and titles instituted by Parliament and authorizing the acceptance of foreign orders and titles;

(k) Exercising the prerogative of mercy;

(l) Deciding issues specially submitted to its jurisdiction by an Act of Parliament.

(2) The Presidential Council of the People's Republic may annul or modify any bylaw, regulation or measure introduced by central or local organs of government, if they infringe the Constitution or are detrimental to the interests of the working people.

(3) The Presidential Council of the People's Republic may dissolve any local organ of government the activities of which infringe the Constitution or are seriously detrimental to the interests of the working people.

(4) When Parliament is not in session, its functions are exercised by the Presidential Council of the People's Republic; that body cannot, however, change the Constitution.

(5) The enactments of the Presidential Council of the People's Republic are law-decrees, which must, however, be submitted to Parliament at its next sitting.

(6) All decisions and measures taken by the Presidential Council of the People's Republic are signed by the president and the secretary of that body; its decrees must be published in the official gazette.

ARTICLE 21. (1) The term of office of the Presidential Council of the People's Republic expires when Parliament elects a new Presidential Council of the People's Republic.

(2) The Presidential Council of the People's Republic is responsible to Parliament and is under the obligation of rendering an account of its activities to Parliament.

(3) Parliament has the right to recall the Presidential Council of the People's Republic or any member of it.

(4) In order to make valid decisions, at least nine members of the Presidential Council of the People's Republic must be present, in addition to the president and the secretary.

(5) The Presidential Council of the People's Republic draws up its own rules of procedure, which must be submitted to Parliament.

SECTION FOUR

THE HIGHEST ORGAN OF STATE ADMINISTRATION

ARTICLE 22. The highest organ of state administration is the Council of Ministers of the Hungarian People's Republic (The Hungarian Revolutionary Workers' and Peasants' Government).

ARTICLE 23. (1) The Council of Ministers consists of

(a) The chairman of the Council of Ministers;

(b) The first deputy chairmen or deputy chairmen of the Council of Ministers;

(c) The minister or ministers of State;

(d) The ministers heading the various ministries, and the president of the National Planning Office.

(2) The Council of Ministers or single members of it are elected to, or relieved of, office by Parliament on the recommendation of the Presidential Council of the People's Republic.

(3) Members of the Council of Ministers who are not members of Parliament may attend the sittings of Parliament and take part in its debates.

ARTICLE 24. The ministries of the Hungarian People's Republic are listed in a special enactment.

ARTICLE 25. (1) The Council of Ministers

(a) Directs the work of the ministries and of the other organs immediately subordinate to it;

(b) Ensures the enforcement of the laws and of the decrees issued by the Presidential Council of the People's Republic;

(c) Ensures the fulfillment of the economic plans;

(d) Deals with all the matters referred, by provision of law, to its jurisdiction.

(2) In the execution of its duties the Council of Ministers may issue decrees which must not, however, infringe the law or the decrees issued by the Presidential Council of the People's Republic.

(3) Decrees issued by the Council of Ministers are signed by its chairman. Such decrees must be published in the official gazette.

(4) The Council of Ministers is empowered to annul or modify any statutory provision or measure of any central or local organ of government if such statutory provisions, regulations or measures infringe the Constitution or are detrimental to the interests of the working people.

ARTICLE 26. (1) The Chairman of the Council of Ministers presides over the meetings of the Council, provides for the execution of the orders and decisions of the Council, and directs the work of the organs immediately subordinate to it.

(2) The ministers direct the branches of state administration entrusted to them and the work of the organs immediately subordinate to them, in accordance with the laws and the decrees and decisions of the Council of Ministers.

(3) In the execution of their duties the chairman of the Council of Ministers and the ministers are empowered to issue decrees, which may not, however, infringe the laws of the People's Republic or the decrees made by the Presidential Council of the People's Republic or its Council of Ministers. Such decrees must be published in the official gazette.

ARTICLE 27. (1) The Council of Ministers is responsible for its activities to Parliament and must render regular accounts of its work to that body.

(2) The chairman of the Council of Ministers (or his deputy) and its members are individually responsible for their actions and conduct. A special law regulates the implementation of this responsibility.

(3) Any member of Parliament may put to the Council of Ministers, its chairman or members, questions relating to any matter within the competence of the persons named and such questions must be answered by them in the House of Parliament.

ARTICLE 28. (1) The Council of Ministers may take measures on any matter touching state administration either directly or through one of its members.

(2) The Council of Ministers is empowered to take under its own immediate control any branch of the state administration and can set up special organs for this purpose.

SECTION FIVE

THE LOCAL ORGANS OF STATE POWER

ARTICLE 29. (1) For purposes of administration the territory of the Hungarian People's Republic is divided up into counties, districts, towns and boroughs. Larger towns and cities may be subdivided into smaller administrative units.

(2) Changes in the territorial jurisdiction of the various administrative organs can be made by the organs of state power.

ARTICLE 30. (1) The local organs of state power are the county council, the district council, the town council, the borough council and the town precinct council.

(2) The members of the councils are elected by the voters in the area in question for a term of four years, in accordance with the principles established in connection with the election of members of Parliament.

(3) The members of the local councils can be recalled by their constituents in accordance with the law.

ARTICLE 31. (1) The local councils exercise their administrative functions in their area of jurisdiction in accordance with the constitutionally created laws, decrees and other enactments and within the limits defined by their superior organs.

(2) Local councils

(a) Direct the economic, social and cultural activities in their area;

(b) Prepare the local economic plan and budget—within the limits imposed by the national economic plan and the state budget—and supervise their fulfillment;

(c) Enforce the laws and the regulations made by superior organs;

(d) Direct and supervise the activities of the state administrative and executive organs subordinate to them;

(e) Ensure the maintenance of public order and the protection of public property;

(f) Protect the rights of the workers;

(g) Direct and supervise the activities of economic enterprises of a local character;

(h) Give support to the cooperative societies of the workers;

(i) Deal with all matters within their competence as defined by a valid enactment.

(3) Local councils can issue regulations within the area of their jurisdiction; but such regulations must not infringe the laws, law-decrees, or decrees issued by

the Council of Ministers, the ministers, or a superior council. The orders issued by local councils must be promulgated according to custom.

(4) Local councils can annul or modify the orders, decisions or measures of the councils subordinate to them, if such orders, decisions or measures infringe the Constitution or a constitutionally created enactment.

ARTICLE 32. (1) The local councils exercise their functions in close contact with the population, ensure the active participation of the workers in the work of local government and encourage initiative and vigilance on their part.

(2) Local councils must give an account of their activities to their constituents not less than twice every year.

ARTICLE 33. (1) The executive and administrative organs of the local councils are the Executive Committees, which they elect from among their own members.

(2) The Executive Committee is presided over by a chairman. Its business is conducted by a secretary subordinate to the chairman. The chairman and his deputy or deputies, and the secretary are elected by the Executive Committee from among its own members.

(3) The Executive Committees are directly responsible to the local council which has elected them, as well as to superior organs of state power, further to the Executive Committees of the superior councils and to the Council of Ministers. In their activities they must comply with the directives of these organs.

(4) Local councils have the right to recall the Executive Committees as a whole or any of their members.

ARTICLE 34. Specific administrative duties within the competence of the local councils are carried out by the branch organs of administration of the Executive Committees; these branch organs are subordinate to the Executive Committees on the one hand, and to the superior branch organs of administration on the other hand.

ARTICLE 35. Detailed regulations relating to the activities of the local councils and executive committees are the subject of a special Act of Parliament.

SECTION SIX
THE JUDICATURE

ARTICLE 36. (1) In the Hungarian People's Republic justice is administered by the Supreme Court of the Hungarian People's Republic, by the county courts and the district courts.

(2) By provision of the law, special courts may be set up to deal with specific groups of cases.

ARTICLE 37. The courts are composed of judges and lay members. The law can establish exceptions from this rule.

ARTICLE 38. The Supreme Court of the Hungarian People's Republic exercises the right of supervising in principle the judicial activities and practice of all other courts. For this purpose the Supreme Court can establish directives and take decisions on questions of principle, which are then binding for all courts.

ARTICLE 39. (1) In the Hungarian People's Republic all judicial offices are filled by election and the elected judges may be recalled.

(2) The judges of the Supreme Court are elected for a period of five years, the judges of the county and district courts for a period of three years.

(3) The president and judges of the Supreme Court are elected by Parliament.

(4) The judges are accountable to their electors in respect of their judicial activities.

(5) The election of the judges of the county courts and district courts is regulated by rules laid down in a special enactment.

ARTICLE 40. (1) The hearings before all courts of law are public unless otherwise prescribed by law.

(2) All those accused before the courts are guaranteed the right of defense during the judicial proceedings.

ARTICLE 41. (1) The Courts of the Hungarian People's Republic punish the enemies of the working people, protect and safeguard the state, the social and economic order and the institutions of the people's democracy and the rights of the workers, and educate the working people in the observance of the rules governing the life of a socialist commonwealth.

(2) Judges are independent and subject only to the law.

SECTION SEVEN
THE PUBLIC PROSECUTOR

ARTICLE 42. (1) The function of the Chief Public Prosecutor of the Hungarian People's Republic is to watch over the observance of the law.

(2) In the exercise of this function the Chief Public Prosecutor supervises the observance of the law by the ministries, the authorities, offices, institutions and other organs, by the local organs of the state executive and by the citizens.

(3) The Chief Public Prosecutor sees to it that all actions detrimental to, or endangering, the social order, security or independence of the Hungarian People's Republic be consistently prosecuted.

ARTICLE 43. (1) The Chief Public Prosecutor of the Hungarian People's Republic is elected by Parliament for a period of six years. Parliament has the right to recall the Chief Public Prosecutor before the expiration of his term of office.

(2) The Chief Public Prosecutor is responsible and accountable to Parliament in respect of his official activities.

(3) Public prosecutors are appointed by the Chief Public Prosecutor of the Hungarian People's Republic.

(4) The organization of public prosecution is under the control and general direction of the Chief Public Prosecutor of the Hungarian People's Republic.

ARTICLE 44. Public prosecutors proceed independently of the administrative organs and of local state power.

SECTION EIGHT

THE RIGHTS AND DUTIES OF CITIZENS

ARTICLE 45. (1) The Hungarian People's Republic guarantees for its citizens the right to work and the right to remuneration in accordance with the quantity and quality of the work done.

(2) This right is implemented by the Hungarian People's Republic by means of the planned development of the forces of production and by a manpower policy based on economic planning.

ARTICLE 46. (1) The Hungarian People's Republic ensures the right of rest and recreation for its citizens.

(2) This right is implemented by the Hungarian People's Republic by means of a legally determined working day, holidays with pay and the organization of the rest and recreation of the workers.

ARTICLE 47. (1) The Hungarian People's Republic protects the health of the workers and assists them in the event of sickness or disability.

(2) The Hungarian People's Republic implements this protection and assistance by means of a comprehensive social insurance scheme and the organization of medical services.

ARTICLE 48. (1) The Hungarian People's Republic ensures the right to education for every worker.

(2) The Hungarian People's Republic implements this right by means of an extension to all of the educational facilities, by means of a free and compulsory general schooling scheme, by the provision of secondary and higher schools, by educational facilities for adult workers and by financial aid to those receiving schooling of any kind.

ARTICLE 49. (1) The citizens of the Hungarian People's Republic are equal before the law and enjoy equal rights.

(2) Discrimination of any kind against any citizen on grounds of sex, religion, or nationality is a severely punishable offense.

(3) The Hungarian People's Republic ensures to all nationalities living within its borders the possibility of education in their native tongue and the possibility of developing their national culture.

ARTICLE 50. (1) In the Hungarian People's Republic women enjoy equal rights with men.

(2) The equal rights of women are implemented by the safeguarding of their working conditions on a par with those of men, maternity leave with pay in the event of pregnancy, increased legal protection of mother and child, and a system of maternity and child welfare institutions.

ARTICLE 51. The Hungarian People's Republic protects the institution of marriage and the family.

ARTICLE 52. The Hungarian People's Republic devotes special care to the education and development of the young and accords them special protection.

ARTICLE 53. The Hungarian People's Republic effectively supports all scientific work serving the cause of the working people, as well as the arts which depict the life and struggle of the people, which describe reality, and proclaim the victory of the people. It gives every support to the emergence of intellectual workers loyal to the people.

ARTICLE 54. (1) The Hungarian People's Republic safeguards the liberty of conscience of all citizens and the freedom of religious worship.

(2) In order to ensure the liberty of conscience, the Hungarian People's Republic separates the church from the state.

ARTICLE 55. (1) In accordance with the interests of the workers the Hungarian People's Republic ensures for its citizens freedom of speech, freedom of the press and freedom of assembly.

(2) In order to implement these freedoms, the state places at the disposal of the workers the material resources required.

ARTICLE 56. (1) In order to develop the social, economic and cultural activities of the workers, the Hungarian People's Republic constitutionally guarantees the right of combination and assembly.

(2) In fulfilling its tasks, the Hungarian People's Republic bases itself on the organizations of the class-conscious workers. In order to defend the people's democracy, promote participation in socialist construction, widen the scope of cultural and educational work, implement the rights of the people and develop international solidarity, the workers establish trade unions, democratic organizations of women and young people as well as other mass organizations and gather the forces of these organizations in the democratic People's Front. In these organizations the close cooperation and democratic unity of the industrial, agricultural and intellectual workers materializes. The leading force in such political and social activities is the working class, led by its vanguard and supported by the democratic unity of the whole people.

ARTICLE 57. The Hungarian People's Republic safeguards the freedom and inviolability of the person, the privacy of the home and the correspondence of its citizens.

ARTICLE 58. (1) The Hungarian People's Republic guarantees these basic freedoms to all workers living within its borders.

(2) Foreign citizens, persecuted for their democratic attitude or their activities in the interests of the liberation of the peoples, enjoy the right of asylum in the Hungarian People's Republic.

ARTICLE 59. It is the fundamental duty of all citizens of the Hungarian People's Republic to defend the property of the people, consolidate social assets, increase the economic strength of the Hungarian People's Republic, raise the living standard and cultural level of the workers and strengthen the people's democratic system.

ARTICLE 60. Military service is the honorable duty of the citizens of the Hungarian People's Republic in accordance with the law on universal military service.

ARTICLE 61. (1) Defense of their country is the sacred duty of all citizens of the Hungarian People's Republic.

(2) Treason, violation of the military oath, desertion to the enemy, espionage and every action detrimental to the military strength of the country—constituting a betrayal of the cause of the country and of the workers—is subject to the severest penalties of the law.

SECTION NINE
THE ELECTORAL SYSTEM

ARTICLE 62. (1) Members of Parliament are elected by the citizens of the Hungarian People's Republic on the basis of universal, equal, and direct suffrage by secret ballot.

(2) The elected members are accountable to their constituents.

(3) The constituents have the right to recall their elected member of Parliament.

ARTICLE 63. (1) All citizens of the Hungarian People's Republic who are of age have the right to vote.

(2) Enemies of the working people and those who are unsound of mind are excluded from the suffrage by law.

ARTICLE 64. At elections every citizen entitled to vote has one vote and all votes are equal.

ARTICLE 65. All citizens who have the vote are eligible for election.

ARTICLE 66. Details of the election and recall of members of Parliament are laid down in a special Act of Parliament.

SECTION TEN
THE COAT OF ARMS, THE FLAG AND THE CAPITAL OF THE HUNGARIAN PEOPLE'S REPUBLIC

ARTICLE 67. The coat of arms of the Hungarian People's Republic is as follows:

An escutcheon of red, white and green stripes, having arched sides, encircled on either side by a wreathed sheaf of wheat and standing in a light blue field. The sheaf of wheat is interwoven with a red-white-and-green ribbon on the left and a red one on the right. Above the escutcheon a five-pointed red star, placed in the middle, casts golden rays onto the field.

ARTICLE 68. The flag of the Hungarian People's Republic is red, white and green.

ARTICLE 69. The capital of the Hungarian People's Republic is the city of Budapest.

SECTION ELEVEN
FINAL PROVISIONS

ARTICLE 70. (1) The Constitution of the Hungarian People's Republic enters into force on the day of its promulgation. Its enforcement is the duty of the Council of Ministers.

(2) The Council of Ministers has the duty of submitting to Parliament the bills required for the implementation of the Constitution.

ARTICLE 71. (1) The Constitution is the fundamental law of the Hungarian People's Republic.

(2) The Constitution as well as all constitutional enactments are obligatory for all organs of state power and all citizens alike.

COMMENTS

Since 1949, the necessity [has arisen] several times for expanding, supplementing and amending some statutes of the Constitution while leaving unchanged the fundamental content of it. The reason for this course lay in the great momentum and rapidity of socialist development which took place in Hungary's social, political and economic system and the interconnected state apparatus.

The text of the foregoing presents the Constitution in accordance with provisions which are valid today, carrying through the changes embodied in the laws amending the Constitution.

In the interest of completeness, a brief summary of the amendments is given here.

1. *Law IV/1950* was passed due to the necessity of coordinating the judicial organization with the council system established at that time. Consequently, the so-called high courts were abolished, and Article 36 [1] and Article 39 were amended, making the administration of justice the right of the Supreme Court, the county courts and the district courts.

2. The membership of the Council of Ministers was complemented by *Law VI/1953* so as to give the Council of Ministers the right to elect the first deputy chairman or first deputy chairmen from among its own members. To this end, Article 23 of the Constitution was amended.

3. *Law VIII/1954* is linked with the development of the council system, and laid the constitutional foundation for framing the new Council Law (X/1954). Consequently, the Constitution was amended, placing the councils under the supervision of the Presidential Council of the Hungarian People's Republic (amendment to Article 20); the right of the Council of Ministers to modify decisions of the councils was abrogated (amendment to Article 25 [4]); the organs of state power were given authority to determine the territorial division for purposes of administration (amendment to Article 29 [2]); the local councils were granted wider powers in defining local economic plans and budgets (amendment to Article 31 [2/b]); the legal status of the Executive Committees of the Councils was clarified and greater autonomy was accorded the local specialized administrative bodies (amendment to Article 33 [3] and Article 34).

4. *Law II/1957* supplemented the appellation of the Council of Ministers to more precisely express its character (Hungarian Revolutionary Workers' and Peasants' Government—amendment to Article 22). A new coat of arms and flag were inaugurated (amendment to Articles 67 and 68). Finally, it was provided that the ministries would not be listed in the Constitution but would be included in a separate law (amendment to Article 24).

5.   From the point of view of the present wording of the Constitution, interim amendments to the Constitution necessitated exclusively by the setting up of new ministries, the merger of several of them and changes in name, have become immaterial and irrelevant.

The new wording of Article 24 removed this issue from the Constitution, as mentioned above, and thus these amendments have become null and void. These amendments were embodied in the following laws: IV/1950; I/1951; I/1952; IV/1953; VI/1953; III/1954; VII/1954; II/1955; III/1956.

SECTION 6

NORTH VIETNAM

CONSTITUTION OF THE DEMOCRATIC REPUBLIC OF VIETNAM[1]

PREAMBLE

Vietnam is a single entity from Lang-Son to Camau.

The Vietnamese people, throughout their thousands of years of history, have been an industrious working people who have struggled unremittingly and heroically to build their country and to defend the independence of their fatherland.

Throughout more than eighty years of French colonial rule and five years of occupation by the Japanese fascists, the Vietnamese people consistently united and struggled against domination by the foreign aggressors in order to liberate their country.

From 1930 onward, under the leadership of the Indochinese Communist Party—now the Vietnam Lao-Dong Party—the Vietnamese revolution advanced into a new stage. The persistent struggle, full of hardship and heroic sacrifice, of our people against imperialist and feudal domination won great success: the August Revolution was victorious; the Democratic Republic of Vietnam was founded; and, on September 2, 1945, President Ho Chi Minh proclaimed Vietnam's independence to the people and the world. For the first time in their history, the Vietnamese people had founded an independent and democratic Vietnam.

On January 6, 1946, the entire Vietnamese people, from north to south, enthusiastically took part in the first general elections to the National Assembly. The National Assembly adopted the first Constitution, which clearly recorded the great successes of our people and highlighted the determination of the entire nation to safeguard the independence and unity of the fatherland and to defend the freedom and democratic rights of the people.

However, the French imperialists, assisted by the U.S. imperialists, again provoked an aggressive war in an attempt to seize our country and once more enslave our people. Under the leadership of the Vietnamese working-class party and the government of the Democratic Republic of Vietnam, our entire people, united as one, rose to fight the aggressors and save their country. At the same time, our people carried out land-rent reduction and land reform with the aim of overthrowing the landlord class and restoring the land to those who till it. The long, hard, and extremely heroic war of resistance of the Vietnamese people, which enjoyed the sympathy and support of the socialist countries, of the oppressed peoples, and of friends of peace throughout the world, won glorious victory. With the Dien Bien

---

[1] Bernard B. Fall, *The Two Viet-Nams: A Political and Military Analysis*, revised edition (New York: Frederick A. Praeger, 1960), pp. 399–431. Reprinted by permission.

Phu victory, the Vietnamese people defeated the French imperialists and the U.S. interventionists. The 1954 Geneva Agreements were concluded; peace was restored in Indochina on the basis of recognition of the independence, sovereignty, unity, and territorial integrity of our country.

This major success of the Vietnamese people was also a common success of the liberation movement of the oppressed peoples, of the world front of peace, and of the socialist camp.

Since the restoration of peace in completely liberated North Vietnam, our people have carried through the national people's democratic revolution. But the South is still under the rule of the imperialists and feudalists; our country is still temporarily divided into two zones.

The Vietnamese revolution has moved into a new position. Our people must endeavor to consolidate the North, taking it toward socialism, and to carry on the struggle for peaceful reunification of the country and completion of the tasks of the national people's democratic revolution throughout the country.

In the last few years, our people in the North have achieved many big successes in economic rehabilitation and cultural development. At present, socialist transformation and construction are being successfully carried out.

Meanwhile, in the South, the U.S. imperialists and their henchmen have been savagely repressing the patriotic movement of our people. They have been strengthening military forces and carrying out their scheme of turning the southern part of our country into a colony and military base for their war preparations. They have resorted to all possible means to sabotage the Geneva Agreements and undermine the cause of Vietnam's reunification. But our southern compatriots have constantly struggled heroically and refused to submit to them. The people throughout the country, united as one, are holding aloft the banner of peace, national unity, independence, and democracy, resolved to march forward and win final victory. The cause of the peaceful reunification of the fatherland will certainly be victorious.

In the new stage of the revolution, our National Assembly must amend the 1946 Constitution in order to adapt it to the new situation and tasks.

The new Constitution clearly records the great revolutionary gains in the recent past and clearly indicates the goal of struggle of our people in the new stage.

Our state is a people's democratic state based on the alliance between the workers and peasants and led by the working class. The new Constitution defines the political, economic, and social system of our country, the relations of equality and mutual assistance among the various nationalities in our country, and provides for the taking of the North toward socialism, the constant improvement of the material and cultural life of the people, and the building of a stable and strong North Vietnam as a basis for the struggle for the peaceful reunification of the country.

The new Constitution defines the responsibilities and powers of the state organs and the rights and duties of citizens with a view to developing the great creative potentialities of our people in national construction and in the reunification and defense of the fatherland.

The new Constitution is a genuinely democratic Constitution. It is a force inspiring the people throughout our country to march forward enthusiastically and win new successes. Our people are resolved to develop further their patriotism, their tradition of solidarity, their determination to struggle and their ardor in work. Our people are resolved to strengthen further solidarity and unity of mind with the brother countries in the socialist camp headed by the great Soviet Union and to strengthen solidarity with the peoples of Asia and Africa and peace loving people all over the world.

Under the clearsighted leadership of the Vietnam Lao-Dong Party, the government of the Democratic Republic of Vietnam, and President Ho Chi Minh, our entire people, broadly united within the National United Front, will surely win glorious success in the building of socialism in North Vietnam and the struggle for national reunification. Our people will surely be successful in building a peaceful, unified, independent, democratic, prosperous, and strong Vietnam, making a worthy contribution to the safeguarding of peace in Southeast Asia and the world.

CHAPTER I

THE DEMOCRATIC REPUBLIC OF VIETNAM

ARTICLE 1. The territory of Vietnam is a single, indivisible whole from north to south.

ARTICLE 2. The Democratic Republic of Vietnam, established and consolidated as a result of victories won by the Vietnamese people in the glorious August Revolution and the heroic Resistance, is a people's democratic state.

ARTICLE 3. The Democratic Republic of Vietnam is a single multinational state.

All the nationalities living on Vietnamese territory are equal in rights and duties. The state has the duty to maintain and develop the solidarity between the various nationalities. All acts of discrimination against, or oppression of, any nationality, all actions which undermine the unity of the nationalities are strictly prohibited.

All nationalities have the right to preserve or reform their own customs and habits, to use their spoken and written languages, and to develop their own national culture.

Autonomous zones may be established in areas where people of national minorities live in compact communities. Such autonomous zones are inalienable parts of the Democratic Republic of Vietnam.

The state strives to help the national minorities to make rapid progress and to keep pace with the general economic and cultural advance.

ARTICLE 4. All power in the Democratic Republic of Vietnam belongs to the people. The people exercise power through the National Assembly and the people's councils, at all levels elected by the people and responsible to the people.

The National Assembly, the people's councils at all levels, and the other organs of state practice democratic centralism.

ARTICLE 5. Election of deputies to the National Assembly and the people's councils at all levels proceeds on the principle of universal, equal, direct, and secret suffrage.

Deputies to the National Assembly and people's councils at all levels may be recalled by their constituent before their term of office expires if they show themselves to be unworthy of the confidence of the people.

ARTICLE 6. All organs of state must rely on the people, maintain close contact with them, heed their opinions, and accept their supervision.

All personnel of organs of state must be loyal to the people's democratic system, observe the Constitution and the law, and wholeheartedly serve the people.

ARTICLE 7. The state strictly prohibits and punishes all acts of treason, opposition to the people's democratic system, or opposition to the reunification of the fatherland.

ARTICLE 8. The armed forces of the Democratic Republic of Vietnam belong to the people; their duty is to safeguard the gains of the revolution and defend the independence, sovereignty, territorial integrity, and security of the fatherland, and the freedom, happiness, and peaceful labor of the people.

CHAPTER II

ECONOMIC AND SOCIAL SYSTEM

ARTICLE 9. The Democratic Republic of Vietnam is advancing step by step from people's democracy to socialism by developing and transforming the national economy along socialist lines, transforming its backward economy into a socialist economy with modern industry and agriculture and an advanced science and technology.

The fundamental aim of the economic policy of the Democratic Republic of Vietnam is continuously to develop the productive forces with the aim of raising the material and cultural standards of the people.

ARTICLE 10. The state leads all economic activities according to a unified plan.

The state relies on the organs of state, trade-union organizations, cooperatives, and other organizations of the working people to elaborate and carry out its economic plans.

ARTICLE 11. In the Democratic Republic of Vietnam, during the present period of transition to socialism, the main forms of ownership of means of production are state ownership, that is, ownership by the whole people; cooperative ownership, that is, collective ownership by the working masses; ownership by individual working people; and ownership by the national capitalists.

ARTICLE 12. The state sector of the economy, which is a form of ownership by the whole people, plays the leading role in the national economy. The state ensures priority for its development.

All mineral resources and waters and all forests, undeveloped land, and other resources defined by law as belonging to the state are the property of the whole people.

ARTICLE 13. The cooperative sector of the economy is a form of collective ownership by the working masses.

The state especially encourages, guides, and helps the development of the cooperative sector of the economy.

ARTICLE 14. The state by law protects the right of peasants to own land and other means of production.

The state actively guides and helps the peasants to improve farming methods and increase production and encourages them to organize producers', supply-and-marketing, and credit cooperatives, in accordance with the principle of voluntariness.

ARTICLE 15. The state by law protects the right of handicraftsmen and other individual working people to own means of production.

The state actively guides and helps handicraftsmen and other individual working people to improve their enterprises and encourages them to organize producers' and supply-and-marketing cooperatives, in accordance with the principle of voluntariness.

ARTICLE 16. The state by law protects the right of national capitalists to own means of production and other capital.

The state actively guides the national capitalists in carrying out activities beneficial to national welfare and the people's livelihood, contributing to the development of the national economy in accordance with the economic plan of the state. The state encourages and guides the national capitalists in following the path of socialist transformation through the form of joint state-private enterprises and other forms of transformation.

ARTICLE 17. The state strictly prohibits the use of private property to disrupt th economic life of society or to undermine the economic plan of the state.

ARTICLE 18. The state protects the right of citizens to possess lawfully earned incomes, savings, houses, and other private means of life.

ARTICLE 19. The state by law protects the right of citizens to inherit private property.

ARTICLE 20. Only when such action is necessary in the public interest does the state repurchase, requisition, or nationalize, with appropriate compensation, means of production in city or countryside, within the limits and in the conditions defined by law.

ARTICLE 21. Labor is the basis on which the people develop the national economy and raise their material and cultural standards.

Labor is a duty and a matter of honor for every citizen.

The state encourages the creativeness and the enthusiasm in labor of workers by hand and brain.

CHAPTER III

FUNDAMENTAL RIGHTS AND DUTIES OF CITIZENS

ARTICLE 22. Citizens of the Democratic Republic of Vietnam are equal before the law.

ARTICLE 23. Citizens of the Democratic Republic of Vietnam who have reached the age of eighteen have the right to vote, and those who have reached the age of twenty-one have the right to stand for election, whatever their nationality, race, sex, social origin, religion, belief, property status, education, occupation, or length of residence, except insane persons and persons deprived by a court or by law of the right to vote and stand for election.

ARTICLE 24. Women in the Democratic Republic of Vietnam enjoy equal rights with men in all spheres of political, economic, cultural, social, and domestic life.

For equal work, women enjoy equal pay with men. The state ensures that women workers and office employees have fully paid periods of the leave before and after childbirth.

The state protects the mother and child and ensures the development of maternity hospitals, crèches, and kindergartens.

The state protects marriage and the family.

ARTICLE 25. Citizens of the Democratic Republic of Vietnam enjoy freedom of speech, freedom of the press, freedom of assembly, freedom of association, and freedom of demonstration. The state guarantees all necessary material conditions for citizens to enjoy these freedoms.

ARTICLE 26. Citizens of the Democratic Republic of Vietnam enjoy freedom of religious belief; they may practice or not practice a religion.

ARTICLE 27. Freedom of the person of citizens of the Democratic Republic of Vietnam is guaranteed. No citizen may be arrested except by decision of a people's court or with the sanction of a people's organ of control.

ARTICLE 28. The law guarantees the inviolability of the homes of the citizens of the Democratic Republic of Vietnam and inviolability of mail.

Citizens of the Democratic Republic of Vietnam enjoy freedom of residence and movement.

ARTICLE 29. Citizens of the Democratic Republic of Vietnam have the right to complain of and denounce to any organ of state any servant of the state for transgression of law. These complaints and denunciations must be investigated and dealt with rapidly. People suffering loss owing to infringement by servants of the state of their rights as citizens are entitled to compensation.

ARTICLE 30. Citizens of the Democratic Republic of Vietnam have the right to work. To guarantee to citizens enjoyment of this right, the state, by planned development of the national economy, gradually creates more employment and better working conditions and wages.

ARTICLE 31. Working people have the right to rest. To guarantee to working people enjoyment of this right, the state prescribes working hours and holidays for workers and office employees and gradually expands material facilities to enable working people to rest and build up their health.

ARTICLE 32. Working people have the right to material assistance in old age and in case of illness or disability. To guarantee to working people enjoyment of this right, the state gradually expands social insurance, social assistance, and public health service.

ARTICLE 33. Citizens of the Democratic Republic of Vietnam have the right to education. To guarantee the citizens enjoyment of this right, the state enforces step by step the system of compulsory education, gradually extends the various types of schools and other cultural institutions, extends the various forms of supplementary cultural, technical, and professional education in public services and factories and and in other organizations in town and countryside.

ARTICLE 34. Citizens of the Democratic Republic of Vietnam enjoy freedom to engage in scientific research, literary and artistic creation, and other cultural pursuits. The state encourages and assists creative work in science, literature, art and other cultural pursuits.

ARTICLE 35. The state pays special attention to the moral, intellectual, and physical education of youth.

ARTICLE 36. The state protects the proper rights and interests of Vietnamese residents abroad.

ARTICLE 37. The Democratic Republic of Vietnam grants the right of asylum to any foreign national persecuted for demanding freedom, for supporting a just cause, for taking part in the peace movement, or for engaging in scientific activity.

ARTICLE 38. The state forbids any person to use democratic freedoms to the detriment of the interests of the state and of the people.

ARTICLE 39. Citizens of the Democratic Republic of Vietnam must abide by the Constitution and the law, uphold discipline at work, keep public order, and respect social ethics.

ARTICLE 40. The public property of the Democratic Republic of Vietnam is sacred and inviolable. It is the duty of every citizen to respect and protect public property.

ARTICLE 41. Citizens of the Democratic Republic of Vietnam have the duty to pay taxes according to law.

ARTICLE 42. To defend the fatherland is the most sacred and noble duty of citizens of the Democratic Republic of Vietnam.

It is the duty of citizens to perform military service in order to defend the fatherland.

CHAPTER IV

THE NATIONAL ASSEMBLY

ARTICLE 43. The National Assembly is the highest organ of state authority in the Democratic Republic of Vietnam.

ARTICLE 44. The National Assembly is the only legislative authority of the Democratic Republic of Vietnam.

ARTICLE 45. The term of office of the National Assembly is four years.

A new National Assembly must be elected two months before the term of office of the sitting National Assembly expires.

The electoral procedure and the number of deputies are prescribed by law.

In the event of war or other exceptional circumstances, the National Assembly may decide to prolong its term of office and take necessary measures to ensure its activities and those of deputies.

ARTICLE 46. The National Assembly meets twice a year, convened by its Standing Committee. The Standing Committee of the National Assembly may convene extraordinary sessions of the National Assembly according to its decisions, or at the request of the Council of Ministers or of a minimum of one-third of the total number of deputies.

The Standing Committee of the National Assembly must convene the new National Assembly not later than two months after the elections.

ARTICLE 47. When the National Assembly meets, it elects a Presidium to conduct its sittings.

ARTICLE 48. Laws and other decisions of the National Assembly require a simple majority vote of all deputies to the National Assembly, except for the case specified in Article 112 of the Constitution.

ARTICLE 49. Laws must be promulgated not later than fifteen days after their adoption by the National Assembly.

ARTICLE 50. The National Assembly exercises the following functions:

1) To enact and amend the Constitution;
2) To enact laws;
3) To supervise the enforcement of the Constitution;
4) To elect the President and Vice President of the Democratic Republic of Vietnam;
5) To choose the Prime Minister of the government upon the recommendation of the President of the Democratic Republic of Vietnam and the vice-premiers and the other component members of the Council of Ministers upon the recommendation of the Prime Minister;
6) To choose the vice president and the other component members of the National Defense Council upon the recommendation of the President of the Democratic Republic of Vietnam;
7) To elect the President of the Supreme People's Court;
8) To elect the Procurator General of the Supreme People's Organ of Control;
9) To remove the President and Vice President of the Democratic Republic of Vietnam, the Prime Minister, the vice premiers and the other component members of the National Defense Council, the president of the Supreme People's Court, and the Procurator General of the Supreme People's Organ of Control;
10) To decide upon national economic plans;
11) To examine and approve the state budget and the financial report;
12) To fix taxes;
13) To decide the establishment and abolition of ministries and of organs having a status equal to that of a ministry;
14) To ratify the boundaries of provinces, autonomous regions, and municipalities directly under the central authority;
15) To decide on general amnesties;
16) To decide on questions of war and peace; and
17) To exercise other necessary functions as defined by the National Assembly.

ARTICLE 51. The Standing Committee of the National Assembly is a permanent executive body of the National Assembly and is elected by it. The Standing Committee is composed of the Chairman; the vice-chairmen; the Secretary General and other members.

ARTICLE 52. The Standing Committee of the National Assembly is responsible to the National Assembly and reports to it.

The National Assembly has power to remove any member of the Standing Committee.

ARTICLE 53. The Standing Committee of the National Assembly exercises the following functions:

1) To proclaim and conduct the election of deputies to the National Assembly;

2) To convene the National Assembly;

3) To interpret the laws;

4) To enact decrees;

5) To decide on referenda;

6) To supervise the work of the Council of Ministers, the Supreme People's Court, and the Supreme People's Organ of Control;

7) To revise or annul decisions, orders, and directives of the Council of Ministers which contravene the Constitution, laws, and decrees; to revise or annul inappropriate decisions issued by the people's councils of provinces, autonomous regions, and municipalities directly under the central authority; and to dissolve the above-mentioned people's councils if they do serious harm to the people's interests;

8) To decide on the appointment or removal of the vice-premiers and the other component members of the Council of Ministers when the National Assembly is not in session;

9) To appoint or remove the vice presidents and judges of the Supreme People's Court;

10) To appoint or remove the deputy procurators general and procurators of the Supreme People's Organ of Control;

11) To decide on the appointment or removal of plenipotentiary diplomatic representatives of the Democratic Republic of Vietnam to foreign states;

12) To decide on the ratification or abrogation of treaties concluded with foreign states, except when the Standing Committee considers it necessary to refer such ratification or abrogation to the National Assembly for decision;

13) To decide on military, diplomatic, and other grades and ranks;

14) To decide on the granting of pardons;

15) To institute and decide on the award of state orders, medals, and titles of honor;

16) To decide, when the National Assembly is not in session, on the proclamation of a state of war in the event of armed attack on the country;

17) To decide on general or partial mobilization;

18) To decide on the enforcement of martial law throughout the country or in certain areas.

Apart from these functions, the National Assembly may, when necessary, invest the Standing Committee with other functions.

ARTICLE 54. The decisions of the Standing Committee of the National Assembly must be approved by a simple majority vote of its members.

ARTICLE 55. The Standing Committee of the National Assembly exercises its functions until a new Standing Committee is elected by the succeeding National Assembly.

ARTICLE 56. The National Assembly elects a commission for examination of the qualifications of deputies to the National Assembly. The National Assembly will base itself on the reports of this commission in deciding on the recognition of the qualifications of deputies.

ARTICLE 57. The National Assembly establishes a law-drafting committee, a planning board and budget commission, and other committees which the National Assembly deems necessary to assist the National Assembly and its Standing Committee.

ARTICLE 58. The National Assembly or its Standing Committee, when the National Assembly is not in session, may, if necessary, appoint commissions of inquiry to investigate specific questions.

All organs of state, people's organizations, and citizens concerned are required to supply all information necessary to these commissions when they conduct investigations.

ARTICLE 59. Deputies to the National Assembly have the right to address questions to the Council of Ministers and to organs under the authority of the Council of Ministers.

The organs to which questions are put are obliged to answer within a period of five days. In the event of investigations having to be carried out, the answer must be given within one month.

ARTICLE 60. No deputy to the National Assembly may be arrested or tried without the consent of the National Assembly or, when the National Assembly is not in session, of its Standing Committee.

CHAPTER V

THE PRESIDENT OF THE DEMOCRATIC REPUBLIC OF VIETNAM

ARTICLE 61. The President of the Democratic Republic of Vietnam is the representative of the Democratic Republic of Vietnam in internal affairs as well as in foreign relations.

ARTICLE 62. The President of the Democratic Republic of Vietnam is elected by the National Assembly of the Democratic Republic of Vietnam. Any citizen of the Democratic Republic of Vietnam who has reached the age of thirty-five is eligible to stand for election as President of the Democratic Republic of Vietnam.

The term of office of the President of the Democratic Republic of Vietnam corresponds to that of the National Assembly.

ARTICLE 63. The President of the Democratic Republic of Vietnam, in pursuance of decisions of the National Assembly or its Standing Committee, promulgates laws and decrees; appoints or removes the Prime Minister, the vice-premiers, and the other component members of the Council of Ministers; appoints or removes the vice president and the other component members of the National Defense Council; promulgates general amnesties and grants pardons; confers orders, medals, and titles of honor of the state; proclaims a state of war; orders general or partial mobilization; and proclaims martial law.

ARTICLE 64. The President of the Democratic Republic of Vietnam receives plenipotentiary representatives of foreign states; and, in pursuance of decisions of the National Assembly or its Standing Committee, ratifies treaties concluded with foreign states, appoints or recalls plenipotentiary representatives of the Democratic Republic of Vietnam to foreign states.

ARTICLE 65. The President of the Democratic Republic of Vietnam is the Supreme Commander of the armed forces of the country and is president of the National Defense Council.

ARTICLE 66. The President of the Democratic Republic of Vietnam has power, when necessary, to attend and preside over the meetings of the Council of Ministers.

ARTICLE 67. The President of the Democratic Republic of Vietnam, when necessary, convenes and presides over the Special Political Conference.

The Special Political Conference is composed of the President and Vice President of the Democratic Republic of Vietnam, the chairman of the Standing Committee of the National Assembly, the Prime Minister, and other persons concerned.

The Special Political Conference examines major problems of the country. The President of the Democratic Republic of Vietnam submits the view of this conference to the National Assembly, the Standing Committee of the National Assembly, the Council of Ministers, or other bodies concerned for their consideration and decision.

ARTICLE 68. The Vice President of the Democratic Republic of Vietnam assists the President in his duties. The Vice President may exercise such part of the functions of the President as the President may entrust to him.

The provisions governing the election and term of office of the President apply also to the election and term of office of the Vice President.

ARTICLE 69. The President and Vice President of the Democratic Republic of Vietnam exercise their functions until the new President and Vice President take office.

ARTICLE 70. Should the President of the Democratic Republic of Vietnam be incapacitated for a prolonged period by reason of ill health, the functions of President shall be exercised by the Vice President.

Should the office of President of the Democratic Republic of Vietnam fall vacant, the Vice President shall fulfill the functions of President until the election of a new President.

CHAPTER VI

THE COUNCIL OF MINISTERS

ARTICLE 71. The Council of Ministers is the executive organ of the highest organ of state authority; it is the highest administrative organ of the Democratic Republic of Vietnam.

The Council of Ministers is responsible to the National Assembly and reports to it or, when the National Assembly is not in session, to the Standing Committee of the National Assembly.

ARTICLE 72. The Council of Ministers is composed of the Prime Minister; the vice-premiers; the ministers; the heads of state commissions; and the Director-General of the National Bank.

The organization of the Council of Ministers is determined by law.

ARTICLE 73. Basing itself on the Constitution, laws, and decrees, the Council of Ministers formulates administrative measures, issues decisions and orders, and verifies their execution.

ARTICLE 74. The Council of Ministers exercises the following functions:

1) To submit draft laws, draft decrees, and other drafts to the National Assembly and the Standing Committee of the National Assembly;

2) To centralize the leadership of the ministries and organs of state under the authority of the Council of Ministers;

3) To centralize the leadership of the administrative committees at all levels;

4) To revise or annul inappropriate decisions of the ministries, and organs of state under the authority of the Council of Ministers; to revise or annul inappropriate decisions of administrative organs at all levels;

5) To suspend the execution of inappropriate decisions of the People's Councils of provinces, autonomous zones, and municipalities directly under the central authority and recommend to the Standing Committee of the National Assembly revision or annulment of these decisions;

6) To put into effect the national economic plans and the provisions of the state budget;

7) To control home and foreign trade;

8) To direct cultural and social work;

9) To safeguard the interests of the state, to maintain public order, and to protect the rights and interests of citizens;

10) To lead the building of the armed forces of the state;

11) To direct the conduct of external relations;

12) To administer affairs concerning the nationalities;

13) To ratify territorial boundaries of administrative areas below the provincial level;

14) To carry out the order of mobilization, martial law, and all other necessary measures to defend the country;

15) To appoint and remove personnel of organs of state, according to provisions of law.

Besides these functions, the National Assembly or its Standing Committee may invest the Council of Ministers with other functions.

ARTICLE 75. The Prime Minister presides over the meetings of the Council of Ministers and leads its work. The vice-premiers assist the Prime Minister in his work and may replace him in the event of his absence.

ARTICLE 76. The ministers and heads of organs of state under the authority of the Council of Ministers lead the work of their respective departments under the unified leadership of the Council of Ministers.

Within the jurisdiction of their respective departments, in accordance with and in pursuance of laws and decrees, decisions, orders, and directives of the Council of Ministers, they may issue orders and directives and supervise their execution.

ARTICLE 77. In the discharge of their functions, members of the Council of Ministers bear responsibility before the law for such acts as contravene the Constitution and the law and do harm to the state or the people.

CHAPTER VII

THE LOCAL PEOPLE'S COUNCILS AND THE LOCAL ADMINISTRATIVE COMMITTEES AT ALL LEVELS

ARTICLE 78. The administrative division of the Democratic Republic of Vietnam is as follows:

The country is divided into provinces, autonomous zones, and municipalities directly under the central authority.

Provinces are divided into districts, cities, and towns.

Districts are divided into villages and townlets.

Administrative units in autonomous zones will be determined by law.

ARTICLE 79. People's councils and administrative committees are established in all the above-mentioned administrative units.

Cities may be divided into wards with a ward people's council and administrative committee, according to decision of the Council of Ministers.

ARTICLE 80. Local people's councils at all levels are the organs of state authority in their respective areas.

People's councils at all levels are elected by the local people and are responsible to them.

ARTICLE 81. The term of office of the people's councils of provinces, autonomous zones, and municipalities directly under the central authority is three years.

The term of office of the people's councils of districts, cities, towns, villages, townlets and wards is two years.

The term of office of the people's councils at all levels in autonomous zones is fixed by law.

The electoral procedure and the number of representatives to people's councils at all levels are determined by law.

ARTICLE 82. The people's councils ensure observance and execution of state laws in their respective areas; draw up plans for local economic and cultural development and public works; examine and approve local budgets and financial reports; maintain public order and security in their areas; protect public property, protect the rights of citizens, and safeguard the equal rights of the nationalities.

ARTICLE 83. The local people's councils issue decisions for execution in their areas on the basis of state law and of decisions taken at higher levels.

ARTICLE 84. The people's councils elect administrative committees and have power to recall members of administrative committees.

The people's councils elect and have power to recall the presidents of the people's courts at corresponding levels.

ARTICLE 85. The people's councils have power to revise or annul inappropriate decisions issued by administrative committees at corresponding levels, as well as inappropriate decisions issued by people's councils and administrative committees at the next lower level.

ARTICLE 86. The people's councils at all levels have power to dissolve people's councils at the next lower level when the latter do serious harm to the people's interests. Such a decision must be ratified by the people's council at the next higher level prior to its application. A decision of dissolution issued by the people's councils of provinces, autonomous zones, and municipalities directly under the central authority is subject to endorsement by the Standing Committee of the National Assembly prior to its application.

ARTICLE 87. The administrative committees at all levels are the executive organs of the local people's councils at corresponding levels and are the administrative organs of state in their respective areas.

ARTICLE 88. The administrative committee is composed of president, one or several vice presidents, a secretary, and a number of committee members.

The term of office of an administrative committee is the same as that of the people's council which elected it.

On the expiration of the term of office of the people's council or in the event of its dissolution, the administrative committee continues to exercise the above functions until a new people's council has elected a new administrative committee.

The organization of administrative committees at all levels is determined by law.

ARTICLE 89. The administrative committees at all levels direct the administrative work in their respective areas, carry out the decisions issued by people's councils at corresponding levels and the decisions and orders issued by organs of state at higher levels.

The administrative committees at all levels, within the limits of the authority prescribed by law, issue decisions and orders and verify their execution.

ARTICLE 90.   The administrative committees at all levels direct the work of their subordinate departments and the work of administrative committees at lower levels.

The administrative committees at all levels have power to revise or annul inappropriate decisions of their subordinate departments and of administrative committees at lower levels.

The administrative committees at all levels have power to suspend the carrying out of inappropriate decisions of people's councils at the next lower level, and to propose to people's councils at corresponding levels the revision or annulment of such decisions.

ARTICLE 91.   The administrative committees at all levels are responsible to the people's councils at corresponding levels and to the administrative organs of state at the next higher level, and shall report to these bodies.

The administrative committees at all levels are placed under the leadership of the administrative committees at the next higher level, and under the unified leadership of the Council of Ministers.

The People's Councils and Administrative Committees in Autonomous Zones

ARTICLE 92.   The organization of the people's councils and administrative committees in autonomous zones are based on the basic principles governing the organization of the people's councils and administrative committees at all levels, as defined above.

ARTICLE 93.   In the autonomous zones where a number of nationalities live together, they are entitled to appropriate representation on the people's councils.

ARTICLE 94.   The people's councils and the administrative committees in autonomous zones work out plans for economic and cultural development suited to the local conditions, administer their local finances, and organize their local self-defense and public security force within the limits of autonomy prescribed by law.

ARTICLE 95.   The people's councils in autonomous zones may, within the limits of autonomy, and basing themselves on the political, economic, and cultural characteristics of the nationalities in their respective areas, draw up statutes governing the exercise of autonomy and regulations concerning particular problems to be put into effect in their areas, after endorsement by the Standing Committee of the National Assembly.

ARTICLE 96.   The higher organs of state must ensure that the people's councils and administrative committees in the autonomous zones exercise their right to autonomy and assist the minority peoples in the full promotion of their political, economic, and cultural development.

CHAPTER VIII

THE PEOPLE'S COURTS AND THE PEOPLE'S ORGANS OF CONTROL

The People's Courts

ARTICLE 97. The Supreme People's Court of the Democratic Republic of Vietnam, the local people's courts, and the military courts are judicial organs of the Democratic Republic of Vietnam.

Special courts may be set up by the National Assembly in certain cases.

ARTICLE 98. The system of elected judges according to the procedure prescribed by law applies to the people's courts.

The term of office of the president of the Supreme People's Court is five years.

The organization of the people's courts is determined by law.

ARTICLE 99. Judicial proceedings in the people's courts must be carried out with the participation of people's assessors according to law. In administering justice, people's assessors enjoy the same powers as judges.

ARTICLE 100. In administering justice, the people's courts are independent and subject only to law.

ARTICLE 101. Cases in the people's courts are heard in public unless otherwise provided for by law.

The right to defense is guaranteed the accused.

ARTICLE 102. The people's courts ensure that all citizens of the Democratic Republic of Vietnam belonging to national minorities may use their own spoken and written languages in court proceedings.

ARTICLE 103. The Supreme People's Court is the highest judicial organ of the Democratic Republic of Vietnam.

The Supreme People's Court supervises the judicial work of local people's courts, military courts, and special courts.

ARTICLE 104. The Supreme People's Court is responsible to the National Assembly and reports to it or, when the National Assembly is not in session, to its Standing Committee. The local people's courts are responsible to the local people's councils at corresponding levels and report to them.

The People's Organs of Control

ARTICLE 105. The Supreme People's Organ of Control of the Democratic Republic of Vietnam controls the observance of the law by all departments of the Council of Ministers, all local organs of state, persons working in organs of state, and all citizens.

Local organs of the People's Organ of Control and military organs of control exercise control authority within the limits prescribed by law.

ARTICLE 106. The term of office of the Procurator General of the Supreme People's Organ of Control is five years.

The organization of the people's organs of control is determined by law.

ARTICLE 107. The people's organs of control at all levels work only under the leadership of their higher control organs and the unified leadership of the Supreme People's Organ of Control.

ARTICLE 108. The Supreme People's Organ of Control is responsible to the National Assembly and reports to it or, when the National Assembly is not in session, to its Standing Committee.

CHAPTER IX
NATIONAL FLAG, NATIONAL EMBLEM, CAPITAL

ARTICLE 109. The national flag of the Democratic Republic of Vietnam is a red flag with a five-pointed gold star in the middle.

ARTICLE 110. The national emblem of the Democratic Republic of Vietnam is round in shape, has a red ground with ears of rice framing a five-pointed gold star in the middle and with a cogwheel and the words 'Democratic Republic of Vietnam' at the base.

ARTICLE 111. The capital of the Democratic Republic of Vietnam is Hanoi.

CHAPTER X
AMENDMENT OF THE CONSTITUTION

ARTICLE 112. Only the National Assembly has power to revise the Constitution. Amendments to the Constitution require a two-thirds majority vote of all deputies to the National Assembly.

EAST GERMANY

CONSTITUTION OF THE GERMAN DEMOCRATIC REPUBLIC AS AMENDED[1]

Adopted by the President of the Provisional People's
Chamber on October 7, 1949, and on August 10, 1950

THE CONSTITUTION DERIVES FROM THE PEOPLE

THE constitution is the basic law of every social and state order; it forms the legal basis for the life of the whole people. What is therefore more natural than that the people itself creates the basis of the state order in which it wishes to live. This great democratic principle of the self-determination of the people has been realized in the creation of the Constitution of the German Democratic Republic to such a high degree as has seldom been achieved in history.

The discussion concerning a new all-German constitution began among responsible Germans as early as September 1946. In November of the same year the executive council of the Socialist Unity Party of Germany approved the draft of a constitution worked out by its constitutional committee and disseminated it among the public.

This draft constitution was considered and discussed into 1948 by the population, in the plants, on the radio and in the press. All political parties and organizations of the toilers, the Free German Trade Union Federation, the Free German Youth, the Democratic Women's Federation of Germany, the Cultural Federation, and others participated in the discussion, worked out proposals for changes, and

---

[1] *The East German Constitution* (Washington, D.C.: U.S. Department of Commerce, Office of Technical Services, Joint Publications Research Service), J.P.R.S. No. 19,648, June 11, 1963. Reprinted by permission.

This is a translation of the brochure *Die Verfassung der Deutschen Demokratischen Republik* (The Constitution of the German Democratic Republic), published by the VEB Deutscher Zentralverlag (People-Owned German Central Publishing House), Berlin and Dresden, 1962, and incorporating all changes up to the publication date. The translation was taken from the *Soviet Zone Constitution and Electoral Law*, published by the Office of the U.S. High Commissioner for Germany, Frankfurt/Main, West Germany, 1951, except for the following passages which have been changed, added, or rescinded since the adoption of the original constitution:

Article 5, last paragraph concerning military service added;

Article 63, one line changed dealing with the power of the People's Chamber to elect the State Council of the Republic (formerly the President);

Articles 71–80 and 84, dealing with the abolished East German Laender Chamber and its powers, rescinded;

Articles 101–108, formerly dealing with the powers of the Presidency, replaced by provisions dealing with the powers of the State Council of the Republic;

Article 112, last paragraph added concerning the military protection of East Germany.

This translation also includes the brochure's propaganda introduction to the constitution and the preambles to the Law Concerning the Dissolution of the Laender Chamber and to the Law Concerning Formation of the State Council of the Republic.

created new drafts. For the first time in history the German people itself took a part in the development of its own constitution.

Meanwhile the German People's Congress emerged from the mass movement for the unity of Germany and a just peace. The German People's Council, formed from this representation of the German people, and especially the constitutional committee established by it, worked out guidelines which took into account all wishes which national-minded forces had to offer toward an all-German constitution.

The German People's Council came before the public with these guidelines, in which the basic ideas of the future constitution had already assumed more solid form. The guidelines were adopted at the fourth congress of the German People's Council on August 3, 1948. The elaboration of the actual constitution could then begin.

In October 1948 the Draft Constitution was approved by the constitutional committee of the German People's Council and presented to the German people for its opinion. The following months became a really historical period. For the second time the Germans themselves spoke out in meetings or the political parties, the democratic mass organizations, the plants, in the newspapers, and on the radio. More than 9,000 meetings which dealt exclusively with the Draft Constitution were conducted. More than 15,000 resolutions were forwarded to the German People's Council. Many hundreds of proposals for amendments were submitted. They numbered 503 exactly. When Otto Grotewohl submitted the new Draft Constitution to the German People's Council in March 1949, 52 of the 144 articles of the Constitution were changed in accordance with the proposals submitted by the population. The German People's Council approved the Draft Constitution on March 19, 1949 and transmitted it to the German People's Congress for ratification.

The German People's Congress, which came about as a result of general, secret, and direct elections, ratified the Constitution on May 30, 1949. After the transformation of the German People's Council into the People's Chamber, the latter, at its constituting session on October 7, 1949, passed the 'Law Concerning the Constitution of the German Democratic Republic,' through which the Constitution was put into effect. The announcement was made in the Collection of Laws [Gesetzblatt] of the German Democratic Republic No. 1 of October 8, 1949.

PREAMBLE

THE German people, imbued with the desire to safeguard human liberty and rights, to reshape collective and economic life in accordance with the principles of social justice, to serve social progress, and to promote a secure peace and amity with all peoples, have adopted this Constitution.

A. FUNDAMENTALS OF STATE AUTHORITY

ARTICLE 1. Germany is an indivisible democratic republic, the foundations of which are the German Laender.

The (German Democratic) Republic decides on all issues which are essential to the existence and development of the German people as a whole, all other issues being decided upon by independent action of the Laender (states).

As a rule, decisions of the Republic are carried out by the Laender.

There is only one German nationality.

ARTICLE 2. The colors of the German Democratic Republic are black, red and gold.

The capital of the Republic is Berlin.

ARTICLE 3. All state authority emanates from the people.

Every citizen has the right and the duty to take part in the formation of the political life of his Gemeinde (community), Kreis (county), Land (state) and of the German Democratic Republic.

This right of co-determination takes the form of voting in popular initiatives and referendums; exercising the right to vote and standing for election; entering upon public offices in general administration and in the administration of justice.

Every citizen has the right to submit petitions to the popular representative body.

State authority must serve the welfare of the people, liberty, peace and the progress of democracy.

Those active in public service are servants of the community as a whole and not of any one party. Their activity is supervised by the popular representative body.

ARTICLE 4. All measures taken by state authority must be compatible with the principles which the Constitution has declared to be contained in state authority. Pursuant to Article 66 of this Constitution, the popular representative body is to decide on the constitutionality of such measures. Everyone has the right and the duty to resist measures contradicting enactments of the popular representative body.

Every citizen is in duty bound to act in accordance with the Constitution and to defend it against its enemies.

ARTICLE 5. The generally recognized rules of international law are binding upon state authority and every citizen.

It is the duty of state authority to maintain and cultivate amicable relations with all peoples.

No citizen may participate in belligerent actions designed to oppress any people.

The service for the defense of the fatherland and the achievements of the toilers is an honorable duty of the citizens of the German Democratic Republic.

B. CONTENTS AND LIMITS OF STATE AUTHORITY

I. Rights of the Citizen

ARTICLE 6. All citizens have equal rights before the law.

Incitement to boycott of democratic institutions or organizations, incitement to attempts on the life of democratic politicians, the manifestation of religious and racial hatred and of hatred against other peoples, militaristic propaganda and warmongering as well as any other discriminatory acts are felonious crimes within the meaning of the Penal Code. The exercise of democratic rights within the meaning of the Constitution is not an incitement to boycott.

Whoever has been convicted of such a crime is disqualified from holding public office or a leading position in economic or cultural life. He also loses the right to vote and to stand for election.

ARTICLE 7. Men and women have equal rights.

All laws and regulations which conflict with the equality of women are abolished.

ARTICLE 8. Personal liberty, inviolability of the home, secrecy of the mail, and the right to take up residence at any place are guaranteed. State authority may restrict or revoke these freedoms only on the basis of a law applicable to all citizens.

ARTICLE 9. All citizens have the right, within the limits of universally applicable laws, to express their opinion freely and publicly and to hold unarmed and peaceful assemblies for that purpose. This freedom shall not be restricted by any service or employment status, and no one may be discriminated against for exercising this right.

There is no press censorship.

ARTICLE 10. No citizen may be turned over to a foreign power by extradition.

Allies shall neither be extradited nor expelled, if, outside this country, they are subject to persecution because of their struggle in support of the principles embodied in this Constitution.

Every citizen has the right to emigrate. This right may be restricted only by a law of the Republic.

ARTICLE 11. Free ethnic development of foreign-language elements of the population of the Republic is to be promoted by legislative and administrative action. In particular, they must on no account be prevented from using their native language in matters of education, internal administration and administration of justice.

ARTICLE 12. All citizens have the right to form associations or societies for purposes not conflicting with criminal law.

ARTICLE 13. Associations that, in accordance with their statutes, aim to bring about, on the basis of this Constitution, a democratic organization of public life and whose executive bodies are determined by their members, are entitled to submit nominations of candidates for election to membership in Gemeinde (community), Kreis (county) and Land (state) popular representative bodies.

Nominations for the People's Chamber may be made only by those associations which, pursuant to their statutes, aim to bring about the democratic organization of public and social life in the entire Republic and which maintain an organization throughout the territory of the Republic.

ARTICLE 14. Everyone is guaranteed the right to organize for the improvement of wages and working conditions. Any agreements and measures intended to restrict this right or impede it are unlawful and prohibited.

(Recognized) trade unions are vouchsafed the right to strike.

ARTICLE 15. (The individual's) capacity for work is protected by state authority.

The right to work is guaranteed. By means of economic control the state ensures to each citizen work and a living. Whenever suitable work cannot be found for him, he shall be provided necessary sustenance.

ARTICLE 16. Every worker is entitled to recreation, to an annual leave with pay and to being provided for in illness and old age.

Sundays, holidays and the first of May are days of rest and are protected by law.

On the principle of autonomous administration by the insured, a unitary and comprehensive social insurance system serves to maintain the health and strength of the working population, to protect motherhood, and to provide against the economic consequences of old age, disability, unemployment and other vicissitudes of life.

ARTICLE 17. Workers and employees shall play a decisive part in the regulation of industrial production, wages, and working conditions in enterprises.

Workers and employees shall exercise these rights through trade unions and Works Councils.

ARTICLE 18. The Republic shall establish uniform labor legislation, a uniform system of labor courts and uniform legislation for the protection of labor, in all of which the working population shall play a decisive part.

Working conditions must be such as to safeguard the health, cultural requirements and family life of the workers.

Remuneration for work must correspond to performance and must provide a worthwhile existence for the worker and those dependents entitled to his support.

Men and women, adults and juveniles, are entitled to equal pay for equal work.

Women enjoy special protection in employment relations. The laws of the Republic shall provide for institutions enabling women to coordinate their tasks as citizens and workers with their duties as wives and mothers.

Juvenile workers shall be protected against exploitation and saved from falling into moral, physical or mental neglect. Child labor is prohibited.

II. The Economic Order

ARTICLE 19. Organization of economic life must conform to the principles of social justice; it must guarantee to all an existence compatible with the dignity of man.

It is incumbent upon the economy to contribute to the benefit of the whole people and to the satisfaction of its wants and to insure that everybody will obtain, in accordance with his performance, a just share in the yield of production.

Freedom (of enterprise in the) economic (field) is guaranteed to the individual within the scope of the above tasks and aims.

ARTICLE 20. Farmers, traders and craftsmen are to be given support in the development of their private initiative. Mutual aid through cooperatives is to be expanded.

ARTICLE 21. In order to secure the basic standard of living for its citizens and to promote their prosperity, the state, acting through its legislative bodies and with the direct participation of its citizens, establishes a public economic plan. It is the task of the popular representative bodies to supervise the implementation of the plan.

ARTICLE 22. Private property is guaranteed by the Constitution. Its scope and its limitations are derived from law and from the obligations toward the welfare of the community at large.

The right of inheritance is guaranteed to the extent provided by civil law. The share of the Government in the estate is determined by law.

Intellectual work and the rights of authors, inventors, and artists enjoy protection, furtherance, and support by the Republic.

ARTICLE 23. Restrictions on private property and expropriations may be imposed only for the benefit of the general public and on a legal basis. They shall take place against reasonable compensation unless the law provides otherwise. If the amount of compensation is in dispute, recourse to the ordinary courts shall be open insofar as a law does not provide otherwise.

ARTICLE 24. Property commits to duties. Its use must not run counter to the public good.

Misuse of property with the intent of establishing an economic ascendancy to the detriment of the public good results in expropriation without compensation and transfer to the people's ownership.

Enterprises owned by war criminals and active National Socialists have been expropriated and will be transferred to the people's ownership (without compensation). The same shall apply to private enterprises offering their services to a warlike policy.

All private monopolistic formations such as cartels, syndicates, combines, trusts and similar private organizations aiming at an increase of profits through the control of production, prices and markets have been abolished and are prohibited.

Privately-owned large estates with an acreage of more than one hundred hectares are dissolved and shall be redistributed without compensation.

Following the accomplishment of the above agrarian reform, ownership of their land shall be guaranteed to the farmers.

ARTICLE 25. All mineral resources, all economically exploitable natural power sources, as well as the mining, iron and steel and electric power industries serving their exploitation, are to be transferred to the people's ownership.

Until such transfer, their use will be supervised by the Laender or by the Republic insofar as the interests of the whole of Germany are involved.

ARTICLE 26. Distribution and utilization of the land shall be supervised, and each abuse thereof shall be prevented. Incremental value of landed property which has accrued without expenditure of labor or capital is to be made of use to the collectivity.

Every citizen and every family shall be assured of a healthy dwelling befitting their needs. Herein special consideration shall be given to victims of fascism, to seriously disabled persons, persons having incurred special war losses and resettlers.

Maintenance and furtherance of assured returns from agriculture will be safeguarded also by means of land planning and conservation.

ARTICLE 27. Private economic enterprises suitable for socialization may be transferred to collective ownership by law under the provisions dealing with expropriation.

The Republic, the Laender (states), the Kreise (counties) and Gemeinden (communities) may be given by law a decisive voice in the management, or otherwise, of enterprises and associations.

Economic enterprises and associations may, by legislation, be combined into autonomous organizations in order to ensure the collaboration of all working elements of the nation, to give workers and employers a share in the management, and to regulate production, manufacture, distribution, utilization, prices, as well as import and export of commodities along the principles of collective economic interests.

Consumer and buying cooperatives, profit-making cooperatives and agricultural cooperatives and their associations shall be integrated into the collective economy while preserving their statutes and characteristic features.

ARTICLE 28. Any alienation or encumbrance of landed property, productive plants or shares therein owned by the people must have the approval of the popular representative body exercising jurisdiction over the title-holding agency. Such approval requires at least a two-thirds majority of the statutory number of members.

ARTICLE 29. Property and income shall be taxed according to progressively increasing rates on the basis of social viewpoints and with particular consideration of family obligations.

Taxation must give special consideration to earned property and income.

III. Family and Motherhood

ARTICLE 30. Marriage and family are the foundations of collective life and are protected by the state.

All laws or statutory provisions by which the equal rights of men and women within the family are impaired are abrogated.

ARTICLE 31. Parents have the natural right to bring up their children in a democratic spirit which will enable them mentally and physically to become responsible individuals, and this is their supreme duty toward society.

ARTICLE 32. During maternity a woman has a rightful claim to particular protection and care by the state.

The Republic shall issue a law for the protection of mothers. Institutions are to be created to protect mother and child.

ARTICLE 33. Extramarital birth is to be no ground for discrimination against either the child or the parents.

Any laws and statutory provisions to the contrary are abrogated.

IV. Education

ARTICLE 34. Art, science, and their teaching, are free.

The state participates in their cultivation and grants them protection, especially against their abuse for purposes which are contrary to the provisions or the spirit of the Constitution.

ARTICLE 35. Every citizen has an equal right to education and to a free choice of his vocation.

Education of youth and adult education of the citizenry in intellectual or technical disciplines are provided by public institutions in all fields of national and social life.

ARTICLE 36. The Laender are responsible for the establishment of a public school system and for the practical operation of school instruction. To this effect the Republic shall issue uniform legislative provisions of a basic character. The Republic may itself establish public educational institutions.

The Republic shall issue uniform provisions for the training of teachers. Such training shall take place in the universities or institutions of equal status.

ARTICLE 37. The school educates the youth in the spirit of the Constitution to be independently thinking and responsibly acting individuals who will be able and willing to take their place in the life of the community at large.

As conveyor of culture, the school has the task of educating the youth to be truly humane in the spirit of peaceful and amicable cooperation in the life of nations and genuine democracy.

The parents shall participate in the school education of their children by councils of parents.

ARTICLE 38. Attendance at school is compulsory for all until completion of the eighteenth year of life. After completion of a primary school course compulsory for all children, training is pursued in a vocational or technical school, in high school or in other public educational institutions. All juveniles under eighteen years of age must attend a vocational or training school unless they attend another (public) school. Private schools as substitutes for public schools (state or municipal) are inadmissible.

Vocational and technical shools afford general and vocational training.

High schools (Oberschule) pave the way for admission to a university. Such admission, however, does not require high school attendance; attendance at other public educational institutions, which shall be extended or created for that purpose, may take its place.

All citizens must be given the opportunity to prepare their admission to a university in special preparatory schools.

Members of all classes of the population shall be given an opportunity to acquire knowledge in colleges of the people without interruption of their occupational activities.

ARTICLE 39. Every child must be given the opportunity fully to develop its physical, mental and moral capacities. The school career of youth must on no account depend on the social or economic position of the parents. Indeed, children who are at a disadvantage because of social conditions are to be given special care. Attendance at vocational school, high school and university must be open to gifted pupils from all classes of the population.

Tuition is free. Textbooks and instructional material used in compulsory schools are furnished without cost: in case of need, attendance at vocational school, high school and university will be promoted through scholarships and other measures.

ARTICLE 40. Religious instruction is a concern of the religious associations. The exercise of this right is guaranteed.

V. Religion and Religious Associations

ARTICLE 41. Every citizen enjoys complete freedom of faith and conscience. The practice of religion without interference enjoys the protection of the Republic.

Any abuse of establishments created by religious associations, of religious acts or religious instruction for purposes which are contrary to the principles of the Constitution or for purposes of party politics is prohibited. However, the right of religious associations to express an attitude in keeping with their own viewpoints toward issues vital for the people shall be uncontested.

ARTICLE 42. Civil or civic rights and duties are neither conditioned nor restricted by the practice of religion.

Exercise of civil or civic rights or the admission to public service is independent of a religious creed.

No one is required to disclose his religious belief. Administrative agencies have the right to make inquiries about a person's membership in a religious association only insofar as rights and duties are connected therewith, or a statistical survey directed by law requires it.

No one may be forced to attend religious rites or celebrations, or to participate in religious exercises, or to use a religious form of oath.

ARTICLE 43. There is no state church. Freedom of membership in religious associations is guaranteed.

Every religious association regulates and administers its affairs autonomously and in accordance with the laws applicable to all.

Religious associations remain public law corporations insofar as they were such heretofore. Other religious associations are granted like rights upon their application, if through their organization and the number of their members they offer a guarantee of permanency. If several such public law religious associations join in a union, this union is also a corporation of public law.

Religious associations having public law status are entitled by levy taxes upon their members on the basis of the governmental tax list according to (the standards of) the general provisions.

Associations whose function is the common cultivation of a philosophy of life have the same status as religious associations.

ARTICLE 44. The right of the church to give religious instruction on school premises is guaranteed. Religious instruction is given by personnel selected by the church. No one may be forced to give, or be prevented from giving, religious instruction. Those entitled to bring up a child shall determine whether the latter shall receive religious instruction.

ARTICLE 45. Public contributions to religious associations, which rest upon law, contract, or special legal title, shall be abrogated by legislation.

Ownership and other rights of the religious associations and religious unions, in respect to their institutions, foundations and other property devoted to purposes of worship, education and charity, are guaranteed.

ARTICLE 46. Insofar as there exists a need for religious service and spiritual guidance in hospitals, penal institutions, or other public institutions, the religious associations are to be given an opportunity for religious exercises. No person may be forced to participate.

ARTICLE 47. Any person wishing to resign from a public-law religious association and to have such resignation become legally effective, shall declare his intention before a court, or submit it in form of a publicly attested individual declaration.

ARTICLE 48. Decision as to whether children up to fourteen years of age shall belong to a religious association rest with the persons entitled to bring them up. Older children shall decide themselves whether or not they wish to be members of an association or organization professing a religious creed or a philosophy of life.

VI. *Effectiveness of Basic Rights*

ARTICLE 49. A basic right may not be violated in its essential content, not even where this Constitution authorizes its restriction by law or makes its further development subject to (specific) legislation.

C. ORGANIZATION OF STATE AUTHORITY

I. *The Popular Representative Body of the Republic*

ARTICLE 50. The supreme authority of the Republic is the People's Chamber.

ARTICLE 51. The People's Chamber is composed of the representatives of the German people.

Representatives are elected in universal, equal, direct and secret ballot for a term of four years, according to the principles of proportional representation.

Representatives serve the people as a whole. They are bound only by their own conscience and are not bound by any instructions.

ARTICLE 52. All citizens who have passed their eighteenth birthday have the right to vote.

All citizens who have passed their twenty-first birthday may stand for election.

The People's Chamber consists of four hundred representatives.

Details are determined by an Electoral Law.

ARTICLE 53. Nominations for the People's Chamber may be submitted only by associations which satisfy the provisions of Article 13, paragraph 2.

Details are determined by a law of the Republic.

ARTICLE 54. Elections are held on a Sunday or legal holiday. Freedom and secrecy of the ballot are guaranteed.

ARTICLE 55. The People's Chamber convenes not later than thirty days after election, unless it is convoked by the previous Presidium for an earlier date.

The President must convoke the People's Chamber if the Government, or at least one-fifth of the representatives in the People's Chamber, so request.

ARTICLE 56. A new Chamber must be elected not later than sixty days after the end of a legislative term, or forty-five days after dissolution of the People's Chamber.

Before the completion of a legislative term, the People's Chamber may be dissolved only upon its own resolution or upon a referendum, except in the case described in Article 95, paragraph 6.

To dissolve the People's Chamber upon its own resolution, the consent of more than one-half of the statutory number of representatives is necessary.

ARTICLE 57. When first convening, the People's Chamber elects the Presidium and adopts Rules of Procedure.

Each parliamentary party is represented in the Presidium, provided that it has at least forty members.

The Presidium consists of the President, his deputies, and of associate members.

The President directs the business of the Presidium and presides over the deliberations of the People's Chamber. Maintenance of order on the premises of the Chamber is his prerogative.

ARTICLE 58. Resolutions of the Presidium are adopted by majority vote.

A quorum exists when at least half of the members of the Presidium are present.

Upon the resolution of the Presidium the acting President convokes the People's Chamber; he also fixes the date for new elections.

The Presidium continues in office until the convening of the new People's Chamber.

ARTICLE 59. The People's Chamber examines the accreditation of its members and decides on the validity of elections.

ARTICLE 60. For the periods when the People's Chamber is not in session, and after a legislative term has expired or the People's Chamber has been dissolved, the People's Chamber appoints three Standing Committees to carry on its functions, namely: a Committee of General Affairs, a Committee of Economic and Financial Affairs, and a Committee of Foreign Affairs.

These Committees have the same rights as investigating committees.

ARTICLE 61. The People's Chamber adopts laws and resolutions by majority vote, unless this Constitution provides otherwise.

A quorum exists when more than half of the members of the Chamber are present.

ARTICLE 62. Deliberations of the People's Chamber and of its committees are open to the public. The public may be excluded from the People's Chamber if two-thirds of the representatives present so request, and from the committees on the demand of the majority of the members of such committees.

True records of public meetings of the People's Chamber or its committees do not entail any responsibility.

ARTICLE 63. The functions of the People's Chamber include

The determination of the principles of governmental policy, and of its implementation;

The confirmation, supervision, and recall of the Government;

The determination of administrative policies and supervision over all governmental agencies;

The right to legislate, except when a (popular) referendum is held;

Decisions on the national budget, on the Economic Plan, on loans and credits of the Republic and the ratification of state treaties;

The granting of amnesties;

The election of the State Council of the Republic;

The election and recall of the members of the Supreme Court of the Republic and of the Prosecutor General of the Republic.

ARTICLE 64. For the purpose of obtaining information, the People's Chamber or any of its committees may request the presence of the Minister President or any other minister, their permanent deputies, or the chiefs of administrative agencies of the Republic. The members of the Government and deputies designated by them are authorized to attend meetings of the People's Chamber and its committees at all times.

If they so request, members of the Government or their deputies must be given the floor during deliberations, regardless of the agenda.

They are subject to the disciplinary authority of the President.

ARTICLE 65. For the purpose of supervising the activities of governmental agencies, the People's Chamber has the right, or, if at least one-fifth of the statutory number of representatives so request, the duty, to appoint investigating committees. These committees take such evidence as they or the representatives having requested the investigation deem necessary. They may for this purpose be represented by persons commissioned by them.

Courts and administrations must comply with the request of these committees, or persons acting on their instructions, for the taking of evidence and, upon demand, present their files for inspection.

In the taking of evidence by the investigating committees the provisions of the Criminal Procedure are applied correspondingly.

ARTICLE 66. For the duration of the legislative term the People's Chamber establishes a Constitutional Committee, in which all parliamentary parties are represented according to their (numerical) strength. To this committee shall also belong three members of the Supreme Court of the Republic as well as three German professors of constitutional law who must on no account be members of the People's Chamber.

Members of the Constitutional Committee are elected by the People's Chamber.

(Only) the Constitutional Committee reviews laws of the Republic as to their constitutionality.

Constitutionality of laws of the Republic may be challenged by not less than one-third of the members of the People's Chamber, by its Presidium, by the President of the Republic, by the Government of the Republic and by the Laender Chamber.

Disputes on constitutional questions between the Republic and the Laender, and the compatibility of Land legislation and legislation of the Republic, are reviewed by the Constitutional Committee, with the assistance of three elected delegates of the Laender Chamber.

Final decision with respect to the report of the Constitutional Committee is reserved to the People's Chamber; the latter's decision is binding on everyone.

The People's Chamber also determines the execution of its decision.

The People's Chamber is, in the exercise of the administrative supervision delegated to it, responsible for determining whether an administrative measure is unconstitutional.

ARTICLE 67. No proceedings, judicial or disciplinary, may at any time be instituted against any member of the People's Chamber for his vote or for any utterance made, in the exercise of his parliamentary functions, nor may he be otherwise called to account outside the Chamber. This does not apply to defamation in the meaning of the Penal Code, if it has been established to be such by an investigating committee of the People's Chamber.

Restraint of personal freedom, house searches, seizures or criminal prosecution may not be instituted against representatives except with the consent of the People's Chamber.

Any criminal proceedings against a representative in the People's Chamber, and any arrest or other restraint of his personal freedom, is suspended for the duration of the session upon demand of the chamber of which the representative is a member.

Members of the People's Chamber have the right to refuse to give evidence concerning persons who confided facts to them in their capacity as representatives, or to whom they have entrusted facts in this capacity, as well as concerning those facts themselves. In respect to seizure of documents, they enjoy the same privileges as persons who have the legal right to refuse testimony.

No search or seizure may be conducted in the premises of the People's Chamber without the consent of the Presidium.

ARTICLE 68. Members of the People's Chamber do not require leave in order to perform their functions.

Persons standing as candidates for a seat in the People's Chamber must be granted such leave as is necessary to prepare for election.

Salaries and wages continue to be paid.

ARTICLE 69. Members in the People's Chamber receive an allowance for expenses, which is tax-exempt.

Renunciation of the allowance for expenses is inadmissible. The claim to the allowance for expenses cannot be transferred or garnished.

ARTICLE 70. Members of the People's Chamber are entitled to free travel in all public transport.

II. Representation of the Laender

ARTICLES 71–80. Rescinded.

III. Legislation

ARTICLE 81. Laws are enacted by the People's Chamber, or directly by the people by means of a referendum.

ARTICLE 82. Bills are introduced by the Government, by the Laender Chamber or by members of the People's Chamber. At least two readings will be held on any bill.

ARTICLE 83. The Constitution may be amended by legislation.

The People's Chamber may enact legislation to amend the Constitution only if at least two-thirds of the representatives are present, and such enactments require a two-thirds majority of those present.

If an amendment to the Constitution is to be adopted by means of a (popular) referendum, the approval of the majority of those entitled to vote is required.

ARTICLE 84. *Rescinded*.

ARTICLE 85. The President of the People's Chamber shall engross all constitutionally enacted laws within the period of one month.

They are promulgated without delay by the President of the Republic in the official gazette of the Republic.

A law cannot be engrossed or promulgated, if it has been declared unconstitutional within one month, as provided for in Article 66.

Unless otherwise provided, laws come into force on the fourteenth day after their promulgation.

ARTICLE 86. Engrossment and promulgation of a law are to be suspended for two months, if one-third of the representatives in the People's Chamber so request.

Upon expiration of this period, the law is to be engrossed and promulgated unless a popular initiative calls for a (popular) referendum against the enactment of the law.

Laws declared urgent by the majority of the representatives in the People's Chamber must be engrossed and promulgated despite such (public) demand.

ARTICLE 87. If the promulgation of a law has been suspended at the instance of at least one-third of the representatives in the People's Chamber, such law is to be submitted to a (popular) referendum upon the demand of one-twentieth of those entitled to vote.

A (popular) referendum shall furthermore be held, if requested by one-tenth of those entitled to vote or by recognized political parties or organized groups which can demonstrate satisfactorily that they represent one-fifth of those entitled to vote (constituting popular initiative).

A popular initiative must be based on a draft law, which law is to be submitted to the People's Chamber by the Government with a statement of the Government's position with respect to this law.

A (popular) referendum will take place only if the desired law has not been adopted by the People's Chamber in a version with which the petitioners or their representations are in agreement.

A (popular) referendum shall not be held on the budget, on tax legislation or on salary schedules.

A law submitted to a (popular) referendum is considered as adopted if it has received the consent of a majority of the votes cast.

A specific law shall regulate the procedures for popular initiative and (popular) referendum.

ARTICLE 88. The budget and the economic plan are adopted by law.

Amnesties require a (specific) law.

State treaties concerning matters of legislation, are to be promulgated as laws.

ARTICLE 89. Laws which have been duly promulgated cannot be reconsidered by the judiciary with respect to their constitutionality.

After the review proceedings provided for in Article 66 have been instituted, all pending court proceedings shall be suspended until the review proceedings have been completed.

ARTICLE 90. General administrative regulations required for the implementation of the laws of the Republic will be issued by the Government of the Republic, unless the law provides otherwise.

IV. The Government of the Republic

ARTICLE 91. The Government of the Republic consists of the Minister President and the Ministers.

ARTICLE 92. The Minister President is appointed by the party with the greatest strength in the People's Chamber; he (the Minister President) forms the Government. All parties having at least forty representatives (in the People's Chamber) are represented by Ministers or State Secretaries in proportion to their strength. State secretaries may attend meetings of the Government in an advisory capacity.

Should one parliamentary party refuse to be included, the Government will be formed without it.

Ministers should be members of the People's Chamber.

The People's Chamber approves the Government and the program submitted by it.

ARTICLE 93. On taking office, members of the Government shall be sworn in by the President of the Republic and pledged to perform their duties impartially for the welfare of the people and in faithful observance of the Constitution and the laws.

ARTICLE 94. The Government, and each of its members, require the confidence of the People's Chamber in order to perform their functions.

ARTICLE 95. The functions of the Cabinet are terminated if and when the People's Chamber passes a motion of no-confidence.

A motion of no-confidence will be voted on only if at the same time a new Minister President and his program are proposed. The motion of no-confidence and these proposals will be considered in one combined vote.

A vote of no-confidence shall not be effective unless the motion is carried by at least one-half (two hundred) of the statutory number of representatives.

A motion of no-confidence must be signed by at least one-fourth of the members of the People's Chamber. A vote on such a motion may not be taken prior to the second day after it has been debated, and not later than one week after its presentation.

Unless the new Government takes office within twenty-one days after the motion of no-confidence has been carried, that motion shall become void.

If the new Government receives a vote of no-confidence, the People's Chamber shall be considered dissolved.

The former Government continues its functions until a new Government has taken office.

ARTICLE 96. A member of the Government who receives a vote of no-confidence from the People's Chamber must resign. Unless decided otherwise by the People's Chamber, he is to continue his functions until his successor takes office.

The provision of Article 95, paragraph 3, is applicable correspondingly.

Any member of the Government may resign at any time. Unless decided otherwise by the People's Chamber, his official functions shall be performed by his deputy until a successor has been appointed.

ARTICLE 97. The Minister President presides over the Government and directs its business under Rules of Procedure to be decreed by the Government and communicated to the People's Chamber.

ARTICLE 98. The Minister President determines governmental policy in accordance with the guiding principles laid down by the People's Chamber. For this, he is responsible to the latter.

Within the framework of these guiding principles, each Minister directs independently the department entrusted to him and is personally responsible to the People's Chamber.

ARTICLE 99. Ministers shall refer to the Government, for deliberation and decision, all bills, any matters which must be referred to it under the Constitution or the law, as well as differences of opinion with respect to matters which fall within the competence of more than one Minister.

ARTICLE 100. The Government makes decisions by majority vote. In case of a tie, the Minister President shall cast the deciding vote.

V. State Council of the Republic

ARTICLE 101. The State Council of the Republic is elected by the People's Chamber for a term of four years.

After the expiration of the election period the State Council carries on its activity until the election of the new State Council by the People's Chamber.

ARTICLE 102. The State Council of the Republic consists of the chairman, six deputy chairmen, sixteen members, and the secretary.

The chairman conducts the work of the State Council.

ARTICLE 103. The chairman, the deputy chairman, the members, and the secretary of the State Council of the Republic take the following oath to the People's Chamber upon entering office:

'I swear to devote my strength to the welfare of the German people, to guard the Constitution and the Laws of the German Democratic Republic, to fulfill my duties conscientiously, and to show justice to all.'

ARTICLE 104. The State Council of the Republic is responsible to the People's Chamber.

The State Council of the Republic proclaims the laws of the Republic.

The signing is carried out by the chairman of the People's Council.

ARTICLE 105. The chairman of the State Council of the Republic swears in the members of the government upon their entry in office.

ARTICLE 106. The State Council of the Republic

Calls the elections to the People's Chamber and convokes the first session of the People's Chamber after the new election;

May carry out a general popular referendum;

Ratifies and gives notice of international treaties of the German Democratic Republic;

Appoints the plenipotentiary representatives of the German Democratic Republic in other states and recalls them;

Accepts the credentials and notices of recall of the diplomatic representatives of other states accredited to it;

Issues generally binding interpretations of the laws;

Issues decisions with the effect of law;

Frames basic decisions on problems of the defense and security of the country;

Confirms basic instructions of the National Defense Council of the German Democratic Republic;

Convokes the members of the National Defense Council of the German Democratic Republic;

Establishes the military service ranks, diplomatic ranks, and other special titles;

Confers orders and other high decorations and titles of honor;

Exercises the right of pardon.

ARTICLE 107. The State Council of the Republic is represented outside by its chairman or his deputy.

The chairman of the State Council represents the Republic under international law.

ARTICLE 108. The chairman, the deputy chairman, the members, and the secretary of the State Council of the Republic may be recalled by decision of the People's Chamber. The decision requires a majority of two-thirds of the legal number of the representatives.

VI. Republic and Laender

ARTICLE 109. Each Land must have a constitution which conforms to the principles of the Constitution of the Republic and under which the Landtag is the supreme and sole popular representative body in the Land.

The popular representative body must be elected, by all citizens entitled to do so, in universal, equal, direct and secret ballot held in accordance with the principles of proportional representation as laid down in the Electoral Law of the Republic.

ARTICLE 110. Any change in the territory of a Land and the formation of a new Land within the Republic requires a law of the Republic amending the Constitution.

Only an ordinary law (of the Republic) is required if the Laender immediately affected concur.

An ordinary law will likewise suffice, even if one of the Laender affected does not concur, provided, however, that the territorial change or the formation of a new Land is demanded by a plebiscite held in the territories concerned.

ARTICLE 111. The Republic may enact uniform legislation in any field. However, in so doing it should confine itself to laying down principles, provided this meets the need for uniform regulation.

To the extent that the Republic does not exercise its legislative power, the Laender shall have such power.

ARTICLE 112. The Republic has the exclusive right to legislate on

Foreign relations;

Foreign trade;

Customs and the free movement of commodities within a unified customs and trade area;

Citizenship; freedom of movement; immigration and emigration; extradition; passport regulations and laws affecting the status of aliens;

Legislation on census and registry (marriage, divorce and status of children);

Civil law; criminal law; the constitution of courts and their procedure;

Labor law;

Transport;

The fields of postal, telecommunication, and radio broadcasting services;

The fields of press and of film production, distribution and display;

Currency and coinage, weights, measures, standards and gauging;

Social insurance; and

War damages, occupation costs and reparations.

Legislation concerning the military defense of the homeland and concerning the defense of the civil population is incumbent upon the Republic.

ARTICLE 113. Legislation in the field of finance and taxation must be of such nature as not to infringe upon the existence of the Laender, the Kreise (counties) and Gemeinden (communities).

ARTICLE 114. Law of the whole of Germany overrides Land law.

ARTICLE 115. As a rule, the laws of the Republic are carried out by the executive agencies of the Laender, unless otherwise provided for in this Constitution or by a law. The Republic, insofar as there is a necessity, establishes its own administrative agencies by law.

ARTICLE 116. The Government of the Republic exercises supervision in those matters with respect to which the Republic has the right to legislate.

The Government of the Republic may issue general instructions where the laws of the Republic are not executed by its (own) administrative authorities. For the supervision of the execution of these laws and instructions, it is authorized to delegate commissioners to the implementing agencies. As for the powers of these commissioners, Article 65 is correspondingly applicable.

Upon the request of the Republic, the Laender governments are bound to remedy deficiencies discovered in the execution of the laws of the Republic.

Any controversies arising therefrom are to be examined and settled in accordance with the procedure specified in Article 66, paragraph 5.

VII. Administration of the Republic

ARTICLE 117. Maintenance of foreign relations is an exclusive concern of the Republic.

The Laender may conclude treaties with foreign states on matters within the competence of Land legislation; such treaties (before taking effect) are subject to the approval of the People's Chamber.

Treaties with foreign states concerning changes of national boundaries are concluded by the Republic, after the consent of the Land thereby affected has been obtained. Boundary changes may be effected only by a law of the Republic, unless a mere rectification of boundaries in uninhabited areas is involved.

ARTICLE 118. Germany forms a single customs and trade area, bounded by a common customs frontier.

Territories of foreign states or parts of such territories may be included in the German customs area by treaty or convention. Parts of the German customs area may be excluded therefrom by law.

Any goods enjoying internal free trade within the German customs area may, within the area, freely be introduced into, or carried in transit across the boundaries of, German Laender and political subdivisions as well as, pursuant to paragraph 2, into, or across the boundaries of, the territories of foreign states or parts of such territories included.

ARTICLE 119. Customs and such taxes as are regulated by laws of the Republic are administered by the Republic.

The power to levy taxes is, normally, vested in the Republic.

The Republic should levy taxes only to the extent required to cover its needs.

The Republic establishes its own agencies for the administration of taxes. In conjunction therewith, arrangements shall be made enabling the Laender to safeguard their special interests in the spheres of agriculture, commerce, handicrafts, trades or professions, manufacture and industry.

To the extent required for the uniform and equitable enforcement of its tax laws, the Republic shall enact legislation on the organization of tax administrations in the Laender, the organization and powers of the authorities entrusted with the enforcement of the tax laws of the Republic, the settlement of accounts with the Laender, and the reimbursement for the administrative costs incurred in the enforcement of the tax laws of the Republic.

ARTICLE 120. Taxes and other levies may be assessed only as provided by law.

Property, income and excise tax legislation are to be kept in a suitable proportion to each other, and to be graduated according to social considerations.

Through sharply progressive tax rates on inheritance, the amassing of socially harmful fortunes should be prevented.

ARTICLE 121. Revenues and expenditures of the Republic must be estimated for each fiscal year and provided for in the budget. The budget is to be enacted by legislation before the beginning of the fiscal year.

ARTICLE 122. The Minister of Finance, in order to secure a discharge for the Government, gives an accounting to the People's Chamber of the revenues of the Republic and their use. The auditing of accounts is regulated by law of the Republic.

ARTICLE 123. Funds may be procured by borrowing only for extraordinary needs. Borrowing of such funds and the guaranteeing of loans as a charge of the Republic may be effected only on the basis of a law of the Republic.

ARTICLE 124. Postal, telecommunication, broadcasting and railroad services are to be administered by the Republic.

The former Reich Autobahnen (auto-highways) and Reich highways as well as all roads for long distance traffic are under the control of the Republic. The same provisions apply to waterways.

ARTICLE 125. Control of merchant shipping and the administration of maritime shipping, and of aids to navigation, are duties of the Republic.

VIII. Administration of Justice

ARTICLE 126. The ordinary administration of justice is exercised by the Supreme Court of the Republic and by courts of the Laender.

ARTICLE 127. In the exercise of their judicial function, the judges are independent and bound only by the Constitution and the Law.

ARTICLE 128. Judges must be persons who, by their qualification and activity, offer the guarantee that they will exercise their office in accordance with the principles laid down in the Constitution.

ARTICLE 129. Through the development of law schools, the Republic provides an opportunity for members of all classes of the population to become qualified for the profession of judge, attorney and public prosecutor.

ARTICLE 130. Laymen are, as much as possible, to be used as judges.

Laymen are elected, on the proposal of democratic parties and organizations, by the competent popular representative bodies.

ARTICLE 131. Judges of the Supreme Court of the Republic, and the Prosecutor General of the Republic, are elected by the People's Chamber upon their nomination by the Government of the Republic.

Judges of the high courts of the Laender, and the prosecutors general of the Laender, are elected by the Landtage upon their nomination by the Land governments.

All other judges are appointed by the Land governments.

ARTICLE 132. Judges of the Supreme Court, and the Prosecutor General of the Republic, may be recalled by the People's Chamber if they violate the Constitution or the laws, or commit a serious breach of their duties as judge or public prosecutor.

This recall is effected after hearing the report of a Committee on Justice to be established in the People's Chamber.

The Committee on Justice is composed of the chairman of the Legal Committee of the People's Chamber, three members of the People's Chamber, two members of the Supreme Court and one member of the Prosecutor General's office. It is presided over by the chairman of the Legal Committee. The other committee members are elected by the People's Chamber for the legislative term. The members of the Supreme Court and the Prosecutor General's office serving on the Committee on Justice cannot be members of the People's Chamber.

Judges elected by a Landtag, or appointed by a Land government, may be recalled by the respective Landtag. Their recall will be effected after hearing the report of a committee on justice to be set up with the respective Landtag. The committee on justice is composed of the chairman of the legal committee of the Landtag, three members of the Landtag, two members of the Land high court and one member of the prosecutor general's office of the respective Land. It is presided over by the chairman of the Legal Committee. The other committee members are elected by the respective Landtag for the duration of the legislative term. The members of the (Land) high court and of the prosecutor general's office, and participating in the committee on justice, cannot be members of the Landtag.

Judges appointed by Land governments may, under the same conditions, be recalled by the respective Land government, provided that the consent of the Landtag committee on justice has been obtained.

ARTICLE 133. All court proceedings are open to the public.

In all matters involving a threat to public safety and order, or to public morals, the court may order the public to be excluded.

ARTICLE 134. No citizen should be deprived of his right to be tried before the judge having lawful jurisdiction in the matter. Extraordinary courts are inadmissible. The legislative authorities may set up courts for special matters only if their competence is to comprise categories of persons or issues defined beforehand and in a general way.

ARTICLE 135. Only such penalties may be imposed as have been provided for by law at the time the punishable act was committed.

No penal law has retroactive force.

Exceptions to this rule are measures and the application of provisions which are adopted for the overcoming of Nazism, fascism and militarism, or which are necessary for the prosecution of crimes against humanity.

ARTICLE 136. In cases of temporary arrest, house searches, and seizures effected in the course of a preliminary investigation, the approval of a judge must be obtained without (undue) delay.

It rests with the judge alone to decide on the admissibility and continuance of an arrest. Persons arrested must be brought before a judge at the latest on the day after their apprehension. If pretrial confinement is ordered by the judge, he must make a periodic review as to whether continued detention is justified.

The reason for the detention is to be communicated to the arrested person at his first examination by a judge and, if he so desires, within an additional twenty-four hours to a person to be named by him.

ARTICLE 137. Execution of sentences is founded on the concept of reforming persons capable of rehabilitation through common productive work.

Article 138. Citizens are protected against unlawful administrative measures by the supervision exercised by the legislature and through recourse to administrative courts.

The structure and jurisdiction of administrative courts are regulated by law.

Principles applying to the election and recall of judges of ordinary courts apply correspondingly to the members of administrative courts.

IX. Administrative Autonomy

Article 139. Gemeinden and Gemeindeverbaende (communities and associated communities) enjoy administrative autonomy subject to the provisions of the laws of the Republic and the Laender.

Autonomy functions include determination and implementation of all policies concerning the economic, social and cultural life of the Gemeinde or Gemeindeverband. Each task is to be accomplished by the lowest (local) administrative unit qualified for this purpose.

Article 140. Gemeinden and Gemeindeverbaende have representative bodies organized on democratic principles.

To assist them, committees are formed in which delegates of the democratic parties and organizations participate responsibly.

The right to vote and the procedure to be followed in (local) elections are governed by the provisions applying to elections to the People's Chamber and to the Landtage.

The right to vote may, however, by Land legislation be predicated on the length of residence in the (respective) locality for a period not to exceed half a year.

Article 141. For the due exercise of their functions, the elected executive authorities of Gemeinden and Gemeindeverbaende require the confidence of the (local) representative bodies.

Article 142. Supervision of the administrative autonomy practiced by Gemeinden and Gemeindeverbaende is limited to a review of the statutory compliance of administrative measures and of the observance of democratic administrative principles.

Article 143. The Republic and the Laender may delegate functions, and the application of laws, to the Gemeinden and Gemeindeverbaende.

X. Transitional and Concluding Provisions

Article 144. All provisions of this Constitution have direct force of law. Any provisions to the contrary are repealed herewith. Provisions superseding them and required to implement the Constitution are to take effect simultaneously with the Constitution. Existing laws are to be interpreted in the meaning of this Constitution.

Constitutional liberties and rights may not be used as arguments against past or future measures adopted for the overcoming of National Socialism and militarism, or to redress wrongs caused by them.

The above Constitution of the German Democratic Republic, worked out with the participation of the entire German People by the German People's Council, passed by it on March 19, 1949, confirmed by the Third German People's Congress on May 30, 1949, and put into effect by a Law of the Provisional People's Chamber dated October 7, 1949, is hereby promulgated.

Berlin, October 7, 1949

The President of the Provisional People's Chamber
of the German Democratic Republic
Dieckmann

PREAMBLE
OF THE LAW CONCERNING THE DISSOLUTION OF THE LAND CHAMBERS OF THE GERMAN DEMOCRATIC REPUBLIC
December 8, 1958

The strengthening of the responsibility of the people's representations as the highest organs of the state power in their fields of competence on the basis of democratic centralism has led to the solidification of the unified system of the state organs of the workers' and peasants' power. The Law of January 17, 1957 concerning the local organs of the state power, the Law of January 17 Concerning the Rights and Duties of the People's Chamber Toward the Local Representations of the People, and the Law of February 11, 1958 concerning the Improvement and Simplification of the Work of the State Apparatus are the basis for the further development of socialist democracy.

These laws guarantee the conscious and direct participation of the toilers in the conduct of the state and the economy in the elected organs of power. The dissolution of the Land Chambers is the result of the solidification of the workers' and peasants' state and the development of socialist democracy.

PREAMBLE
OF THE LAW CONCERNING THE FORMATION OF THE STATE COUNCIL OF THE GERMAN DEMOCRATIC REPUBLIC
September 12, 1960

The population of our Republic and the whole German people have suffered a great and painful loss in the passing of the President of the German Democratic Republic, Wilhelm Pieck, sustained by the great responsibility for the maintenance of peace, for the socialist future of the German Democratic Republic, the formation of the State Council of the German Democratic Republic is resolved for the further development of the socialist order of society and for the rebirth of Germany and a peace-loving, democratic, and unified state.

The amplifications and amendments established in the Law on the Expansion of the Constitution of September 26, 1955 (GB1 I S.867), and in the Law Concerning the Formation of the State Council of the German Democratic Republic of September 12, 1960 (GB1 S.505), have been taken into account in the subject text.

The preambles of the Laws of December 8, 1958 and the Law of December 12, 1960 are printed at the conclusion of this edition because of their significance.

LAW
ON THE CONSTITUTION OF THE GERMAN DEMOCRATIC REPUBLIC
dated October 7, 1949

ARTICLE 1. The Constitution of the German Democratic Republic, created with the participation of the entire German people, passed on March 19, 1949, by the German People's Council and confirmed on May 30, 1949, by the Third German People's Congress is hereby put into effect.

ARTICLE 2. This Law comes into effect on its adoption. It is engrossed and promulgated by the President of the Provisional People's Chamber.

Engrossed and promulgated in Berlin, on October 7, 1949.

The President of the Provisional People's Chamber
of the German Democratic Republic
Dieckmann

8. 1

CONSTITUTION
OF THE DEMOCRATIC
PEOPLE'S REPUBLIC OF KOREA[1]

Adopted by the Supreme People's Assembly at Its First Session
September 8, 1948,
with amendments adopted at the Seventh, Eighth and Ninth Sessions

CHAPTER I
BASIC PRINCIPLES

ARTICLE 1.   Our state is the Democratic People's Republic of Korea.

ARTICLE 2.   The state power of the D.P.R.K. belongs to the people.

The representative organs through which the people exercise power are the Supreme People's Assembly and the local people's assemblies at all levels.

ARTICLE 3.   All the representative organs of state power from *ri* people's assemblies to the Supreme People's Assembly are elected by the free will of the people.

The elections to the organs of state power are conducted by the citizens of the D.P.R.K. on the basis of universal, equal and direct suffrage by secret ballot.

ARTICLE 4.   Deputies to all the organs of state power are responsible to their electors for their activities.

The electors may recall their deputies before the expiration of the term of office in case the deputies betray their confidence.

ARTICLE 5.   In the D.P.R.K. the ownership of the means of production takes the following forms: state ownership; cooperative ownership; ownership by private natural or by private juridical person.

Mines and other mineral wealth, forests, waters, major enterprises, banks, rail, water and air transport, communication, waterworks, natural energy, as well as all the property which formerly belonged to the Japanese government, the Japanese nationals or pro-Japanese elements, are owned by the state.

Foreign trade is conducted by the state or under its supervision.

ARTICLE 6.   The land owned by the Japanese government and the Japanese nationals as well as the Korean landlords is confiscated.

The tenancy system is abolished forever.

Only those who till land with their own labor are allowed to own it.

---

[1] *Constitution of the Democratic People's Republic of Korea* (Pyongyang: New Korea Press, 1956).

Maximum extent of land ownership is [from] five [to] twenty *jungbo*.

Maximum extent of land ownership is specially prescribed by law according to locality and conditions.

[Besides] the private ownership of land, the state and cooperative organizations are allowed to own land.

No limit is imposed upon the acreage owned by the state and cooperative organizations.

The state protects in particular the interests of the working peasants and gives them help in various forms insofar as the economic policy permits.

ARTICLE 7. In the areas in Korea where the land reform has not yet been effected, it is to be carried out at the date fixed by the Supreme People's Assembly of the D.P.R.K.

ARTICLE 8. The private ownership prescribed by law of land, draft cattle, farm implements and other means of production, medium and small industrial enterprises, medium and small trade, raw materials and manufactured goods, residences and outhouses, articles of domestic economy, income and savings is protected by law.

The right to inherit private property is ensured by law.

Creative initiative in private economy is encouraged.

ARTICLE 9. The state encourages the development of the cooperative organizations of the people.

The property of the cooperative organizations is protected by law.

ARTICLE 10. With a view to utilizing rationally in the interests of the people all the domestic economic resources and all potential resources, the state works out a uniform national economic plan, and strives accordingly for the restoration and development of the national economy and culture.

The state carries out the national economic plan on the basis of state and cooperative ownership, and allows privately owned economy to participate in it.

CHAPTER II

FUNDAMENTAL RIGHTS AND DUTIES OF CITIZENS

ARTICLE 11. All citizens of the D.P.R.K., irrespective of sex, nationality, religious belief, specialty, property status or education, have equal rights in all spheres of government, political, economic, social and cultural activity.

ARTICLE 12. All citizens of the D.P.R.K. who have reached the age of twenty, irrespective of sex, nationality, social origin, religious belief, length of residence, property status or education, have the right to elect and be elected to organs of state power.

Citizens serving in the Korean People's Army have the right to elect and be elected to organs of state power on equal terms with other citizens.

Persons who are deprived of the electoral right by the decision of a court, insane persons, and the pro-Japanese elements have no right to elect and be elected.

ARTICLE 13. Citizens of the D.P.R.K. have freedom of speech, the press, association, assembly, mass meetings and demonstration.

Citizens are guaranteed the right to organize and unite in democratic political parties, trade unions, cooperative organizations, sports, cultural, technical, scientific and other societies.

ARTICLE 14. Citizens of the D.P.R.K. have freedom of religious belief and of conducting religious services.

ARTICLE 15. Citizens of the D.P.R.K. have the right to equal pay for equal work in the state organs, cooperative organizations, and in the privately owned enterprises.

ARTICLE 16. Citizens of the D.P.R.K. have the right to rest.

The right to rest is ensured by the establishment of an eight-hour working day for workers and office employees and by the institution of paid vacations.

ARTICLE 17. Citizens of the D.P.R.K. who are entitled to the benefit of social insurance have the right to material assistance in old age and in case of sickness or disability.

This right is ensured in the form of medical service and material assistance in accordance with social insurance provided by the state.

ARTICLE 18. Citizens of the D.P.R.K. have the right to education.

Elementary education is universal and compulsory.

The state ensures free education for the children of poor citizens.

A system of state stipends is applied to the majority of students of technical and higher educational institutions.

Education is conducted in the national language.

ARTICLE 19. Citizens of the D.P.R.K. have freedom of running medium and small industrial enterprises and engaging in commerce.

ARTICLE 20. Citizens of the D.P.R.K. have freedom of engaging in scientific and artistic pursuits.

Copyright and patent right of invention are protected by law.

ARTICLE 21. The inviolability of the homes of citizens and privacy of correspondence are protected by law.

ARTICLE 22. Women in the D.P.R.K. are accorded equal rights with men in all spheres of government, political, economic, social and cultural activity.

The state protects especially mothers and children.

ARTICLE 23. The state protects marriage and the family.

Duties of parents to the child born out of wedlock are equal with the duties to the child born in wedlock.

The child born out of wedlock has equal rights with the child born in wedlock.

Juridical relations of marriage and the family are specially prescribed by law.

ARTICLE 24. Citizens of the D.P.R.K. are guaranteed inviolability of the person.

No citizen may be placed under arrest except by decision of a court or with the sanction of a procurator.

ARTICLE 25. Citizens of the D.P.R.K. have the right to submit petition and make complaints to the organs of state power.

Citizens have the right to make complaints to any government authority against transgression of the law in the discharge of duty by any government employee and the right to compensation for the loss sustained as a result of infringement of their rights.

ARTICLE 26. The D.P.R.K. affords the right of asylum to foreign nationals persecuted for fighting for democratic principles or national liberation movements, or for the interests of the working people or for freedom of scientific and cultural activities.

ARTICLE 27. Citizens of the D.P.R.K. must abide by the Constitution and the law.

It is the most heinous of crimes against the state to abuse the rights granted by the Constitution for the purpose of altering or undermining the lawful order provided for in the Constitution, and is punishable by law.

ARTICLE 28. It is the duty of every citizen of the D.P.R.K. to defend the homeland.

To defend the homeland is the highest duty and honor of every citizen of the D.P.R.K.

It is the most heinous of crimes to betray the homeland and the people, and the criminal is subject to severe punishment.

ARTICLE 29. It is the duty of every citizen of the D.P.R.K. to pay taxes according to his economic status.

ARTICLE 30. It is the duty of every citizen of the D.P.R.K. to work.

Work is a matter of honor for the Korean people.

In the D.P.R.K. work constitutes a foundation for the development of the national economy and culture.

ARTICLE 31. The national minorities who have the citizenship of the D.P.R.K. are guaranteed equal rights with the Korean citizens.

They have freedom to use their mother tongues and develop their own national culture.

CHAPTER III

THE HIGHEST ORGAN OF STATE POWER

SECTION I

THE SUPREME PEOPLE'S ASSEMBLY

ARTICLE 32. The Supreme People's Assembly is the highest organ of state power in the D.P.R.K.

ARTICLE 33. The legislative power of the state is exercised exclusively by the Supreme People's Assembly of the D.P.R.K.

ARTICLE 34. The Supreme People's Assembly is composed of deputies elected on the basis of universal, equal and direct suffrage by secret ballot.

ARTICLE 35. The Supreme People's Assembly is elected at the ratio of one deputy for every 50,000 of the population.

ARTICLE 36. Deputies of the Supreme People's Assembly are elected for a term of four years.

ARTICLE 37. The Supreme People's Assembly exercises the supreme power of the state, with the exception of the rights vested by the Constitution in the Presidium of the Supreme People's Assembly and in the Cabinet.

The following powers are exercised exclusively by the Supreme People's Assembly:

1) To approve and amend the Constitution;
2) To establish basic principles of the domestic and foreign policies;
3) To elect the Presidium of the Supreme People's Assembly;
4) To form the Cabinet;
5) To pass laws and to approve major decrees adopted by the Presidium of the Supreme People's Assembly when the Supreme People's Assembly is not in session;
6) To approve the national economic plan;
7) To approve the state budget;
8) To establish or revise the status and boundaries of provinces, cities, counties and *ri*, towns or workers' settlements;
9) To exercise the right of amnesty;
10) To elect the Supreme Court;
11) To appoint the Procurator General.

ARTICLE 38. The Supreme People's Assembly convenes ordinary and extraordinary sessions.

Ordinary sessions are convened twice a year.

Ordinary sessions are convened by the decision of the Presidium of the Supreme People's Assembly.

Extraordinary sessions are convened by the Presidium of the Supreme People's Assembly when it deems necessary or on the demand of over one-third of the deputies.

ARTICLE 39. The Supreme People's Assembly elects a chairman and two vice-chairmen.

The chairman presides over the sittings in accordance with the regulations adopted by the Supreme People's Assembly.

ARTICLE 40. Attendance of a simple majority of [all] deputies is required to hold sessions of the Supreme People's Assembly.

Laws are adopted by a majority vote of the deputies present at the session.

ARTICLE 41. The law passed by the Supreme People's Assembly is published over the signatures of the chairman and the secretary-general of the Presidium of the Supreme People's Assembly within a period not exceeding five days.

ARTICLE 42. The Supreme People's Assembly may organize appropriate committees to consider in advance matters for discussion.

The committees are entitled to supervise the organs of state power and the organs subordinate to them.

ARTICLE 43. The Supreme People's Assembly establishes a Legislative Bills Committee to draw up or consider draft laws to be submitted to the Supreme People's Assembly for approval.

ARTICLE 44. Deputies of the Supreme People's Assembly are ensured inviolability as deputies.

No deputy of the Supreme People's Assembly may be arrested or punished except in case of a flagrant offense without the consent of the Supreme People's Assembly or, when the Supreme People's Assembly is not in session, without the consent of the Presidium of the Supreme People's Assembly.

ARTICLE 45. Prior to the expiration of the term of office of the Supreme People's Assembly, its Presidium shall arrange the holding of elections to the succeeding Supreme People's Assembly.

In the event of the dissolution of the Supreme People's Assembly, new elections must be carried out within a period not exceeding two months from the date of its dissolution.

ARTICLE 46. Should extraordinary circumstances arise, the sitting Supreme People's Assembly may exercise its powers exceeding the term of office provided for in the Constitution as long as the circumstances continue.

The Supreme People's Assembly, in such event, may decide upon its dissolution before its term of office expires.

SECTION 2

THE PRESIDIUM OF THE SUPREME PEOPLE'S ASSEMBLY

ARTICLE 47. The Presidium of the Supreme People's Assembly is the highest organ of state power when the Supreme People's Assembly is not in session.

ARTICLE 48. The Presidium of the Supreme People's Assembly is elected by the Supreme People's Assembly and composed of a chairman, vice-chairmen, a secretary-general and its members.

ARTICLE 49. The Presidium of the Supreme People's Assembly exercises the following functions:

1) To convene the Supreme People's Assembly;
2) To supervise the execution of the Constitution and laws, and interpret the laws in operation and issue decrees;
3) To annul decisions and orders of the Cabinet where these contravene the Constitution or laws;
4) To promulgate laws adopted by the Supreme People's Assembly;
5) To exercise the right of pardon;
6) To appoint and remove ministers upon recommendation by the Premier when the Supreme People's Assembly is not in session, subject to subsequent confirmation by the Supreme People's Assembly;
7) To award orders and medals and confer titles of honor;

8) To ratify or annul treaties concluded with foreign states;

9) To appoint or recall ambassadors and ministers to foreign states;

10) To receive the letters of credence and recall of diplomatic representatives accredited to it by foreign states.

ARTICLE 50. The Presidium of the Supreme People's Assembly is responsible to the Supreme People's Assembly for its activities, and the Supreme People's Assembly reelects, whenever it deems necessary, some or all of the members of the Presidium of the Supreme People's Assembly.

ARTICLE 51. In the event of dissolution of the Supreme People's Assembly, the Presidium of the Supreme People's Assembly exercises its functions until a new Presidium of the Supreme People's Assembly is elected.

CHAPTER IV

THE CENTRAL EXECUTIVE ORGAN OF STATE POWER

SECTION I
THE CABINET

ARTICLE 52. The Cabinet of the D.P.R.K. is the highest executive organ of state power.

ARTICLE 53. The Cabinet of the D.P.R.K. has the right to promulgate decisions and orders in accordance with the Constitution and laws.

The decisions and orders promulgated by the Cabinet are binding throughout the territory of the D.P.R.K.

ARTICLE 54. The Cabinet of the D.P.R.K. controls and directs the work of all ministries and other organs subordinate to it.

ARTICLE 55. The Cabinet of the D.P.R.K. exercises the following functions:

1) To conduct general guidance in the sphere of relations with foreign states and conclude treaties with foreign states;

2) To control foreign trade;

3) To direct local organs of state power;

4) To organize the monetary and credit system;

5) To draw up a uniform state budget and to fix taxation and other revenue included in the state and local budgets;

6) To direct state industrial and commercial establishments, agricultural enterprises and state transport and communication facilities;

7) To adopt measures for the maintenance of public order, for the protection of the interests of the state and for the safeguarding of the rights of citizens;

8) To establish basic principles concerning the utilization of land, mineral wealth, forests and waters;

9) To direct the educational, cultural, scientific, artistic and public health work;

10) To establish political, economic and social measures for the improvement of economic and cultural standards of the people;

11) To direct the formation of the Korean People's Army; to appoint and remove high-ranking officers of the Korean People's Army;

12) To appoint and remove vice-ministers, managers of major industrial enterprises and rectors of universities.

ARTICLE 56. The Cabinet of the D.P.R.K. has the right to annul ordinances and regulations of the ministries, decisions and directives of the provincial people's committees where these contravene the Constitution, laws and decrees or decisions and orders issued by the Cabinet.

ARTICLE 57. The decisions of the Cabinet are adopted by a majority vote.

The decisions adopted by the Cabinet are published over the signatures of the Premier and the ministers concerned.

ARTICLE 58. The Cabinet of the D.P.R.K. is composed of the following persons: (1) the Premier; (2) the Vice-Premiers; (3) the ministers; (4) the chairmen of the committees.

The organization of the Cabinet is specially determined by law.

ARTICLE 59. The Premier is the head of the government of the D.P.R.K.

The Premier convenes and presides over the Cabinet meetings.

The Vice-Premier is under the direction of the Premier, and should the Premier be absent from the office for [any] reason the Vice-Premier acts in behalf of the Premier.

When the Vice-Premier acts in behalf of the Premier, the Vice-Premier exercises equal rights with the Premier.

ARTICLE 60. The Cabinet of the D.P.R.K. is subordinate to the Supreme People's Assembly in its work and is responsible to the Presidium of the Supreme People's Assembly when the Supreme People's Assembly is not in session.

ARTICLE 61. The Premier, Vice-Premiers and ministers take the following oath before the Supreme People's Assembly:

'I pledge myself to serve faithfully the Korean people and the Democratic People's Republic of Korea, to fight solely for the welfare of the entire people and the country through my activities in the capacity of a member of the Cabinet, to observe strictly the Constitution and the laws of the Democratic People's Republic of Korea, and to dedicate all my power and ability to the safeguarding of the sovereignty of the Democratic People's Republic of Korea and democratic freedoms.'

ARTICLE 62. Deputies to the Supreme People's Assembly may address questions to the Cabinet or to the ministers.

The Cabinet or a minister to whom a question is addressed is obliged to furnish answers in accordance with the procedure prescribed by the Supreme People's Assembly.

THE MINISTRIES

ARTICLE 63. The ministries are the executive organs of state power in their respective branches.

ARTICLE 64. The functions of the ministries are to direct their respective branches of the state administration within the jurisdiction of the Cabinet.

ARTICLE 65. The minister is the head of the ministry.

The minister is a member of the Cabinet with a vote and is subject to the Cabinet in discharging his duties.

ARTICLE 66. The minister may, within the limits of his authority, issue ministerial ordinances or regulations whose execution is binding.

ARTICLE 67. Should the minister for reasons be unable to perform his duties, the vice-minister exercises the functions on his behalf. The vice-minister is under the direction of the minister.

CHAPTER V
THE LOCAL ORGANS OF STATE POWER

ARTICLE 68. The local organs of state power in provinces, cities, counties or city districts and *ri*, towns or workers' settlements are the respective people's assemblies.

ARTICLE 69. The people's assemblies at all levels are composed of the deputies elected on the basis of universal, equal and direct suffrage by secret ballot.

The provincial people's assemblies are elected for a term of four years and the people's assemblies of cities, counties or city districts and *ri*, towns or workers' settlements for a term of two years.

The elections to the people's assemblies at all levels are specially provided for by law.

ARTICLE 70. The local people's assemblies at all levels ensure the observance and execution of laws in their respective areas; direct all activities in economic, public and cultural fields; approve local budgets; ensure the protection of state and public property, the maintenance of public order and the rights of citizens.

ARTICLE 71. The local people's assemblies at all levels adopt decisions within the limits of the powers vested in them by law.

ARTICLE 72. The people's committees of provinces, cities, counties or city districts and *ri*, towns or workers' settlements are the executive organs of the people's assemblies at corresponding levels and the local administrative organs of the state.

ARTICLE 73. The people's committees at all levels each consist of a chairman, vice-chairmen, a secretary-general and committee members elected by the people's assemblies at corresponding levels.

ARTICLE 74. The people's committees at all levels carry out all administrative affairs of the state in the areas under their jurisdiction in pursuance of decisions and directives of the people's assemblies at corresponding levels and the organs at higher levels.

ARTICLE 75. The people's committees at all levels are responsible in their activities to the people's assemblies at corresponding levels and the people's committees at higher levels.

All the people's committees are under the unified leadership of, and subordinate to, the Cabinet.

ARTICLE 76. The people's committees at higher levels have the right to annul or revise decisions and directives of the people's committees at lower levels, and to suspend decisions of the people's assemblies at lower levels.

ARTICLE 77. The people's assemblies at higher levels have the right to annul or revise decisions and directives of the people's assemblies and the people's committees at lower levels.

ARTICLE 78. The people's committees at all levels, even after the expiration of the term of office of the people's assemblies at corresponding levels, continue to perform their functions until new people's committees are elected.

ARTICLE 79. The people's committees of provinces, cities and counties or city districts are provided with adequate departments for the direction of their affairs.

These departments are specially provided for by law.

ARTICLE 80. The heads of departments of the people's committees of provinces, cities and counties or city districts are subordinate to the people's assemblies and the people's committees to which they belong, and to the corresponding departments of the people's committees at higher levels and to the ministries concerned.

ARTICLE 81. The people's assemblies and the people's committees at all levels must always secure a broad participation of the local population in the discharge of their duties and rely upon their initiative.

CHAPTER VI

THE COURTS AND THE PROCURATOR'S OFFICE

ARTICLE 82. In the D.P.R.K., cases are tried by the Supreme Court, the courts of provinces, cities and counties, and the special courts.

Judgment is passed and executed in the name of the D.P.R.K.

ARTICLE 83. The courts are organized through elections.

The Supreme Court is elected by the Supreme People's Assembly.

The courts of provinces, cities and counties are elected by the people's assemblies at corresponding levels by secret ballot.

The organization of the special courts is specially provided for by law.

Judges or people's assessors are removed only by means of recall of the organs which elected them.

ARTICLE 84. The first trial is conducted with the participation of the people's assessors who have equal rights with judges.

ARTICLE 85. Every citizen who has electoral right has the right to be a judge or a people's assessor.

Those who served as judges or procurators under Japanese rule are deprived of the right to be judges or procurators.

ARTICLE 86. Cases are tried in public, and the accused is guaranteed the right to defense.

Cases may be closed to the public by the decision of a court only in cases otherwise provided for by law.

ARTICLE 87. Judicial proceedings are conducted in the Korean language.

Persons not knowing this language are guaranteed the opportunity of fully acquainting themselves with the records of the case through an interpreter and likewise the right to use their own language in court.

ARTICLE 88. Judges are independent and subject only to the law in exercising judicial authority.

ARTICLE 89. The Supreme Court is the highest judicial organ of the D.P.R.K.

The Supreme Court supervises the judicial work of all courts.

ARTICLE 90. Procurators exercise supervision to ensure precise and honest observance and execution of the law by all ministries and institutions and organizations subordinate to them as well as by officials and citizens.

ARTICLE 91. Procurators supervise if the ordinances and regulations of all ministries and the decisions and directives of local organs of state power conform with the Constitution, laws and decrees, as well as with the decisions and orders of the Cabinet.

ARTICLE 92. The head of the Supreme Procurator's Office is the Procurator General appointed by the Supreme People's Assembly.

ARTICLE 93. Procurators of provinces, cities and counties are appointed by the Procurator General.

ARTICLE 94. Procurators are independent in the discharge of their duties without being subject to the local organs of state power.

CHAPTER VII

THE STATE BUDGET

ARTICLE 95. The fundamental aim of the state budget is to organize a mighty national economy by consolidating all the state property, enhance the cultural and living standards of the people, and strengthen the national defense.

ARTICLE 96. The state budget is annually drawn up by the Cabinet and subject to approval by the Supreme People's Assembly.

ARTICLE 97. The state revenue and expenditure are consolidated in a uniform state budget.

ARTICLE 98.   No organ of state power is allowed to make any outlay not stipulated in the state budget.

All the organs of state power must observe the financial discipline and consolidate the financial system.

ARTICLE 99.   To practice economy on, and make rational utilization of, the state finance is the fundamental principle of financial activities.

CHAPTER VIII

NATIONAL DEFENSE

ARTICLE 100.   The Korean People's Army is formed for the defense of the D.P.R.K.

The mission of the Korean People's Army is to safeguard the sovereignty of the fatherland and freedom of the people.

CHAPTER IX

STATE EMBLEM, NATIONAL FLAG, CAPITAL

ARTICLE 101.   The state emblem of the D.P.R.K. is a grand hydroelectric power station under the beaming light of a red star, framed with ears of rice bound with a band bearing the inscription 'The Democratic People's Republic of Korea.'

ARTICLE 102.   The national flag of the D.P.R.K. is of three colors—a broad, red horizontal stripe in the center with a five-pointed red star in a white circle near the staff, and white and blue stripes over and under the red stripe. The ratio of the width to the length is 1:2.

ARTICLE 103.   The capital of the D.P.R.K. is the City of Seoul.

CHAPTER X

PROCEDURE FOR AMENDING THE CONSTITUTION

ARTICLE 104.   The Constitution of the D.P.R.K. may be amended only by the Supreme People's Assembly. Adoption of the draft laws for amendments to the Constitution requires the approval by a majority of not less than two-thirds of the deputies of the Supreme People's Assembly.

9. 1

ON THE CUBAN CONSTITUTIONAL PROBLEM

by Theodore Draper

CUBA is the only Communist party-state which does not, as yet, have a constitution.

In its origins, the movement headed by Fidel Castro pledged itself to the restoration of the 1940 Cuban Constitution. In his 'History Will Absolve Me' speech, delivered at his trial in October 1953 after the abortive attack on the Moncada army post in Santiago de Cuba, Fidel Castro summed up the program which he had intended to put into effect had his attempt succeeded. 'The first revolutionary law would have restored sovereignty to the people and proclaimed the Constitution of 1940 as the true supreme law of the state until the people should decide to modify or change it,' he said.[1] This remained the official position of his 26th of July Movement until the end of 1958, when the Batista regime fell.

The first post-Batista government, headed by President Manuel Urrutia, implicitly recognized the validity of the 1940 Constitution, if only because it issued decrees which formally amended the Constitution. Five such amendments were of such a fundamental character—such as the suspension of the right of *habeas corpus*—that it is questionable whether the Constitution was recognized in spirit as well as in letter. In any case, the ambiguous status of the 1940 Constitution was soon resolved by the adoption of a new document, the Fundamental Law of the Republic of Cuba, on February 7, 1959.[2]

In effect, the Fundamental Law replaced the Constitution of 1940. This operation was accomplished not by writing a new document, but by changing the operative sections of the old constitution while carrying over other sections of a more abstract nature.

However, the Fundamental Law soon was amended so frequently and so drastically that actual legislation has had little relation to the Law, and the Cuban regime has operated on the basis of a proliferation of decrees rather than a legislative process governed by a written constitution.

One step was taken in October 1965: Blas Roca, former editor of the newspaper *Hoy*, which had by then ceased publication, was appointed chairman of a Commission of Constitutional Studies 'on which to build the entire judicial system of the Socialist State.' Presumably this commission is the first step toward providing Communist Cuba with its own constitution.

---

[1] *La Historia Me Absolverá* (Havana: Editora Politica, 1964), p. 79.

[2] *Fundamental Law of Cuba 1959* (Washington, D.C.: Organization of American States, Pan American Union, General Secretariat, 1959).

THE CONSTITUTIONAL
LEGISLATION OF CUBA[1]

I. INTRODUCTION

THE constitutional history of Cuba may be divided into five periods: the first covers the colonial period up to the promulgation of the 1902 Constitution; the second goes from that date until July 8, 1940 when the Constitution of that year was adopted; the third reaches from that date until 1952; the fourth period begins on March 10, 1952 and ends on December 31, 1958. This period coincides with Batista's coup d'état and his abdication of power. The fifth period begins with the advent of Castro's regime.

This chapter will merely deal with the constitutional structure of Cuba during the last of these five periods. Nevertheless, it must be mentioned that in its sixty years of existence as an independent country, the Republic of Cuba has on two occasions only been governed by a constitution freely expressing the will of the people. The first occasion was in 1901, following the War of Independence against Spain. That Constitution came into force on May 20, 1902. The other period of free constitutional development was entered by Cuba on July 8, 1940, the date of the publication of the second Constitution in the *Gaceta Oficial*.

II. THE 1940 CONSTITUTION

The 1940 Constitution governed the life of Cuba for twelve years. During that period three Presidents of the Republic followed each other through free elections. They were Fulgencio Batista, Emilio Grau San Martin and Carlos Prio Socarras. This period was the only time in the history of Cuba when its political representatives have been elected on a democratic basis. There were considerable and undoubted evils and defects in this period, but the observance of the will of the people by the rulers should not be denied. This brief period of democratic experience was interrupted on March 10, 1952, and the legal continuity of the political system acquired in 1940 was broken. The establishment of Batista's personal rule, his dictatorial methods and the growing political tension in Cuba resulted in armed resistance. The declared purpose of this strife against Batista was to restore the 1940 Constitution—an idea that united and harmonized all opposition groups. Whether it was to stimulate active strife or to promote passive resistance, the 1940 Constitution became the banner under which the citizens of Cuba fought and ultimately forced out Batista.

---

[1] *Cuba and the Rule of Law* (Geneva: International Commission of Jurists, 1962), pp. 78–113. Reprinted by permission.

What were the most noteworthy characteristics of the 1940 Constitution? Drafted with the collaboration of practically all the sectors representing the Cuban political opinion, it is characterized by the rare balance it established between republican, liberal and democratic postulates on one hand and the demands of social justice and economic advancement on the other. It comprises 286 articles, grouped in nineteen titles. It also lays down several transitional provisions, the value of which from the viewpoint of constitutional law is rather dubious.

A. DOGMATIC PART OF THE CONSTITUTION

The dogmatic part of the Constitution, laying down the principles that will govern the life of the Republic and establishing individual rights, constitutional guarantees, the rights of the family and education, the right to work and to own property, and the right of suffrage, comprises 117 articles.

Title I of the 1940 Constitution defines 'The Nation, its Territory and Form of Government.' It states that 'Cuba is an independent and sovereign Nation organized as a unitary and democratic republic, for the enjoyment of political liberty, social justice, individual and collective welfare, and human solidarity' (Article 1). Article 2 stipulates that 'Sovereignty rests in the people and from the people all public powers emanate.' Title II deals with Nationality, the right to citizenship in Cuba; Title III refers to Alienage, general rules about aliens. Title IV is concerned with the definition of Fundamental Rights (Section I). The main articles are: equality before the law (Art. 20); non-retroactive nature of criminal law; prohibition of the confiscation of property (Arts. 21 and 22); prohibition of the death penalty for civilians, except in the case of spying on behalf of the enemy in time of war (Art. 25); the right to be tried (Arts. 27 and 28); the right of habeas corpus (Art. 29); freedom of movement (Art. 30); the right of asylum (Art. 31); inviolability of mails (Art. 32); freedom of thought and speech (Art. 33); inviolability of domicile (Art. 34); freedom of worship (Art. 35); right to petition authorities (Art. 36); freedom to meet and to form associations for lawful purposes (Art. 37).

Section II of Title IV refers to Constitutional Guarantees and states that in cases where the security of the State should require it the above guarantees may be suspended for a period of not more than forty-five days.

Title V deals with the Family and Culture. In Section I, it declares that the family, maternity, and marriage have the protection of the Nation. It is stated that matrimony is the legal basis of the family which rests on absolute equality of rights for husband and wife. The principle of full civil rights of women is admitted. Marriage may be dissolved by agreement between husband and wife or upon petition by either party, in accordance with the law (Art. 43).

With regard to culture (Section II), it is stated that free and compulsory primary education shall be granted (Art. 48). Freedom of teaching is recognized. Special mention is made of the need to eliminate and prevent illiteracy by means of rural schools (Art. 49). In addition, the autonomy of the University of Havana is guaranteed (Art. 53), and private universities are recognized (Art. 54).

Title VI refers to Labor and Property. Section I states that 'labor is an inalienable right of the individual' (Art. 60). The State assumes responsibility for full employment. Foundations are laid for a minimum wage, and the principle of equal pay for equal work is adopted (Art. 62). Payment of wages in promissory notes or in kind is prohibited (Art. 64). Social security for workers is established (Art. 65). A maximum working day of eight hours and a working week of forty-four hours are guaranteed (Art. 66). The right to a paid vacation of one month for each eleven months' work is proclaimed (Art. 67). No difference may be made between married and unmarried women with regard to work (Art. 68). Employers, salaried employees and wage earners are granted the right to form trade unions for the sole purpose of social and economic activity (Art. 69). Obligatory official association is established for the exercise of professions requiring university degrees (Art. 70). The 1940 Constitution recognizes the right of workers to strike and of employers to stop work under conditions stated in law (Art. 71). The system of collective labor contracts, subject to regulation by law, is also introduced (Art. 72). Cubans by birth are entitled to preferential treatment in work, with regard both to the category of employment and to salaries and wages (Art. 73). The constitutional bases for the Ministry of Labor and for the Ministry of Health and Social Assistance are established (Art. 74 and 80). The dismissal of workers without previous notice is forbidden unless it occurs for specified causes (Art. 77). The State assumes responsibility for promoting the building of inexpensive housing for workers (Art. 79). For the case of disputes in relations between management and workers, conciliation committees with equal membership from both parties are set up (Art. 84).

In Section II, the Constitution recognizes the existence and legitimacy of private property 'in its broadest concept as a social function' (Art. 87). The subsoil belongs to the Nation (Art. 88). Article 90 prohibits large land ownership *(Latifundio)*. It is stated that legislation will lay down the maximum land holding permissible for any person or entity, having regard to the particular use and characteristics of such property. The principle is stated that acquisition and possession of land by foreign persons and companies shall be restrictively limited by law which shall provide measures tending to restore the land to Cubans.

The contents and the extent of the above principles in themselves constitute the best definition of the spirit of the 1940 Constitution. They express the desire of the great majority of the Cuban people and thereby constitute their national political objective.

B. ORGANIC PART OF THE CONSTITUTION

As explained above, Cuba was organized as a united and democratic republic (Art. 1). The organs of the State as provided for under the 1940 Constitution were the legislative, executive and judicial branches. Their functions were set up in Titles IX-XIV. The legislative power was exercised by two bodies, the House of Representatives and Senate respectively. Jointly they were called Congress (Art. 119). The executive power was a combination of a presidential and parliamentary system. The President of the Republic was the chief of the Nation and represented it. Article 138 stated: 'The executive power is exercised by the President of the Republic with the cabinet in accordance with what is established in this Constitution.'

The President of the Republic shall be elected, according to the 1940 Constitution, 'by universal, equal, direct, and secret suffrage, on a single day, for a period of four years, in accordance with the procedure to be established by law ' (Art. 140). The 1940 Constitution also organized a cabinet. Article 151 established: 'For the exercise of the executive power, the President of the Republic shall be assisted by a cabinet, composed of the number of members determined by law. One of these ministers shall have the category of Prime Minister, by designation of the President of the Republic, and can act as such with or without portfolio.' Article 164 determined the relations between Congress and the Government: 'The Prime Minister and the cabinet are responsible for their acts of government, before the House and the Senate. These bodies can grant confidence to or withhold it from the Prime Minister, a minister, or the cabinet as a whole, in the manner specified in this Constitution.'

Administratively, the Republic of Cuba was divided into municipalities and provinces. Since this is a classic principle of modern constitutional law, details regarding the separation of powers and the respective functions of the Legislature, the Executive or the Judiciary shall be omitted. Specific reference will be made to the sections of the Constitution amended by the Fundamental Law of, and other subsequent amending legislation issued by, the Castro regime.

The municipality is autonomous, the municipal council being vested with all powers needed to perform freely the local functions of society. The Constitution lays down a detailed system of protection of municipal autonomy (Title XV).

The provincial system is organized at length by Title XVI of the 1940 Constitution. The governor is elected by direct and secret vote and is the official representative of the province. A Council assists the governor.

Title XVII refers to the national treasury, defining the resources and property of the State, providing for procedures regarding the budget, and establishing the Tribunal of Accounts responsible for controlling the income and expenditure of the State, of the provinces and municipalities. It is stated that 'the Nation shall orient the national economy for the benefit of the people, in order to insure to each individual a decorous existence' (Art. 271). The State is responsible for promoting national agriculture and industry by bringing about 'the diversification thereof as sources of public wealth and collective benefit' (Art. 271).

Title XVIII of the 1940 Constitution deals with the state of emergency. Upon request by the Cabinet, the Congress may, by means of extraordinary legislation, declare a state of national emergency. This consists of authorizing the Cabinet to exercise exceptional powers when the external security or domestic order of the Nation is in danger (Art. 281). During the emergency period, a permanent Commission of Congress shall meet to watch over the use of exceptional facilities granted to the Cabinet. At the end of the emergency period the Cabinet shall give an account of the use of the exceptional facilities before the Congress (Arts. 283 and 284).

Finally, Title XIX stipulates the procedure applicable for amending the Constitution. Two methods are laid down. The first, emanating from the initiative of the people, requires that not less than 100,000 electors able to read and write should propose a constitutional amendment to the Congress. Then the Congress must meet in joint session and vote without debate on a bill to call elections of delegates or a popular referendum. The second method is through the initiative of the Congress, the motion requiring the support of not less than one-fourth of the members of the Senate or of the Chamber of Representatives.

A reform to the Constitution may be specific, partial or comprehensive.

III. CHANGES IN THE CONSTITUTIONAL ORDER

On March 10, 1952 a coup d'état took place in Cuba, overthrowing the constituted government, whose term of office was due to end seven months later, on October 10, 1952.

On the same day a proclamation was addressed to the people of Cuba, in which Fulgencio Batista attempted to justify his recourse to violence in overthrowing the Government by 'the absence of guarantees for the life and property of the inhabitants of this country and general political and administrative corruption.' He referred also to 'the imminence of a coup d'état plotted by the retiring President' with the purpose of preventing presidential elections scheduled for June 1, 1952.[2]

A. THE CONSTITUTIONAL ACT OF 1952

The new regime issued on April 4, 1952 a constitutional Act which was to govern the country.[3] An accurate remark about this constitutional Act was made by Fidel Castro in his speech in his own defense before Batista's court following the assault on the Moncada barracks on October 16, 1953:

> The Constitution is understood to be the basic and supreme law of the land—to define the country's political structure, regulate the functioning of government agencies and determine the boundaries of their activities. It must be *sui generis*, stable, enduring —and to a certain extent inflexible. The Statutes (of April 4th) fulfill none of these qualifications. To begin with, they harbor a monstrous, shameless and brazen contradiction in regard to the most vital subject—the integration relation of the republican structure and the principle of national sovereignty.
>
> Article I says: 'Cuba is a sovereign and independent state constituted as a democratic Republic. . . .' Article II says: 'Sovereignty resides in the will of the people, and all powers derive from this source.'
>
> But then comes Batista's Article 118, which says: 'The President will be nominated by the Cabinet'. So it is *not* the people who choose the president, but rather the Cabinet chooses him. And who chooses the Cabinet?
>
> Batista's Article 120, section 13: 'The President will be authorized to nominate and reappoint the members of the Cabinet and to replace them when the occasion arises.' So, after all, who nominates whom? Is this not the old classic of the chicken and the egg that no one has ever been able to solve?[4]

An analysis of Castro's own Fundamental Law, which will follow below, reveals that while setting up an identical system, Castro too was unable to solve the problem of the chicken and the egg.

---

[2] *Gaceta Oficial*, special edition, March 10, 1952.
[3] *Gaceta Oficial*, special edition, April 4, 1952.
[4] Fidel Castro, *History Will Absolve Me*, New York: Liberal Press, Inc., 1959, p. 69.

Another correct criticism by Fidel Castro of the Constitutional Act of 1952 focused on the usurpation of popular sovereignty. He said:

> Batista's statutes contain an article that has not received much attention but which furnishes the key to this situation and is the one from which we shall derive decisive conclusions. I refer specifically to the modifying clause included in Article 257, which reads: 'This constitutional law is open to reform by the Council of Ministers (Cabinet) by a two-thirds quorum vote.' Here mockery reached its maximum. Not only did they exercise sovereignty in order to impose upon the people a Constitution without the people's consent and to install a régime which concentrates all power in its own hands; but also, through Article 257, they assume the most essential attribute of sovereignty—the power to change the basic and supreme Law of the Land. And they have already changed it several times since the 10th of March. Yet, with the greatest gall, they assert in Article II 'that sovereignty resides in the will of the people and that the people are the source of all power. . . .'

Castro concluded this paragraph by saying, 'Such a power recognizes no limits. Under its aegis, any article, any chapter, any clause—even the whole law—can be modified. . . .'

The Constitutional Act of Batista was reformed twice before the return to the 1940 Constitution. In connection with the constitutional legislation of Castro's regime, it will be seen that the Fundamental Law of 1959 authorized its own reform by the Council of Ministers. The constituent power, 'the most essential attribute of sovereignty,' to use Castro's own words, was used by his government five times to alter the 1940 Constitution, once in order to issue the Fundamental Law and sixteen times later to modify it, all in the course of two and a half years.

B. THE SHORT-LIVED RESTORATION OF THE 1940 CONSTITUTION

Article 256 of the Constitutional Act of 1952 states, in accordance with the amendment under Legislative Decree No. 1133 of October 30, 1953,[5] that the 1940 Constitution would be restored as soon as the president-elect took office. The presidential elections were held on November 1, 1954, and Fulgencio Batista was elected. Batista was the only candidate in this election, which was preceded by confused political maneuvers. . . . On February 24, 1955, Batista took the oath and resumed office as President of the Republic. Automatically, in accordance with the above-quoted clause on the reinstatement of the Constitution, the 1940 Constitution came once more into force.

After almost two years of growing and violent opposition to the Batista regime, on December 2, 1956 a contingent of men under the leadership of Fidel Castro landed on the shore of the province of Oriente, an event which marked the beginning of the armed uprising against Batista. On the same day the Executive issued Presidential Decree No. 3230, suspending the constitutional guarantees in the provinces of Oriente, Camaguey, Las Villas and Pinar del Rio. This suspension was ordered for a period of forty-five days. The Congress of the Republic ratified the decree. From that time onward, every forty-five days until December 1958, the Government renewed the suspension of the constitutional guarantees. There were

---

[5] *Gaceta Oficial*, special edition, No. 90, November 6, 1953.

only two brief periods during which the suspension was lifted: one from April 17 to August 1, 1957, the other from April 2 to May 17, 1958, when Special Act No. 2 declared a state of national emergency. This practice of ignoring the Constitution ended on January 1, 1959, when Batista escaped to the Dominican Republc.

IV. CONSTITUTIONAL VARIATIONS UNDER THE CASTRO REGIME

On January 1, 1959, following the abdication of power by Batista and his collaborators, Fidel Castro took over peacefully. The oft-proclaimed standard of the 1940 Constitution once again began to rule the destinies of Cuba. Once more it was to last a very short while before it underwent substantial modifications. On January 13, 1959, the process of constitutional reforms began. From then until 1959 the 1940 Constitution was amended five times. On February 7, 1959 it was directly replaced by the so-called Fundamental Law. The analysis of Castro's constitutional work has therefore to begin with a survey of the five amendments, then consider the Fundamental Law and finally examine the sixteen amendments to the Fundamental Law itself.

A. AMENDMENTS TO THE 1940 CONSTITUTION

On January 5, 1959, in a proclamation to the people of Cuba, President Manuel Urrutia Lleo declared that it was necessary to 'provide for the exercise of the legislative power properly belonging to the Congress of the Republic, in accordance with the 1940 Constitution.' This implicit recognition of the Constitution was confirmed by its subsequent modifications.

a) The first amendment to the 1940 Constitution[6] suspended the application of the constitutional provisions establishing requirements as to minimum age and minimum experience in professional activity for the discharge of public functions.

Article 2 suspended the irremovability of members of the Tribunal of Accounts until such times as it was reorganized.

This apparently harmless reform introduced the use of constituent power by the Council of Ministers. The introductory clauses state:

'The Revolutionary Government, fulfilling its obligations to the people of Cuba, interpreting the people's will and feelings and faced by the urgent necessity to use the constituent power in order to provide force for legislation enabling the acts required of the Revolution to be performed, using the full powers placed in the Revolution, agrees to approve, sanction and proclaim the following constitutional reform.'

This determination to use unrestricted constituent power 'in order to give force to legislation enabling the acts required by the Revolution to be performed' marks the beginning of the end of what might be considered as the restoration of the 1940 Constitution or, in the final analysis, of any written and stable constitutional system. From then on everything was to be 'constitutional.'

---

[6] *Gaceta Oficial*, special edition, No. 4, January 13, 1959.

b) The second amendment to the Constitution was equally of [sic] January 13, 1959.[7] For a period of thirty days, the Council of Ministers suspended the irremovability of the judiciary established in Article 200 of the Constitution, as well as the irremovability of the Public Prosecutor and the Electoral Court.

Article 3 suspends for a period of three months the transitional provisions of the 1940 Constitution referring to irremovability of administrative officials.

c) The constituent power was used by the Council of Ministers on the third occasion to establish retroactivity of criminal law, to introduce the penalty of confiscation of property and to extend the death penalty. This amendment took place on January 14, 1959.[8]

This amendment modified Article 21 of the 1940 Constitution which stated: 'Penal laws shall have retroactive effect when they are favorable to the delinquent. There are excluded from this benefit, in cases where fraud was involved, public officers or employees who commit a crime in the exercise of their office, and those responsible for electoral crimes and crimes against the individual rights guaranteed by this Constitution. Those who commit these crimes shall have applied to them the penalties and qualifications according to the law in force at the time the crime was committed.'

The amendment was to add to the text of the above-quoted section the following paragraph:

> In cases of offenses committed in the service of the dictatorship overthrown on December 31, 1958, those responsible may be tried in accordance with criminal legislation to be issued for that purpose.

The establishment of retroactivity of criminal law in Cuba constitutes in its tragic consequences one of the worst violations of Article 10 of the Universal Declaration of Human Rights proclaimed by the General Assembly of the United Nations on December 10, 1948.

Under the above-cited provisions, death sentences and penalties of confiscation of property were meted out by the revolutionary courts.

Article 2 of the amendment modifies Article 24 of the 1940 Constitution which provided as follows:

> Confiscation of property is prohibited. No one can be deprived of his property except by competent judicial authority and for a justified cause of public utility or social interest, and always after payment of the corresponding indemnity in cash, as fixed by court. Noncompliance with these requisites shall determine the right of the person whose property has been expropriated, to be protected by the courts, and, if the case calls for it, to have his property restored to him.
>
> The existence of a cause of public utility or social interest, and the need for the expropriation, shall be decided by the courts in case of impugnation.

The amendment inserted after the sentence stating 'confiscation of property is prohibited' the following words:

> However, confiscation is authorized in the case of property of natural persons or corporate bodies liable for offenses against the national economy or the public treasury committed during the tyranny which ended on December 31, 1958, as well as in the case of property of the tyrant and his collaborators.

---

[7] *Gaceta Oficial*, special edition, No. 4, January 13, 1959.

[8] *Gaceta Oficial*, special edition, No. 5, January 14, 1959.

The rest of the article retains the original wording.

It will be shown further how the confiscation of property was gradually extended to other fields by means of subsequent amendments, making it increasingly easy for Castro's regime to exercise direct repressive action.

Article 3 of the amending legislation modified Article 25 of the 1940 Constitution, which stated:

> The death penalty cannot be imposed. Exception is made as to members of the armed forces, for crimes of a military character, and as to persons guilty of treason, or of espionage in favor of the enemy at a time of war with a foreign nation.

After the amendment, Article 25 had the following wording:

> The death penalty may not be imposed. An exception shall apply in the case of members of the armed forces, of the repressive bodies under the dictatorship, of the auxiliary groups organized by the dictatorship, of spies guilty of offenses of a military nature or committed for the purpose of the installation or defense of the regime overthrown on December 31, 1958, and the persons guilty of treason or subversion against the established order or of espionage on behalf of the enemy in time of war with a foreign power.

From the constitutional point of view, this amendment, then, meant a substantial alteration of the three principles contained in the fundamental rights safeguarded under the 1940 Constitution: *(a)* retroactivity of criminal law was sanctioned; *(b)* confiscation of property was authorized in the case of specific persons; and *(c)* the death penalty for political causes was introduced. This modification in the dogmatic part of the Constitution enabled the Castro regime to pursue the course of violence and repression.

d) On January 20, 1959, the Council of Ministers once again referred to its constituent power in order to do away with the system established by the 1940 Constitution for provincial and municipal government.[9]

The municipal system was organized by the 1940 Constitution on a basis of autonomy. Title XV contained twenty-three articles setting up detailed provisions on the scope of municipal administration and the safeguards applying thereto.

As to the provincial system, Title XVI of the Constitution regulated the operation of the provinces in nineteen articles. The governor was elected by direct and secret vote and represented the province.

The amendment consisted of providing that

> The provinces and municipalities shall be governed by organs established by the Council of Ministers and the constitutional and legal provisions regulating the provincial and municipal systems shall remain in force notwithstanding. The new authorities governing the provinces and municipalities shall exercise the same functions as those held respectively by governors, councils of mayors, mayors and town councils.

The *Gaceta Oficial* published in its No. 16 of February 2, 1959 the texts of Acts Nos. 36 and 37, referring to the provincial and municipal systems respectively.

Act No. 36 provided that the government of each province should be controlled by an officer appointed by the Ministry of the Interior. Article 2 stated that this officer should have the powers granted to the governor and to provincial councillors under the existing legislation establishing provincial administration.

---

[9] *Gaceta Oficial*, January 20, 1959.

Article 3 stated that 'decisions by the officer may be quashed or suspended by the Minister of the Interior, if he finds them prejudicial to the public interest.'

This provision brought about the administrative centralization of the provincial system. It was strengthened by Act. No. 37, establishing the system of administration for each municipality. It was provided that each municipality shall be controlled by three officers appointed by the Minister of the Interior. These officers came under the Minister of the Interior, who could quash or suspend their decisions 'whenever he finds this necessary on grounds of their conflict with public interests.'

e) The fifth amendment of the 1940 Constitution took place on January 30, 1959.[10]

Article 1 suspends for a period of ninety days, beginning with publication of this amendment in the *Gaceta Oficial*, the application of Articles 27, 29, 196 and 197 of the 1940 Constitution, containing important procedural guarantees of human rights.

This suspension affected the following persons: *(a)* persons subject to the jurisdiction of the revolutionary courts governed by the penal system of the Rebel Army; *(b)* members of the armed forces; *(c)* members of the repressive groups organized by the tyranny overthrown on December 31, 1958; *(d)* members of groups armed privately and organized to defend the tyranny; *(e)* spies; *(f)* persons held by military authorities for purposes of questioning and charged with offenses of a military character; *(g)* persons in the same situation as under *(f)* above charged with offenses aimed at establishing or defending the tyranny; *(h)* persons in the same situation charged with offenses against the national economy or the public treasury.

The articles suspended with regard to persons listed above read:

Article 27. Every arrested person shall be placed at liberty, or delivered to the competent judicial authority, within twenty-four hours following his arrest.

Every arrest shall be set aside or shall be converted into imprisonment, by a judicial decision stating the reasons for it, within seventy-two hours after the arrested person is placed at the disposition of the competent judge. The interested person shall within the same period be notified of the decision rendered.

Persons imprisoned but not yet convicted shall be kept in places distinct and completely separate from those utilized for serving sentences, and those so imprisoned cannot be compelled to do any work whatever or be subjected to the prison regulations for those serving sentences.

The text of the above article makes any comment superfluous. With regard to persons listed, the suspension of the above constitutional guarantee means that they may remain under arrest for an unlimited period of time without being brought before the competent magistrate within seventy-two hours, as established under the 1940 Constitution. This is exactly what has been happening in Cuba ever since Castro came to power.

Article 29. Everyone who is arrested or imprisoned outside of the cases or without the formalities and guarantees specified by the Constitution and the law shall be placed at liberty, on his own request or that of any other person, without the necessity of a

---

[10] *Gaceta Oficial*, special edition, No. 16, February 2, 1959.

power of attorney or the services of a lawyer, by means of summary *habeas corpus* proceedings before the regular courts.

The court cannot decline its jurisdiction, or consider questions of competency in any case or for any reason, or defer its decision, which shall have preference over any other matter.

Presentation, before the court which issued the writ of *habeas corpus*, of every arrested or imprisoned person, regardless of the authority or officer, person, or entity holding him, is absolutely obligatory, and no allegation of due obedience can be made.

All provisions that impede or retard the presentation of the person deprived of liberty, as well as those causing any delay in the *habeas corpus* proceedings, shall be null, and the judicial authority shall so declare on its own initiative.

When the arrested or imprisoned person is not presented before the court hearing the *habeas corpus* proceedings, that court shall order the arrest of the violator, who shall be judged as provided by law.

Judges or justices who refuse to admit an application for a writ of *habeas corpus*, or who do not comply with the other provisions of this Article, shall be removed from their respective offices by the government section of the Supreme Court.

Suspension of *habeas corpus* started off as a transitional step of exceptional character. But as opposition to Castro's regime increased it very soon became permanent and general. This development is discussed in detail in Part Three relating to criminal legislation under the Castro regime.

This deprivation of legal protection for persons listed in Article 1 of the constitutional amending legislation of January 30 was supplemented by the suspension of Article 196 and 197 of the 1940 Constitution. Article 196 stated:

The regular courts shall take cognizance of all suits, causes, or matters, whatever be the jurisdiction to which they pertain, with the sole exception of those resulting from military crimes or acts which occur in the armed service, which are subject to the military jurisdiction.

When these crimes are committed jointly by members of the armed forces and persons who are not members thereof, they shall pertain to the jurisdiction of the regular courts.

The effect of suspending this article was to provide a legitimate basis for the operation of the revolutionary courts, which are exceptional military courts, with regard to the persons listed in the above-quoted Article 1 of this constitutional amendment.

Article 197 followed the line of the preceding article and stated that:

There cannot be created in any case courts, commissions, or bodies of any kind to which special jurisdiction is granted to take cognizance of acts, suits, causes, proceedings, questions, or matters within the jurisdictions attributed to the regular courts.

These last two sections were incompatible with the operation of the revolutionary courts; consequently, the moderate provisions of the 1940 Constitution fell over again under the pressure of extremist tendencies.

Article 2 of this constitutional amendment closes the way to any legal escape for persons listed in Article 1, since it suspends, also for ninety days, the application of Article 174 *(d)* and Article 182 *(a)* of the 1940 Constitution. Their provisions applied in cases where the constitutionality of government enactments were raised by persons listed in Article 1.

Section 174 *(d)* stated:

In addition to the other attributes which this Constitution and the law specify for it, the Supreme Court shall have the following: . . . *(d)* To decide on the constitutionality of laws, decree-laws, decrees, regulations, resolutions, orders, provisions, and other acts of any body, authority, or officer.

Section 182 *(a)* stated:

The court of constitutional and social guarantees is competent to take cognizance of the following matters: *(a)* unconstitutionality appeals against laws, decree-laws, decrees, resolutions, or acts that deny, diminish, restrict, or impair the rights and guarantees specified in this Constitution or that impede the unrestricted functioning of government bodies.

This last action completed the gradual abolition of constitutional guarantees of personal freedom. The right to be brought before a judge within seventy-two hours of arrest was suspended. The right of *habeas corpus* was suspended. The constitutional provision whereby special courts may not be set up was likewise suspended. The operation of the so-called revolutionary courts was thereby legalized. Finally, the right to raise the constitutionality of such measures before the Supreme Court of Justice and the Court of Constitutional and Social Guarantees was suspended.

B. THE FUNDAMENTAL LAW OF THE REPUBLIC OF CUBA OF FEBRUARY 7, 1959

One month and seven days after taking power, Castro's regime, which professed to have fought for the restoration of the 1940 Constitution, proceeded to repeal it. Although the Fundamental Law, like the Constitutional Act of 1952, repeats most of the articles of the 1940 Constitution almost word for word, the emphasis is not on what was retained from the earlier text but on what was altered.

An analysis of the Fundamental Law reveals the two contradictory elements which characterized the Cuban Revolution in its first months. On the one hand, there are the articles and provisions which merely transcribe the 1940 Constitution. On the other hand, there are 'transitional and exceptional' provisions and reforms of the organs of the State that pave the way for the trend that was to prevail only a few months later.

a) The *dogmatic part* of the Fundamental Law is practically identical with the 1940 Constitution, with the sole exception of the articles amended by the Provisional Revolutionary Government since January 1959 (see above).

The innovations introduced by the Fundamental Law which have so serious an effect on the constitutional guarantees of individual liberty and on the very basis of Cuban criminal law do naturally affect the spirit of the law. The provisions which remained in force thus inevitably become of lesser importance. The emphasis throughout is on exceptions. For example, the Fundamental Law emphatically repeats that criminal laws shall have retroactive effect when this is favorable to the offender. However, retroactive criminal legislation is authorized under Article 21 when it is clearly to the disadvantage of the offender. The confiscation of property is rohibited, but it is authorized in the case of persons listed in Article 24. Article 25 states that the death penalty shall not be imposed; however the death penalty is authorized for the military or civilian personnel listed in the same Article. The Fundamental Law established a summary procedure of *habeas corpus* in respect of all persons detained without the formalities and guarantees provided for under the Fundamental Law; however, this provision was first suspended for ninety days and its application was later denied by the Cuban criminal legislation to an ever-increasing number of persons.

Though there is little purpose in repeating the sections which are merely taken over from the 1940 Constitution, it should be pointed out once more that Article 1 of the Fundamental Law restates that:

> Cuba is an independent and sovereign State, organized as a unitary and democratic republic, for the enjoyment of political liberty, social justice, individual and collective welfare, and human solidarity.

Article 2 proclaims that 'sovereignty rests in the people, and from the people all public powers emanate.'

Like the 1940 Constitution, Title I of the Fundamental Law refers to 'The Nation, its Territory and Form of Government,' Title II deals with Nationality, Title III with Alienage, Title IV relates to Fundamental Rights, Title V to the Family and Culture, Title VI to Labor and Property, Title VII to Suffrage and Public offices.

Article 97 of that title (Title VII) states the principle of universal, equal and secret suffrage 'as a right, duty and function' of all Cuban citizens. Article 102 declares that political parties and associations may be freely organized. This is the counterpart to Article 38 of the Fundamental Law stating, 'Every act which prohibits or limits the participation of citizens in the political life of the nation is declared punishable.'

However, the fifth transitory provision to Title IV adds:

> Notwithstanding the provisions of Article 38 of this Fundamental Law, laws may be promulgated that limit or prohibit the participation in the political life of the Nation to those citizens who as a result of their public action and their participation in the electoral process under the Tyranny, have aided the maintenance thereof.

The provisions on rights and guarantees laid down in the 1940 Constitution and reproduced above should be reread in order to contrast the legal and political principles that inspired the 1940 Constitution with the provisions of the Fundamental Law.

b) The *organic part* of the Fundamental Law retains the semblance of division of State functions between the legislative, executive and judicial branches (Title VIII). Nevertheless, an analysis of the organization of the power of the Castro regime shows that there is no such actual division of power and that a supreme and omnipotent power has been set up concentrating the executive, legislative and even constituent functions. This supreme organ is the Council of Ministers.

The Council of Ministers. In accordance with the Fundamental Law, the Council of Ministers discharges the following functions: first, legislative power (Article 119); second, assistance to the President of the Republic in the exercise of his executive functions (Article 135); third, direction, through the Prime Minister, of the general government policy and, in conjunction with the President of the Republic, dispatch of administrative matters (Article 146); fourth, in case of absence, incapacity or death of the President of the Republic, designation by the Council of Ministers of the person who shall succeed him either temporarily or permanently (Article 134); fifth, authority to amend the Fundamental Law either partially or completely (Article 232 and 233).

1) As a legislative organ the Council of Ministers took unto itself the functions assigned to the Legislature under the 1940 Constitution. Title IX of the Fundamental Law refers to the legislative powers of the Council of Ministers, and enumerates in Article 120 the following powers properly vested in the Council of Ministers:

(a) To approve the appointments made by the President of the Republic of the permanent chiefs of diplomatic missions and of other officials whose appointment requires approval according to law.

(b) To authorize Cubans to enter the military service of a foreign country or to accept from another Government an employment or honor that carries with it authority or jurisdiction of its own.

(c) To approve the treaties negotiated by the President of the Republic with other countries.

(d) Any other powers emanating from this Fundamental Law.

The Fundamental Law stipulates in Article 121 that the Council of Ministers as legislative organ has the following powers which may not be delegated:

(a) To draw up the codes and laws of a general character; to determine the system of conducting elections; to enact provisions relative to the national, provincial, and municipal administrations; and to enact all other laws and resolutions that it deems suitable concerning any other matters of public interest or that are necessary to make effective this Fundamental Law.

(b) To levy the taxes and imposts of national character that are necessary for the needs of the State.

(c) To discuss and approve the budget of expenditures and revenues of the State.

(d) To resolve upon the annual reports submitted by the Tribunal of Accounts with respect to the liquidation of the budget, the condition of the public debt, and the national currency.

(e) To borrow money, and also to authorize the granting of a guarantee by the State for credit operations.

(f) To enact pertinent provisions concerning the coinage of money, determining its standard, fineness, value, and denomination, and to enact what it deems necessary concerning the issuance of fiduciary devices and concerning the banking and financial system.

(g) To regulate the system of weights and measures.

(h) To enact provisions for the regimen and development of foreign trade; of agriculture and industry, insurance for labor and old age, maternity, and unemployment.

(i) To regulate communications services, taking care of the system of railroads, highways, canals and ports, and land, air, and sea traffic, creating those which public convenience requires.

(j) To fix the rules and procedures for obtaining naturalization and regulating the status of aliens.

(k) To grant amnesties in accordance with this Fundamental Law.

(l) To fix the strength of the armed forces and determine their organization.

(m) To declare war and approve peace treaties negotiated by the President of the Republic.

(n) To enact all laws directed by this Fundamental Law and those which carry out the principles contained in its precepts.

2) In accordance with Title XI, the Council of Ministers assists the President of the Republic in the exercise of executive power. Article 135 states that the Council of Ministers shall consist of 'the number of members determined by law.' It further states that one of these ministers shall have the function of Prime Minister. The power of appointing him belongs to the President.

Article 140 provides that Ministers 'shall deliberate and decide upon all questions of general interest that are not attributed to other agencies or authorities.'

The Prime Minister and the other Ministers take the oath before the President of the Republic and undertake to fulfill the obligations of their posts and to observe and enforce the Fundamental Law and the other legislation of the Republic.

Article 147 states that the functions of Ministers are

(a) To comply with and enforce the Fundamental Law, the laws, decree-laws, decrees, regulations, and all other resolutions and provisions.

(b) To draft proposed laws, regulations, decrees, and any other resolutions and present them for consideration by the Government.

(c) To countersign, jointly with the Prime Minister, the laws and other documents authorized by the signature of the President of the Republic, except decrees appointing or removing Ministers.

3) Article 146 states, 'It shall be the function of the Prime Minister to direct the general policy of the Government, to dispatch administrative matters with the President of the Republic accompanied by the ministers, upon the matters of the respective departments.'

4) As was already pointed out, the Council of Ministers is empowered to decide who shall succeed the President of the Republic in case of death, incapacity or absence. This appointment may be either temporary or permanent. This power is of major importance if it is borne in mind that the Fundamental Law contains no provisions with regard to procedure for election of the President of the Republic or to his term of office. Article 140 of the 1940 Constitution said in this connection:

> The President of the Republic shall be elected by universal, equal, direct, and secret suffrage, on a single day, for a period of four years, in accordance with the procedure to be established by law.

This Article was not retained in the Fundamental Law. The power to appoint the President was already exercised by the Council of Ministers upon the resignation of the first provisional President of Cuba, Manuel Urrutia Lleo. He presented his resignation to the Council of Ministers, which accepted it on July 17, 1959 and at the same session appointed Osvaldo Dorticos Torrado to succeed him.[11]

---

[11] Declaration of the Secretary to the President and of the Council of Ministers, *Gaceta Oficial*, special edition, No. 9, July 18, 1959, appendix.

From the constitutional point of view, the provisions described above imply that the first provisional President of Cuba in 1959 came to power by spontaneous generation. He then appointed his ministers, and selected one of them as Prime Minister. They made up the Council of Ministers. The provisional President presented his resignation to the Council, which thereupon appointed the new President.

Under Article 129 *(m)*, 'the President of the Republic freely appoints and removes the Ministers of Government and replaces them when proper in accordance with this Fundamental Law.' This [provision] clearly reveals the process of reciprocal appointment practiced by Fidel Castro and his immediate collaborators, at least until December 1, 1961, the date of this Marxist-Leninist proclamation of collective leadership.

In his 'History Will Absolve Me' speech, Castro stated:

> One day eighteen rogues got together. Their plan was to assault the Republic and loot its 350-million-dollar annual budget. Treacherously and surreptitiously they succeeded in their purpose. 'And what do we do next?' they wondered.
>
> One of them said to the rest: 'You name me Prime Minister and I will make you general.' As soon as this was done, he rounded up a clique of twenty men and told them: 'I will make you my Cabinet and you will make me President.'
>
> In this fashion they nominated each other generals, ministers and president and then took over the treasury and government, lock, stock, and barrel.[12]

These were Castro's comments concerning the tyrant Batista, but the similarity with his own procedure could not be more striking.

5) The Council of Ministers has the power to amend the Fundamental Law either partially or in its entirety. This means that at any time the Fundamental Law can be modified in accordance with circumstances that require it. There is no limit whatsoever to this procedure and the Council of Ministers as the constituent organ is thereby empowered to dispose of the lives, freedom and property of citizens or inhabitants of Cuba without any limitations by positive law. Once again, the words should be quoted with which Castro condemned the Constitutional Act for the Republic of Cuba proclaimed by Batista and his Council of Ministers in April 1952.[13]

Article 232 of the Fundamental Law states: 'The Fundamental Law may be amended by the Council of Ministers, by a roll-call vote of two-thirds of its members, ratified by a similar vote at three successive meetings, and with the approval of the President of the Republic.'

The only difference from the text of Article 257 in Batista's Act which Fidel Castro calls a 'maximum of mockery' is that the Fundamental Law requires ratification by a similar vote at three successive meetings of the Council of Ministers. This formal requirement is so obviously superfluous that the *Gaceta Oficial* contains no record of its having ever been applied.

Castro concluded the lengthy section he devoted to this subject by saying:

> Since these changes can be brought about by a vote of two-thirds of the Cabinet and the Cabinet is named by the President, then the right to make and break Cuba

---

[12] Fidel Castro, *op. cit.*, p. 69.

[13] See above, pp. 261–62.

is in the hands of one man. . . . Such a power recognizes no limits. Under its aegis, any article, any chapter, any clause—even the whole law—can be modified. . . . Batista and his cabinet under the provisions of Article 257 can modify all these other articles. They can say that Cuba is no longer to be a Republic but a hereditary monarchy and he, Batista, can anoint himself King. He can dismember the national territory and sell a province to a foreign country, as Napoleon did with Louisiana. He can suspend the right to life itself, and, like Herod, order the decapitation of newborn children. All of these measures would be legal and you, my friends, would have to incarcerate all those who opposed them, just as you now intend to do with me.

This extensive quotation from Castro's defense speech before Batista's court in 1953 illustrates correctly the sad and humiliating situation prevailing in the constitutional practice of Cuba today.

Since other organs established by the Fundamental Law—such as the municipal system, the provincial system, the budget—maintain the letter of the 1940 Constitution, consideration will next be given to the *Additional Transitory Provisions*.

The Additional Transitory Provisions set the tone of Castro's regime and, far from being transitional, have remained in force until now. A brief analysis is sufficient to give an approximate idea of the legal insecurity existing in Cuba.

The first such provision states that

All legal and regulatory criminal, civil and administrative provisions promulgated by the High Command of the Rebel Army during the progress of the armed struggle against the tyranny overthrown on December 31, 1958, shall continue in effect throughout the territory of the Nation until the Government installs popular elections, unless subsequently modified or repealed.

It will be noted that this additional provision incorporates 'all legal provisions' proclaimed by the High Command of the Rebel Army, without specifying any particular item whatsoever or stating any order. What are these legal provisions? Have they been published in the *Gaceta Oficial*? In order to answer these questions the second additional transitory provision was adopted, stating that 'in order that they (the legal provisions of the Rebel Army) shall become widely known, provision is made for publication in the Official Gazette. . . .' No such publication has yet taken place. Many of these laws and regulations passed by the Rebel Army have been incorporated into new laws by the Castro regime. It is pointed out in the chapter on criminal legislation in Cuba that on one occasion there was modified by law a provision of the Rebel Army that had not even been published in the *Gaceta Oficial*. In other words, an Act which did not exist as such was amended. This was the case of Act No. 33 amending Regulation No. 1 of the Rebel Army.[14]

The second observation regarding the first Additional Transitory Provision is that these laws and regulations cited in general terms are to apply in Cuba 'until the Government installs popular elections.' As Prime Minister Fidel Castro proclaimed that there was no need to call elections, the condition stated by the first Additional Transitory Provision may never be fulfilled. Consequently, the provisions quoted will remain in force as long as Castro's regime so desires.

---

[14] *Gaceta Oficial*, special edition, No. 10, January 30, 1959.

The third, fourth and fifth Additional Transitory Provisions incorporated in the text of the Fundamental Law the amendment of the 1940 Constitution made on January 13 and 14, 1959.

V. AMENDMENTS TO THE FUNDAMENTAL LAW

Between February 7, 1959 and August 23, 1961, the Fundamental Law was amended sixteen times.

1. Three months after its proclamation, the first such measure took place, extending the third and fourth Additional Transitory Provisions for a further ninety days. These related to suspension for ninety days of application of Articles 27, 29, 174 and 175 of the Fundamental Law, whose text is identical to that of Articles 27, 29, 196 and 197 of the 1940 Constitution. (See above pages 258, 267).[15]

2. The second amendment of the Fundamental Law came through the adoption of the Agrarian Reform, Act 3 (June 3, 1959). This Act substantially affects the sections of the Fundamental Law referring to property, in particular Articles 24 and 87. The first constitutional modification was in fact contained in the Fundamental Law itself (third Transitory Provision relating to Section I of Title IV of the Fundamental Law), authorizing compensation for expropriation by 'other means of payment, provided they meet the necessary guarantees.' However, Article 31 of the Agrarian Reform Act referred directly to 'agrarian reform bonds.'

Any contradiction there might be between the Agrarian Reform Act and the Fundamental Law was always to be decided in favor of the former, since the final additional provision of this Act states:

> In pursuance of the constituent power vested in the Council of Ministers, this Act is declared an integral part of the Fundamental Law of the Republic, which is thereby amended.

In consequence, this Act has constitutional force and validity.

In a case concerning the constitutional compatibility of the Agrarian Reform Act, the Court of Constitutional and Social Guarantees found that the argument that Articles 24 and 87 of the Fundamental Law were violated should be rejected, since 'it is also the doctrine of this Court that such standards regulating the right of property cannot be invoked with regard to property falling under the special system of the agrarian reform, which is subject to special provisions laid down by that Act which is on an equal footing with the Constitution.'

With regard to Article 52 of this Act, the delegates of agrarian development areas may not be denied the power to occupy property affected by the Act; they are not required to apply to the organs of ordinary jurisdiction, nor are there provisions for prior compensation to the owners.

The Court further found that 'the Agrarian Reform Act, by virtue of the vital importance of its aims, the validity of its provisions and the extent of its coverage, constitutes a dynamic and flexible system which is brought into action through

---

[15] *Gaceta Oficial*, May 6, 1959.

those appointed to implement it, whose function it is to administer its provisions within the broad limits in which it was conceived.'[16]

3.   On June 29, 1959, the Council of Ministers met once more to amend the Fundamental Law. Article 25 was modified to include in what was already a large list of persons liable to the death penalty 'those guilty of counterrevolutionary offenses and those harming the national economy or the public treasury.'[17]

This amendment was followed by Act No. 425 of July 9, 1959, defining 'counter-revolutionary' offenses. . . .

4.   The fourth amendment of the Fundamental Law took place on November 2, 1959, and restored the operation of the revolutionary courts on a constitutional basis.[18] Its object was to make permanent the suspension of constitutional guarantees decreed for a period of ninety days under the amendment of January 30, 1959.

Article 1 modified Article 174 of the Fundamental Law, stating with regard to the item under consideration:

> Notwithstanding, the revolutionary courts whose operation is restored shall be competent to hear cases arising through offenses defined by the law as counter-revolutionary, whether committed by civilians or by members of the armed forces.

This constitutional amendment was followed by Act No. 634, restoring summary trials according to the procedure fixed in the Procedural Act of the Republic of Cuba under Arms of July 28, 1896. . . .

5.   Twenty days later, on November 22, 1959, the Council of Ministers again used its constituent power to amend Article 24 of the Fundamental Law.[19] This time it was to extend the number of persons liable to confiscation of property. In addition to the persons listed in Article 24 of the Fundamental Law, this penalty was extended to (1) persons found guilty of offenses defined by law as counter-revolutionary; (2) persons evading the action of the revolutionary courts by leaving the national territory in any manner whatsoever; and (3) persons who, having left the national territory, perform conspiratorial acts abroad against the Revolutionary Government.

On the next day Act No. 664 was issued, Article 1 of which stated that in all cases of counterrevolutionary offenses the court should order total confiscation of property.

6.   The Fundamental Law was again amended on March 14, 1960.[20] This reform modified Articles 61, 84 and 160 *(e)*, bringing about substantial changes in the constitutional foundations of labor law. Article 61 reads, 'A law shall establish the manner of periodical payment of minimum wages by means of Conciliation Commissions for each branch of employment.'

---

[16] Judgment No. 45 of the Court of Constitutional and Social Guarantees. *Gaceta Oficial*, No. 109, June 7, 1961. These arguments exclude *a priori* any attack on the constitutionality of the Agrarian Reform Act.

[17] *Gaceta Oficial*, No. 122, July 6, 1959.

[18] *Gaceta Oficial*, No. 207, November 2, 1959.

[19] *Gaceta Oficial*, special edition, No. 58, December 22, 1959.

[20] *Gaceta Oficial*, No. 50, March 14, 1960.

The amendment consisted of eliminating the word 'periodical' and the reference to 'Conciliation Commissions.'

Article 84 of the Fundamental Law provided that disputes arising between labor and management should be brought before 'Conciliation Commissions with equal numbers of representatives of employers and workers.' The reform deletes the reference to the Conciliation Commissions and mentions merely 'administrative and judicial authorities.' These were to be set up under special legislation.

Finally, Article 160 *(e)* was amended. This stated that the Court of Constitutional and Social Guarantees had the jurisdiction to hear '. . . *(e)* Juridico-political questions and questions of social legislation which the Fundamental Law and the Law submit to its consideration.' The amendment now reads, ' . . . *(e)* Juridico-political questions and questions of social legislation which the law expressly submits to its consideration subject to the provisions on procedure and appeal laid down in the same law.'

The intention of this amendment is clear: by deleting the reference to the Fundamental Law, it created the legal instrument to limit the competence of the Court of Constitutional and Social Guarantees by means of a simple law.

This amendment was followed by the adoption of Act No. 795 establishing the procedure to be followed with regard to labor disputes.[21]

7. On June 29, 1960 there were deleted Articles 210, 212, 216 and 221 *(b)* and amended Articles 116, 203, 206, 209 and 211 of the Fundamental Law.[22]

Article 116 had set up an autonomous authority known as the Public Offices Tribunal. The function of this Tribunal was to deal with questions relating to public offices. The amendment eliminated the constitutional basis by stipulating that 'questions concerning public offices and public officials, employees and workmen shall be dealt with according to the law.'

Article 203 of the Fundamental Law stated the conditions subject to which property owned by the State might be sold. These conditions were *(a)* consent of the Council of Ministers through special legislation for a reason of social necessity of convenience and subject to agreement by two-thirds of its members; *(b)* that the sale should be by public auction except in two exceptions stated by the law; and *(c)* that the proceeds of such sale should be devoted to creating employment opportunities or providing public welfare. The amendment deleted the whole article and substituted another as follows: 'The law shall determine the conditions for sale or lease of property owned by the State.'

Once again the clear and precise constitutional provisions of the Fundamental Law were replaced by ambiguous reference to future legislation without any constitutional safeguards.

Article 3 of the amending Act dealt with Article 206 of the Fundamental Law, which referred to the annual budget. Article 206 stated:

---

[21] *Gaceta Oficial*, special edition, No. 7, March 15, 1960.
[22] *Gaceta Oficial*, special edition, No. 10, June 29, 1960.

All revenues and expenditures of the State, with the exception of those mentioned below, shall be provided for and fixed in annual budgets and shall be in force only during the year for which they are approved.

The moneys, special funds, or private assets of entities authorized by the Fundamental Law or by law, and destined for social security, public works development of agriculture, and the regulation of industrial livestock, commercial or professional activities, and in general to the development of the national wealth, are excepted from the provisions of the preceding paragraph. These funds or their taxes are to be turned over to the autonomous entity and administered by it, in accordance with the law that created them, subject to audit by the Court of Accounts.

This exemption was now abolished, which meant that such assets shall henceforth all be brought within the national budget.

Article 209 of the Fundamental Law stated that the Executive should prepare and submit the annual budget of the State, but that the Council of Ministers should approve or modify it in its legislative capacity. The article laid down a detailed procedure for the Executive to follow in drafting the budget.

The amendment eliminated all such constitutional guarantees, stating simply that 'the legislation establishing budgets shall cover the drafting, approval, execution, liquidation and auditing of budgets, within the limits stated in this Fundamental Law.'

Article 211 of the Fundamental Law provided that 'allotments specified in the statement of expenses in the budget shall fix the maximum amounts allotted to each service, which may not be increased or transferred by the Executive Power without prior authorization from the Council of Ministers.' The amendment deleted the whole paragraph. This left within the hands of the Executive, without any control whatsoever, the possibility of appropriating funds or granting additional credits in the following cases: *(a)* war or imminent danger of war; *(b)* serious disturbance of public law and order; *(c)* public disasters. The Fundamental Law provided that the Executive should grant extraordinary credits in the cases mentioned above 'when the Council of Ministers is not in session.'[23]

By eliminating the requirement that in order to authorize the Executive to appropriate extraordinary credits the Council of Ministers should not be in session, the amendment of Article 211 makes a rule out of what used to be an exception. And the contingency which the commentator believed could never arise becomes reality. The Executive of Cuba can grant whatever extraordinary credits it considers appropriate. In this respect the legal situation is worse than that set up under Batista's Statutes in 1952.

The sixth Article of this Amending Act deleted Article 221 *(b)*, which granted the Tribunal of Accounts the power 'to take cognizance of orders of the State for

---

[23] This provision gave rise to the following comment by the *Folletos de Divulgacion Legislativa* (Havana, 1959, Vol. II, p. 109), which published the legislation issued under the Castro regime: 'The text of the 1940 Constitution was transcribed in so literal and mechanical a manner into the Fundamental Law of the Revolution that it was not noticed how absurd it was to enable the Executive to grant extraordinary credits when the Council of Ministers is not in session. We do not believe this contingency could ever arise, since it would imply the exercise of personal power completely incompatible with a democratic regime born out of the revolution. By rare coincidence, Article 211 of the Fundamental Law reproduces almost word for word Article 233 of the 1952 Statutes.' The author of this interesting comment refers here to the Batista Constitutional Act, 1952.

advancement of money in order to approve the placement of funds in accordance with the budget, in such a way that the provisions of the Fundamental Law are complied with and that the orders are handled without preference or preterition.' Since this provision meant a limitation of executive power, the regime found no better solution than to eliminate it altogether.

Finally, Article 7 deleted Articles 210, 212 and 216 of the Fundamental Law. Article 210 reproduced the exact wording of Article 259 of the 1940 Constitution and provided, apart from certain formal budgetary requirements, that 'the Law of Bases shall establish, with respect to the foregoing articles, the rules relative to the manner in which the amount or amounts fixed for payments during the budget period shall be prorated among creditors with liquidated claims.'

Article 212 of the Fundamental Law stated the obligation to submit annual State accounts, laying down detailed provisions to be followed by the Ministry of Finance in submitting its annual report to the Tribunal of Accounts. It also required the Executive to submit monthly statements of State income and expenditure to the Council of Ministers. It seems incredible that this article of the Fundamental Law should have been deleted, since such measure enables the Executive to administer public funds without any legal control. Yet this is now a constitutional principle in Cuba, by reason of the constituent power wielded by the Council of Ministers.

Article 216 provided for publication in the *Gaceta Oficial* of the liquidation of any appropriations of government funds for the execution of any public work or service. This liquidation had to be published in full, following approval by the Ministry concerned.

Similarly, the instrument of approval for any public work either totally or partially undertaken with State funds was required to be published in the *Gaceta Oficial*. This elementary requirement of publicity for administration of public funds was also eliminated.

This meant that the administration of the finances of the State remained in the hands of the Executive, without any control and without any legal duty for publication of the use made of such funds.

8.   On July 5, 1960, the Council of Ministers referred once more to its constituent power in order to alter again the disputed Article 24 of the Fundamental Law.[24] At the same time Articles 30 and 147 *(c)* were amended. This time, the amendment to Article 24 was not to extend the number of persons against whom general confiscation of property could be ordered but rather to alter the last paragraph which had not been affected by the preceding reforms. It stated:

> No other natural or juridical person can be deprived of his property except by competent judicial authority and for a justifiable reason of public benefit or social interest and always after payment of appropriate compensation in cash, fixed by court action. Noncompliance with these requirements shall give the person whose property has been expropriated the right to protection by the courts and, if the case so warrants, to restitution of his property.

---

[24] See above pp. 264, 274–75.

The reality of the grounds for public benefit or social interest and the need for expropriation shall be decided by the courts in the event of challenge.

The amendment consisted of substituting the following paragraph for the above:

No other natural or juridical person can be deprived of his property except by competent authority and for a justifiable cause of public utility or social or national interest. The law shall regulate the procedure for expropriation and shall establish legislation and forms of payment and shall determine the competent authority to declare the case to be of public utility or social or national interest and that expropriation is necessary.

The effect of this amendment is perfectly clear. Where the Fundamental Law says 'competent judicial authority,' the amending Act has 'competent authority,' in other words, any authority, not necessarily judicial. Where the Fundamental Law says 'for a justifiable cause' the amendment says 'for a cause.' This means that the cause of expropriation does not call for any justification to a judicial authority. The amendment adds to the causes which may lead to expropriation instances 'of national interest'.

The amending legislation deleted further the provisions under which the expropriated party may appeal to the courts and, if appropriate, have his or its property returned. Similarly, the courts of law no longer have power to decide in case of dispute whether the cause for and necessity of expropriation exist. The constitutional amendment merely states that 'the law shall regulate the procedure for expropriation and shall establish legislation and forms of payment and shall determine the authority competent to declare the case to be of public utility or social or national interest and that expropriation is necessary.' This is one more proof of the way in which the right of property was stripped of all constitutional protection.

9.   On September 28, 1960, a new constitutional change took place.[25] The Council of Ministers amended Article 107 *(a)* of the Fundamental Law, substituting for the words 'ambassadors, extraordinary envoys and ministers plenipotentiary' the words 'members of the foreign service of the Republic in all branches in which it is constituted.' All such persons are thus brought under the provisions relating to 'offices of a political and confidential nature.'

This extension might be considered as a privilege anywhere else than in Cuba. Article 106 of the Fundamental Law states the irremovability of public officials, employees and workmen attached to any authority under the State, and provides that 'their irremovability is guaranteed by this Fundamental Law, with the exception of those holding office of a political or confidential nature.' The amendment means that any member of the foreign service of the Republic may be dismissed without the Fundamental Law protecting him.

10.   On October 14, 1960, the Urban Reform Act was issued.[26] This Act which in itself constitutes an independent organic structure, directly and adversely affects the right of property and the freedom of contract. For instance, Article 2

[25] *Gaceta Oficial*, special edition, No. 21, September 28, 1960.
[26] *Gaceta Oficial*, special edition, No. 23, October 14, 1960.

of the Urban Reform Act states: 'Leasing of urban property is prohibited; any contract which implies the transfer of the use of an urban property is also prohibited.' The Act only permits leases of hotels, motels, pensions and houses or apartments in summer places. In these cases the rent is fixed by the National Institute of Tourist Industries. Article 5 declares null and without legal effect all leases of urban property which existed at the time of publication of the Urban Reform Act. Article 1 and Article 9 order the compulsory selling of urban houses and apartments. The sales price of such property is fixed by its rent value over a period of from five to twenty years. The Urban Reform Act sets up the administrative agencies authorized by the Urban Reform Act to fix prices and resolve all conflicts which may arise from the enactment of this Act (Articles 7, 8, 9, 15, 16, 17, 19, 38, 39, 40, 41, 42 and 43).

Under the provisions of the Urban Reform Act, houses or apartments cannot be sold, transferred or changed to [sic] other persons without the consent of the Council of Urban Reform (Article 29). The Council of Ministers, instead of co-ordinating this Act with the Fundamental Law, which it affects in some of its principles, preferred to raise it to an equal footing with the Constitution. In the same way as for the Agrarian Reform Act, the Urban Reform Act contains an additional provision stating:

> In pursuance of the constituent power vested in the Council of Ministers, this Act is declared an integral part of the Fundamental Law of the Republic, to which it is thereby added. Consequently, this Act shall have constitutional force and validity from the date of its publication in the *Gaceta Oficial*.

Thus the Urban Reform Act came to be included in this study of constitutional legislation in Cuba.

11. On December 20, 1960, nine Articles of the Fundamental Law were amended, and the irremovability of officials of the judiciary once more [was] suspended.[27]

The amendments affect Articles 22, 23, 65, 150, 159, 160 and 186, and alter the heading of the third section of Title XII of the Fundamental Law.

Article 22 of the Fundamental Law read:

> No other laws shall have retroactive effect, unless the law itself so specifies for reasons of public order, of social utility, or national necessity expressly stated in the law, approved by a vote of two-thirds of the total number of members of the Council of Ministers.

This first part of Article 22 was retained, but the passage quoted below, which completed that section in the Fundamental Law, was deleted. Its text suffices to explain the reasons for its suppression:

> If the grounds for retroactivity are impugned as unconstitutional, the Court of Constitutional and Social Guarantees shall decide thereon, and it cannot for technical reasons or any other motive, refrain from doing so.
> In every case, the law itself must establish the degree, manner, and form in which indemnity shall be paid for damages, if any, which the retroactivity causes to rights legitimately acquired in accordance with previous legislation.

---

[27] *Gaceta Oficial*, special edition, No. 26, December 2, 1960.

A law approved in accordance with this Article shall not be valid if it produces effects contrary to the provisions of Article 24 of this Fundamental Law.

It should be recalled here that Article 24 dealing with the confiscation of property was modified in various ways referred to elsewhere in this chapter.

Article 23 of the Fundamental Law stated that

> Obligations of a civil character arising from contracts or other acts or omissions producing them cannot be annulled or altered by either the Legislative power or the Executive power, and consequently laws cannot have retroactive effect with respect to such obligations.

The amendment consisted of inserting the following words after the words 'Executive power':

> . . . unless the law provides otherwise for reasons of public order, social utility or national necessity expressly stated in the law by a two-thirds majority of the Council of Ministers.

This means that the firm declaration in Article 23 that civil obligations arising from contracts or other acts of commission or omission may not be cancelled or altered by the Legislature or by the Executive is deprived of its meaning, since it is made subject to the condition that any Act may 'provide otherwise.'

Article 65 of the Fundamental Law established social security as an inalienable right. The administration of the institutions set up by laws, such as retirement pensions and survivors' grants, was placed under the authority of 'joint bodies elected by management and workers including a representative of the State. . . .' The amendment substituted the simple statement: 'The administration and regulation of the social security system shall be under the authority of the State, and determined by law.'

The final paragraph of Article 65 stated that funds or reserves under the social insurance scheme should not be transferred or disposed of for purposes other than those which led to their establishment. This last part was deleted.

The amendments to Articles 150, 156, 158, 159, 160 (c) and 186 directly affect the organization of judicial power in Cuba. Article 150 of the Fundamental Law established that 'The Supreme Court of Justice is composed of such divisions as the law may provide. One of these divisions shall constitute the Court of Constitutional and Social Guarantees. When it tries constitutional matters it shall be presided over by the President of the Supreme Court and shall not consist of less than fifteen Magistrates.'

The new amendment reads:

> The Supreme Court of Justice is composed of such divisions as the law may provide. One of these divisions will be called Division of Constitutional and Social Guarantees and shall be presided over by the President of the Supreme Court.

The amendment substituted for the Court of Constitutional and Social Guarantees a division of the Supreme Court. Consequently, the amendment deleted the last sentence of Article 150 of the Fundamental Law stating that the number of Justices should be 'no less than fifteen.'

Article 156 of the Fundamental Law determined the competence of the Government Division of the Supreme Court and read as follows: 'The Government Division of the Supreme Court shall determine, classify, and publish any merits that have been awarded to judicial officials in each category, for purposes of promotion.' The amendment consists in adding the following enumeration of the members of the Government Division: 'The Government Division of the Supreme Court shall be composed of the President of the Supreme Court, the President of the Division, the Attorney and one magistrate appointed by each of the Divisions among their members.' Then follows the original text of article 156.

Article 158 was also amended. This article refers to the procedure of appointing judges of the Supreme Court. It establishes the system of appointment by the President of the Republic from a list of three names proposed by an electoral college of nine members. Members of this electoral college were chosen as follows: four by the full bench of the Supreme Court among its members; three by the President of the Republic; two by the Law Faculty of the University of Havana. All of them were required to have the qualifications set out in the Fundamental Law for Magistrates of the Supreme Court. According to Article 158, 'the President of the Supreme Court and the presidents of its divisions shall be appointed by the President of the Republic on proposal of the full bench of the Court. These appointments and those of the Magistrates of the Supreme Court must receive the approval of the Council of Ministers.'

Article 6 of the Amendment Act alters Article 158 of the Fundamental Law as follows:

> The President (of the Supreme Court), the presidents of the divisions, the Magistrates of the Supreme Court and the Presidents of the Audiences shall be appointed by the President of the Republic with the assistance of the Council of Ministers.

Through this reform, the procedure established in the Fundamental Law for the nomination of judges of the Supreme Court was over-simplified and put directly into the hands of the President of the Republic and the Council of Ministers.

Article 7 of the Amendment Act concerns Article 159. This article established that 'appointments, promotions, transfers, exchanges, suspensions, disciplinary action, retirement leaves, and eliminations of positions shall be effected by a special Government Division composed of the President of the Supreme Court and six members thereof, elected annually from among the presidents of divisions and Magistrates of the Court.'

The composition of the Government Division was already modified by Article 5 of the Amendment Act as was shown above when the amendment of Article 156 was explained. Article 7 refers only to the first part of Article 159 and reads as follows: 'Transfers and exchanges of presidents of divisions [and] Magistrates of the Supreme Court shall be effected by the President of the Republic assisted by the Council of Ministers at the proposal of the Government Division.'

Article 7 of the Amendment Act modifies further the already amended Article 160 *(e)* (see above pp. 275–76). Article 160 *(e)* determined: 'The Court of Constitutional and Social Guarantees is competent to take cognizance of the following matters: . . .*(e)* Juridico-political questions and questions of social legislation which the law expressly submits to its consideration subject to the provisions on procedure and appeal laid down in the same law.'

The amended text now reads: 'The Division of Constitutional and Social Guarantees is competent to take cognizance of the following matters: . . . *(e)* Juridico-political questions and questions of social and agrarian legislation. . . .'

Article 9 of the Amendment Act modified Article 186 of the Fundamental Law which provides the procedure to be enforced in cases of criminal liability and causes for removal that may be incurred by the President, presidents of divisions, and Magistrates of the Supreme Court of Justice. The Fundamental Law establishes that 'the Council of Ministers shall be the competent body to take cognizance of denunciations against the said officials,' and establishes the following procedure:

> When a denunciation is received, the Council shall appoint a committee to study it, and the committee shall submit its report to the Council. If by a vote of two-thirds of its members, by secret ballot, the Council finds that there is a basis for the denunciation, appropriate proceedings shall be opened before a tribunal to be known as the Grand Jury, composed of thirteen members designated in the following manner:
> The President of the Supreme Court shall forward to the Council of Ministers a complete list of the members of that body who are not affected by the accusation.
> The Rector of the University of Havana shall send to the Council of Ministers a complete list of the full professors of its Law Faculty.
> The President of the Republic shall send to the Council of Ministers a list of fifty lawyers who have qualifications to be a Magistrate of the Supreme Court, freely designated by him.
> When these lists have been received by the Council of Ministers, it shall proceed to select the members of the Grand Jury by lot:
> Five from the Supreme Court. If there are none, or the number is insufficient, it shall be completed by the same procedure from a list composed of the President and magistrates of the Havana Court of Appeals, submitted to the Council of Ministers by the President of that Court.
> Five members of the Law Faculty of the University of Havana.
> Three members from the list of fifty lawyers.
> This tribunal shall be presided over by the judicial official of highest rank and in lieu thereof by the one having greatest seniority among those composing it.
> When the Grand Jury has been named, the Council of Ministers shall submit the denunciation to it for appropriate action. When a decision has been rendered, the Grand Jury shall dissolve.

This long article was replaced by the following:

> The full bench of the Supreme Court of Justice shall take cognizance of the criminal liability and causes for removal that may be incurred by the President, the Attorney, the presidents of divisions, and the Magistrates of the Supreme Court of Justice.

It may be mentioned here that this clause was made under the pressure of the final and greatest crisis of the judiciary in Cuba, in November 1960. . . . This is the apparent reason for replacing the Grand Jury by the Supreme Court of Justice whose remaining members were ideologically identified with the regime of Fidel Castro.

Article 10 of the Amendment Act refers to the heading of Title XII, Section III, of the Fundamental Law and changing the name of the *Court* of Constitutional and Social Guarantees to *Division*.

Finally, to recognize the Judiciary after the crisis of November 1960, the Amendment Act suspended for forty-five days the irremovability of the functionaries of the Judiciary. The President of the Republic with the assistance of the Council of Ministers may now dismiss any of the members of the Judiciary.

12.   Fifteen days after the above amendment on January 4, 1961, the Council of Ministers used its powers as a constitutent organ for the twelfth time, in order to amend Article 15 of the Fundamental Law and, once again, Article 24[28]

The first Article of this amending legislation modified Article 15, which listed the cases in which Cuban citizenship might be forfeited, namely if the person concerned entered the military service of another nation or performed functions subject to foreign jurisdiction; however, such deprivation of Cuban citizenship 'would not be effective other than through a binding decision by court of law as provided for under the law.' This provision also applied to naturalized Cuban subjects who resided for three consecutive years in their country of birth.

The amendment consisted in eliminating this passage and in completing the article as follows:

> The law may determine offenses and grounds of unworthiness producing loss of citizenship through binding decision by the competent courts.

Article 2 of the Amending Act once again rewrote Article 24 of the Fundamental Law. This time it was to extend further the categories of persons against whom confiscation of property may be ordered. In addition to the wide terms of reference already existing (see pp. 278–79, above), the following passage was included: '. . . as well as those (cases) deemed necessary by the Government in order to prevent acts of sabotage, terrorism or any other counterrevolutionary activities.'

Act No. 923 [was] promulgated on the day of the above amendment, . . . 'authorizing through the Ministry of Finance, action to confiscate property where this is deemed necessary by the Government in order to prevent acts of sabotage, terrorism or any other counterrevolutionary activities.'[29]

13.   On January 19, 1961,[30] Castro's regime amended Article 13 of the Fundamental Law, by adding to the paragraphs listing Cubans by naturalization the following paragraph *(d)*: 'A foreigner citizen of an American nation in which exceptional conditions exist as recognized by express agreement of the Council of Ministers.'

There must be no confusion between this constitutional amendment and the text of Article 12 *(e)* defining 'Cubans by birth.' The latter states that 'foreigners' who fought against Batista's regime in the Rebel Army for not less than two years and who have held the rank of Major for not less than one year 'shall be deemed Cubans by birth.' This article 12 *(e)* was so conceived as to recognize Ernesto

---

[28] *Gaceta Oficial*, special edition, No. 1, January 4, 1961.
[29] *Gaceta Oficial*, No. 1, January 4, 1961.
[30] *Gaceta Oficial*, special edition, No. 3, January 19, 1961.

Guevara, of Argentine origin, as a native Cuban citizen. Hence the text of the paragraph, which is practically a thumbnail biography of the chief beneficiary.

14. In pursuance of its constitutional powers, the Council of Ministers incorporated in the Fundamental Law the provisions of the so-called Nationalization of Education Act.[31] It follows the same pattern as the Agrarian and Urban Reform Acts, in that the text affects vitally the constitutional rights and guarantees under the Fundamental Law. Article 1 declares that the function of education is a public one and that it is the responsibility of the State to deal with this matter through the governmental agencies. Article 2 determines the nationalization of all centers of education existing in Cuba at the time of publication of this act. All buildings, properties, instruments of teaching are transferred to the State. Article 4 authorizes the Minister of Education to decide what indemnity will owners of educational institutions receive and who among them will be eligible for it. To decide this point the Minister of Education will have to consider the attitude of the owners of these educational institutions, or their professors, toward the interests of the Cuban revolution and of the fatherland. Contradictions between these provisions and the rights guaranteed in titles IV, V and VI of the Fundamental Law are covered over by the final provision to the effect that:

> In pursuance of the constituent power of the Council of Ministers this Act is declared to be an integral part of the Fundamental Law of the Republic, whereby it has constitutional force and validity.

15. On August 1, 1961, legislation was adopted amending Articles 69, 70 and 185 of the Fundamental Law.[32] Articles 69 and 70 regulate the setting up of associations, while Article 185 deals with the incompatibility of public functions.

16. On August 23, 1961, the Council of Ministers amended Article 134 of the Fundamental Law.[33] Article 134 gave the Council of Ministers the power to appoint the person to succeed the President of the Republic in case of absence, incapacity or death. The amendment provides that in cases of incapacity or death of the President, the Council of Ministers should retain the power to appoint the successor but in the case of temporary absence of the President from the national territory the Prime Minister should take his place during the interim period.

This constitutional amendment concludes the survey of the sixteen amendments to the Fundamental Law of Cuba enacted as of the end of August 1961.

VI. CONCLUSIONS

1. Between January 1, 1959 and August 23, 1961 (the date of the last document referred to in this part) the Council of Ministers used its constituent power on twenty-two occasions. This means that this power [was] exercised approximately once every forty-six days.

2. The amendments were caused by the desire to overcome obstacles arising for the Castro regime from the Fundamental Law which it had itself promulgated.

[31] *Gaceta Oficial*, No. 109, June 7, 1961.
[32] *Gaceta Oficial*, special edition, August 3, 1961.
[33] *Gaceta Oficial*, August 24, 1961.

3. In most cases the amendments of the Fundamental Law were in answer to circumstantial problems. Reference has been made to a body of legislation adopted immediately after each constitutional reform. In other words, in the face of a concrete situation it was necessary to take specific action. Since such action was prohibited by the Fundamental Law, the first step was to reform that Fundamental Law. Immediately afterward, legislation adapted to the government's needs was issued and based on the precedent amendment of the Fundamental Law.

4. All the amendments to the Fundamental Law reveal a single purpose, namely to concentrate arbitrary power in the hands of the ruling group. On the one hand, every legal guarantee for the freedom, property and life of Cuban citizens is being eliminated. On the other hand, the number of persons covered by 'counter-revolutionary offenses' is being gradually increased. With regard to administration of State funds a similar pattern is followed. Legal means of controlling the administration of public funds are gradually eliminated, while ever greater powers are being granted to the Government. The same course was observed in the case of labor legislation, where joint worker-management councils to decide labor disputes were eliminated and this function vested directly in the State. Education is nationalized, and brought under the exclusive responsibility of the State.

5. The mechanism of the legislative process in Cuba is as follows: the Council of Ministers, acting as the *constituent* organ, amends the Fundamental Law, whereupon the same Council of Ministers, in its *legislative* capacity, issues a law which one of its members will subsequently have the *executive* authority to implement.

6. The five reforms to the 1940 Constitution, the proclamation of the Fundamental Law and the sixteen subsequent amendments bear witness to the chaotic legal situation in Cuba.

7. Examination of the amendments to the Fundamental Law reveals the transformation in Castro's government and the final triumph of the extremist and totalitarian tendencies observed from the earliest days of the Revolutionary Government.

8. Examination of constitutional changes in Cuba shows that many of the changes incorporated in the Constitution or the Fundamental Law since January 1959 violated the Universal Declaration of Human Rights.

9. Careful examination of constitutional legislation in Cuba as well as of actual events shows that the constitutional chaos described above set the stage for the arbitrary despotism now controlling Cuba.

9.3

QUESTIONS AND ANSWERS CONCERNING CONSTITUTIONAL PRINCIPLES APPLIED[1]

WE would like to ask the column 'Aclaraciones' (Explanations) for an answer to the following questions:

By what Constitution do we rule ourselves? Is it the modified Constitution of 1940? Is it the revolutionary laws without constitution, in the hope that the Socialist Constitution will be worked out and approved?

We ask these questions because during the sugarcane harvest we had a discussion on the subject and the question was not quite clear.

SIGNED: Gilberto Sanchez Castro, employee of the Consolidated Enterprise of Nonferrous Metallurgy.

We answer these questions as follows:

We govern ourselves by the Constitution of 1940, which has been amended by a new edition of certain articles, and by laws of a constitutional character which were added to the text of the Constitution and have the same legal strength and category as the Constitution.

If we can say that formally we are governed by the modified Constitution of 1940, we can say that in reality, in fact, the determinant elements in our development are the revolutionary laws which regulate our socialist creation.

The part of the Constitution of 1940 which is actually in effect is relatively small.

This is logical, because the Cuban society has suffered a radical transformation, a complete transformation at its economic base in terms of property relationships.

Although the Constitution of 1940 was progressive at its time, it maintained the principles of the defense of private capitalist property and protected the bourgeois system.

Although the Constitution of 1940 proclaims 'the social function of property,' the 'banishment of large estates,' the obligation to carry out an 'agrarian reform,' and the obligation of the state to guarantee paid employment to all Cubans who lack such employment, its starting point was the maintenance and defense of capitalist private property, the confiscation of which was expressly prohibited in Article 24. An expropriation for reasons of public utility or socialist interest could be ordered only on the basis of a court decision and always with the provision that indemnification is to be paid in advance.

---

[1] Translation of an unsigned article that appeared in the Spanish-language daily, *Hoy* (Havana, April 24, 1964), p. 2.

These principles cannot govern our society of today, a society which develops on the basis of the principles which regulate the transition from capitalism to socialism.

The laws and rules which originate in our state do not intend to preserve or defend bourgeois private property, but rather to eliminate such property in all its forms and to replace it with collective socialist property. These rules and laws are in open conflict with the essence, with the essential starting point of the Constitution of 1940. It is their principles which govern us in reality.

Nor are we governed in fact by the articles of the Constitution which refer to the organization of the state, since together with the political organs of the tyranny we have eliminated its congress, its municipal councils, its mayors, its provincial governments, etc.

Instead of the old apparatus which concealed the pro-imperialist, bourgeois-latifundist dictatorship, we have today various organs—some of which are still at the initial stage in the process of formation—which represent the revolutionary power of workers and peasants:

> JUCEIS [Juntas de Coordinacion, Ejecucion e Inspeccion—Coordination, Execution, and Inspection Boards] and other forms of local power;
>
> Council of Ministers, which has executive, legislative, and constitutional functions;
>
> Far-reaching transformation of the ministers and of their role, and creation of entirely new ministries;
>
> Institutes such as the Institute of Agrarian Reform, Institute of Hydraulic Resources, Institute of Mineral Resources, etc., which have leading functions in the economy;
>
> Central Planning Board, which is an organ of top management and control of the economic activities of the country.

None of these organizations is governed or could be governed by the Constitution of 1940, which is becoming more and more obsolete every day in view of the advancement of the creation of socialism in our country, the progress of the socialist society, the new production relations, the new property relations established in Cuba.

The revolutionary laws govern various aspects of the life of the country, they regulate and stimulate socialist transformation. These laws have a constitutional character, even though they are not a constitution.

At the appropriate moment, our country, acting under the leadership of the United Party of Socialist Revolution and on the basis of the experience obtained during these years, will give itself a constitution which will correspond to the new realities: it will give itself its Socialist Constitution.

9. 4

THE DEVELOPMENT OF
THE SOCIALIST COUNTRIES[1]

'WHAT is the difference between the Democratic German Republic, the People's Republic of China, the Soviet Union, and other socialist countries, and Cuba? I refer to the difference in name to designate the same system, because I understand that the variations in the systems are due to the different characteristics of each country. But I want to know the difference between the countries I have named. What is the system we are building now in Cuba similar to in the socialist bloc?'

This is what Maria Rosa Medina of Cienfuegos, Las Villas, says in her letter. Let us start by saying that the expression 'socialist bloc' should not be used to designate the aggregate of countries that have built or are building socialism. 'Bloc' is used to indicate countries that are joined by some military or other similar treaty.

It is well known that the imperialists follow a policy of blocs, promoting aggressive agreements against socialist nations and the peoples who fight for their liberation, as well as agreements aimed against the interests of rival imperialists.

We are accustomed to call the aggregate of the social[ist] countries the socialist camp. The camp does not exist because there are or are not military treaties between the socialist countries, but because these nations are naturally and spontaneously related by the same socialist regime that is building or that already has built itself on the basis of Marxist-Leninist ideology.

The socialist countries constitute a world community because of the economic, political, ideological, and other kinds of roots and relations that they maintain with each other, these roots and relations being based on the principles of the international proletariat, socialist solidarity, equality among the socialist countries, and mutual respect for the rights of each state.

The existence of this community, its economic and military power, and its development, have created a new balance of power between imperialism and socialism, the advantage being with the latter.

The result of this new balance of power and the existence of the socialist community is that any country in the world, whatever its size, whatever its geographical situation, now has the possibility of carrying forward a revolution, of embarking on the socialist road, of building a socialist society, without being hindered by the imperialists. The Cuban revolution is the historic example of transcendent importance that confirms this thesis.

Cuba is building socialism in the American hemisphere, ninety miles from the imperialism of the United States. And it has all the political and economic possibil-

---

[1] This translation of an unsigned article that appeared in the 'Aclaraciones' column of the Spanish-language daily, *Hoy* (Havana), June 29, 1963, p. 2, is reprinted from *Translations on Cuba* (Washington, D.C.: U.S. Department of Commerce, Office of Technical Services, Joint Publications Research Service), No. 65, August 7, 1963, pp. 3–5.

ities to do so thanks to the existence of the socialist community and to the new relationship between world powers.

The possibility of making a revolution and of building socialism can be converted into reality only to the extent that the people and the revolutionary leaders of each country show their determination to do so, to the extent that the people and their leaders are capable of appreciating those possibilities, of understanding them, of taking advantage of them with audacity and firmness.

As for the questions in the letter, they seem somewhat confused. We understand that what is asked is why have the socialist countries adopted different names to designate their nations? The names are related to two things: first, to the form adopted by the different socialist states, and second, to the peculiarities of the politico-revolutionary process of each country and to the circumstances existing at the moment of triumph of each of them. As we know, the Soviets were a kind of worker and peasant power that arose during the October Revolution. Though the Soviet workers were organized for the first time in 1905, their power was revealed only in 1917. The Soviets gave their country the name of Union of Soviet Socialist Republics.

The process by which East Germany came to adopt socialism determined the name of that country also. When Germany was divided into two states (by the action of the imperialists), the essential question was the following: What road will Germany take, that of neofascist monopolist reaction, or the democratic road to the complete liquidation of Nazism and of the monopolies that were the prime movers of the war? The German Democratic Republic decided on the second course and adopted its present name as an expression of it. In forming the new state, an effort was made to create no obstacles, not even in the name, to the reuniting of the two German states. The imperialists and the revanchists have made such a reunion impossible. The Democratic German Republic, sure of its future, has passed from the state of liquidation of the monopolies to that of the building of socialism, without the need to change its name.

The name of the People's Republic of China comes from the course of the revolutionary struggle, of the way in which it developed, and from conditions existing at the time of victory. Its regime is also socialist; it is now in the process of building socialism.

Cuba has conserved the name of Republic of Cuba also as a result of the way in which the revolutionary process developed. In addition to the differences of name, there are also differences as to the form of the state institutions, the ways in which various economic and social problems are solved, etc. These differences spring from the traditions of each country, from its historic process, from the differences in its socio-economic development, and so on.

Lenin foresaw that there would be differences in the forms of government and the developments toward socialism, saying, 'All countries will arrive at socialism; this is inevitable. But they will not all arrive by the same route. Each will carry with it its own features in one or another form of democracy, in one or another form of the dictatorship of the proletariat, in one or another rhythm in the socialist transformations within the different social strata.'

SECTION 10

MONGOLIA

10. 1

CONSTITUTION OF THE
MONGOLIAN PEOPLE'S REPUBLIC[1]

Adopted by the First Great Huruldan[2]
November 26, 1924

IN conformity with the interests of the broad masses who manifested their will during the revolution of the eleventh year (1921), by which revolution the foreign oppressors were driven out by the revolutionary people, and also in consideration of the death of the hitherto head of state Bogda Khan Damba Hutuktu on the seventeenth day of the fourth month (May 24), the government, elected by the revolutionary people, decided:

1.   To entrust the seal of Bogda Khan to the custody of the government.

2.   To adopt in the country a republican constitution, without president as head of state, which will vest the highest authority in the People's Great Huruldan and in the government elected by it (Great Huruldan).

3.   To commemorate each year the era of the Mongolian People's Republic together with the day of the establishment of the Mongolian State on the sixth day of the sixth month.

4.   To rename the period of government of Olana Ergugdeksen from this date (10 July 1924) of this fourteenth year to such and such successive year of the Mongolian State.

The Great Huruldan of the whole nation, at this its first convention, confirms the above fundamental decrees of the government and the following Fundamental Law [Constitution] of the Mongolian People's Republic.

The above-mentioned Fundamental Law shall be made public by the central and local authorities and posted in all public places.

The Great Huruldan commits to the government the teaching of the fundamental regulations of this constitution in schools and to the military forces.

PROCLAMATION OF RIGHTS OF THE
MONGOLIAN WORKING CLASSES

1.   Mongolia is declared an independent Republic, in which all power belongs to the working classes. The people exercise their supreme power through the Great Huruldan of the entire nation and through the government elected thereby.

---

[1] Translated for this volume from Iwan Jakowlewitsch Korostovetz and Erich Hauer, *Von Cinggis Khan zur Sowjetrepublik* (Berlin and Leipzig: Walter de Gruyter & Co., 1926), pp. 344–51.

[2] Assembly.

2. The fundamental task of the Mongolian Republic is to obliterate the remains of the feudo-theocratic system and to consolidate the new republican order on the principle of a more complete democratization of the government.

3. In order to realize the authority of the people in the government and to confirm this Constitution, the following fundamental principles are established:

(a) In accordance with the Mongolian way of life which is consistent with the principles of the prevailing order, all the land and all the wealth contained therein, with its mineral resources, forests, and waters are property of the people. Private ownership thereon is not permitted; everything is at the disposal of the working people.

(b) All international treaties and commitments regarding loans, entered into by the Mongolian authorities before the revolution of the eleventh year (1921), as imposed by force, are declared null and void.

(c) Inasmuch as debts of private persons and institutions to foreign usurers, contracted at the time of foreign dominion and based on reciprocal guarantees, proved to be a very heavy burden on the economy of the country and on the people, the government decree of the present fourteenth year regarding cancellation of the balance of the above-mentioned debts and the decree of the eleventh year regarding abolition of the reciprocal guarantees system are confirmed.

(d) A uniform economic policy of the country is concentrated in the hands of the state; a state monopoly of foreign trade is introduced as one of the preliminary conditions of liberation of the masses and confirmation of the authority of the people.

NOTE: The state monopoly of foreign trade will be gradually introduced and to such extent as feasible.

(e) In order to protect the absolute power of the working classes and to eliminate every possibility of the restoration of power of foreign or domestic exploiters, the armament of the workmen will be maintained by the organization of a Mongolian revolutionary army, as well as by military training of the young people of the working class.

(f) In order to guarantee freedom of conscience of the working people, the Church is separated from the state, and religion is declared a personal matter.

(g) In order to guarantee the right of free expression of the workers, the Mongolian People's Republic organizes the press; it will be turned over to the working people.

(h) In order to guarantee the real freedom of assembly, meetings, and [street] processions, the state places at the disposal of the working people halls for public meetings with accommodations and equipment.

(i) In order to guarantee the right of forming associations, the Mongolian People's Republic helps the poorer working classes (arats and craftsmen) to unite and form organizations by procuring material and other assistance.

(j) In order to enable the working masses to acquire education, the Mongolian People's Republic takes upon itself to organize a general educational system, free of charge.

(k) The Mongolian People's Republic recognizes the equality of rights of its citizens, irrespective of their nationality, religion or race.

(l) The Mongolian People's Republic, in the interests of the working masses, may deprive individual persons or groups of their rights or limit these rights should they be exercised to the detriment of the interests of the Republic.

(m) Titles and ranks of former ruling princes and taijis [overlords] as well as rights to govern of hutuktus and hubilgane[3] are abolished.

(n) Taking into consideration that the workers of the whole world are striving to overthrow capitalism and to establish communism, the People's Republic of workmen must shape its foreign policy in a way consistent with the interests and fundamental tasks of the oppressed smaller nations and revolutionary workers of the whole world.

NOTE: It is not impossible, however, depending on circumstances, to establish friendly relations with another power; on the other hand, every attempt to undermine the independence of the Mongolian People's Republic should be met with determined resistance.

STRUCTURE OF THE ORGANS OF HIGHEST AUTHORITY

4. The highest authority in the Mongolian People's Republic is vested in the People's Great Huruldan; during the interval between sessions of the Great Huruldan—in the Little Huruldan; and in the interval between sessions of the latter—in the Presidium [of the Little Huruldan] and in the government.

5. The jurisdiction of the highest organs of authority extends to:

(a) Representation of the Republic in international relations, control over diplomatic relations, conclusion of political, commercial and other treaties with [foreign] countries.

(b) Alteration of boundaries of the Mongolian state, declaration of war and of peace, ratification of international treaties.

(c) Conclusion of loans, foreign and domestic, payment of interest on capital and [repayment] of the principal, extension of these loans, as well as granting of external loans.

(d) Supervision of foreign trade and establishment of a system of internal trade.

(e) Planning of the economy of the Republic, granting, revising and abolishing concession and monopoly rights.

(f) Organization of transport and of the post and telegraph system.

---

[3] Reincarnated saints.

(g) Organization of and control over the armed forces of the Mongolian Republic.

(h) Approval of the state budget, establishment of taxes and revenues.

(i) Organization of the money and credit system, issue of paper money and minting of coins.

(j) Establishment of basic principles in the field of agriculture, as well as establishment of boundaries for the aimaks[4] and hosun,[5] promulgation of decrees concerning utilization of mineral resources, forests and other natural resources.

(k) Establishment of principles of judicial organization, judicial procedure, and penal and civil codes of the Republic.

(l) Legislation concerning national education.

(m) General measures in the field of national health protection.

(n) Establishment of a weights and measures system.

(o) Organization of statistics of the Republic.

6.   Approval and revision of the fundamental laws of the Republic rest solely with the Great Huruldan.

THE GREAT HURULDAN

7.   The Great Huruldan is composed of deputies of the aimaks, townspeople, and armed forces. The number of deputies is proportionate to the population of the electoral district. Deputies are elected for the term of one year.

NOTE 1:   If for any reason the aimak meeting does not take place, deputies of the hosun will be delegated.

NOTE 2:   The procedure for the election to the Great Huruldan is governed by regulations set forth in the decree concerning elections to the Great Huruldan.

8.   Regular sessions of the Great Huruldan are convened once a year by the Little Huruldan.

9.   Extraordinary sessions of the Great Huruldan are convened by the Little Huruldan in its official capacity, or upon demand of [not less than] one-third of the members of the Great Huruldan, or upon demand of the voters of the aimaks representing [not less than] one-third of the [entire] population of the Republic.

10.   The Great Huruldan elects the Little Huruldan, which consists of thirty members.

11.   The Little Huruldan is totally responsible to the Great Huruldan.

---

[4] Provinces.   [5] Districts.

THE LITTLE HURULDAN

12. The Little Huruldan promulgates laws, decrees and orders, combines in itself the work of supervision of higher organs of the Republic, determines the field of activities of the Presidium of the Little Huruldan and of the government; gives a general direction concerning the activities of the government, and exercises control over the putting into effect of the Constitution of the Republic and the carrying out of the decrees of the Little Huruldan.

13. The Little Huruldan convenes at least twice a year.

14. Extraordinary sessions of the Little Huruldan are convened by the Presidium of the Little Huruldan on the motion of the government or upon demand of [not less than] one-third of the members of the Little Huruldan.

15. The Little Huruldan elects at its sessions a permanent Presidium consisting of five members; it also elects the government and, when necessary, working committees.

16. The Little Huruldan is accountable to the Great Huruldan for all its activities and keeps the Great Huruldan informed of its general policy and of its particular problems.

17. Members of the Little Huruldan work in the Presidium or in other offices by order of the chairman [sic].

NOTE: A special decree will be issued by the Presidium concerning the rights of the members of the Little Huruldan.

PRESIDIUM OF THE LITTLE HURULDAN

18. The Presidium of the Little Huruldan governs at the sessions of the Little Huruldan.

19. It prepares materials for the sessions of the Little Huruldan.

20. It presents to the plenary sessions of the Little Huruldan bills for approval.

21. It exercises control over the carrying out of the decrees of the Little Huruldan.

22. It exercises control over the government in the spheres of local and other problems; it deals with the respective agencies through the government [Council of Ministers] and in especially important cases it deals directly with the agencies.

23. It makes decisions regarding general and partial amnesty.

24. In the interval between the sessions of the Little Huruldan, the Presidium confirms laws and decrees, returns them to the Council of Ministers for amendment, or suspends them to present them for decision at the following plenum of the Little Huruldan, and appoints and dismisses individual ministers.

25. Any problems and differences of opinion between the ministers or complaints against them are settled by the Presidium of the Little Huruldan.

26. The Presidium of the Little Huruldan is accountable to the Little Huruldan for all its activities.

COUNCIL OF MINISTERS

27. The Council of Ministers is in charge of the management of the affairs of the Mongolian People's Republic. The following are members of the government: the Chairman of the Council of Ministers, the Vice-Chairman, Deputies of the War and Economic Councils, the Commander-in-Chief, the State Controller, the Minister of Domestic Affairs, the Minister of Foreign Affairs, the Minister of Military Affairs, the Minister of Finance, the Minister of Agriculture, the Minister of Justice, and the Minister of Education.

28. The Council of Ministers is in charge of all matters which are mentioned in the decree concerning questions within its province.

THE ECONOMIC COUNCIL

29. In compliance with a special decree an Economic Council of the Mongolian Republic will be appointed in order to coordinate policies regarding economic and agricultural measures.

SELF-GOVERNMENT

30. Local huruldans of aimaks, hosun, somun, baksi, and zenthöfe and towns are established in conformity with laws concerning self-government.

31. For the current work of economic and administrative nature local huruldans elect, for the term of one year, from their own members the executive organs of aimaks, hosun, somun, baksi, zenthöfe and towns authorities.

32. The executive organs are responsible to the local huruldans by which they have been elected.

33. The assemblies of the aimaks, hosun, somun, baksi, zenthöfe and their executive organs are governed by, and their duties are set forth in, the decree concerning local self-government.

THE PASSIVE AND ACTIVE RIGHT TO VOTE

34. The following categories of citizens of the Republic (both men and women) who were eighteen years of age on the day of the election have the right to vote and to be elected in the assemblies (the Great Huruldan, the Little Huruldan and the local ones):

(a) Those who earn their living, as well as persons who are self-employed.

(b) Ciriks[6] of the national revolutionary army.

35. Those who cannot vote or be elected:

---

[6] Soldiers.

(a) Persons who make their living solely by exploiting others in order to derive obvious profit.

(b) Businessmen and usurers who live on the work of others, on interest on capital, or on their private income, etc.

(c) Former princes, hutuktus, and those clergymen who permanently live in monasteries.

(d) Persons who are legally declared insane or feeble-minded.

(e) Persons who have been convicted by the courts for self-seeking or dishonorable offenses.

36.   The conduct of the elections, verification, and so on, are in accordance with a special electoral law.

THE BUDGET LAW

37.   Government revenues and expenditures of the Mongolian Republic are combined in an overall state budget.

38.   The state budget is confirmed by the Great Huruldan or, in exceptional cases, by the Little Huruldan.

39.   The state budget is submitted for approval of the highest organs of authority at least two months before the beginning of the budgetary period.

40.   If the state budget is not approved by the beginning of the budgetary period, the government makes use of the credits in the budget of the preceding year; [this may be done] however only during the first four months of the new fiscal year.

41.   The government cannot make any disbursement whatsoever of state funds unless such expenditure is provided for by the state budget or authorized by a special decree.

42.   Funds provided by the state budget are expended in accordance with their allocation within the limits of the established estimates and only within the stated budget subdivision and will not be used to serve any other needs unless by special decree of the government.

43.   The Great Huruldan and the Little Huruldan determine what kinds of revenues and taxes are designated for the state budget and which are allocated for the needs of local self-governments.

44.   General state needs will be met by general state funds. To satisfy regional needs, organs of local self-governments may assess taxes in accordance with one of the decrees enacted by the central government.

45.   Local organs prepare half-yearly and yearly budgets covering local needs. The budgets of the somun are determined by the hosun committees, the budgets of the hosun administration—by the aimak committees, the budgets of the aimaks committees—by the government in yearly and half-yearly state budgets.

46. Local administration organs will apply to the appropriate ministry for expenditures which have not been provided for in the budgets, as well as for supplementary credits for general state needs, should this be necessary.

THE STATE SEAL, EMBLEM AND FLAG

47. The seal of the Great Huruldan, the government, the ministries and other authorities is quadrangular; in the middle on the obverse of the seal is the word 'Soyunba' and on both sides of the seal the inscription of the name of the authority in question.

48. The state emblem consists of the above-mentioned word 'Soyunba' and a lotus flower depicted below the word.

49. The flag is red with the national emblem in the middle.

50. The Great and the Little Huruldans convene in Ulan Bator Hoto (Urga).

This Constitution was confirmed at 4:17 on the 30th day of the 10th month of the 14th year of the State of Mongolia (November 26, 1924) at the 14th session of the Great Huruldan of the Mongolian Republic.

> The chairman of the Huruldan: (signed) Dscha Damba
> The assistant to the chairman: (signed) Badaraho
> The secretaries: (signed) Geleksengge, Dogarschantsan

NOTE: In the first paragraph of the protocol of the fourteenth session of the Great Huruldan it was decided that 'the number of deputies of the Great Huruldan should not be less than the present membership of ninety-five persons.'

10. 2

CONSTITUTION OF THE MONGOL PEOPLE'S REPUBLIC AS AMENDED[1]

Adopted June 30, 1940, and amended in February 1949 and February 1952; amended also in 1957 and 1959, by the Great People's Khural

CHAPTER I

SOCIAL ORGANIZATION

ARTICLE 1. The Mongol People's Republic is an independent state of workers (Arat cattle raisers, workers, and intelligentsia), who have annihilated the imperialistic and feudal yoke, ensuring a noncapitalistic approach to the development of the country to pave the way to socialism in the future.

ARTICLE 2. The khurals of Arat workers, which came into being as a result of the overthrow of the feudal order and the seizure of political power by the people, the abolition of privilege and arbitrary law, the political and economic subjugation and exploitation, which were inflicted upon the broad masses of the Arats by the feudal overlords (khans, vans, guns, taidzhis, khutukhta, and khubilgans)—constitute the political foundation of the Mongol People's Republic.

ARTICLE 3. In the Mongol People's Republic all power belongs to the urban and rural workers as represented by the workers' khurals.

ARTICLE 4. The development of the Mongol People's Republic along noncapitalistic lines and the transition in the future to socialism are guaranteed by the achievement, in accordance with the state plan, of reforms in the economic, cultural, and social life of the Mongol People's Republic, that is, by assistance on the part of the state, in every way possible, toward the development and improvement of the Arat labor economy, by assistance on the part of the state to the voluntary and collective organizations of Arat workers, by the development of a network of stations for mowing machines drawn by horses, by the development in the country of cattle raising, industry, transport and communications.

The development of the national economy of the Mongol People's Republic is being carried out with the aim of increasing the public wealth, of steadily improving the material welfare and the cultural level of the working people, of consolidating national independence and the defensive capacity of the country.

---

[1] Translation from *Soviet Press Translations*, published by the Far Eastern and Russian Institute, University of Washington (Seattle, Washington), Vol. III, No. 1, 1948, pp. 3–14. Reprinted by permission.

ARTICLE 5.   All the land and its natual resources, the forests, the waters, and all the wealth contained therein, the factories, mills, mines, gold production, the railroad, automobile, water and air transport, means of communication, banks, mowing-machine stations, and state enterprises are state property, that is, they belong to the people as a whole.

Private ownership of the above is forbidden.

ARTICLE 6.   The right of citizens to private ownership of cattle, agricultural implements and other tools of production, raw material, manufactured products, dwelling houses and outhouses, yurts, and household articles, incomes and savings, as well as the right of inheritance of private property, is protected by law.

ARTICLE 7. Public enterprises in the cooperative organizations and the Arat associations, together with their equipment and stock, their manufactured products, as well as their voluntarily socialized property, cattle, agricultural implements, and public buildings, constitute public ownership of these cooperative organizations and Arat associations.

ARTICLE 8.   The land, being state property, that is the common property of the people, is given free of charge to citizens as well as to voluntary associations of workers for use as pastures and agricultural tracts.

ARTICLE 9.   Honest and conscientious labor is the basis of the development of the people's economy, of the consolidation of the defensive capacity, and of the further growth of the well-being of the workers of the Mongol People's Republic, and is the honorable duty of every able-bodied citizen.

CHAPTER II
THE ORGANIZATION OF THE STATE

ARTICLE 10.   The jurisdiction of the Mongol People's Republic, as represented by its highest organs of authority and organs of government, extends to

 (a) Representation of the Mongol People's Republic in international relations; the conclusion and ratification of treaties with other states.

 (b) General control over the domestic policy of the Mongol People's Republic and the development of its economic and cultural life.

 (c) The organization of defense, control over the armed forces, and the preservation of the independence of the Mongol People's Republic.

 (d) The fixing and alteration of state boundaries.

 (e) Questions of war and peace.

 (f) Control over the observance of the Constitution.

 (g) Establishment of the administrative divisions of the Republic.

 (h) The guarantee of the political, economic, and cultural development of the people who inhabit the Mongol People's Republic, in accordance with their national peculiarities.

(i) Foreign trade on the basis of a state monopoly, and control over the system of domestic trade.

(j) Maintenance of the security of the state, of order, and the rights of citizens.

(k) Approval of the national economic plan.

(l) Control over the monetary and credit system, approval of the state budget, and the establishment of taxes, levies, and revenues.

(m) Administration of state banks, industries, agricultural and trade enterprises, and institutions.

(n) Organization of the state, as well as of social insurance.

(o) Conclusion and approval of foreign loans and the issue of domestic loans.

(p) Control of transport and the organs of communications.

(q) Organization of the protection and exploitation of the natural resources of the country and the establishment of regulations for the use of the land. pastures, forests, waters, and the wealth contained therein.

(r) Organization and administration of the development of cattle raising and agriculture.

(s) Establishment of a system of weights and measures.

(t) Organization of the state inventory, accounts, and statistics.

(u) Administration of dwelling houses and communal economy, of construction and public utilities in the cities and of road construction in the country.

(v) Administration of national education and culture, public health, scientific, and physical culture organizations.

(w) Organization of court organs and of the organs of the procurators.

(x) Award of orders, certificates of merit, and the conferring of honorable titles of the Mongol People's Republic.

(y) Legislation concerning citizenship in the Mongol People's Republic.

(z) Issuance of regulations concerning amnesty and pardon.

ARTICLE 11. The Mongol People's Republic consists of aimaks: the Central, Kentei, Eastern, East-Gobi, South-Gobi, Uburkhangai, Arakhangai, Dzapkhyn, Kobdos, Khubsugul, Bulgan, Selengin, Ubsanur, and the city of Ulan Bator.[2]

ARTICLE 12. The aimaks are divided for administrative purposes into somons. The somons, in their turn, are divided into bags. The city of Ulan Bator is divided into khorons, and the khorons into khorins.

---

[2] At the 24th session of the Little Khural of the Mongol People's Republic (February 1941) it was decided: 'In connection with the formation of the Bain-Ulegei and Gobi-Altai aimaks, to revise Article 11 of the Constitution of the Mongol People's Republic as follows:

'ARTICLE 11. The Mongol People's Republic consists of aimaks [regions]: the Central, Kentei, Eastern, East-Gobi, South-Gobi, Uburkhangai, Arakhangai, Gobi-Altai, Dzapkhyn, Kobdos, Bain-Ulegei, Khubsugul, Bulgan, Ubsanur, Selengin, and the city of Ulan Bator.'

CHAPTER III

THE GREAT PEOPLE'S KHURAL

ARTICLE 13. The highest organ of state authority of the Mongol People's Republic is the Great People's Khural.

ARTICLE 14. The Great People's Khural is composed of deputies of the urban workers, the aimaks and the armed forces of the People's Revolutionary Army, elected by the urban and aimak Khurals, on the basis of one deputy for every 1,500 of the population.

ARTICLE 15. The Great People's Khural is convened by the Little Khural once in three years. Special (extraordinary) sessions of the Great People's Khural are convened at the discretion of the Little Khural, or upon the demand of the local organs of authority representing not less than one-third of the entire population.

ARTICLE 16. The exclusive jurisdiction of the Great People's Khural extends to

(a) Approval and revision of the Constitution (Fundamental Law) of the Mongol People's Republic.

(b) Establishment of basic principles and measures in the sphere of foreign and domestic policy.

(c) Election of members of the Little Khural.

ARTICLE 17. In the interval between sessions of the Great People's Khural, the highest authority in the Mongol People's Republic is vested in the Little Khural.

CHAPTER IV

THE LITTLE KHURAL AND THE
PRESIDIUM OF THE LITTLE KHURAL

ARTICLE 18. The Little Khural is elected by the Great Khural for a term of three years, on the basis of one member for every 10,000 of the population.

ARTICLE 19. The jurisdiction of the Little Khural extends to:

(a) Convocation of the Great People's Khural.

(b) Formation of the Council of Ministers, confirmation of the newly organized ministries, or the reorganization of existing ministries and the central organs of the state administration.

(c) Annulment, whenever necessary, of the decisions and orders of the Council of Ministers.

(d) Confirmation of laws and regulations adopted by the Presidium of the Little Khural in the interval between the sessions of the Little Khural.

(e) Examination and confirmation of the state budget.

(f) Receiving the reports of the Presidium of the Little Khural and the Council of Ministers, and the examinations of questions of state, economic, and cultural development.

(g) Election of the Supreme Court of the Mongol People's Republic.

(h) Appointment of the Procurator of the Mongol People's Republic.

ARTICLE 20. Regular sessions of the Little Khural are convened once a year. Special, extraordinary sessions may be convened by the Presidium of the Little Khural at its discretion, as well as upon the demand of not less than one-third of the members of the Little Khural.

ARTICLE 21. For the conduct of current business, the Little Khural elects from its own members a Presidium consisting of seven members: a president, vice president, secretary, and four members.

ARTICLE 22. The Presidium of the Little Khural, in the interval between the sessions of the Little Khural, is the highest organ of state authority.

ARTICLE 23. The Presidium of the Little Khural

(a) Exercises control over the putting into effect of the Constitution of the Mongol People's Republic and the carrying out of the decisions of the Great People's Khural and the Little Khural.

(b) Convenes sessions of the Little Khural.

(c) Passes new laws, subject to the subsequent confirmation of the Little Khural; interprets existing laws.

(d) Suspends, when it deems necessary, the decisions of the Council of Ministers and submits proposals for their annulment for the confirmation of the Little Khural.

(e) Appoints and removes ministers from their duties upon representation of the Chairman of the Council of Ministers, subject to the subsequent confirmation of the Little Khural.

(f) Makes decisions as to amnesty and exercises the right of pardon.

(g) Awards decorations and certificates of merit of the Mongol People's Republic, and confers titles of honor.

(h) Receives the credentials and letters of recall of diplomatic representatives accredited to it by foreign states.

(i) Appoints and recalls plenipotentiary representatives of the Mongol People's Republic to foreign states.

(j) Ratifies treaties and agreements with other states.

(k) In the interval between the sessions of the Little Khural proclaims a state of war, in the event of an armed attack on the Mongol People's Republic, and likewise whenever necessary to fulfill international treaty obligations concerning mutual defense against aggression.

(l) Orders general or partial mobilization.

(m) Exercises control over admission to citizenship in the Mongol People's Republic.

(n) Annuls, when it deems necessary, the decisions of local Khurals.

ARTICLE 24. The Presidium of the Little Khural is accountable to the Little Khural for all its activities.

ARTICLE 25. The President of the Presidium of the Little Khural presides over the Little Khural and exercises jurisdiction over its internal organization.

ARTICLE 26. The members of the Little Khural may not be prosecuted or arrested without the consent of the Little Khural, and—during the interval between sessions of the Little Khural—without the consent of the Presidium of the Little Khural.

CHAPTER V

THE COUNCIL OF MINISTERS OF THE MONGOL PEOPLE'S REPUBLIC

ARTICLE 27. The highest executive and administrative organ of state authority of the Mongol People's Republic is the Council of Ministers of the Mongol People's Republic.

ARTICLE 28. The Council of Ministers of the Mongol People's Republic is responsible for its activities to the Great People's Khural and to the Little Khural, and in the interval between sessions of the latter, to the Presidium of the Little Khural.

ARTICLE 29. The Council of Ministers of the Mongol People's Republic issues decrees and orders on the basis and in pursuance of existing laws, and supervises their execution.

ARTICLE 30. Decrees and orders of the Council of Ministers of the Mongol People's Republic are binding throughout the territory of the Mongol People's Republic.

ARTICLE 31. The Council of Ministers of the Mongol People's Republic

(a) Coordinates and directs the work of the ministers of the Mongol People's Republic and other agencies under its jurisdiction.

(b) Adopts measures for the carrying out of the national economic plan, state and local budgets, taxes, and the credit system.

(c) Exercises general guidance in respect to relations with foreign states.

(d) Exercises general supervision over defense and the building up of the armed forces of the country, and likewise determines the annual contingent of citizens to be called up for military service.

(e) Adopts measures for the maintenance of public order, for the protection of the interests of the state, and for the safeguarding of the personal and property rights of citizens.

(f) Directly supervises and controls the work of the aimak and Ulan Bator autonomous institutions and other local khurals and their presidiums.

(g) Revises and annuls orders, instructions, and decrees of the agencies directly subordinate to the Council of Ministers, the Ministers, and the local organs of authority.

(h) Sets up, when it deems necessary, central administrative agencies under the Council of Ministers of the Mongol People's Republic to deal with economic and cultural development.

(i) Approves patterns and issues the permit for the preparation of the state seal for the use of organs and institutions of the government.

ARTICLE 32. The Council of Ministers of the Mongol People's Republic is appointed by the Little Khural and consists of
The Chairman of the Council of Ministers of the Mongol People's Republic;
The Vice-Chairman of the Council of Ministers of the Mongol People's Republic;
The head of the Commission on State Planning Inventory, and Control;
The Ministers of the Mongol People's Republic.

ARTICLE 33. The following Ministries are functioning in the Mongol People's Republic: War, Foreign Affairs, Cattle Raising and Agriculture, Industry and Construction, Transport, Trade, Finance, Domestic Affairs, Education, Public Health, and Justice.

ARTICLE 34. Directly subordinate to the Council of Ministers of the Mongol People's Republic are *(a)* The Commission on Planning, Inventory, and Control, *(b)* The Commission on Communications, *(c)* The Committee on the Arts, *(d)* The Committee on Science, *(e)* The State Publishing House.[3]

ARTICLE 35. The Ministers and chairmen of the central agencies of the Mongol People's Republic each direct a corresponding branch of state administration and assume full responsibility for it before the Council of Ministers.

ARTICLE 36. The Ministers of the Mongol People's Republic and chairmen of the central government agencies, within the limits of their competence, issue orders and instructions, and also supervise their execution. Orders and instructions are issued on the basis of, and in conformity with, the existing laws, decrees, and orders of the Council of Ministers of the Mongol People's Republic.

---

[3] At the 24th session of the Little Khural of the Mongol People's Republic (February 1941) it was decided: 'In view of the elimination of the Handicrafts Industrial Union from the Ministry of Industry and Construction, and the organization of the Central Council of the Handicrafts Industrial Cooperative, directly subordinate to the Council of Ministers, to revise Article 34 of the Constitution (Fundamental Law) of the Mongol People's Republic, as follows:

'ARTICLE 34. Directly subordinate to the Council of Ministers of the Mongol People's Republic are (a) The Commission on Planning, Inventory, and Control; (b) The Commission on Communications; (c) The Committee on the Arts; (d) The Committee on Science; (e) The State Publishing House; (f) The Central Council of the Handicrafts Industrial Cooperative.'

CHAPTER VI

LOCAL ORGANS OF STATE AUTHORITY

ARTICLE 37. The highest organs of authority in the aimaks, in Ulan Bator, in the somons, khorons, khorins, and bags are the Khurals of Arat workers.

ARTICLE 38. The aimak, somon, and khoron khurals, as well as the Khural of the city of Ulan Bator, are composed of deputies in conformity with the below-mentioned khurals, which are elected on the basis of: in the city of Ulan Bator, one deputy for every 200 of the population; in the aimaks, one deputy for every 400 of the population; in the somons and khorons, one deputy for every 50 of the population. The bag and khorin khurals are composed of all citizens of the bag and khorin who have the right to vote.

ARTICLE 39. Regular sessions of the aimak khurals of workers, and of the khural of workers of the city of Ulan Bator, are convened once in three years. Regular sessions of the somon, khoron, bag, and khorin khurals of workers are convened once a year. Special sessions of the workers' khurals are convened upon the demand of not less than half of all the voters of the aimak, somon, bag, khoron, or khorin, or upon the demand of not less than two-thirds of the members of the elected khural, and also upon the recommendation of the Presidium of the Little Khural of the Mongol People's Republic.

ARTICLE 40. The aimak, somon, khoron, khorin, and bag khurals, as well as the Khural of the city of Ulan Bator, receive the reports of the organs of administration subordinate to them, and conduct elections of local organs of administration and of deputies to the above-mentioned khurals.

ARTICLE 41. In the interval between sessions of the khurals of the aimaks and the city of Ulan Bator, the highest organs of authority in the aimaks and in the city of Ulan Bator are the little khurals, elected by the workers' khurals of the aimaks and the city of Ulan Bator for a term of three years, on the basis of one deputy for every 1,000 of the population.

ARTICLE 42. The khurals of the aimaks and of the city of Ulan Bator are convened twice a year.

ARTICLE 43. For the conduct of current business, the little khurals of the aimaks and the city of Ulan Bator elect from their own members a Presidium of from seven to thirteen persons, consisting of a chairman, vice-chairman, and members.

ARTICLE 44. The executive and administrative organs of the somon, khoron, bag, and khorin khurals of workers elect local, self-governing bodies of from three to thirteen persons, each consisting of a chairman, a secretary, and members of the self-governing body, for a term of one year. The Chairmen of the self-governing bodies direct all the business, convene sessions of the self-governing bodies, and preside over them.

ARTICLE 45. The little khurals of the aimaks and of the city of Ulan Bator and their Presidiums, as well as the somon and khoron self-governing bodies *(a)* Direct cultural-political and economic development in their territories.

(b) Draw up the local budget.

(c) Direct the work of the organs of administration subordinate to them.

(d) Ensure the maintenance of public order, the observance of the laws and protection of the rights of the citizens.

(e) Annul the decrees and orders of the below-mentioned organs of authority, in the event that they are at variance with the laws of the Mongol People's Republic.

ARTICLE 46. The little khurals of the aimaks and of the city of Ulan Bator and their presidiums, the somon, khoron, bag, and khorin self-governing bodies, pass resolutions and give orders, within the limits of the powers vested in them by the laws of the Mongol People's Republic.

ARTICLE 47. The presidiums of the little khurals of the aimaks, and of the city of Ulan Bator, as well as of the somon, khoron, bag, and khorin self-governing bodies, are directly accountable to their khurals, elected by the workers, and to the above-mentioned organs of administration.

ARTICLE 48. The presidiums of the little khurals of the aimaks and of the city of Ulan Bator have the following departments: Cattle Raising and Agriculture, Finance, Public Health, Education, War.

CHAPTER VII

THE COURTS AND THE PROCURATOR'S OFFICE

ARTICLE 49. In the Mongol People's Republic justice is administered by the Supreme Court of the Republic, by the city court of Ulan Bator, by the aimak courts, and by the district people's courts.

ARTICLE 50. Judicial proceedings in all the courts are conducted by permanent judges, with the participation of People's assessors, with the exception of cases specially provided for by law.

ARTICLE 51. The Supreme Court of the Mongol People's Republic is the highest judicial organ. The Supreme Court is charged with the supervision of the judicial activities of all the judicial organs of the Mongol People's Republic. The Supreme Court directly tries the most important cases submitted to its consideration by the Procurator of the Republic, and likewise reviews complaints and protests, in the capacity of a court of appeal and supervision, of cases tried by the courts mentioned below.

ARTICLE 52. The Chairman and members of the Supreme Court and the special courts are elected by the Little Khural of the Mongol People's Republic for a term of four years.

ARTICLE 53. The city, aimak, and district people's courts are elected by the city and aimak little khurals for a term of three years.

ARTICLE 54. Judicial proceedings are conducted in the Mongol language, persons unfamiliar with the language being ensured an opportunity to become fully acquainted with the proceedings through an interpreter, and likewise the right to use their own language in court.

ARTICLE 55. In all courts, cases are heard in public, the accused being guaranteed the right to be defended by counsel. Closed judicial sessions are permitted in cases specially provided for by law.

ARTICLE 56. Judges are independent and are subject only to the law.

ARTICLE 57. Supreme supervisory power over the strict execution of the laws by all the Ministries, central organs and agencies subordinate to them, as well as by public servants and citizens of the Mongol People's Republic, is vested in the Procurator of the Republic.

ARTICLE 58. The Procurator of the Mongol People's Republic is appointed by the Little Khural for a term of five years.

ARTICLE 59. In the cities, somons, and bags, the Procurator's power is exercised by the city and aimak procurators, who are appointed by the Procurator of the Mongol People's Republic for a term of four years.

ARTICLE 60. Local procurators exercise their functions independently of any local organs whatsoever, being subordinate solely to the Procurator of the Republic.

CHAPTER VIII
THE BUDGET OF THE MONGOL PEOPLE'S REPUBLIC

ARTICLE 61. The entire financial policy of the Mongol People's Republic is directed toward the betterment and well-being of the broad masses of workers, the decisive restriction and dislodging of the exploiting elements and, at the same time, the strengthening by every possible means of the authority of the workers, as well as the independence and defensive capacity of the country.

ARTICLE 62. Government revenues and expenditures of the Mongol People's Republic are combined in the overall state budget.

ARTICLE 63. The state budget is prepared by the Ministry of Finance and examined by the Council of Ministers. The budget as approved by the Council of Ministers is subject to the confirmation of the Little Khural of the Mongol People's Republic.

ARTICLE 64. The Little Khural of the Mongol People's Republic elects the budget committee, which reports to the Little Khural its conclusions on the state budget of the Mongol People's Republic.

ARTICLE 65. There can be no disbursement whatsoever of state funds, unless it is provided for by the state budget, or unless such expenditure is authorized by a special decree of the Presidium of the Little Khural or the Council of Ministers. The funds provided for by the state budget are expended solely in accordance with their direct allocation, within the limits of the established estimates.

ARTICLE 66. The Little Khural distributes the revenues among the state and local budgets.

ARTICLE 67. Laws regarding taxes and levies are passed by the Presidium of the Little Khural, subject to the subsequent confirmation of the Little Khural of the Mongol People's Republic. No other organs of authority have any right whatsoever to introduce taxes and levies.

ARTICLE 68. Somon estimates of revenues and expenditures are confirmed by the Little Khural of the aimak or its Presidium, the estimates of the khorons—by the Little Khural of the city of Ulan Bator or its Presidium, aimak estimates and the estimates of the city of Ulan Bator—by the Presidium of the Little Khural of the Mongol People's Republic.

ARTICLE 69. The report on the execution of the state budget, after its examination by the Council of Ministers, is approved by the Little Khural of the Mongol People's Republic.

CHAPTER IX

THE ELECTORAL SYSTEM OF THE
MONGOL PEOPLE'S REPUBLIC

ARTICLE 70. Elections of all organs of authority are conducted in the khural by voice vote. Each member of the khural may nominate candidates for membership in the executive organs and candidates as deputies for the above-mentioned khurals. The name of each candidate nominated must be submitted for discussion in the khural prior to the voting. Each member of the khural is guaranteed the right of free expression *for* or *against* the candidate nominated. Candidates who have received a simple majority of votes are considered elected.

ARTICLE 71. All citizens of the Mongol People's Republic who have reached the age of eighteen have the right to participate in elections and to be elected, irrespective of their sex, nationality, religion, education, nomadic or settled mode of life, and property status, with the exception only of exploiters who hire workers for profit, usurers, former khutukhta, khubilgans, higher Lamas, active dzasak and nadzasak, khans, vans, beili, beisi, guns, and also those who have had slaves and cruelly oppressed their slaves, government officials, who managed the khoshun and shabin institutions, influential shamans, active participants in the White Army and counterrevolutionary uprisings, as well as the insane and persons convicted by the court, whose sentence includes deprivation of electoral rights.

ARTICLE 72. In elections all voters have equal rights; each voter has one vote. Members of the armed forces have the right to participate in the elections on an equal footing with all citizens.

ARTICLE 73. Women have the right to elect and be elected on equal terms with men.

ARTICLE 74. For the conduct of elections, central and local electoral commissions are appointed, which act in accordance with instructions and regulations approved by the Presidium of the Little Khural.

CHAPTER X

FUNDAMENTAL RIGHTS AND DUTIES OF CITIZENS

ARTICLE 75. The Constitution of the Mongol People's Republic consolidates the right won by the people to free use of pastures, in order to promote the greater development of cattle raising, as well as the application by the citizens of their knowledge and labor in all branches of state economic and cultural development.

ARTICLE 76. Citizens of the Mongol People's Republic have the right to rest. This right is ensured by the reduction of the working day to eight hours for employees and workers, the institution of annual vacations with full pay for workers and employees, and the provision of theaters, clubs, sanatoriums, and rest homes for the accommodation of the working people.

ARTICLE 77. Citizens of the Mongol People's Republic have the right to education. This right is ensured by education free of charge, by the development of a network of schools, technical schools, and by instruction in schools in the native language.

ARTICLE 78. Citizens of the Mongol People's Republic and hired laborers have the right to material assistance in old age, as well as in the event of illness and loss of the capacity to work. This right is ensured by a system of social insurance for workers and employees at the expense of the state or employer, free medical service for the working people, and the development of a network of health resorts.

ARTICLE 79. All citizens of the Mongol People's Republic, irrespective of their nationality, have equal rights in all spheres of the state, economic, cultural, and socio-political life of the country. All direct or indirect restrictions on the rights of citizens, the manifestation of imperialistic chauvinism, discrimination, and propaganda on nationalistic grounds, are punishable by law.

ARTICLE 80. Women in the Mongol People's Republic are accorded equal rights with men in all spheres of economic, state, cultural, and socio-political life. The opportunity to exercise these rights is ensured by granting women equal rights with men in regard to work, rest, social insurance, education, state protection of the interests of the mother and child, and by granting hired women pre-maternity leave with full pay.

Interference, in any way whatsoever, with the emancipation and equal rights of women, that is, marrying them off before they have come of age, taking them in marriage, giving or receiving ransom for a bride, polygamy, preventing them from attending school or from participating in the economic, state, cultural, and socio-political life, etc., is punishable by law.

ARTICLE 81. In the Mongol People's Republic religion is separated from the state and the school. Citizens of the Mongol People's Republic have freedom of religion and of antireligious propaganda.

ARTICLE 82. In conformity with the interests of the workers, and in order to develop the organizational initiative and political activity of the working masses, citizens of the Mongol People's Republic are ensured the right to unite in public organizations: trade unions, cooperative associations, youth organizations, sport and defense organizations, cultural, technical, and scientific societies; and the most active and politically-conscious citizens in the ranks of the workers, Arat workers, and intelligentsia, are united in the Mongol People's Revolutionary Party, which is the vanguard of the working people in their struggle to strengthen and develop the country along noncapitalistic lines into a party which is the foremost nucleus of all organizations of workers, both public and state.

ARTICLE 83. Every citizen of the Mongol People's Republic has the right freely to submit written or oral complaints or declarations against the unlawful acts of the organs of authority, or against individual officials in the corresponding organs of the government and administration, up to the very highest. All organs of authority and officials are obligated to examine forthwith the declarations and complaints submitted, and to give the complainant a reply bearing upon the declaration or complaint.

ARTICLE 84. All citizens of the Mongol People's Republic have the right to move about freely, and to select a place of residence.

ARTICLE 85. In conformity with the interests of the workers, and in order to develop and strengthen the state system of the Mongol People's Republic, citizens of the Mongol People's Republic are guaranteed by law (1) freedom of speech, (2) freedom of the press, (3) freedom of assembly and meetings, (4) freedom of street processions and demonstrations.

ARTICLE 86. Citizens of the Mongol People's Republic are guaranteed inviolability of the person. No person may be placed under arrest, except by decision of a court or with the sanction of a procurator.

ARTICLE 87. The inviolability of the homes of citizens and privacy of correspondence are protected by law.

ARTICLE 88. The Mongol People's Republic affords the right of asylum to foreign citizens persecuted for defending the interests of the workers, or for their struggle for national liberation.

ARTICLE 89. It is the duty of every citizen of the Mongol People's Republic to abide by the Constitution (Fundamental Law) of the Mongol People's Republic, to observe the laws, to maintain labor discipline, to promote in every way possible the economic, cultural, and political development of the country, and to perform his public duties honestly.

ARTICLE 90. Compulsory military service is the law of the land. Military service in the Mongol People's Revolutionary Army is obligatory for citizens of the Mongol People's Republic.

ARTICLE 91. The defense of the motherland is the sacred duty of every citizen of the Mongol People's Republic. Treason to the motherland—the violation of the oath of allegiance, desertion to the enemy, impairment of the military power of the state, and espionage—is punishable as the most heinous of crimes.

CHAPTER XI

ARMS, FLAG, CAPITAL

ARTICLE 92. The State Emblem of the Mongol People's Republic consists of a circle, in which is depicted an Arat with a lariat in his hands, galloping on horseback toward the sun.

Inside the circle is depicted a typical Mongol landscape (a forested steppe, a desert, mountains).

Around the edge of the circle, which is framed in green, on two sides there are depicted in small circles the heads of a sheep, a cow, a camel, and a goat. At the base of the circle is the ornament 'Alkha' in one line.

In the center of the upper part of the circle is a five-pointed star. At the base of the circle is a bunch of greens tied with a ribbon, with the inscription 'The Mongol People's Republic.'

ARTICLE 93. The flag of the Mongol People's Republic consists of a red cloth with the State Emblem depicted in the center, and with the inscription on either side 'Mongol People's Republic.'

ARTICLE 94. The capital of the Mongol People's Republic is Ulan Bator.

CHAPTER XII

PROCEDURE FOR AMENDING THE CONSTITUTION OF THE MONGOL PEOPLE'S REPUBLIC

ARTICLE 95. The Constitution of the Mongol People's Republic is amended only by the decision of the Great People's Khural, adopted by not less than a two-thirds majority vote.

THE CONFERRING OF ELECTORAL RIGHTS UPON PERSONS DEPRIVED OF THESE RIGHTS BY ARTICLE 71 OF THE CONSTITUTION OF THE MONGOL PEOPLE'S REPUBLIC

Decree of the Presidium of the Little Khural of the
Mongol People's Republic September 28, 1944

WITH a view to the further expansion of democracy to all citizens of the Mongol People's Republic, and also with the object of strengthening the people's revolutionary order in our country and the development of the political consciousness and activity of the working people, taking into consideration in this connection that:

  (a) Whereas persons deprived of electoral rights do not represent at the present time an organized force in opposition to the people's revolutionary order, and do not constitute a threat to its existence, especially since their number in the Republic is insignificant and amounts only to 0.08 percent of the entire population of the Mongol People's Republic;

  (b) Whereas the overwhelming majority of persons deprived of electoral rights have for more than the past ten years been occupied in useful public work and in reality are workers;

  (c) Whereas, in depriving individual citizens of their electoral rights, local organs of authority have in many cases acted without due consideration, as a result of which the interests of the Arat workers were injured;

Therefore, the Presidium of the Little Khural of the Mongol People's Republic decrees:

  1) That electoral rights be granted to all those citizens of the Mongol People's Republic heretofore deprived of these rights by Article 71 of the Constitution of the Mongol People's Republic, with the exception of the insane, and persons deprived of political rights by the court, which will promote the further strengthening of the people's revolutionary order.

  2) That Article 71 of the Constitution (Fundamental Law) of the Mongol People's Republic be amended to read as follows:

     'ARTICLE 71. All citizens of the Mongol People's Republic, who have reached the age of eighteen, have the right to participate in elections and to be elected, irrespective of their sex, nationality, religion, education, nomadic or settled mode of life, and property status, with the exception of the insane and persons convicted by the court, whose sentence includes deprivation of electoral rights.'

     That the changes indicated be submitted for approval to the regular session of the Little Khural of the Mongol People's Republic and the regular session of the Great People's Khural of the Mongol People's Republic.

10. 3

CONSTITUTION OF THE
MONGOLIAN PEOPLE'S REPUBLIC[1]

Ratified by the Great People's Khural[2]
July 1961

PREAMBLE

THE Great October Socialist Revolution, that laid the foundation of mankind's transition from capitalism to communism, marked a turning point in the history of the age-old struggle of the Mongolian people for liberation that provided them with an opportunity to establish their own independent, sovereign people's democratic state.

The Mongolian People's Republic emerged and became established as a result of the victorious popular revolution of 1921, when the Mongolian people abolished the rule of the imperialist colonialists, overthrew the power of the feudal lords, and put an end to serfdom.

The Mongolian People's Republic grew and gained strength with the fraternal socialist aid of the Soviet Union and as a result of the consolidation of its political and economic independence in a stubborn struggle against imperialist aggression and internal reaction, as a result of overcoming the evil consequences of the former system of national and social oppression, the abolition of the feudal class and the creation of a socialist economy and culture.

In the course of the transition from feudalism to socialism, bypassing the capitalist stage of development in accordance with the teachings of Lenin, radical revolutionary, socio-economic reforms were made in the Mongolian People's Republic, a new socialist economy was built up, socialist production relations became victorious throughout the national economy, and tremendous achievements were recorded in promoting the welfare and culture of the working people.

The Mongolian People's Republic sets itself the aim of completing socialist construction and of building, in the future, communist society.

The Mongolian People's Republic pursues a foreign policy aimed at ensuring durable peace, friendship and cooperation between all peoples on the basis of the principles of peaceful coexistence, consolidating the fraternal relations, close cooperation and mutual assistance that have been established and are developing between the nations of the socialist world, founded on the principle of proletarian internationalism.

---

[1] *Constitution of the Mongolian People's Republic* (Ulan Bator, n.d.). Translation supplied by the Permanent Mission of the Mongolian People's Republic to the United Nations.
[2] Assembly.

The supreme duty of the M.P.R., the most important prerequisite for its prosperity and the strengthening of its independence, is to promote an ever-growing unity and solidarity between the peoples of the socialist countries on the basis of Marxist-Leninist principles.

In the M.P.R., the guiding and directing force of society and of the state is the Mongolian People's Revolutionary Party, which is guided in its activities by the all-conquering theory of Marxism-Leninism.

CHAPTER ONE

THE NATURE AND GENERAL PRINCIPLES OF STATE ORGANIZATION

ARTICLE 1. The M.P.R. is a socialist state of workers, arats (herdsmen and farmers) organized in cooperatives, and working intellectuals, based on the alliance of the working class and the arats.

ARTICLE 2. The Mongolian People's Republic is a socialist state in the form of a People's Democracy.

ARTICLE 3. All power in the Mongolian People's Republic is vested in the working people who implement that power through the state representative bodies—the Khurals of People's Deputies.

ARTICLE 4. The Khurals of People's Deputies are elected by citizens of the M.P.R. on the basis of universal, equal and direct suffrage by secret ballot.

The system of election of deputies to the organs of state power is laid down in a special ordinance.

ARTICLE 5. Democratic centralism is the fundamental principle of the organization and functioning of all state bodies.

The state bodies are duty bound to draw support from the working masses and constantly to strengthen their ties with them.

ARTICLE 6. The Khurals of People's Deputies are responsible and accountable to their electors.

Every deputy is duty bound to give an account of his work and the work of the Khurals of People's Deputies to the electorate and may be recalled by the electorate at any time in the manner provided by the law.

ARTICLE 7. The state bodies are duty bound to abide exactly by the Constitution and the laws of the M.P.R.

CHAPTER TWO

THE FUNDAMENTAL ECONOMIC PRINCIPLES AND FUNCTIONS OF THE STATE

ARTICLE 8. The economic basis of the M.P.R. is the socialist system of economy and the socialist ownership of the means of production established as a result of the long and arduous struggle of the working people and realized as a result of the abolition of the private ownership of the means of production and the elimination of the exploitation of man by man.

ARTICLE 9. Socialist property in the M.P.R. has two forms: state property (belonging to the entire people) and cooperative property (belonging to agricultural associations and other types of cooperatives).

ARTICLE 10. The land, its mineral resources, the forests, the waters and their wealth, state factories, mines, power stations, rail, road, water and air transport, arterial roads, communications, banks, state-owned agricultural enterprises (stage farms, machine and livestock stations, etc.), municipal enterprises, and the bulk of the dwelling houses in the towns and other inhabited centers, raw materials, the materials and produce of state enterprises, state trading establishments and warehouses, scientific and cultural establishments and also the property of all state organizations and institutions are state property, i.e., the property of the whole people.

ARTICLE 11. The socialized enterprises of the agricultural associations and other cooperative organizations with all their machinery and equipment, their produce, buildings, tractors, harvester combines and other farm machines and implements, transport facilities, livestock and other socialized property are the socialist property of those associations and cooperative organizations.

Every family in an agricultural association obtains its main income from personal participation of each of its members in the social production of the association and has a personal subsidiary husbandry of a size fixed by the rules of the association.

ARTICLE 12. The land occupied by an agricultural association is allotted to it for its permanent use free of charge.

ARTICLE 13. The law protects the personal property right of citizens in respect of their incomes and savings from work, their dwelling houses and personally owned small holdings, livestock and articles of domestic use, as well as the right of citizens to inherit personal property. The right to own personal property shall not be used to the detriment of state and public interests.

ARTICLE 14. The socialist state protects and strengthens socialist property, ensures the active participation of members of society in economic and cultural activities, in every way strengthens socialist labor discipline, and organizes the defense of the country against imperialist aggression.

ARTICLE 15. The economic life of the Mongolian People's Republic is determined and directed by a single state economic plan with a view to ensuring the continuous growth and development of the country's productive forces, the uninterrupted expansion of socialist reproduction and a continuous rise in the living standard and cultural level of the working people.

State economic policy serves the purpose of correctly reflecting the requirements of the economic laws of socialism in the national economic plan.

The economic plan of the M.P.R., approved by the Great National Khural, has the force of a law.

The guidance of the economy by the state must invariably be accompanied by the strictest accounting and by control over production and distribution, over the measure of labor and the measure of consumption.

ARTICLE 16.   The finance and credit policy of the M.P.R. has as its purpose the regular growth of the economic might of the country, the development and consolidation of socialist property, the development of socialist culture and the improvement of the living standard of the working people.

The state draws up its annual finance plan in the form of a state budget in accordance with the national economic plan, and it is approved and published as a law.

The basic source of budget revenue is the income from socialist economy and its accumulation.

ARTICLE 17.   The purpose of socialist production in the M.P.R. and its motive force is the creation of a social product of regularly increasing dimensions for the accumulation of a national income necessary for the maximum satisfaction of the constantly growing personal and collective needs of the members of socialist society.

The entire national income of the M.P.R.—after deducting the social fund which is used for the expansion of socialist production, the creation of reserves, the development of education and the health services, the maintenance of the aged and the disabled, as well as for other collective needs of the members of society—is distributed among the members of society in accordance with the quality and quantity of labor expended on the socialist principle 'from each according to his ability, to each according to his work.'

Labor in the M.P.R. is an essential condition and the basis of the realization of extended socialist reproduction; it is the source of the material and spiritual benefits necessary for a constant improvement in the living standard of the working people.

CHAPTER THREE

THE HIGHER ORGANS OF STATE POWER

(A) THE GREAT NATIONAL KHURAL OF THE M.P.R.

ARTICLE 18.   The highest organ of state power in the Mongolian People's Republic is the Great National Khural.

ARTICLE 19.   Legislative power in the M.P.R. is exercised exclusively by the Great National Khural. The right to initiate legislation is vested in the Standing Committees of the Great National Khural of the M.P.R., the Presidium of the Great National Khural of the M.P.R., the Council of Ministers of the M.P.R., the Supreme Court of the M.P.R. and deputies to the Great National Khural of the M.P.R.

ARTICLE 20.   The Great National Khural of the M.P.R. exercises the full measure of state power. In particular, the following come within the jurisdiction of the Great National Khural:

(a) Approval and amendment of the Constitution of the M.P.R.;

(b) The passing of laws;

(c) The determination of basic principles and measures in the sphere of domestic and foreign policy;

(d) Election of the Presidium of the Great National Khural;

(e) The formation of the Council of Ministers;

(f) Approval of newly organized, abolished or reorganized ministries and other central state administrative bodies that go to make up the Council of Ministers of the M.P.R.;

(g) The examination and approval of the economic plan of the Republic;

(h) The examination and approval of the State budget and the report on its realization;

(i) The confirmation of decrees adopted by the Presidium of the Great National Khural in the period between sessions of the Great National Khural and subject to the approval of the Great National Khural;

(j) The promulgation of acts of amnesty;

(k) Decisions on questions of peace and the defense of the socialist fatherland.

ARTICLE 21.   The Great National Khural is elected by citizens of the Mongolian People's Republic, election districts of four thousand people each electing one deputy.

ARTICLE 22.   The Great National Khural is elected for a term of three years.

ARTICLE 23.   The election of new Great National Khural of the M.P.R. is ordered by the Presidium of the Great National Khural two months before the expiration of the term of office of the Great National Khural.

ARTICLE 24.   The newly elected Great National Khural is convened by the Presidium of the outgoing Great National Khural not later than two months after its election.

ARTICLE 25.   Regular sessions of the Great National Khural are convened once a year.

Extraordinary sessions of the Great National Khural may be convened both on the initiative of the Presidium of the Great National Khural and on the demand of not less than one-third of the deputies.

ARTICLE 26.   The Great National Khural elects a Chairman of the Great National Khural and four Vice-Chairmen. The Chairman presides at sessions of the Great National Khural and takes charge of all proceedings.

ARTICLE 27.   The Great National Khural elects a Credentials Committee which verifies the credentials of the deputies to the Great National Khural of the M.P.R.

ARTICLE 28.   The Great National Khural appoints the Budget and Economy, Legislative Proposals, Foreign Affairs and Nationalities Standing Committees.

In case of necessity the Great National Kural appoints Select Committees. The terms of reference of the committees are laid down by the Great National Khural.

Article 29. The Great National Khural elects the Presidium of the Great National Khural consisting of Chairman, Vice-Chairman, Secretary and six members.

Article 30. A law is considered adopted if passed by the Great National Khural of the M.P.R. by a simple majority vote.

Laws and decisions adopted by the Great National Khural are published over the signatures of the Chairman and Secretary of the Presidium of the Great National Khural of the M.P.R. with the exception of the decision on the election of the Presidum of the Great National Khural, which is published over the signature of the Chairman of the Great National Khural.

Article 31. Deputies to the Great National Khural and also deputies to the local Khurals have the right to question members of the relevant state administrative bodies on matters coming within their jurisdiction. The administrative body concerned must reply to the deputy's question.

Article 32. A deputy to the Great National Khural of the M.P.R. may not be arrested or prosecuted without the sanction of the Great National Khural, or, in the period between sessions, without the sanction of its Presidium.

(B) THE PRESIDIUM OF THE GREAT NATIONAL KHURAL

Article 33. The Presidium of the Great National Khural is the highest organ of state power in the period between sessions of the Great National Khural.

Article 34. The Presidium of the Great National Khural

(a) Exercises control over the application of the Constitution and the laws of the M.P.R.;

(b) Orders elections to the Great National Khural;

(c) Convenes sessions of the Great National Khural;

(d) Interprets operative laws;

(e) Issues decrees;

(f) Conducts nationwide polls (referendums);

(g) Annuls decisions and orders of the Council of Ministers of the M.P.R. and of local Khurals of People's Deputies in the event of their being unconstitutional;

(h) Establishes new and abolishes or reorganizes existing ministries and other central state administrative bodies, such acts to be subsequently submitted to the Great National Khural for approval;

(i) Appoints ministers and other members of the government or releases them from posts held on the representation of the Chairman of the Council of Ministers, such acts to be subsequently submitted to the Great National Khural for approval;

(j) Exercises the right of pardon;

(k) Institutes orders and medals and also honorary, military and other titles of the M.P.R.;

(l) Awards orders and medals of the M.P.R. and confers honorary titles on the representation of the Council of Ministers of the M.P.R.;

(m) Appoints and recalls diplomatic representatives of the M.P.R. to foreign states;

(n) Receives the letters of credence and recall of diplomatic representatives accredited to the Presidium by foreign states;

(o) Authorizes the Council of Ministers to conclude treaties and agreements with other states;

(p) Ratifies and denounces treaties and agreements with other states;

(q) In the intervals between sessions of the Great National Khural proclaims a state of war in the event of an armed attack on the M.P.R. and also when necessary to fulfill international treaty obligations in respect of mutual defense against aggression;

(r) Orders general or partial mobilization;

(s) Grants citizenship of the M.P.R. and permits the relinquishing of citizenship of the M.P.R.;

(t) On the representation of the Council of Ministers approves the formation or abolition of aimaks[3] (towns), somons[4] (horons),[5] and also their administrative subdivisions.

ARTICLE 35. On the expiration of the term of office of the Great National Khural of the M.P.R., its Presidium remains in office until the newly elected Great National Khural forms a new Presidium of the Great National Khural of the M.P.R.

ARTICLE 36. The Presidium of the Great National Khural is responsible and accountable to the Great National Khural for all its activities.

CHAPTER FOUR

THE HIGHER AND CENTRAL ORGANS
OF STATE ADMINISTRATION

ARTICLE 37. The highest executive body of state administration in the Mongolian People's Republic is the Council of Ministers of the M.P.R.

ARTICLE 38. The Council of Ministers of the M.P.R. is responsible and accountable for its activities to the Great National Khural, or, in the intervals between sessions of the latter, to the Presidium of the Great National Khural.

ARTICLE 39. The Council of Ministers of the M.P.R. issues decisions and orders on the basis and in pursuance of operative laws and verifies their execution.

---

[3] Aimak—region.   [4] Somon—rural district.   [5] Horon—urban district.

ARTICLE 40.   The decisions and orders of the Council of Ministers of the M.P.R. are binding throughout the territory of the M.P.R.

ARTICLE 41.   The Council of Ministers of the Mongolian People's Republic:

(a) Coordinates and directs the work of the ministries of the M.P.R. and other bodies under its jurisdiction in their guidance of state, economic and cultural organization;

(b) Guides the planning of the economy, adopts measures for the implementation of the state economic plan and of the state and local budgets, and exercises control over the implementation of finance and credit policy;

(c) Exercises general direction in the sphere of relations with foreign states, exercises a monopoly in foreign trade;

(d) Exercises general guidance in matters concerning the defense of the country and the organization of the armed forces and determines the contingent of citizens to be conscripted for military service;

(e) Adopts measures to protect the interests of the state and to protect and consolidate socialist property as the economic basis of the socialist state;

(f) Adopts measures to ensure public order and protect the personal and property rights of citizens;

(g) Directs and guides the work of the aimak (town) executive boards of the khurals of people's deputies;

(h) In case of necessity amends or annuls the orders and instructions of the ministries and of the bodies under the jurisdiction of the Council of Ministers, and other administrative bodies;

(i) When necessary sets up departments and institutions under the Council of Ministers to deal with economic and cultural development;

(j) Approves designs and grants permits for the manufacture of state seals for the organs and institutions of state power.

ARTICLE 42.   The Council of Ministers of the M.P.R. is set up by the Great National Khural and consists of the chairman of the Council of Ministers of the M.P.R., the vice-chairmen of the Council of Ministers of the M.P.R., and the ministers of the M.P.R.

ARTICLE 43.   The ministries and departments are the central organs of state administration of the M.P.R.

The ministers and heads of departments of the M.P.R. guide the relevant branches of state administration and are fully responsible for their condition and their activities to the Council of Ministers. The work of the Ministries and departments of the M.P.R. is organized on the principle of personal managerial responsibility and the collective discussion of questions, and is based on a rising level of individual responsibility on the part of every worker.

ARTICLE 44.   The competency of each ministry and department is defined in the relevant regulations which are drawn up on the basis of the laws and are approved by the Council of Ministers of the M.P.R.

ARTICLE 45.   The ministers of the M.P.R. and the heads of departments issue orders and instructions within the limits of their competency and verify their execution. These orders and instructions are issued on the basis and in pursuance of the operative laws of the M.P.R. and the orders and decisions of the Council of Ministers of the Mongolian People's Republic.

CHAPTER FIVE

THE LOCAL ORGANS OF STATE POWER AND STATE ADMINISTRATION

ARTICLE 46.   The territory of the M.P.R. is divided administratively [into] aimaks and towns. The aimaks are subdivided into somons and the towns into horons.

ARTICLE 47.   The organs of state power in the aimaks, towns, somons and horons are the khurals of people's deputies elected by the population of the respective territorial divisions for a term of two years.

ARTICLE 48.   The number of members of the local khurals of people's deputies per administrative unit is laid down by the Presidium of the Great National Khural of the M.P.R.

ARTICLE 49.   Regular sessions of aimak and town khurals of people's deputies are convened by their executive boards at least twice a year.

Sessions of somon and horon khurals of people's deputies are convened by their executive boards at least three times a year.

Extraordinary sessions of local khurals of people's deputies are convened on the demand of at least one-half of the deputies to the khural or on the initiative of the executive board and also on the orders of the Presidium of the Great National Khural.

The executive board of a local khural informs the population in good time of the date and agenda of a regular session of the khural and ensures the participation of the people's representatives in the work of the session of the khural.

ARTICLE 50.   A chairman and a secretary are elected for each session to conduct meetings of the aimak, town, somon and horon khurals of people's deputies.

ARTICLE 51.   Aimak and town khurals of people's deputies elect, as their administrative organs, executive boards of seven to eleven deputies consisting of a chairman, vice-chairmen, an executive secretary and members.

ARTICLE 52.   The administrative bodies of the somon and horon khurals of people's deputies are the executive boards of five to nine deputies which they elect and which consist of a chairman, a vice-chairman, a secretary and members.

ARTICLE 53.   The chairman of the executive board guides the work of the board, convenes its sittings and presides at them.

ARTICLE 54. On the expiration of the term of office of the aimak, town, somon and horon khurals of people's deputies, their executive boards remain in office until new executive bodies are again elected by the khurals.

ARTICLE 55. The aimak, town, somon and horon khurals of people's deputies and their executive boards

(a) Guide economic, cultural and political development within their own territorial subdivisions;

(b) Guide and control the work of economic and cooperative organizations;

(c) Approve the economic plan and the local budget and adopt measures for their implementation;

(d) Guide the activities of the administrative bodies under their jurisdiction;

(e) Ensure adherence to the rules of the socialist way of life, the protection of the rights and interests of state enterprises and institutions, agricultural associations and other cooperative organizations and also the protection of the rights of citizens;

(f) Ensure the exact observance of the laws and also the strict implementation of the decisions of higher organs;

(g) Ensure the extensive participation of the working people in all fields of state, economic and cultural development.

ARTICLE 56. The local khurals of people's deputies adopt decisions within the limits of the powers vested in them by the law.

ARTICLE 57. The higher khurals of people's deputies have the right to amend or annul decisions of lower khurals of people's deputies as well as the decisions and orders of their executive boards.

ARTICLE 58. The higher executive boards of khurals of people's deputies have the right to amend or annul the decisions and orders of lower executive boards to suspend decisions of lower khurals of people's deputies.

ARTICLE 59. The executive board of a local khural of people's deputies is directly accountable to the khural of people's deputies that elected it and to the executive body of a higher khural of people's deputies.

ARTICLE 60. The local khural of people's deputies set up standing committees for various branches of their activities and ensure the participation of an extensive group of working people in their activities.

ARTICLE 61. For the guidance of the different branches of work, aimak and town executive boards set up divisions and departments. In their work they are under the jurisdiction of the executive board of the aimak or town khural of people's deputies as well as the relevant ministry or department of the M.P.R.

ARTICLE 62. Deputies of local khurals of the M.P.R. may not be arrested or arraigned without the sanction of the khural concerned, or, between sessions of the Khural, without the sanction of the executive body concerned.

CHAPTER SIX

THE COURTS AND THE PROCURATOR'S OFFICE

(A) THE COURTS

ARTICLE 63. Justice in the M.P.R. is administered in accordance with the laws by the Supreme Court of the Republic, aimak and town courts, special courts of the M.P.R. and district people's courts.

ARTICLE 64. All courts cases are tried by permanent judges sitting with people's assessors, except in cases for which special provision is made in the law.

ARTICLE 65. The Supreme Court of the M.P.R. is the highest judicial body. The Supreme Court is charged with the guidance of all judicial bodies in the M.P.R. and also with supervision over their judicial activities.

ARTICLE 66. The Supreme Court of the M.P.R. is elected by the Great National Khural for a term of three years. The Supreme Court is responsible and accountable to the Great National Khural of the M.P.R. and its Presidium.

ARTICLE 67. Town and aimak courts are elected by the town and aimak khurals of people's deputies for a term of two years.

ARTICLE 68. People's courts are elected by the citizens of the aimak, somon, town or horon concerned, on the basis of universal, direct and equal suffrage by secret ballot for a term of two years. Citizens who have reached the age of twenty-three and have never been convicted by a court may be elected judges and people's assessors.

ARTICLE 69. Court proceedings are conducted in the Mongolian language, persons not knowing that language being guaranteed the right to acquaint themselves fully with the material of the case through an interpreter and likewise the right to use their own language in court.

ARTICLE 70. All cases are heard in public and the accused are guaranteed the right to defense. Courts may sit *in camera* in cases for which special provision is made in the law.

ARTICLE 71. Judges are independent in their examination of cases and are subject only to the law.

(B) THE PROCURATOR'S OFFICE

ARTICLE 72. Supreme supervisory power over the strict observance of the law by all ministries and other central administrative bodies and the institutions and organizations subordinated to them, by local state bodies and also all public and cooperative organizations as well as people in office and citizens of the M.P.R. is vested in the Procurator of the Republic.

ARTICLE 73. The Procurator of the M.P.R. is appointed by the Great National Khural for a term of three years. The Procurator of the M.P.R. is responsible and accountable to the Great National Khural of the M.P.R. and its Presidium.

ARTICLE 74. Procuratorial supervision in the localities is vested in the aimak, town and district procurators appointed by the Procurator of the M.P.R. for a term of three years.

ARTICLE 75. Local procurators are subordinated only to the procurator of higher rank in fulfilling their functions.

CHAPTER SEVEN

THE FUNDAMENTAL RIGHTS AND LIBERTIES
OF CITIZENS AND HOW THEY ARE ENSURED

ARTICLE 76. Citizens of the M.P.R. enjoy equal rights irrespective of sex, race and nationality, religion or social origin and position.

ARTICLE 77. Citizens of the M.P.R. have the right to work and to payment for their work in accordance with its quantity and quality.

This right is ensured by the advantages accruing from the socialist system of economy established in the M.P.R., which gives each citizen every opportunity to employ his knowledge and labor in any branch of economy and culture without let or hindrance, and to receive a guaranteed recompense according to the labor expended.

ARTICLE 78. Citizens of the M.P.R. have the right to leisure.

This right is ensured by the establishment of a maximum working day of eight hours, the reduction of the working day in a number of special trades, the establishment of a weekly rest-day and annual paid holidays for factory, office and professional workers, and by placing at the disposal of the working people sanatoria, holiday homes, theaters, clubs and other welfare institutions.

The policy of the M.P.R. is directed toward increasing, in the future, as the productive forces of the country develop, the amount of free time available to the working people by reducing working time and by improving social services and placing them more within the reach of the working people so that they may employ their leisure for recuperation, for their physical and spiritual growth and for the improvement of their knowledge.

ARTICLE 79. Citizens of the M.P.R. have the right to maintenance in old age, in cases of disability, in cases of sickness or the loss of the breadwinner.

This right is ensured by the granting of assistance through the social insurance system, by state pensions, through the special funds of cooperative organizations, as well as by extending the network of medical institutions and holiday resorts, by free medical attention for the people and by the development of the labor protection system.

ARTICLE 80. Citizens of the M.P.R. have the right to education. This right is ensured by free tuition, the extension of the network of schools providing general education, special secondary schools and higher educational establishments, and by a system for improving trade qualifications as well as by a state system of scholarship grants for students of special secondary schools and higher educational establishments.

ARTICLE 81. Citizens of the M.P.R. have the right to participate freely in the administration of the state and society and also in guiding the economic life of the country both directly and through their representative bodies. This right is ensured by granting all citizens the real possibility to play an extensive part in all spheres of the country's political, economic and cultural life, in particular, to participate in elections, referendums, the organization of various democratic societies, etc.

All citizens of the M.P.R. who have attained the age of eighteen, with the exception of those found insane, are granted the right to vote in elections and be elected to all organs of state power.

ARTICLE 82. Citizens of the M.P.R. have the right to unite in public organizations: trade unions, cooperative associations, youth, sports and other organizations, cultural and scientific societies, and also societies for strengthening world peace, etc.

The more active and politically conscious citizens in the ranks of the working class, members of cooperatives and working intelligentsia unite in the Mongolian People's Revolutionary Party, which is the vanguard and leader of all state and other mass organizations of the working people.

ARTICLE 83. Citizens of the M.P.R., irrespective of their nationality, have equal rights in all spheres of economic, cultural, social and political life of the country.

Any direct or indirect restriction of the rights of citizens on account of their nationality or race and the advocacy of the ideas of chauvinism or nationalism are forbidden by law. The M.P.R. ensures representatives of all nationalities living on the territory of the Republic the opportunity to develop their national culture and to receive tuition and conduct business in their own native language.

The M.P.R. grants the right of asylum to foreign citizens persecuted for their defense of the interests of the working people, for participation in the national liberation movement, for their activities to strengthen peace, and for scientific activities.

ARTICLE 84. Women in the M.P.R. are accorded the same rights as men in all spheres of economic, state, cultural, social and political life. The realization of these rights is ensured by according women the same conditions of work, leisure, social insurance and education as men, by the state promotion of mother-and-child welfare, state assistance for mothers of large families, leave of absence from work before and after confinement with full pay, and the extension of the network of maternity hospitals, nurseries and kindergartens.

The infringement, in any form whatsoever, of the equal rights of men and women is forbidden by law.

ARTICLE 85. Every citizen of the Mongolian People's Republic has the right freely to apply to any of the organs of state power and administration and to submit written or verbal complaints and statements concerning illegal acts on the part of state organs or people in office, and concerning facts of bureaucratic treatment or red tape. State organs and people in office shall, without delay, examine all complaints and statements submitted, adopt measures to check infringements of law and order and give an answer on the substance of the statement or complaint.

ARTICLE 86. Religion in the M.P.R. is separated from the state and from the school. Citizens of the M.P.R. are granted freedom of worship and freedom of antireligious propaganda.

ARTICLE 87. In conformity with the interests of the working people, and in order to strengthen the socialist state system of the M.P.R., its citizens are guaranteed by law (1) freedom of speech; (2) freedom of the press; (3) freedom of assembly, including mass meetings; (4) freedom to hold demonstrations and processions.

These freedoms are ensured by placing at the disposal of the working people and their organizations the material requisites for their realization.

ARTICLE 88. Citizens of the Mongolian People's Republic are guaranteed inviolability of the person and the home and privacy of correspondence. No person may be arrested except by order of the court or with the sanction of the Procurator.

CHAPTER EIGHT

THE FUNDAMENTAL DUTIES OF CITIZENS

ARTICLE 89. It is the duty of every citizen of the M.P.R.

(a) To devote all his efforts and knowledge to the building of socialism, remembering that honest and conscientious work for the benefit of society is the source of the increasing wealth and might of the socialist state and of the rising living standard of the working people;

(b) To conform strictly to the Constitution of the M.P.R., abide strictly by the laws and observe labor discipline, adhere to the rules of the socialist way of life and struggle actively against all antisocial manifestations;

(c) To ensure the unity of personal and social interests and give priority to social and state interests;

(d) To safeguard, as something dear to him, the sacred and inviolable foundation of the socialist system—public socialist property—and to do everything to strengthen and increase it;

(e) To regard the strengthening of international friendship between peoples as an objective necessity, and in his own practical work to promote greater friendship and solidarity among the working people, to promote the unity and solidarity of the peoples of the socialist camp, headed by the Soviet Union, to struggle with determination against all manifestations detrimental to this sacred friendship and unity;

(f) To train the rising generation in a spirit of industry, discipline and organization, collectivism and respect for the interests of society, in a spirit of a communist attitude to labor and to socialist property, a spirit of unbounded loyalty to the socialist fatherland, the ideas of communism and the principles of proletarian internationalism, in a spirit of respect for all working people regardless of their nationality;

(g) To promote the consolidation of the people's democratic system, to preserve strictly state secrets and to be vigilant in respect of enemies;

(h) To defend the socialist fatherland from its enemies as something sacred. Military service in the People's Army of the M.P.R. is the honorable duty of citizens of the M.P.R.;

(i) To fulfill impeccably all his civic duties and to demand the same of other citizens.

CHAPTER NINE

ARMS, FLAG, CAPITAL

ARTICLE 90. The coat of arms of the Mongolian People's Republic reflects the nature of the state and the idea of the friendship of the peoples, and displays the national and economic peculiarities of the country.

The arms of the M.P.R. consists of a circle surrounded by ears of corn whose stalks are affixed to a cogwheel. They are bound with a red and blue ribbon bearing the inscription 'M.P.R.'

In the center of the circle is the symbolic figure of a working man on horseback galloping toward the sun—communism—against the background of a landscape typical for the M.P.R. (mountains, forest-steppe and desert).

Where the ears of corn meet in the upper part of the circle, a red five-pointed star is depicted, with the 'Soyombo' sign inscribed on it.

ARTICLE 91. The state flag of the Mongolian People's Republic is based on the state coat of arms and consists of red and blue stripes, the center stripe of the flag, one-third in width, being sky-blue and the two other stripes flanking it being red.

In the upper part of the red stripe nearest the flagpole is a golden five-pointed star below which is the 'Soyombo' symbol, also golden in color. The ratio of width to length is 1:2.

ARTICLE 92. The capital of the Mongolian People's Republic is the city of Ulan Bator.

CHAPTER TEN

PROCEDURE FOR AMENDING AND ABOLISHING THE CONSTITUTION OF THE M.P.R.

ARTICLE 93. The Constitution of the Mongolian People's Republic may be amended only by a decision of the Great National Khural adopted by a majority of no less than two-thirds.

ARTICLE 94. As various functions of the state gradually cease to exist under communism they will be effaced from the Constitution.

The Constitution of the M.P.R. will be abolished when there is no longer any need for the existence of the state, the chief instrument for the building of socialism and communism, when the state will be replaced by a communist association of working people.

POLAND

11. 1

CONSTITUTION OF THE POLISH
PEOPLE'S REPUBLIC AS AMENDED[1]

Adopted by the Legislative Seym on July 22, 1952

Amended September 25, 1954; December 13, 1957;

December 22, 1960; May 15, 1961; and December 19, 1963

THE Polish People's Republic is a republic of the working people.

The Polish People's Republic carries on the most glorious progressive traditions of the Polish nation and gives effect to the liberation ideals of the working masses.

The Polish working people under the leadership of the heroic working class, and on the basis of the alliance between workers and peasants, fought for many decades for the liberation from national enslavement imposed upon the nation by the Prussian, Austrian and Russian conquerors and colonizers, just as they fought for the abolition of exploitation by the Polish capitalists and landlords.

During the occupation, the Polish nation waged an unflinching heroic fight against the murderous Nazi invasion. The historic victory of the Union of Soviet Socialist Republics over fascism liberated Polish soil, enabled the Polish working people to take power into their own hands, and established conditions for the national rebirth of Poland within new and just frontiers. The Regained territories were restored to Poland forever.

By carrying out the memorable directives of the Manifesto of the Polish Committee of National Liberation of July 22, 1944, and by developing the principles laid down in the programme of that Manifesto, people's power—thanks to the selfless and creative efforts of the Polish working people in the fight against the bitter resistance of the remnants of the old capitalist-landlord system—has accomplished great social changes. As a result of revolutionary struggles and transformations, the power of the capitalists and landlords has been overthrown, a State

---

[1] *Constitution of the Polish People's Republic* (Warsaw: Polonia Publishing House, 1964).

TRANSLATOR'S NOTE: This text of the Constitution (published in the *Journal of Laws*, No. 33, item 232) includes the changes introduced by

1) The law of September 25, 1954, regarding a change in the Constitution of the Polish People's Republic (*Journal of Laws*, No. 43, item 190);

2) The law of December 13, 1957, regarding a change in the Constitution of the Polish People's Republic (*Journal of Laws*, No. 61, item 329);

3) The law of December 22, 1960, regarding a change in the Constitution of the Polish People's Republic (*Journal of Laws*, No. 57, item 322);

4) The law of May 15, 1961, regarding a change in the number of members of the Council of State (*Journal of Laws*, No. 25, item 120);

5) The law of December 19, 1963, regarding a change in term of office of the People's Councils (*Journal of Laws*, No. 57, item 306).

of People's Democracy has been firmly established, and a new social system, in accord with the interests and aspirations of the great majority of the people, is taking shape and growing in strength.

The legal principles of this system are laid down by the Constitution of the Polish People's Republic.

The basis of people's power in Poland today is the alliance between the working class and the working peasants. In this alliance, the leading role belongs to the working class—the leading class of the people, the class based on the revolutionary gains of the Polish and international working class movement, and on the historic experience of victorious socialist construction in the Union of Soviet Socialist Republics, the first state of workers and peasants.

Implementing the will of the Polish nation, the Legislative Seym of the Republic of Poland, in accordance with its purpose, solemnly adopts the present Constitution as the fundamental law by which the Polish nation and all organs of power of the Polish working people shall be guided, in order:

To consolidate the People's State as the fundamental power assuring to the Polish nation the highest degree of prosperity, its independence and sovereignty;

To accelerate the political, economic and cultural development of the fatherland, and the growth of its resources;

To strengthen the patriotic feelings, the unity and solidarity of the Polish nation in its struggle still further to improve social conditions, to eliminate completely the exploitation of man by man, and to put into effect the great ideals of socialism;

To strengthen friendship and cooperation between nations, on the basis of the alliance and brotherhood which today link the Polish nation with the peace-loving nations of the world for the attainment of their common aim—to make aggression impossible and to consolidate world peace.

CHAPTER I

POLITICAL STRUCTURE

ARTICLE 1. 1. The Polish People's Republic is a State of People's Democracy.

2. In the Polish People's Republic the power belongs to the working people of town and country.

ARTICLE 2. 1. The working people exercise the authority of the State through their representatives elected to the Seym of the Polish People's Republic, and to the People's Councils, on the basis of universal, equal and direct suffrage by secret ballot.

2. The people's representatives in the Seym of the Polish People's Republic, and in the People's Councils, are responsible to their constituents and may be recalled by them.

ARTICLE 3. The Polish People's Republic

1) Safeguards the achievements of the Polish working people of town and country and secures their power and freedom against forces hostile to the people;

2) Secures the development and continuous growth of the productive forces of the country through its industrialization and through elimination of economic, technical and cultural backwardness;

3) Organizes a planned economy on the basis of undertakings constituting social property;

4) Places restrictions on, gradually ejects and abolishes those classes of society which live by exploiting the workers and peasants;

5) Ensures a continual rise in the level of the wellbeing, health and cultural standards of the people;

6) Secures the development of national culture in all its aspects.

ARTICLE 4. 1. The laws of the Polish People's Republic express the interests and the will of the working people.

2. Strict compliance with the laws of the Polish People's Republic is the fundamental duty of every organ of the State and of every citizen.

3. All organs of state power and administration act on the basis of law.

ARTICLE 5. All organs of state power and administration are supported in the exercise of their functions by the conscious and active cooperation of the broadest masses of the people, and they are bound

1) To account to the nation for their work;

2) To examine carefully and take into consideration, in accordance with existing legislation, reasonable proposals, complaints and wishes of the citizens;

3) To interpret to the working people the basic aims and guiding principles of the policy of the people's authorities in the various fields of state, economic and cultural activity.

ARTICLE 6. The armed forces of the Polish People's Republic safeguard the sovereignty and independence of the Polish nation, its security and peace.

CHAPTER II

SOCIAL AND ECONOMIC STRUCTURE

ARTICLE 7. 1. The Polish People's Republic promotes, on the basis of socialized means of production, trade, transportation and credit, the economic and cultural life of the country in accordance with the national economic plan and, in particular, through the expansion of socialist state industry, which is the decisive factor in the transformation of social and economic relations.

2. The State has the monopoly of foreign trade.

3. The principal aim of the planned economic policy of the Polish People's Republic is the constant development of the productive forces of the country, the continuous raising of the standard of living of the working people, and the strengthening of the power, defense capacity and independence of the fatherland.

ARTICLE 8. The national wealth, that is, the mineral deposits, waters, state forests, mines, roads, rail, water and air transport, means of communication, banks, state industrial establishments, state farms and state machine stations, state commercial enterprises and communal enterprises and utilities, is the subject of special care and protection by the State and by all citizens.

ARTICLE 9. 1. The Polish People's Republic strengthens, according to plan, the economic bond between town and country founded on brotherly cooperation between workers and peasants.

2. For this purpose, the Polish People's Republic secures a continuous increase in the output of State industry, serving to meet the all-round needs of the rural population in their capacity as producers and consumers, at the same time exerting a planned influence on the constant growth of production of agricultural commodities which supplies industry with raw materials and the urban population with foodstuffs.

ARTICLE 10. 1. The Polish People's Republic protects the individual farms of working peasants and assists them with a view to safeguarding them against capitalist exploitation, to increasing production, to raising the technical level of agriculture and to improving their welfare.

2. The Polish People's Republic gives special support and all-round aid to the cooperative farms, set up on the basis of voluntary membership, as forms of collective economy. By applying methods of the most efficient collective cultivation and mechanized work, collective farming enables the working peasants to reach a turning point in production and contributes to the complete elimination of exploitation in the countryside and to a rapid and considerable improvement in the level of its well-being and culture.

3. The principal forms of state support and help for cooperative farms are the state machine stations, which make it possible to employ modern technology, and low-interest state credits.

ARTICLE 11. The Polish People's Republic promotes the development of various forms of the cooperative movement in town and country and gives it every help in the fulfillment of its tasks, while extending special care and protection to cooperative property constituting social property.

ARTICLE 12. The Polish People's Republic recognizes and protects, on the basis of existing laws, individual property and the right to inherit land, buildings and other means of production belonging to peasants, craftsmen and home workers.

ARTICLE 13. The Polish People's Republic guarantees to citizens full protection of personal property and the right to inherit such property.

ARTICLE 14. 1. Work is the right, the duty and a matter of honor of every citizen. By their work, by the observance of work discipline, by work emulation and the perfecting of methods of work, the working people of town and country add to the strength and power of the fatherland, raise the level of prosperity of the people and expedite the full realization of the socialist system.

2. Exemplary workers enjoy the respect of the whole nation.

3. The Polish People's Republic gives increasing practical effect to the principle: 'From each according to his ability, to each according to his work.'

CHAPTER III

THE SUPREME ORGANS OF STATE POWER

ARTICLE 15.　1. The highest organ of state power is the Seym of the Polish People's Republic.

2. The Seym, which is the highest representative of the will of the working people of town and country, realizes the sovereign rights of the nation.

3. The Seym passes laws and exercises control over the functioning of other organs of state power and administration.

ARTICLE 16.　1. The Seym is made up of 460 deputies.[2]

2. The validity of the election of a deputy is confirmed by the Seym.

3. No deputy may be either prosecuted or arrested, without the consent of the Seym, and when the Seym is not in session, without the consent of the Council of State.

ARTICLE 17.　1. The Seym meets in sessions. The sessions of the Seym are convened by the Council of State at least twice a year. The Council of State is also bound to convene a session on a written motion by one-third of the total number of deputies.

2. The first session of a newly elected Seym must be convened within a period of one month after the date of the elections.

ARTICLE 18.　1. The Seym elects from among its members a Marshal, deputy marshals and committees.

2. The marshal or his deputy presides over the debates and supervises the course of the work of the Seym.

3. The debates of the Seym are open to the public. The Seym may vote the holding of a secret meeting if the interests of the State require it.

4. The order of work of the Seym, the nature and number of committees, are defined by rules of procedure adopted by the Seym.

ARTICLE 19.　1. The Seym adopts the national economic plans for a period of a number of years.

2. The Seym adopts every year the State budget.

ARTICLE 20.　1. The right to propose legislation is vested in the Council of State, the Government and the deputies.

2. Laws passed by the Seym are signed by the Chairman of the Council of State and its Secretary. Laws are published in the Journal of Laws by order of the Chairman of the Council of State.

ARTICLE 21.　The Seym may appoint a commission to examine a specified matter. The terms of reference and the procedure of the commission are determined by the Seym.

---

[2] The original text of Article 16, Paragraph 1 of the Constitution read as follows: 'Deputies to the Seym are elected by the citizens in electoral districts, in the proportion of one deputy to 60,000 inhabitants.' It was changed by the law of December 22, 1960 (Journal of Laws, No. 57, item 322).—TR.

ARTICLE 22. The Chairman of the Council of Ministers or individual ministers are bound to give an answer within seven days to an interpellation by a deputy.

ARTICLE 23. 1. The Seym is elected for a term of four years.

2. The Council of State orders the holding of elections to the Seym not later than one month before the expiry of the term of office of the Seym, the date of elections to be fixed on a work-free day within two months after the expiry of the term of office of the Seym.

ARTICLE 24. 1. At its first sitting, the Seym elects from among its members the Council of State, consisting of the Chairman of the Council of State; four deputy chairmen; the Secretary of the Council of State; eleven members.[3]

2. The Marshal and deputy marshal of the Seym may be elected to the Council of State as deputy chairmen or as members.

3. After the expiry of the term of office of the Seym, the Council of State acts until the election of a Council of State by the newly elected Seym.

ARTICLE 25. 1. The Council of State

1) Orders the holding of elections to the Seym;

2) Convenes sessions of the Seym;

3) Lays down universally binding interpretation of laws;

4) Issues decrees having the force of law;

5) Appoints and recalls plenipotentiary representatives of the Polish People's Republic in other states;

6) Receives letters of credence and of recall of diplomatic representatives of other states accredited to the Council of State;

7) Ratifies and denounces international treaties;

8) Fills civilian and military posts specified by law;

9) Awards orders and decorations, and confers titles of honor;

10) Exercises the right of pardon;

11) Exercises other functions vested in the Council of State by the Constitution or assigned to it by law.

2. The Council of State is accountable to the Seym for all its activities.

3. The Council of State acts as a collective body.

4. The Council of State is represented by its Chairman or his deputy.

ARTICLE 26. 1. In the intervals between the sessions of the Seym, the Council of State issues decrees having the force of law. The Council of State submits its decrees for approval to the next session of the Seym.

---

[3] The original text of Article 24, paragraph 1 of the Constitution read as follows: 'At its sitting, the Seym elects from among its members the Council of State, consisting of the Chairman of the Council of State; four deputy chairmen; the Secretary of the Council of State; nine members.' It was changed by the law of May 15, 1961 (*Journal of Laws*, No. 25, item 120).—TR.

2. Decrees issued by the Council of State are signed by the Chairman of the Council of State and its Secretary. Decrees are published in the Journal of Laws by order of the Chairman of the Council of State.

ARTICLE 27. The Council of State exercises ultimate supervision over the People's Councils. Specific powers of the Council of State in this respect are determined by law.

ARTICLE 28. 1. A decision concerning the declaration of a state of war may be adopted only in the event of armed aggression having been committed against the Polish People's Republic, or if, in pursuance of international agreements, the necessity of common defense against aggression should arise. Such a decision is voted by the Seym or, if the Seym is not in session, by the Council of State.

2. The Council of State may, should considerations of the defense or security of the State so require, proclaim martial law in parts or in the entire territory of the Polish People's Republic. For similar reasons the Council of State may proclaim partial or general mobilization.

CHAPTER IIIa[4]

THE SUPREME CONTROL CHAMBER

ARTICLE 28a. 1. The function of the Supreme Control Chamber is to exercise supervision over the economic, financial and organizational-administrative activity of the higher and local organs of state administration, as well as of agencies subordinate to them, from the point of view of legality, good management, utility and honesty.

2. The Supreme Control Chamber may also carry out supervision over social organizations and institutions as well as nonsocialized units of the economy with regard to tasks indicated by the State, and also in other cases defined by law.

ARTICLE 28b. 1. The Supreme Control Chamber comes under the jurisdiction of the Seym.

2. The Council of State exercises supervision over the Supreme Control Chamber in the realm specified by law.

ARTICLE 28c. 1. The Chairman of the Supreme Control Chamber is appointed and recalled by the Seym.

2. The Supreme Control Chamber functions as a collective body, in accordance with the provisions of the law.

3. The organizational structure and the way of operation of the Supreme Control Chamber are defined by law.

ARTICLE 28d. The Supreme Control Chamber presents its opinions to the Seym regarding the execution of the state budget and of the national economic plan, and submits motions of approval for the Government in this regard.

---

[4] Chapter IIIa (Articles 28a–d) was included in the Constitution by the law of December 13, 1957, regarding a change in the Constitution of the Polish People's Republic (*Journal of Laws*, No. 61, item 329).—TR.

CHAPTER IV

THE SUPREME ORGANS OF STATE ADMINISTRATION

ARTICLE 29. 1. The Seym appoints and recalls the Government of the Polish People's Republic—the Council of Ministers or its individual members.

2. In the intervals between sessions of the Seym, the Council of State, on the motion of the Chairman of the Council of Ministers, appoints and recalls members of the Council of Ministers. The Council of State submits its decisions for approval to the next session of the Seym.

ARTICLE 30. 1. The Council of Ministers is the supreme executive and administrative organ of state power.

2. The Council of Ministers is responsible and accountable to the Seym for its work, and when the Seym is not in session, to the Council of State.

ARTICLE 31. The Council of Ministers consists of the Chairman of the Council of Ministers, who presides; the vice-chairmen of the Council of Ministers; the chairmen of such commissions and committees as are specified by law, and fulfill the functions of the highest organs of state administration.

ARTICLE 32. The Council of Ministers

1) Coordinates the activities of ministries and other organs under its jurisdiction and gives directives as to their work;

2) Adopts yearly and submits to the Seym the state budget estimates, adopts and submits to the Seym the draft of the national economic plan for a period of a number of years;

3) Adopts the yearly national economic plans;

4) Ensures the execution of laws;

5) Supervises the execution of the national economic plan and of the state budget;

6) Presents to the Seym an annual report on the execution of the state budget;

7) Ensures the protection of public order, of the interests of state and of the rights of citizens;

8) In pursuance of laws and in order to give them effect, issues regulations, adopts decisions and supervises their execution;

9) Exercises general guidance in the sphere of relations with other states;

10) Exercises general guidance regarding the defense capacity of the country and the organization of the Armed Forces of the Polish People's Republic, and establishes the annual contingent of citizens to be called up for military service;

11) Directs the work of the presidia of the People's Councils.

ARTICLE 33. 1. Ministers direct specified branches of state administration. The sphere of competence of ministers is determined by law.

2. Ministers issue orders and regulations in pursuance of laws and for the execution of laws.

3. The Council of Ministers may rescind an order or a regulation issued by a minister.

CHAPTER V

THE LOCAL ORGANS OF STATE POWER

ARTICLE 34. 1. The organs of state power in rural communities in towns, in boroughs of larger towns, in settlements[5] and voivodeships are the People's Councils.

2. The People's Councils are elected by the population for a term of four years.[6]

ARTICLE 35. The People's Councils express the will of the working people, and develop their creative initiative and activity in order to increase the strength, prosperity and culture of the nation.

ARTICLE 36. The People's Councils strengthen the links between the state authorities and working people of town and country, drawing increasing numbers of the working people into participation in governing the State.

ARTICLE 37. The People's Councils direct, within the limits of their jurisdiction, economic, social and cultural activities, linking local requirements with the general tasks of the State.

ARTICLE 38. The People's Councils take constant care of the everyday needs and interests of the population, combat any manifestations of arbitrary and bureaucratic attitude toward citizens, exercise and promote social supervision over the activities of offices, enterprises, establishments and institutions.

ARTICLE 39. The People's Councils ensure the maintenance of public order and watch over the observance of the people's rule of law, protect social property, safeguard the rights of citizens, and cooperate in strengthening the defense capacity and security of the State.

ARTICLE 40. The People's Councils fully exploit all local resources and possibilities for the general economic and cultural development of the area, for meeting to an increasing extent the needs of the population with regard to supply and services, as well as for the expansion of communal institutions and facilities connected with public services, education, culture, sanitation and sport.

ARTICLE 41. The People's Councils adopt local economic plans and local budgets.

---

[5] The words 'in rural communities (in the sense of the Polish word *gromady*), in settlements' were incorporated in the Constitution by the law of September 25, 1954, at the same time the word 'in rural communities' (in the sense of the Polish word *gminy*) were deleted (*Journal of Laws of 1954*, No. 43, item 190).—TR.

[6] The original text of Article 34, paragraph 2 of the Constitution provided for the election of the People's Councils for a term of three years. It was changed by the law of December 19, 1963 (*Journal of Laws*, No. 57, item 306).—TR.

ARTICLE 42.   1. The People's Councils meet in sessions.

2.   The presidia elected by the People's Councils are the executive and administrative organs of those councils.

3.   The presidium of a People's Council is responsible to the People's Council by which it has been elected, and to the presidium of the People's Council of a higher level.

ARTICLE 43.   The People's Councils appoint committees for various spheres of their activity. The committees of the People's Councils maintain constant and close links with the population, mobilize it for cooperation in implementing the council's tasks, exercise social supervision on behalf of the council and submit proposals to the council and its organs.

ARTICLE 44.   1. A People's Council rescinds the decision of a People's Council of a lower level or of the presidium of such council, if that decision is at variance with the law or incompatible with the basic line of the policy of the State.

2.   The presidium of a People's Council may suspend the execution of a decision of a People's Council of a lower level and submit the case for decision at the next meeting of its own People's Council.

ARTICLE 45.   The details of composition as well as the terms of reference and the rules of procedure of the People's Councils and their organs are established by law.

CHAPTER VI

THE COURTS AND THE PUBLIC PROSECUTOR'S OFFICE

ARTICLE 46.   1. The administration of justice in the Polish People's Republic is carried out by the Supreme Court, voivodeship courts, district courts and special courts.

2.   Organization, jurisdiction and procedure of the courts are established by law.

ARTICLE 47.   The courts pronounce judgment in the name of the Polish People's Republic.

ARTICLE 48.   The courts are the custodians of the political and social system of the Polish People's Republic; they protect the achievements of the Polish working people, safeguard the people's rule of law, social property and the rights of citizens, and punish offenders.

ARTICLE 49.   People's assessors take part in the hearing of cases and the pronouncement of judgment, except in cases specified by law.

ARTICLE 50.   1. Judges and people's assessors are elected.

2.   The procedure of election and the term of office of judges and assessors of voivodeship and district courts are established by law.

3.   The procedure of appointment of judges of special courts is established by law.

ARTICLE 51. 1. The Supreme Court is the highest judicial organ and supervises the activity of all other courts concerning the pronouncement of judgment.

2. The procedure for the exercise of supervision by the Supreme Court is established by law.

3. The Supreme Court is elected by the Council of State for a term of five years.

ARTICLE 52. Judges are independent and subject only to the law.

ARTICLE 53. 1. Cases in all courts of the Polish People's Republic are heard in public. The law may specify exceptions to this principle.

2. The accused is guaranteed the right to legal defense. He may have a defense counsel, either of his own choice or appointed by the court.

ARTICLE 54. 1. The Prosecutor General of the Polish People's Republic safeguards the people's rule of law, watches over the protection of social property and ensures that the rights of citizens are respected.

2. The Prosecutor General supervises, in particular, the prosecution of offenses endangering the political and social system, security and independence of the Polish People's Republic.

3. The limits of jurisdiction and the scope of activity of the Prosecutor General are established by law.

ARTICLE 55. 1. The Prosecutor General of the Polish People's Republic is appointed and recalled by the Council of State.

2. The mode of appointing and recalling prosecutors subordinate to the Prosecutor General, is, together with the principles of the organization and procedure of organs of the Prosecutor's Office, established by law.

3. The Prosecutor General is accountable to the Council of State for the activity of the Prosecutor's Office.

ARTICLE 56. The organs of the Prosecutor's Office are subordinate to the Prosecutor General of the Polish People's Republic and in the exercise of their functions are independent of local organs.

CHAPTER VII

FUNDAMENTAL RIGHTS AND DUTIES OF CITIZENS

ARTICLE 57. The Polish People's Republic, by consolidating and multiplying the gains of the working people, strengthens and extends the rights and liberties of the citizens.

ARTICLE 58. 1. Citizens of the Polish People's Republic have the right to work, that is, the right to employment paid in accordance with the quantity and quality of work done.

2. The right to work is ensured by the social ownership of the basic means of production, by the development of a social and cooperative system in the country-

side, free from exploitation; by the planned growth of the productive forces; by the elimination of sources of economic crises and by the abolition of unemployment.

ARTICLE 59. 1. Citizens of the Polish People's Republic have the right to rest and leisure.

2. The right to rest and leisure is assured to manual and office workers by reduction of working hours through the application of the eight-hour working day and shorter work time in cases specified by law, by the institution according to law of days off work and by annual holidays with pay.

3. The organization of workers' holiday schemes, the development of the tourist movement, of health resorts, sports facilities, houses of culture, clubs, recreation rooms, parks and other leisure-time facilities, create possibilities for healthy and cultural relaxation for an increasing number of working people in town and country.

ARTICLE 60. 1. Citizens of the Polish People's Republic have the right to health protection and to aid in the event of sickness or incapacity for work.

2. Effect is being given to this right on an increasing scale through

1) The development of social insurance for manual and office workers to cover sickness, old age and incapacity for work, as well as through the expansion of various forms of social assistance;

2) The development of the state-organized protection of the health of the population, the expansion of sanitation services and the raising of the health standards in town and country, consistent improvement of safety conditions, protection and hygiene of work, a wide campaign for the prevention of and fighting disease, increasing access to free medical attention, the development of hospitals, sanatoria, medical aid centers, rural health centers, and care for the disabled.

ARTICLE 61. 1. Citizens of the Polish People's Republic have the right to education.

2. This right is ensured on an increasing scale by

1) Universal, free and compulsory primary schools;

2) A constant development of secondary schools, providing general or vocational education, and of schools of academic level;

3) The help of the State in raising the skill of citizens employed in industrial establishments and other places of employment in town and country;

4) A scheme of state scholarship, the development of hostels, boarding schools and students' homes, together with other forms of material aid for the children of workers, working peasants and intelligentsia.

ARTICLE 62. 1. Citizens of the Polish People's Republic have the right to benefit from cultural achievements and to participate in the development of national culture.

2. This right is ensured on an increasing scale by developing and making accessible to the working people in town and country libraries, books, press, radio,

cinemas, theaters, museums and exhibitions, houses of culture, clubs and recreation rooms; by a general fostering and promoting of the cultural creative activity of the people and of the development of creative talents.

ARTICLE 63. The Polish People's Republic fosters the all-round development of science and learning based on the achievements of the most advanced thought of mankind and of Polish progressive thought—the development of science and learning in the service of the nation.

ARTICLE 64. The Polish People's Republic encourages the development of literature and art which express the needs and aspirations of the nation and which are in accord with the best progressive traditions of Polish creative thought.

ARTICLE 65. The Polish People's Republic extends special protection to the creative intelligentsia—to those working in science, education, literature and art, as well as to pioneers of technical progress, to rationalizers [sic] and inventors.

ARTICLE 66. 1. Women in the Polish People's Republic have equal rights with men in all spheres of public, political, economic, social and cultural life.

2. The equality of rights of women is guaranteed by

1) Equal rights with men to work and pay according to the principle 'equal pay for equal work,' the right to rest and leisure, to social insurance, to education, to honors and decorations, to hold public office;

2) Mother-and-child care, protection of expectant mothers, paid holidays during the period before and after confinement, the development of a network of maternity homes, crèches and nursery schools, the extension of a network of service establishments and restaurants and canteens.

ARTICLE 67. 1. Marriage and the family are under the care and protection of the Polish People's Republic. The State gives particular care to families with many children.

2. A child born out of wedlock suffers no loss of rights.

ARTICLE 68. The Polish People's Republic gives particularly careful attention to the education of youth and guarantees them the most extensive possibilities for development.

ARTICLE 69. 1. Citizens of the Polish People's Republic, irrespective of nationality, race or religion, enjoy equal rights in all spheres of public, political, economic, social and cultural life. Infringement of this principle by any direct or indirect granting of privileges or restriction of rights on account of nationality, race or religion is punishable by law.

2. The spreading of hatred or contempt, the provocation of strife or the humiliation of man on account of national, racial or religious differences is forbidden.

ARTICLE 70. 1. The Polish People's Republic guarantees freedom of conscience and religion to citizens. The church and other religious bodies may freely exercise their religious functions. It is forbidden to prevent citizens from taking part in religious activities or rites. It is also forbidden to coerce anybody to participate in religious activities or rites.

2. The church is separated from the state. The principles of the relationship between church and state are, together with the legal and patrimonial position of religious bodies, determined by law.

3. The abuse of the freedom of conscience and religion for purposes prejudicial to the interests of the Polish People's Republic is punishable.

ARTICLE 71. 1. The Polish People's Republic guarantees its citizens freedom of speech, of the press, of meetings and assemblies, of processions and demonstrations.

2. The making available to the working people and their organizations of the use of printing shops, stocks of paper, public buildings and halls, means of communication, the radio and other indispensable material means, serves to give effect to this freedom.

ARTICLE 72. 1. In order to promote the political, social, economic and cultural activity of the working people of town and country, the Polish People's Republic guarantees to citizens the right of association.

2. Political organizations, trade unions, associations of working peasants, cooperative associations, youth, women's, sports and defense organizations, cultural, technical and scientific associations, as well as other working people's social organizations, unite the citizens for active participation in political, social, economic and cultural life.

3. The setting up of, and participation in, associations the aims or activities of which are directed against the political or social system or against the legal order of the Polish People's Republic are forbidden.

ARTICLE 73. 1. Citizens have the right to approach all organs of the State with complaints and grievances.

2. Citizens' complaints and grievances are to be examined and settled in an expeditious and just manner. Those guilty of protraction or of displaying a soulless and bureaucratic attitude toward citizens' complaints and grievances will be called to responsibility.

ARTICLE 74. 1. The Polish People's Republic guarantees to citizens inviolability of the person. A citizen may be deprived of his freedom only in cases specified by law. A detained person must be set free unless, within forty-eight hours from the moment of his detention, a warrant of arrest issued by the court or the prosecutor has been served on him.

2. The law protects the inviolability of the home and the privacy of correspondence. Search of the home is permissible only in cases specified by law.

3. Property may be seized only in cases established by law, by virtue of a final judgment.

ARTICLE 75. The Polish People's Republic grants asylum to citizens of foreign countries persecuted for defending the interests of the working people, for struggling for social progress, for activity in defense of peace, for fighting for national liberation or for scientific activity.

ARTICLE 76. It is the duty of every citizen of the Polish People's Republic to abide by the provisions of the Constitution and of the laws, to maintain socialist work discipline, to respect the rules of social intercourse and to discharge conscientiously [his] duties toward the State.

ARTICLE 77. 1. It is the duty of every citizen of the Polish People's Republic to safeguard and strengthen social property, which is the unshakable foundation of the development of the State, the source of the wealth and might of the country.

2. Persons who commit sabotage, subversion, inflict damage, or . . . otherwise injure social property, are punishable with all the severity of law.

ARTICLE 78. 1. To defend the country is the most sacred duty of every citizen.

2. Military service is an honorable patriotic duty of citizens of the Polish People's Republic.

ARTICLE 79. 1. Vigilance against the enemies of the nation and the diligent guarding of state secrets is the duty of every citizen of the Polish People's Republic.

2. High treason—espionage, undermining of the Armed Forces, desertion to the enemy—is punishable as the gravest of crimes with all the severity of law.

CHAPTER VIII

PRINCIPLES OF ELECTORAL LAW

ARTICLE 80. Elections to the Seym and to the People's Councils are universal, equal, direct and carried out by secret ballot.

ARTICLE 81. Every citizen who has reached the age of eighteen has, irrespective of sex, nationality and race, religion, education, length of residence, social origin, profession or property, the right to vote.

ARTICLE 82. Every citizen who has reached the age of eighteen is eligible for election to the People's Councils and every citizen who has reached the age of twenty-one is eligible for election to the Seym.

ARTICLE 83. Women have all electoral rights on equal terms with men.

ARTICLE 84. Citizens serving in the armed forces have all electoral rights on equal terms with civilians.

ARTICLE 85. Electoral rights are denied only to insane persons and to persons deprived by court decision of public rights.

ARTICLE 86. Candidates for the Seym and candidates for the People's Councils are nominated by political and social organizations in town and country.

ARTICLE 87. It is the duty of deputies to the Seym and of members of People's Councils to report to the electors on their work and on the activity of the body to which they have been elected.

ARTICLE 88. The procedure for nomination of candidates and for holding elections, as well as the procedure for the recall of deputies to the Seym and of members of People's Councils, are established by law.

CHAPTER IX

COAT OF ARMS, COLORS AND CAPITAL
OF THE POLISH PEOPLE'S REPUBLIC

ARTICLE 89. 1. The coat of arms of the Polish People's Republic is the image of a white eagle on a red field.

2. The colors of the Polish People's Republic are white and red.

3. The details are established by law.

ARTICLE 90. The capital of the Polish People's Republic is Warsaw—city of heroic traditions of the Polish nation.

CHAPTER X

PROCEDURE FOR AMENDING THE CONSTITUTION

ARTICLE 91. The Constitution may be amended only by an act of the Seym of the Polish People's Republic, passed by a majority of not less than two-thirds of the votes, not less than half the total number of Deputies being present.

CONSTITUTIONAL LAW
of July 22, 1952

REGULATIONS REGARDING THE INTRODUCTION
OF THE CONSTITUTION OF THE
POLISH PEOPLE'S REPUBLIC[7]

ARTICLE 1. The Constitution of the Polish People's Republic goes into effect on July 22, 1952.

ARTICLE 2. 1. The President of the Republic continues in office, within the limits of the rights applicable to date, until the election of the Council of State by the newly elected Seym of the Polish People's Republic.

2. On the day that this election takes place, the functions of the President of the Republic provided for by laws in effect until now—unless in line with the Constitution and this law they do not come within the scope of activity of the Council of State—are taken over by the Council of Ministers.

ARTICLE 3. The Council of State appointed on the basis of Article 15 of the Constitutional Law of February 19, 1947 continues to function, within the limits of rights applicable to date, until the Council of State is chosen by the newly elected Seym of the Polish People's Republic.

---

[7] This law was published in the *Journal of Laws*, No. 33, item 233.—TR.

ARTICLE 4.   1. The Government is empowered to issue decrees with the force of law during the interval between the end of the term of office of the Legislative Seym and the opening of the first session of the Seym of the Polish People's Republic, according to the provisions of Article 4 of the Constitutional Law of February 19, 1947.

2.   The Government shall submit the decrees issued on the basis of Paragraph 1 [hereof] to the first session of the Seym.

ARTICLE 5.   Until the time that the new law on the system of the courts goes into effect, the regulations concerning the judiciary remain in force, with the following changes:

1) The courts pronounce judgment in the name of the Polish People's Republic;

2) The rights of the President to appoint judges, provided for by the laws of the judiciary in effect until now, shall be taken over by the Council of State on the day it is elected by the Seym of the Polish People's Republic.

ARTICLE 6.   Until the time that the new law regarding state control comes into force, the Supreme Control Chamber is to exercise its function within the limits of its rights in effect to date.

ARTICLE 7.   Within a week after the expiry of the term of office of the Legislative Seym, the Council of State (Article 3) shall order the holding of elections to the Seym of the Polish People's Republic, fixing the date of election on a work-free day within three months after the expiry of this term of office.

ARTICLE 8.   The law goes into effect on the day of its publication—July 22, 1952.

12. 1

CONSTITUTION OF THE PEOPLE'S REPUBLIC OF RUMANIA[1]

Adopted April 13, 1948

TITLE I

THE PEOPLE'S REPUBLIC OF RUMANIA

ARTICLE 1. The People's Republic of Rumania is a popular, unitary, independent and sovereign state.

ARTICLE 2. The People's Republic of Rumania was created in the struggle waged by the people, headed by the working class, against fascism, reaction and imperialism.

ARTICLE 3. In the People's Republic of Rumania, the whole power of the state is derived from the people and belongs to the people.

The people exercise their power through representative bodies elected on the basis of universal, direct and equal suffrage by secret ballot.

ARTICLE 4. The people's representatives in all the bodies of state power are responsible to the people and are liable to be revoked upon the will of the electors in conditions established by law.

TITLE II

SOCIAL AND ECONOMIC STRUCTURE

ARTICLE 5. In the People's Republic of Rumania, the means of production belong either to the state, being the possession of the whole people, or to cooperative organizations, or to private physical or juridical persons.

ARTICLE 6. All mineral resources, mines, forests, waters, sources of natural power, communication lines by rail, land, water and sea, post, telegraph, telephone and radio belong to the state, as common possessions of the people.

The method of passing into the property of the state any of the resources specified in the preceding paragraph which were in private hands on the day the present Constitution came into force, will be laid down in law.

ARTICLE 7. The common possessions of the people constitute the material basis of the economic progress and national independence of the People's Republic of Rumania.

---

[1] *The Constitution of the People's Republic of Rumania* (Washington, D.C.: Legation of the People's Republic of Rumania, n.d.).

It is the duty of every citizen to defend and develop the common possessions of the people.

ARTICLE 8.   Private property and the right of inheritance are acknowledged and guaranteed by law.

Private property acquired through work and savings enjoys special protection.

ARTICLE 9.   The land belongs to those who work it.

The state protects the working peasant's holdings. It encourages and gives support to village cooperation.

In order to stimulate the improvement of agriculture the state may create state-owned agricultural enterprises.

ARTICLE 10.   Expropriations for reasons of public utility can be made in accordance with the law and under payment of rightful compensation as established by law.

ARTICLE 11.   When required in the general interest, the means of production, banks and insurance companies which are the property of private physical or juridical persons may become state property, i.e. the possession of the people, under conditions established by law.

ARTICLE 12.   Work is the fundamental factor of the economic life of the state. It is the duty of every citizen. The state grants support to all working people in order to defend them against exploitation and to raise their standard of living.

ARTICLE 13.   The state grants protection to private initiative which serves the general interest.

ARTICLE 14.   The internal and foreign trade is regulated and controlled by the state, and it is carried out through state, private and cooperative commercial enterprises.

ARTICLE 15.   The state directs and plans the national economy in order to develop the economic power of the country, to ensure the welfare of the people, and to safeguard the national independence.

TITLE III

FUNDAMENTAL RIGHTS AND DUTIES OF THE CITIZENS

ARTICLE 16.   All citizens of the People's Republic of Rumania, irrespective of sex, nationality, race, religion or educational qualifications, are equal before the law.

ARTICLE 17.   Any advocacy or manifestation of racial or national hatred is punishable by law.

ARTICLE 18.   All citizens, irrespective of sex, nationality, race, religion, educational qualifications, profession, including servicemen, magistrates and civil servants, have the right of electing and of being elected to all the organs of the state.

All citizens who have reached the age of eighteen have the right to vote, and all citizens who have reached the age of twenty-three have the right to be elected.

Disqualified persons, deprived of civil and political rights—if pronounced as such by the qualified authorities in accordance with the law—do not enjoy the right to vote.

ARTICLE 19.   The citizens have the right to work. The state gradually insures this right by the planned organization and development of the national economy.

ARTICLE 20.   The citizens have the right to leisure. This right to leisure is ensured by regulating working hours, by paid vacations, in accordance with the law, by organizing rest homes, sanatoriums, clubs, parks, sport grounds, and institutions especially designed for this purpose.

ARTICLE 21.   Women are accorded equal rights with men in all spheres of public, economic, social, cultural, private-law and political life.

For equal work women have the right to equal pay as men.

ARTICLE 22.   In the People's Republic of Rumania all citizens have the right to education.

The state ensures the achievement of this right by organizing and developing elementary education, compulsory and free of charge, by state scholarships granted to meritorious pupils and students, and by organizing and developing vocational and technical education.

ARTICLE 23.   The state encourages and supports the development of science and art and organizes research institutes, libraries, printing houses, theaters, museums, and music academies.

ARTICLE 24.   In the People's Republic of Rumania, the right of using their native language and of organizing education of every grade in their own language is ensured to all nationalities living in the country. Administrative and judicial authorities in the districts inhabited also by nationalities other than Rumanian will also use, orally and in writing, the language of the nationality concerned, and will appoint officials from the nationality concerned, or from another nationality who know the language of the local population.

The teaching of the Rumanian language and literature is compulsory in schools of every grade.

ARTICLE 25.   The state takes care of public health by creating and developing health services and by encouraging and protecting physical training.

The state assures social protection and medical care in cases of sickness, accidents and disablements resulting from or occurring at work, or in the defense services of the country, as well as maintenance in old age, both for civil servants and for employees of private enterprises, whose contribution and rights are established by law.

ARTICLE 26.   Marriage and the family enjoy the protection of the state.

Mothers and children under eighteen years of age enjoy special protection as established by law.

The parents have the same duties toward children born out of wedlock as toward those born in wedlock.

All acts affecting the civil status are valid only if contracted before the state authorities.

ARTICLE 27. Freedom of conscience and freedom of religious worship are guaranteed by the state.

Religious creeds are free to organize themselves and can freely function, provided their ritual and practice are not contrary to the Constitution, public security, or morality.

No religious denomination, congregation or community can open or maintain institutions of general education, but may only run special schools for training personnel necessary to the cult under state control.

The Rumanian-Orthodox Church is autocephalous and unitary in its organization.

The way of organizing and functioning of the religious creeds will be established by law.

ARTICLE 28. The individual liberty of the citizen is guaranteed.

No person may be placed under arrest and imprisoned longer than forty-eight hours without a warrant of the public prosecutor, or of the examining magistrature as established by law, or under an authorization of the judicial authorities, in accordance with the law.

ARTICLE 29. The domicile is inviolable. No person may enter the home or residence of a citizen without his consent, except in his presence and on the basis of a written warrant from the appropriate authority, or in case of flagrante delicto.

ARTICLE 30. No person may be sentenced or detained to serve a sentence except under a judicial decision according to the law.

ARTICLE 31. Freedom of the press, of speech, of assembly, of mass meetings, of street processions and demonstrations is guaranteed.

The exercising of these rights is ensured by the fact that the means of printing, the paper and meeting halls are placed at the disposal of the working people.

ARTICLE 32. The citizens have the right of association and organization, if the aims pursued are not directed against the democratic order established by the Constitution.

Any association of fascist or antidemocratic character is forbidden and punishable by law.

ARTICLE 33. The secrecy of correspondence is guaranteed. Only in the case of court instruction, under martial law, or in case of mobilization, correspondence may be inspected.

ARTICLE 34. Every citizen has the right to petition, as well as the right to ask the legislature to bring suit against any civil servant for offenses committed in the exercise of duty.

ARTICLE 35. The People's Republic of Rumania grants the right of refuge to all foreigners persecuted for their democratic activities, for their struggle for national liberation, for their scientific or cultural activities.

ARTICLE 36. The defense of their country is a duty of honor for all citizens.

Military service is obligatory for all citizens according to the law.

High treason—violating the oath of allegiance, entering the service of the enemy, impairing the military power of the state—constitutes the gravest crime against the people and is punishable with all the severity of the law.

TITLE IV

THE SUPREME ORGAN OF STATE AUTHORITY

ARTICLE 37. The supreme organ of state authority in the People's Republic of Rumania is the Great National Assembly of the People's Republic of Rumania.

ARTICLE 38. The Great National Assembly of the People's Republic of Rumania is the only legislative body of the People's Republic of Rumania.

ARTICLE 39. Within the direct competence of the Great National Assembly of the People's Republic of Rumania fall:

1) The electing of the Presidium of the Great National Assembly of the People's Republic of Rumania.

2) The forming of the government of the People's Republic of Rumania.

3) The amending of the Constitution.

4) The establishing of the number, attribution and appellation of ministries, and the abolishing, merging or giving new appellation to the existing ministries.

5) The voting of the state budget and of the closing of the budgetary year, the fixing of taxes and of the ways of their collection.

6) The questions of war and peace.

7) The decision to consult the people by referendum.

8) The granting of amnesty.

ARTICLE 40. The Great National Assembly elects from its members the Presidium of the Assembly.

The Presidium is elected by one-half plus one of the total number of deputies.[2]

ARTICLE 41. The Presidium of the Great National Assembly of the People's Republic of Rumania consists of one president, three vice presidents, one secretary, and fourteen members directly elected by the Great National Assembly.

ARTICLE 42. The Presidium as a whole, or any of its members, may be removed at any time by the Great National Assembly by a majority as laid down in Article 40.

ARTICLE 43. The Presidium of the Great National Assembly of the People's Republic of Rumania is responsible for its whole activity to the Great National Assembly.

ARTICLE 44. The Presidium of the Great National Assembly of the People's Republic of Rumania has the following functions:

---

[2] TRANSLATOR'S NOTE: The deputies are the people's representatives. (See Article 47.)

1) To summon the Great National Assembly of the People's Republic of Rumania in ordinary and special sessions;

2) To issue decrees;

3) To enact the laws passed by the Great National Assembly of the People's Republic of Rumania;

4) To exercise the right of pardon and to commute punishments;

5) To confer the decorations and medals of the People's Republic of Rumania;

6) To represent the People's Republic of Rumania in international relations;

7) To appoint and recall, at the proposal of the government, the diplomatic representatives of the People's Republic of Rumania.

8) To receive the credentials and the letters of recall from the diplomatic representatives of foreign countries accredited to it;

9) To appoint and remove ministers on the recommendation of the Prime Minister during the intervals between the sessions of the Great National Assembly of the People's Republic of Rumania;

10) To establish military ranks, diplomatic ranks and honorary titles on the recommendation of the government;

11) To make and sanction civil service appointments on recommendation of the ministers concerned or of the government, in accordance with the law;

12) To declare—in the interval between sessions of the Great National Assembly of the People's Republic of Rumania, on the recommendation of the government—a state of war and partial or general mobilization, in case of aggression against the People's Republic of Rumania, or against another state toward which she has mutual defense obligations ensuing from international treaties;

13) To ratify or denounce international treaties on the recommendation of the government;

14) To settle any question submitted to it by the Great National Assembly of the People's Republic of Rumania and to carry out any functions which may be vested in it by law.

ARTICLE 45. The Presidium of the Great National Assembly of the People's Republic of Rumania takes valid decisions by simple majority of its members.

Decrees will be signed by the president and the secretary of the Presidium of the Great National Assembly of the People's Republic of Rumania. If they are prevented from signing, the president will be replaced by one of the vice presidents, and the secretary by one of the members designated by the Presidium from its ranks.

ARTICLE 46. After the mandate of the Great National Assembly of the People's Republic of Rumania expires or in case of its dissolution before term, the Presidium of the Great National Assembly of the People's Republic of Rumania continues until the election of a new Presidium.

ARTICLE 47. The Great National Assembly of the People's Republic of Rumania is elected for a period of four years. It is composed of representatives of the people (deputies), elected according to the procedure established by electoral law.

ARTICLE 48. The Great National Assembly of the People's Republic of Rumania meets in ordinary sessions at least twice a year, each session lasting until the end of the proceedings.

The Assembly is convened by decree of the Presidium of the Great National Assembly of the People's Republic of Rumania.

ARTICLE 49. The Great National Assembly of the People's Republic of Rumania may be convened in extraordinary sessions by decree of the Presidium, at the request of not less than one-third of the deputies.

ARTICLE 50. After the validation of the deputies the Great National Assembly of the People's Republic of Rumania elects a bureau which will conduct the proceedings, consisting of one president, three vice presidents, and secretaries. The Bureau of the Great National Assembly of the People's Republic of Rumania is elected for each session of the Great National Assembly of the People's Republic of Rumania.

The proceedings of the Great National Assembly will be presided over by the president, or by one of the vice presidents of the bureau, in accordance with the regulations drawn up by the Great National Assembly of the People's Republic of Rumania.

ARTICLE 51. The presence of one-half plus one of the total number of deputies will constitute a quorum. Valid decisions will be taken by simple majority of deputies present, except in cases where the Constitution or the regulations of the Great National Assembly of the People's Republic of Rumania provide for a different number.

ARTICLE 52. Voting may be done by secret vote, by raising of hands or by acclamation, according to the decision of the Great National Assembly of the People's Republic of Rumania.

ARTICLE 53. The Great National Assembly of the People's Republic of Rumania declares the validity of the election of deputies. The vote of a deputy is valid even prior to the examination of the validity of his mandate.

ARTICLE 54. Deputies whose mandate has been declared valid, take the following oath to the Great National Assembly of the People's Republic of Rumania: 'I swear to serve the people and the People's Republic of Rumania with all my devotion and capacity to work, to defend and respect the Constitution and the laws of the country; to keep state secrets and defend the interests of the people and the state, the democratic liberties and the independence of the country.'

The same oath will be taken by members of the Presidium and the members of the government on taking up office.

ARTICLE 55. The legislative initiative belongs to the government. Not less than one-fifth of the total number of deputies may also introduce legislation.

ARTICLE 56. The laws, after having been voted by the Great National Assembly of the People's Republic of Rumania, are signed by the president and secretary of the Presidium, and are published in the official monitor. A law comes into effect on the day indicated in the text, or three days after its publication in the official monitor.

ARTICLE 57. The sessions of the Great National Assembly are public, except in cases where the Assembly decides to hold secret sessions.

ARTICLE 58. The Great National Assembly of the People's Republic of Rumania has the right to investigate and inquire into any sphere of the People's Republic of Rumania, by means of commissions elected from its ranks.

All state authorities and organs, as well as private persons, are bound to give every information and to put at the disposal of such commissions any document required by them.

ARTICLE 59. No deputy can be detained, arrested or prosecuted, without the consent of the Great National Assembly of the People's Republic of Rumania during the sessions, or of the Presidium of the Great National Assembly of the People's Republic of Rumania between sessions, for any offense, except in such cases of flagrante delicto, and [such] in cases the authorization of the Great National Assembly or of the Presidium must be obtained forthwith.

ARTICLE 60. The Great National Assembly of the People's Republic of Rumania is considered dissolved on the expiration of the mandate on which it was elected. The Great National Assembly of the People's Republic of Rumania can dissolve before this date.

ARTICLE 61. In case of war or in other exceptional circumstances, the Great National Assembly of the People's Republic of Rumania can prolong its mandate for the duration of the exceptional situation.

ARTICLE 62. In case war breaks out, or another exceptional circumstance arises, during the time when the Great National Assembly of the People's Republic of Rumania is dissolved, the Presidium of the dissolved Great National Assembly of the People's Republic of Rumania will convene it again, and the Assembly thus convened may prolong its mandate in accordance with Article 61.

ARTICLE 63. Elections for a new Great National Assembly of the People's Republic of Rumania must be held not later than three months after dissolution.

ARTICLE 64. Deputies receive a salary fixed by the Great National Assembly of the People's Republic of Rumania.

ARTICLE 65. Every deputy has the right of addressing questions or interpellating the government or each of the ministers. The Prime Minister or the minister thus questioned or interpellated must reply at the same sitting or at another, fixed by Great National Assembly of the People's Republic of Rumania.

TITLE V

THE ORGANS OF STATE ADMINISTRATION:
THE COUNCIL OF MINISTERS AND THE MINISTRIES

ARTICLE 66. The highest executive and administrative organ in the People's Republic of Rumania is the government.

The government consists of the president of the Council of Ministers (Prime Minister), one or more vice presidents and ministers, who together form the Council of Ministers.

ARTICLE 67. The ministries and their functions are determined by the Great National Assembly of the People's Republic of Rumania in accordance with Article 39, paragraph 4.

ARTICLE 68. The Presidium of the Great National Assembly of the People's Republic of Rumania, on the recommendation of the Council of Ministers, may appoint assistant ministers for any ministry.

ARTICLE 69. The government is responsible and accountable to the Great National Assembly of the People's Republic of Rumania for its activities, and in the interval between sessions, to the Presidium of the Great National Assembly of the People's Republic of Rumania.

ARTICLE 70. The members of the government take the oath to the Presidium of the Great National Assembly of the People's Republic of Rumania.

ARTICLE 71. Ministers will be appointed from the deputies or from persons not belonging to the ranks of the Great National Assembly of the People's Republic of Rumania. Ministers who are not appointed from the ranks of the Great National Assembly of the People's Republic of Rumania may take part in the debates of the Assembly, but are not allowed to vote.

ARTICLE 72. The government is in charge of the conduct of the state administration.

It coordinates and gives general instructions to the departments concerned, directs and plans the national economy, draws up the state budget, maintains public order and the security of the state.

The government conducts the general policy of the state in the sphere of international relations.

It organizes and equips the armed forces. The government may organize and conduct special services of any kind for certain spheres of activity, directly depending on the Council of Ministers.

The Council of Ministers may annul ministerial decisions which are not in accordance with the Constitution or the laws.

The Presidium of the Great National Assembly of the People's Republic of Rumania may annul decisions taken by the Council of Ministers which are not in accordance with the Constitution or the laws.

The decisions of the Council of Ministers are obligatory over the whole territory of the People's Republic of Rumania.

ARTICLE 73. Ministers are responsible for unlawful acts committed in the execution of their duties.

A special law will regulate the method of prosecuting and judging ministers.

ARTICLE 74. Ministers conduct their departments on the basis of the general instructions given by the Council of Ministers. Ministers make decisions in accordance with the laws which are binding on all citizens.

TITLE VI

LOCAL ORGANS OF STATE POWER

ARTICLE 75. The territory of the People's Republic of Rumania is divided for administrative purposes into communes, districts, counties and regions.

Modifications of these divisions can be made by law.

ARTICLE 76. The local organs of the state power are the local people's councils.

ARTICLE 77. The local people's councils are representative organs, elected for a four-year term by universal, direct, equal, and secret ballot.

ARTICLE 78. The local people's councils direct and conduct the local economic, social and cultural activities, in accordance with the laws and instructions issued by the superior administrative organs.

The local people's councils draw up and put into practice the economic plan and the local budget, taking into consideration the national general plan and the general budget of the state; they ensure the good administration of local assets and enterprises, maintain public order, defend the rights of the citizens, ensure the application and respect of the laws, as well as take the necessary measures for improving the local administration.

ARTICLE 79. In carrying out their duties the local people's councils rely on the initiative and wide participation of the popular masses.

ARTICLE 80. The local people's councils report to the people.

ARTICLE 81. The local people's councils meet in ordinary and extraordinary working sessions.

ARTICLE 82. The directing and executive organs of the local people's councils are the executive committees. These are elected from the ranks of the respective local people's councils, and are formed and function as established by law.

ARTICLE 83. The executive committees are responsible to the respective local people's councils.

ARTICLE 84. The people's councils and the local executive committees carry out their activities in accordance with the laws. They are subordinate to the superior people's councils and the superior executive committees, as well as to the central administrative organs of the state.

ARTICLE 85. Sections of the people's councils to deal with various activities may be created, but their activities will be subordinate to the people's councils and the executive committees under which they function. Regarding special technical guidance, they will be subordinate to the corresponding sections of the superior people's councils as well as to the appropriate central administrative organs of the state.

TITLE VII

JUDICIAL ORGANS AND THE OFFICE OF THE PUBLIC PROSECUTOR

ARTICLE 86. The judicial instances are: the Supreme Court, one for the whole country, the courts of appeal, the tribunals, and the people's courts.

ARTICLE 87. Certain special instances may be created by law for specific purposes.

ARTICLE 88. In all instances, except in the Supreme Court, the judicial proceedings take place with the assistance of people's assessors, except in cases where the law provides otherwise.

ARTICLE 89. The First President, the presidents and the members of the Supreme Court are appointed by the Presidium of the Great National Assembly of the People's Republic of Rumania, on the recommendation of the government.

ARTICLE 90. The Supreme Court supervises the activities of all judicial instances and organs as established by law.

ARTICLE 91. In all judicial instances proceedings are public, except in cases or circumstances provided by law.

ARTICLE 92. The right of defense before all instances is guaranteed.

ARTICLE 93. The judges of all grades must, in the exercise of their duties, be guided only by the law and apply the law equally to all citizens.

ARTICLE 94. The organization and the functioning of the judicial instances, as well as the way of appointing and removing judges at all stages, will be determined by law.

ARTICLE 95. In the People's Republic of Rumania the Office of the Public Prosecutor supervises the observance of penal laws, both by civil servants and by the other citizens.

ARTICLE 96. The Office of the Public Prosecutor especially supervises the prosecution and punishment of crimes committed against the democratic order and liberties, economic interests, national independence and sovereignty of the Rumanian State.

ARTICLE 97. The Office of the Public Prosecutor consists of one General Public Prosecutor of the People's Republic of Rumania and several public prosecutors.

The organization, the competence, and the functioning of the Office of the Public Prosecutor will be determined by law.

ARTICLE 98. The General Public Prosecutor is appointed by the Presidium of the Great National Assembly of the People's Republic of Rumania, on the recommendation of the government.

TITLE VIII

COAT OF ARMS, SEAL, FLAG AND CAPITAL

ARTICLE 99. The coat of arms of the People's Republic of Rumania represents mountains covered with forests, over which the sun rises. In the center there is an oil derrick, and around the coat of arms there is a crown made of spikes of wheat.

ARTICLE 100. The state seal bears the coat of arms of the country.

ARTICLE 101. The flag of the People's Republic of Rumania is made of the colors blue, yellow and red, in vertical stripes. In the center is the coat of arms of the country.

ARTICLE 102. The capital of the People's Republic of Rumania is the city of Bucharest.

TITLE IX

AMENDMENT OF THE CONSTITUTION

ARTICLE 103. The Constitution of the People's Republic of Rumania may be amended in part or as a whole on the recommendation of the government or of one-third of the members of the Great National Assembly of the People's Republic of Rumania.

ARTICLE 104. The bill amending the Constitution is considered passed if voted by two-thirds of all members of the Great National Assembly of the People's Republic of Rumania.

TITLE X

TRANSITORY DISPOSITIONS

ARTICLE 105. All existing codes and laws will be revised to agree with the Constitution.

From the day the Constitution comes into force by its publication in the official monitor, all provisions of the law, decrees, regulations and all other provisions contrary to the stipulations of the Constitution are abolished.

12. 2

CONSTITUTION OF THE
RUMANIAN PEOPLE'S REPUBLIC

September 24, 1952[1]

INTRODUCTORY CHAPTER

THE Rumanian People's Republic is a state of the working people from town and village. The Rumanian People's Republic came into being as a result of the historic victory of the Soviet Union over German fascism and of the liberation of Rumania by the glorious Soviet army; this liberation enabled the working people—with the working class led by the Communist Party at the helm—to fell the fascist dictatorship, to destroy the power of the exploiting classes, and to create a state [regime] of people's democracy which corresponds fully with the interests and aspirations of the popular masses of Rumania.

In this way it was possible to crown with an historic victory the century-long struggle carried on by the Rumanian people for freedom and independence—the heroic battles of the working class allied with the working peasantry for the felling of the capitalist landlord regime and the shaking off of the imperialist yoke.

The creation and strengthening of the state of people's democracy, the friendship and alliance with the great Soviet Union, and its brotherly support and assistance, guarantee the independence, state sovereignty, development and prosperity of the Rumanian People's Republic.

The military forces of the Rumanian People's Republic stand guard over the boundaries of the country, the sovereignty and independence of the Rumanian people, their security and peace.

The foreign policy of the Rumanian People's Republic is a policy of defense of peace, of friendship and alliance with the Union of Soviet Socialist Republics and the countries of people's democracy, and a policy of peace and friendship with all peace-loving people.

The national minorities of the Rumanian People's Republic enjoy full equality in rights with the Rumanian people. In the Rumanian People's Republic, territorial administrative autonomy is insured to the Hungarian population of the Szekler districts, where it forms a compact mass.

The present Constitution of the Rumanian People's Republic reflects the results already obtained by the working people, led by the working class, in the enterprise of building a socialist society in our country.

The policy of the state of people's democracy is directed toward liquidation of exploitation of man by man and toward the building of socialism.

---

[1] Translated for this volume by Ladis Kristof, Hoover Institution, 1967, from 'Konstitutsiia rumynskoi narodnoi respubliki, 24 sentiabria 1952 g.' in *Konstitutsii evropeiskikh stran narodnoi demokratii* (Moscow: Gosulitizdat, 1954), pp. 153–79.

CHAPTER I

THE SOCIAL SYSTEM

ARTICLE 1. The Rumanian People's Republic is a state of working people from town and village.

ARTICLE 2. The foundation of popular power in the Rumanian People's Republic is the alliance of the working class with the working peasantry, in which the leading role belongs to the working class.

ARTICLE 3. The Rumanian People's Republic was born and strengthened as a result of the country's liberation from the yoke of fascism and imperialist domination by the armed forces of the Union of Soviet Socialist Republics—and as a result of the felling of the power of the landlords and of the capitalists by the popular masses from town and village—led by the working class with the Rumanian Communist Party at its helm.

ARTICLE 4. In the Rumanian People's Republic power belongs to the working people from town and village, who exercise it through the Great National Assembly and the people's councils.

The people's councils constitute the political foundation of the Rumanian People's Republic.

ARTICLE 5. The national economy of the Rumanian People's Republic comprises three social-economic sectors: the socialist sector, the sectors of small-scale commodity production, and the private capitalist sector.

ARTICLE 6. The foundation of the social-economic socialist sector is the socialist ownership of the means of production, either in the form of state property (asset of the whole people), or in the form of cooperative collective property (property of collective farms or of cooperative organizations).

In the socialist sector of the national economy, exploitation of man by man has been liquidated.

The socialist sector, to which belongs the leading role in the national economy of the Rumanian People's Republic, is the foundation for development of the country along the socialist road. The state of people's democracy, proclaiming the building of socialism as its principal task, continually strengthens and broadens this socialist sector, insuring the continual growth of the material well-being and cultural level of the working people.

ARTICLE 7. All wealth of the subsoil, the factories, plants and mines, the forests, the waters, the sources of natural energy, all ways of communication, means of transportation by rail, river, sea and air, the banks, post, telegraphs, telephone, radio, means of printing, cinemas and theater, the state farms, the machine and tractor stations, and communal enterprises, as well as the nationalized part of the fund of dwelling houses in towns, are state property and are an asset of the whole nation.

ARTICLE 8. The land of the People's Republic of Rumania belongs to those who work it.

ARTICLE 9. The animate and inanimate inventory of the collective farms and cooperatives, their output as well as all their enterprises and buildings, are the communal property of the collective farms and of the cooperatives.

The peasant members of the collective farms hold for personal use a plot of land next to their dwellings and, as their personal property, the husbandry on that plot, a dwelling house, productive animals, poultry, and small agricultural implements—this in accordance with the collective farm statute.[2]

ARTICLE 10. The small-scale production of commodities in the Rumanian People's Republic includes small and medium-size farms of peasants holding the land in private on the basis of the producers' own labor, as well as the workshops of the craftsmen and handicraftsmen who do not exploit the work of others. The state protects on the basis of the laws in force the right to private ownership of the land of peasants with small and medium-size farms.

The people's democratic state supports the peasants with small and medium-size farms, as well as the craftsmen and handicraftsmen, with the aims of protecting them from capitalist exploitation, increasing their production, and raising their well-being.

ARTICLE 11. The private capitalist formation in the Rumanian People's Republic includes wealthy [kulak] farms, private commercial enterprises, and the small non-nationalized industrial enterprises based on the exploitation of wage labor.

The people's democratic state systematically follows a policy of isolating and eliminating the capitalist elements.

ARTICLE 12. The rights of the citizens of the Rumanian People's Republic to private property, to incomes and savings originating from work, to a dwelling house and auxiliary husbandry around the house, to household objects and items of personal use, as well as to inheritance of personal property, are protected by law.

ARTICLE 13. The economic and cultural life of the Rumanian People's Republic develops on the basis of the state plan for the national economy, in the interests of building socialism, continually raising the material and cultural well-being of the working people, and strengthening the independence and defensive capacity of the country.

ARTICLE 14. In the Rumanian People's Republic foreign commerce is a monopoly of the state.

ARTICLE 15. In the Rumanian People's Republic work is a duty and a question of honor for every citizen able to work, this according to the principle he who does not work shall not eat. In the Rumanian People's Republic the principle of socialism —from each according to his abilities, to each according to his work—is being realized on an ever widening scale.

---

[2] According to Gheorghiu-Dej, thirty of 18,836 suggested amendments to the draft constitution (published July 18, 1952) were incorporated in the final text. Of these, the most important eliminated peasants' personal property rights to their household plots and extended instead the privilege of personal use of this land—ED.

CHAPTER II

THE STATE SYSTEM

ARTICLE 16. The state system of the Rumanian People's Republic is one of people's democracy, which represents the power of the working people.

ARTICLE 17. The Rumanian people's democratic state, a unitary, sovereign and independent state:

(a) Defends the independence and sovereignty of the Rumanian people; the gains which the working people of town and village have achieved; the rights, freedoms and power of the laboring man against the enemies of the working people;

(b) Ensures the strengthening and development of the productive forces of the country through socialist industrialization, through liquidation of economic, technical and cultural backwardness and through gradual socialist transformation of agriculture on the basis of the free consent of the working peasant;

(c) Organizes and develops the planned economy on the basis of state and cooperative enterprises;

(d) Organizes the defense of the republic from foreign enemies and leads the armed forces of the country;

(e) Ensures the internal security of the citizens, and renders harmless and represses the enemies of the people;

(f) Directs the monetary and credit system, and elaborates and realizes the state budget; determines taxes, levies and other revenues necessary to cover the needs of the state;

(g) Administers the banks, as well as the industrial, agricultural and commercial state enterprises and institutions;

(h) Directs public education at all levels;

(i) Ensures the steady growth of the health and well-being of the masses of people from town and village;

(j) Ensures the development of culture—socialist in content, nationalist in form—of the Rumanian people and of the national minorities;

(k) Oversees the application and observance of the Constitution and laws of the Rumanian People's Republic, these being the expression of the will and of the interests of the working people.

The Constitution and the laws of the land prevail over the whole territory of the republic, and consequently their exact observance and application is the principal duty of every state institution and of every citizen.

ARTICLE 18. The administrative-territorial division of the Rumanian People's Republic is as follows:

The regions of Arad, Bacău, Baia Mare, Bârlad, Braşov, Bucharest, Cluj, Constanţa, Craiova, Galaţi, Hunedoara, Iaşi, Oradea, Piteşti, Ploeşti, Stalin, Suceava, Timişoara, and the Autonomous Hungarian Region.

ARTICLE 19. The Autonomous Hungarian Region of the Rumanian People's Republic is defined by the territory occupied by the compact Hungarian Szekely population and has an autonomous administration elected by the population of the autonomous region.

The Autonomous Hungarian Region includes the districts of Ciuc, Gheorgheni, Odorhei, Reghin, Sângeorgiu de Padure, Sft. Gheorghe, Târgu-Mureş, Târgu-Sâcuesc, Topliţa.

The administrative center of the Hungarian Autonomous Region is the town of Tărgu-Mureş.

ARTICLE 20. The laws of the Rumanian People's Republic, as well as the decisions and directives of the central organs of the state, are obligatory on the territory of the Autonomous Hungarian Region.

ARTICLE 21. The statute of the Hungarian Autonomous Region is drawn up by the people's council of the autonomous region and submitted for approval to the Great National Assembly of the Rumanian People's Republic.

CHAPTER III

THE SUPREME ORGAN OF STATE POWER OF THE RUMANIAN PEOPLE'S REPUBLIC

ARTICLE 22. The supreme organ of state power of the Rumanian People's Republic is the Great National Assembly of the Rumanian People's Republic.

ARTICLE 23. The Great National Assembly is the sole legislative organ of the Rumanian People's Republic.

ARTICLE 24. The direct competence of the Great National Assembly includes:

(a) Election of the Presidium of the Great National Assembly of the Rumanian People's Republic;

(b) Formation of the Government of the Rumanian People's Republic;

(c) Modification of the Constitution;

(d) Decision upon questions of war and peace;

(e) Determination of plans for the national economy;

(f) Approval of the state budget, and of the report on fulfillment of the state budget, and determination of taxes and revenues designated for the state budget;

(g) Determination of the number and names of ministries, as well as the fusion and abolition of ministries;

(h) Modification of the regional divisions of the Rumanian People's Republic;

(i) Granting of amnesty;

(j) General control over application of the Constitution.

ARTICLE 25. The Great National Assembly is elected by workers, citizens of the Rumanian People's Republic, on the basis of electoral districts providing one deputy for every 40,000 of population.

The Great National Assembly is elected for a four-year term.

ARTICLE 26. A law is considered adopted if it is passed by a simple majority of the Great National Assembly.

ARTICLE 27. Laws adopted by the Great National Assembly are then signed by the President and Secretary of the Presidium and published in the official bulletin of the Great National Assembly.

Observance of laws adopted by the Great National Assembly is obligatory for all citizens of the Rumanian People's Republic.

ARTICLE 28. Sessions of the Great National Assembly are held twice a year. The Great National Assembly is convened by its Presidium.

ARTICLE 29. The Great National Assembly may be convened in extraordinary session by its Presidium or on demand of one-third of the total number of deputies.

ARTICLE 30. The Great National Assembly elects for each of its sessions a president and two vice presidents who conduct the meetings according to the internal rules of procedure.

ARTICLE 31. The Great National Assembly validates the mandates of its elected deputies.

In order to verify the circumstances under which each deputy was elected, the Great National Assembly [appoints a] commission of validation. This commission submits its report for approval to the Great National Assembly, which then validates or nullifies the election of every deputy.

ARTICLE 32. The Great National Assembly may name commissions of inquiry and investigation into various problems.

All authorities and state employees have the obligation to put at the disposition of these commissions the necessary information and documents.

The Great National Assembly determines the powers and mode of functioning of every individual commission.

ARTICLE 33. Every deputy has the right to direct questions, or to interpellate the government or any individual minister. The government or the minister to whom the question was directed has the obligation to answer, verbally or in writing, within three days.

ARTICLE 34. No deputy may be brought to court or arrested without permission of the Great National Assembly during the sessions, or of the Presidium of the Great National Assembly during the recesses.

ARTICLE 35. The Great National Assembly of the Rumanian People's Republic elects its [own] Presidium, consisting of a president, two vice presidents, one secretary and thirteen members.

ARTICLE 36. The Presidium of the Great National Assembly is responsible for all its activity to the Great National Assembly of the Rumanian People's Republic.

ARTICLE 37. The Presidium of the Great National Assembly of the Rumanian People's Republic has the following competences:

(a) To convene sessions of the Great National Assembly;

(b) To issue decrees;

(c) To interpret the laws in force in the Rumanian People's Republic;

(d) To decide on the holding of a national consultation (referendum);

(e) To set aside the decisions and dispositions of the Council of Ministers in case these contravene the laws;

(f) In the interval between the sessions of the Great National Assembly, to release and name ministers of the Government on the recommendation of the President of the Council of Ministers, subject to subsequent approval by the Great National Assembly;

(g) To institute decorations, medals and honorific titles of the Rumanian People's Republic;

(h) To confer decorations, medals and honorific titles of the Rumanian People's Republic; to establish military and diplomatic ranks and other special titles;

(i) In the interval between the sessions of the Great National Assembly of the Rumanian People's Republic, to declare, on the recommendation of the Government, the state of war in case of an armed aggression directed against the Rumanian People's Republic or against another state toward which the Rumanian People's Republic has mutual defense obligations arising from international treaties;

(j) To name and to recall the supreme commander of the armed forces of the Rumanian People's Republic;

(k) To declare a state of partial or general mobilization;

(l) To exercise the right of pardon and commutation of punishments [sentences];

(m) To ratify and to denounce international treaties of the Rumanian People's Republic;

(n) To accredit and to recall plenipotentiary representatives of the Rumanian People's Republic in foreign countries;

(o) To accept letters of accreditation and recall of diplomatic representatives of foreign countries accredited to the Presidium;

(p) In the interest of the defense of the Rumanian People's Republic or of the securing of public order and security of the state, to proclaim a state of emergency in certain localities or on the entire territory of the country.

ARTICLE 38. The authority of the Great National Assembly ceases with the expiration of the term for which it was elected.

ARTICLE 39. After the expiration of the mandate of the Great National Assembly of the Rumanian People's Republic, the Presidium of the Great National Assembly orders new elections within a maximum period of three months from the day of the expiration of the mandate of the Great National Assembly.

The Presidium in office retains its powers until the election of a new Presidium by the new Great National Assembly of the Rumanian People's Republic.

ARTICLE 40. In case of war or other exceptional circumstances, the Great National Assembly can prolong its mandate for the duration of the state of emergency.

ARTICLE 41. The newly elected Great National Assembly is convoked by the Presidium in office within a maximum period of three months after the elections.

CHAPTER IV

THE ORGANS OF STATE ADMINISTRATION OF THE RUMANIAN PEOPLE'S REPUBLIC

ARTICLE 42. The supreme executive and administrative organ of state power of the Rumanian People's Republic is the Council of Ministers of the Rumanian People's Republic.

ARTICLE 43. The Council of Ministers is appointed by the Great National Assembly of the Rumanian People's Republic and consists of:

The president of the Council of Ministers of the Rumanian People's Republic;

The vice presidents of the Council of Ministers of the Rumanian People's Republic;

The president of the State Planning Committee;

The president of the State Control Commission;

The ministers of the Rumanian People's Republic;

The president of the State Committee on the Stocking of Agricultural Products;

The president of the State Committee for Architecture and Construction.

ARTICLE 44. The Council of Ministers is responsible to and accounts for its activities before the Great National Assembly and before the Presidium of the Great National Assembly in the intervals between the sessions of the Great National Assembly.

ARTICLE 45. The Council of Ministers of the Rumanian People's Republic issues decisions and dispositions on the basis of laws in force and with the view of carrying them into effect, and it controls their execution.

ARTICLE 46. The application of the decisions and dispositions of the Council of Ministers of the Rumanian People's Republic is obligatory throughout the territory of the Rumanian People's Republic.

ARTICLE 47. The Council of Ministers of the Rumanian People's Republic has the following competences:

(a) To coordinate and guide the activities of the ministries and of the other subordinate institutions;

(b) To take measures for the realization of the national economic plan, of the state budget, and for the consolidation of the monetary and credit system;

(c) To take measures with view of assuring public order, the defense of state interests and protection of the rights of citizens;

(d) To exercise overall direction in the domain of relations with foreign states;

(e) To establish the annual contingents of citizens to be called for the fulfillment of active military service; and to direct the general organization of the country's armed forces;

(f) To establish according to need special committees and commissions as well as general administrative departments attached to the Council of Ministers for economic, cultural, juridical and military affairs.

ARTICLE 48. The Council of Ministers of the Rumanian People's Republic can annul orders and instructions of ministers which do not conform to laws and decisions of the Council of Ministers.

ARTICLE 49. Within the limits of the jurisdiction of the ministries they direct, the ministers give orders and instructions on the basis of, and with view of executing the laws in force and the decisions and dispositions of the Council of Ministers, and they exercise control over their application.

ARTICLE 50. The ministries of the Rumanian People's Republic are the following:

The Ministry of Foreign Affairs;
The Ministry of Internal Affairs;
The Ministry of Agriculture and Forestry;
The Ministry of Railways;
The Ministry of Foreign Trade;
The Ministry of Internal Trade;
The Ministry of Construction and of the Building Materials Industry;
The Ministry of Religions;
The Ministry of Culture;
The Ministry of Electrical Energy and Electro-technical Industry;
The Ministry of Finance;
The Ministry of Armed Forces;
The Ministry of Communal Economy and Local Industry;
The Ministry of Food Industry;
The Ministry of Coal Industry;
The Ministry of Chemical Industry;
The Ministry of Metallurgical and Machine Building Industry;
The Ministry of Oil Industry;
The Ministry of Forest, Paper and Cellulose Industry;

The Ministry of Light Industry;

The Ministry of Public Education;

The Ministry of Justice;

The Ministry of Post and Telecommunication;

The Ministry of Social Insurance;

The Ministry of Health;

The Ministry of Water and Air Transport.

CHAPTER V

THE ORGANS OF LOCAL STATE POWER

ARTICLE 51. The organs of state power in the regions, districts, towns, and rural localities are the people's councils of the working people from towns and villages.

ARTICLE 52. The people's councils consist of deputies elected for a two-year term by the working men, citizens of the Rumanian People's Republic from the given region, district, town and rural locality.

The quota of representation in the People's Councils is established by law.

ARTICLE 53. The people's councils guide the work of the administrative organs subordinate to them, direct the local economic and cultural activities, assure the maintenance of public order as well as observance of laws and protection of the rights of citizens, and draw up the local budget.

ARTICLE 54. The people's councils organize the active participation of the working people in the management of state and social affairs and in the building of socialism.

ARTICLE 55. The people's councils take decisions and issue dispositions within the limits of the jurisdiction granted them by the laws of the Rumanian People's Republic.

ARTICLE 56. The executive and administrative organs of the people's councils on the regional, district, town and rural level are executive committees elected by the people's councils and consisting of president, vice president, a secretary, and members.

ARTICLE 57. The organ of state power of the Hungarian Autonomous Region is the people's council of the region.

The executive organ of the people's council of the Autonomous Hungarian Region is the executive committee elected by it.

ARTICLE 58. The people's council of the Hungarian Autonomous Region is elected, according to the norms established by law, for a two-year term by the working people of the Hungarian Autonomous Region, citizens of the Rumanian Peoples Republic.

ARTICLE 59. The executive and administrative organ of the people's councils in small communities is composed of the president, vice president, and a secretary, elected by the deputies of the respective people's council.

ARTICLE 60. The executive and administrative organs of the people's councils give account of their activities to the people's council which has elected them, as well as to the executive committee of the immediately superior [higher] people's council.

ARTICLE 61. The people's councils of regions, districts and towns organize sections of the executive committees.

The organization, mode of functioning, and activities of the sections is determined by law.

ARTICLE 62. The sections of the executive committees of the people's councils are subordinated to their respective people's council and executive committee as well as to corresponding sections of the executive committee of the immediately superior people's council and to the respective ministries.

ARTICLE 63. After the expiration of the mandate of the people's councils, the executive committees retain their competences until new executive organs are formed by the newly elected people's councils.

CHAPTER VI
THE JUDICIAL INSTITUTIONS AND THE PROCURATOR'S OFFICE

ARTICLE 64. Justice is administered in the Rumanian People's Republic by the Supreme Court of the Rumanian People's Republic, the regional courts and the people's courts, as well as by special courts as established by law.

The organization, competences and procedure of the courts are established by law.

ARTICLE 65. The courts defend the regime [system] of people's democracy and the gains of the working people; they secure rule of law for the people, public property and the rights of the citizens.

ARTICLE 66. Except when law provides otherwise, people's assessors participate in the trials at all court levels.

ARTICLE 67. The Supreme Court of the Rumanian People's Republic is elected by the Great National Assembly for a term of five years.

The judges and people's assessors are elected in conformance with the procedure established by law.

The manner of appointment of judges of special courts is also established by law.

ARTICLE 68. The judicial procedure is conducted in the Rumanian People's Republic in the Rumanian language; in regions and districts inhabited by a population of a different nationality from the Rumanian, the use of the mother tongue of that population is ensured.

Parties who do not speak the language in which the judicial process is conducted are assured of the possibility of acquainting themselves, through a translator, with the documentary evidence, and of speaking in court and presenting conclusions in their mother tongue.

ARTICLE 69. Except for cases foreseen by law, the judicial procedure at all courts is public.

The accused is guaranteed the right of defense.

ARTICLE 70. The judges are independent and subject only to the law.

ARTICLE 71. The judges pronounce the verdicts in the name of the people.

ARTICLE 72. The Supreme Court of the Rumanian People's Republic supervises the judiciary activities of all courts in the Rumanian People's Republic.

ARTICLE 73. The Procurator General of the Rumanian People's Republic exercises higher supervision over the observance of laws by ministries and other central organs of the state, and by local organs of state power and administration as well as by state functionaries and other citizens.

ARTICLE 74. The Procurator General of the Rumanian People's Republic is appointed by the Great National Assembly for a term of five years.

The deputies [substitutes] of the Procurator General of the Rumanian People's Republic and the procurator of the local units of the Procurator's Office are appointed by the Procurator General for a term of four years.

ARTICLE 75. The Procurator General is responsible to the Great National Assembly of the Rumanian People's Republic, and—in the intervals between the sessions—before the Presidium of the Great National Assembly and before the Council of Ministers.

ARTICLE 76. The organs of the Procurator's Office are independent from the local organs and subordinate themselves only to the Procurator General of the Rumanian People's Republic.

CHAPTER VII

THE FUNDAMENTAL RIGHTS AND DUTIES OF CITIZENS

ARTICLE 77. The citizens of the Rumanian People's Republic are assured of the right to work, that is the right to obtain guaranteed work paid according to its quantity and quality.

The right to work is ensured through the existence and development of the socialist sector of the national economy, through uninterrupted and systematic growth of the productive forces of the Rumanian People's Republic, through the elimination of the possibility of economic crises, and through the elimination of unemployment.

ARTICLE 78. The citizens of the Rumanian People's Republic have the right to rest.

The right to rest is ensured through establishment of an eight-hour work day for workers and office employees; reduction of the work day to less than eight hours in certain professions in which working conditions are arduous and in certain sectors in which these conditions are especially arduous; establishment of paid yearly vacations for workers and office employees; putting at the disposal of working men rest homes, sanatoria and cultural institutions.

ARTICLE 79. The citizens of the Rumanian People's Republic have the right to material security in old age and in case of sickness or employment disability.

This right is guaranteed by a broad development of social insurance of workers and office employees financed at the state expense, by free medical assistance extended to those who work, and by putting at the disposal of the working people spas and climatic [health] resorts.

ARTICLE 80. The citizens of the Rumanian People's Republic have the right to education.

This right is ensured through universal, compulsory and free elementary education; through a system of state scholarships extended to deserving students and pupils of the higher, secondary and elementary educational system [establishment]; through organization on the part of industrial enterprises, state farms, machine and tractor stations, and collective farms of free vocational instruction for those who work [for them].

Education of all levels is state education.

The state concerns itself with the development of science, literature and art.

ARTICLE 81. The working people, citizens of the Rumanian People's Republic, without distinction of nationality, race or sex, are assured of full equality of rights in all domains of economic, political and cultural life.

Any direct or indirect restriction of the rights of the working people, citizens of the Rumanian People's Republic, or establishment of direct or indirect privileges on the basis of race or nationality to which citizens belong, or any manifestation of chauvinism, race or national hatred as well as chauvinist nationalistic propaganda, is punishable by law.

ARTICLE 82. In the Rumanian People's Republic the national minorities are ensured the free use of the mother tongue, as well as education at all levels, books, newspapers and theaters in the mother tongue. In all constituencies inhabited by a nationality other than Rumanian, all the authorities and institutions will use, in word and in writing, also the language of the respective nationality and will appoint functionaries from the ranks of the respective nationality or from among other local people who are familiar with both the language and way of life of the local population.

ARTICLE 83. The woman in the Rumanian People's Republic has equal rights with the man in all the domains of economic, political, state and cultural life.

The woman has equal rights with the man to work, pay, rest, social insurance and education.

The state protects marriage and family and the interests of the mother and child. The state grants aid to mothers with many children and those who are heads of households, and paid vacations to pregnant women; it organizes maternity homes, nurseries and children's homes.

ARTICLE 84. The freedom of conscience is guaranteed to all citizens of the Rumanian People's Republic.

Religious cults are free to organize and function. The free exercise of religion is guaranteed to all citizens of the Rumanian People's Republic.

The school is separated from the church. No religious confession, congregation or community can open or maintain general educational institutions but only special schools for the training of [their] religious personnel.

The mode of organization and functioning of religious confessions is regulated by law.

ARTICLE 85. In conformity with the interests of the working people and with view of strengthening the regime of people's democracy, the citizens of the Rumanian People's Republic are guaranteed by law:

(a) Freedom of speech;

(b) Freedom of the press;

(c) Freedom of assembly and of [mass] meetings;

(d) Freedom of street processions and demonstrations.

These rights are ensured by means of putting at the disposition of the working masses and their organizations printing presses, stocks of paper, public buildings, streets, and means of communication, as well as other material prerequisites necessary for the exercise of these rights.

ARTICLE 86. In conformity with the interests of those who work and for the purpose of developing the political and public activities of the popular masses, the citizens of the Rumanian People's Republic are ensured the right to form public organizations, professional unions, cooperative societies, women's and youth organizations, sports organizations, and cultural, technical and scientific associations.

Any association with a fascist or antidemocratic character is prohibited. Participation in such associations is punished by law.

The most active and conscious elements from the ranks of the working class and other strata of working people unite in the Rumanian Workers' Party, which is the vanguard of the workers in their struggle for the strengthening and development of the people's democratic system and the building of a socialist society.

The Rumanian Workers' Party is the leading force of the organizations of the working people, as well as of the state organs and institutions. Around it unite together all the organizations of the working people in the Rumanian People's Republic.

ARTICLE 87. The citizens of the Rumanian People's Republic are guaranteed inviolability of the person.

No one can be arrested except on the basis of a decision of the court or of the procurator, conforming to the provisions of the law.

ARTICLE 88. Inviolability of the citizen's home and the secrecy of the mail are protected by law.

ARTICLE 89. The Rumanian People's Republic grants the right of asylum to foreign citizens persecuted for defending the interests of the working people, for scientific activity, or for participation in the struggle of national liberation or in defense of peace.

ARTICLE 90. It is the duty of every citizen of the Rumanian People's Republic to observe the Constitution and the laws of the state of people's democracy; to guard, strengthen and develop public socialist property; to observe labor discipline; actively to contribute to the strengthening of the regime of people's democracy and the flourishing of the country's economy and culture.

ARTICLE 91. Military service is obligatory. Military service in the ranks of the armed forces of the Rumanian People's Republic is a duty of honor for the citizens of the Rumanian People's Republic.

ARTICLE 92. To defend the fatherland is a sacred duty of every citizen of the Rumanian People's Republic. Betrayal of the fatherland, violation of the oath, going over to the side of the enemy, prejudicing the defensive capacity of the state, [and] espionage constitute the gravest crimes toward the people and state, and are punished by law with all severity.

CHAPTER VIII

THE ELECTORAL SYSTEM

ARTICLE 93. The elections of the deputies to the Great National Assembly and the people's councils take place by universal, equal, direct, and secret vote.

ARTICLE 94. The right to participate in the election of deputies is vested in all the working people, citizens of the Rumanian People's Republic, who have reached the age of eighteen years, without distinction of race, nationality, sex, religion, level of culture, profession or length of domicile, with the exception of the insane, of persons deprived of electoral right by court sentence, and of those declared unworthy by law.

Any working man, a citizen of the Rumanian People's Republic, who is in possession of the right to vote and has reached the age of twenty-three years, may be elected a deputy of the Great National Assembly.

ARTICLE 95. All working people, citizens of the Rumanian People's Republic, take equal part in the elections, each having the right to one vote.

ARTICLE 96. Women enjoy equal right with men to elect and to be elected to the Great National Assembly and to the People's Councils.

ARTICLE 97. Citizens serving in the ranks of the armed forces of the Rumanian People's Republic have the right to elect and be elected on equal terms with all the working people, citizens of the Rumanian People's Republic.

ARTICLE 98. The election of deputies is [by] direct [suffrage]. The working people, citizens of the Rumanian People's Republic, participate by direct vote in the elections to the Great National Assembly and all the people's councils.

ARTICLE 99. The election of deputies takes place by secret vote.

ARTICLE 100. The registration of candidates for the election of deputies takes place by electoral districts, according to the norms established by law.

The right to put forward candidates is ensured to all organizations of the working people: organizations of the Rumanian Workers' Party, trade unions, cooperatives, youth and other mass organizations, and cultural societies.

ARTICLE 101. Every deputy is obliged to account to his electors for his activities and the activities of the elected body of which he is a member.

The mandate of the deputy can be recalled at any time on the basis of a decision of the majority of the electors, in conformity to the procedure established by law.

CHAPTER IX

THE [COAT OF] ARMS, FLAG, AND CAPITAL OF THE RUMANIAN PEOPLE'S REPUBLIC

ARTICLE 102. The [coat of] arms of the Rumanian People's Republic represents forested mountains above which the sun rises. In the left [foreground] is an [oil] derrick. The [coat of] arms is framed by a wreath of wheat ears. In the upper part of the arms is a five-pointed star.

In the bottom part, the ears of wheat are entwined with a tricolor ribbon on which are written the letters R.P.R.

ARTICLE 103. The flag of the Rumanian People's Republic bears the colors red, yellow, and blue, arranged vertically with the blue next to the staff. In the middle [of the flag] is placed the [coat of] arms of the Rumanian People's Republic.

ARTICLE 104. The capital of the Rumanian People's Republic is Bucharest.

CHAPTER X

THE PROCEDURE FOR AMENDING THE CONSTITUTION OF THE RUMANIAN PEOPLE'S REPUBLIC

ARTICLE 105. The Constitution of the Rumanian People's Republic can be amended only by law voted by the Great National Assembly.

A bill amending the Constitution is considered adopted when at least two-thirds of the total membership of the Great National Assembly of the Rumanian People's Republic have voted for it.

12. 3

CONSTITUTION OF THE SOCIALIST REPUBLIC OF RUMANIA[1]

Adopted by the Grand National Assembly

August 20, 1965

THE SOCIALIST REPUBLIC OF RUMANIA

ARTICLE 1. Rumania is a socialist republic.

The Socialist Republic of Rumania is a sovereign, independent and unitary state of the working people of the towns and villages. Its territory is inalienable and indivisible.

ARTICLE 2. The whole power in the Socialist Republic of Rumania belongs to the people, free and masters of their destiny.

People's power is based on the worker-peasant alliance. In close union, the working class—the leading class of society—the peasantry, the intelligentsia and the other categories of working people, regardless of nationality, build the socialist system, creating the conditions for transition to communism.

ARTICLE 3. In the Socialist Republic of Rumania, the leading political force of the whole of society is the Rumanian Communist Party.

ARTICLE 4. The sovereign holder of power, the people, exercise this power through the Grand National Assembly and the People's Councils, bodies elected by universal, equal, direct and secret vote.

The Grand National Assembly and the People's Councils are the basis of the whole system of state bodies.

The Grand National Assembly is the supreme body of state power, under whose conduct and control all the other state bodies carry on their activities.

ARTICLE 5. The national economy of Rumania is a socialist economy, based on the socialist ownership of the means of production.

In the Socialist Republic of Rumania, man's exploitation by man has been abolished forever and the socialist principle of distribution according to the quantity and quality of work is implemented.

Work is a duty of honor for each citizen who is fit to work.

ARTICLE 6. Socialist ownership of the means of production is either state property —goods belonging to the whole people—or cooperative property—goods belonging to each cooperative organization.

---

[1] *Constitution of the Socialist Republic of Rumania* (Bucharest: Meridiane Publishing House, 1965). Text supplied by the Embassy of the Rumanian People's Republic, Washington, D.C.

ARTICLE 7. The wealth of the subsoil, whatever its nature, the mines, the state land, the forests, waters, sources of natural power, the factories and mills, the banks, the state farms, the machine-and-tractor stations, the means of communication, the state means of transport and telecommunication, the state buildings and dwellings, the material basis of state socio-cultural institutions belong to the whole people and are state property.

ARTICLE 8. Foreign trade is a state monopoly.

ARTICLE 9. The land of the agricultural production cooperatives, the animals, implements, installations and buildings belonging to them are cooperative property.

The plot of land which, according to the rules of the agricultural production cooperatives, is being used by the family household of the cooperative farmers is cooperative property.

The dwelling and the ancillary farm buildings, the land on which they stand and, according to the rules of the agricultural production cooperatives, the productive livestock and small agricultural dead stock are the personal property of the cooperative farmers.

The tools, machines, installations and constructions of the handicraft cooperatives and of the consumer cooperatives are cooperative property.

ARTICLE 10. The agricultural production cooperatives, a socialist form of agricultural organization, secure the conditions for the intensive cultivation of the land and the application of advanced science and contribute, by increasing output, to the development of the national economy, to the continuous raising of the living standard of the peasantry and of the whole people.

The state gives support to the agricultural production cooperatives and protects their property. The state also gives support to the other cooperative organizations and protects their property.

ARTICLE 11. In the conditions of cooperativized agriculture, the state guarantees, according to the law, to the peasants who cannot associate themselves in agricultural production cooperatives ownership of the land which they themselves and their families are working as well as ownership of the implements they use with this purpose.

The handicraftsmen are also guaranteed ownership of their own workshops.

ARTICLE 12. Land and buildings can be expropriated only for work of public interest and on payment of an equitable compensation.

ARTICLE 13. In the Socialist Republic of Rumania the whole of state activity has as its purpose the development of the socialist system, the continuous growth of the people's living standard and cultural level, the ensurance of the freedom and dignity of man, the many-sided affirmation of the human person.

For this purpose, the Rumanian socialist state:

Organizes, plans and conducts the national economy;

Defends the socialist property;

Guarantees the full exercise of citizen rights, assures socialist legality and defends the rule of law;

Develops education at all levels, ensures the conditions for the development of
science, the arts and culture, carries out public health protection;

Ensures defense of the country and organizes its armed forces;

Organizes relations with other states.

ARTICLE 14. The Socialist Republic of Rumania maintains and develops relations
of friendship and fraternal collaboration with the socialist countries, promotes
relations of collaboration with countries having other socio-political systems,
activates in international organizations with a view to ensuring peace and understanding among the peoples.

The foreign relations of the Socialist Republic of Rumania are based on the
principles of observance of sovereignty and national independence, equal rights
and mutual advantage, noninterference in internal affairs.

ARTICLE 15. The territory of the Socialist Republic of Rumania is organized in
territorial-administrative units: regions, districts, towns and villages.

The regions of the Socialist Republic of Rumania are:

Argeş, Bacău, Banat, Braşov, Bucharest, Cluj, Crişana, Dobruja, Galaţi,
Hunedoara, Jassy, Maramureş, Mureş—Magyar Autonomous, Oltenia, Ploieşti and
Suceava.

The capital of the Socialist Republic of Rumania is the city of Bucharest.

ARTICLE 16. Rumanian citizenship is acquired and lost according to the law.

CHAPTER II

THE FUNDAMENTAL RIGHTS AND
DUTIES OF THE CITIZENS

ARTICLE 17. The citizens of the Socialist Republic of Rumania, irrespective of
nationality, race, sex or religion, have equal rights in all fields of economic, political,
juridical, social and cultural life.

The state guarantees the equal rights of the citizens. No restriction of these
rights and no difference in their exercise on the grounds of nationality, race, sex or
religion are permitted.

Any expression aiming to establish such restrictions, nationalist-chauvinist
propaganda, the fanning of racial or national hatred are punished by the law.

ARTICLE 18. In the Socialist Republic of Rumania, the citizens have the right to
work. Each citizen is given the possibility to carry on, according to his training, an
activity in the economic, administrative, social or cultural field and is remunerated
according to its quantity and quality. For equal work there is equal pay.

The law establishes the measures for the protection and safety of labor as well
as special measures for the protection of the work of women and young people.

ARTICLE 19. The citizens of the Socialist Republic of Rumania have the right
to leisure.

The right to leisure is guaranteed to those who work by the establishment of the
maximum duration of the working day at eight hours, of weekly rest and of annual
paid holidays.

In the sectors of arduous and very arduous work, the working day is reduced to less than eight hours, without any reduction in pay.

ARTICLE 20. The citizens of the Socialist Republic of Rumania have the right to material security in case of old age, sickness or incapacity to work.

The right to material security is implemented for factory and office workers through pensions and sickness benefits paid by the state social insurance system, and for the members of the cooperative organizations or of other public organizations through the forms of insurance organized by these organizations. The state ensures medical assistance through its health units.

Paid maternity leave is guaranteed.

ARTICLE 21. The citizens of the Socialist Republic of Rumania have the right to education.

The right to education is ensured by general and compulsory eight-year elementary education, by the fact that education at all levels is free and by the system of state scholarships.

Education in the Socialist Republic of Rumania is state education.

ARTICLE 22. In the Socialist Republic of Rumania the co-inhabiting nationalities are ensured the free utilization of their native language as well as books, papers, magazines, theaters and education at all levels in their own language. In districts also inhabited by a population of non-Rumanian nationality, all the bodies and institutions use the language of the respective nationality in speech and in writing and appoint officials from its ranks or from the ranks of other citizens who know the language and way of life of the local population.

ARTICLE 23. In the Socialist Republic of Rumania women have equal rights with men.

The state protects marriage and the family and defends the interests of mother and child.

ARTICLE 24. The Socialist Republic of Rumania ensures to young people the conditions required for the development of their physical and intellectual aptitudes.

ARTICLE 25. The citizens of the Socialist Republic of Rumania have the right to elect and to be elected to the Grand National Assembly and the People's Councils.

The vote is universal, equal, direct and secret. All citizens who have reached the age of eighteen years have the right to vote.

Citizens with the right to vote who have reached the age of twenty-three years can be elected as deputies to the Grand National Assembly and to the People's Councils.

The right to nominate candidates is ensured to all organizations of the working people: the organizations of the Rumanian Communist Party, the trade unions, the cooperatives, the youth and women's organizations, the cultural associations and other mass and public organizations.

The electors have the right to recall their deputy at any time, according to the same procedure under which he has been nominated and elected.

Mentally alienated and deficient people have no right to elect and to be elected, [not have] persons deprived of these rights during the period laid down by a court of law in its sentence.

ARTICLE 26.   The most advanced and conscious [sic] citizens from the ranks of the workers, peasants, intellectuals and other categories of working people unite in the Rumanian Communist Party, the highest form of organization of the working class, its vanguard detachment.

The Rumanian Communist Party expresses and loyally serves the aspirations and vital interests of the people, implements the role of leader in all the fields of socialist construction, and directs the activity of the mass and public organizations and of the state bodies.

ARTICLE 27.   The citizens of the Socialist Republic of Rumania have the right to associate themselves in trade union, cooperative, youth, women's and socio-cultural organizations, in creative unions, scientific, technical, sports associations and other public organizations.

The state gives support to the activity of the mass and public organizations, creates conditions for the development of the material basis of these organizations and defends their property according to the law.

The mass and public organizations ensure the large participation of the mass of the people in the political, economic, social and cultural life of the Socialist Republic of Rumania and in the exercise of public control—an expression of the democratic spirit of the socialist system. Through the mass and public organizations the Rumanian Communist Party achieves an organized link with the working class, the peasantry, the intelligentsia and the other categories of working people, mobilizes them in the struggle for the completion of the building of socialism.

ARTICLE 28.   The citizens of the Socialist Republic of Rumania are guaranteed freedom of speech, of the press, of reunion, of meeting and demonstration.

ARTICLE 29.   The freedom of speech, of the press, reunion, meeting and demonstration cannot be used for aims hostile to the socialist system and to the interests of the working people.

Any association of a fascist or anti-democratic character is prohibited. Participation in such associations and propaganda of a fascist or anti-democratic character are punished by the law.

ARTICLE 30.   Freedom of conscience is guaranteed to all the citizens of the Socialist Republic of Rumania.

Anybody is free to share or not to share a religious belief. The freedom of exercising a religious cult is guaranteed. The religious cults organize and function freely. The way of organization and functioning of the religious cults is regulated by law.

The school is separated from the Church. No religious confession, congregation or community can open or maintain any other teaching establishments than special schools for the training of servants of the Church.

ARTICLE 31.   The citizens of the Socialist Republic of Rumania are guaranteed inviolability of their person.

No person can be detained or arrested if there are no well-grounded proofs or indications that he has committed a deed listed and punished by the law. The organs of inquiry can order the detention of a person for a maximum of twenty-four hours. No one can be arrested except on the basis of an order of arrest issued by a court or the Procurator.

ARTICLE 32. The domicile is inviolable.

No one can enter the dwelling of a person without the latter's consent, except in the cases and conditions specially laid down by the law.

ARTICLE 33. The secret [sic] of correspondence and of telephone conversations is guaranteed.

ARTICLE 34. The right to petition is guaranteed. The state bodies have the obligation to resolve, according to the law, the petitions of the citizens concerning personal or public rights and interests.

ARTICLE 35. Those harmed in a right of theirs by an illegal act of a state body can ask the competent bodies, in the conditions provided by the law, to annul the act and repair the damage.

ARTICLE 36. The right to personal property is protected by the law.

Objects of the right to personal property can be income and savings derived from work, the dwelling house, the household around it and the land on which they stand, as well as the goods of personal use and comfort.

ARTICLE 37. The right to inheritance is protected by the law.

ARTICLE 38. The Socialist Republic of Rumania grants the right of refuge to foreign citizens persecuted for their activity in defense of the interests of the working people, for their participation in the fight for national liberation or in defense of peace.

ARTICLE 39. Every citizen of the Socialist Republic of Rumania is bound to respect the Constitution and the laws, to defend socialist property, to contribute to the strengthening and development of the socialist system.

ARTICLE 40. Military service in the ranks of the armed forces of the Socialist Republic of Rumania is compulsory and is a duty of honor of the citizens of the Socialist Republic of Rumania.

ARTICLE 41. To defend the homeland is the sacred duty of each citizen of the Socialist Republic of Rumania. Violation of the military oath, treason to the homeland, desertion to the enemy, prejudice to the defensive capacity of the state are the greatest crimes against the people and are punished by the law with the utmost severity.

CHAPTER III

THE SUPREME BODIES OF STATE POWER

The Grand National Assembly

ARTICLE 42. The Grand National Assembly, the supreme body of state power, is the sole legislative body of the Socialist Republic of Rumania.

ARTICLE 43. The Grand National Assembly has the following main attributions:

1) It adopts and amends the Constitution of the Socialist Republic of Rumania;

2) It regulates the electoral system;

3) It approves the State Plan of the National Economy, the State Budget and the general final account of the budgetary exercise;

4) It organizes the Council of Ministers, the ministries, and the other central bodies of state administration;

5) It regulates the organization of courts and the Procurator's Office;

6) It establishes the norms for the organization and functioning of the people's councils;

7) It establishes the administrative organization of the territory;

8) It grants amnesty;

9) It ratifies and denounces international treaties that imply modification of laws;

10) It elects and recalls the State Council;

11) It elects and recalls the Council of Ministers;

12) It elects and recalls the Supreme Court and the Procurator General;

13) It exercises general control of the application of the Constitution (it is only the Grand National Assembly that decides on the constitutionality of the laws);

14) It controls the activity of the State Council;

15) It controls the activity of the Council of Ministers, of the ministries and of the other central bodies of state administration;

16) It hears reports on the activity of the Supreme Court and controls its directive decisions;

17) It controls the activity of the Procurator's Office;

18) It exercises general control of the activity of the People's Councils;

19) It establishes the general line of foreign policy;

20) It proclaims, in the interest of the country's defense, of public order or state security, the state of urgency in some localities, or throughout the country's territory;

21) It orders partial or general mobilization;

22) It declares the state of war. The state of war can be declared only in case of armed aggression directed against the Socialist Republic of Rumania or against another state toward which the Socialist Republic of Rumania has mutual defense obligations arising from international treaties, if a situation has come about for which the obligation of declaring a state of war has been laid down;

23) It appoints and recalls the Supreme Commander of the Armed Forces.

ARTICLE 44. The deputies to the Grand National Assembly are elected in constituencies with the same number of inhabitants. The constituencies are established by decrees of the State Council.

One deputy is elected for every constituency.

The Grand National Assembly is made up of 465 deputies.

ARTICLE 45. The Grand National Assembly is elected for a term of four years, reckoned from the date the mandate of the previous Grand National Assembly has expired.

The mandate of the Grand National Assembly cannot cease before the term it has been elected for has expired.

In case it finds that there are circumstances which make [it] impossible to hold elections, the Grand National Assembly can decide to prolong its mandate for the duration of these circumstances.

ARTICLE 46. Elections to the Grand National Assembly are held on one non-working day in the last month of every legislature. The date of elections is established at least sixty days before.

The newly-elected Grand National Assembly is convened during the three months following the expiration of the mandate of the previous Grand National Assembly.

ARTICLE 47. The Grand National Assembly verifies the legality of the election of every deputy, deciding on the validation or annulment of his election.

In the case of an annulled election, the rights and duties of the deputy cease from the moment of annulment.

ARTICLE 48. The Grand National Assembly adopts its rules of functioning.

ARTICLE 49. The Grand National Assembly establishes its annual budget, which is included in the State Budget.

ARTICLE 50. The Grand National Assembly elects, for the duration of the legislature, the Bureau of the Grand National Assembly, formed of the Chairman of the Grand National Assembly and four vice-chairmen.

ARTICLE 51. The Chairman of the Grand National Assembly conducts the proceedings of the sessions of the Grand National Assembly.

The Chairman of the Grand National Assembly can designate any one of the four vice-chairmen to fulfill some of his attributions.

ARTICLE 52. The Grand National Assembly elects standing commissions formed of deputies.

The standing commissions draw up reports or opinions on bills or matters sent to them for study, according to their competence, by the Chairman of the Grand National Assembly.

At the request of the State Council, the standing commissions draw up opinions on the draft of decrees with the power of law.

The Grand National Assembly can elect temporary commissions for any problem or field of activity, establishing the authority and mode of activity for each of these commissions.

All the state bodies and officials are obliged to put at the disposal of the commissions of the Grand National Assembly the requested information and documents.

ARTICLE 53. In exercising control of the constitutionality of laws, the Grand National Assembly elects a Constitutional Commission for the duration of the legislature.

Experts who are not deputies, members of the Supreme Court, teachers of higher education and scientific researchers, can be elected to the Constitutional Commission; their number must not exceed one-third of the total membership of the Commission.

The Commission presents to the Grand National Assembly reports and opinions at its own initiative or at the intimation of the bodies provided for by the rules of the Grand National Assembly.

ARTICLE 54. The Grand National Assembly works in sessions.

Ordinary sessions of the Grand National Assembly are convened twice a year.

The Grand National Assembly is convened, whenever necessary, in special sessions, at the initiative of the State Council or of at least one-third of the total number of deputies.

ARTICLE 55. The Grand National Assembly works only if at least one-half plus one of the total number of deputies are present.

ARTICLE 56. The Grand National Assembly adopts laws and decisions.

The laws and decisions are adopted by a majority vote of the deputies to the Grand National Assembly.

The Constitution is adopted and amended by the vote of at least two-thirds of the total number of deputies to the Grand National Assembly.

The laws and decisions of the Grand National Assembly are signed by the Chairman or vice-chairman of the Grand National Assembly who conducted the meeting.

ARTICLE 57. After their adoption by the Grand National Assembly, the laws are published in the Official Bulletin of the Socialist Republic of Rumania within a maximum of ten days, signed by the President of the State Council.

ARTICLE 58. Every deputy to the Grand National Assembly has the right to put questions and address interpellations to the Council of Ministers or to any of its members.

Within the framework of the control exercised by the Grand National Assembly, a deputy can put questions and address interpellations to the president of the Supreme Court and to the Procurator General.

The person to whom a question or interpellation has been put is obliged to reply orally or in writing in a maximum of three days, and in any case during the same session.

ARTICLE 59. In preparation of the discussions of the Grand National Assembly or of interpellations, the deputy has the right to ask for the necessary information from any state body applying for this purpose to the Bureau of the Grand National Assembly.

ARTICLE 60. Every deputy is obliged to report periodically to the electorate on his activity and on that of the Grand National Assembly.

ARTICLE 61. No deputy to the Grand National Assembly can be detained, arrested or sent for trial without the previous consent of the Grand National Assembly during session and of the State Council between sessions.

Only in case of flagrant infraction can a deputy be detained without this consent.

The State Council

ARTICLE 62. The State Council of the Socialist Republic of Rumania is the supreme body of state power with a permanent activity; it is subordinated to the Grand National Assembly.

ARTICLE 63. The State Council permanently exercises the following main attributions:

1) It establishes the date of elections to the Grand National Assembly and People's Councils;

2) It appoints and recalls the heads of central bodies of state administration who are not on the Council of Ministers;

3) It establishes the military ranks; it grants the ranks of general, admiral and marshal;

4) It institutes and confers decorations and honorary titles; it authorizes the wearing of decorations conferred by other states;

5) It grants pardon;

6) It grants citizenship, approves renunciation of citizenship and withdraws the Rumanian citizenship;

7) It grants the right of refuge;

8) It ratifies and denounces international treaties, with the exception of those whose ratification and denouncement is within the competence of the Grand National Assembly;

9) It establishes the ranks of diplomatic missions, appoints and recalls diplomatic representatives of the Socialist Republic of Rumania;

10) It receives letters of credence and of recall of diplomatic representatives of other states;

11) In international relations the State Council, through its President, represents the Socialist Republic of Rumania.

ARTICLE 64. The State Council exercises, in the interval between the sessions of the Grand National Assembly, the following main attributions:

1) It convenes the sessions of the Grand National Assembly;

2) It establishes, without being able to change the Constitution, norms with the power of law. The norms with the power of law are tabled, at the first session, for discussion to the Grand National Assembly according to the procedure for the adoption of laws. The State Plan of the National Economy, the State Budget as well as the general final account of the

budgetary exercise, can be approved by the State Council if the Grand
National Assembly cannot meet due to exceptional circumstances;

3) It appoints and recalls the Council of Ministers, the Supreme Court and
   the Procurator General if the Grand National Assembly cannot meet
   because of exceptional circumstances;

4) It gives the laws in force a general and compulsory interpretation;

5) It grants amnesty;

6) It controls the application of laws and decisions of the Grand National
   Assembly, the activity of the Council of Ministers, of the ministries and of
   the other central bodies of state administration as well as the activity of the
   Procurator's Office; it listens to the reports of the Supreme Court and controls its directive decisions; it controls the activity of the people's councils;

7) It appoints and recalls the members of the Council of Ministers at the
   proposal of its Chairman;

8) It appoints and recalls the President and members of the Supreme Court;

9) In the interest of defending the Socialist Republic of Rumania, of ensuring
   public order or state security, it proclaims in case of emergency, in some
   localities or throughout the country's territory, the state of urgency;

10) It orders, in case of emergency, partial or general mobilization;

11) It declares, in case of emergency, the state of war. The state of war can be
    declared only in the event of armed aggression directed against the Socialist
    Republic of Rumania or against another state toward which the Socialist
    Republic of Rumania has mutual defense obligations arising from
    international treaties, if a situation has come about for which the obligation
    of declaring a state of war has been laid down;

12) It appoints and recalls the Supreme Commander of the Armed Forces.

ARTICLE 65. The State Council is elected by the Grand National Assembly from
among its members for the duration of the legislature in its first session. The State
Council functions up to the election of the new State Council in the following
legislature.

ARTICLE 66. The State Council is formed of the President of the State Council,
three vice presidents and fifteen members.

The State Council elects a secretary from among its members.

ARTICLE 67. The State Council carries on its activity according to the principle of
collective leadership.

ARTICLE 68. The State Council issues decrees and adopts decisions.

The decrees and decisions are signed by the President of the State Council.
The decrees with the power of law are published in the Official Bulletin of the
Socialist Republic of Rumania.

ARTICLE 69. The State Council reports to the Grand National Assembly on the
exercise of its attributions, as well as on the observance and execution in state
activity of the laws and decisions of the Grand National Assembly.

The State Council as a whole and every one of its members are responsible to the Grand National Assembly. The members of the State Council answer both for their own activity and for the entire activity of the State Council.

CHAPTER IV

THE CENTRAL BODIES OF STATE ADMINISTRATION

ARTICLE 70. The Council of Ministers is the supreme body of state administration.
The Council of Ministers exercises the general conduct of the executive activity for the whole territory of the country and has the following main attributions:

1) It establishes general measures for the implementation of the state's home and foreign policy;

2) It organizes and ensures the application of the laws;

3) It guides, coordinates and controls the activity of the ministries and of the other central bodies of state administration;

4) It takes measures with a view to ensuring public order, defending the interests of the state and protecting the rights of the citizens;

5) It works out the draft of the State Plan and the draft [of the] State Budget; it draws up the general final account of the budgetary exercise;

6) It establishes measures for the implementation of the State Plan and the State Budget;

7) It sets up enterprises, economic state organizations and institutions of republican interest;

8) It establishes the annual contingents of citizens to be called up for military service; it takes measures for the general organization of the armed forces;

9) It exercises the general conduct in relations with other states and takes measures for the conclusion of international agreements;

10) It suspends the decisions of the regional people's councils which are not in accordance with the law;

11) It exercises the conduct, direction and general control of the activity of the executive committees of all people's councils.

ARTICLE 71. The Council of Ministers is elected by the Grand National Assembly for the duration of the legislature in its first session. The Council of Ministers functions [until] the election of the new Council of Ministers in the following legislature.

ARTICLE 72. In the fulfillment of its attributions, the Council of Ministers adopts decisions on the basis and in view of the application of the laws.

The decisions of a normative character are published in the Official Bulletin of the Socialist Republic of Rumania.

ARTICLE 73. The Council of Ministers is formed of the Chairman of the Council of Ministers, the vice-chairmen of the Council of Ministers, of whom one or more can be first vice-chairmen; ministers, as well as heads of other central bodies of state administration provided for by law.

ARTICLE 74. The Council of Ministers carries on its activity according to the principle of collective leadership, ensuring the unity of political and administrative action of the ministries and of the other central bodies of state administration.

ARTICLE 75. The Council of Ministers as a whole, and every one of its members, is responsible to the Grand National Assembly and in the interval between sessions [of the Grand National Assembly], to the State Council. Every member of the Council of Ministers is answerable both for his own activity and for the entire activity of the Council of Ministers.

ARTICLE 76. The ministries and the other central bodies of state administration implement the state policy in the branches or fields of activity for which they have been set up.

ARTICLE 77. The ministers and the heads of the other central bodies of state administration issue, on the basis and in view of applying the laws and the decisions of the Council of Ministers, instructions and orders as well as other acts provided for by law; their acts of a normative character are published in the Official Bulletin of the Socialist Republic of Rumania.

ARTICLE 78. The ministers and the other heads of central bodies of state administration are responsible to the Council of Ministers for the activity of the body which they lead.

CHAPTER V

THE LOCAL BODIES OF STATE POWER AND THE LOCAL BODIES OF STATE ADMINISTRATION

ARTICLE 79. The People's Councils are the local bodies of state power in the regions, districts, towns, and villages.

The People's Councils conduct the local activity, securing the economic, socio-cultural and administrative development of the territorial-administrative units in which they have been elected, the maintaining of public order, socialist legality and the protection of citizen rights.

The People's Councils organize the participation of the citizens in the solution of state and public affairs on the local level.

ARTICLE 80. The People's Council exercises the following main attributions:

1) It adopts the local budget and economic plan, approves the final account of the budgetary exercise;

2) It elects and recalls the executive committee of the People's Council;

3) It establishes enterprises, economic organizations and state institutions of local interest;

4) It conducts, directs and controls the activity of its executive committee, of the local specialized bodies of the state administration, of the subordinated enterprises and institutions;

5) It controls the acts of hierarchically inferior People's Councils.

ARTICLE 81. The People's Councils are formed of deputies elected by the constituencies, one deputy being elected for each constituency.

The constituencies formed for the election of the deputies to a People's Council have the same number of inhabitants.

The mandate of the People's Council is of four years, except that of the village People's Council which is of two years. The mandate is reckoned from the date of the end of the mandate of the preceding People's Council.

The new elections are held on the one of the non-working days during the last month of the mandate of the People's Council.

ARTICLE 82. The People's Councils elect from among the deputies standing commissions which help them in the fulfillment of their tasks.

ARTICLE 83. The People's Councils work in sessions; the convocation of sessions is made by the executive committee of the People's Council.

Special sessions are called at the initiative of the executive committee or at the demand of at least one-third of the total number of deputies.

ARTICLE 84. The People's Councils work in the presence of at least one-half plus one member of the total number of deputies. At each session the People's Council elects a presidium to conduct its proceedings.

ARTICLE 85. Each deputy is obliged to present periodically to the electorate reports on his activity and on that of the People's Council to which he has been elected.

ARTICLE 86. The People's Councils adopt decisions.

A decision is adopted if it receives the vote of the majority of the People's Council deputies.

Decisions of a normative character are communicated to the citizens in the forms provided for by the law.

ARTICLE 87. The executive committee of the People's Council is the local body of state administration with general competence in the territorial-administrative unit in which the People's Council has been elected.

ARTICLE 88. The executive committee of the People's Council has the following principal attributions:

1) It carries out the laws, decrees and decisions of the Council of Ministers and the other acts of the superior bodies;

2) It applies the decisions of the People's Council which has elected it;

3) It works out the drafts of the local budget and economic plan; it elaborates the final account of the budgetary exercise;

4) It carries out the local budget and economic plan;

5) It conducts, directs and controls the activity of the specialized local bodies of the state administration and of the subordinated institutions and enterprises;

6) It conducts, directs and controls the activity of the executive committees of the People's Councils which are hierarchically inferior to the People's Council which has elected it;

7) It suspends the decisions of the People's Councils directly subordinated to the People's Council that has elected it which are not in accordance with the law.

ARTICLE 89. The members of the executive committee are elected by the People's Council from among its deputies at the first session after the elections for the duration of the mandate of the People's Council.

After the expiry of the mandate of the People's Council, the executive committee continues to function up to the election of the new executive committee.

ARTICLE 90. The executive committee of the People's Council is formed of a chairman, vice-chairmen and a number of members established by the law.

The executive committee carries on its activity according to the principle of collective leadership.

ARTICLE 91. In the exercise of its attributions, the executive committee of the People's Council issues decisions on the basis of and with a view to the implementation of the law.

Decisions of a normative character are communicated to the citizens in the forms provided for by the law.

ARTICLE 92. The executive committee is responsible for its activity to the People's Council which has elected it.

The executive committee is also responsible to the executive committee of the hierarchically superior People's Council; the executive committee of the regional People's Council is responsible to the Council of Ministers.

ARTICLE 93. Specialized local bodies of the state administration attached to the executive committees of the regional, district and city People's Councils are organized and function according to the law.

CHAPTER VI
THE COURTS

ARTICLE 94. In the Socialist Republic of Rumania the law is administered by the Supreme Court, regional courts, people's courts and by military courts established according to the law.

ARTICLE 95. By their judiciary activity, the courts defend the socialist system and the rights of persons, educating the citizens in the spirit of respect for the law.

In applying penal sanctions, the courts aim to reform and re-educate infractors and to prevent the commission of new infractions.

ARTICLE 96. The courts try civil, penal and any other cases in their competence.

In the cases provided for by the law, the courts exercise control over the decisions of administrative or public bodies having a jurisdictional activity.

The courts try the demands of those harmed in their rights by administrative acts and can, in the conditions provided for by the law, also give their views on the legality of these acts.

ARTICLE 97. The Supreme Court exercises general control over the judicial activity of all the courts. The way of exercising this control is established by law.

With a view to the uniform application of the laws in judicial activity, the Supreme Court, in its plenum, issues decisions of direction.

ARTICLE 98. The Supreme Court is elected by the Grand National Assembly for the duration of the legislature in its first session.

The Supreme Court functions up to the election of the new Supreme Court in the following legislature.

ARTICLE 99. The Supreme Court is responsible for its activity to the Grand National Assembly, and between sessions to the State Council.

ARTICLE 100. The organization of the courts, their competence and judicial procedure are established by law.

Cases in the first instance at the people's courts, the regional courts and the military courts are tried with the participation of people's jurors, unless otherwise provided for by law.

ARTICLE 101. Judges and people's jurors are elected in accordance with the procedure established by law.

ARTICLE 102. In the Socialist Republic of Rumania judicial procedure is in the Rumanian language and, in the regions and districts inhabited by a population of another nationality than Rumanian, the use of the mother tongue of that population is assured.

The parties who do not speak the language in which the trial is held are given the possibility of becoming acquainted through an interpreter with the files and the right to speak in court and to sum up in the mother tongue.

ARTICLE 103. Trials are held in public sessions unless otherwise provided for by law.

ARTICLE 104. In their judicial activity the judges and the people's jurors are independent and subject only to the law.

ARTICLE 105. The right to defense is guaranteed throughout the trial.

CHAPTER VII

THE ORGANS OF THE PROCURATOR'S OFFICE

ARTICLE 106. The Procurator's Office of the Socialist Republic of Rumania exercises the supervision of the observance of the law by the ministries and the other central bodies of the state administration, the local bodies of the state administration, the penal prosecution organs and the courts, as well as by the officials and other citizens.

ARTICLE 107. The Procurator's Office is conducted by the Procurator General. The organs of the Procurator's Office are the Procurator General's Office, the Procurator's regional, district and city offices and the Procurator's military office.

The organs of the Procurator's Office are hierarchically subordinated.

ARTICLE 108. The Procurator General is elected by the Grand National Assembly for the duration of the legislature in its first session and functions up to the election of the new Procurator General in the first session of the following legislature.

The procurators are appointed by the Procurator General.

ARTICLE 109. The Procurator General is responsible to the Grand National Assembly for the activity of the Procurator's Office, and between sessions to the State Council.

CHAPTER VIII

THE INSIGNIA OF THE SOCIALIST REPUBLIC OF RUMANIA

ARTICLE 110. The emblem of the Socialist Republic of Rumania represents wooded mountains over which the sun is rising. In the left part of the emblem there is an oil derrick. The emblem is surrounded by a wreath of wheat ears. The emblem is surmounted by a five-pointed star. At the base of the emblem the sheaves are bound with a tricolor ribbon bearing the words 'Republica Socialistă România.'

ARTICLE 111. The state seal bears the country's emblem, around which are the words 'REPUBLICA SOCIALISTĂ ROMÂNIA.'

ARTICLE 112. The flag of the Socialist Republic of Rumania bears the colors red, yellow and blue, placed vertically, with the blue stripe next to the flag staff. The emblem of the Socialist Republic of Rumania is placed in the center.

ARTICLE 113. The anthem of the Socialist Republic of Rumania is approved by the Grand National Assembly.

CHAPTER IX

FINAL AND TRANSITORY PROVISIONS

ARTICLE 114. The present Constitution comes into force on the date of its adoption.

ARTICLE 115. The Constitution of September 24, 1952, and any provisions of laws, decrees and other normative acts that are contrary to the provisions of the present Constitution are abrogated on the same date.

ARTICLE 116. The banknotes and coins with the imprint of the present name of the state 'Republica Populară Română' and 'Banca Republicii Populare Române—Banca de stat' will continue to have full power of circulation.

They will be withdrawn from circulation only as they wear out.

The banknotes and coins that will be put into circulation according to legal provisions with the new name of the state 'Republica Socialistă România' and the new name of the Bank 'Banca Naţională a Republicii Socialiste România' will circulate simultaneously with the current money.

SECTION 13

CZECHOSLOVAKIA

13. 1

CONSTITUTION OF THE
CZECHOSLOVAK REPUBLIC[1]

(Constitutional Act of May 9, 1948)

Promulgated on June 9, 1948, as No. 150 of the
Collection of Acts and Orders of the Czechoslovak Republic[2]

THE Constituent National Assembly of the Czechoslovak Republic has enacted the following Constitutional Act:

DECLARATION

We, the Czechoslovak People, declare that we are firmly resolved to build up our liberated state as a People's democracy which will ensure to us a peaceful road to socialism.

We are determined to defend with all our strength the achievements of our national and democratic revolution against all the endeavors of domestic and foreign reaction, as we have proved afresh before the whole world by the action we took in defense of the People's Democratic Order in February 1948.

We mutually pledge ourselves that our two nations shall labor at this great task together, hand in hand, thus continuing the progressive and humanitarian traditions of our history.

The Czechs and Slovaks, two brotherly nations,[3] members of the great Slav family of nations, lived already a thousand years ago jointly in a single state, and jointly accepted from the East the highest achievement of the culture of that era—Christianity. As the first in Europe they raised on their standards, during the Hussite revolution, the ideas of liberty of thought, government of the people, and social justice.

For centuries on, the Czech and Slovak people fought the feudal exploiters and the German Hapsburg Dynasty for social and national liberation. The thoughts of freedom, progress and humanity were the guiding ideas of our two nations when in the nineteenth century, they entered, by the joint effort of Slovak and Czech intellectual pioneers who had sprung from the people, upon the era of national revival. Under this flag also both our nations began their joint struggle against German imperialism during the First World War, and, inspired by the great Octo-

---

[1] *The Constitution of the Czechoslovak Republic* (Prague: Czechoslovak Ministry of Information, 1948).

[2] This Constitutional Act became operative on the day of promulgation.

[3] The term 'nation' *(národ)* denotes throughout the linguistically and culturally distinct Czech and Slovak ethnic groups respectively; the term 'People' *(lid)* denotes the entire population as a political unit. Hence, 'national' *(národní)* means 'pertaining to the Czech (or Slovak) nation' and is not synonymous, as in current English usage, with 'of or pertaining to the state' (cf. also esp. Part V).—TR.

ber Revolution, they created after centuries of subjection, on October 28, 1918, their common state—the democratic Republic of Czechoslovakia.

Already then, during the first resistance movement, our people, inspired by the great example of the revolutionary struggle of the Russian workers and peasants, longed for a better social order, for socialism. But this progressive endeavor, true to our best traditions, was shortly brought to naught, when, upon the split of the workers' movement in December 1920, the numerically weak section of capitalists and landowners succeeded in turning back, in spite of the democratic Constitution, the progressive development of our Republic, and in establishing the capitalist economic order with all its attendant evils, above all the nightmare of unemployment.

When before long a new imperialist expansion, in the foul likeness of German nazism, threatened both our nations with destruction, then once again, as the nobility had betrayed the people in the Hussite wars, now the latter-day ruling class, the bourgeoisie, allied itself in the time of greatest peril with the enemy against the people and thus enabled world imperialism to settle its differences, albeit temporarily, at the expense of both our nations, by the shameful Munich Pact.

Thus the road was cleared for the rape of our peace-loving country by the ancient enemy, with the zealous assistance of the descendants of alien colonists settled in our midst and enjoying, equally with us, full democratic rights in accordance with our Constitution. The dreadful events of the Second World War saw our two nations again united in the common struggle for liberation, a struggle which, at the cost of the lives of countless of our best sons and with the aid of the Allies, above all the great Slav Power, the Union of Soviet Socialist Republics, reached its climax through the Slovak and Czech risings of 1944 and 1945 with the national and democratic revolution of our people, and was brought to a victorious conclusion in the liberation of Prague by the Red Army, on May 9, 1945.

We have decided now that our liberated state shall be a national state, rid of all hostile elements, living in brotherly harmony with the family of Slav states and in friendship with all peace-loving nations of the world. We wish it to be a People's democratic state where the People not only make the laws through their representatives, but also carry them into effect through their representatives. We wish it to be a state in which the entire economy shall serve the people and be so directed that general prosperity should grow, that there should be no economic crises and that the national income should be justly distributed. Along this road we wish to attain to a social order in which exploitation of man by man shall be completely abolished—to socialism.

In this spirit we have laid down in the second part of this Constitution its Fundamental Articles, and in the third we have expounded them in detail, whereby we propose to give a firm foundation to the legal order of our People's democracy.

FUNDAMENTAL ARTICLES
OF THE CONSTITUTION

ARTICLE 1.   1. The Czechoslovak State is a People's democratic Republic.

2. The People are the sole source of all power in the state.

ARTICLE 2. 1. The Czechoslovak Republic is a unitary state of two Slav nations possessing equal rights, the Czechs and the Slovaks.

2. The territory of the state forms a single and indivisible whole.

ARTICLE 3. 1. The People's democratic Republic recognizes no privileges; work for the benefit of the community and participation in the defense of the state is the duty of all.

2. The state guarantees to all its citizens, men and women alike, freedom of the person and its expression and takes care that every citizen receive the same possibilities and the same opportunities.

3. All citizens have the right to education, the right to work, to a just reward for work done, and to leisure after work. National insurance shall provide for all citizens in cases of incapacity for work.

ARTICLE 4. 1. The sovereign people discharge the state power through representative bodies which are elected by the people, controlled by the people and accountable to the people.

2. The franchise to the representative bodies is universal, equal, direct, and secret. Every citizen has the right to vote on reaching the age of eighteen. Every citizen may be elected on reaching the age of twenty-one.

3. To deal with public matters and to exercise their democratic rights the people form voluntary associations, in particular political, trade union, cooperative, cultural, women's, youth, and gymnastic associations.

ARTICLE 5. The supreme organ of legislative power is the National Assembly of one Chamber. It has three hundred members (deputies), elected for a term of six years.

ARTICLE 6. At the head of the state is the President of the Republic, elected by the National Assembly for a term of seven years.

ARTICLE 7. The supreme organ of governmental and executive power is the Government. It is accountable to the National Assembly. It is appointed and recalled by the President of the Republic.

ARTICLE 8. 1. The state power in Slovakia is vested in and carried into effect, and the national individuality of the Slovak nation is represented by the Slovak National Organs.

2. The Slovak National Organs ensure, in the spirit of the People's democracy, the equality of the Czechs and Slovaks. All organs of the Republic shall endeavor, in harmony with the Slovak National Organs, to ensure that equally favorable conditions be created for the economic, cultural and social life of both nations.

ARTICLE 9. 1. The national organ of legislative power in Slovakia is the Slovak National Council. It has one hundred members (deputies), elected in Slovakia for a term of six years.

2. The national organ of governmental and executive power in Slovakia is the Board of Commissioners. It is accountable to the Slovak National Council and to the Government of the Republic. It is appointed and recalled by the Government of the Republic.

ARTICLE 10. The State power in parishes, districts, and regions[4] is vested in and carried into effect and the rights and liberties of the People are safeguarded by the National Committees.

ARTICLE 11. 1. The judicial power is exercised by independent courts.

2. The judges are both judges by profession and lay judges; they are both equal in any decision.

3. The judges discharge their office independently, being bound solely by the legal order of the people's democracy.

ARTICLE 12. 1. The economic system of the Czechoslovak Republic rests

On the nationalization of mineral wealth, industry, the wholesale trade and of finance;

On the ownership of the land in accordance with the principle 'The land belongs to those who till it';

On the protection of small and medium-sized enterprise, and on the inviolability of personal property.

2. The entire national economy of the Czechoslovak Republic shall serve the People. In this public interest the State directs all economic activity by a Uniform Economic Plan.

DETAILED PROVISIONS OF THE CONSTITUTION

PART I
RIGHTS AND DUTIES OF CITIZENS

Equality
SECTION 1. 1. All citizens are equal before the law.

2. Men and women shall hold equal position in the family and in the community and shall have equal access to education, and to all professions, offices and honors.

Personal Freedom
SECTION 2. Personal freedom is guaranteed. It may be restricted or withheld only on the basis of the law.

SECTION 3. 1. No one shall be prosecuted, except in cases permitted under the law, and then only by a court or authority competent by law, and in the manner prescribed by law.

---

[4] 'Parish' *(obec)*—the basic local government and administrative unit, i.e., any town or village, irrespective of size (e.g., *Pražská obec*—the Parish of Prague). The term implies no reference to the organization of the church.—'District' *(okres)*—second local government and administrative unit, consisting of a district town and surrounding area.—'Region' *(kraj)*: instead of the present three 'provinces' *(země)*, Bohemia, Moravia-Silesia, Slovakia, there will be approximately fifteen regions. At the same time, Slovakia will continue to represent a distinct unit by virtue of its national organs.—TR.

2. No one shall be arrested, [unless] he be caught in the act itself, except on a written circumstantiated warrant granted by a judge. This warrant shall be served at the time of the arrest, or, if this is not possible, within forty-eight hours thereafter.

3. No one shall be taken into custody by a public functionary, except in such cases as are prescribed by law, whereupon he shall either be released within forty-eight hours or brought before a court or such authority as may be competent, according to the nature of the case, to deal with it further.

Inviolability of Domicile

SECTION 4. The inviolability of the domicile is guaranteed. It may be restricted only on the basis of the law.

SECTION 5. 1. The premises of no one may be searched, except in cases permitted under the law, and then only by a court or public functionary competent by law, and in the manner prescribed by law.

2. A search may be carried out, unless the law directs otherwise, only on the strength of a written circumstantiated warrant granted by a judge or competent authority. This warrant shall be served at the time of the search, or, if this is not possible, within forty-eight hours thereafter.

3. The functionary carrying out the search shall produce his authority, and furnish the person whose premises he has searched, at the request of that person, at the time of the search, or, if this is not possible, within forty-eight hours thereafter, with a written statement giving the reasons for the search, and the result thereof, and a list of all articles seized.

Privacy of Mails and Privacy of Communicated News

SECTION 6. No one shall violate the privacy of letters under cover or other written matter, whether they be kept in a private place or dispatched by mail or other means of transport, except in cases authorized by law and in the manner prescribed by law. The privacy of news communicated by telephone, telegraph, or other similar public means of communication, is likewise protected.

Freedom of Residence

SECTION 7. 1. Every citizen may take up domicile or sojourn anywhere within the territory of the Czechoslovak Republic. This right may be restricted only in the public interest on the basis of the law.

2. The right to emigrate abroad may be restricted only on the basis of the law.

Right of Property

SECTION 8. Within general statutory limits every citizen may anywhere within the territory of the Czechoslovak Republic acquire real and other property and carry on gainful activity there.

SECTION 9. 1. Private ownership may be restricted only by law.

2. Expropriation shall be possible only on the basis of the law and on payment of compensation except in such cases as there is or shall be prescribed by law that no compensation be given.

3. No one shall misuse the right of property to the detriment of the community.

Protection of the Family and of Youth

SECTION 10. 1. The institution of marriage, the family and motherhood are under the protection of the state.

2. The state shall ensure that the family be the sound foundation of the development of the nation. Large families shall be granted special relief and assistance.

SECTION 11. 1. To children the state shall ensure special care and protection. In particular the state shall take systematic measures in the interest of the increase of the population within the nation.

2. The rights of a child shall not be prejudiced by virtue of its origin. Details shall be prescribed by act.

3. To youth the state shall ensure all opportunities for full physical and mental development.

Right to Education

SECTION 12. 1. All citizens have the right to education.

2. The state shall ensure that everyone receives education and training in accordance with his natural abilities and with a view toward the needs of the community.

SECTION 13. 1. All schools shall be state schools.

2. Basic education shall be uniform, compulsory and free.

3. Details and exceptions shall be prescribed by act.

SECTION 14. 1. All education and all instruction shall be so provided as to be in accordance with the results of scientific research, and so as not to be inconsistent with the people's democratic order.

2. The supreme direction of all education and of all instruction, as well as the supervision thereof, shall be the competence of the state.

Freedom of Conscience and of Religious Denomination

SECTION 15. 1. Freedom of conscience is guaranteed.

2. No one shall suffer prejudice by virtue of his views, philosophy, faith or convictions; neither may any such views, philosophy, faith or convictions be a ground for anyone to refuse to fulfill the civil duties laid upon him by law.

SECTION 16. 1. Everyone shall be entitled to profess privately and publicly any religious creed or to be without denomination.

2. All religious denominations as well as the absence thereof shall be equal before the law.

SECTION 17. 1. Everyone shall be at liberty to carry out the acts connected with any religious denomination or absence thereof. The exercise of this right shall not, however, be inconsistent with public order and morality. This right shall not be misused for nonreligious ends.

2. No pressure, direct or indirect, shall be put upon anyone to take part in such acts.

Freedom of Expression and Protection of Cultural Assets

SECTION 18. 1. Freedom of expression is guaranteed.

2. Everyone may, within the limits of the law, express his opinion by word of mouth, in writing, print, pictorially, or in any other manner whatsoever. No one shall suffer prejudice by virtue of the exercise of this right.

SECTION 19. 1. Freedom of creative mental work is guaranteed. Scientific research and the promulgation of the results thereof, as well as art and its expressions are free, provided they do not violate the penal law.

2. Cultural assets are under the protection of the state. The state shall ensure that these assets be available to all, and support science and the arts in the interest of the development of the national culture, of progress, and of the general welfare; in particular the state shall ensure to creative workers favorable conditions for their work.

SECTION 20. 1. Everyone shall have the right to bring his views and the fruits of his creative mental work to the general notice, and to distribute and perform them in any manner whatever.

2. This right may be restricted by law only with a view to the public interest and to the cultural needs of the people.

SECTION 21. 1. Freedom of the press is guaranteed. It shall therefore not be permitted, as a rule, to subject the press to preliminary censorship.

2. Who shall be entitled, and on what conditions, to publish periodical journals, in particular with regard to the principle that profit should not be the aim of such publication, shall be prescribed by act.

3. The manner of the planned direction of the issue and distribution of non-periodical publications, in particular books, musical scores, and reproductions of works of art, while maintaining the freedom of science and the arts and with a view to the protection of valuable works, shall be prescribed by act.

SECTION 22. 1. The right to produce, distribute, publicly exhibit, as well as to import and export motion pictures shall be reserved to the state.

2. Broadcasting and television shall be the exclusive right of the state.

3. The exercise of these rights shall be regulated and exceptions prescribed by acts.

Right of Petition

SECTION 23. Everyone shall be entitled to petition with any public authority whatsoever.

Right to Assemble and to Form Associations

SECTION 24. 1. The right to assemble and to form associations is guaranteed, provided that the people's democratic order or public law and order are not threatened thereby.

2. The exercise of these rights shall be regulated by acts.

SECTION 25. 1. In order to protect their rights, employed persons may associate together in a United Trade Union Organizaton and be entitled to defend their interests through the instrumentality thereof.

2. The United Trade Union Organization shall be ensured a wide participation in the control of the economy and in dealing with all matters relating to the interests of the working population.

3. The interests of the employed persons in individual works and offices shall be represented by the United Trade Union Organization and its bodies.

Social Rights

SECTION 26. 1. All citizens shall have the right to work.

2. This right shall be secured especially by the organization of work directed by the state in pursuance of the planned economy.

3. Women shall be entitled to special regulation of conditions of work, in view of the circumstances of pregnancy, maternity and child care.

4. Special conditions of work in respect of young persons, in consideration of the requirements of their physical and mental development, shall be prescribed by act.

SECTION 27. 1. All working members of the population shall be entitled to a just remuneration for work done.

2. This right shall be secured by the wage policy of the state, pursued in concurrence with the United Trade Union Organization and directed toward the constant raising of the standard of living of the working population.

3. In assessing the remuneration for work done, the decisive factors shall be the quality and quantity of the work done, as well as its benefit to the community.

4. On the same conditions of work, men and women shall be entitled to equal remuneration for equal work.

SECTION 28. 1. All working members of the population shall have the right to leisure.

2. This right shall be secured by the regulation of hours of work and of holidays with pay by act, as well as by the care of the recreation of working members of the population.

SECTION 29. 1. Everyone shall be entitled to the protection of health. All citizens shall be entitled to medical care and to provision in old age, incapacity for work and loss of livelihood.

2. Women shall be entitled to special care in the events of pregnancy and maternity; children and young persons shall be entitled to all facilities for a full physical and mental development.

3. These rights shall be secured by the acts relating to national insurance, as well as by the public health and social welfare services.

4. The protection of life and health at work shall be ensured in particular by state supervision and by regulations issued in respect of safety precautions in places of work.

Fundamental Duties of the Citizen Toward the State
and the Community

SECTION 30. 1. It is the duty of every citizen to be loyal to the Czechoslovak Republic, to uphold the Constitution and the laws and in all his actions to be sensible of the interests of the state.

2. In particular it is the patriotic duty of every citizen to assist in the maintenance and furtherance of the national property and to guard against its being diminished or damaged.

SECTION 31. It is the duty of citizens to discharge all public functions to which they have been called by the people conscientiously and honestly in the spirit of the people's democratic order.

SECTION 32. It is the duty of every citizen to work in accordance with his abilities and to contribute by his work to the common weal.

SECTION 33. Taxes and public duties may be levied only on the basis of the law. Likewise the public authority may demand personal services only on the basis of the law.

SECTION 34. 1. The defense of the state and of the people's democratic order is the supreme duty of every citizen. Service in the people's democratic army of the Czechoslovak Republic is the supreme honor for every citizen.

2. It is the duty of every citizen to undergo military training, to take part in military service, and to obey any call to the defense of the state.

3. For the purpose of the defense of the state and for the preparation of such defense, cooperation and material contributions may be demanded from, and restrictions and material services imposed upon every one.

4. Public authorities and executive officers shall in the exercise of their official function, by virtue of their authority, take care also of the interests of the defense of the state.

5. Details shall be prescribed by act.

General Provisions

SECTION 35. Penalties may be threatened or imposed only on the basis of the law.

SECTION 36. 1. It is the duty of all public authorities to act in the discharge of their office or duty in accordance with the law and with the principles of the people's democratic order.

2. If any public functionary offends against this duty he shall be liable to punishment according to law.

SECTION 37. 1. Statements and acts that constitute a threat to the independence, entirety and unity of the state, the Constitution, the republican form of government and the people's democratic order are punishable according to law.

2. The misuse of civil rights and liberties to such ends is inadmissible. In particular it is forbidden to spread, in any manner and in any form whatever, nazism and fascism, racial and religious intolerance, or chauvinism.

SECTION 38. What restrictions may be imposed upon the rights and liberties of citizens in time of war, or when events occur that threaten in increased measure the independence, entirety and unity of the state, the Constitution, the republican form of government and the people's democratic order, or public law and order, shall be prescribed by act.

PART II
THE NATIONAL ASSEMBLY

SECTION 39. 1. The seat of the National Assembly shall be Prague.

2. Temporarily the National Assembly may be summoned to another place.

SECTION 40. 1. Details in respect of the conditions of the franchise, of the exercise thereof and of the carrying out of the election of deputies of the National Assembly, shall be prescribed by act.

2. What activity and which public functions are incompatible with the function of deputy, shall be prescribed by act.

SECTION 41. 1. The National Assembly shall verify the validity of the election of the individual deputies and decide upon the incompatibility of the function of deputy with another function.

2. Verification shall be carried out within six months after the Chamber has been constituted, or within three months after the day on which a substitute member, replacing a deputy, has taken the pledge.

SECTION 42. 1. At his first sitting in the National Assembly a deputy shall take the following pledge: 'I pledge myself that I will be loyal to the Czechoslovak Republic and her People's Democratic Order. I will uphold her laws and discharge my mandate according to the best of my knowledge and conscience, to the benefit of the people and of the state.'

2. Refusal to take the pledge or a pledge taken with reservations shall involve the direct loss of the mandate.

SECTION 43. The deputies shall discharge their mandate personally. They may resign at any time.

SECTION 44. The deputies may not be prosecuted at all for voting in the National Assembly or in the committees of the Chamber. For statements made there in the exercise of the mandate they shall be amenable only to the disciplinary power of the National Assembly.

SECTION 45. 1. In order that criminal or disciplinary proceedings might be taken against a deputy in respect of any other offense or omission, the assent of the

National Assembly shall first be obtained. If the National Assembly refuses this assent, no proceedings shall be taken in respect of that offense or omission then or ever after.

2. This provision does not apply to the penal liability incurred by a deputy as the responsible editor of a journal.

SECTION 46. 1. If a deputy be apprehended and arrested in the criminal act itself, the court or other competent authority shall be liable to notify the Chairman of the National Assembly at once of the arrest.

2. Unless the National Assembly make known within fourteen days its assent to further custody, the deputy shall be released.

3. If the Chamber is not in session at the time of the arrest, the consent of the Presidium of the National Assembly shall be required. If the Presidium assents to further custody, the National Assembly shall decide in respect of the matter within fourteen days after the date of its next sitting. This decision shall be final.

SECTION 47. Deputies shall have the right to refuse testimony in respect of matters confided to them in their capacity as members of the National Assembly, and shall be so entitled even after they have ceased to be such members. Excepted shall be cases relating to inducement to a misuse of the mandate.

SECTION 48. 1. A deputy in public or private employment shall be entitled to leave-of-absence from the day on which he takes the pledge throughout the duration of the mandate.

2. The deputies shall be entitled during the exercise of the mandate to compensation, the amount whereof shall be prescribed by act.

3. Further details in respect of the position of deputies, in particular in respect of their claim to salary (if in public or private employment) shall be prescribed by act.

SECTION 49. 1. It shall be the duty of the President of the Republic to summon the National Assembly for two ordinary sessions in each year, being the spring session and the autumn session. The spring session shall begin in March and the autumn session shall begin in October.

2. The President of the Republic shall prorogue the National Assembly at the end of each session. He may adjourn it for not longer than one month and not more often than once a year.

3. The President of the Republic shall summon the National Assembly for extraordinary sessions, if necessary. If an absolute majority of all the deputies apply to the Prime Minister that the National Assembly be recalled, making known to him at the same time the subject of proceedings, the President of the Republic shall summon the National Assembly so that it may convene within a fortnight after the application has been lodged. Should the President of the Republic fail to do so, the National Assembly shall convene within the following fortnight at the summons of its Presidium.

SECTION 50. 1. The President of the Republic shall have the right to dissolve the National Assembly. He shall not be entitled to exercise this right during the last six months of his term of office.

2. New elections to the National Assembly shall be carried out within sixty days after the expiry of the election term of the National Assembly or after it has been dissolved by the President.

3. By virtue of a dissolution of the National Assembly, criminal proceedings initiated under sections 78 or 91 shall not be discontinued.

SECTION 51. The fundamental rules relating to the proceedings of the National Assembly, its relations with the Government and with the outside world in general shall be laid down in the National Assembly Standing Orders Act. Subject to the provisions of this act, the National Assembly may regulate its internal affairs and lay down additional rules of procedure by autonomous resolution.

SECTION 52. 1. The sittings of the National Assembly shall be presided over by the Chairman of the National Assembly.

2. The Presidium of the National Assembly may appoint additional officers for the carrying out of specific parliamentary tasks.

SECTION 53. 1. The sittings of the National Assembly shall as a rule be public.

2. Non-public sittings may take place only in cases provided for in the Standing Orders.

SECTION 54. 1. The quorum of the National Assembly shall consist of not less than one-third of the deputies. The enactments of the National Assembly shall be valid if adopted by a simple majority of votes.

2. Enactments whereby the Constitution is amended, a Constitutional act is adopted, or a decision in respect of a declaration of war is taken, shall be valid if adopted by a three-fifths majority of all the deputies. The same majority shall be required for the validity of an enactment whereby a conviction is brought in a criminal action against the President of the Republic or against members of the Government.

SECTION 55. 1. The Prime Minister and the other members of the Government shall be entitled at any time to take part in the sittings of the National Assembly or of any of its committees. They shall be permitted to speak whenever they so request.

2. A member of the Government shall appear before the Chamber in person at the request of the National Assembly, its Presidium or any of its Committees.

3. At other times a member of the Government may be represented by officials of his department.

SECTION 56. 1. The National Assembly shall be entitled to interpellate the Prime Minister and the other members of the Government in respect of matters of their competence. It shall be the duty of the Prime Minister and the other members of the Government to reply to the interpellations of deputies.

2. The National Assembly may adopt addresses and resolutions.

SECTION 57. 1. Bills may be moved on the conditions laid down in the Standing Orders, either by the Government or by deputies.

2. Every bill moved by deputies shall be accompanied by an estimate of the financial import of the bill and by a proposal for revenue to cover the expenditure involved.

SECTION 58. The President of the Republic shall have the right to return enactments of the National Assembly with his comments within one month after the day on which the enactment was submitted to the Prime Minister.

SECTION 59. 1. If the National Assembly in a ballot taken by roll call re-enact a returned enactment by an absolute majority of votes, it shall be promulgated as an act.

2. Where the enactment is such that its adoption is subject to the affirmative vote of a three-fifths majority of all the deputies, the re-enactment (after having been returned by the President) shall be subject to that same majority.

3. If the election term of the National Assembly expires or if the National Assembly is dissolved before being able to decide in respect of the returned enactment, this decision may be taken by the newly elected National Assembly.

SECTION 60. 1. There shall be set out in every act which member of the Government is to be charged with its implementation.

2. An act shall be signed by the President of the Republic, the Chairman of the National Assembly, the Prime Minister, and the Minister charged with its implementation. If the President is prevented or ailing and if there is no Vice President (section 72, subsection 2), the Prime Minister shall sign for the President.

3. Members of the Government may for the purpose of signing acts be represented by other members of the Government.

SECTION 61. 1. In order to be valid, an act shall be promulgated in the manner prescribed by act.

2. Acts shall be promulgated by means of the following introductory clause: 'The National Assembly of the Czechoslovak Republic has enacted the following Act.'

3. An act shall be promulgated within eight days after having been signed by the President of the Republic, or after lapse of the period set out in section 58. If, however, the President makes use of his right as there set out, the act shall be promulgated within eight days after its re-enactment by the National Assembly (section 59) has been notified to the Prime Minister.

SECTION 62. 1. The National Assembly shall be competent to enact the State Budget Act and to audit the final state accounts. The estimates bill and the final accounts shall be laid before the National Assembly be the Government. The state budget shall be uniform. Further provision shall be made by act.

2. The control of the public finances shall be regulated uniformly by act for the entire territory of the state.

The Presidium of the National Assembly

SECTION 63. 1. The National Assembly shall elect a Presidium of twenty-four from among the deputies.

2. The Presidium of the National Assembly shall consist of the Chairman of the National Assembly, the vice-chairmen, and the other members.

3. The Chairman of the National Assembly may be represented by one of the vice-chairmen, subject to the provisions of the Standing Orders.

SECTION 64. 1. The Presidium of the National Assembly shall always be elected for a term of one year. The Chairman of the National Assembly and the vice-chairmen shall be elected by separate vote.

2. The first election shall take place as soon as the newly elected National Assembly is constituted. At subsequent elections the members of the Presidium shall remain in office until the new Presidium has been elected. If the election term of the National Assembly has expired or if the National Assembly has been dissolved, the members of the Presidium shall remain in office until such time as the new National Assembly elects its Presidium, and the provisions of sections 43 to 48 shall continue to apply to them.

3. If for any reason the seat of any member of the Presidium falls vacant prior to the expiry of the term of office of the Presidium, a by-election shall be held for the remainder of the term.

4. The National Assembly may recall its Presidium or the individual members thereof at any time.

SECTION 65. 1. The Presidium of the National Assembly shall, where a matter at issue is controversial, give a binding interpretation of acts and decide exclusively whether an act or an Act of the Slovak National Council is contrary to the Constitution or whether an order is contrary to an act.

2. The implementation of the foregoing provision shall be regulated by act.

SECTION 66. 1. At a time when the National Assembly is not in session, because (1) it has been prorogued or adjourned, or (2) its election term has expired, or (3) it has been dissolved, or (4) its convention is made impossible by exceptional circumstances, the Presidium of the National Assembly shall remain in office (section 64, subsection 2). The provisions of section 55 shall at such a time apply to the sittings of the Presidium, mutatis mutandis.

2. The Presidium of the National Assembly shall during this time take urgent measures, including such measures as would otherwise require an act. The Presidium shall at such a time be competent to deal with all matters appertaining to the competence of the National Assembly, with the exception of the matters set out in subsections 3 and 4 below.

3. If the National Assembly is not in session because its convention has been made impossible by exceptional circumstances (subsection 1, paragraph [provision] 4), the Presidium of the National Assembly shall not be entitled *(a)* to elect the President of the Republic or the Vice President; [or] *(b)* to amend the Constitution or Constitutional Acts.

4. If the National Assembly is not in session for any of the reasons set out in subsection 1, paragraph [provision] 1 to 3, the Presidium of the National Assembly shall not be entitled *(a)* to elect the President of the Republic or the Vice President; *(b)* to amend the Constitution or Constitutional Acts; *(c)* to extend military service, or to impose permanent charges upon the state finances; *(d)* to take decision in respect of a declaration of war.

5. In respect of measures which would otherwise require an act, or in order to sanction expenditure or revenue not provided for in the budget, the agreement

of the absolute majority of all members of the Presidium shall be necessary. In respect of other matters the presence of one-half of the members of the Presidium and the assent of a simple majority of present members shall be sufficient.

6. Urgent measures which would otherwise require an act may be proposed only by the Government. Such measures shall possess the temporary validity of an act and shall be promulgated with reference to section 66 of the Constitution in accordance with section 61, mutatis mutandis. They shall be signed by the President of the Republic, the Chairman of the National Assembly, the Prime Minister, and not less than one-half of the members of the Government. Measures which the President of the Republic or the Prime Minister refuse to sanction shall not be promulgated.

7. As soon as the National Assembly is again in session the Chairman shall report to the National Assembly on the proceedings of the Presidium. If a new National Assembly has in the meantime been elected, this report shall be made during the inaugurating session by the Chairman of the former National Assembly or by one of its vice-chairmen, even if they are not members of the newly elected National Assembly.

8. Measures not ratified by the National Assembly within two months of its convention shall cease to be valid.

PART III

THE PRESIDENT OF THE REPUBLIC

SECTION 67. 1. Every citizen of the state who is eligible to the National Assembly and who has reached the age of thirty-five may be elected President of the Republic.

2. The chief seat of the President shall be Prague.

SECTION 68. 1. The President of the Republic shall be elected by the National Assembly.

2. The election of the President of the Republic shall be valid if an absolute majority of deputies is present at the sitting. A candidate shall be elected if he secures a three-fifths majority of the votes of those present.

3. Should no decision be reached after two votes, a final ballot shall decide between those candidates who secure the greatest number of votes in the second ballot. The candidate who secures the greatest number of votes shall be elected. In the event of an even vote, decision shall be made by lot.

4. Details shall be prescribed by act.

SECTION 69. 1. The term of office shall be seven years, and shall begin on the day on which the newly elected President takes the pledge.

2. Where the newly elected President takes the pledge before the acting President's term of office expires, and provided that this is not a case under section 72, subsection 1, the newly elected President's term of office shall be deemed to run from the day on which the former President's term of office expires.

3. The election shall take place within the last four weeks of the acting President's term of office.

SECTION 70. 1. No one may be elected more than twice in succession. Who has been President of the Republic for two successive terms of office shall not again be eligible until seven years have elapsed since the end of his second term of office.

2. These provisions shall not apply to the second President of the Czechoslovak Republic.

SECTION 71. 1. The President of the Republic shall not at the same time be a member of the National Assembly, or a member of the Government.

2. If a deputy or a member of the Government is elected President of the Republic, he shall cease to discharge that function from the day of the election. His mandate, or membership in the Government, shall lapse on the day on which he takes the pledge.

SECTION 72. 1. If the President of the Republic dies, or resigns during the term of office, or loses his office under section 78, a new President shall be elected for a full term of office. The National Assembly shall to this end be summoned within fourteen days.

2. Until such time as a new President is elected and has taken the pledge, or where the President is prevented or ailing so as to be unable to discharge his office, the discharge of his function shall appertain to the Government, which may delegate certain specific acts to the Prime Minister; the supreme command of the armed forces shall during this time be held by the Prime Minister.

SECTION 73. 1. If the President has been prevented or ailing for a period exceeding six months (section 72, subsection 2), and provided that the Government so decides, the National Assembly shall elect a Vice President, who shall remain in office until the impediment passes.

2. A member of the National Assembly who has been elected Vice President may not discharge his mandate while he is Vice President.

SECTION 74. 1. The President of the Republic

1) Shall represent the state externally. He shall negotiate and ratify international treaties. Political treaties, and economic treaties of a general character, as well as such treaties as require an act to be carried into effect, shall require enactment by the National Assembly prior to ratification. Treaties involving alteration of the state boundaries shall be enacted by the National Assembly in the form of a Constitutional Act (section 166). The negotiation of international treaties and agreements which do not require enactment by the National Assembly and where ratification is not a condition, may be delegated by the President to the Government and, with the consent of the Government, to individual members thereof. On what conditions economic treaties of a general character may be carried into effect even prior to the sanction of the National Assembly being expressed, shall be prescribed by act;

2) Shall receive and appoint envoys;

3) Shall summon, adjourn and dissolve the National Assembly and prorogue it at the end of a session;

4) Shall sign the acts of the National Assembly and the measures taken by the Presidium of the National Assembly under section 66, and shall have the right to return enactments with his comments;

5) May submit to the National Assembly oral or written reports regarding the condition of the Republic, and recommend to the Assembly such measures as he considers necessary and expedient;

6) Shall appoint the Prime Minister and the other members of the Government, prescribe the number of members of the Government and determine which of them shall direct a certain ministry, recall the Government if it resigns, as well as its individual resigning members;

7) Shall have the right to be present and to take the chair at meetings of the Government, to invite the Government or individual members thereof to conferences, and to request reports from the Government and individual members thereof, on all matters within their sphere of competence. He may give notice of a report thus obtained to the Prime Minister and suggest to him that the Government consider taking appropriate measures;

8) Shall appoint all university professors, further judges by profession from the fifth grade of functional salary upwards, and officers of the armed forces, as well as other civil servants from the third grade upwards;

9) Shall award decorations, unless he empowers another organ to do so, and grant permission to Czechoslovak citizens to accept foreign decorations and titles of honor;

10) Shall award, on recommendation of the Government, honorary gifts and allowances, as well as charitable gifts and allowances;

11) Shall have the right to proclaim an amnesty, to grant a pardon or to mitigate a sentence or the legal consequences of a criminal court conviction and to order the abolition or suspension of criminal proceedings save in the case of acts suable by private persons. These rights shall not be exercised by a President against whom proceedings are about to be initiated under section 78, or in respect of a President charged or convicted under section 78, or of members of the Government charged or convicted under section 91;

12) Shall hold the supreme command of the armed forces, and proclaim, in pursuance of a Government decision, a state of war, and declare war in pursuance of a decision of the National Assembly.

2. All governmental and executive power, insofar as it is not or shall not be by the Constitution or other acts explicitly reserved to the President of the Republic, shall be vested in the Government.

SECTION 75. The President of the Republic shall take the following pledge before the National Assembly: 'I pledge myself upon my faith and honor that I shall discharge my duties in the spirit of the people's democratic order in pursuance of the will of the people and in the interest of the people, that I shall cherish the welfare of the Republic and abide by the Constitution and the other laws.'

SECTION 76. The President of the Republic shall not be accountable in respect of the exercise of his office. For any pronouncements made by him in connection with the office of President of the Republic, the Government shall be accountable.

SECTION 77. Any act of governmental or executive power performed by the President of the Republic, in order to be valid, shall be countersigned by a responsible member of the Government.

SECTION 78. 1. The President may be proceeded against only on a charge of treason. The indictment against the President shall be brought by the Presidium of the National Assembly, and he shall be tried by the National Assembly. No penalty may be awarded save the loss of the presidential office and of the fitness to regain it thereafter.

2. Details shall be prescribed by act.

SECTION 79. The provisions relating to the President of the Republic shall also apply to a vice president.

PART IV
THE GOVERNMENT

SECTION 80. 1. The Government shall consist of the Prime Minister, the deputy prime ministers and the other members of the Government (ministers and state secretaries).

2. What functions are incompatible with the function of members of the Government shall be prescribed by act.

3. The regular seat of the Government shall be Prague.

SECTION 81. The members of the Government shall deliver the following pledge into the hands of the President of the Republic: 'I pledge myself upon my faith and honor that I shall be loyal to the Czechoslovak Republic and her people's democratic order. I will carry out my duties conscientiously and impartially in accordance with the will of the people and in the interest of the people. I will abide by the Constitution and the other laws.'

SECTION 82. Having been appointed by the President of the Republic, it shall be the duty of the Government to come before and present its program to the National Assembly and to ask for a vote of confidence.

SECTION 83. 1. The Government shall be accountable to the National Assembly throughout its term of office. The National Assembly may pass a vote of no-confidence upon the Government.

2. A motion of no-confidence shall be signed by not less than a hundred deputies and shall be submitted to the Presidium of the National Assembly, which shall report upon it within eight days. The vote shall be valid if an absolute majority of all the deputies is present, and if a majority of votes be obtained in a ballot taken by roll call.

3. The Government may at any time move a vote of confidence in the National Assembly. The motion shall be dealt with without being submitted to the Presidium.

SECTION 84. 1. The Government may resign and shall in that case tender its resignation into the hands of the President of the Republic.

2. If the National Assembly passes a vote of no-confidence upon the Government, or rejects a Government motion of confidence, the Government shall be bound to tender its resignation into the hands of the President of the Republic.

3. If the resignation of the Government takes place at a time when the Government discharges the office of the President of the Republic (section 72, subsection 2), the resignation shall be accepted by the Presidium of the National Assembly.

SECTION 85. A Government that has resigned shall continue to discharge the function of government transitionally until such time as the National Assembly expresses its confidence to a newly appointed Government.

SECTION 86. 1. A member of the Government may resign and shall in that case tender his resignation into the hands of the President of the Republic.

2. The National Assembly may also pass a vote of no-confidence upon an individual member of the Government. In that event, that member of the Government shall be bound to tender his resignation into the hands of the President of the Republic.

3. The provisions of section 83, subsection 3, shall apply, mutatis mutandis, to the motion of a vote of no-confidence and the manner of voting thereupon.

SECTION 87. 1. Where an individual member of the Government resigns, the President of the Republic shall prescribe which of the remaining members of the Government shall provisionally discharge the functions of the resigning member, until such time as the Government is brought up to strength.

2. If the resignation of a member of the Government takes place at a time when the Government discharges the office of the President of the Republic (section 72, subsection 2), the Presidium of the National Assembly shall accept the resignation and make temporary provision.

SECTION 88. 1. The Prime Minister shall direct the work of the Government, summon and preside over its sittings and determine the order of business. He shall coordinate the activity of all central departments and supervise the implementation of the Government program.

2. The Prime Minister may appoint one of the deputy prime ministers or another member of the Government to represent him.

SECTION 89. 1. The Government shall decide in council which shall be deemed to form a quorum, provided that not less than one-half of the total number of members is present.

2. The Government shall decide in council regarding in particular:

    1) All more important matters of a political character;

    2) The appointment of judges, civil servants and officers of the armed forces from the fifth grade of salary upwards, provided that such appointment appertains to the central authorities, and in respect of proposals for the appointment of functionaries the appointment of whom appertains to the President of the Republic;

3) The appointment and recall of the Chairman of the Board of Commissioners and individual commissioners;

4) Government bills to be moved in the National Assembly;

5) Proposals that the President of the Republic use his right to return enactments with his comments (section 58);

6) Acts of the Slovak National Council, submitted to the Government by the Prime Minister under section 110, subsection 2;

7) Government orders.

SECTION 90. 1. The Government may issue orders for the implementation of a certain act and within the limits of that act. Orders may also be issued by individual ministers provided that they are empowered thereto by that act.

2. A Government order shall be signed by the Prime Minister or the acting Deputy Prime Minister and the members of the Government charged with carrying the said order into effect. An order issued by a minister shall, in order to be valid, require to be countersigned by the Prime Minister or the acting Deputy Prime Minister. Ministers may, for the purpose of signing orders, be represented by other members of the Government.

3. An act and a Government order within the limits of that act may delegate detailed provision to be made by the general statutory regulations of individual ministries, national committees, as well as other authorities.

SECTION 91. 1. If a member of the Government, whether with intent or from gross negligence, violates the Constitution or other laws in the exercise of his function, he shall be held criminally liable.

2. The indictment shall be brought by the Presidium of the National Assembly; the case shall be tried before the House.

SECTION 92. 1. Ministries shall be created by act, which may delegate detailed regulation, in particular in respect of their competence, to a Government order.

2. Other authorities competent to perform the public administration shall likewise be created (section 124, subsection 2) and their competence regulated by act, which may delegate detailed regulation to a Government order.

3. The power to issue orders shall include the power to set up and regulate the function of public bodies not vested with sovereign power.

PART V

SLOVAK NATIONAL ORGANS

SECTION 93. The Slovak national organs shall under the Constitution discharge the legislative, governmental and executive power within the territory of Slovakia.

SECTION 94. The Slovak National Council shall discharge the legislative power (section 96) in matters of a national or regional character, provided that these matters require special regulation so as to ensure the full development of the material and spiritual forces of the Slovak nation, and provided that the said matters are not such as require uniform regulation by act.[5]

SECTION 95. 1. The Board of Commissioners (individual commissioners) shall in principle discharge all governmental and executive power in Slovakia (subsection 2 of this section), save for matters of foreign affairs, national defense and foreign trade.

2. Save for the exercise of the governmental and executive power within the sphere of the legislative power of the Slovak National Council (section 96, subsection 1), this power shall be vested in the Board of Commissioners (individual commissioners) as in the executive organ of the Government (individual ministers), in the following departments:

1) General internal administration;
2) Financial administration;
3) Health administration;
4) Social welfare and labor administration;
5) Technical administration;
6) Justice;
7) Food;
8) Agriculture;
9) Industry;
10) Internal trade;
11) Education, popular culture and information;
12) Transport and postal services.

3. Orders issued by the Government and by ministers for the implementation of an act (section 90) shall be valid throughout the territory of the state.

The Slovak National Council

SECTION 96. 1. The legislative power of the Slovak National Council shall consist in

1) The care of the development of the national culture, that is, science, the arts of literature, drama, music and the dance, the fine arts, and the film; the care of historic monuments; all matters pertaining to libraries and museums; the care of specialized training in the sphere of home-industry and popular art; the care of matters pertaining to Slovak cultural workers;

2) The care of national, secondary, technical and art education under the relevant acts; of nursery schools and crèches; of popular adult education, sports, physical culture, the tourist trade and rambling [sic];

---

[5] 'Act' *(zákon)* denotes an act of the National Assembly, valid throughout the territory of the state; the enactments of the Slovak National Council, which are valid in the territory of Slovakia only, are specifically designated as 'Acts of the Slovak National Council' *(zákony Slovenské národní rady)*.— Cf. the terms 'Deputy' (of the National Assembly) and 'Deputy of the Slovak National Council'.—TR.

3) The public health service and social welfare, save for such matters as are or shall be uniformly regulated by acts valid throughout the territory of the state;

4) Funds and endowments, provided that the scope thereof is restricted to Slovakia only;

5) The merging and division of parishes and districts, and the regulation of their boundaries; topography;

6) The technical aspects of the construction of towns and villages and building regulations, save for matters within the scope of the Uniform Economic Plan; the construction and maintenance of roads, highways and bridges not under the administration of the state; hydro-economic matters not within the scope of the Uniform Economic Plan, in particular the maintenance of riverbeds and streams, reservoirs and other waterworks, as well as the construction of fisheries, water supply lines and drainage installations;

7) The maintenance and development of the land, save for matters within the scope of the Uniform Economic Plan; the protection of agriculture and forestry from pests and natural catastrophes; veterinary care and the care of the breeding of domestic cattle; fruit-growing and pastures, hunting and fishing; the protection of land and forest property;

8) Handicrafts and the retail trade, insofar as the operator's personal labor predominates, as well as matters of local markets (provided the uniform regulation of labor law is not infringed thereby), as well as the regulation of distribution, commerce and trade;

9) Statistics and research in the sphere of special Slovak interests;

10) Matters of guardianship and the care of orphans.

2. The Slovak National Council shall further decide by way of acts of the Slovak National Council on matters the regulation of which has been delegated to the Slovak National Council by an act.

SECTION 97. 1. The seat of the Slovak National Council shall be Bratislava.

2. The Slovak National Council may be summoned temporarily to another place.

SECTION 98. 1. Details in respect of the conditions of the franchise for the Slovak National Council, of the exercise thereof, and of the carrying out of the election of deputies of the Slovak National Council shall be prescribed by act.

2. What activity and which public functions are incompatible with the function of deputy of the Slovak National Council shall be prescribed by act.

SECTION 99. 1. The Slovak National Council shall verify the validity of the election of individual deputies of the Slovak National Council and decide upon the incompatibility of the function of deputy of the Slovak National Council with other functions.

2. The verification shall be carried out within a period not exceeding six months after the Slovak National Council has been constituted, or within a period not exceeding three months after the day on which a substitute member, replacing a deputy of the Slovak National Council, takes the pledge.

SECTION 100. 1. During his first sitting a deputy shall take the following pledge: 'I pledge myself that I shall be loyal to the Czechoslovak Republic, to her People's Democratic Order and to the heritage of the Slovak National Rising. I will abide by her laws and discharge my mandate according to the best of my knowledge and conscience, to the benefit of the people, the state and the Slovak nation.'

2. Refusal to take the pledge or a pledge taken with reservations shall involve the direct loss of the mandate.

SECTION 101. 1. The deputies of the Slovak National Council shall discharge their mandate personally. They may resign at any time.

2. They shall be entitled to compensation during the exercise of the mandate, the amount whereof shall be prescribed by act of the Slovak National Council.

3. In respect of the discharge of the mandate of deputies of the Slovak National Council, their immunity and their right to refuse testimony, their entitlement to leave-of-absence and to continued payment of salary (if in public or private employment), the provisions relating to deputies (sections 44 to 47, and section 48, subsections 1 and 3) shall apply, mutatis mutandis.

SECTION 102. 1. The Slovak National Council shall be summoned for sessions by the Prime Minister. It shall be the duty of the Prime Minister to summon the National Council to its first sitting not later than four weeks after the day of the elections.

2. The Prime Minister may adjourn the sessions of the Slovak National Council for not more than three months and not more often than twice a year. If during that time the absolute majority of deputies of the Slovak National Council applies to the Prime Minister that the Slovak National Council be recalled, it shall be the duty of the Prime Minister to recall the Slovak National Council so as to convene within a fortnight after lodgment of the application.

3. The Slovak National Council shall be dissolved by the Prime Minister on the authority of a decision of the Government.

4. New elections shall be carried out within sixty days after the expiry of the election term of the Slovak National Council or after it has been dissolved.

SECTION 103. 1. The Slovak National Council shall elect a presidium from among the deputies of the Slovak National Council.

2. The presidium shall direct the work of the Slovak National Council and deal with its internal affairs.

SECTION 104. 1. The fundamental rules relating to the proceedings of the Slovak National Council and its relations with the Board of Commissioners shall be laid down in the Slovak National Council Standing Orders Act which shall be enacted by the Slovak National Council. Subject to the provisions of this act the Slovak National Council may regulate its internal affairs and lay down additional rules of procedure by autonomous resolution.

2. The sittings of the Slovak National Council shall be presided over by the Chairman or one of the vice-chairmen.

3. The sittings of the Slovak National Council shall as a rule be held in public. Non-public sittings may be held only in cases provided for in the Standing Orders.

4. The quorum of the Slovak National Council shall consist of not less than one-half of the total number of deputies of the Slovak National Council. The enactments of the Slovak National Council shall be valid if adopted by a simple majority of votes.

SECTION 105. The Prime Minister and the other members of the Government shall have the right at any time to take part in the sittings of the Slovak National Council. They shall be permitted to speak whenever they so request.

SECTION 106. 1. The chairman and the other members of the Board of Commissioners shall have the right at any time to take part in the sittings of the Slovak National Council. They shall be permitted to speak whenever they so request.

2. It shall be the duty of a member of the Board of Commissioners to appear before the Chamber in person whenever the Slovak National Council, its presidium or any of its committees so request.

3. At other times a member of the Board of Commissioners may be represented by officials of his department.

SECTION 107. 1. The Slovak National Council shall be entitled to interpellate the chairman and the other members of the Board of Commissioners in respect of matters within their sphere of competence. It shall be the duty of the chairman and the other members of the Board of Commissioners to reply to the interpellations of the deputies of the Slovak National Council.

2. The Slovak National Council may adopt addresses and resolutions.

SECTION 108. 1. Bills of the Slovak National Council may be moved, subject to the provisions of the Standing Orders, either by the Government or by the Board of Commissioners or by the deputies of the Slovak National Council.

2. Each bill of the Slovak National Council shall be accompanied by an estimate of the financial import of the bill and by a proposal regarding revenue to cover the expenditure involved, from that portion of the Uniform State Budget which is allocated to Slovakia, and that in accordance with the Budget Act.

3. There shall be indicated in each act of the Slovak National Council which member of the Board of Commissioners is to be charged with its implementation.

SECTION 109. Acts of the Slovak National Council, insofar as they infringe the Constitution or other laws, shall be void.

SECTION 110. 1. Acts of the Slovak National Council shall be signed by the Prime Minister, the chairman of the Slovak National Council, the chairman of the Board of Commissioners, and the commissioner charged with the implementation of the act.

2. Where the Prime Minister is of opinion that an enactment of the Slovak National Council submitted to him for signature infringes the Constitution or a Constitutional act, or exceeds the powers of the Slovak National Council or is inconsistent with the Uniform Economic Plan, or the Budget Act, he shall submit the said enactment to the Government, which shall decide in respect thereof with final validity within two months.

SECTION 111. 1. All acts of the Slovak National Council shall, in order to be valid, be promulgated in the manner prescribed by act.

2. The acts of the Slovak National Council shall be promulgated by means of the following introductory clause: 'The Slovak National Council has enacted the following act.'

3. The acts of the Slovak National Council shall be promulgated within eight days after having been signed by the Prime Minister.

SECTION 112. The Slovak National Council shall, where a matter at issue is controversial, give a binding interpretation of the acts of the Slovak National Council. Such interpretation shall require the approval of the Prime Minister in order to be valid.

The Board of Commissioners

SECTION 113. 1. The Board of Commissioners shall consist of the chairman and of the other members (commissioners).

2. The usual seat of the Board of Commissioners shall be Bratislava.

3. Commissioners' departments shall be created by act, which may delegate detailed regulation, in particular respecting their function, to a Government order.

SECTION 114. 1. The chairman and the other members of the Board of Commissioners shall be appointed and recalled by the Government, which shall also determine which commissioner shall direct a certain department.

2. The Board of Commissioners and its individual members may resign and shall in that case tender their resignation into the hands of the Prime Minister.

SECTION 115. 1. A member of the Board of Commissioners may not be a member of the Government.

2. Which other functions are incompatible with the function of member of the Board of Commissioners, shall be prescribed by act.

SECTION 116. The members of the Board of Commissioners shall deliver the following pledge into the hands of the Prime Minister: 'I pledge myself that I shall be loyal to the Czechoslovak Republic, to her People's Democratic Order and to the heritage of the Slovak National Rising. I will discharge my duties conscientiously and impartially in accordance with the will of the people and in the interest of the people, the state and the Slovak nation. I will abide by the Constitutional and other laws as well as by the orders and directives of the Government.'

SECTION 117. 1. The Board of Commissioners and the members thereof shall be accountable to the Government.

2. It shall be the duty of the Board of Commissioners and of its members to abide by the directives and instructions of the Government, as it shall also be the duty of individual commissioners to abide by the directives and instructions of the competent ministers.

3. A minister shall however be entitled, with the knowledge of the competent commissioner, to exercise his authority in Slovakia also directly.

SECTION 118. Within the sphere of the legislative power of the Slovak National Council the Board of Commissioners shall, in the matters set out in section 96, subsection 1, be accountable also to the Slovak National Council.

SECTION 119. 1. The Board of Commissioners (individual commissioners) shall issue orders within the sphere of the legislative power of the Slovak National Council (section 96) and shall take appropriate measures within the territory of Slovakia.

2. The provisions of section 90 shall apply, mutatis mutandis, to the limits of the power of the Board of Commissioners (individual commissioners) to issue orders and to the manner of signing orders.

SECTION 120. The Board of Commissioners shall decide in council, which shall be deemed to form a quorum provided that not less than one-half of the members of the Board of Commissioners are present.

SECTION 121. 1. In respect of the appointment of university professors, judges and other civil servants in Slovakia which appertains to the President of the Republic, the Board of Commissioners shall submit appropriate proposals to the Government. The Government may return the said proposals to the Board of Commissioners insofar as they are not consistent with the uniform state personnel policy.

2. The appointment of judges and other civil servants which otherwise appertains to the Government shall in Slovakia be the function of the Board of Commissioners, which shall, however, obtain the preliminary approval of the Government.

3. The appointment of civil servants and employees, which is otherwise the function of a minister, shall in Slovakia be the function of a commissioner, who shall, however, as a rule obtain the preliminary approval of the competent minister.

4. The competence of the Board of Commissioners and of individual commissioners in the matters set out in subsections 1 to 3 of this section shall be inoperative in respect of the appointment of civil servants and other employees in the National Security Corps and in those departments in which under section 95, subsection 1 the governmental and executive power is not vested in the Board of Commissioners, as also in respect of the appointment of civil servants and other employees attached to departments the competence of which extends throughout the territory of the state.

SECTION 122. 1. Where an order, decision or measure of the Board of Commissioners (regulation or measure of a commissioner), exceeds the competence of the Board of Commissioners (individual commissioner), or infringes the Constitution, an act, an act of the Slovak National Council, a Government order or the order of a minister, the Government may declare it void. The same right shall appertain to the Government where a decision or measure of the Board of Commissioners is inconsistent with a decision of the Government.

2. In the cases set out in subsection 1 of this section, a minister may stay the execution of a commissioner's measure pending a decision of the Government, which may declare the commissioner's measure void.

PART VI

NATIONAL COMMITTEES

SECTION 123. In accordance with the administrative system of the Czechoslovak Republic, National Committees shall be (1) local, (2) district, (3) regional.

SECTION 124. 1. National committees shall discharge within the territory for which they have been elected, the public administration in all its branches, in particular the general internal administration, the administration of education and popular culture, labor administration and the administration of the health and social welfare services, as well as, subject to special provisions, the financial administration.

2. Other organs shall be competent to discharge the public administration only exceptionally and by virtue of an act.

SECTION 125. The national committees, being the organs of the Uniform People's Administration, shall in particular have the following tasks:

To protect and strengthen the People's Democratic Order;

To participate in tasks connected with the defense of the state;

To care for the public safety;

To support the maintenance and increase of the national property;

To take part in the preparation and implementation of the Uniform Economic Plan;

Subject to the provisions of the Uniform Economic Plan, to plan and direct economic, social and cultural development within their territory, to take steps to ensure the constant flow of agricultural and economic production, and to care for supplies and the feeding of the population;

To care for the maintenance of public health;

To administer law within their sphere of jurisdiction; in particular, to discharge within the limits of the law the criminal judicial power.

SECTION 126. 1. The national committees shall in discharging their tasks lean on the direct participation and initiative of the people and shall be subject to control by the people. The members of the national committees and the members of the organs thereof shall be accountable to the people for their activity.

2. The manner in which the people shall exercise this control and carry into effect the said responsibility shall be prescribed by act.

SECTION 127. 1. The number of members of the national committees shall be prescribed by act.

2. Details regarding the conditions and the exercise of the right to elect the members of the national committees as also regarding the holding of the elections shall be prescribed by act.

SECTION 128. 1. The members of the national committees shall take the following pledge before entering office: 'I pledge myself that I shall be loyal to the people and to the Republic, that I shall by my work protect and strengthen the People's Democratic Order and that I shall abide by the laws and orders.'

2. Refusal to take the pledge or a pledge taken with reservations shall directly involve the loss of the mandate.

SECTION 129. 1. The organizational principles of the national committees as well as the principles of their activity and the proceedings before them shall be prescribed by act.

2. The organization of the People's Administration in the capital of the Republic shall be prescribed by special act.

SECTION 130. 1. The entire public administration shall be effectively decentralized.

2. The competence and territorial jurisdiction of the national committees shall in accordance with their instances be so regulated as to enable them to deal without delay and effectively with all material and personnel matters of the public administration, inasmuch as these said matters do not affect the interests of higher units.

SECTION 131. 1. It shall be the duty of the national committees to abide by the acts and orders and in the interest of the uniform public administration and the uniform state policy to respect the directives and instructions of superior organs.

2. A national committee of a lower instance shall be subordinate to a national committee of a higher instance.

3. The national committees shall be subordinate to the organs of governmental and executive power, in particular to the Ministry of the Interior.

SECTION 132. 1. A national committee may be dissolved, in particular where it does not discharge its duties or where its activity endangers the proper operation of the public administration.

2. New elections shall be held within the period prescribed by act.

SECTION 133. The financial administration of the national committees shall be regulated by act and within the framework of the public economy subject to the requirements of the Uniform Economic Plan in such a way as to enable the national committees adequately to discharge their tasks.

PART VII

THE JUDICIARY

SECTION 134. No one shall be withheld from his lawful judge.

SECTION 135. 1. The jurisdiction in matters of civil law shall be discharged by civil courts, which may be regular courts or special courts or courts of arbitration.

2. The jurisdiction in matters of criminal law shall be discharged by criminal courts, save where the general regulations prescribe that criminal cases shall be dealt with by administrative criminal proceedings.

3. In criminal proceedings extraordinary courts may be established and may be established only for a limited period and only in cases specified in advance by act.

SECTION 136. 1. The jurisdiction of military criminal courts shall be regulated by special act.

2. The authority of military courts may be under an act extended to the civilian population only in time of war or of national emergency and only in respect of acts committed in such a time.

SECTION 137. 1. There shall be established for the whole territory of the Czechoslovak Republic (1) the Supreme Court, (2) the Supreme Military Court, (3) the Administrative Court.

2. The composition, organization and competence of these said courts and the manner of proceedings before them shall be regulated by act.

SECTION 138. 1. The judiciary in all its instances shall be separated from the administration.

2. The manner of settling disputes between the courts and the administrative authorities in matters of competence shall be regulated by act.

SECTION 139. The organization of the courts, their competence and territorial jurisdiction as well as proceedings before them shall be regulated by act.

SECTION 140. 1. The courts shall as a rule discharge their power through benches.

2. The bench of courts of the second instance shall be constant for the whole year. Exceptions shall be prescribed by act.

3. The bench shall as a rule consist of judges by profession and lay judges. Details and exceptions shall be prescribed by act.

SECTION 141. 1. The conditions of obtaining the qualification for the office of judge by profession as well of the conditions of service of such judges shall be prescribed by act.

2. Judges by profession shall always be appointed permanently; they may be transferred, dismissed or pensioned against their will only in cases of a reorganization of the judiciary, for a limited period prescribed by act, or by virtue of a valid disciplinary finding; they may be pensioned also upon reaching a prescribed age or upon completion of a prescribed period of service. Details of the foregoing provisions as well as the circumstances in which judges by profession may be suspended from office shall be prescribed by act.

3. Judges by profession may not undertake other paid functions, permanent or temporary, save where exceptions are provided for by act.

SECTION 142. 1. Lay judges shall be appointed by the competent national committee, save in special cases otherwise provided for by act.

2. Provisions relating to the qualification for the office of lay judge, the appointment and recall of such judges, their legal position and accountability and the exercise of their office shall be laid down by act.

SECTION 143. Judges shall declare on oath that they will abide by the laws and orders, interpret them in the light of the Constitution and of the principles of the People's Democratic Order, and pronounce judgment impartially.

SECTION 144. 1. Proceedings at court shall as a rule be oral and public. The public may be excluded from the proceedings only in cases prescribed by act.

2. Judgment shall be pronounced in the name of the Republic.

3. Judgment in criminal cases shall always be pronounced in public.

4. Proceedings at criminal courts shall be based upon the principle of public prosecution. The accused shall be guaranteed the right to be defended by counsel.

SECTION 145. The liability of the state and the judge in respect of damages arising out of a violation of the law committed by the judge in the discharge of his office shall be prescribed by act.

PART VIII

THE ECONOMIC SYSTEM

SECTION 146. The means and instruments of production shall be either national property, or the property of people's cooperatives, or in the private ownership of individual producers.

SECTION 147. National property shall in particular include also economic assets nationalized under special acts (section 153), as well as all public assets serving the common weal.

SECTION 148. There shall be exclusively national property:

Mineral wealth and the mining thereof; sources of natural energy and power plants; coal mines and foundries; natural therapeutic sources; the production of goods serving the health of the people; undertakings of not less than fifty employees or persons engaged therein, save for the undertakings of People's Cooperatives; banks and insurance institutions; public rail transport and regular road and air transport; postal services, public telegraph services and telephone services; broadcasting, television and motion pictures (section 22).

SECTION 149. 1. National property shall as a rule be the tenure of the state (state ownership).

2. Portions of the national property which are not of national significance and serve wholly or chiefly the inhabitants of a certain administrative unit (parish, district, region), may be the tenure of the units of the people's administration (communal ownership).

SECTION 150. The state shall administer the national property either directly or through the instrumentality of national enterprises (section 155).

SECTION 151. Economic enterprise shall be either public (in particular enterprise of the state or of the units of the people's administration), or people's cooperatives, or private.

SECTION 152. 1. The right to economic enterprise shall be vested in the state exclusively

1) In the sphere of exclusively national property (section 148), provided the said property is not under an act the tenure of the units of the people's administration (section 149, subsection 2);

2) Under the Nationalization Acts (section 153);

3) Under the acts relating to the regulation of internal and foreign trade, as well as to the international forwarding trade.

2. The state may, in consideration of the public interest and of the requirements of the national economy, surrender the exploitation of certain economic or other assets to the units of the people's administration or to people's cooperatives, or to other bodies corporate.

SECTION 153. 1. Which sectors of the economy and which economic and other assets are or shall be nationalized and to what extent shall be prescribed by act.

2. The extent of nationalization carried out under Nationalization Acts cannot be restricted.

3. By nationalization the ownership of the affected enterprises and other economic units and property rights shall pass to the state.

SECTION 154. Nationalized enterprise shall as a rule be organized by the state in the form of national enterprises.

2. In this form the state may organize also other sectors or units of state enterprise, as well as economic assets that have been or shall in future be acquired by it otherwise than by nationalization.

SECTION 155. 1. National enterprises shall be a part of the national property and shall be subject to the supreme direction and supervision of the state.

2. National enterprises shall be autonomous bodies corporate.

SECTION 156. The economy of the people's administrative units shall be directed by the national committees. This economy or portions thereof may be organized in a form analogous to that of national enterprises.

SECTION 157. 1. People's cooperatives shall be associations of workers for common activity, the aim of which is the raising of the standard of living of the members and the rest of the working population, not however to derive the greatest possible profit from the capital invested.

2. The state shall support the people's cooperative movement in the interest of the development of the national economy and the general welfare.

SECTION 158. 1. The private ownership of small and medium enterprises up to fifty employees is guaranteed.

2. The personal property of the citizens is inviolable. This provision shall in particular relate to household utensils and articles of personal use, family dwelling houses and savings derived from personal labor as well as the rights of inheritance connected therewith.

SECTION 159. 1. The largest area of land which may be held in private ownership by individual or joint owners or by a family working together shall be fifty hectares.

2. The private ownership of land in respect of farmers who till the land in person, shall be guaranteed up to the limit of fifty hectares.

3. Details shall be prescribed by act.

SECTION 160. The state shall, with the active participation of the farmers, so direct the agricultural policy that the technical level of agricultural production be gradually raised and the social and cultural gap between town and country be bridged.

SECTION 161. Private monopoly organizations operating for profit, in particular cartels, trusts and syndicates, are prohibited.

The Uniform Economic Plan

SECTION 162. The state shall direct all economic activity by means of the Uniform Economic Plan, in particular production, trade and transport, in such a way that an effective level of national consumption be ensured, that the quantity, quality and fluency of production be increased and the standard of living of the population thus be gradually raised.

SECTION 163. 1. The Uniform Economic Plan shall always be drawn up for a certain period of time and shall be promulgated by act.

2. The preparation and implementation of the Uniform Economic Plan shall be one of the primary functions of the Government. In this task the Government shall base its work upon the creative initiative of the working population and its associations.

3. The Government shall submit to the National Assembly at regular intervals reports respecting the implementation of the Uniform Economic Plan.

SECTION 164. 1. It is the duty of everyone who is alloted any task whatever in the operation and implementation of the Uniform Economic Plan to carry out the said tasks conscientiously and economically to the best of his personal and economic capacity.

2. It shall be the duty of persons and bodies corporate to adapt their economic activity to the Uniform Economic Plan.

PART IX
GENERAL PROVISIONS

SECTION 165. 1. State citizenship in the Czechoslovak Republic shall be one and uniform.

2. The conditions upon which state citizenship is acquired and lost shall be prescribed by act.

SECTION 166. The frontiers of the Czechoslovak Republic may be altered only by Constitutional act.

SECTION 167. 1. Territorial administrative units shall be created with a view toward the requirements of the national economy and the cultural and social needs of the people.

2. The administration of the Republic shall be based upon the regional administrative system. Regions shall be divided into districts, districts into parishes.

SECTION 168. The capital of the Czechoslovak Republic shall be Prague.

SECTION 169. 1. The colors of the Republic shall be white, red and blue.

2. The coat of arms and the flags shall be prescribed by act.

PART X
CONCLUDING AND TRANSITIONAL PROVISIONS

SECTION 170. The Constitution shall become operative upon the day of promulgation.

SECTION 171. 1. All parts of this Constitution (the Declaration, Fundamental Articles and Detailed Provisions) shall be valid as a whole.

2. The interpretation of the individual provisions of this Constitution shall rest on the spirit of this whole and on the principles upon which it is based.

3. The interpretation and application of all other provisions of the legal order shall always be consistent with the Constitution.

SECTION 172. 1. The Constitution may be amended and supplemented only by acts which are designated as Constitutional acts and are enacted under the relevant provisions (section 54, subsection 2).

2. Acts issued after the date set out in section 170 shall, insofar as they are inconsistent with this Constitution or with Constitutional acts, be void.

SECTION 173. 1. As from the day on which this Constitution becomes operative, the Constitutional Charter of the Czechoslovak Republic introduced by the Act No. 121 Sb.,[6] dated February 29, 1921, and all the parts thereof shall cease to be valid.

2. As from the same day, all Constitutional and other acts insofar as they are inconsistent with this Constitution or the principles of the People's Democratic Order, or regulate matters at variance with this Constitution shall cease to be valid.

3. The provisions of the foregoing subsection of this section shall not apply to the acts relating to nationalization and land reform which became valid before this Constitution becomes operative.

SECTION 174. 1. The National Assembly elected under the Constitutional Act No. 74 Sb.[7] relating to the transitional regulation, pending the operation of the new Constitution, of the election and competence of the National Assembly and the activity of the Constituent National Assembly, dated April 16, 1948, shall be deemed a National Assembly elected in accordance with this Constitution. The election term of this National Assembly shall be deemed to run from the date of the election.

2. If the National Assembly set out in the preceding subsection of this section is constituted before this Constitution becomes operative, the changes required by this Constitution shall be carried out within fourteen days after the Constitution becomes operative. Within the same period the members (deputies) of the National Assembly shall take the pledge under this Constitution irrespective of whether they have already taken the pledge under the provisions previously in force.

3. Until such time as the National Assembly Standing Orders Act (section 51) becomes operative, the provisions of the Act No. 140 Sb., relating to the Standing Orders of the Constituent National Assembly, dated July 2, 1947, shall apply, mutatis mutandis.

SECTION 175. 1. The Slovak National Council as at present constituted, or supplemented in accordance with the result of the elections to the National Assembly (section 174, subsection 1) shall exercise the power which is under this Constitution vested in the Slovak National Council, until such time as a Slovak National Council is constituted which has been elected under the new Election Act (section 98,

---

[6] Sb. = *Sbírka zákonů a nařízení státu Československého* (Collection of Acts and Orders of the Czechoslovak State).

[7] Sb. = *Sbírka zákonů a nařízení republiky Československé* (Collection of Acts and Orders of the Czechoslovak Republic).—TR.

subsection 1). Until such time as the act of the Slovak National Council relating to the Standing Orders of the Slovak National Council (section 104, subsection 1) is issued, the provisions of the present Standing Orders of the Slovak National Council shall apply, mutatis mutandis.

2. The orders of the Slovak National Council issued prior to the date set out in section 170 shall be deemed acts of the Slovak National Council, even where these orders exceed the power vested in the Slovak National Council by this Constitution, provided that the said orders are not in discord with the provisions of this Constitution.

SECTION 176. 1. Until such time as the acts anticipated by this Constitution, relating to the principles of the organization, the procedure and proceedings (section 129), the financial administration (section 133), and the manner of popular control (section 126), of the national committees become operative, the regulations hitherto operating shall apply.

2. The national committees in their present composition or supplemented shall discharge their authority until such time as national committees are constituted under the new act (section 127).

3. An act shall prescribe the day on which the regional national committees will begin to function and the present provincial national committees will cease to exist; this shall also be the date on which the national committees will begin to perform the function of the public administration in those departments which have not hitherto been part of their authority (section 124).

SECTION 177. 1. The competence which has under regulations hitherto valid been exercised by the Presidium of the Government, shall on the date set out in section 170, pass to the Prime Minister.

2. The Constitutional acts relating to the regulation of state citizenship and matters connected therewith shall on the day lose the character of Constitutional acts.

SECTION 178. The Constitution shall be implemented by the Government.

(signed) Gottwald

Also as representing the President of the Republic in accordance with Section 60 of the Constitutional Charter of 1920

(signed)	Široký	(signed)	Kopecký
	Laušman		Fierlinger
	Zápotocký		Ďuriš
	Dr. Clementis		Krajčír
	Arm. Gen. Svoboda		Petr
	Dr. Ševčík		Dr. Ing. Šlechta
	Dr. Gregor		Dr. Neumann
	Nosek		Erban
	Dr. Dolanský		Plojhar
	Dr. Nejedlý		Ing. Jankovcová
	Dr. Čepička		Dr. Šrobár

13. 2

CONSTITUTION OF THE
CZECHOSLOVAK SOCIALIST REPUBLIC[1]

Adopted by the National Assembly of the Czechoslovak Republic
July 11, 1960

DECLARATION

I

WE, the working people of Czechoslovakia, solemnly declare:

The social order for which whole generations of our workers and other working people fought, and which they have had before them as an example since the victory of the Great October Socialist Revolution, has become a reality in our country, too, under the leadership of the Communist Party of Czechoslovakia.

Socialism has triumphed in our country!

We have entered a new stage in our history, and we are determined to go forward to new and still higher goals. While completing the socialist construction of our country, we are proceeding toward the construction of an advanced socialist society and gathering strength for the transition to communism.

We shall continue along this road hand in hand with our great ally, the fraternal Union of Soviet Socialist Republics, and all the other friendly countries of the world socialist system, of which our Republic is a firm part.

We desire to live in peace and friendship with all nations of the world and contribute to peaceful co-existence and to good relations among countries with different social systems. Through a consistently peaceful policy and through the comprehensive development of our country we shall help to convince all nations of the advantages of socialism, which alone can bring well-being for all mankind.

II

Fifteen years ago, in 1945, our working people, following their liberation by the heroic Soviet Army from the yoke of fascist occupation, decided in the light of their experience with a bourgeois republic to build up their newly liberated country as a people's democracy whose objective would be to ensure peaceful development toward socialism. The Communist Party of Czechoslovakia, the proved vanguard of the working class, steeled in struggle under the bourgeois Republic and during the occupation, took its stand at the head of the Republic. The last major attempt of international and domestic reaction to reverse this development was defeated by the determined action of the working people in February 1948.

---

[1] *Constitution of the Czechoslovak Socialist Republic* (Prague: *Orbis*, 3d edition, 1964).

Thus our working people first freed themselves from the shackles of foreign rule and then from capitalist exploitation and became masters of their country. In the last fifteen years they have, by their work and purposeful efforts, achieved successes in all fields of human endeavor which would be inconceivable under capitalism. The advantages of the socialist system have been demonstrated clearly and convincingly in this country, too.

The face of our country has undergone a fundamental transformation. Our economy is expanding as never before. Production is increasing from year to year and the living standard of all working people is constantly rising. There are no longer any exploiting classes, exploitation of man by man has been eliminated forever. There are no longer economic crises or unemployment. Education and culture are becoming the common property of all the working people.

The two nations, Czechs and Slovaks, which created the Czechoslovak Republic, live in fraternal harmony. By building socialism together they have made it possible for Slovakia rapidly to overcome its former backwardness and achieve an advanced level of industry and agriculture.

The Czechoslovak State, into which the working people led by the working class organized itself, has become a people organization in the truest sense of the word—a socialist state.

In our country all the main tasks of the transition from capitalist to socialist society have already been solved. Emancipated human labor has become the basic factor throughout our society. It is now not only a duty but a matter of honor for every citizen. We are already practicing the socialist principle:

'From each according to his ability, to each according to his work.'

People's democracy, as a way to socialism, has fully proved its worth; it has led us to the victory of socialism.

III

All our efforts are now directed at creating the material and moral conditions for the transition of our society to communism.

While developing socialist statehood we shall perfect our socialist democracy by increasing the direct participation of the working people in the administration of the state and in the management of the economy, consolidating the political and moral unity of our society, safeguarding the defense of our country, cherishing the revolutionary achievements of the people and providing conditions for the development of all their creative abilities.

At a later stage, in which work becomes the primary necessity of life, it is our intention to expand the forces of production and multiply the wealth of society to such a degree that it will be possible to provide for all the growing requirements of society and for the full development of each of its members. It will then be possible to proceed to the realization of the highest principle of distribution—the principle of communism:

'From each according to his ability, to each according to his needs.'

In order to consolidate the results achieved by the struggle and labor of our people, and at the same time to show our unbreakable will to advance to still higher objectives, we enact this day the following socialist Constitution of our Republic.

CHAPTER ONE
THE SOCIAL ORDER

ARTICLE 1. 1. The Czechoslovak Socialist Republic is a socialist state founded on the firm alliance of the workers, farmers and intelligentsia, with the working class at its head.

2. The Czechoslovak Socialist Republic is a unitary state of two fraternal nations possessing equal rights, the Czechs and the Slovaks.

3. The Czechoslovak Socialist Republic is part of the world socialist system; it works for friendly relations with all nations and to ensure lasting peace throughout the world.

ARTICLE 2. 1. All power in the Czechoslovak Socialist Republic shall belong to the working people.

2. The working people shall exercise state power through representative bodies which are elected by them, controlled by them, and accountable to them.

3. Representative bodies of the working people in the Czechoslovak Socialist Republic shall be the National Assembly, the Slovak National Council, and national committees. The authority of other state organs shall be derived from them.

4. Representative bodies and all other state organs shall rely in their activity on the initiative and direct participation of the working people and their organizations.

ARTICLE 3. 1. The right to elect all representative bodies shall be universal, equal, direct and by secret ballot. Every citizen shall have the right to vote on reaching the age of eighteen. Every citizen shall be eligible for election on reaching the age of twenty-one.

2. Members of representative bodies, deputies, shall maintain constant contact with their constituents, shall heed their suggestions, shall be accountable to them for their activity, and shall report to them on the activity of the body of which they are members.

3. A member of any representative body may be recalled by his constituents at any time.

ARTICLE 4. The guiding force in society and in the state is the vanguard of the working class, the Communist Party of Czechoslovakia, a voluntary militant alliance of the most active and most politically conscious citizens from the ranks of the workers, farmers and intelligentsia.

ARTICLE 5. For the development of joint activities, for full and active participation in the life of society and the state, and to ensure the exercise of their rights, the working people form voluntary associations, particularly the Revolutionary Trade Union Movement, cooperative, youth, cultural, physical training and other organizations; some of the duties of the state organs shall gradually be transferred to these organizations of the people.

ARTICLE 6. The National Front of Czechs and Slovaks, into which the people's organizations are associated, is the political expression of the alliance of the working people of town and country, led by the Communist Party of Czechoslovakia.

ARTICLE 7. 1. The economic foundation of the Czechoslovak Socialist Republic shall be the socialist economic system, which excludes every form of exploitation of man by man.

2. The socialist economic system, in which the means of production are socially owned and the entire national economy directed by plan, ensures, with the active cooperation of all citizens, a tremendous development of production and a continuous rise in the living standard of the working people.

3. Labor in a socialist society is always labor for the benefit of the community, and at the same time for the benefit of the worker himself.

ARTICLE 8. 1. Socialist ownership has two basic forms: state ownership, which is ownership by the people as a whole (national property), and cooperative ownership (property of people's cooperatives).

2. National property is particularly the mineral wealth and basic sources of power; the main areas of forests, rivers, natural therapeutic sources; means of industrial production, public transport and communications; banks and insurance institutions; broadcasting, television and motion picture enterprises, and the most important social institutions, such as health facilities, schools and scientific institutes.

3. Land joined for the purpose of joint cooperative cultivation shall be in the joint use of unified agricultural cooperatives.

ARTICLE 9. Within the limits of the socialist economic system small private enterprises, based on the labor of the owner himself and excluding exploitation of another's labor power, shall be permitted.

ARTICLE 10. 1. The citizen's personal ownership of consumer goods, particularly articles of personal and domestic use, family houses, as well as savings derived from labor, shall be inviolable.

2. Inheritance of such personal property shall be guaranteed.

ARTICLE 11. 1. The state shall establish economic organizations, particularly national enterprises, which shall, as independent legal persons, be entrusted with the administration of part of the national property.

2. Unified agricultural cooperatives shall be voluntary associations of working farmers for joint socialist agricultural production. The state shall support their development in every way and shall effectively assist cooperative farmers to advance large-scale socialist agricultural production, making use of modern science and technology. The state shall support the development of other people's cooperatives in accordance with the interests of society.

3. All economic activity of state and other socialist economic organizations is carried out in mutual harmony and directed according to the principle of democratic centralism. At the same time, the participation and enterprise of the working people and their organizations, particularly the Revolutionary Trade Union Movement, shall be exercised in full measure and systematically at all levels of management.

ARTICLE 12. 1. The entire national economy shall be directed by the state plan for the development of the national economy, which shall be drawn up and implemented with the widest active participation of the working people.

2. The plan for the development of the national economy and culture, usually worked out for a period of five years, shall be promulgated as law and shall be binding for that period as the basis of all planning activity by state organs and economic organizations.

3. A state budget shall be drawn up each year in conformity with the state plan for the development of the national economy, and promulgated as law.

ARTICLE 13. 1. Every organization and every citizen who is allotted any task connected with the fulfillment of the state plan for the development of the national economy shall exert every effort and show the utmost initiative to carry out this task with the maximum success.

2. All economic organizations shall systematically create the material, technological and organizational conditions for their activity, in accordance with the long-term plans for the development of the national economy, in such a way that their planned tasks may be fulfilled.

ARTICLE 14. 1. The state shall direct its entire policy, and particularly its economic policy, so that the all-round development of production on the basis of the continuous advance of science and technology and increasing labor productivity shall secure the full development of socialist society and create the conditions for the gradual transition to communism. Particular attention shall be paid to eliminating the substantial differences between physical and mental labor and between town and country.

2. The realization of these aims is made possible by fraternal cooperation between the Czechoslovak Socialist Republic and the Union of Soviet Socialist Republics and the other countries of the world socialist system. The Czechoslovak Socialist Republic shall systematically develop and strengthen this cooperation, which is based on mutual assistance and the international socialist division of labor.

ARTICLE 15. 1. The state shall carry out an economic, health, social and cultural policy enabling the physical and mental capabilities of all the people to develop continuously together with the growth of production the rise in the living standard, and the gradual reduction of working hours.

2. The state shall make provision for the conservation of nature and the preservation of the beauties of the country so as to create an increasingly rich source of benefit to the people and suitable surroundings for the working people with a view to their health and their right to recreation.

ARTICLE 16. 1. The entire cultural policy of Czechoslovakia, the development of all forms of education, schooling and instruction shall be directed in the spirit of the scientific world outlook, Marxism-Leninism, and closely linked to the life and work of the people.

2. The state, together with the people's organizations, shall give all possible support to creative activity in science and art, shall endeavor to achieve an increasingly high educational level of the working people and their active participation in scientific and artistic work, and shall see to it that the results of this work serve all the people.

3. The state and the people's organizations shall systematically endeavor to free the minds of the people from surviving influences of a society based on exploitation.

ARTICLE 17. 1. All citizens and all state and people's organizations shall direct all their activity according to the legal order of the socialist state, and shall see to the full enforcement of socialist legality in the life of society.

2. People's organizations, in fulfilling their purpose, shall guide citizens to uphold the law, to maintain working discipline and the rules of socialist conduct, and shall endeavor to forestall and prevent their violation.

ARTICLE 18. 1. The central direction of society and the state in accordance with the principle of democratic centralism shall be effectively combined with the broad authority and responsibility of lower organs, drawing on the initiative and active participation of the working people.

2. In conformity with the scientific world outlook, the results of scientific research shall be fully applied in the direction of the society of the working people and in planning its further development.

CHAPTER TWO
RIGHTS AND DUTIES OF CITIZENS

ARTICLE 19. 1. In a society of the working people in which exploitation of man by man has been abolished, the advancement and interests of each member are in accord with the advancement and interests of the whole community. The rights, freedoms and duties of citizens shall therefore serve both the free and complete expression of the personality of the individual and the strengthening and growth of socialist society; they shall be broadened and deepened with its development.

2. In a society of the working people the individual can fully develop his capabilities and assert his true interests only by active participation in the development of society as a whole, and particularly by undertaking an appropriate share of social work. Therefore, work in the interests of the community shall be a primary duty and the right to work a primary right of every citizen.

ARTICLE 20. 1. All citizens shall have equal rights and equal duties.

2. The equality of all citizens without regard to nationality and race shall be guaranteed.

3. Men and women shall have equal status in the family, at work and in public activity.

4. The society of the working people shall ensure the equality of all citizens by creating equal possibilities and equal opportunities in all fields of public life.

ARTICLE 21. 1. All citizens shall have the right to work and to remuneration for work done according to its quantity, quality and social importance.

2. The right to work and to remuneration for work done is secured by the entire socialist economic system, which does not experience economic crises or unemployment and guarantees a continuous rise in the real value of remuneration.

3. The state shall follow a policy which, as production and productivity increase, will permit the gradual reduction of working hours without reduction in wages.

ARTICLE 22. 1. All working people shall have the right to leisure after work.

2. This right shall be secured by the legal regulation of working hours and paid holidays, as well as by the attention paid by the state and people's organizations to ensuring the most fruitful use of the free time of the working people for recreation and for cultural life.

ARTICLE 23. 1. All working people shall have the right to the protection of their health and to medical care, and to material security in old age and when incapable of work.

2. The state and people's organizations shall secure these rights by the prevention of disease, the whole health system, the provision of medical and social facilities, by continuous expansion of free medical services and by the organization of safety measures at work, by health insurance and pension security.

ARTICLE 24. 1. All citizens shall have the right to education.

2. This right shall be secured by compulsory free basic school education for all children up to the age of fifteen years, and by a system of free education which shall to an increasing extent provide complete secondary education, general or specialized, and university-level education. The organization of courses for employed persons, free specialized training in industrial enterprises and agricultural cooperatives and the cultural and educational activities undertaken by the state and the people's organizations shall serve further to advance the level of education.

3. All education and schooling shall be based on the scientific world outlook and on close ties between school and the life and work of the people.

ARTICLE 25. The state shall ensure citizens of Hungarian, Ukrainian and Polish nationality every opportunity and all means for education in their mother tongue and for their cultural development.

ARTICLE 26. 1. Motherhood, marriage and the family shall be protected by the state.

2. The state and society shall ensure that the family provides a sound foundation for the development of young people. Large families shall be granted special relief and assistance by the state.

3. Society shall ensure to all children and youth every opportunity for full physical and mental development. This development shall be secured through the care provided by the family, the state and the people's organizatons, and by the special adjustment of working conditions for young people.

ARTICLE 27. The equal status of women in the family, at work and in public life shall be secured by special adjustment of working conditions and special health care during pregnancy and maternity, as well as by the development of facilities and services which will enable women fully to participate in the life of society.

ARTICLE 28. 1. Freedom of expression in all fields of public life, in particular freedom of speech and of the press, consistent with the interests of the working people, shall be guaranteed to all citizens. These freedoms shall enable citizens to further the development of their personalities and their creative efforts, and to take an active part in the administraton of the state and in the economic and cultural development of the country. For this purpose freedom of assembly, and freedom to hold public parades and demonstrations shall be guaranteed.

2. These freedoms shall be secured by making publishing houses and printing presses, public buildings, halls, assembly grounds, as well as broadcasting, television and other facilities available to the working people and their organizations.

ARTICLE 29. Citizens and organizations shall have the right to submit their proposals, suggestions and complaints to representative bodies and to other state organs; it shall be the duty of state organs to take responsible and prompt action.

ARTICLE 30. 1. Inviolability of the person shall be guaranteed. No one shall be prosecuted except in cases authorized by law and by due process of law. No one shall be taken into custody except in cases prescribed by law and on the basis of a decision of the court or the Procurator.

2. Offenders can be punished only by due process of law.

ARTICLE 31. Inviolability of the home, the privacy of the mails and all other forms of communication, as well as freedom of domicile shall be guaranteed.

ARTICLE 32. 1. Freedom of confession shall be guaranteed. Everyone shall have the right to profess any religious faith or to be without religious conviction, and to practice his religious beliefs insofar as this does not contravene the law.

2. Religious faith or conviction shall not constitute grounds for anyone to refuse to fulfill the civic duties laid upon him by law.

ARTICLE 33. The Czechoslovak Socialist Republic shall grant the right of asylum to citizens of a foreign state persecuted for defending the interests of the working people, for participating in the national liberation movement, for scientific or artistic work, or for activity in defense of peace.

ARTICLE 34. Citizens shall be in duty bound to uphold the Constitution and other laws, and in all their actions to pay heed to the interests of the socialist state and the society of the working people.

ARTICLE 35. Citizens shall be in duty bound to protect and strengthen socialist ownership as the inviolable foundation of the socialist social order and the source of the welfare of the working people, the wealth and strength of the country.

ARTICLE 36. Citizens shall be in duty bound to discharge the public functions entrusted to them by the working people conscientiously and honestly, and to consider their fulfillment in the interests of society as a matter of honor.

ARTICLE 37. 1. The defense of the country and its socialist social order shall be the supreme duty and a matter of honor for every citizen.

2. Citizens shall be in duty bound to serve in the armed forces as prescribed by law.

ARTICLE 38. An essential part of the duty of every citizen shall be respect for the rights of his fellow citizens and the careful observance of the rules of socialist conduct.

CHAPTER THREE
THE NATIONAL ASSEMBLY

ARTICLE 39. 1. The National Assembly shall be the supreme organ of state power in the Czechoslovak Socialist Republic. It shall be the sole statewide legislative body.

2. The National Assembly shall consist of 300 deputies, who shall be elected by the people, shall be accountable to the people, and may be recalled by the people.

3. The National Assembly shall be elected for a term of four years.

4. Provisions regarding the exercise of the right to elect and be elected to the National Assembly and the manner in which the election and recall of deputies shall be conducted, shall be prescribed by law.

The Competence of the National Assembly

ARTICLE 40. 1. The National Assembly shall discuss and decide on fundamental questions of the home and foreign policy of the state.

2. All the activity of the National Assembly and the work of its organs and deputies shall be directed towards fulfilling the tasks of the socialist state.

ARTICLE 41. 1. The National Assembly shall enact the Constitution and other laws, and shall supervise their implementation. It shall in particular approve the long-term plans for the development of the national economy and the state budget, investigate their fulfillment, and discuss the reports of the Government on the fulfillment of annual plans and the state financial account.

2. The National Assembly shall see to it that the Constitution is upheld. It may annul a law of the Slovak National Council, an order or decision of the Government and a generally binding order of a regional national committee if they contravene the Constitution or another law.

ARTICLE 42. The National Assembly shall approve international political treaties, economic treaties of a general nature and such treaties as require implementation by legislation.

ARTICLE 43. 1. The National Assembly shall elect the President of the Republic. The President of the Republic shall be responsible to it for the discharge of his office.

2. The President of the Republic shall have the right to speak in the National Assembly whenever he requests it.

ARTICLE 44. 1. After being appointed by the President of the Republic, the Government shall present its program to the National Assembly and ask for its approval.

2. The National Assembly shall supervise and control the activities of the Government and its members. The Government, and its members as well, shall be accountable for their activities to the National Assembly, which shall debate their statements of policy and reports.

3. The National Assembly may propose to the President of the Republic recall of the Government or of its individual members.

ARTICLE 45. 1. The National Assembly shall be entitled to question the Premier and the other members of the Government regarding matters within their competence. The Premier and the other members of the Government shall be required to answer the questions of deputies.

2. A member of the Government shall be required to appear in person at a meeting of the National Assembly, of the Presidium or of a committee at the request of the National Assembly, the Presidium, or any of its committees.

3. The Premier and other members of the Government shall be entitled to take part in meetings of the National Assembly, its Presidium, or any of its committees, and shall have the right to speak if they so request.

ARTICLE 46. 1. The National Assembly shall elect the Supreme Court and may recall its members.

2. The Procurator General shall be responsible to the National Assembly for the exercise of his office. The National Assembly may propose to the President of the Republic that he recall the Procurator General.

3. The National Assembly shall discuss reports of the Supreme Court and the Procurator General on the state of socialist legality.

ARTICLE 47. The National Assembly shall enact laws establishing ministries and other central organs.

ARTICLE 48. The National Assembly, as the supreme representative body in the Republic, shall consider the suggestions of the national committees, discuss their activities, draw general conclusions from their experience and pass measures to improve their structure and methods of work.

ARTICLE 49. The National Assembly shall have the power to declare war in case of an attack on the Czechoslovak Socialist Republic or in fulfillment of international treaty obligations concerning joint defense against aggression.

Sessions of the National Assembly

ARTICLE 50. 1. The President of the Republic shall convene the National Assembly at least twice a year. The National Assembly must be convened if at least one-third of the deputies request it.

2. The President of the Republic shall prorogue the session of the National Assembly.

ARTICLE 51. 1. A majority of the deputies to the National Assembly shall constitute a quorum.

2. Enactments of the National Assembly shall require a straight majority vote of deputies present.

3. Adoption or amendment of the Constitution, a declaration of war, changes in the state boundaries and election of the President shall require a three-fifths majority of all the deputies.

4. The meetings of the National Assembly shall as a rule be public.

5. The principles of work of the National Assembly shall be laid down in the National Assembly Rules of Procedure and Work.

Laws

ARTICLE 52. 1. Bills may be introduced by deputies of the National Assembly, its committees and its Presidium, the President of the Republic, the Government and the Slovak National Council.

2. Laws shall be signed by the President of the Republic, the Chairman of the National Assembly and the Premier.

3. A law shall take effect only when promulgated in the manner prescribed by law. Laws shall be promulgated by the Presidium of the National Assembly within fourteen days after their adoption.

Committees of the National Assembly

ARTICLE 53. 1. The National Assembly shall establish committees for the principal sectors of state and social activity as its working and initiatory organs.

2. The National Assembly shall elect the chairman and the other members of its committees and shall have the power to recall them at any time.

3. The committees of the National Assembly shall supervise and discuss the fulfillment of economic and cultural tasks and make recommendations for the activity of state organs.

ARTICLE 54. 1. The committees of the National Assembly shall rely in their activities on the cooperation of the working people and their organizations.

2. The committees shall have the right to invite members of the Government and representatives of other state organs to their meetings and request from them information and reports.

3. The committees shall invite scientists, innovators, technicians and other leading workers in economic and cultural life to participate in their work.

Deputies of the National Assembly

ARTICLE 55. The National Assembly shall verify the validity of the election of its deputies. It shall do so on the recommendation of the Mandates Committee, which it shall elect.

ARTICLE 56. A deputy of the National Assembly shall take the following oath at the first meeting of the National Assembly which he attends: 'I swear on my honor and conscience to be loyal to the Czechoslovak Socialist Republic and to the cause of socialism. I will respect the will and the interests of the people, uphold the Constitution and the other laws of the Republic and work for their implementation.'

ARTICLE 57. 1. It shall be the duty of a deputy of the National Assembly to work in his constituency, maintain constant contact with his constituents, heed their suggestions and account to them regularly for his activity. A deputy shall cooperate with the national committees in his constituency and help them to fulfill their tasks.

2. It shall be the duty of a deputy of the National Assembly to take an active part and show initiative in the work of the National Assembly. As a general rule it shall be the duty of every deputy to serve on one of the committees of the National Assembly.

ARTICLE 58. No penal or disciplinary proceedings shall be instituted against a deputy, nor can he be taken into custody, without the assent of the National Assembly.

The Presidium of the National Assembly

ARTICLE 59. 1. The National Assembly shall elect a Presidium of thirty from the deputies. The Presidium shall consist of the Chairman of the National Assembly, the vice-chairmen, the chairmen of the committees, and other members.

2. The Presidium shall be elected for the entire electoral term of the National Assembly. It shall remain in office after the expiration of the electoral term until a new National Assembly has elected its Presidium.

3. The Presidium of the National Assembly and its members shall be accountable for their activity to the National Assembly. The National Assembly shall have the power to recall the Presidium and its members at any time.

4. Decisions of the Presidium of the National Assembly shall require an absolute majority of all its members.

ARTICLE 60. 1. The Presidium shall direct the work of the National Assembly.

2. At a time when the National Assembly is not in session because it has been adjourned or because its electoral term has expired, the Presidium shall exercise the competence of the National Assembly. It shall not, however, be competent to elect the President of the Republic or to amend the Constitution. It may make a decision regarding a declaration of war only if the convening of the National Assembly is prevented by exceptional circumstances; such a decision shall require the approval of three-fifths of all members of the Presidium. Measures of the Presidium of the National Assembly resulting from the exercise of this competence must be approved at the next session of the National Assembly; otherwise they shall become null and void. Measures which require legislation shall take the form of legal measures of the Presidium and shall be signed by the President of the Republic, the Chairman of the National Assembly and the Premier; they shall be promulgated in the same manner as laws.

3. At a time when the Government is discharging the office of President of the Republic, the Presidium of the National Assembly shall be competent to appoint and recall the Government and its members and invest in them the direction of ministries and other central organs.

4. The Presidium of the National Assembly shall order elections to the National Assembly and general elections to representative bodies.

CHAPTER FOUR

THE PRESIDENT OF THE REPUBLIC

ARTICLE 61. 1. At the head of the State shall be the President of the Republic, elected by the National Assembly as the representative of state power.

2. The President shall be accountable to the National Assembly for the discharge of his office.

ARTICLE 62.   1. The President of the Republic shall

1) Represent the state in foreign relations, negotiate and ratify international treaties. The negotiation of international treaties and agreements which do not require approval of the National Assembly may be delegated by the President to the Government or, with its approval, to its individual members;

2) Receive and accredit envoys;

3) Summon and prorogue sessions of the National Assembly;

4) Sign laws of the National Assembly and legal measures of its Presidium;

5) Have the right to submit to the National Assembly reports on the state of the Republic and on important political questions, recommend necessary measures, and be present at meetings of the National Assembly;

6) Appoint and recall the Premier and the other members of the Government and entrust them with the direction of ministries and other central organs;

7) Have the right to be present and to take the chair at meetings of the Government, to request reports from the Government and its individual members, and to discuss with the Government or its members matters requiring action;

8) Appoint high state officials in cases laid down by law; appoint and promote generals;

9) Award decorations unless he authorizes another organ to do so;

10) Have the right to proclaim an amnesty, to grant a pardon or mitigate a sentence imposed by a criminal court and order the cancellation or suspension of criminal proceedings;

11) Be the Commander-in-Chief of the Armed Forces;

12) Proclaim a state of war on the recommendation of the Government and declare war in pursuance of a decision of the National Assembly if Czechoslovakia is attacked or in fulfillment of international treaty obligations concerning joint defense against aggression.

2. The President of the Republic shall also exercise authority which is not explicitly reserved to him in the Constitution if the laws so provides.

ARTICLE 63.   1. Any citizen of the state who is eligible for election to the National Assembly may be elected President of the Republic. A candidate shall be declared elected if he receives three-fifths of the votes of all the deputies of the National Assembly.

2. The President of the Republic shall be elected for a term of five years. He shall assume his function by taking the oath of office.

3. The President of the Republic may not at the same time be a deputy of the National Assembly, the Slovak National Council, or of a national committee or a member of the Government.

4. If a deputy or a member of the Government is elected President of the Republic he shall cease to exercise his previous office from the day of his election. His mandate or membership in the Government shall lapse on the day on which he takes the oath of office.

ARTICLE 64. The President of the Republic shall take the following oath before the National Assembly: 'I swear upon my honor and conscience to be loyal to the Czechoslovak Socialist Republic and the cause of socialism. I will discharge my duties in accordance with the will of the people and in the interests of the people. I will cherish the welfare of the Republic and abide by the Constitution and the other laws of the socialist State.'

ARTICLE 65. If the office of the President of the Republic has been vacated and a new President has not yet been elected and has not taken the oath of office, or if the President is unable to exercise his function for serious reasons, the exercise of his function shall fall to the Government. The Government shall have the authority in such an event to delegate some of the powers of the President to the Premier; the supreme command of the armed forces shall, during this time, pass to the Premier.

CHAPTER FIVE

THE GOVERNMENT

ARTICLE 66. 1. The Government shall be the supreme executive organ of state power in the Czechoslovak Socialist Republic.

2. The Government and its members are accountable for the exercise of their office to the National Assembly.

ARTICLE 67. The Government shall consist of the Premier, the vice-premiers, and the ministers.

ARTICLE 68. The Government shall organize and ensure fulfillment of the economic and cultural tasks of socialist construction, the raising of the standard of living of the working people, strengthening of the country's security, and pursuance of a peaceful foreign policy.

To this end it shall, specifically,

1) Unify, direct and control the activities of the ministries and other central organs of state administration;

2) Direct and control the work of the national committees;

3) Prepare long-term plans for the development of the national economy and the state budget and ensure and control their fulfillment, it shall set forth annual plans necessary for the carrying out of the long-term plans for development of the national economy and submit reports to the National Assembly on their fulfillment;

4) Ensure observance of the laws and the maintenance of state discipline, the protection of the rights of citizens and the interests of the state;

5) Issue decisions and orders on the basis of laws and for their implementation, and supervise their execution;

6) Have the right to introduce bills in the National Assembly and drafts of legal measures to the Presidium of the National Assembly;

7) Appoint state officials and heads of economic organizations where provided by law and propose officials who are appointed by the President of the Republic.

ARTICLE 69. Members of the Government shall take the following oath administered by the President: 'I swear upon my honor and conscience to be loyal to the Czechoslovak Socialist Republic and to the cause of socialism. I will perform my duties in accordance with the will of the people and in the interests of the people. I will abide by the Constitution and other laws and work for their implementation.'

ARTICLE 70. 1. The National Assembly may propose that the President of the Republic recall the Government or any of its members. In such an event the President of the Republic shall recall the Government or the member concerned.

2. The Government and its members shall fulfill their tasks in close cooperation with the National Assembly and its organs.

ARTICLE 71. After being appointed by the President of the Republic, the Government shall present its program to the National Assembly and ask for its approval.

ARTICLE 72. Ministries and other central organs of state administration may on the basis of laws and government orders and in pursuance of them issue generally binding legal regulations.

CHAPTER SIX
THE SLOVAK NATIONAL COUNCIL

ARTICLE 73. 1. The Slovak National Council shall be the national organ of state power and administration in Slovakia.

2. The Slovak National Council shall be composed of deputies of the Slovak National Council, who shall be elected by the people of Slovakia, shall be accountable to the people and may be recalled by the people.

3. The Slovak National Council shall be elected for a term of four years.

4. The number of deputies of the Slovak National Council, provisions regarding the exercise of the right to elect and be elected to the Slovak National Council and the manner in which the election and recall of deputies shall be conducted shall be prescribed by law of the Slovak National Council.

5. The seat of the Slovak National Council shall be Bratislava.

Competence of the Slovak National Council

ARTICLE 74. The Slovak National Council shall have the competence to

(a) Enact, in conformity with state-wide legislation, laws of the Slovak National Council concerning matters of a national or regional nature where special legislation is required to ensure the full economic and cultural development of Slovakia;

(b) Enact laws of the Slovak National Council where empowered to do so by law of the National Assembly;

(c) Participate in the drawing up of the state plan for the development of the national economy and discuss, within the limits of the state plan, the overall economic and cultural development of Slovakia;

(d) Discuss and approve the budget of the Slovak National Council, of its organs and of institutions in Slovakia under its immediate jurisdiction;

(e) Introduce bills in the National Assembly;

(f) Exercise control within the limits of its own authority;

(g) Ensure, in the spirit of equality, favorable conditions for the full development of the life of citizens of Hungarian and Ukrainian nationality;

(h) Elect a presidium and from its members commissioners of the Slovak National Council;

(i) Discuss reports of the presidium, of the commissions, and of commissioners of the Slovak National Council.

Sessions of the Slovak National Council

ARTICLE 75. 1. The presidium of the Slovak National Council shall convene the Slovak National Council at least twice a year. The Slovak National Council must be convened if at least one-third of the deputies request it.

2. The presidium of the Slovak National Council shall prorogue the session of the Slovak National Council.

ARTICLE 76. 1. A majority of the deputies of the Slovak National Council shall constitute a quorum. Enactments shall require a straight majority vote of deputies present.

2. Meetings of the Slovak National Council shall, as a rule, be public.

3. The fundamental rules of procedure of the Slovak National Council shall be set forth in the Slovak National Council Rules of Procedure and Work.

Laws of the Slovak National Council

ARTICLE 77. 1. Bills of the Slovak National Council may be introduced by deputies, commissions, and the presidium of the Slovak National Council.

2. Laws shall be signed by the chairman of the Slovak National Council.

3. A law shall take effect only when promulgated in the manner prescribed by law of the Slovak National Council. Laws shall be promulgated by the presidium of the Slovak National Council within fourteen days after their adoption.

Commissions of the Slovak National Council

ARTICLE 78. 1. The Slovak National Council shall establish commissions for the particular sectors of its activities as its initiatory, controlling and executive organs.

2. Commissions of the Slovak National Council shall supervise the carrying out of tasks evolving from the economic and cultural development of Slovakia,

discuss them and make decisions concerning them, help to execute them and submit their decisions and recommendations to the Slovak National Council and its presidium.

3. Commissions of the Slovak National Council shall rely in their activities on the cooperation of the working people and their organizations.

4. Members of the commissions of the Slovak National Council shall be elected by the Slovak National Council from among its deputies and from the ranks of political, economic, cultural and other workers in Slovakia. The Slovak National Council shall as a rule elect commissioners of the Slovak National Council to be chairmen of commissions.

Deputies of the Slovak National Council

ARTICLE 79. The Slovak National Council shall verify the validity of the election of its deputies. It shall do so on the recommendation of the Mandates Commission, which it shall elect.

ARTICLE 80. A deputy of the Slovak National Council shall take the following oath at the first meeting of the Slovak National Council which he attends: 'I swear on my honor and conscience to be loyal to the Czechoslovak Socialist Republic, the cause of socialism and the heritage of the Slovak National Uprising. I will respect the will and interests of the people, uphold the Constitution and the other laws of the Republic, and work for their implementation.'

ARTICLE 81. 1. It shall be the duty of a deputy of the Slovak National Council to work in his constituency, maintain constant contact with his constituents, heed their suggestions and account to them regularly for his activity. He shall cooperate with the national committees in his constituency and help them to fulfill their tasks.

2. It shall be the duty of a deputy of the Slovak National Council to take an active part in the work of the Slovak National Council and its organs. As a general rule it shall be the duty of every deputy to serve on one of the commissions of the Slovak National Council.

3. A deputy of the Slovak National Council may also be a deputy of the National Assembly.

ARTICLE 82. Penal or disciplinary proceedings shall not be instituted against a deputy of the Slovak National Council, nor can he be taken into custody, without the assent of the Slovak National Council.

The Presidium of the Slovak National Council

ARTICLE 83. 1. The Presidium of the Slovak National Council shall have sixteen members. It shall consist of the chairman of the Slovak National Council, the vice-chairmen and other members.

2. The presidium of the Slovak National Council shall be elected by the Slovak National Council from among its members for the entire electoral term. The presidium shall remain in office after the expiration of the electoral term until a new Slovak National Council has elected its presidium.

3. The presidium of the Slovak National Council and its members shall be accountable for their activity to the Slovak National Council. The Slovak National Council shall have the power to recall the presidium and its members at any time.

4. A member of the presidium of the Slovak National Council may also be a member of the Government.

ARTICLE 84. 1. The presidium shall be the executive organ of the Slovak National Council within the limits of the latter's authority. It shall ensure the implementation of laws and shall particularly see to the balanced fulfillment of the tasks of the state economic plan in Slovakia in complete conformity with the plan.

2. The presidium of the Slovak National Council shall direct and coordinate the work of the commissions and the commissioners of the Slovak National Council, discuss their reports and prepare recommendations for the sessions of the Slovak National Council.

3. The presidium of the Slovak National Council shall issue decisions and orders on the basis of laws of the Slovak National Council and in pursuance of them.

4. The presidium of the Slovak National Council shall appoint and propose state officials for Slovakia within limits set by the Government.

ARTICLE 85. 1. The Slovak National Council shall elect commissioners of the Slovak National Council from among the members of the presidium of the Slovak National Council. The council shall have the power to recall a commissioner of the Slovak National Council at any time.

2. Commissioners of the Slovak National Council shall hold office in those branches of the state administration laid down by law.

3. Commissioners shall discharge the tasks entrusted to them within the limits of the authority of the Slovak National Council. They shall discharge other tasks connected with the economic and cultural life of Slovakia within limits set by the Government.

CHAPTER SEVEN
THE NATIONAL COMMITTEES

ARTICLE 86. 1. The national committees—the broadest organization of the working people—are the organs of state power and administration in the regions, districts and localities.

2. The national committees shall be composed of deputies who shall be elected by the people, shall be accountable to the people and may be recalled by the people.

3. The national committees shall be elected for a term of four years.

4. Provisions regarding the exercise of the right to elect and be elected to the national committees and the manner in which the election and recall of deputies shall be conducted shall be prescribed by law.

ARTICLE 87. 1. The national committees shall rely in all their work on the constant and active participation of the working people of their area. In this way they shall gain the fullest cooperation of the working people in the administration of the state, draw on their experience and learn from it.

2. The national committees shall work closely with other organizations of the working people, rely on their cooperation and help them fulfill their tasks.

ARTICLE 88. 1. The national committees and their deputies shall be accountable to their constituents for their activities.

2. It shall be the duty of a deputy of a national committee to work in his constituency, maintain constant contact with his constituents, take their advice, heed their suggestions, account to them for his activity and report to them on the work of the national committee.

3. It shall be the duty of a deputy of a national committee to take an active part in the work of the national committee and to work in one of its commissions.

4. A deputy of a national committee shall take the following oath at the first meeting of the national committee which he attends: 'I swear on my honor and conscience to be loyal to the Czechoslovak Socialist Republic and to the cause of socialism. I shall respect the will and the interests of the people, uphold the Constitution and the laws of the Republic and work for their implementation.'

ARTICLE 89. The national committees shall, with the broadest participation of the citizens,

Direct, organize and ensure in a planned manner the development of their area as regards economic affairs, culture, health and social services; their primary responsibilities shall include satisfaction of the material and cultural requirements of the working people to a continuously increasing degree; to this end they shall establish economic institutions and cultural, health and social institutions and direct their work;

Ensure the protection of socialist ownership and all the achievements of the working people, the maintenance of socialist order in society, see that the rules of socialist conduct are upheld, and strengthen the defense potential of the Republic;

Ensure the implementation of laws and see to their observance, ensure the protection and realization of the rights and the assertion of the true interests of the working people and of socialist organizations.

ARTICLE 90. 1. The national committees shall be guided in their work by the state plan for the development of the national economy. They shall take part in drafting and carrying it out. They shall draw up the plan of development for their areas in accordance with and on the basis of the state plan.

2. They shall have at their disposal the necessary material and financial resources to carry out the planned tasks and shall employ them as responsible managers.

3. The basis of the financial management of the national committees shall be their budgets, which they shall draft and which shall be part of the state budget.

ARTICLE 91. National committees shall be regional, district, and municipal or local in localities. In Prague there shall be the National Committee of the City of Prague; for the districts of Prague and of certain other cities there shall be district national committees.

ARTICLE 92. The authority and responsibility of the national committees at the various levels shall be laid down so that they may, most effectively and with the broadest possible participation of the working people, ensure the economic and cultural advancement and satisfy the requirements of the citizens of their areas.

ARTICLE 93. 1. The national committees shall combine in their work the fulfillment of the state-wide tasks with satisfaction of the special needs of their areas and the interests of their citizens.

2. The national committees shall be guided by the principle that the interests of all the people of the Czechoslovak Socialist Republic stand above sectional and local interests, and shall in all their activity educate citizens for the politically conscious and voluntary fulfillment of their responsibilities toward society and the state.

ARTICLE 94. In the exercise of their functions, the national committees may issue generally binding orders for their respective districts.

ARTICLE 95. 1. National committees shall establish a council, commissions and other organs and direct their work.

2. The council shall, under the direction of the national committee, direct and coordinate the work of the other organs of the national committee and its organizations and institutions. The council shall be elected by the national committee from among its members for the whole term of office. The council and its members shall be accountable to the national committee, which may recall the council or its individual members at any time.

3. The commissions shall be the initiatory, controlling and executive organs of the national committee for individual fields or branches of its activity. They shall be furnished with the necessary authority to this end. The commissions, to which a national committee shall elect its members and other citizens, shall systematically intensify the participation of the working people in the activity of the national committee. The commissions shall be accountable to the national committee and its council.

ARTICLE 96. 1. National committees of superior levels shall guide and direct the work of national committees of subordinate levels. In so doing they shall respect the authority and responsibility of the latter. They shall rely on their initiative and experience and carry out their tasks in constant cooperation with them.

2. National committees shall be guided in their activity by the laws and orders and the decisions of the Government, as well as the decisions and directives of higher state organs; decisions of national committees of a subordinate level which conflict with these may be annulled by a national committee of a superior level or by the Government.

CHAPTER EIGHT

THE COURTS AND THE OFFICE OF THE PROCURATOR

ARTICLE 97. 1. The courts and the office of the Procurator shall protect the socialist state, its social order and the rights and true interests of its citizens and of the organizations of the working people.

2. The courts and the Procurator's office shall in all their activity educate citizens to be loyal to their country and the cause of socialism, to abide by the laws and the rules of socialist conduct, and honorably to fulfill their duties toward the state and society.

The Courts

ARTICLE 98. 1. The execution of justice in the Czechoslovak Socialist Republic shall be vested in elected and independent people's courts.

2. The courts shall be the Supreme Court, regional courts, district courts, military courts and local people's courts.

ARTICLE 99. 1. The Supreme Court shall be the highest court; it shall supervise the judicial activities of all other courts. Judges of the Supreme Court shall be elected by the National Assembly.

2. Judges of the regional courts shall be elected by regional national committees.

3. Judges of the district courts shall be elected by citizens by universal, direct, equal vote and by secret ballot.

4. The Supreme Court, regional and district courts shall be elected for a term of four years.

5. Military courts shall be elected under special regulations.

ARTICLE 100. 1. The courts shall, as a rule, make decisions through benches.

2. Benches of the Supreme Court, regional, district and military courts shall be composed both of judges who carry out their function as a profession and of judges who carry it out in addition to their regular employment. Both categories of judges are equal in making decisions.

ARTICLE 101. 1. To ensure increased participation of the working people in the work of the judiciary, local people's courts shall be elected in the localities and at places of work.

2. Local people's courts shall contribute to the consolidation of socialist legality, to the safeguarding of social order and the rules of socialist conduct.

3. The extent of the jurisdiction of the local people's courts, the manner of their installment, their electoral term and the principles of their organization and proceedings shall be prescribed by law.

ARTICLE 102. 1. Judges shall be independent in the discharge of their office and shall be bound solely by the legal order of the socialist state. They shall be in duty bound to act in accordance with the laws and other legal regulations and to interpret them in the spirit of socialist legality.

2. Judges shall be in duty bound to submit reports on the activities of the courts of which they are members to their electors or to the representative body that has elected them. Judges may be recalled by their electors or by the representative body that has elected them; the conditions for and manner of recall of judges shall be prescribed by law.

Article 103.   1. The courts shall proceed so that the true facts of the case shall be determined and shall base their judgments on these findings.

2. All court proceedings shall in principle be oral and public. The public may be excluded only in cases prescribed by law.

3. The accused shall be guaranteed the right of defense.

4. Judgments shall be pronounced in the name of the Republic and shall always be pronounced in public.

The Office of the Procurator

Article 104.   The supervision of the precise fulfillment and observance of the laws and other legal regulations by ministries and other organs of state administration, national committees, courts, economic and other organizations and by individual citizens, shall rest with the office of the Procurator, headed by the Procurator General.

Article 105.   1. The Procurator General shall be appointed and recalled by the President of the Republic.

2. The Procurator General shall be accountable to the National Assembly.

Article 106.   The organs of the Procurator's office shall be subordinated to the Procurator General only and shall discharge their functions independently of local organs. In all their activities they shall rely on the initiative of the working people and their organizations.

CHAPTER NINE

GENERAL AND CONCLUDING PROVISIONS

Article 107.   1. The territory of the Czechoslovak Socialist Republic shall constitute a single and indivisible whole.

2. The state frontiers may be altered by constitutional law only.

3. The territorial organization of Czechoslovakia shall be determined with a view to the economic, political, social and cultural needs of the whole of society, so as to aid its further development in every way and ensure the widest possible participation of the working people in the administration of the state and the direction of economic and cultural construction.

Article 108.   Conditions for the acquisition and loss of state citizenship shall be prescribed by law.

Article 109.   The capital of the Czechoslovak Socialist Republic shall be Prague.

Article 110.   1. The state emblem of the Czechoslovak Socialist Republic shall consist of a red escutcheon in the form of a Hussite shield with a five-pointed star in the upper part, with a white, two-tailed lion bearing a red shield on its chest showing a blue outline of Kriváň Mountain and a golden fire of freedom. The emblem is outlined in gold.

2. The flag of the Czechoslovak Socialist Republic shall consist of a lower red field and an upper white field, with a blue wedge between them extending from the hoist to the center of the flag.

3. Details of the state emblem and state flag and their proper display shall be enacted by law.

ARTICLE 111. 1. The Constitution may be amended by constitutional law only.

2. Laws and other legal regulations may not contravene the Constitution. Interpretation and application of all legal regulations must be in conformity with the Constitution.

ARTICLE 112. 1. The Constitution shall take effect from the day of enactment by the National Assembly.

2. As from that day the previous Constitution and all previous constitutional laws which amended and supplemented it shall cease to have effect.

SECTION 14

YUGOSLAVIA

14. 1

CONSTITUTION OF THE FEDERATIVE PEOPLE'S REPUBLIC OF YUGOSLAVIA[1]

Adopted by the Presidium of the Constituent Assembly
of the Federative People's Republic of Yugoslavia,

1946

RESOLUTION of the Constituent Assembly of the Federative People's Republic of Yugoslavia on the Promulgation of the Constitution of the Federative People's Republic of Yugoslavia.

THE Constituent Assembly of the Federative People's Republic of Yugoslavia, being the supreme representative of the sovereignty of the people and the expression of the unanimous will of all the peoples of the Federative People's Republic of Yugoslavia, at a joint session of both Houses, the Federal Assembly and the Assembly of Nationalities,

resolves:

That the Constitution of the Federative People's Republic of Yugoslavia, enacted by the Federal Assembly and the Assembly of Nationalities, be promulgated and proclaimed to the peoples and citizens of the Federative People's Republic of Yugoslavia.

CONSTITUTION

PART ONE
FUNDAMENTAL PRINCIPLES

CHAPTER I
THE FEDERATIVE PEOPLE'S REPUBLIC OF YUGOSLAVIA

ARTICLE I. The Federative People's Republic of Yugoslavia is a federal people's state, republican in form, a community of peoples equal in rights who, on the basis of the right to self-determination, including the right of separation, have expressed their will to live together in a federative state.

---

[1] *Constitution of the Federative People's Republic of Yugoslavia* (Belgrade: Official Gazette of the Federative People's Republic of Yugoslavia, 1946).

ARTICLE 2.   The Federative People's Republic of Yugoslavia is composed of the People's Republic of Serbia, the People's Republic of Croatia, the People's Republic of Slovenia, the People's Republic of Bosnia and Herzegovina, the People's Republic of Macedonia and the People's Republic of Montenegro.

The People's Republic of Serbia includes the autonomous province of Vojvodina and the autonomous Kosovo-Metohijan region.

ARTICLE 3.   The state coat of arms of the Federative People's Republic of Yugoslavia represents a field encircled by ears of corn. At the base the ears are tied with a ribbon on which is inscribed the date 29-XI-1943. Between the tops of the ears is a five-pointed star. In the center of the field five torches are laid obliquely, their several flames merging into one single flame.

ARTICLE 4.   The state flag of the Federative People's Republic of Yugoslavia consists of three colors: blue, white and red, with a red five-pointed star in the middle. The ratio of the width to the length of the flag is as one to two. The colors of the flag are placed horizontally in the following order from above: blue, white and red. Each color covers one-third of the flag's width. The star has a regular five-pointed shape and a gold (yellow) border. The central point of the star coincides with the intersection point of the diagonals of the flag. The upmost point of the star reaches half way up the blue field of the flag, so that the lower points of the star occupy corresponding positions in the red field of the flag.

ARTICLE 5.   The principal town of the Federative People's Republic of Yugoslavia is Belgrade.

CHAPTER II

THE PEOPLE'S AUTHORITY

ARTICLE 6.   All authority in the Federative People's Republic of Yugoslavia derives from the people and belongs to the people.

The people exercise their authority through freely elected representative organs of state authority, the people's committees, which, from local people's committees up to the assemblies of the people's republics and the People's Assembly of the F.P.R.Y., originated and developed during the struggle for national liberation against fascism and reaction, and are the fundamental achievement of that struggle.

ARTICLE 7.   All the representative organs of state authority are elected by the citizens on the basis of universal, equal and direct suffrage by secret ballot.

The people's representatives in all organs of state authority are responsible to their electors. It will be determined by law in which cases, under what conditions and in what way the electors may recall their representatives even before the end of the period for which they were elected.

ARTICLE 8.   The organs of state authority exercise their power on the basis of the Constitution of the F.P.R.Y., the constitutions of the people's republics, the laws of the F.P.R.Y., the laws of the people's republics and the general regulations issued by the higher organs of state authority.

All acts of the state administration and judiciary organs must be founded on law.

CHAPTER III

FUNDAMENTAL RIGHTS OF THE PEOPLES AND
THE PEOPLE'S REPUBLICS

ARTICLE 9. The sovereignty of the people's republics composing the Federative People's Republic of Yugoslavia is limited only by the rights which by this Constitution are given to the Federative People's Republic of Yugoslavia.

The Federative People's Republic of Yugoslavia protects and defends the sovereign rights of the people's republics.

The Federative People's Republic of Yugoslavia protects the security and the social and political order of the people's republics.

ARTICLE 10. Any act directed against the sovereignty, equality and national freedom of the peoples of the Federative People's Republic of Yugoslavia and their people's republics is contrary to the Constitution.

ARTICLE 11. Each people's republic has its own constitution.

The people's republic makes its constitution independently.

The constitution of the people's republic reflects the special characteristics of the republic and must be in conformity with the Constitution of the F.P.R.Y.

ARTICLE 12. The People's Assembly of the F.P.R.Y. determines the boundaries between the people's republics.

The boundaries of a people's republic cannot be altered without its consent.

ARTICLE 13. National minorities in the Federative People's Republic of Yugoslavia enjoy the right to and protection of their own cultural development and the free use of their own language.

CHAPTER IV

SOCIAL-ECONOMIC ORGANIZATION

ARTICLE 14. Means of production in the Federative People's Republic of Yugoslavia are either the property of the entire people, i.e., property in the hands of the state or the property of the people's cooperative organizations, or else the property of private persons or legal entities.

All mineral and other wealth underground, the waters, including mineral and medicinal waters, the sources of natural power, the means of rail and air transport, the posts, telegraphs, telephones and broadcasting are national property.

The means of production in the hands of the state are exploited by the state itself or given to others for exploitation.

Foreign trade is under control of the state.

ARTICLE 15. In order to protect the vital interests of the people, to further the people's prosperity and the right use of all economic potentialities and forces, the state directs the economic life and development of the country in accordance with a general economic plan, relying on the state and cooperative economic sectors, while achieving a general control over the private economic sector.

In carrying out the general economic plan and economic control, the state relies on the cooperation of syndicalist organizations of workmen and employees and other organizations of the working people.

ARTICLE 16. The property of the entire people is the mainstay of the state in the development of the national economy.

The property of the entire people is under the special protection of the state.

The administration and disposal of the property of the entire people are determined by law.

ARTICLE 17. The state devotes special attention to the people's cooperative organizations and offers them assistance and facilities.

ARTICLE 18. Private property and private initiative in economy are guaranteed.

The inheritance of private property is guaranteed. The right of inheritance is regulated by law.

No person is permitted to use the right of private property to the detriment of the people's community.

The existence of private monopolist organizations, such as cartels, syndicates, trusts and similar organizations created for the purpose of dictating prices, monopolizing the market and damaging the interests of the national economy, is forbidden.

Private property may be limited or expropriated if the common interest requires it, but only in accordance with the law. It will be determined by law in which cases and to what extent the owner shall be compensated.

Under the same conditions individual branches of national economy or single enterprises may be nationalized by law if the common interest requires it.

ARTICLE 19. The land belongs to those who cultivate it.

The law determines whether and how much land may be owned by an institution or a person who is not a cultivator.

There can be no large landholdings in private hands on any basis whatsoever.

The maximum size of private landholdings will be determined by law.

The state particularly protects and assists poor peasants and peasants with medium-sized holdings by its general economic policy, its low rates of credit, and its tax system.

ARTICLE 20. By economic and other measures the state assists the working people to associate and organize themselves for their protection against economic exploitation.

The state protects persons who are engaged as workers or employees especially, by assuring them the right of association, by limiting the working day, by ensuring the right to paid annual holidays, by controlling working conditions, by devoting attention to housing conditions and social insurance.

Minors in employment enjoy the special protection of the state.

CHAPTER V

THE RIGHTS AND DUTIES OF CITIZENS

ARTICLE 21. All citizens of the Federative People's Republic of Yugoslavia are equal before the law and enjoy equal rights regardless of nationality, race and creed.

No privileges on account of birth, position, property status or degree of education are recognized.

Any act granting privileges to citizens or limiting their rights on grounds of difference of nationality, race and creed, and any propagation of national, racial and religious hatred and discord are contrary to the Constitution and punishable.

ARTICLE 22. The citizens of the Federative People's Republic of Yugoslavia are bound to comply with the Constitution and laws.

ARTICLE 23. All citizens, regardless of sex, nationality, race, creed, degree of education or place of residence, who are over eighteen years of age, have the right to elect and be elected to all organs of state authority.

Citizens in the ranks of the Yugoslav Army have the same right to elect and be elected as other citizens.

The suffrage is universal, equal and direct and is carried out by secret ballot.

The suffrage is not enjoyed by persons under guardianship, persons deprived of electoral rights by sentence of a court of law for the duration of the sentence, and persons who have lost their electoral rights in accordance with Federal law.

ARTICLE 24. Women have equal rights with men in all fields of state, economic and social-political life.

Women have the right to the same pay as that received by men for the same work, and as workers or employees they enjoy special protection.

The state especially protects the interests of mothers and children by the establishment of maternity hospitals, children's homes and day nurseries and by the right of mothers to a leave with pay before and after childbirth.

ARTICLE 25. Freedom of conscience and freedom of religion are guaranteed to citizens.

The Church is separate from the state.

Religious communities, whose teaching is not contrary to the Constitution, are free in their religious affairs and in the performance of religious ceremonies. Religious schools for the education of priests are free and are under the general supervision of the state.

The abuse of the Church and of religion for political purposes and the existence of political organizations on a religious basis are forbidden.

The state may extend material assistance to religious communities.

ARTICLE 26. Matrimony and the family are under the protection of the state. The state regulates by law the legal relations of marriage and the family.

Marriage is valid only if concluded before the competent state organs. After the marriage, citizens may go through a religious wedding ceremony.

All matrimonial disputes come within the competence of the people's courts.

The registration of births, marriages and deaths is conducted by the state.

Parents have the same obligations and duties to children born out of wedlock as to those born in wedlock. The position of children born out of wedlock is regulated by law.

Minors are under the special protection of the state.

ARTICLE 27. Citizens are guaranteed the freedom of the Press, freedom of speech, freedom of association, freedom of assembly, the freedom to hold public meetings and demonstrations.

ARTICLE 28. Citizens are guaranteed inviolability of person.

No person may be detained under arrest for longer than three days without the written and motivated decision of a court of law or of a public prosecutor. The longest period of arrest is determined by law.

No person may be punished for a criminal act except by sentence of a competent court on the basis of the law establishing the competence of the court and defining the offense.

Punishments may be determined and pronounced only on the basis of the law.

No person, if within the reach of the state authorities, may be tried without being given a lawful hearing and duly invited to defend himself.

Punishments for infringements of legal prescriptions may be pronounced by the organs of the state administration only within the limits set by law.

No citizen of the Federative People's Republic of Yugoslavia may be banished from the country.

Only in cases defined by law may a citizen be expelled from his place of residence.

Federal law determines in which cases and in what manner citizens of the Federative People's Republic of Yugoslavia may be deprived of their citizenship.

Citizens of the Federative People's Republic of Yugoslavia in foreign countries enjoy the protection of the Federative People's Republic of Yugoslavia.

ARTICLE 29. The dwelling is inviolable.

Nobody may enter another person's dwelling or premises, or search them against the occupant's will without a legal search warrant.

A search may only be made in the presence of two witnesses. The occupant of the premises has the right to be present during the search of his dwelling or premises.

ARTICLE 30. The privacy of letters and other means of communication is inviolable except in cases of criminal inquiry, mobilization or war.

ARTICLE 31. Foreign citizens persecuted on account of their struggle for the principles of democracy, for national liberation, the rights of the working people or the freedom of scientific and cultural work, enjoy the right of asylum in the Federative People's Republic of Yugoslavia.

ARTICLE 32. It is the duty of every citizen to work according to his abilities; he who does not contribute to the community cannot receive from it.

ARTICLE 33. All public offices are equally accessible to all citizens in accordance with the conditions of the law.

It is the duty of citizens to perform conscientiously the public duties to which they have been elected or which are entrusted to them.

ARTICLE 34. The defense of the fatherland is the supreme duty and honor of every citizen.

High treason is the greatest crime toward the people.

Military service is universal for all citizens.

ARTICLE 35. The state ensures disabled ex-servicemen a decent living and free occupational training.

The children of fallen soldiers and of war victims are under the special care of the state.

ARTICLE 36. The state promotes the improvement of public health by organizing and controlling health services, hospitals, pharmacies, sanatoria, nursing and convalescent homes and other health institutions.

The state extends its care to the physical education of the people, especially of young people, in order to increase the health and the working capacity of the people and the power of defense of the state.

ARTICLE 37. The freedom of scientific and artistic work is assured.

The state assists science and art with a view to developing the people's culture and prosperity.

Copyright is protected by law.

ARTICLE 38. In order to raise the general cultural standard of the people, the state ensures the accessibility of schools and other educational and cultural institutions to all classes of the people.

The state pays special attention to the young and protects their education.

Schools are state-owned. The founding of private schools may be permitted only by law, and their work is controlled by the state.

Elementary education is compulsory and free.

The School is separate from the Church.

ARTICLE 39. Citizens have the right to address requests and petitions to the organs of the state authorities.

Citizens have the right of appeal against the decisions of the organs of the state administration and the irregular proceedings of official persons. The procedure for lodging an appeal will be prescribed by law.

ARTICLE 40. Every citizen has the right to file a suit against official persons before a competent tribunal on account of criminal acts committed by them in their official work.

ARTICLE 41. Subject to conditions prescribed by law, citizens have the right to seek indemnity from the state and from official persons for damage resulting from the illegal or irregular discharge of official functions.

ARTICLE 42. All citizens shall pay taxes in proportion to their economic capacity.

Public taxes and duties and exemptions from them are established only by law.

ARTICLE 43. With a view to safeguarding the civic liberties and democratic organization of the Federative People's Republic of Yugoslavia, established by this Constitution, it is declared illegal and punishable to make use of civic rights in order to change or undermine the constitutional order for anti-democratic purposes.

PART TWO
ORGANIZATION OF THE STATE

CHAPTER VI
THE FEDERATIVE PEOPLE'S REPUBLIC OF YUGOSLAVIA AND THE PEOPLE'S REPUBLICS

ARTICLE 44. The Federative People's Republic of Yugoslavia exercises all the rights vested in it by the Constitution.

Under the jurisdiction of the Federative People's Republic of Yugoslavia as represented by the highest federal organs of state authority and the organs of state administration are included:

1) Amendments to the Constitution of the F.P.R.Y., control over the observance of the Constitution, and the ensuring of the conformity of the Constitutions of the people's republics with the Constitution of the F.P.R.Y.;

2) The admission of new republics and approval of the foundation of new autonomous provinces and autonomous regions;

3) The delimitation of boundaries between the republics;

4) The representation of the Federative People's Republic of Yugoslavia in international relations; international treaties;

5) Questions of war and peace;

6) The general direction and control of commercial relations with foreign countries;

7) National defense and the security of the state;

8) Traffic by rail, air, river and sea and navigational affairs of national importance;

9) Posts, telegraphs, telephones and wireless;

10) Federal citizenship;

11) Matters connected with emigration and immigration; the legal status of foreigners;

12) The general economic plan of the state; statistics;

13) The Federal budget; the passing of the general state budget and of final accounts; supreme control over the administration of the general state budget;

14) The monetary and credit system; Federal loans; foreign exchange and currency transactions; insurance; customs; state monopolies;

15) Patents, trade marks, models, samples, measures, weights, precious metals;

16) Care for disabled ex-servicemen;

17) Amnesty and pardon in cases of acts violating Federal laws;

18) Financial, industrial, mining, building, commercial, forestry and agricultural concerns of national importance;

19) Roads, rivers, canals and ports of national importance;

20) Control over the carrying out of Federal laws;

21) Legislation concerning the distribution of revenues to the Federal budget, the budgets of the republics and those of autonomous and administrative-territorial units; legislation concerning public loans and taxes;

22) Legislation concerning the organization of the law courts, public prosecution, advocateship; criminal law; commercial, exchange and check law;

maritime law; legislation concerning civil procedure litigious and non-litigious, executive, bankruptcy, criminal and general administrative procedure; the personal status of citizens;

23) Basic legislation concerning labor, enterprises and social insurance; co-operative societies; civil rights;

24) The establishment of general principles for the legislation and admini-stration of the republics in the domains of agriculture, mining, forestry, hunting, water power; building; economic administration; regulation of prices; health and physical culture; education; social welfare and the organization of state authority.

The republics may issue their own prescriptions in these matters until general principles are laid down by the Federative People's Republic of Yugoslavia.

Outside these matters the people's republics exercise their authority inde-pendently.

ARTICLE 45. The territory of the Federative People's Republic of Yugoslavia consists of the territories of its republics and forms a single state and economic area.

ARTICLE 46. Federal laws are valid throughout the territory of the Federative People's Republic of Yugoslavia.

In case of discrepancy between Federal laws and the laws of the republics, Federal law shall be applied.

ARTICLE 47. The traffic of goods between republics is free and cannot be restricted by the laws of any republic.

Acts and documents issued by organs of state administration and organs of justice of one republic have the same validity in every republic.

ARTICLE 48. A single Federal citizenship is established for the citizens of the Federative People's Republic of Yugoslavia. Every citizen of a people's republic is at the same time a citizen of the Federative People's Republic of Yugoslavia.

Every citizen of a republic enjoys in every republic the same rights as the citizens of that republic.

CHAPTER VII

THE SUPREME FEDERAL ORGANS OF STATE AUTHORITY

(a)   The People's Assembly of the Federative People's Republic of Yugoslavia

ARTICLE 49. The People's Assembly of the Federative People's Republic of Yugoslavia is the representative of the sovereignty of the people of the Federative People's Republic of Yugoslavia.

ARTICLE 50. The People's Assembly is the supreme organ of state authority of the Federative People's Republic of Yugoslavia and exercises all those rights belonging to the Federative People's Republic of Yugoslavia which are not trans-ferred by the Constitution to the jurisdiction of other Federal organs of state authority and state administration.

ARTICLE 51. The People's Assembly of the F.P.R.Y. exercises exclusively the power of legislation in all matters within the jurisdiction of the Federative People's Republic of Yugoslavia.

ARTICLE 52. The People's Assembly of the F.P.R.Y. consists of two Houses—the Federal Council and the Council of Nationalities.

ARTICLE 53. The Federal Council is elected by all citizens of the Federative People's Republic of Yugoslavia. For every 50,000 inhabitants one deputy is elected.

ARTICLE 54. The Council of Nationalities is elected in the republics, autonomous provinces and autonomous regions. The citizens of each republic elect thirty, the autonomous provinces twenty, and the autonomous regions fifteen representatives.

ARTICLE 55. No person can be a deputy in both houses of the People's Assembly of the F.P.R.Y. at the same time.

ARTICLE 56. The People's Assembly of the F.P.R.Y. is elected for a term of four years.

ARTICLE 57. Both houses of the People's Assembly of the F.P.R.Y. have equal rights.

ARTICLE 58. The houses of the People's Assembly of the F.P.R.Y. sit, as a rule, separately.

The sessions of the Federal Council and the Council of Nationalities open and close simultaneously.

ARTICLE 59. The Federal Council elects a president, two vice presidents and three secretaries.

The Council of Nationalities elects a president, two vice presidents and three secretaries.

The presidents conduct the meetings of the houses and their work according to the rules of procedure.

ARTICLE 60. The sessions of the People's Assembly of the F.P.R.Y. are regular or extraordinary and are convened by a decree of the Presidium of the People's Assembly of the F.P.R.Y.

Regular sessions are convened twice a year: on the 15th of April and on the 15th of October. If the People's Assembly is not convened on these dates it can meet even without the decree of the Presidium.

Extraordinary sessions are convened whenever the Presidium of the People's Assembly of the F.P.R.Y. considers it necessary, whenever one of the republics requests it through its supreme organ of state authority, or if one-third of the deputies of one house request it.

ARTICLE 61. Both houses of the People's Assembly of the F.P.R.Y. sit in joint meeting only when this Constitution expressly provides for it or when both houses so decide.

Joint meetings of the People's Assembly of the F.P.R.Y. are presided over alternatively by the presidents of the houses.

At a joint meeting of the People's Assembly of the F.P.R.Y. resolutions are carried by a majority of votes. For the passing of resolutions the presence of the majority of the deputies of each house is required.

ARTICLE 62.   Each house prescribes its own rule of order, and the People's Assembly of the F.P.R.Y. prescribes the rule of procedure for joint meetings.

ARTICLE 63.   The Government of the F.P.R.Y., the members of the Government of the F.P.R.Y. and the deputies of both houses have the right to introduce bills.

A bill may be introduced in either house of the People's Assembly of the F.P.R.Y.

No bill may become law unless it receives a majority of votes in both houses during a meeting at which a majority of the deputies of each house is present.

ARTICLE 64.   Each house of the People's Assembly of the F.P.R.Y. has the right to propose amendments to a bill already accepted in one house. Thus amended, the bill is returned for confirmation to the house in which it originated.

If agreement is not reached, the matter is submitted to a coordinating committee of the People's Assembly of the F.P.R.Y., which comprises an equal number of members of both houses.

If the coordinating committee does not reach an agreement or if one of the houses rejects the solution proposed by the coordinating committee, the houses will reconsider the whole matter.

If again no agreement is reached, the People's Assembly of the F.P.R.Y. shall be dissolved.

The dissolution decree shall also embody the order for holding new elections.

ARTICLE 65.   Laws and other general prescriptions of the Federative People's Republic of Yugoslavia are published in the languages of the people's republics.

ARTICLE 66.   A law comes into force on the eighth day after its publication in the 'Official Gazette of the F.P.R.Y.,' unless the law itself provides otherwise.

ARTICLE 67.   Each house elects committees to which it entrusts specific matters.

Each house at its first meeting elects a verification committee which examines the deputies' mandates.

On the proposal of its committee each house confirms or annuls the deputies' mandates.

ARTICLE 68.   The People's Assembly of the F.P.R.Y. and each of its houses may, through their enquiry committees, carry out enquiries on any matter of general significance.

It is the duty of all state organs to comply with the demands of enquiry committees for the establishment of facts and collection of evidence.

ARTICLE 69.   Deputies of the People's Assembly of the F.P.R.Y. enjoy rights of immunity.

Deputies may not be arrested nor may criminal proceedings be instituted against them without the approval of the house to which they belong or of the Presidium of the People's Assembly of the F.P.R.Y., unless taken in the act of committing an offense, in which case the Presidium of the People's Assembly must immediately be informed.

ARTICLE 70. In case of war or similar extraordinary circumstances the People's Assembly of the F.P.R.Y. may prolong the duration of its mandate as long as such circumstances exist.

The People's Assembly of the F.P.R.Y. may decide to dissolve even before the end of the period for which it was elected.

ARTICLE 71. Elections for a new People's Assembly of the F.P.R.Y. must be announced before the expiry of the last day of the period for which the outgoing People's Assembly was elected.

Not less than two and not more than three months shall elapse between the date of dissolution of the People's Assembly of the F.P.R.Y. and the date of elections for a new People's Assembly of the F.P.R.Y.

ARTICLE 72. The People's Assembly of the F.P.R.Y. passes amendments to the Constitution.

A proposal to amend the Constitution may be submitted by the Presidium of the People's Assembly of the F.P.R.Y., by the Government of the F.P.R.Y. or by one-third of the deputies of one of the houses.

A proposed amendment to the Constitution must be approved by a majority of votes in each house.

The proposed amendment to the Constitution is adopted if an absolute majority of the total number of deputies in each house votes in its favor.

An adopted amendment to the Constitution is promulgated by the People's Assembly of the F.P.R.Y. at a joint meeting of both houses.

(b) The Presidium of the People's Assembly of the Federative People's Republic of Yugoslavia

ARTICLE 73. The People's Assembly of the F.P.R.Y. elects the Presidium of the People's Assembly of the F.P.R.Y. at a joint meeting of both houses.

The Presidium of the People's Assembly of the F.P.R.Y. consists of a President, six vice presidents, a secretary and not more than thirty members.

ARTICLE 74. The Presidium of the People's Assembly of the F.P.R.Y. performs the following functions:

1) Convenes the sessions of the People's Assembly of the F.P.R.Y.;

2) Dissolves the People's Assembly of the F.P.R.Y. in the event of disagreement of the houses over a bill;

3) Orders elections for the People's Assembly of the F.P.R.Y.;

4) Gives the ruling as to whether a law of the republics is in conformity with the Constitution of the F.P.R.Y. and with the Federal laws, subject to the ratification of the People's Assembly of the F.P.R.Y., at the request of the Government of the F.P.R.Y., the presidium of the people's assemblies of the republics, the Supreme Court of the F.P.R.Y., the Public Prosecutor of the F.P.R.Y., or on its own initiative;

5) Gives obligatory interpretations of Federal laws;

6) Proclaims laws which have been passed; issues decrees;

7) Exercises the right of pardon according to the provisions of the law;

8) Awards decorations and confers honorary titles of the Federative People's Republic of Yugoslavia according to the provisions of the Federal law;

9) Ratifies international treaties;

10) Appoints and recalls ambassadors, envoys extraordinary and ministers plenipotentiary to foreign countries on the proposal of the Government of the F.P.R.Y.;

11) Receives the credentials and letters of recall of diplomatic representatives accredited to it by foreign countries;

12) Declares general mobilization and state of war in the event of an armed attack against the Federative People's Republic of Yugoslavia, or in case of necessity for the immediate fulfillment of international obligations of the Federative People's Republic of Yugoslavia toward the international peace organization or toward an allied country;

13) On the proposal of the President of the Government of the F.P.R.Y. and subject to ratification by the People's Assembly of the F.P.R.Y., appoints and relieves of their office individual members of the Government during the period between two sessions of the People's Assembly of the F.P.R.Y.;

14) Appoints the deputies of members of the Government on the proposal of the President of the Government of the F.P.R.Y.;

15) Modifies, unites and abolishes existing ministries and commissions on the proposal of the President of the Government of the F.P.R.Y., during the period between sessions of the People's Assembly of the F.P.R.Y. and subject to ratification by the latter;

16) Determines, upon the proposal of the Government of the F.P.R.Y., what enterprises and institutions are of national significance and come under the direct administration of the Federal Government;

17) Orders a people's referendum on matters within the jurisdiction of the Federative People's Republic of Yugoslavia on the basis of a resolution of the People's Assembly of the F.P.R.Y. or on the proposal of the Government of the F.P.R.Y.;

The decrees of the Presidium of the People's Assembly of the F.P.R.Y. are signed by the President and the secretary.

ARTICLE 75. The Presidium of the People's Assembly of the F.P.R.Y. is responsible for its work to the People's Assembly of the F.P.R.Y. The People's Assembly of the F.P.R.Y. may recall the Presidium and elect a new one, and also relieve individual members of their functions and elect new ones even before the end of the term for which they have been elected.

ARTICLE 76. When the People's Assembly of the F.P.R.Y. is dissolved, the Presidium carries out its duty until the Presidium of the new People's Assembly of the F.P.R.Y. is elected.

The newly elected People's Assembly of the F.P.R.Y. shall meet within one month of the conclusion of the elections.

CHAPTER VIII

FEDERAL ORGANS OF STATE ADMINISTRATION

ARTICLE 77. The highest executive and administrative organ of state authority of the Federative People's Republic of Yugoslavia is the Government of the F.P.R.Y.

The Government of the F.P.R.Y. is appointed and relieved of its functions by the People's Assembly of the F.P.R.Y. at a joint meeting of both houses.

The Government of the F.P.R.Y. is responsible to and accountable for its work to the People's Assembly of the F.P.R.Y. In the interval between two sessions of the People's Assembly of the F.P.R.Y. the Government is responsible and accountable for its work to the Presidium of the People's Assembly of the F.P.R.Y.

ARTICLE 78. The Government of the F.P.R.Y. acts on the basis of the Constitution and Federal laws.

The Government of the F.P.R.Y. issues regulations for the application of laws and regulations on the basis of legal authorization, as well as instructions and orders for the execution of Federal laws. The Government of the F.P.R.Y. sees to the execution of Federal laws and supervises their application.

Regulations, instructions, orders and decisions of the Government of the F.P.R.Y. are signed by the President of the Government and by the responsible minister.

ARTICLE 79. Regulations, instructions, orders and decisions of the Government of the F.P.R.Y. are binding throughout the territory of the Federative People's Republic of Yugoslavia.

ARTICLE 80. The Government of the F.P.R.Y. directs and coordinates the work of its ministries, commissions and committees.

The Government of the F.P.R.Y. sees to the preparing and carrying out of the national economic plan and budget; draws up and carries out the annual economic plans; controls the credit and monetary system; undertakes all necessary measures for the safeguarding and protection of the constitutional order and of the rights of citizens; directs the general organization of the Yugoslav Army; directs the maintenance of relations with foreign states; sees to the carrying out of international treaties and obligations; decides upon bills presented by individual members of the Government to the People's Assembly of the F.P.R.Y.; prescribes the internal organization of ministries and of subordinate institutions; appoints committees, commissions and institutions for the carrying out of economic, defensive and cultural measures.

ARTICLE 81. The Government of the F.P.R.Y. consists of the President, vice presidents, ministers, the chairman of the Federal Planning Commission and the chairman of the Federal Control Commission.

The Government of the F.P.R.Y. may also include ministers without portfolio.

ARTICLE 82. The members of the Government of the F.P.R.Y., before taking up their duties, take the oath before the Presidium of the People's Assembly of the F.P.R.Y.

ARTICLE 83. The President of the Government of the F.P.R.Y. represents the Government, presides over the meetings and directs the work of the Government.

ARTICLE 84. Members of the Government of the F.P.R.Y. are responsible under criminal law if, in the execution of their official duties, they trespass against the Constitution and laws.

They are responsible for any damage which they cause to the state by illegal acts.

More explicit provisions concerning the responsibility of members of the Government of the F.P.R.Y. are laid down by Federal law.

ARTICLE 85. The ministers of the Government of the F.P.R.Y. direct the branches of the state administration which come within the competence of the Federative People's Republic of Yugoslavia.

The ministers of the Federal Government, the chairman of the Federal Planning Commission and the chairman of the Federal Control Commission issue rules, instructions and orders on the basis of and for the application of the Federal laws, regulations, instructions and orders of the Federal Government.

The ministers see to the proper execution of the Federal laws, regulations, instructions and orders of the Federal Government and are responsible for their application within the branch of state administration under their direction.

ARTICLE 86. The ministries of the Government of the F.P.R.Y. are either Federal or Federal-republican.

Federal ministries are the Ministry of Foreign Affairs; the Ministry of National Defense; the Ministry of Communications; the Ministry of Shipping; the Ministry of Posts; the Ministry of Foreign Trade.

Federal-republican ministries are the Ministry of Finance; the Ministry of the Interior; the Ministry of Justice; the Ministry of Industry; the Ministry of Mines; the Ministry of Commerce and Supplies; the Ministry of Agriculture and Forestry; the Ministry of Labor; the Ministry of Public Works.

ARTICLE 87. The Federal ministries administer, as a rule directly through their own organs, a given branch of state administration throughout the territory of the Federative People's Republic of Yugoslavia.

The Federal ministries in order to carry out those affairs for which they are responsible may appoint their representatives to the governments of the republics and set up departments and sections attached to the people's committees.

ARTICLE 88. The Federal-republican ministries direct a determined branch of state administration indirectly through the corresponding ministries of the people's republics, and can administer directly only specified affairs, enterprises and institutions of national significance.

ARTICLE 89. The Government of the F.P.R.Y. includes committees concerned with education and culture, public health and social welfare and appointed for the general direction of these branches of state administration.

Such committees may be formed for other affairs of state administration.

CHAPTER IX

SUPREME ORGANS OF STATE AUTHORITY OF THE PEOPLE'S REPUBLICS

ARTICLE 90. The supreme organ of state authority of a people's republic is the people's assembly of the republic.

The people's assembly of a republic is elected by the citizens of the republic for a period of four years according to the terms of the constitution and the laws of the republic.

ARTICLE 91. The People's Assembly of a republic exercises the sovereign rights of the republic in the name of the people on the basis of the constitution of the republic and in conformity with the Constitution of the F.P.R.Y. It deals with all matters within the jurisdiction of the republic insofar as they are not transferred by the constitution of the republic to the competence of the presidium of the people's assembly of the republic or to the government of the republic.

ARTICLE 92. Legislative power in the republic is exercised exclusively by the people's assembly of the republic.

ARTICLE 93. The people's assembly of the republic elects a president, a vice president and secretaries to conduct its sessions.

ARTICLE 94. The people's assembly elects the presidium of the people's assembly of the republic, consisting of a president, one or more vice presidents, a secretary and members, whose number is determined by the constitution of the republic.

The competence of the presidium of the people's assembly of the republic is determined by the constitution of the republic.

ARTICLE 95. The people's assembly of the republic appoints the government of the republic and relieves it of its functions.

CHAPTER X

ORGANS OF STATE ADMINISTRATION OF THE PEOPLE'S REPUBLICS

ARTICLE 96. The highest executive and administrative organ of state authority of a people's republic is the government of the people's republic.

The government of a people's republic is responsible to the people's assembly of the republic, to which it gives account for its work. In the interval between two sessions of the people's assembly, the government of the republic is responsible and accountable for its work to the presidium of the people's assembly of the republic.

ARTICLE 97. The government of a republic acts on the basis of the Constitution of the F.P.R.Y., the constitution of the republic, the Federal laws, the laws of the republic, and the regulations, instructions and orders of the Federal Government.

The government of a republic issues regulations for the application of the Federal laws, the laws of the republic, the regulations, instructions and orders of the Federal Government; it issues regulations on the basis of legal authorization and also instructions and orders for the application of Federal laws and the laws of the republic and controls their application.

ARTICLE 98. The ministers of a republic have the right to issue rules, orders and instructions on the basis of and for the execution of the Federal laws, the laws of the republic, and the regulations, instructions and orders of the Federal Government and the government of the republic.

The ministers of the republic supervise the proper execution of the Federal laws, the laws of the republic and the regulations, instructions and orders of the Federal Government and the government of the republic.

ARTICLE 99. The ministries of a republic are Federal-republican or republican.

ARTICLE 100. Federal-republican ministries in a people's republic direct specified branches of state administration and, in addition to matters within their own competence, deal with matters in the competence of the Federal-republican ministries of the Federal Government, on the basis of their rules, instructions, orders and decisions.

ARTICLE 101. The republican ministries direct independently certain specified branches of state administration which come within the competence of the people's republic concerned.

ARTICLE 102. The ministries of a republic are determined by the constitution of the republic in conformity with the Constitution of the F.P.R.Y.

The presidium of the people's assembly of a republic may change, unite or abolish the existing ministries in conformity with the Constitution of the F.P.R.Y., the constitution of the republic, the Federal laws and the decisions of the Presidium of the People's Assembly of the F.P.R.Y.

CHAPTER XI

ORGANS OF STATE AUTHORITY OF AUTONOMOUS PROVINCES AND AUTONOMOUS REGIONS

ARTICLE 103. The rights and the scope of the autonomy of autonomous provinces and autonomous regions are determined by the constitution of the republic.

ARTICLE 104. The statute of an autonomous province or of an autonomous region is drawn up in conformity with the constitution of the F.P.R.Y. and the constitution of the republic by the highest organ of state authority of the autonomous province or autonomous region, and is confirmed by the people's assembly of the republic.

ARTICLE 105. The highest organ of state authority of an autonomous province is the people's assembly of the autonomous province, which is elected by the citizens of the autonomous province for a period of three years and meets in accordance with the provisions of the constitution of the republic.

The people's assembly of an autonomous province elects the principal executive committee of the autonomous province as its executive and administrative organ.

ARTICLE 106. The highest organ of state authority of an autonomous region is the regional people's committee, which is elected by the citizens of the autonomous region for a period of three years and holds its assemblies in accordance with the provisions of the constitution of the republic.

The regional people's committee elects the regional executive committee as its executive and administrative organ.

CHAPTER XII

ORGANS OF STATE AUTHORITY
OF ADMINISTRATIVE-TERRITORIAL UNITS

ARTICLE 107. The people's committees are the organs of state authority in localities (villages, small towns), districts, town-wards, towns, departments and regions.

The people's committees of localities are elected by the citizens for a term of two years and the people's committees of districts, town-wards, towns, departments and regions are elected by the citizens for a term of three years.

The people's committees of districts, town-wards, towns, departments and regions hold their regular assemblies within terms prescribed by the constitution of the people's republic.

ARTICLE 108. The people's committees direct the work of subordinate organs of administration and economic and cultural development in their sphere of action; they ensure the maintenance of public order, the execution of the laws and the protection of the rights of citizens; they draw up their own budgets.

The people's committees issue, within the framework of their competence, general rules (decisions) on the basis of the Federal Constitution, the constitution of the republic, the Federal laws, the laws of the republic and the general rules of higher organs of state authority.

ARTICLE 109. It is the duty of the people's committees, in the execution of their general and local duties, to rely on the initiative and wide participation of the masses of the people and the workers' organizations.

ARTICLE 110. The executive and administrative organs of the people's committees, except in smaller villages, are the executive committees. An executive committee consists of a president, vice president, secretary and members.

Executive committees are elected by the people's committees from among their members.

ARTICLE 111. The executive organ of the people's committee of a smaller village consists of a chairman and a secretary.

ARTICLE 112. The local people's committee convenes, within the time limits set by law, a local meeting of the electors to whom they are accountable for their work. The rights and duties of the local meeting of electors are determined by law.

ARTICLE 113. The executive and administrative organs of the people's committees are subordinate both to their own people's committees and also to executive and administrative organs of state authority of higher rank.

ARTICLE 114. A people's committee may have, under the control of its executive committee, departments or sections to deal with individual branches of administration. The departments and sections are subordinate in their work to the executive committee and at the same time to the corresponding department of the higher people's committee and to the competent ministry of the republic.

CHAPTER XIII

THE PEOPLE'S COURTS

ARTICLE 115. The organs of justice in the Federative People's Republic of Yugoslavia are the Supreme Court of the F.P.R.Y., the supreme courts of the republics and autonomous provinces, the departmental and district courts.

The organization and competence of military tribunals are regulated by Federal law.

Special courts for specified categories of disputes may be set up by law.

ARTICLE 116. The law courts are independent in their dispensing of justice and mete out justice according to the law.

The courts are separate from the administration in all instances.

Higher courts have, within the limits of the law, the right of supervision over lower courts.

ARTICLE 117. The law courts dispense justice in the name of the people.

ARTICLE 118. Proceedings in the law courts are as a rule public.

The resolutions of a court may only be altered by a competent higher court.

The accused is guaranteed the right of defense before a court.

ARTICLE 119. All courts as a rule judge in council.

The councils of district and departmental courts, when judging in the first instance, consist of judges and judges-jurors, who have equal rights in the court's proceedings.

ARTICLE 120. Judicial proceedings in the courts are conducted in the languages of the republics, autonomous provinces and autonomous regions where the courts are located. Citizens not speaking the language in which the proceedings are conducted may use their own language. Such citizens are guaranteed the right to acquaint themselves with all the legal material and to follow the proceedings of the court through an interpreter.

ARTICLE 121. Judges of the Supreme Court of the F.P.R.Y. are elected and released from their functions by the People's Assembly of the F.P.R.Y. at a joint meeting of both houses.

Judges of the supreme court of a republic or autonomous province are elected and released from their functions by the people's assembly of the republic or by the people's assembly of the autonomous province.

Judges and judges-jurors of a departmental court in a department or town are elected and released from their functions by the people's committee of the department or town.

Judges and judges-jurors of a district court in a district or town are elected and released from their functions by the people's committee of the district or town.

ARTICLE 122. The Supreme Court of the F.P.R.Y. is the highest organ of justice of the Federative People's Republic of Yugoslavia.

It is determined by Federal law in what cases the Supreme Court of the F.P.R.Y. shall judge in the first and in what cases in the second instance.

ARTICLE 123. The Supreme Court of the F.P.R.Y. decides on the legality of the judgments of all courts in the Federative People's Republic of Yugoslavia from the point of view of the application of Federal laws.

The supreme courts of republics and autonomous provinces ascertain the legality of the judgments of all courts of the republic or autonomous province.

CHAPTER XIV

PUBLIC PROSECUTION

ARTICLE 124. The public prosecution is the organ of the People's Assembly of the F.P.R.Y. for supervising the proper application of the law by all ministries and other administrative organs and institutions subordinate to them in the Federative People's Republic of Yugoslavia and in the people's republics, by public officials and by all citizens.

ARTICLE 125. The Public Prosecutor of the F.P.R.Y. and his deputies are elected and released from their functions by the People's Assembly of the F.P.R.Y. at a joint meeting of both houses.

The public prosecutors of the people's republics and their deputies are appointed and released from their functions by the Public Prosecutor of the F.P.R.Y.

The public prosecutors of autonomous provinces, autonomous regions, regions, departments and districts are appointed and released from their functions by the public prosecutor of the republic subject to the confirmation of the Public Prosecutor of the F.P.R.Y.

ARTICLE 126. Public prosecutors are independent in their work and are subordinate only to the Public Prosecutor of the F.P.R.Y.

ARTICLE 127. Public prosecutors have the right to enter appeals and suits, the right of legal intervention in the course of judicial and administrative proceedings, the right to institute criminal proceedings and the right to file a demand for the defense of legality against valid resolutions of law courts and administrative organs.

ARTICLE 128. The military prosecutor of the Yugoslav Army and other military prosecutors are appointed by the Commander-in-Chief of the Yugoslav Army.

The organization and competence of the military prosecution will be determined by Federal law.

CHAPTER XV

RELATIONS BETWEEN THE ORGANS OF STATE AUTHORITY AND THE ORGANS OF STATE ADMINISTRATION

ARTICLE 129. The Presidium of the People's Assembly of the F.P.R.Y. has the right to annul or abolish the regulations, instructions, orders and decisions of the Federal Government if they are not in conformity with the Constitution and Federal laws.

The Federal Government has the right to annul or abolish the rules, orders, instructions and decisions of members of the Federal Government, if they are not in conformity with the Constitution, the Federal laws and the regulations, instructions, orders and decisions of the Federal Government.

ARTICLE 130. The presidium of the people's assembly of a republic has the right to annul or abolish the regulations, instructions, orders and decisions of the government of the republic if they are not in conformity with the Constitution of the F.P.R.Y., the constitution of the republic, the Federal laws and the laws of the republic.

The government of the republic has the right to annul or abolish the rules, orders, instructions and decisions of the ministers of the republic if they are not in conformity with the Federal Constitution, the constitution of the republic, Federal laws, the laws of the republic and the regulations, instructions, orders and decisions of the government of the republic.

ARTICLE 131. In matters within Federal competence, the Federal Government has the right to suspend the acts of the government of a republic and abolish the acts of the ministers of a republic, if they are not in conformity with the Federal Constitution, the constitution of the republic, the Federal laws, the laws of the republic, the regulations, instructions and orders of the Federal Government, or the rules, orders and instructions of a member of the Federal Government.

Under the same conditions the members of the Federal Government have the right to suspend the acts of the ministers of the republic.

ARTICLE 132. The presidium of the people's assembly of a republic or the people's assembly of an autonomous province and the people's committees of higher rank have the right to annul or abolish illegal and irregular acts of people's committees of lower rank.

The government of a republic, its individual ministers and the principal executive committee of an autonomous province have the right within the limits of their competence to annul or abolish the illegal or irregular acts of executive committees. The executive committees of people's committees of higher rank have the same rights toward executive committees of lower rank.

A people's committee has the right to annul or abolish illegal and irregular acts of its executive committee.

The executive committee of a people's committee of higher rank or the principal executive committee of an autonomous province and the government of a republic have the right to suspend the execution of illegal and irregular acts of a people's committee of lower rank and to propose to its own people's committee or to the people's assembly of the autonomous province or to the presidium of the people's assembly of the republic respectively to annul or abolish them.

ARTICLE 133. A people's committee of higher rank, the people's assembly of an autonomous province or the presidium of the people's assembly of a republic has the right to dissolve any people's committee of lower rank and to order elections for a new people's committee to be held. A people's committee of higher rank, the people's assembly of an autonomous province or the presidium of the people's assembly of a republic has the right to release from its functions the executive committee of any people's committee of lower rank and to order elections for a new executive committee to be held.

CHAPTER XVI

THE YUGOSLAV ARMY

ARTICLE 134. The Yugoslav Army is the armed force of the Federative People's Republic of Yugoslavia. Its duty is to safeguard and defend the independence of the state and the freedom of the people. It is the guardian of the inviolability of the state frontiers and serves the maintenance of peace and security.

ARTICLE 135. The Commander-in-Chief of [the] Yugoslav Army is appointed by the People's Assembly of the F.P.R.Y. at a joint meeting of both houses. The Commander-in-Chief directs the entire military and armed forces of the Federative People's Republic of Yugoslavia.

PART THREE

TRANSITIONAL AND CONCLUDING PROVISIONS

ARTICLE 136. On the day when [this] Constitution comes into force all laws and other legal dispositions contrary to the Constitution are abolished.

Resolutions, laws and regulations confirmed by the decision of the Constituent Assembly of December 1, 1945, remain in force until a final resolution with regard to them is made.

The legislative committees of both houses of the People's Assembly of the F.P.R.Y. are authorized, within a period of six months from the day when the Constitution comes into force, to examine all resolutions, laws and regulations confirmed by the decision of the Constituent Assembly of December 1, 1945, to bring them into conformity with the Constitution and to issue laws deciding which of those resolutions, laws and regulations shall remain in force without modification or to issue laws for the modification and amplification of those resolutions, laws, and regulations. These laws, issued by the legislative committees of both houses of the People's Assembly of the F.P.R.Y., are promulgated by a decree of the Presidium of the People's Assembly of the F.P.R.Y. and are submitted for confirmation to the People's Assembly of the F.P.R.Y. at its first subsequent session. The proposals of resolutions, laws and regulations shall, in order to be brought into conformity with the Constitution, be transmitted by the President of the Government of the F.P.R.Y. to the legislative committees.

ARTICLE 137. All persons under the age of eighteen, who have been entered in the lists of electors for the Constituent Assembly, shall retain the electoral right thus acquired.

ARTICLE 138. Existing ministries which are not provided for by the Constitution in the composition of the Government of the F.P.R.Y. may remain in the composition of the Government until a resolution with regard to them is passed in accordance with Article 74, § 15, of the Constitution.

ARTICLE 139. The Constitution comes into force by promulgation at a joint meeting of both houses of the Constituent Assembly.

Given at Belgrade,
the principal town of the Federative People's
Republic of Yugoslavia,
January 31, 1946.

The Presidium of the Constituent Assembly of the Federative People's Republic of Yugoslavia

Secretary,   *President,*

(Signed) Mile Peruničić.   (Signed) Dr. Ivan Ribar.

Vice presidents,

(Signed): Moša Pijade, Josip Rus, Dimitar Vlahov, Filip Lakuš, Djuro Pucar, Marko Vujačić.

Members,

(Signed): Josip Broz-Tito, Bane Andrejev, Dr. Vlado Bakarić, Dušan Brkić, Josip Vidmar, Milovan Djilas, Edvard Kardelj, Sreten Žujović, Dr. Siniša Stanković, Vlada Zečević, Dr. Stevan Jakovljević, Blažo Jovanović, Dr. Dragoljub Jovanović, Boris Kidrič, Sava Kosanović, Lazar Kuliševski, Dr. Blagoje Nešković, Jaša Prodanović, Aleksandar Ranković, Dr. Zlatan Sremec, Dobrosav Tomašević, Frane Frol, Andrija Hebrang, Avdo Humo, Rodoljub Čolaković, Vlado Šegrt.

14. 2

CONSTITUTION OF THE SOCIALIST FEDERAL REPUBLIC OF YUGOSLAVIA[1]

Adopted by the Federal People's Assembly

April 7, 1963

CONSIDERING THE HISTORICAL FACT that the working people of Yugoslavia, under the leadership of the Communist Party, overthrew the former class society based on exploitation, political oppression and national inequality by their struggle in the People's Liberation War and Socialist Revolution in order to found a community in which human labor and man will be delivered from exploitation and arbitrariness and each of the peoples of Yugoslavia and all of them together will find conditions for free and comprehensive development;

Aware that such changes have been brought about in the development of the material basis of the country and of socialist social relations as supersede the present Constitution;

Desirous of consolidating these achievements and of securing conditions for the further development of socialist and democratic relations and for comprehensive progress and freedom of the people by uniform constitutionality;

The Federal People's Assembly, as the supreme representative body of the working people and of all the peoples of Yugoslavia,

Establishes:

THE CONSTITUTION OF THE SOCIALIST FEDERAL REPUBLIC OF YUGOSLAVIA

INTRODUCTORY PART
BASIC PRINCIPLES

I

The peoples of Yugoslavia, on the basis of the right of every people to self-determination, including the right to secession, on the basis of their common struggle and their will freely declared in the People's Liberation War and Socialist Revolution, and in accord with their historical aspirations, aware that the further consolidation of their brotherhood and unity is to their common interest, have united in a federal republic of free and equal peoples and nationalities and have founded a socialist federal community of working people, the Socialist Federal Republic of

---

[1] *The Constitution of the Socialist Federal Republic of Yugoslavia* (Belgrade: Secretariat of Information of the Federal Executive Council, 1963).

477

Yugoslavia, in which, in the interests of each people and of all of them together, they are achieving and developing:

Socialist social relations and the protection of the socialist system of society;

National freedom and independence;

Brotherhood and unity among the peoples and solidarity among the working people;

Possibilities and freedom for the comprehensive development of the human personality and for close communion of the people in accord with their interests and aspirations to create an ever richer culture and civilization in socialist society;

Unity and coordination of efforts to develop the material basis of the social community and the prosperity of the people;

Association of their own aspirations with the progressive strivings of mankind;

Common foundations of an economic and political system in which common interests and equality are achieved among the people.

The working people and the peoples of Yugoslavia exercise their sovereign rights in the Federation when the Constitution determines this to be in the common interest and exercise all other relations in the socialist republics.

II

The socialist system in Yugoslavia is based on relations between people acting as free and equal producers and creators, whose work serves exclusively to satisfy their personal and common needs.

Accordingly, the inviolable foundation of the position and role of man lies in

Social ownership of the means of production, which precludes the restoration of any system of exploitation of one man by another, and which, by eliminating the separation of man from the means of production and other working conditions, provides the conditions necessary for management by the working people in production and in the distribution of the products of labor, and for social guidance of economic development;

Emancipation of work, which supersedes the historically conditioned inequality and dependence of people in work, which is assured by the abolition of wage-labor relations, by self-management of the working people, by comprehensive development of the productive forces, by the diminishing of the socially necessary labor time, by the development of science, culture, and technology, and by the continual expansion of education;

The right of man, both as an individual and as a member of the working collective, to enjoy the fruits of his work and of the material progress of the social community, in accordance with the principle, 'From each according to his abilities; to each according to his work,' along with the obligation of man to assure the development of the material foundations of his own and of socially organized work and to contribute to the satisfaction of other social needs;

Self-management by the working people in the working organization; free association of the working people, of working and other organizations and of social-political communities in order to satisfy common needs and interests; self-government in the commune and in the other social-political communities so as to assure the direct participation of the citizens in the determination of the course of social development, in the exercise of power and in the decisions on other social affairs;

The democratic political relations that enable man to achieve his interests, to realize his right of self-government and other rights and mutual relations, and to develop his personality by direct activity in social life, especially in the organs of self-government, in the social-political organizations and associations, which he himself creates and through which he influences the development of social consciousness and expands the conditions for his activity and for the attainment of his interests and rights;

Equality of rights, duties and responsibilities of the people in conformity with uniform constitutionality and legality;

Solidarity and cooperation of the working people and working organizations, their interest and their unrestricted initiative in developing production and other social and personal activities in behalf of man and his social community;

Economic and social security of man.

It is from this position of man that the social-economic and political system derives, and it is man and his role in society that it serves.

Any form of management of production and of other social activities [or] any form of distribution that distorts the social relations based on this position of man, whether in the form of bureaucratic arbitrariness and privileges based on monopoly position or in the form of private-ownership selfishness and particularism, is contrary to the individual and common interests of the working man and to the social-economic and political system determined by the Constitution.

III

The socially owned means of production, being the common, inalienable basis of socially organized work, serve to satisfy the personal and common needs and interests of the working people and to develop the material foundations of the social community and socialist social relations. The socially owned means of production are managed directly by the working people, who work with these means on their own behalf and on behalf of the social community and are responsible to each other and to the social community.

Since no one has the right of ownership over the socially owned means of production, the social-political community or the working organization or the working man may [not] appropriate in any form of ownership the product of socially organized work, nor manage and dispose of socially owned means of production and work, nor arbitrarily determine the terms of distribution.

Work is the only grounds for the appropriation of the product of socially organized work, and the foundation of management of social means.

The social product serves to restore and expand the material basis for socially organized work, and directly to satisfy the personal and common needs of the working people, in conformity with the principle of distribution according to work.

That part of the social product which is set aside for the renewal and expansion of the material basis of socially organized work provides the foundation for social-economic growth, which the working people realize in their working organizations, and through the mutual cooperation of these organizations, as well as in the social-political communities.

A uniform system of distribution shall assure that the working organizations will employ the funds for social-economic growth in proportion to their share in creating them, subject to their ability to make the most effective use of them within the framework of the social division of labor determined by the social plans.

In order to attain self-management and to realize the individual and common interests of the working people, in order to stimulate their initiative and create the most favorable conditions for the development of the productive forces, to equalize the working conditions, to achieve distribution according to work, and to develop socialist relations, the social community plans the development of the economy and the material foundations of other social activities. Planning is done in the working organizations by the working people as the bearers of production and of socially organized work, and by the social-political communities in the performance of their social-economic functions.

The social plan of Yugoslavia coordinates the basic relations in production and distribution. Within the framework of these relations and a unified economic system, the working people in the working organizations and social-political communities autonomously plan and develop the material bases for their activities.

In order to equalize the material conditions in social life and in the work of the working people, in order to achieve harmonious economic development as a whole, and in order to create the material basis for equality among the peoples of Yugoslavia, the social community, acting in the common interest, devotes special attention to the rapid development of the productive forces in those republics and areas with inadequate economic development, and to this end it provides the necessary funds and undertakes other measures.

Social ownership of the means of production is the foundation of personal ownership acquired by personal work, and serves to satisfy the personal needs and interests of man.

In order to develop socialist relations in agriculture and to promote agricultural production, conditions are assured for the development of production on the basis of socially owned means and socially organized work, and for association among farmers and their cooperation with the working organizations on a voluntary basis.

Having the constitutional right of ownership to arable land, the farmers have the right and obligation to utilize the land in order to promote agricultural production in their own interests and in the interests of the social community.

IV

Every form of government, including political power, is created by the working class and by all the working people for themselves in order to organize society as a free community of producers, which is assured

By social self-government as the basis of the social-political system;

By decision of the citizens on all social matters, either directly or through delegates whom they elect to the representative bodies of the social-political communities and to other bodies of social self-government;

By the establishment and development of equal and democratic relations among the citizens, and by the attainment of human and civil freedoms and rights in accord with the strengthening of solidarity, the citizens' performance of their social duties, and the material and social development of the socialist community;

By the personal responsibility of all holders of public office, especially those with functions of power, and by the responsibility of the political-executive and administrative organs to the representative body of the social-political community and to the public;

By judicial supervision of constitutionality and legality; and by social supervision of the work of state organs, organs of social self-government, and organizations dealing with matters of public concern;

By the social and political activity of the socialist forces organized in social-political organizations.

The functions of power determined by the Constitution are vested in the representative bodies of the social-political communities as the territorial organs of social self-government. These representative bodies are constituted and removable delegations elected in the communes by all the citizens, and in the working communities by the working people.

With the exception of the functions of power and the general affairs of social self-government, which they discharge through the representative bodies and bodies accountable to them, the citizens decide on social affairs in their working and other autonomous organizations and by forms of direct determination; and they attain other common interests also in their social-political organizations and associations, which they found themselves.

In the socialist social relations and conditions of social self-government, the working people voluntarily unite in trade unions in order to cooperate as directly as possible in the development of socialist social relations and social self-government, to coordinate their personal and common interests with the general interests, to realize the principles of distribution according to work, and to adapt the worker for work and for management, as well as to take the initiative and undertake measures to protect their rights and interests and to improve their living and working conditions, to develop solidarity, to coordinate opinions and mutual relations, and to solve other questions of common interest.

The citizens are the source of initiative for social activities directly and through their social-political organizations and associations; they exercise supervision over the work of the organs of government and other holders of public office, they determine the norms for mutual relations and they lend their support to the state organs, the organs of social self-government, and organizations dealing with affairs of public concern.

In order to realize self-government and the other rights of the citizens, the public working of the state organs, organs of social self-government, organizations, and holders of public office shall be assured, and conditions shall be created so that the citizen may be fully informed and capable of discharging public affairs.

The principle of limitation of reelection and renomination to particular offices assures the removability of holders of government and of other public offices, in order to allow the widest possible participation of citizens in the discharge of public functions, and to consolidate and develop democratic relations in society.

V

The Socialist Alliance of the Working People of Yugoslavia, founded during the People's Liberation War and Socialist Revolution as a voluntary democratic alliance of the citizens, is the broadest base of social-political activity and social self-government of the working people.

In the Socialist Alliance of the Working People of Yugoslavia the citizens

Discuss social-political questions from all provinces of social life, coordinate opinions and pass political resolutions dealing with the solution of these questions, the course of social development and the strengthening of self-government, the attainment of the rights and interests of man and citizen, and the promotion of socialist and democratic relations;

Give their opinions and judgments on the work of state organs, organs of social self-government, organizations, and holders of public office, and exercise social supervision over their work, especially to render their work public and themselves responsible for it;

Strive for the creation and protection of every form of social-political life stimulating socialist and democratic development; take the political initiative in every province of public life; and ensure the fullest possible realization of their voting and other rights;

Provide conditions for the comprehensive participation of youth and its organizations in social and political life;

Strive for human relations among people, for the development of socialist consciousness and for the norms of a socialist way of life, and for the elimination of manifestations that impede the development of socialist and democratic social relations or otherwise harm them.

VI

The League of Communists of Yugoslavia, initiator and organizer of the People's Liberation War and Socialist Revolution, owing to the necessity of historical development, has become the leading organized force of the working class and working people in the development of socialism and in the attainment of solidarity among the working people and of the brotherhood and unity of the peoples.

Under the conditions of socialist democracy and social self-government, the League of Communists, with its guiding ideological and political work, is the prime mover of the political activity necessary to protect and to promote the achievements of the Socialist Revolution and socialist social relations, and especially to strengthen the socialist social and democratic consciousness of the people.

VII

Whereas peaceful coexistence and active cooperation between states and peoples, irrespective of differences in their social systems is indispensable to peace and social progress in the world, Yugoslavia bases its international relations on the principles of respect of national sovereignty and equality, noninterference in the internal affairs of other countries, peaceable settlement of international disputes, and socialist internationalism. In its international relations Yugoslavia adheres to the principles of the United Nations Charter, fulfills its international commitments, and actively participates in the work of the international organizations to which it is affiliated.

In order to realize these principles, Yugoslavia strives

For the establishment and development of every form of international co-operation that helps to consolidate peace, to strengthen mutual respect and friendship between peoples and states, and to bring about their rapprochement; for the broadest and freest exchange of material and intellectual wealth, for the freedom of mutual information, and for the development of other relations that contribute to the realization of common economic, cultural and other interests of states, nations and people, and especially to the development of democratic and socialist relations in international cooperation, and general social progress;

For the repudiation of the use or threat of force in international relations; and for general and complete disarmament;

For the right of every people to determine freely and to develop its own social and political system by ways and means of its own free choosing;

For the right of peoples to self-determination and national independence and for their right to wage liberation struggle to attain these just aims;

For international support to peoples waging a just struggle for national independence and liberation from colonialism and national oppression;

For the development of such international cooperation as assures equality in economic relations in the world, sovereign exploitation of national resources and the creation of conditions conducive to the more rapid development of the underdeveloped countries.

In pledging itself to comprehensive political, economic and cultural cooperation with other peoples and states, Yugoslavia, as a socialist community of peoples, holds that this cooperation should contribute to the creation of new democratic forms of association between states, nations and people which will answer to the interests of peoples and social progress, and in this respect it is an open community.

VIII

The social-political relations and the forms determined by the Constitution are aimed at broadening the conditions for the further development of socialist society, the elimination of its contradictions, and for such social progress as, on the basis of the comprehensive development of the productive forces, high productivity of labor, an abundance of products, and comprehensive development of man as an emancipated being, will bring about the development of social relations in which the communist principle, 'From each according to his abilities, to each according to his needs,' will be realized.

To this end all the state organs, organs of social self-government, organizations and citizens are enjoined, in all their activities

To expand and strengthen the material basis of society and the life of the individual by developing the productive forces, raising the productivity of labor, and continually promoting socialist social relations;

To create conditions in which the social-economic differences between intellectual and physical work will be eliminated and in which human work will become an ever fuller expression of creativity and of the human personality;

To expand and develop every form of social self-government and socialist democracy, especially in those fields in which the functions of political power predominate; to limit coercion and promote the conditions for its elimination; and to establish relations among people based on awareness of common interests and on the unrestricted activity of man;

To contribute to the realization of human freedoms and rights, to the humanization of the social environment and man's personality, to the strengthening of solidarity and humanity between people, and respect for man's dignity;

To develop comprehensive cooperation and rapprochement with all peoples in keeping with the progressive strivings of mankind to develop a free community of all the peoples in the world.

IX

In expressing the basic principles of the socialist community and the principles for its progress, this section of the Constitution is also the basis for the interpretation of the Constitution and law and for the work of each and every [individual].

PART ONE
THE SOCIAL AND POLITICAL SYSTEM

CHAPTER I
INTRODUCTORY PROVISIONS

ARTICLE 1. The Socialist Federal Republic of Yugoslavia is a federal state of voluntarily united and equal peoples and a socialist democratic community based on the powers of the working people and on self-government.

ARTICLE 2. The Socialist Federal Republic of Yugoslavia comprises the socialist republics of Bosnia and Herzegovina, Croatia, Macedonia, Montenegro, Serbia and Slovenia.

The territory of the Socialist Federal Republic of Yugoslavia is unified, consisting of the territories of the socialist republics.

ARTICLE 3. The coat-of-arms of the Socialist Federal Republic of Yugoslavia is a field encircled with ears of wheat. At the bottom the ears of wheat are tied together with a scroll bearing the inscription 29. XI 1943. Between the tops of the ears of wheat, there is a five-pointed red star. In the field are six torches, set obliquely, whose flames blend into a single flame.

ARTICLE 4. The state flag of the Socialist Federal Republic of Yugoslavia shall consist of three colors: blue, white and red, with a red five-pointed star in the center. The ratio of the width to the length of the flag shall be one to two. The colors of the flag shall extend horizontally; starting from the top, the order is blue, white and red. Each color shall occupy one-third of the width of the flag. The star shall have a regular five-pointed form and a golden (yellow) border. The central point of the star shall coincide with the point in which the diagonals of the flag intersect. The top point of the star shall extend as far as the middle of the blue stripe of the flag, the lower points of the star assuming equivalent places in the red stripe of the flag.

ARTICLE 5. The capital of the Socialist Federal Republic of Yugoslavia shall be Belgrade.

CHAPTER II

SOCIAL-ECONOMIC ORGANIZATION

ARTICLE 6. The basis of the social-economic system of Yugoslavia is free, associated work with socially owned means of labor, and self-management of the working people in production and in distribution of the social product in the working organization and social community.

ARTICLE 7. Only work and the results of work shall determine man's material and social position.

No one may gain material or other advantage directly or indirectly by exploiting the work of others.

ARTICLE 8. The means of production and the other means of socially organized work, as well as mineral and other natural resources, are social property.

The employment of the means of production and other socially owned means, and all other rights over these and other means shall be regulated by law in accordance with their nature and purpose.

ARTICLE 9. Self-management in the working organization shall include in particular the right and duty of the working people

1) To manage the working organization directly or through organs of management elected by themselves;

2) To organize production or other activity, to attend to the development of the working organization, and to determine plans and programs of work and development;

3) To decide on commerce in products and services and on other business matters of the working organization;

4) To decide on the use of socially owned means and their disposal, and to employ these means with economic expediency so as to gain the greatest return for the working organization and the social community;

5) To distribute the income belonging to the working organization and to provide for the development of the material basis for their work; to distribute income among the working people; to meet the working organization's obligations to the social community;

6) To decide on the admission of working people into the working organization, the cessation of their work, and other labor relations; to determine working hours in the working organization in accordance with general working conditions; to regulate other matters of common concern; to secure internal supervision and to render their work public;

7) To regulate and promote their working conditions, to organize labor safety and recreation, to provide conditions for their education, and to advance their own and the general standard of living;

8) To decide on dissociation of a part of the working organization and its establishment into a separate organization, and to decide on merger and association of the working organization with other working organizations.

In attaining self-government, the working people in the social-political communities shall decide on the course of economic and social development, on the distribution of the social product, and on other matters of common concern.

Citizens and representatives of organizations concerned and of the social community may participate in the management of a working organization in affairs of special concern to the social community.

In order to secure the uniform social-economic position of the working people, provision shall be made in law and statute determining the rights of self-management of the working people employed in the state administration [and in] social-political organizations or associations, in accord with the nature of the work of these organs and organizations.

The working people shall exercise self-management in the unified social-economic system in accordance with the Constitution, law and statute, and shall be held accountable for their work.

Any act violating the right of self-management of the working people is unconstitutional.

ARTICLE 10. The working people in the working organization, as members of the working community, shall establish working relations with each other and shall be equals in management.

The organization of work, and management in the working organization must enable the working people at every level and in every part of the working process which constitutes a whole to decide as directly as possible on matters of work, organization of mutual relations, distribution of income, and on other matters affecting their economic position, at the same time assuring the working organization as a whole the most favorable conditions for its work and business.

ARTICLE 11. The product of socially organized work, created in the working organizations, as the foundation for social economic growth and for the satisfaction of social needs and personal and common needs of the working people, shall be divided according to a uniform system of distribution and on the basis of uniform conditions and standards assuring social economic growth, distribution according to work, and social self-government.

The working organization, after providing the means to renew the value of the resources expended in work, and after allocating a part of the created value of the product for equalization of working conditions and acquisition of income, shall apportion the income of the working organization into a fund to expand the material basis for work and a fund to satisfy the personal and common needs of the working people.

The working organization shall be assured a part of the created value of the product to expand the material basis of its work, proportionate to its share in producing the means of social economic growth, and in non-economic activities, a part consistent with the tasks of the working organization and in accordance with social needs. The working organization shall be entitled to a part of the created value of the product for the satisfaction of personal and common needs of the working people proportionate to the productivity of work of the working people, and subject to the business success of the working organization, and in non-economic activities, proportionate to the results of the work done to satisfy social needs.

The means of the working organization allocated for the renewal and expansion of the material basis of work, as common means of social economic growth, shall be used to expand the material basis of the working organization of the social community as a whole. The working organization shall employ these means in accordance with uniform principles of utilization of the means of social economic growth determined by federal law, and in accordance with conditions and standards determined by the regulations coordinating economic development and the attainment of the other basic relations envisaged by the social plans.

To expand the material basis of its work, the working organization shall be assured other social means, apart from those it has created by its own work, under equal conditions and in accordance with the uniform principles of the credit system.

ARTICLE 12. In accordance with the principle of distribution according to work, every working man in the working organization shall be entitled to a personal income proportionate to the results of his work and to the work of his department and of the working organization as a whole.

ARTICLE 13. Working organizations may be founded in accordance with law by social-political communities, by working and other organizations and by citizens.

The working organization shall be founded as an enterprise or other economic organization for economic activities, or as an institution or other organization for activities in the fields of education, science, culture, health, social welfare, or other social services.

The working organizations, irrespective of the founder, shall have an identical status.

The conditions under which working organizations may amalgamate, or particular departments become independent, or separate, may be determined by law.

ARTICLE 14. Working people who by personal work perform independent cultural, professional or other similar activities shall in principle have the same social economic status and the same fundamental rights and duties as the working people in the working organization.

Working people with occupations of this type may associate and form temporary or permanent working communities, which shall have the same fundamental status as the working organizations, and in which the working people shall have the same fundamental rights and duties as the working people in working organizations.

The conditions under which these working people and their working communities shall realize their rights and fulfill their obligations, and the conditions under which they may utilize and manage social means in the performance of their activities shall be prescribed by law.

ARTICLE 15. The working organization is an independent and autonomous organization.

The working organization is a juristic person and possesses certain rights in relation to the socially owned means managed by it. The working organization may not be dispossessed of these rights nor may they be restricted, unless this is required by the general interest determined by federal law and in accordance with procedure prescribed by law, and with equivalent compensation being made in return.

The working organization shall preserve undiminished the value of the social means in its possession.

The working organization shall be responsible for its obligations with the social means in its possession.

ARTICLE 16. The general conditions under which working organizations shall discharge activities of special social concern may be prescribed by law.

The conditions under which products and services may be exchanged in internal commerce may be prescribed only on the basis of federal law.

The conditions of commerce in commodities and services and the business conditions of working organizations in their relations with other countries shall be established by federal law.

ARTICLE 17. Cooperatives may be founded as working organizations to carry on and stimulate socially organized work and cooperation among working people who work with their own means of labor in agriculture and in other fields of the economy, with the aim of linking these activities with the social economy and expanding socialist social relations in these provinces.

Membership in the cooperatives shall be voluntary.

Provision may be made in law and in the statute of the cooperative or other working organization according to which the working people who work with their own means of labor and permanently cooperate economically with the working organization may take part in the management of the working organization in those affairs in which they cooperate.

Provision may be made in law determining that farmers who work with their own means of labor shall associate or cooperate with a working organization in order to carry out land improvements, to further the exploitation of land so improved, to exploit water resources and to raise defenses against damage by water, to protect land from erosion, and to regulate torrential streams, or whenever the social interest in the province of cultivation and exploitation of forests, or in the promotion of agricultural production on certain lands so requires.

ARTICLE 18. Subject to the conditions and procedure provided by federal law, an economic organization may be dissolved if it is unable to renew the means of production and other means of work which it manages, or to meet other legal obligations.

An economic organization, under the conditions and in accordance with the procedure provided by federal law, may be placed under temporary emergency administration if in its work it has gravely damaged social interests.

Subject to the conditions and in accordance with the procedure provided by law, an institution may be dissolved if it no longer fulfills the conditions determined by law or if it lacks the conditions to do its work.

ARTICLE 19. In order to bring about an efficient division of labor and to carry on activities of common concern, working organizations may form business corporations.

Working organizations may also associate in order to promote production or other activities, to cooperate with each other and to examine and solve other matters of common concern.

Management of amalgamated working organizations shall be based on the principle of self-management of the working people in the working organizations so associated.

Working organizations may pool their resources in order to promote and develop their activities, and conclude other agreements concerning joint activities and business.

In accordance with federal law, chambers and business corporations may be founded, and the conditions prescribed for the obligatory association of particular types of working organizations in chambers and business corporations.

ARTICLE 20. Land is a resource of common concern.

All land shall be utilized in accordance with the general conditions determined by law to assure the efficient utilization of land and other general interests.

Forests and woodland shall have special protection determined by law.

ARTICLE 21. The social community shall provide the material and other conditions for the establishment and development of agricultural working organizations based on social ownership of land and socially organized work, and for cooperation of farmers with the cooperatives and other working organizations.

Farmers shall be guaranteed right of ownership to arable land up to a maximum area of ten hectares to the household.

The limits and conditions under which farmers may have right of ownership to other land, and the limits and conditions under which other citizens may have right of ownership to agricultural and other land shall be determined by law.

The right of ownership to forests and woodland shall be determined by law.

ARTICLE 22. Subject to the restrictions and under the conditions provided by law, citizens may by personal work perform agricultural, handicraft and other services or similar activities in order to gain income.

The extent and the conditions under which citizens may have right of ownership to the means of work and business premises to perform agricultural, handicraft and other services or similar activities by personal work, shall be determined by law.

No one shall employ the work of others to gain income.

Subject to the restrictions and conditions determined by law, the work of other persons may be employed in agricultural production, the handicraft trades and in other services or similar activities carried on by citizens with their own means of work.

ARTICLE 23. Citizens shall be guaranteed right of ownership to objects for personal consumption and use or for the satisfaction of cultural and other personal needs.

Citizens may have right of ownership to dwelling houses and dwellings for the satisfaction of their personal and family needs; and for occupations based on personal work in accordance with the right of citizens guaranteed by the Constitution and subject to the conditions determined by law.

The limits of the right of ownership to dwelling houses and dwellings shall be determined by federal law.

ARTICLE 24. The conditions under which social-political organizations and associations of citizens may own real estate and other objects that serve to satisfy the common interests of their members and to perform the tasks of the organizations, and the conditions under which they may use social means for these purposes shall be determined by law.

ARTICLE 25. If the general interest determined by federal law so requires, real estate to which citizens and juristic persons have right of ownership may be expropriated, with fair compensation being given in return, or this right may be restricted.

The right of ownership to objects of special cultural value may be restricted in accordance with law, if the general interest so requires.

ARTICLE 26. In order to secure conditions for the most favorable economic and social development, to equalize general conditions of work and the acquisition of income, to determine general standards of distribution, to realize the principle of distribution according to work, and to develop socialist social relations, the social-political communities shall undertake, in accordance with their rights and duties, measures to develop a unified economic system, to plan economic development and the material bases of other activities, and to this end they shall adopt social plans. In order to achieve the relations determined by the social plans, the social-political communities shall pass regulations and other general decisions, set up social funds and social reserves, and undertake economic and other measures.

The social-political communities are juristic persons.

ARTICLE 27. The means of social economic growth acquired on the territory of the social-political communities, as common means of social economic growth, shall be used in these communities in proportion to the effort made by the working people to produce them. These means shall be used in accord with the uniform principles for using the means of social economic growth and under the conditions and standards determined by the regulations coordinating economic development and the attainment of other relations envisaged by the social plans.

Other social means shall also be used to develop the material basis of the social-political communities in accordance with the uniform principles of the credit system.

To meet social needs of their territories, the social-political communities shall be entitled to means acquired from personal incomes and from other sources determined by federal law, in accordance with the principle of distribution according to work, and they shall autonomously determine the amount of these means and their disposal.

The social community shall provide the inadequately developed republics and regions with the material and other conditions necessary for more rapid economic development, and for the creation of the material bases of social activities.

ARTICLE 28. The territory of Yugoslavia is a unified economic and customs area.

Commerce in goods and services shall be unrestricted on the whole territory of Yugoslavia and may be restricted only in accordance with federal law.

The working organizations may carry on economic and other activities on the whole territory of Yugoslavia under conditions of equality.

ARTICLE 29. Money and the credit system shall be uniform. Financial transactions shall be carried on in accordance with uniform principles.

The working and other autonomous organizations, the social-political communities and their organs, and anyone else in possession of socially owned means shall make all payments, carry out all other financial operations, and deposit money in a manner prescribed by federal law.

The working organizations and social-political communities shall be entitled to banking credits under equal conditions determined by federal law.

Banks are economic organizations whose business is of special social concern. The position, the rights and duties and the business of the banks shall be determined by federal law.

The status of the National Bank of Yugoslavia shall be determined by federal law.

ARTICLE 30. Merger or association between working organizations, or any other activity of an organization or state organ aimed at preventing or restricting free commerce in goods and services for the purpose of material and other advantages not based on work, or violating socialist economic relations, or promoting other relations of inequality in business, or causing damage to the general interest determined by federal law, shall be prohibited.

ARTICLE 31. Control and supervision over the use of socially owned means, as well as supervision over the meeting of obligations by the working and other autonomous organizations and social-political communities, shall be performed by a unified social accounting service.

The social accounting service shall be autonomous in its work.

CHAPTER III

THE FREEDOMS, RIGHTS AND DUTIES OF MAN AND CITIZEN

ARTICLE 32. The freedoms and rights of man and citizen are an inalienable part and expression of the socialist and democratic relations which are protected by the Constitution, and through which man is being emancipated from every exploitation and arbitrariness, and [through which man] by his personal and socially organized work is creating the conditions for comprehensive development, for the unrestricted expression and protection of his personality and the attainment of his human dignity.

The freedoms and rights shall be achieved in solidarity among the people and by the fulfillment of their duties toward one another.

ARTICLE 33. The citizens are equal in rights and duties, regardless of differences in nationality, race, religion, sex, language, education or social position.

All shall be equal before the law.

ARTICLE 34. The right of the citizen to social self-government shall be inviolable. In order to achieve social self-government, the citizen shall have

1) The right to decide directly on social affairs at meetings of the electorate, and at meetings of the working people in the working communities, by referendum and by other forms of direct determination;

2) The right to decide on social affairs as a member of an organ of social self-government, as a lay judge, or in other public function;

3) The right to elect and to stand for election to the organs of management of the working organization, the representative bodies of the social-political communities and the other organs of self-government, to nominate candidates for election to these bodies and organs, to initiate recall and to decide on the recall of elected delegates;

4) The right to initiate the convocation of meetings of the electorate and meetings of the working people in the working communities, the right to initiate the calling of a referendum, and the right to initiate actions of social supervision;

5) The right to be informed about the work of the representative bodies and their organs, the organs of social self-government, and organizations carrying on affairs of public concern, and in particular, in the working organization in which he works and in other organizations in which he realizes his interests, the right to be informed about material and financial conditions, the fulfillment of plans, and business, with the obligation that he keep business and other secrets;

6) The right to examine the work of the state organs, the organs of social self-government and the organizations that discharge affairs of public concern, and to express his opinions on their work;

7) The right to petition and present proposals to the representative bodies and other organs, to receive an answer to them, and to undertake political and other initiatives of general concern.

ARTICLE 35. Every citizen who is eighteen years of age shall have suffrage. In realizing this right, the citizen shall nominate candidates and elect delegates to the representative bodies and organs of social self-government and may stand for election to these bodies and organs.

Every member of a working community shall be eligible to elect the organs of management of the working organization and to stand for election to them.

ARTICLE 36. The right to work and the freedom to work are guaranteed.

The community shall provide ever more favorable conditions toward the realization of the right to work, especially by developing the productive forces and the material bases of other socially organized activities, and by promoting concern for the interests of the working man in regard to work.

Everyone shall be free to choose an occupation and employment.

Forced labor shall be prohibited.

Every citizen shall have access, under conditions of equality, to every job and every office in the community.

Working relations may cease against the worker's will only under conditions and in a manner determined by federal law.

The right to material security during temporary unemployment shall be guaranteed under conditions determined by law.

The rights acquired on the basis of work shall be inalienable.

The social community shall create conditions to improve the capacities of citizens who are not fully capable of working, as well as conditions for their adequate employment.

The social community shall lend assistance to citizens who are incapable of working and have no means of livelihood.

Whoever will not work, though he is fit to do so, shall not enjoy the rights and the social protection that man enjoys on the basis of work.

ARTICLE 37. The worker shall be entitled to a limited working time.

A maximum working week of forty-two hours shall be guaranteed. The conditions under which the working time may be shortened may be determined by law. In exceptional cases provision may be made determining that in certain occupations or in other cases determined by law the working time may for a limited period be longer than forty-two hours in the week if the particular nature of the work so requires.

The worker shall be entitled to daily and weekly rest and, under conditions determined by law, to a paid annual vacation of not less than fourteen working days.

The working man's right to personal safety and to health and other protection at work shall be assured.

Youth, women and disabled persons shall enjoy special protection at work.

Workers shall be guaranteed a minimum personal income determined by federal law.

ARTICLE 38. In accordance with the principle of mutualism and solidarity, the workers shall be insured within a uniform system of social security established by federal law.

On the basis of obligatory social security, workers shall be provided with health protection and other rights against illness, reduced working ability or loss of working ability, and old age.

In the event of the death of the insured person, health protection and rights, as well as other rights arising from social security, shall be provided the members of the family of the worker, subject to conditions determined by law.

Provision also shall be made in law determining security for the health protection and other rights arising from social security for other citizens.

The social security service shall be managed by the insured directly and through bodies which they shall elect and may recall of their own accord.

ARTICLE 39. Freedom of thought and determination shall be guaranteed.

ARTICLE 40. Freedom of the press and other media of information, freedom of association, freedom of speech and public expression, freedom of meeting and other public assemblage shall be guaranteed.

The citizens shall have the right to express and publish their opinions through the media of information, to inform themselves through the media of information, to publish newspapers and other publications, and to disseminate information by other media of communication.

These freedoms and rights shall not be used by anyone to overthrow the foundations of the socialist democratic order determined by the Constitution: to endanger the peace, international cooperation on terms of equality, or the independence of the country; to disseminate national, racial, or religious hatred or intolerance; or to incite to crime; [nor shall they be used] in any manner that offends public decency.

The cases and conditions in which the utilization of these freedoms and rights in a manner contrary to the Constitution shall entail restriction or prohibition shall be determined by federal law.

The press, radio and television shall truthfully and objectively inform the public and publish and broadcast [those] opinions and information of organs, organizations, and citizens which are of interest to public information.

The right to correction of information that has violated the rights or interests of man or organization shall be guaranteed.

In order to assure the widest possible information of the public, the social community shall promote conditions conducive to the development of appropriate activities.

ARTICLE 41. The citizen shall be guaranteed the freedom to express his nationality and culture, as well as the freedom to speak his language.

No one shall have to declare himself as to nationality or determine himself for one of the nationalities.

The dissemination or pursuance of national inequality, as well as all incitement to national, racial and religious hatred or intolerance, is unconstitutional and shall be punishable.

ARTICLE 42. The languages of the peoples of Yugoslavia and their scripts shall be equal.

Members of the peoples of Yugoslavia on the territories of republics other than their own shall have the right to school instruction in their own languages, in conformity with republican law.

As an exception, in the Yugoslav People's Army, commands, military drill and administration shall be in the Serbo-Croatian language.

ARTICLE 43. With the view of attaining the freedom of the citizen to express his nationality and culture, every nationality/national minority, shall have the right to use its language freely, to develop its culture, and to found organizations to this end, and it shall enjoy the other rights determined by the Constitution.

In the schools for the members of the nationalities, instruction shall be in the languages of those nationalities.

The other rights of the nationalities on the territories on which they live shall be determined by the constitutions and laws of the republics.

ARTICLE 44. The citizens shall be entitled, under equal conditions determined by law, to acquire knowledge and training in any type of school and in any other educational institution.

Eight years of elementary education shall be obligatory. Longer obligatory education may be determined by law.

The social community shall provide the material and other conditions necessary to found and maintain schools and other educational institutions and to advance their work.

ARTICLE 45. Scientific and artistic creativity shall be unrestricted.

The authors of scientific and artistic works, as well as of scientific discoveries and technical inventions, shall have the moral and material rights in their products. The scope, duration and protection of these rights shall be determined by federal law.

The social community shall provide conditions for the development of scientific, artistic and other cultural activities.

ARTICLE 46. Religious confession shall not be restricted and shall be man's private affair.

The religious communities shall be detached from the state and shall be free to perform religious affairs and religious rites.

The religious communities may found religious schools in which to train their clergy.

Abuse of religion and religious work for political purposes is unconstitutional.

The social community may give material assistance to the religious communities.

The religious communities may have the right of ownership to real estate within the limits determined by federal law.

ARTICLE 47. Life and the freedom of man shall be inviolable.

Exceptionally, capital punishment may be provided for by federal law for the gravest criminal offenses, and it may be pronounced only for the most serious forms of these offenses.

Arrest shall be based on law. Every unlawful arrest shall be punishable.

The inviolability of life and other privacy rights of the person shall be guaranteed.

ARTICLE 48. During criminal proceedings, the accused may be arrested and held under arrest only if this is provided by law and is indispensable to the criminal proceedings; or for reasons of public safety.

Custody shall be reduced to the shortest necessary time.

Custody shall be determined by a court of law; only in exceptional cases prescribed by law may custody be determined by another authority empowered by law, and then for not more than three days.

Custody by decision of a court of the first instance may last not more than three months, but in exceptional cases prescribed by law the superior court may by decision extend custody for another six months. If upon the expiration of these periods no indictment has been made, the prisoner shall be released.

A fully documented written warrant shall be brought in matters of custody, which shall be served on the person concerned at the moment of arrest or not later than twenty-four hours after arrest.

The court shall adopt a decision immediately or not later than forty-eight hours on a complaint against a warrant of arrest.

ARTICLE 49. No one shall be punished for any act that before its commission was not defined by law or by prescript based on law as a punishable offense, or for which no penalty had been provided.

Criminal offenses and punitive sanctions may be determined only by law.

Offenses of an economic nature and punitive sanctions for such offenses may be determined by law or by decree adopted on the basis of law.

Sanctions may be pronounced for criminal offenses or offenses of an economic nature only by the decision of a competent court reached in accordance with the procedure determined by law.

Organs of the administration may pronounce punitive sanctions only for misdemeanors and only within the limits and according to the procedure provided by law.

ARTICLE 50. No one shall be deemed to have committed a criminal offense until this has been ascertained by valid conviction.

Respect of person and dignity are guaranteed in criminal and in all other proceedings as well as during enforcement of a penalty.

No one within the reach of the court or other body of authority competent to conduct proceedings shall be sentenced if he has not been heard in accordance with law or if he has not been given the opportunity to defend himself.

The right to defense is guaranteed.

During criminal proceedings, the accused shall be entitled to have defense counsel, who shall be enabled, in accordance with the law, to defend and protect the rights of the accused. Provision shall be made in law determining when the accused in criminal proceedings must have defense counsel.

Any person who has been unjustifiably sentenced for a criminal offense or who has been arrested without grounds shall be entitled to compensation from social sources for the damage that has been done to him.

ARTICLE 51. The citizens shall enjoy freedom of movement and abode.

Limitation of the freedom of movement or abode may be prescribed by law, but only in order to assure the execution of criminal proceedings, to prevent the spread of infectious diseases, or to preserve the public order, or when the interests of the country's defense so require.

ARTICLE 52. The dwelling shall be inviolable.

No one shall enter any dwelling or other premises or search them against the will of the owner without a warrant issued in accordance with law.

The person whose dwelling or other premises are being searched, or the members of his family or his representative, shall be entitled to be present during the search.

A search may be carried out only in the presence of two witnesses.

Subject to the conditions determined by law, a person in an official capacity may enter a dwelling or premises without a warrant from the competent authority and carry out a search in the absence of witnesses if this is indispensable for the direct apprehension of a criminal offender, or for the safety of life and property, or if it is beyond doubt that evidence in criminal proceedings cannot be secured otherwise.

Illegal entry and search of a dwelling or premises are prohibited and shall be punishable.

ARTICLE 53. The privacy of letters and of other means of communication shall be inviolable.

Provision may be made only by federal law to depart, in accordance with the decision of a competent authority, from the principle of inviolability of privacy of letters and of other means of communication, if this is indispensable for the execution of criminal proceedings, or for the security of the country.

ARTICLE 54. Every citizen of Yugoslavia shall have the protection of the Socialist Federal Republic of Yugoslavia abroad.

No citizen of Yugoslavia shall be deprived of his citizenship, exiled or extradited.

A citizen who is absent from the country may in accordance with law be deprived of Yugoslav citizenship only exceptionally, if by his work he causes harm to the international or other general interests of Yugoslavia, or if he declines to perform his basic civil duties and holds citizenship in another country.

ARTICLE 55. The right of inheritance is guaranteed.

No one shall have real estate and means of work on grounds of inheritance in excess of the limit determined by the Constitution or law.

ARTICLE 56. Every citizen shall be entitled to the protection of his health.

The cases in which uninsured citizens shall be entitled to the protection of their health from social means shall be determined by law.

The social community shall provide conditions for the founding of health institutions and to promote the health protection of the citizens.

The social community, particularly the commune and the working organization, shall provide conditions for the development of physical culture and for the rest and recreation of the citizens, and shall support the initiative of the citizens and their associations in these provinces.

ARTICLE 57. The social community shall provide special protection for the mother and child.

Minors without parental care and other persons unable to provide for themselves and to safeguard their own rights and interests shall enjoy the special protection of the social community.

Disabled war veterans shall be provided with vocational rehabilitation, disability rights and other forms of protection.

ARTICLE 58. The family shall have the protection of the social community. Marriage and legal relations in marriage and in the family shall be regulated by law.

Marriage shall be validly contracted by persons entering into marriage in accordance with their free will before a competent authority.

It shall be the right and duty of parents to raise and to educate their children.

Children born out of marriage shall have the same rights and duties toward their parents as children born in marriage.

ARTICLE 59. Relations among people shall be based on mutual cooperation and on respect for man and for his freedoms and rights.

It shall be the duty of every person to come to the assistance and help of any person in danger, and to participate in the elimination of general danger.

ARTICLE 60. The defense of the country is the right and the supreme duty and honor of every citizen.

ARTICLE 61. Every citizen shall conscientiously discharge any public or other social office vested in him, and shall be personally accountable for discharging it.

ARTICLE 62. Every citizen shall contribute, under equal conditions determined by law, to the satisfaction of the material requirements of the social community.

ARTICLE 63. Everyone shall abide by the Constitution and law.

Provision shall be made in law determining the conditions under which failure to discharge duties determined by the Constitution shall be punishable.

ARTICLE 64. Aliens in Yugoslavia shall enjoy basic freedoms and human rights, and shall have other rights and duties determined by law and by international agreements.

ARTICLE 65. Citizens of other countries and persons without citizenship who are persecuted for their defense of democratic ideas and political movements, social emancipation and national liberation, the freedom and the rights of the human personality or of the freedom of scientific or artistic creativity, shall be guaranteed right of asylum.

ARTICLE 66. Every arbitrary act violating or restricting the rights of man, by whomsoever committed, is unconstitutional and punishable.

No one shall employ coercion or restrict the rights of any person, except in cases and proceedings provided by law and in accord with the Constitution.

ARTICLE 67. Every person shall be entitled to equal protection of his rights in proceedings before a court, administrative and other state organs and organizations which decide on his rights and obligations.

The social community shall provide the conditions for legal assistance through the legal profession as an autonomous socially organized service, and through other forms of legal assistance.

ARTICLE 68. Everyone shall be guaranteed the right of appeal or other legal expedient against court decisions and decisions of other state organs and organizations which deliberate on his rights or his lawful interests.

ARTICLE 69. Everyone shall be entitled to damages for the unlawful or faulty execution of an office or action by a person or officer of a state organ or organization carrying on affairs of public concern.

The damages shall be paid by the social-political community or organization in which the service or action is performed. The claimant shall be entitled, under conditions determined by law, to damages also directly from the person responsible for the damage.

ARTICLE 70. The freedoms and rights guaranteed by the Constitution are inalienable and shall not be restricted by any act.

These freedoms and rights shall be attained on the basis of the Constitution itself. The manner of attaining particular freedoms and rights may be prescribed only by law, and only when this is envisaged by the Constitution or when it is indispensable for their attainment.

The freedoms and rights guaranteed by the Constitution shall be provided judicial protection.

CHAPTER IV

THE SOCIAL-POLITICAL SYSTEM

ARTICLE 71.   The working people shall be the sole holder of power and government of social affairs.

The citizens shall attain self-government directly at meetings of the electorate, by referendum, or by other forms of direct decision in the working organization, commune, and other social-political communities, and indirectly through their delegates, whom they shall elect to the organs of management of the working and other autonomous organizations and to the representative bodies of the social-political communities.

ARTICLE 72.   No one shall exercise public powers unless they have been vested in him, in accordance with the Constitution, by the citizens or by the bodies elected by them.

ARTICLE 73.   Self-government by the citizens in the commune is the political foundation of the uniform social-political system.

The forms of social self-government from which the organs discharging the functions of power derive shall be founded and realized in the commune.

The uniformity of the social-political system shall be secured by the realization of the rights and duties of all the social-political communities, and by their mutual relations as determined by the Constitution and law.

ARTICLE 74.   The functions of power and government of social affairs shall be exercised by representative bodies, as the general organs of social self-government of the social-political communities, and by the organs responsible to them.

The judicial power shall be executed by courts as autonomous organs of the social community.

The protection of constitutionality shall be vested in constitutional courts.

ARTICLE 75.   The assembly shall be the representative body of the social-political community; it shall consist of delegates of the citizens and of the working people in the working communities.

ARTICLE 76.   The communal assembly shall comprise the communal chamber and the chamber of the working communities. The constitutions of the republics may provide for the formation of several chambers of working communities.

The members of the communal chamber shall be elected directly by the citizens the members of the chamber of the working communities shall be elected by th working people who are engaged in working organizations, state organs, and social political organizations and associations, by farmer-members of cooperatives c

other working organizations, and by other citizens working on the territory of the commune determined by law.

Any citizen with suffrage shall be eligible for election to the communal chamber. Any working man eligible to elect the members of a chamber of working communities, any member of an organ of management of a working organization or working community, any member of an organ of management of an association of working organizations, and any trade union officer or official of a social-political organization in the commune shall be eligible for election to the chamber of the working communities.

The members of the assemblies of the district, the republic and the Federation shall be elected on the principle of communal delegation, the commune being the basic community of citizens and working people.

ARTICLE 77. Direct elections for members of the representative bodies of the social-political communities shall be held on the basis of general and equal suffrage.

The members of all the representative bodies shall be elected and removed by secret ballot.

ARTICLE 78. The assembly shall be the supreme organ of government and organ of social self-government within the framework of the rights and duties of the social-political community.

The assembly shall determine policy and decide on other basic matters of importance for political, economic and cultural life and social development, pass regulations, the social plan and budget and other general acts, establish the bases for the organization and the powers of its organs, elect public officials, examine the state of affairs and the general problems of the judiciary, and exercise budget supervision, supervision over the work of the political-executive and administrative authorities, and social supervision.

The assembly shall form a commission to consider matters pertaining to the election and nomination of members of the assembly bodies and other officials and to propose motions to the assembly. This commission shall also examine general personnel matters.

The commission shall comprise members of the assembly and representatives of the social-political organizations.

Matters of general interest for the social-political community may be examined by the assembly together with representatives of the social-political organizations and other associations sitting as a general convention.

ARTICLE 79. Collegial political-executive organs of the assembly shall be formed in the social-political community in accordance with the Constitution, law and statute. The Constitution may determine that certain political-executive affairs shall also be discharged by the chambers of the representative bodies.

The political-executive organs shall attend to the execution of policy, the enforcement of law, and the fulfillment of social plans and other assembly enactments; advance proposals determining assembly policy and for the adoption of assembly decisions, pass regulations for which they are authorized; determine the general course of work of the administrative organs; and perform other political-executive affairs.

The political-executive organs shall be elected and dismissed by the assembly.

The political-executive organs shall be responsible for their work to the assembly that has elected them.

ARTICLE 80. The assembly of the social-political community shall establish administrative organs in accordance with the Constitution, law and statute.

The administrative organs shall enforce the law, carry out the social plans and other decisions of the assembly, execute the established policy, follow the state of affairs in particular fields of life, organize and discharge particular services, deliberate on administrative matters, exercise administrative supervision and perform other administrative business, prepare acts, and perform other expert services for the assemblies and their political-executive organs.

The administrative organs shall cooperate with other administrative organs and with working and other organizations in matters of common concern, inform each other about their work, and by their work enable the citizens and organizations to realize their rights and interests efficaciously.

Within the framework of their legal powers, the administrative organs shall be autonomous, and they shall be accountable for their work to the assembly and to its political-executive organs.

ARTICLE 81. The members of the assembly shall be elected for a term of four years.

Half the members of each chamber of the assembly shall be elected every second year.

The term of the members of the assembly may be extended only by decision of the assembly in cases provided by the Constitution.

ARTICLE 82. No one shall be twice consecutively a member of the same chamber of the same assembly or of an executive council.

No one shall at the same time be a member of the Federal Assembly and of the assembly of a republic, or a member of two chambers of the same assembly. A member of the Chamber of Nationalities of the Federal Assembly shall keep his seat in the assembly that has sent him.

A member of the Chamber of Nationalities may be returned for a further term of four years as a deputy of the republic or as a federal deputy; but during his second term he shall not again be a member of the Chamber of Nationalities.

Subject to procedure determined by the Constitution, certain members of the executive council may be returned to this office for a further consecutive term of four years.

A member of a communal assembly who has been elected member of the district assembly may be returned to the communal assembly for a further consecutive term of four years, but he shall not be returned to the district assembly for that term.

ARTICLE 83. The federal secretaries of state, federal secretaries and officers determined by law, as well as equivalent republican officers determined by republican constitution, shall not hold office for longer than four years, nor shall they be appointed to the same office during the next four years.

Subject to special procedure determined by the Constitution, some of these officers may be nominated to one of these offices for not more than an additional consecutive four years.

Provision [also] may be made in law introducing the principle of reelection or renomination after a definite period for other holders of public functions.

A member of the assembly shall not at the same time be a nominated officer or official of an equivalent state organ responsible to the assembly. The positions of judge and member of the assembly which elects him are incompatible.

ARTICLE 84. The assemblies, their political-executive organs and their administrative organs shall discharge their affairs on the basis of and within the restrictions of the Constitution and law.

State organs, organizations or officers vested with public powers shall perform their functions only within the limits of authorization determined by the Constitution and law.

The state organs shall have only the rights determined by the Constitution in relation to the working and other autonomous organizations.

ARTICLE 85. The relations between the organs of various social-political communities shall be based on the rights and duties determined in accordance with the Constitution.

With respect to the supervision of execution of republican and federal regulations the rights and duties of the federal administrative organs toward the republican administrative organs, and the rights and duties of the federal and republican administrative organs toward the district and communal administrative organs may be determined by law in accordance with the rights and duties of the Federation and republics.

ARTICLE 86. A holder of public or other social office shall be personally accountable for its execution.

The types and conditions of responsibility of all holders of public and other social offices shall be determined by law.

A holder of public office may resign from his office and may give his reason for doing so.

ARTICLE 87. The work of the state organs, organs of social self-government and organizations carrying on affairs of public concern shall be public, and the public shall be informed about their work.

The manner in which their work will be made public shall be determined by law and statute. Provision shall be made in law determining what information must be kept secret or may not be made public.

In order to render the work of the state organs, organs of social self-government, organizations discharging affairs of public concern, and social-political communities public and responsible to the community, the representative body exercising social supervision shall examine general matters pertaining to the utilization of social funds and distribution of income and to the manner in which these organs and organizations exercise their rights and duties.

The representative bodies shall exercise social supervision in cooperation with the organs of self-government and shall develop responsibility and socialist norms in self-government, business, and utilization of social funds.

The rights of the organs, organizations and citizens determined by the Constitution and law shall not be restricted by social supervision, nor shall their rights and interests founded on law be violated.

ARTICLE 88. At the meeting of the electorate the citizens shall examine matters of significance for the life and work of the locality and commune and other matters of social concern, initiate and submit proposals for the solution of these matters, directly decide on affairs determined by law and by the communal statute, and nominate candidates for election to the representative bodies.

At their meetings in the working communities, the working people shall nominate candidates for election to the representative bodies and carry out other affairs of management determined by law and by statute.

ARTICLE 89. The assembly of a social-political community may hold a referendum to obtain the preliminary views of the citizens concerning certain matters in its jurisdiction, or to sanction laws and other of its decisions.

The cases in which matters shall be decided by referendum in the working organizations shall be determined by law and by the statutes of the working organizations.

The decisions brought by referendum shall be binding.

Referendum shall be regulated by law.

ARTICLE 90. In exercising management in the working organization, the working people shall entrust, in keeping with the Constitution, law and statute, certain powers of management to the organs of the working organization: the workers' council, the managing board and the director, or other equivalent organs of management. Special supervisory, specialized and other organs of management may be established in a working organization in accordance with law and statute.

Interested citizens and the representatives of organizations and of the social community concerned shall participate, in accordance with law, in the management of certain affairs in a working organization carrying out work or affairs of special social concern as members of the organ of managment in the working organization, or in some other manner determined by law and by the statute.

The organization of work and the distribution of income in a working organization of this type shall be decided upon only by the organs of management elected by the members of the working community. Provision may be made in law determining the general conditions and standards for the distribution of income, and prescribing that a certain organ of management of the working organization, another organization or a state organ must approve certain decisions pertaining to the distribution of income or decisions pertaining to the process of work when these decisions are of special social concern.

ARTICLE 91. In accordance with the Constitution and law, the working organization shall adopt a statute and make other general decisions regulating relations in the working organization.

The statute shall determine the internal organization, jurisdiction and responsibility of the organs of management, the position of the working departments and the rights of the working people in the management of these departments, the working and other internal relations, and the manner of doing business, as well as other matters of importance for management in the working organization and for its affairs. The statute may also grant business autonomy for certain departments of the working organization.

The statute of the working organization, before it is finally adopted, shall be presented for examination to the communal assembly. Provision may be made in law determining that the statute of certain working organizations shall be submitted for examination to the republican assembly or to the assembly of some other social-political community.

The obligation of the working organization to pass certain general decisions and the procedure for the adoption of the statute and other general acts may be established by law. Certain powers may be granted by law to the competent organ of the social-political community to confirm or approve the statute or other general decisions as a whole, or certain parts of them.

ARTICLE 92.   The worker's council shall adopt a statute and other general decisions, determine plans and a program of work and development of the working organization, and decide on other general matters.

The members of the workers' council shall be elected by the working people directly.

A working community with a small number of members shall directly carry out the functions of the workers' council.

The managing board shall decide on the affairs of the working organization.

The members of the managing board of the working organization shall be elected by the workers' council or working community. It may be provided by law or by statute that a working community with a small number of members shall directly execute the functions of the managing board also.

The members of the workers' council shall be elected for a term of two years and the members of the managing board for a term of one year.

No one shall be elected twice consecutively to the worker's council or more than twice consecutively to the managing board.

One-half the members of the workers' council shall be elected every year.

ARTICLE 93.   The director of the working organization shall be in charge of the business of the working organization, execute the decisions of the workers' council and other organs of management and represent the organization. The director shall be independent in his work and shall be personally accountable to the working community and to the organs of management of the working organization, and shall also be responsible to the social-political community for the legality of the work of the working organization and for the fulfillment of its legally determined obligations.

The director shall be nominated by the workers' council on the basis of a public competition, upon the proposal of the appointments commission, subject to the conditions and procedure determined by law. The appointments commission shall be composed of a legally determined number of representatives of the working community and of the commune or other equivalent social-political community.

Some other manner of nominating the director of a working organization which performs work of special social concern may be prescribed by law.

The director of the working organization shall be nominated for a term determined by law, and he may be renominated in accordance with the same procedure.

The conditions under which the workers' council or other competent body may dismiss the director before the expiration of the term for which he has been nominated may be determined by law.

ARTICLE 94. An arbitration commission shall be set up in accordance with the law to eliminate and settle collective disputes between the working people of parts of a working organization, or between the working people of a working organization and the organs of the social-political community.

ARTICLE 95. Affairs of common concern in the management of housing, and in other fields of social life shall be discharged by the citizens directly or through bodies which they themselves elect and which shall be accountable to them for their work.

CHAPTER V

THE SOCIAL-POLITICAL COMMUNITIES

1. The Commune

ARTICLE 96. Directly and through their organs of social self-government in the commune, being the basic social-political community, the citizens shall

Provide the material and other conditions necessary for the work and development of productive forces; guide and coordinate economic development and the development of the social services; determine and distribute the means for common communal requirements; create the conditions required to satisfy the material, social, cultural and other common needs of the citizens; coordinate individual and common interests with the general interests;

Exercise direct social self-government; organize the organs of government, social self-government and social services of common concern; provide conditions for the realization of the freedoms and rights of the citizens; regulate relations of direct concern to the citizens in the commune; determine the general conditions to discharge the business of the communal and similar organizations; safeguard legality and the security of the people and property; maintain public peace and order; exercise social supervision;

Execute other powers of the social community, with the exception of the powers determined by the Constitution as being the rights and duties of the republics or of the Federation.

The rights and duties of the commune shall be determined by the Constitution, by law, and by statute.

The rights and duties of the commune shall be discharged by the citizens at the meetings of the electorate and through other forms of direct decision, by the communal assembly, its organs, and the local communities. The rights and duties of the commune shall be realized by the organs of the commune and local community, with the participation of and in cooperation with other organs of social self-government in the commune.

ARTICLE 97. The territories of the communes shall be determined by republican law in accordance with the conditions determined by republican constitution.

ARTICLE 98. Every commune shall independently adopt a statute.

The communal statute, within the framework of the Constitution and law, shall determine the rights and duties of the commune and the manner in which they shall be exercised; the province, organization and rights of the local communities, and other forms of self-government in localities; the relations between citizens, working and other organizations in the solution of matters of common concern; the manner in which the work of the organs and organizations in the commune shall be rendered public; the organization of the communal and other services; the rights of the citizens, working organizations and other autonomous organizations in the use of funds, social and other services, resources in general use and other social means managed by the commune; the organization of the communal assembly and other communal organs and their rights, duties and powers.

ARTICLE 99. In order to discharge its rights and duties the commune shall autonomously pass regulations, and the social plan and budget, and shall establish its own funds.

In conformity with legally determined sources and types of revenue, the commune shall autonomously determine and use its revenues.

In accordance with law, the commune shall directly discharge the functions of the social community in regard to the regulation and utilization of land resources in general use, the construction and utilization of housing and the regulation of communal housing relations.

ARTICLE 100. Subject to conditions determined by republican constitution and law, a commune that is unable to finance its work and the work of the social services shall be allocated additional resources from republican revenues to finance social services and other services in the commune.

ARTICLE 101. The communal authorities shall attend to the enforcement of federal and republican laws and shall directly enforce them, unless the Constitution or law has placed their enforcement in the jurisdiction of the district, republican or federal authorities.

ARTICLE 102. In towns with more than one commune, organs of self-government may be established by town statute in accordance with republican constitution and law for affairs of general concern to the town as a whole, and these bodies may be given definite communal and district rights and duties.

ARTICLE 103. The communes shall cooperate with each other; they may freely pool their resources to discharge particular affairs within their jurisdiction or to create the conditions to satisfy needs of common concern; found common organs, organizations and services, undertake joint actions and exchange experiences.

ARTICLE 104. In the local community, as an autonomous community of citizens of rural and urban localities, the citizens shall directly exercise self-government in areas directly satisfying the needs of the working people and their families.

The communal statute may provide that the local community shall discharge other affairs in order to satisfy communal, social and other common needs of the citizens, and it may determine the manner in which these affairs shall be financed.

The local community is a juristic person.

2. The District

ARTICLE 105. Districts shall be founded to discharge affairs of common concern to two or more communes.

The republican constitution may provide that only communes shall be founded in a republic.

ARTICLE 106. The Federation and the republics, within the framework of their rights and duties, may determine by constitution and law the rights and duties of the district.

The republican constitution may provide that definite rights exercised in relation to the communal organs by the republican organs may be exercised by the district organs.

By decision of their assemblies, the communes may entrust to the district the execution of affairs of common concern to the communes, and the district may be bound by decision of the republican assemblies to discharge these affairs.

ARTICLE 107. The members of the district assembly shall be elected by the communal assemblies from among their members.

Every district shall have a statute.

Provision shall be made in republican law determining the manner of financing districts.

3. The Socialist Republic

ARTICLE 108. The republic is a socialist democratic state community based on the power of the working people and on self-government.

The working people in the republic shall exercise social self-government, regulate social relations, determine the course of economic development and of the development of the social services, provide for the realization of the rights of the citizens and for constitutionality and legality, and discharge all social affairs of common concern for political, economic, and cultural life and social development in the republic, with the exception of the affairs determined by the Constitution to be the rights and the duties of the Federation.

The rights and duties of the republic shall be determined by republican constitution in accordance with the principles of this Constitution.

ARTICLE 109. The territory of a republic shall not be altered without the consent of the republic concerned.

The boundaries between the republics may be changed only on the basis of agreement between the respective republican assemblies.

ARTICLE 110. The republics shall cooperate with each other in affairs of common concern and develop mutual relations.

In order to attain objectives of common concern, the republics shall found common organizations, undertake common measures and promote the exchange of experiences and other forms of economic and other cooperation.

The decisions, papers and other documents issued by state organs and authorized organizations in one republic shall have equal validity in the other republics.

ARTICLE 111. A republic may found autonomous provinces in accordance with the constitution in areas with distinctive national characteristics or in areas with other distinguishing features, on the basis of the express will of the population of these areas.

The foundation or dissolution of an autonomous province shall take effect when this is sanctioned by the Constitution of Yugoslavia.

In the Socialist Republic of Serbia there are the autonomous provinces of Vojvodina and Kosovo and Metohija, established in 1945 by decision of the People's Assembly of the People's Republic of Serbia in accordance with the express will of the population of these areas.

ARTICLE 112. The autonomous provinces are social-political communities within the republic.

The autonomous rights and duties and the basic principles of organization in the autonomous provinces shall be determined by republican constitution.

4. The Federation

ARTICLE 113. In the Socialist Federal Republic of Yugoslavia the peoples and the citizens shall realize and safeguard the sovereignty, territorial integrity, security and defense of Yugoslavia, the international relations of Yugoslavia, the unity of the social-economic and political system, the economic unity of the country, the course and coordination of general economic development, and the basic freedoms and rights of man and the citizen; and they shall coordinate their political, economic, cultural and other common interests.

In order to realize these common interests, the Constitution determines the rights and the duties of the Federation.

The citizens shall also realize their political, social-economic, cultural and other common interests by means of social-political and other organizations which are active on the whole territory of Yugoslavia.

In exercising its rights and duties the Federation shall have the cooperation of the republics and other social-political communities, and social-political and other organizations.

ARTICLE 114. The Federation shall protect the sovereign rights and equality of the peoples and the socialist social and political organization of the republics.

ARTICLE 115. The Federation shall be directly responsible for the sovereignty, independence, territorial integrity, security and defense of Yugoslavia and for its international relations.

In these provinces, as well as in other provinces in which the Constitution determines it to be directly responsible, the Federation shall have the exclusive right and duty to pass laws and other regulations and directly to enforce them, and it shall be responsible for their enforcement even when the execution of some of these affairs is placed in the jurisdiction of other state organs and organizations.

Within the province of the exclusive rights and duties of the Federation, the federal organs shall adopt regulations for the enforcement of federal law.

The republics may pass laws of their own in this province and in other provinces determined by the Constitution to be regulated exclusively by federal law only if the republics are authorized to do so by federal law.

ARTICLE 116. It shall be the right and duty of the Federation to provide unity of the economic system and of the system of distribution of the social product. The Federation shall safeguard the unity of the political system, the system of social self-government and the basic freedoms and rights of man and the citizen.

ARTICLE 117. The Federation shall provide for the unity of the monetary and credit systems, determine the policy according to which money shall be issued, and assure supervision of money circulation.

Paper money and coin shall be issued by the National Bank of Yugoslavia.

The Federation shall prescribe the obligatory bank deposits to be held by the federal banks, and the conditions and manner in which foreign currency and similar reserves and deposits shall be used.

ARTICLE 118. The citizens of Yugoslavia shall have common Yugoslav citizenship.

Every citizen of a republic shall also be a citizen of Yugoslavia.

The citizens of one republic shall enjoy on the territory of another republic the same rights and duties as a citizen of that republic.

ARTICLE 119. In order to exercise its rights and duties determined by the Constitution, and to provide uniform foundations for the legal system, the Federation shall enact complete, basic and general laws.

The federal laws and other general federal acts shall be binding on the whole territory of Yugoslavia unless these regulations and acts prescribe that they shall be enforced on a lesser territory.

In the provinces in which the Federation passes complete laws the republics may regulate certain matters if federal law is lacking or if they are authorized by federal law to do so.

In the provinces in which the Federation passes basic laws, the republics shall regulate relations which have not been regulated by federal law, and may fully regulate all relations in these provinces if federal law is lacking.

The provisions of republican law pertaining to matters regulated by federal law shall cease to be valid on the day on which the federal law, passed after the republican law, takes effect, unless federal law determines otherwise.

A republic may be authorized by complete and by basic federal law to regulate certain questions in a different manner in its own law.

ARTICLE 120. The Federation, within the framework of its rights and duties, may adopt general laws in the fields of education and culture, health, and social welfare and in other provinces in which the Constitution does not provide that the Federation shall pass other federal laws.

The general laws shall determine the general principles regulating relations of concern for the basic unity of the social and political system.

General laws may also be passed in provinces in which it is provided that the Federation shall pass basic laws.

The republics shall pass laws of their own in conformity with the principles determined by the general law, and shall bring their laws into conformity with subsequently passed general laws.

The general laws shall not be directly enforceable.

ARTICLE 121. The Federation shall determine the general course of the country's economic development and the basic relations in the distribution of the social product, coordinate economic development and relations between industrial branches and areas, determine the course and conditions of trade with foreign countries, equalize the general working conditions and acquisition of income so as to realize the principle of distribution according to work, and promote the most favorable general conditions for the realization of the common interests of the working people, the activities of the working organizations, and the functions of the social-political communities in the province of social-economic relations.

ARTICLE 122. The Federation shall determine the sources and the amount of the resources required to carry out its tasks and discharge its affairs determined by the Constitution and law.

The resources of the Federation shall serve

1) To keep the market in full supply, and to expand trade with other countries;

2) To intervene in the economy in order to coordinate relations between different occupations, to equalize working conditions and the acquisition of income, to provide for the stability of the economy and keep the market in full supply, and to expand trade with other countries;

3) To finance rapid economic development in the economically underdeveloped republics and areas;

4) To take part in investments of essential importance to the coordination and course of Yugoslavia's economic development, and in investments determined by international agreements.

ARTICLE 123. A special federal fund shall be established to finance the rapid economic development of the inadequately developed republics and areas.

Federal law shall provide permanent sources of finances for this fund and special credit terms, and shall determine the manner of operation of the fund.

The Federation shall provide the means for a republic that is unable to finance social and other services with funds of its own, subject to conditions determined by law.

ARTICLE 124. The Federation may

1) Prescribe as obligatory that the working organizations and social-political communities shall form reserve social resources and that the working organizations shall utilize part of their freely disposable income to develop the material bases of their work, or of economic and social development, if this is necessary for economic stability or for the attainment of the basic material relations established by the social plan of Yugoslavia;

2) Temporarily prohibit the use of certain social resources by the working organizations and social-political communities, when this is indispensable in order to prevent or eliminate major disturbances in the economy and major disproportions in the fulfillment of the social plan of Yugoslavia, or when the needs of national defense or other special needs of the country so enjoin;

3) Prescribe obligations for the working organizations and social-political communities of concern for national defense.

These measures may be prescribed only by law.

ARTICLE 125. The sources and types of revenue for the social-political communities shall be determined by federal law.

In order to guarantee the equal position of the working people and of working organizations in business and in the distribution of the social product, or in order to realize the basic material relations established by the social plan of Yugoslavia, the Federation may determine the limits within which the social-political communities may determine their own revenues and other resources.

ARTICLE 126. The republics shall adopt regulations to enforce federal law if the republican organs of state are competent to enforce it, and if federal law has not provided that the regulations for the enforcement of the law shall be adopted by federal organs, or if the republic in question is authorized by federal law to pass such regulations.

The republics shall be responsible for the enforcement on their territories of the federal laws and other federal regulations.

The republic shall ensure the enforcement of federal law and other federal regulations through its organs if the competent communal organs do not enforce them.

ARTICLE 127. In accordance with law, the Federation may found administrative organs on the territories of the republics and of other social-political communities to carry out certain administrative affairs within the province of the exclusive rights and duties of the Federation, and it may prescribe the obligation of the republics and other social-political communities to found administrative organs to discharge such affairs or affairs of concern to the whole country.

The republican, district and communal authorities shall attend to the enforcement of the laws, acts and measures of the federal authorities within these provinces, and to this end they shall cooperate with all the authorities requiring such cooperation in accordance with federal law.

Only in accordance with federal law may it be provided that in the execution of certain affairs in the province of the exclusive rights and duties of the Federation the federal administrative organs may stay the execution of general acts of the republican administrative organs which are at variance with federal law or with other federal regulations adopted in accordance with law, and hear appeals against administrative decisions of the republican administrative organs. Provision may be made in federal law determining that in these affairs and in other affairs of concern to the country as a whole, the federal administrative organs shall have the right to issue instructions binding the republican administrative organs, to supervise their work, and to exercise other powers in order to secure the carrying out of these affairs.

Through its organs the Federation may provide for the enforcement of federal laws and other federal regulations for whose enforcement the organs of other social-political communities are competent, if these organs do not enforce the regulations in question or until they do so.

Affairs of concern to the country as a whole are those affairs designated by law whose execution shall be the responsibility of the federal organs even when these affairs are discharged by the republican organs directly.

The federal authorities shall communicate with the organs of the other social-political communities in the republics through the equivalent republican authorities and they may also communicate with them directly in affairs within the province of the exclusive rights and duties of the Federation and in other cases designated by federal law.

ARTICLE 128. If certain matters of enforcement of federal laws within the province of the exclusive rights and duties of the Federation are transferred to the jurisdiction of the republican, district or communal authorities, the Federation shall be responsible to provide the resources or the sources of revenue necessary to discharge these relegated affairs.

ARTICLE 129. The federal organs in charge of inspection or supervision may perform these tasks, in accordance with federal law, on the whole territory of Yugoslavia, in order to supervise the enforcement of federal laws and to protect legality and the rights of citizens and organizations.

ARTICLE 130. In order to realize the rights and duties of the Federation, the Constitution and federal law shall determine the jurisdiction of the federal organs and the province of the organizations in charge of affairs within the framework of the rights and duties of the Federation.

The federal organs and these organizations shall carry on the activities in their jurisdiction, within the framework of the rights and duties of the Federation established by the Constitution.

The federal organs and these organizations shall carry on the activities in their jurisdiction, within the framework of the rights and duties of the Federation established by the Constitution.

ARTICLE 131. The federal laws and other general acts of the federal organs shall be made public in the official gazette of the Federation, in the authentic texts in the languages of the peoples of Yugoslavia: in Serbo-Croatian and Croato-Serbian, Slovene and Macedonian.

In official communication the organs of the Federation shall abide by the principle of equality of languages of the peoples of Yugoslavia.

CHAPTER VI

THE COURTS AND THE PUBLIC PROSECUTION

ARTICLE 132. The judicial functions shall be discharged within a uniform judicial system.

The judicial system shall comprise courts of general jurisdiction and courts of special jurisdiction, which shall be established to hear definite cases within court jurisdiction.

The courts of general jurisdiction shall be the communal courts, the county courts, the republican supreme courts and the Supreme Court of Yugoslavia.

Economic cases and other legal matters of concern for the economy shall be heard by economic courts.

Criminal offenses committed by military personnel and certain criminal offenses committed by other persons, and other legal matters pertaining to cases involving service in the Yugoslav People's Army shall be heard by military courts.

The courts of special jurisdiction shall be established by law.

ARTICLE 133. Subject to conditions determined on the basis of federal law, judicial functions may be discharged by courts of arbitration or by arbitration commissions.

Conciliation councils and other institutions to settle disputes between citizens or organizations may be founded in accordance with law.

ARTICLE 134. The jurisdiction of the courts shall be established and altered only by law.

ARTICLE 135. The courts shall judge basic personal, property, labor and other rights of the citizens and their obligations as well as property and other rights and obligations of organizations and social-political communities; pronounce penalties and other measures over criminal and economic offenders; judge in administrative litigation the legality of individual acts of the state organs and of organizations that discharge public powers; and decide on other relations when this is provided by law.

The courts shall follow and study social relations and manifestations of interest for the discharge of their functions, and shall advance proposals to prevent socially dangerous and harmful manifestations and to consolidate legality.

Within their jurisdiction courts shall have the right and duty to inform the assembly of the pertinent social-political community about the enforcement of law and about problems in the work of the courts.

ARTICLE 136. The courts shall be autonomous in the performance of their judicial functions and shall hear cases in accordance with the Constitution and law.

ARTICLE 137. Cases shall be heard by judges and lay judges.

Provision may be made in federal law determinating that only judges shall sit in certain courts and hear certain cases.

The judges and lay judges shall be chosen by the assembly of the corresponding social-political community. Provision may be made in law determining that the judges and lay judges of some courts shall be elected directly by the citizens.

The judges and lay judges may be removed from office only by the representative body that has elected them, under the conditions and in accordance with the procedure prescribed by law.

ARTICLE 138. A judge or lay judge shall not be called to account for an opinion given in the performance of judicial functions.

A judge or lay judge may not be placed under arrest for a criminal offense committed in the performance of his judicial duty without the approval of the competent assembly.

ARTICLE 139. Rulings in the first instance shall be passed by communal or county courts unless some other court has been given jurisdiction to hear in the first instance.

Appeals and other legal expedients against court decisions shall be heard by the competent court.

Only the competent court may amend, annul or set aside a court decision.

ARTICLE 140. Courts shall sit in council.

Provision may be made in law determining that certain cases shall be heard by a single judge.

ARTICLE 141. Court hearings shall be public.

The law shall designate those cases in which the public may be barred from court hearings in order to safeguard secrets, or to protect public decency, or in the interest of minors, or to safeguard other particular interests of the social community.

ARTICLE 142. The public prosecution is an autonomous organ entrusted with criminal prosecution. The public prosecution shall also undertake measures determined by law and legal expedients to assure the uniform enforcement of law and to protect legality.

The public prosecution shall discharge its functions in accordance with law and pursuant to the policy of the Federal Assembly.

The function of public prosecution in the Yugoslav People's Army shall be exercised by the military prosecution.

ARTICLE 143. The federal public prosecutor shall be nominated and removed by the Federal Assembly.

The public prosecutor of the republic shall be appointed and removed by the federal public prosecutor with the approval of the republican executive council. All other public prosecutors shall be appointed by the public prosecutor of the republic.

ARTICLE 144. Superior public prosecutors shall have the right and duty to issue instructions binding subordinate public prosecutors in their work.

The superior public prosecutor may discharge certain tasks which are within the jurisdiction of a subordinate public prosecutor.

CHAPTER VII

CONSTITUTIONALITY AND LEGALITY

ARTICLE 145. Constitutionality and legality shall be safeguarded in order to secure the constitutionally and legally established social-economic and political relations and unity of the legal order, as well as to protect the freedoms and rights of man and the citizen, the rights to self-government, and other rights of the organizations and social-political communities.

ARTICLE 146. Constitutionality and legality shall be the concern of the courts and other state organs, the organs of self-government and everyone who discharges public or other social functions.

The constitutional courts, as the safeguard of constitutionality, shall secure legality in accordance with the Constitution.

ARTICLE 147. Every regulation and other general act must be in conformity with the Constitution of Yugoslavia.

Every regulation and other general act enacted in the republic must also be in accord with the republican constitution.

ARTICLE 148. The republican constitution shall not be at variance with the Constitution of Yugoslavia.

Republican law shall conform to federal law.

All other regulations and other general acts passed by the state organs shall be in conformity with law.

The statutes of the social-political communities, as well as the statutes and other general decisions adopted by the working and other autonomous organizations shall conform to the Constitution and law.

ARTICLE 149. If the republican constitution is at variance with the Constitution of Yugoslavia, the Constitution of Yugoslavia shall be binding.

If republican law is not in accord with federal law, federal law shall be binding, pending the decision of the Constitutional Court of Yugoslavia.

Whenever a court deems that a law which it must enforce does not conform to the Constitution, it shall propose to the competent supreme court to institute proceedings to assess the conformity of such a law with the Constitution.

ARTICLE 150. Constitutional courts shall decide on the conformity of law with the constitution and the conformity of other regulations and general acts with the constitution and law.

The constitutional courts, pursuant to law, shall also safeguard the rights of self-government and other basic freedoms and rights established by the constitution whenever these freedoms and rights have been violated by any decisions or action and court protection has not been provided.

ARTICLE 151. Pending the decision of the Constitutional Court of Yugoslavia, the Federal Executive Council shall have the right to stay enforcement of a regulation or other general act of the republican executive council when this regulation or act is at variance with the Constitution of Yugoslavia or federal law.

Pending the decision of the constitutional court, the republican executive council shall have the right to stay enforcement of a regulation or other general act of a communal or district assembly or of any of their organs when such regulation or act is at variance with the Constitution or law. If the republican executive council does not stay enforcement of a regulation or other act which is at variance with the Constitution of Yugoslavia or federal law, the Federal Executive Council may do so.

Pending the decision of the constitutional court, the communal assembly shall have the right to stay enforcement of general decisions of an autonomous organization when these decisions are at variance with the Constitution or law. Provision may be made in law determining that the enforcement of general decisions of certain autonomous organizations may be stayed under the same conditions by the organ of another social-political community.

ARTICLE 152. Laws and other regulations and general acts shall be made public before they take effect.

Federal laws and other regulations and general acts shall become effective not before the eighth day after publication.

Only with special justification may a federal law or other regulation or general act become effective within a period shorter than eight days after publication.

ARTICLE 153. International agreements shall be applied on the day they take effect, unless the instrument of ratification, or the agreement based on the authority of the competent organ determines otherwise.

The court shall directly apply the international agreements that have been made public.

ARTICLE 154. No regulation or other general act shall have retroactive force.

Only by the law in question may provision be made that certain of the law's provisions and the regulations passed in accordance with such provisions shall have retroactive force.

Criminal offenses and economic misdemeanors and offenses shall be ascertained and the penalties for these acts executed according to the law in force at the time when they were committed, unless a subsequent law is more lenient toward the offender.

ARTICLE 155. Every decision and measure of the administrative organs and of other state organs discharging political-executive and administrative business, as well as every decision adopted by organizations in the exercise of their public functions, shall be based on law or on other legally adopted regulations.

ARTICLE 156. State organs and organizations exercising public powers may in particular matters decide on rights and duties, or, on the basis of law, apply measures of coercion or restriction only in accordance with the procedure prescribed by law, in which everyone concerned shall be able to defend his rights and interests and appeal or employ other legal expedients provided by law against the decision that has been adopted.

Administrative organs may bind particular organizations in their work only if they are explicitly authorized by law to do so and in accordance with the procedure prescribed by law.

ARTICLE 157. Ignorance of the language in which proceedings are being conducted shall not be a hindrance for defense and the realization of the rights and justified interests of citizens and organizations.

Every person shall be entitled to speak his own language in proceedings before court or before other state organs and organizations which in exercising public powers decide on the rights and duties of citizens, and during these proceedings every person shall be informed of the facts in his own language.

ARTICLE 158. An appeal may be filed with the competent authority against the decisions and other acts passed by judicial, administrative and other state organs in the first instance, and against such decisions passed by organizations which exercise public powers.

If the protection of rights and legality has been provided for in some other manner, appeal may be ruled out in certain cases in accordance with law.

ARTICLE 159. The legality of individual final decisions by which state organs or organizations exercising public powers decide on rights or duties shall be judged by court in administrative litigation, unless other judicial protection has been provided by law for the case in question.

Only by federal law in exceptional cases, may administrative litigation be ruled out in certain types of administrative cases.

PART TWO

ORGANIZATION OF THE FEDERATION

CHAPTER VIII

JURISDICTION OF THE FEDERAL ORGANS

ARTICLE 160. The exclusive jurisdiction of the Federation shall comprise:

1) Protection of the independence and territorial integrity of Yugoslavia, organization of the armed forces, and affairs pertaining to the defense of the country;

2) Protection of the constitutional order (state security); protection of the constitutionality established by the Constitution;

3) Representation of the Socialist Federal Republic of Yugoslavia; political, economic and other relations with other states and interstate organizations; international agreements; matters of war and peace;

4) Yugoslav citizenship; security and control of the boundaries; the legal status and sojourn of aliens in Yugoslavia; organization of the supervision over foreign-trade and foreign-exchange affairs and other economic relations with other countries; customs; determination of policy for issuing money, and regulation and supervision of money circulation; supervision of security of air traffic; supervision of passenger traffic across the frontier; supervision of traffic in goods across the frontier; supervision of international transport and communications;

5) Organization of the Federation and execution of tasks and affairs for which only the Federation is competent in accordance with the Constitution.

ARTICLE 161. The jurisdiction of the Federation in the legislative field shall comprise:

1) Complete laws concerning social ownership; ownership rights; obligatory and other basic property-law relations; expropriations; money and other media of payment; payment transactions; credit and banking; the social accounting service; weights and measures, standards and technical norms, patents, trade marks, samples, models and copyrights; the maritime code; the code for air traffic; the personal status of the citizen; suffrage; the manufacture of and traffic in narcotic drugs and poisons, and traffic in medicaments; the criminal code; economic offenses; the enforcement of criminal sentences; public security; weapons and explosives; the organization of economic courts; the organization of the public prosecution; court procedures; general administrative procedure; administrative litigation; civil defense; protection of veterans and disabled veterans; other relations of concern for the unity

of the economic area, and those relations which are to be regulated only by federal law, as determined by the Constitution;

2) Basic laws concerning economic organizations; the association of economic organizations; business affairs; work and safety at work; the distribution of the social product; income taxes, revenues and other public dues; public loans; budgets and funds; land, forests and water resources, roads and exploitation of natural resources and other natural potential; commerce in goods and services; social planning; transport and communications and traffic safety; designs and construction; assemblage and other public gatherings; the press and other media of information; associations of the citizens; social security; marriage, the family and guardianship; health protection of concern to the whole country; protection of livestock and vegetation of concern to the whole country; protection against elemental adversity; misdemeanors; the organization of the courts; the internal affairs service and other services whose activity is of concern to the whole country; the legal profession; public prosecution and legal representation; the legal status of religious communities; statistics, supervision and data of concern to the whole country; other relations of concern for the unity of the economic system, basic relations of concern for the political system and concerning those relations provided by the Constitution to be regulated by law;

3) General laws.

ARTICLE 162. The jurisdiction of the Federation shall include:

1) Determination of policy for the enforcement of federal law and other acts of the Federal Assembly, attendance to their enforcement and execution, as well as other political-executive and administrative affairs within the framework of the rights and duties of the Federation; administrative jurisdiction in the direct execution of these regulations and other acts, when this has been provided in accordance with federal law for matters of concern to several republics or of concern to the whole country; the securing of enforcement of international agreements;

2) Provision for the uniform enforcement of federal law and uniform punitive policy in the judicial field;

3) Statistics and supervision of concern to the whole country;

4) Other activities and measures to secure the realization of the rights and the discharge of the duties of the Federation;

5) Organization of a social accounting service and supervision over its work;

6) Other affairs determined by the Constitution.

CHAPTER IX

THE FEDERAL ASSEMBLY

1. Its Position and Jurisdiction

ARTICLE 163. The Federal Assembly is the supreme organ of power and organ of social self-government within the framework of the rights and duties of the Federation.

The Federal Assembly shall discharge its rights and duties on the basis of and in accordance with the Constitution and law.

ARTICLE 164. Being the basic holder of the rights and duties of the Federation, the Assembly shall, directly and exclusively,

1) Decide on a change of the Constitution of Yugoslavia;

2) Pass federal laws, call referendums; issue authentic interpretations of federal law; grant amnesty for criminal offenses determined by federal law;

3) Adopt the social plans of Yugoslavia, the federal budget and the federal annual financial statement;

4) Decide on political matters and determine the foundations of internal and foreign policy; determine the duties of the federal authorities and organizations in charge of those affairs of the Federation related to the enforcement of laws and other acts and policy of the assembly;

5) Elect the President of the Republic and the Vice President of the Republic;

6) Elect and remove the president and the members of the Federal Executive Council; elect and remove the presidents and the judges of the Constitutional Court of Yugoslavia, the Supreme Court of Yugoslavia, and the Supreme Economic Court; appoint and remove the federal secretaries of state, the federal secretaries, the secretary of the Federal Executive Council, and the deputy commander-in-chief, as well as the officers and members of organs of management of organizations designated by the Constitution or federal law, or by other assembly decisions;

7) Exercise political supervision over the work of the political-executive and administrative organs of the Federation; exercise supervision over the enforcement of the social plans of Yugoslavia, the federal budget and the financial plans of the federal funds; exercise social supervision; take positions in principle concerning the reports it may examine;

8) Decide on alterations of the boundaries of the Socialist Federal Republic of Yugoslavia;

9) Decide on war and peace; ratify international agreements concerning political and military cooperation and international agreements requiring enactment of additional laws or the amendment of laws in force;

10) Debate the reports of the federal courts and the federal public prosecution concerning the enforcement of federal law and the general problems of the judiciary; debate the reports of the autonomous organizations and other organs of the Federation designated by federal law;

11) Discharge other affairs determined by the Constitution;

The assembly may enact declarations and resolutions and make recommendations to the state organs and autonomous organizations, giving its opinions on matters of general concern.

2. *Composition and Election*

ARTICLE 165. The Federal Assembly shall comprise the Federal Chamber as a chamber of delegates of the citizens in the communes and republics; and the Economic Chamber, the Chamber of Education and Culture, the Chamber of Social Welfare and Health, and the Organizational-Political Chamber as chambers of delegates of the working people in the working communities.

The members of the Federal Chamber elected by the republican assemblies and the assemblies of the autonomous provinces shall constitute the Chamber of Nationalities, which shall have certain rights and duties under the Constitution for safeguarding the equality of the peoples of Yugoslavia and the rights of the republics, as determined by the Constitution.

ARTICLE 166. Each chamber shall have one hundred twenty deputies, who shall be elected in the ratio of one deputy to an equal number of inhabitants, so that one or several communes, as a constituency, shall elect one deputy to each chamber.

The republican chamber of every republican assembly shall elect ten deputies to the Federal Chamber from among its members. In a republic incorporating autonomous provinces, the provincial council of each autonomous province shall elect an additional five deputies as members of the republican delegation to the Federal Chamber, either from among its members or from among those members of the republican chamber of the republican assembly who have been elected on the territory of the autonomous province.

ARTICLE 167. The deputies of the Federal Chamber shall be elected by the communal assemblies and citizens directly.

The deputies to the chambers of the Federal Assembly which represent working communities shall be elected by the communal assemblies.

The candidates for membership to the Federal Chamber shall be nominated by the citizens at their meetings of the electorate or by groups of citizens, and the candidates for membership to the various chambers representing the working communities shall be nominated by the working people in the working communities depending on their field of work.

ARTICLE 168. Every citizen who enjoys suffrage shall be eligible to election to the Federal Chamber.

Every working man or member of an organ of management of a working organization or working community in the corresponding field of work, every member of an organ of management of an association of working organizations, and every trade-union officer in the corresponding field of work shall be eligible to election to the Economic Chamber, the Chamber of Education and Culture, and the Chamber of Social Welfare and Health.

Every member of an organ of management of a working organization or working community, every member of an organ of management of an association of working organizations, and every official of a social-political organization or association whose activities concern matters in the field of the social-political system shall be eligible to election to the Organizational-Political Chamber.

Any other citizen occupied in a corresponding field shall be eligible to election to any of the chambers representing the working communities, subject to the conditions determined by law.

Only a citizen who enjoys general suffrage shall be eligible to election to the chambers representing the working communities.

ARTICLE 169.   A candidate shall become a member of the Federal Chamber when he is elected in the communal assembly or communal assemblies by a legally determined majority and when after that election he receives the vote of the majority of all the voters in the constituency; and if several candidates are elected, that candidate shall become a member who has received the largest number of votes in the constituency.

A candidate shall become a member of the Economic Chamber, the Chamber of Education and Culture, the Chamber of Social Welfare and Health, or the Organizational-Political Chamber when he is elected by a legally determined majority in the communal assembly or communal assemblies.

ARTICLE 170.   A federal deputy shall be deemed recalled when a majority of the electorate determined by federal law have declared themselves for his recall.

ARTICLE 171.   Elections for new deputies shall be held not later than fifteen days before the expiration of the term of the deputies whose term is expiring.

Elections for deputies shall be called by the President of the Assembly.

If an assembly chamber is dissolved, elections shall be held not later than fifteen days from the day of its dissolution.

. The term of the newly elected chamber shall last until the term of the members of the dissolved chamber would have expired.

Not more than two months nor less than one month shall elapse from the day the elections are called until the day the elections are held.

The functions of the deputies whose terms are expiring shall cease on the day when the credentials of the new deputies are verified.

ARTICLE 172.   Under special circumstances the assembly may extend the term of the federal deputies for the duration of those circumstances. Elections shall be called immediately upon the cessation of the circumstances owing to which the term of the deputies has been extended.

3. Province and Work

ARTICLE 173.   Affairs within the jurisdiction of the assembly shall be discharged by the Federal Chamber acting with the other competent chamber on terms of equality.

Certain affairs in the jurisdiction of the assembly shall be discharged by each chamber independently.

The assembly shall discharge certain affairs in its jurisdiction at joint sessions of all the chambers.

The assembly shall discharge certain affairs in its jurisdiction in committees, commissions and other bodies of the chambers and assembly.

ARTICLE 174. The Federal Chamber, acting on terms of equality with the Economic Chamber, shall

Consider affairs of concern to the working communities in the economic sphere, as well as other matters in the fields of economy and finance;

Pass laws and other acts in these fields;

Pass the social plans of Yugoslavia.

ARTICLE 175. The Federal Chamber, acting on terms of equality with the Chamber of Education and Culture, shall

Consider affairs of concern to the working communities in the fields of education, science, art and other cultural fields as well as in the field of physical culture, and consider other affairs in these fields;

Pass laws and other acts in these fields.

ARTICLE 176. The Federal Chamber, acting on terms of equality with the Chamber of Social Welfare and Health, shall

Consider affairs of concern to the working communities in the fields of health and social security and in other fields of social welfare, and consider other affairs in these fields;

Pass laws and other acts in these fields.

ARTICLE 177. The Federal Chamber, acting on terms of equality with the Organizational-Political Chamber, shall

Consider affairs in the fields of the social-political system and in other fields in the jurisdiction of the assembly, with the exception of matters which in accordance with the Constitution fall equally into the jurisdiction of the other chambers or into the independent jurisdiction of one of the other chambers;

Pass laws and other acts unless they fall equally into the jurisdiction of other chambers or are the independent jurisdiction of the Federal Chamber;

Pass the federal budget and the annual financial statement.

ARTICLE 178. The Federal Chamber shall, independently,

Consider affairs in the field of foreign policy, national defense and state security, and affairs of general internal policy;

Pass laws and other acts and ratify international agreements in the fields of international political relations, national defense and state security;

Elect and remove the president and the members of the Federal Executive Council; elect and remove the presidents and the judges of the Constitutional Court of Yugoslavia, the Supreme Court of Yugoslavia and the Supreme Economic Court; nominate and remove the federal secretaries of state, the federal secretaries, the secretary of the Federal Executive Council, and the deputy commander-in-chief, as well as the officials and members of the organs of management of organizations designated by the Constitution, federal law or other assembly decision; exercise the rights of the assembly with regard to the responsibilities of the political-executive organs and federal officers to the assembly;

Pass decisions concerning the compensation to be paid the federal deputies and officers whom the assembly elects or nominates;

Discharge other affairs in the jurisdiction of the assembly which do not fall equally into the jurisdiction of the other chambers or the independent jurisdiction of one of the other chambers.

ARTICLE 179. Each of the chambers of the working communities, in its jurisdiction, may autonomously debate affairs pertaining to the enforcement of federal law and other assembly decisions, and other affairs of common concern to the working and other autonomous organizations and working communities in the corresponding field of work, in order to coordinate their relations and to develop mutual cooperation. The chambers shall be entitled to make recommendations concerning these affairs to the relevant autonomous organizations, working organizations and state organs.

Each of the chambers, in its jurisdiction, may require reports from the Federal Executive Council and address questions to it.

Each of the chambers, in its jurisdiction, may require reports and explanations from the federal secretaries of state, the federal secretaries and other officers in charge of the administrative organs.

ARTICLE 180. At a joint session of all the chambers the assembly shall elect the President of the Republic and the Vice President of the Republic, and the president and vice presidents of the assembly; it shall decide about extending the term of the deputies, and it shall establish when the circumstances cease owing to which the term of the deputies has been extended.

ARTICLE 181. Each chamber shall pass valid decisions by a majority vote at sessions attended by a majority of the members of the chamber in question, unless in accordance with the Constitution a special majority shall be required to pass certain decisions.

The assembly at a joint session of all its chambers shall pass valid decisions by a majority vote unless in accordance with the Constitution a special majority shall be required. The adoption of decisions at the joint sessions shall require the presence of a majority of the members of each chamber.

ARTICLE 182. Every deputy in his own chamber, the Federal Executive Council, and any committee of a chamber shall have the right to introduce bills and other draft acts.

Any chamber may also introduce bills and other draft acts within the jurisdiction of some other chamber.

The motion for the introduction of a bill may also come from autonomous organizations, from social-political organizations and associations, and from citizens.

ARTICLE 183. Every chamber shall have the right to discuss a bill, the draft social plan and the budget, as well as any other affair in the jurisdiction of another chamber, and to offer its opinions to the competent chamber on the bill or affair in question, if the bill or affair in question also pertains to a province in its own jurisdiction.

The competent chamber may require an opinion from the other chambers on a bill, the draft social plan, the budget or other matters.

The competent chamber shall debate the opinions of the other chambers and take a position on them.

ARTICLE 184. The competent chambers may resolve to place a bill before public discussion, or they may invite the representatives of autonomous organizations and social-political organizations and associations to give their opinions and proposals during the debate on a bill or draft act.

ARTICLE 185. Each chamber shall sit and deliberate separately in its sessions; but the chambers may also decide to sit and work together.

Two chambers participating on terms of equality in the enactment of a law or other act may decide to debate the law or act or to pass it at a joint session.

Two or more chambers may resolve to debate affairs of common concern at a joint session.

If the chambers resolve to vote at a joint session, the members of each chamber shall vote separately.

Voting shall be by acclamation, unless the assembly or the chamber, in accord with the rules of procedure, determines that it shall be by ballot.

ARTICLE 186. The assembly shall have rules of procedure, which shall be adopted at a joint session.

Each chamber shall adopt rules of procedure for its own work.

ARTICLE 187. Each chamber shall independently verify credentials and decide on matters relating to the credentials and parliamentary immunity of its members.

4. The Relations of the Chambers

ARTICLE 188. A law or other act in whose enactment two chambers participate on terms of equality shall be enacted when the two chambers have passed its identical text.

If unanimity is not reached concerning the identical text of a bill or other draft act even after two consecutive discussions of the matter in dispute, the chambers shall form a joint commission composed of an equal number of members from the two chambers, and this commission shall be entrusted with the formulation of a recommendation to settle the dispute.

Should the joint commission fail to reach unanimity, or should either chamber refuse to accept the text recommended by the commission, the bill or other draft act shall be placed before a joint session of the two chambers.

Should the two chambers not reach unanimity at the joint session, the controversial bill shall be removed from the agenda of the assembly, and it may again be placed on the agenda, upon the recommendation of one of the chambers or of the Federal Executive Council, only upon the lapse of six months from the day it has been removed from the agenda. By decision of the two chambers the controversial

l may again be placed on the agenda before this term expires.

ARTICLE 189. If owing to dispute between the Federal Chamber and another competent chamber the social plan of Yugoslavia or the federal budget has not been passed by the time when it should take effect, the two chambers shall be dissolved and the social plan or the budget shall be deemed to have been passed in the text passed by the Federal Chamber.

The newly elected chambers may pass a new social plan or budget.

If owing to dispute between the Federal Chamber and another competent chamber, a bill whose enactment is held by the President of the Republic or by the Federal Executive Council to be indispensable and urgent has not been passed even after the procedure provided for the attainment of unanimity has been followed, the two chambers shall be dissolved. The President of the Republic may decree the temporary application of the bill in the text passed by the Federal Chamber pending the decision of the newly elected chambers.

5. *The Rights of the Chamber of Nationalities*

ARTICLE 190. The Chamber of Nationalities shall meet by obligation when a motion to change the Constitution of Yugoslavia is on the agenda of the Federal Chamber.

The Chamber of Nationalities may meet when a bill or other draft act, or other matters concerning the equality of the peoples and republics, or pertaining to the rights of the republics established by the Constitution are on the agenda of the Federal Chamber. The Chamber of Nationalities shall meet whenever a majority of the delegates of one republic, ten of its own members, or the president of the assembly so requires.

ARTICLE 191. The Chamber of Nationalities may introduce an amendment to a bill or other draft act, or move that a bill or other draft act shall not be passed, if it considers that the bill or other draft act violates the equality of the peoples or republics or other constitutional rights of the republics.

If the Federal Chamber does not accept the motion of the Chamber of Nationalities, the Chamber of Nationalities may again debate the matter in dispute.

If the Chamber of Nationalities stands by its original position and again no accord is reached on the matter in dispute with the Federal Chamber, the two chambers shall form a joint commission composed of an equal number of members from each chamber, and this commission shall be entrusted with the formulation of a recommendation to settle the dispute.

If the joint commission does not reach unanimity, or if the Federal Chamber or the Chamber of Nationalities declines to accept the recommendation of the commission, further debate on the motion in dispute shall cease, and it shall not be placed on the agenda of the Federal Chamber again before the lapse of one year from the date on which the debate was closed.

The Federal Chamber shall debate and pass decisions always as a unified chamber.

ARTICLE 192. If owing to dispute between the Federal Chamber and the Chamber of Nationalities the social plan of Yugoslavia or the federal budget has not been passed by the date when it should take effect, the Federal Chamber shall be dissolved and the social plan or the budget shall be deemed to have been passed in the text passed by the Federal Chamber.

6. *The President of the Assembly and the Presidents of the Chambers*

ARTICLE 193. The assembly shall have a president and one or more vice presidents, who shall be elected from among the members of the Federal Chamber.

Each chamber and the Chamber of Nationalities shall have a president.

The president and vice president of the assembly and the presidents of the chambers who have been in office for four years may not be returned to the same office for a consecutive period of four years.

The assembly shall have a secretary, who shall be appointed and removed by the Federal Chamber.

ARTICLE 194. The president of the assembly shall represent the assembly; he shall convene joint sessions of the chambers; he shall preside over them and he shall attend to the enforcement of the assembly rules of procedure.

ARTICLE 195. The president of the assembly, with the vice president of the assembly and the presidents of the chambers, shall interpret those provisions of the rules of procedure of the assembly and chambers related to the jurisdiction of the chambers and assembly committees, and shall resolve upon other positions pertaining to other affairs of common concern in the work of the chambers, as determined by the assembly rules of procedure.

The president of the assembly shall countersign the decree promulgating law; he shall sign decisions passed at the joint sessions of the chambers; and together with the presidents of the relevant chambers he shall sign the assembly decisions passed by the chambers.

The president of the assembly may convene all the chambers in a joint session to deliberate questions of general political importance.

The president of the assembly shall convene all the chambers in a joint session upon the motion of the President of the Republic or of not less than three chambers of the assembly, and he shall convene a joint session of two or more chambers on the motion of two chambers.

ARTICLE 196. The president of each chamber shall convene the sessions of the chamber in accordance with the decision of the chamber concerned, or of his own accord, and he shall convene a session upon the motion of the president of the assembly or of the Federal Executive Council, and in other circumstances determined by the Constitution.

If the president of the chamber does not convene a session of the chamber when this is determined by the Constitution, the chamber shall meet when it is convened by twenty of its members or by the president of the assembly.

7. The Rights and Duties of the Deputies

ARTICLE 197. Every deputy shall have the right to introduce bills, decisions, recommendations, declarations and resolutions, in the chamber in which he is a member, and to move other questions in the jurisdiction of the chamber.

ARTICLE 198. Every deputy shall have the right to propose to the chamber of which he is a member the examination of matters pertaining to the policy and work of the Federal Executive Council, the enforcement of law or the work of the federal administrative organs.

A determined number of deputies shall have the right, pursuant to the rules of procedure, to move the election, nomination and removal of officers elected or nominated by the assembly, unless this is determined otherwise by the Constitution.

Every deputy shall have the right to question the Federal Executive Council or the officers in charge of the federal administrative organs on matters pertaining to their work and on matters in the jurisdiction of the organ concerned.

ARTICLE 199. Every deputy shall have the right to require information from the federal officers in charge of autonomous federal administrative organs.

The officer in question shall give the required information.

ARTICLE 200. Every deputy shall be accountable to his electorate and shall inform the electorate in his constituency about his work and the work of the chamber of which he is a member.

Every federal deputy shall have the right to take part in the work of the assembly of the commune in which he has been elected.

Every deputy shall inform the communal assembly, if it so requires, about his work and about the work of the chamber of which he is a member. On the request of the communal assembly he shall present the proposals or opinions of the communal assembly to the chamber of which he is a member on matters in the chamber's jurisdiction.

In order to discharge his duties, a deputy shall have the right to require information necessary for his work in the assembly from state organs and from working and other autonomous organizations in the constituency in which he has been elected.

ARTICLE 201. No member of the Federal Chamber shall at the same time be an officer or employee of a state organ.

The conditions under which a member of the Federal Chamber shall be entitled to return to his former place of work or to some equivalent place of work, and the conditions under which he shall have the rights that are acquired on the basis of work, may be determined by law.

ARTICLE 202. Every deputy shall enjoy parliamentary immunity in the assembly and outside it.

No deputy shall be called to account, arrested or punished for an opinion expressed or vote cast in the assembly.

No deputy shall be arrested without the approval of the chamber of which he is a member, nor may criminal proceedings be instituted against him without the approval of the chamber of which he is a member if he invokes parliamentary immunity.

A deputy may be arrested without the approval of the chamber only if he has been found in the act of committing a criminal offense for which a penalty of more than five years of strict imprisonment may be pronounced. In this event the state authority that has arrested the deputy shall notify the president of the assembly, who shall bring the matter up before the relevant chamber to decide whether proceedings shall continue, i.e., whether the warrant of arrest shall remain effective.

The chamber may also grant parliamentary immunity to a deputy who has not invoked it if this is necessary for him to discharge his duties as deputy.

If the chamber is not sitting, permission to arrest and to institute or continue criminal proceedings against a deputy may be granted or the invoking of parliamentary immunity may be resolved upon by the Credentials and Privileges Commission of the relevant chamber, subject to later confirmation by the chamber.

8. *The Committees and Commissions*

ARTICLE 203. Standing committees shall be set up to consider general affairs of policy and to introduce motions pertaining to these matters in the assembly, to consider bills and other assembly acts, and to consider other matters in the jurisdiction of the Federal Chamber.

These committees shall be founded and their jurisdiction determined by decision of the Federal Chamber.

ARTICLE 204. The standing committees of the Federal Chamber, within their several jurisdictions, shall

Discuss the state of affairs in different provinces of social life, attend to the work of the federal authorities and the enforcement of law and other assembly acts, and propose policy and measures to the assembly and the Federal Executive Council for the enforcement of federal law and other assembly acts;

Study bills and other draft acts and other matters in the jurisdiction of the assembly, and present their findings and proposals to the Federal Chamber;

Determine bills and other draft acts of the assembly, and have the right to require the federal administrative organs to prepare bills and other acts of the assembly.

ARTICLE 205. A standing committee of the Federal Chamber may require the Federal Executive Council to explain, through its spokesman, its position on certain matters on the agenda of a committee session, or forward its opinion concerning a bill or other draft act.

A committee may require federal officers to explain the state of affairs in their respective departments of administration and to present reports concerning the enforcement of federal laws and other federal regulations and concerning other matters in the jurisdiction of the pertinent administrative organs, and to answer questions either orally or in writing, and to give other information and explanations.

ARTICLE 206. A standing committee of the Federal Chamber may hold inquiries and hearings and to this purpose may require data, files and documents from all the state organs and organizations. The committee shall have no judicial powers of inquiry.

A committee may summon the representatives of organizations in order to hear their opinions and proposals, or their advice on particular matters.

ARTICLE 207. The Economic Chamber, the Chamber of Education and Culture and of Social Welfare and Health, and the Organizational-Political Chamber may found committees of their own to examine bills and other draft acts and to examine other matters in their respective jurisdictions.

ARTICLE 208. A commission for matters pertaining to elections and nominations shall be set up in the assembly.

The chairman and the majority of the members of the commission shall be elected by the Federal Chamber and other chambers, from among the federal deputies, while a certain number of the members shall be delegated by the Socialist Alliance of the Working People of Yugoslavia.

The commission shall consider all matters pertaining to elections, nominations, and dismissals in the jurisdiction of the assembly, as well as general matters pertaining to personnel.

ARTICLE 209. The assembly and its chambers may also set up other standing and *ad hoc* commissions and other bodies to study particular matters, to prepare bills and other draft acts, and to carry out inquiries. The members of these commissions shall be elected from among the deputies, although members of individual commissions may be nominated from among experts and figures prominent in public life.

The assembly may also set up specialized, advisory and similar staffs necessary for the work of the assembly.

9. *The Changing of the Constitution*

ARTICLE 210. The changing of the Constitution of Yugoslavia shall be decided upon by the Federal Chamber and the Chamber of Nationalities in accordance with the procedure determined by the Constitution.

A motion to change the Constitution may be introduced by not less than thirty members of the Federal Chamber, by the Chamber of Nationalities, by the President of the Republic or by the Federal Executive Council.

The Federal Chamber and the Chamber of Nationalities shall first resolve whether or not deliberations on a change of constitution should be commenced.

If after two consecutive debates the Federal Chamber and the Chamber of Nationalities do not reach unanimity to commence deliberations on a change of constitution, a motion to change the Constitution may not be introduced before the lapse of one year from the date on which the debate was closed.

ARTICLE 211. Before the debate is held on a motion to change the Constitution, the Federal Chamber shall forward the motion to the Economic Chamber, the Chamber of Education and Culture, the Chamber of Social Welfare and Health, and the Organizational-Political Chamber.

The chambers shall consider the motion to change the Constitution and shall give their opinions to the Federal Chamber.

Upon receiving the opinions of the other chambers, the Federal Chamber shall commence debate on the motion to change the Constitution.

ARTICLE 212. Before the debate takes place in the Federal Chamber, the motion to change the Constitution shall be debated by the Chamber of Nationalities.

During the debate on the motion to change the Constitution, the Federal Chamber shall also form an opinion on the views held by the other assembly chambers.

The motion to change the Constitution shall be deemed to have been passed if an identical text has been passed by the Federal Chamber and the Chamber of Nationalities.

If the Federal Chamber does not accept the opinion of the Chamber of Nationalities concerning the motion to change the Constitution, the debate shall be postponed for two months.

Upon the lapse of this period, only two additional consecutive debates may be held on the matters in dispute between the Federal Chamber and the Chamber of Nationalities. If after these two consecutive debates unanimity is not reached, the Federal Chamber and the Chamber of Nationalities may decide to place the matter in dispute before a referendum. If the two chambers do not agree to place the matter in dispute before a referendum, the Federal Chamber shall be dissolved.

ARTICLE 213. The motion to change the Constitution shall be deemed to have been passed in the Federal Chamber and in the Chamber of Nationalities if it has received the vote of two-thirds of the members of the two chambers.

ARTICLE 214. If not later than fifteen days after the adoption of the motion to change the Constitution in the Federal Chamber and the Chamber of Nationalities, at least three of the other chambers of the assembly do not agree to the accepted text of the motion to change the Constitution, the motion to change the Constitution shall be placed before a referendum.

The referendum on the motion to change the Constitution shall be called by the president of the assembly. The referendum shall be held not later than two months from the date on which the motion to change the Constitution has been passed in the Federal Chamber and the Chamber of Nationalities.

The motion to change the Constitution shall be deemed to have been passed by referendum if a majority of the electorate on the territory of Yugoslavia has voted for the motion.

The motion to change the Constitution shall be proclaimed by the Federal Chamber.

CHAPTER X

THE PRESIDENT OF THE REPUBLIC

ARTICLE 215. The President of the Republic shall represent the Socialist Federal Republic of Yugoslavia at home and abroad, and shall discharge other political-executive duties determined by the Constitution.

The President of the Republic shall be commander-in-chief of the armed forces of Yugoslavia.

ARTICLE 216. The President of the Republic shall propose one of the members of the Federal Assembly to the assembly as president of the Federal Executive Council, who shall propose election of the Federal Executive Council.

The President of the Republic may convene sessions of the Federal Executive Council and place certain matters on the agenda of its sessions. The President of the Republic shall preside over sessions which he attends.

ARTICLE 217. The President of the Republic shall,

  1) Promulgate federal laws by decree;

  2) Promulgate the decision of the Federal Assembly on the election of the Federal Executive Council; propose election of the president and judges of the Constitutional Court of Yugoslavia, propose election and removal of the members of the Council of the Federation, propose nomination and removal of the deputy commander-in-chief;

3) Appoint and recall by decree ambassadors and ministers of the Socialist Federal Republic of Yugoslavia, and accept the letters of credence and letters of recall of foreign diplomatic representatives accredited to him; issue instruments of ratification of international agreements;

4) Confer decorations;

5) Grant pardons, in accordance with federal law for criminal offenses provided by federal law;

6) Declare a state of war if the Federal Assembly is unable to meet;

7) Found pertinent staffs to discharge affairs in his jurisdiction;

8) Exercise other rights and duties determined by the Constitution.

The President of the Republic, upon the proposal of the Federal Executive Council, shall during a state of war or in the event of immediate danger of war pass decrees with the force of law on matters in the jurisdiction of the Federal Assembly. The President of the Republic shall submit these decrees to the assembly for approval as soon as it is able to meet.

Particular provisions of the Constitution of Yugoslavia pertaining to the freedoms and rights of the citizens and to the rights of autonomous organizations, or to the composition of political-executive and administrative organs and their powers, may in exceptional cases be suspended by decree with the force of law passed during a state of war for the duration of this emergency, if the interests of the country's defense so require.

ARTICLE 218. The President of the Republic shall have the right to stay any decree and any other regulation of general political significance passed by the Federal Executive Council before the decree or regulation is promulgated.

If the President of the Republic stays a regulation of the Federal Executive Council, he shall immediately place the matter in dispute before the Federal Chamber for a decision.

ARTICLE 219. The President of the Republic shall exercise his rights and duties in accordance with and within the restrictions of the Constitution and federal law.

The President of the Republic shall have presidential immunity, and shall be accountable to the Federal Assembly in accordance with the Constitution and federal law.

The President of the Republic shall cease to be a deputy if he has been elected from among the deputies.

ARTICLE 220. The President of the Republic shall be elected for a term of four years and may be re-elected for one further consecutive term.

No limitation of tenure of office of President of the Republic shall apply to Josip Broz-Tito.

ARTICLE 221. The Federal Assembly shall elect the President of the Republic not later than one month before the expiration of the term of the President of the Republic then in office.

A candidate for President of the Republic may be proposed to the assembly by not less than thirty deputies, of their own accord or in accordance with a proposal made by the Federal Board of the Socialist Alliance of the Working People of Yugoslavia. Not less than five of the nominators shall be from each of the republics, and half the nominators shall be members of the Federal Chamber.

That candidate shall be elected President of the Republic who has received the vote of a majority of all the federal deputies.

Upon being elected, the President of the Republic shall make his affirmation before the Federal Assembly.

ARTICLE 222. The President of the Republic shall give the assembly information on the state and on problems of internal and foreign policy and may propose that the assembly discuss certain matters and pass decisions.

ARTICLE 223. During absence of the President of the Republic, his powers shall be exercised by the Vice President of the Republic. The President of the Republic may charge the Vice President to represent him in certain affairs.

The Vice President of the Republic shall be elected to a term of four years and shall not be re-elected Vice President for a consecutive term.

The Federal Assembly shall elect the Vice President of the Republic immediately upon electing the President of the Republic, in accordance with the same procedure.

If he has been elected from among the federal deputies, the Vice President of the Republic shall retain his seat as deputy.

ARTICLE 224. The President of the Republic shall convene the Council of the Federation in order to consider matters of state policy and the work of the political-executive and administrative organs.

The members of the Council of the Federation shall be elected by the Federal Chamber upon the proposal of the President of the Republic, from among federal officers and officials of the republics and from among officials of the social-political and other organizations.

CHAPTER XI

THE POLITICAL-EXECUTIVE AND ADMINISTRATIVE ORGANS OF THE FEDERAL ASSEMBLY

(a) The Federal Executive Council

ARTICLE 225. The Federal Executive Council shall be the organ of the Federal Assembly . . . entrusted with political-executive powers within the framework of the rights and duties of the Federation.

The Federal Executive Council shall be responsible for the execution of the Federation's policy, the foundations of which shall be established by the Federal Assembly.

ARTICLE 226. The Federal Executive Council shall consist of a president and a definite number of members.

The president and the members of the Federal Executive Council shall be elected by the Federal Chamber on the proposal of a deputy whom the President of the Republic has proposed for president of the Federal Executive Council, and in accordance with the opinion of the Elections and Nominations Commission. The members of the Federal Executive Council shall be elected from among the members of the assembly, with due consideration being given to its composition in terms of nationality.

The presidents of the executive councils of the republics, the federal secretaries of state, the federal secretaries, and the secretary of the Federal Executive Council, as well as other federal officers designated by the assembly at the time of their nomination, shall be members of the Federal Executive Council by virtue of their office.

ARTICLE 227. In exceptional cases, the Federal Chamber may elect a deputy as president or member of the Federal Executive Council who has just held this office for four years, if there are justified reasons for doing so, but he may not hold this office longer than for the next four years. With regard to the president of the Federal Executive Council, a decision to this effect shall be passed by the Federal Chamber on the proposal of the President of the Republic, and with regard to a member of the Federal Executive Council, on the proposal of the president of the Federal Executive Council or the deputy who presents the proposal for the election of the Federal Executive Council.

Before the vote is taken, the Federal Chamber shall decide by a majority vote on the justifiability of the reasons for departing from the principle of limitation of re-election.

The President of the Federal Executive Council shall have the right to propose to the Federal Chamber the removal of members of the Federal Executive Council and election of new members.

The removal of the president of the Federal Executive Council or the resignation of a majority of the members of the council shall entail the resignation of the whole council.

ARTICLE 228. The Federal Executive Council shall

1) Propose internal and foreign policy to the Federal Assembly and attend to the implementation of the policy determined by the assembly; attend to the enforcement of federal law, the social plan of Yugoslavia, the federal budget, and other assembly decisions; supervise the work of the federal administrative organs and give them general instructions in their work;

2) Introduce bills and other draft acts in the assembly, and have the right to give its opinions on bills introduced in the assembly by the assembly chambers, the committees of the chambers or the deputies;

3) Prepare a draft of the social plan of Yugoslavia and a draft of the federal budget and the annual financial statement;

4) Pass decrees, and decisions and directives for the enforcement of federal law and other general acts of the Federal Assembly, if it is authorized to do so by law or by these acts;

5) Determine the general principles of internal organization and work of the federal administrative organs;

6) Set up federal administrative organs which are not set up by law, as well as specialized staffs necessary for the council's work, and found working organizations and other organizations to discharge affairs of interest for the council and other federal organs, in conformity with the law;

7) Set aside the regulations of the federal administrative organs when these are at variance with federal law, decree, or other regulations of the Federal Executive Council;

8) Ratify international agreements whose ratification is not within the jurisdiction of the assembly;

9) Propose to the Federal Chamber the election and removal of the presidents and judges of the Supreme Court of Yugoslavia and the Supreme Economic Court, and propose the nomination and dismissal of the federal public prosecutor and other federal officers designated by law;

10) Appoint officers of the council and federal administrative organs and directors of institutions and organizations designated by law;

11) Manage, within the provisions of the Constitution and federal law, certain funds of the Federation;

12) Discharge other affairs provided for by federal law within the rights and duties of the Federation.

ARTICLE 229. At its sessions the Federal Executive Council shall decide on affairs in its jurisdiction.

All the members of the council shall deliberate on general matters and matters of principle and on matters of common concern to all the administrative organs.

Other matters in the jurisdiction of the council shall be deliberated by designated members of the councils and by the federal secretaries of state.

The organization of the Federal Executive Council and the manner in which it shall decide on matters in its jurisdiction shall be determined by law.

The Federal Executive Council may set up committees and other bodies to coordinate the work of the federal administrative organs and to consider matters of common concern to two or more administrative organs.

Federal secretaries and other officers may be nominated in the Federal Executive Council who shall independently discharge affairs.

ARTICLE 230. The president of the Federal Executive Council shall represent the council, and shall attend to the enforcement of the decisions and to the implementation of the policy of the Federal Executive Council.

The president of the council shall convene the council on his own initiative or on the proposal of the President of the Republic, or on the proposal of no fewer than five members of the council.

The president of the council shall coordinate the work of the federal administrative organs in order to implement the general policy of the council.

ARTICLE 231. The Federal Executive Council shall discharge the affairs in its jurisdiction in accordance with and within the limits of the Constitution and law.

The Federal Executive Council shall be responsible for its work to the Federal Assembly.

The assembly may rescind or cancel any regulation or other decision of the Federal Executive Council that is at variance with the Constitution or law.

ARTICLE 232. The Federal Executive Council shall inform the Federal Assembly about its work.

The Federal Executive Council may propose to the competent assembly chambers to postpone debate on a bill or other decision, or to form a joint commission of members of the competent assembly chamber and of its own members in order to debate a certain matter, or to convene a session of the competent assembly chamber at which the Federal Executive Council shall state its position.

If the assembly passes a bill or draft act at variance with the position of the Federal Executive Council, the council may submit its collective resignation to the Federal Chamber if it considers that it is not in a position to secure the enforcement of the law or other act.

The council which has resigned shall remain in office pending election of a new federal executive council.

(b) The Federal Administration

ARTICLE 233. Secretariats of state, federal secretariats and other federal administrative organs shall be founded to discharge the affairs of the state administration in the jurisdiction of the Federation.

Secretariats of state shall be founded only for those departments of administration which in accordance with the Constitution fall wholly within the exclusive jurisdiction of the federal organs.

Federal secretariats and other federal administrative organs shall be founded to discharge the affairs of the state administration in other provinces that are in the jurisdiction of the Federation.

Councils and other federal organs and organizations may be founded to discharge certain specialized, administrative and other affairs in the jurisdiction of the Federation.

ARTICLE 234. The secretariats of state shall be the Secretariat of State for Foreign Affairs and the Secretariat of State for National Defense.

The province of the secretariats of state shall be determined and altered by law.

The federal secretariats and the other autonomous federal administrative organs and councils, as well as organizations discharging affairs of concern to the whole country, shall be founded and dissolved and their jurisdiction determined by law.

ARTICLE 235. The federal administrative organs shall autonomously discharge affairs in their jurisdiction in accordance with and within the restrictions of the Constitution and federal law.

In the performance of the duties within their jurisdiction the federal administrative organs shall also abide by other federal regulations.

The federal administrative organs shall provide for the enforcement of federal law and other federal regulations, of the policy determined by the Federal Assembly and general instructions of the Federal Executive Council.

ARTICLE 236. The federal secretaries of state, the federal secretaries, the secretary of the Federal Executive Council, and other federal officers designated by law shall be nominated and dismissed by the Federal Assembly upon the proposal of the president of the Federal Executive Council acting on behalf of the council.

An officer who has held one of the enumerated offices for four years may be appointed to that office for no more than an additional consecutive four years if justified reasons so require. Upon the proposal of the president of the Federal Executive Council, the assembly shall first determine by a majority vote whether or not the reasons given for making an exception to the principle of limitation of renomination are justified.

ARTICLE 237. The federal officers who are at the head of the federal administrative organs shall be personally responsible for the work of the respective organs and for the execution of the tasks and affairs in their jurisdiction.

The federal officers at the head of the federal administrative organs may adopt regulations and issue ordinances and instructions for the enforcement of law and the regulations of the Federal Executive Council if they are authorized to do so by law or by a regulation issued by the Federal Executive Council.

ARTICLE 238. The federal officers at the head of the federal administrative organs shall inform the Federal Assembly and the Federal Executive Council about the state of affairs in their respective fields of administration and about the work of the administrative organs in their charge.

Upon the request of the chambers, committees and commissions of the assembly, these officers shall provide information and explanations concerning matters in the jurisdiction of the organs in their charge, and give answers to questions asked by deputies.

CHAPTER XII

THE SUPREME COURT OF YUGOSLAVIA

ARTICLE 239. The Supreme Court of Yugoslavia shall

1) Pass basic rulings and legal judgments in matters of significance for the uniform enforcement of federal law by the courts of general jurisdiction and courts of special jurisdiction;

2) Decide on regular legal expedients against the decisions of the republican supreme courts, when this is provided by federal law;

3) Decide on special legal expedients against valid decisions of the courts which violate federal law, in cases provided by law;

4) Decide on administrative litigation against administrative decisions passed by federal organs or organizations discharging public powers on the territory of Yugoslavia;

5) Resolve conflicts of jurisdiction between courts on the territories of different republics;

6) Discharge other business provided by federal law within the rights and duties of the Federation.

ARTICLE 240. The jurisdiction and organization of the Supreme Court of Yugoslavia shall be determined by federal law.

CHAPTER XIII

THE CONSTITUTIONAL COURT OF YUGOSLAVIA

ARTICLE 241. The Constitutional Court of Yugoslavia shall

1) Decide on the conformity of law with the Constitution of Yugoslavia;

2) Decide on the conformity of republican law with federal law;

3) Decide on the conformity of other regulations and other general decisions of organs and organizations with the Constitution of Yugoslavia, federal law and other federal regulations;

4) Resolve disputes on rights and duties between the Federation and a republic, between republics, and between other social-political communities on the territories of two or more republics, if the jurisdiction of some other court has not been provided by law for the settlement of these disputes; resolve disputes concerning the boundaries between republics;

5) Resolve conflict of jurisdiction between courts and federal organs, and between courts and other state organs on the territories of two or more republics;

6) Discharge other business placed by the Constitution or federal law in its jurisdiction, in conformity with the constitutional rights and duties of the Federation.

The Constitutional Court of Yugoslavia shall also decide on the protection of the rights of self-government and other basic freedoms and rights established by the Constitution if these freedoms and rights have been violated by an individual decision or action of the federal organs, and in other instances determined by federal law for which other court protection has not been provided.

ARTICLE 242. The Constitutional Court of Yugoslavia shall keep itself informed about manifestations of interest for the attainment of constitutionality and legality, and on these grounds shall offer to the Federal Assembly its opinions and proposals to pass laws and to undertake other measures to secure constitutionality and legality and to protect the rights of self-government and the other freedoms and rights of the citizens and organizations.

ARTICLE 243. The Constitutional Court of Yugoslavia shall consist of a president and ten judges.

The president and the judges of the constitutional court shall be elected for a term of eight years, and they may be re-elected only for one more consecutive term of eight years. Half the number of judges of the constitutional court shall be elected every four years.

The president and the judges of the constitutional court shall not at the same time be members of the republican assemblies or of the Federal Assembly, or of their political-executive organs, nor [shall they be] officers or employees of the state administrative organs, or of any other court.

The president and the judges of the constitutional court may be dismissed from office before their terms expire, in accordance with federal law, only if they request to be relieved, or if for a criminal offense they have been sentenced to imprisonment, or if they have lost legal capability or if they have become permanently disabled physically and cannot discharge their duties.

The president and the judges of the constitutional court shall have immunity like the federal deputies.

ARTICLE 244. The Constitutional Court of Yugoslavia shall advise the Federal Assembly as to whether the constitution of a republic is at variance with the Constitution of Yugoslavia.

ARTICLE 245. Whenever the Constitutional Court of Yugoslavia determines that a federal law does not conform to the Constitution, the Federal Assembly shall bring the law into conformity with the Constitution not later than six months from the date of publication of the decision of the constitutional court.

If the assembly does not bring the law into conformity with the Constitution within this period, the law or those of its provisions that do not conform to the Constitution shall cease to be valid, and the Constitutional Court of Yugoslavia shall declare them invalid by its decision.

If in a case of conflict between a republican law and a federal law, the Constitutional Court of Yugoslavia finds that the federal law in question does not conform to the Constitution of Yugoslavia, it shall decide that, pending adoption of a final decision, the provisions of the federal law that do not conform to the Constitution shall be inoperative.

ARTICLE 246. Whenever the Constitutional Court of Yugoslavia finds that a republican law does not conform to the Constitution of Yugoslavia or to federal law, the republican assembly shall bring the republican law into conformity with the Constitution or with federal law not later than six months from the date of publication of the decision of the Constitutional Court of Yugoslavia.

If the republican assembly does not bring the republican law into conformity with the Constitution or with federal law within this period, the republican law or those of its provisions that do not conform to the Constitution of Yugoslavia or to federal law shall cease to be valid, and the constitutional court shall declare them invalid by its decision.

Whenever the Constitutional Court of Yugoslavia finds that a republican law does not conform to the Constitution of Yugoslavia or to federal law, it shall decide that, pending adoption of a final decision, the provisions of the republican law that do not conform to the Constitution or to federal law shall be inoperative. The Constitutional Court of Yugoslavia may forthwith annul a republican law if it clearly violates the rights of the Federation.

ARTICLE 247. Whenever the Constitutional Court of Yugoslavia finds that a provision other than law, or some other general act, does not conform to the Constitution of Yugoslavia or to federal law, it shall annul or set aside the provision or act or regulation that does not conform to the Constitution or to federal law.

ARTICLE 248.   If a point of constitutionality or legality has been raised with regard to a provision or other general act which is at variance both with the Constitution of Yugoslavia or federal law and with the republican constitution or republican law, a ruling on constitutionality and legality shall be given on that point by the republican constitutional court, which shall judge only the conformity of the regulation or other general act in question with the republican constitution or republican law.

If the republican constitutional court decides that the regulation or general act in question conforms to the republican constitution or republican law, it shall forward the matter to the Constitutional Court of Yugoslavia to judge the conformity of the regulation or general act in question with the Constitution of Yugoslavia or federal law.

The Constitutional Court of Yugoslavia may raise a point of constitutionality or legality with regard to such a provision or other general act even before the proceedings before the republican constitutional court terminate, if the regulation or general act in question clearly violates the rights of the Federation.

ARTICLE 249.   A point of constitutionality and legality may be raised before the Constitutional Court of Yugoslavia by

1) The Federal Assembly and the republican assemblies;

2) The Federal Executive Council and the republican executive councils, except when the constitutionality of laws passed by their assemblies is being judged;

3) The Supreme Court of Yugoslavia and the other supreme courts of the Federation, as well as the republican supreme courts, if the point of constitutionality and legality ensues in court proceedings;

4) The federal public prosecutor, if the point of constitutionality and legality ensues in the work of the public prosecution;

5) The republican constitutional courts;

6) The assembly of a social-political community, or a working or other autonomous organization, if any of their rights established by the Constitution of Yugoslavia have been violated.

A point of constitutionality and legality may be raised by the Constitutional Court of Yugoslavia of its own initiative.

The conditions under which other state organs, organizations and citizens may institute proceedings or move the institution of proceedings raising a point of constitutionality and legality before the Constitutional Court of Yugoslavia shall be determined by federal law.

ARTICLE 250.   If in proceedings on a point of constitutionality and legality the Constitutional Court of Yugoslavia finds that the law or other provision in question is not at variance with the Constitution of Yugoslavia or with federal law, it may for purposes of enforcement of the provision establish the interpretation which conforms to the Constitution or federal law.

ARTICLE 251. The jurisdiction and procedure of the Constitutional Court of Yugoslavia, and the legal scope of its decisions, shall be determined in detail by federal law.

The Constitutional Court of Yugoslavia shall autonomously determine its organization and work.

CHAPTER XIV

NATIONAL DEFENSE AND THE YUGOSLAV PEOPLE'S ARMY

ARTICLE 252. It is the inalienable right and duty of the peoples of Yugoslavia to safeguard and defend the independence and territorial integrity of the Socialist Federal Republic of Yugoslavia.

Defense of the country shall be the right and duty of the citizens, of the working and other organizations, and of the Federation, republic, commune, and other social-political communities.

The Federation shall be responsible for the preparation and organization of the Yugoslav People's Army, and the Federation, republic, commune and other social-political communities shall be responsible for the organization of civil defense, preliminary military training and the general preparation and organization of the defense of the country.

In matters of national defense the rights, duties and responsibilities of the citizens and of the working and other organizations shall be determined by federal law.

ARTICLE 253. Military service of the citizens shall be universal.

The beginning of service in the Yugoslav People's Army and the cessation of service, as well as the special rights and duties of the members of the Yugoslav People's Army in regard to service in the Army shall be determined by federal law.

ARTICLE 254. No one shall have the right to sign or to acknowledge capitulation or the occupation of the country on behalf of the Socialist Federal Republic of Yugoslavia. Such an action is unconstitutional and shall be punishable by law.

High treason is a crime against the people and shall be punished as a grave criminal offense.

ARTICLE 255. The Yugoslav People's Army is the basic armed force of national defense of Yugoslavia.

The Yugoslav People's Army shall protect the independence, constitutional order, inviolability and integrity of the territory of the Socialist Federal Republic of Yugoslavia.

ARTICLE 256. The commander-in-chief of the armed forces of Yugoslavia shall command and be in charge of the Yugoslav People's Army, and shall determine the bases of plans and preparatory measures for the defense of the country.

The commander-in-chief shall appoint, promote and relieve of duty generals and admirals and other military officers designated by federal law.

The commander-in-chief shall appoint and remove the president, judges and lay judges of military courts, as well as the military prosecutors.

The commander-in-chief may have a deputy, who shall act in his stead in those affairs of command and jurisdiction over the Yugoslav People's Army designated by the commander-in-chief.

ARTICLE 257. The Council of National Defense shall attend to the organization and mobilization of the resources and forces of the country for the requirements of national defense.

The members of the Council of National Defense shall be nominated and removed by the Federal Chamber upon the proposal of the President of the Republic.

The President of the Republic shall be chairman of the Council of National Defense.

PART THREE
TRANSITIONAL AND CONCLUDING PROVISIONS

ARTICLE 258. A special constitutional law shall be enacted to implement the Constitution and to provide for transition to its application.

ARTICLE 259. The Constitution shall be promulgated by the Federal People's Assembly.